FREE MOVEMENT
OF GOODS
IN THE E.E.C.

Second Edition

FREE MOVEMENT OF GOODS IN THE E.E.C.
UNDER ARTICLES 30 to 36 OF THE ROME TREATY

Second Edition

by
PETER OLIVER
Barrister-at-Law
Middle Temple

LONDON
EUROPEAN LAW CENTRE LIMITED
1988

European Law Centre Limited,
4 Bloomsbury Square, London WC1A 2RL

First edition 1982
Second edition 1988

© Peter Oliver 1988

Index compiled by
Jane Milward
M.A., LL.B. (Cantab)

A CIP catalogue record for this book is available from the British Library

ISBN 0-907451-20-9

Typeset in Garamond and
Printed in Great Britain by
The Eastern Press Ltd. of London and Reading

CONTENTS

CONTENTS

CHAPTER VI

Measures of equivalent effect: General

CHAPTER VII

Measures of equivalent effect: II

CONTENTS

CHAPTER VIII

The main exception: Article 36 EEC and the 'mandatory requirements'   166

CONTENTS
CHAPTER IX
Other exception clauses

CHAPTER X
Agriculture

CHAPTER XI
State monopolies of a commercial character

CHAPTER XII
Community legislation relating to the free movement of goods

CHAPTER XIII
The Single European Act

CONTENTS

CHAPTER XIV

Conclusion

Preface

Since the first edition of this book appeared in 1982, the developments in this area of the law have been immense: the Court has delivered some 100 judgments relating to Articles 30 to 36, including such significant cases as *Campus Oil* and *E.C. Commission* v. *Germany* (beer); much important legislation has been passed; and, last but by no means least, the Single European Act has been adopted. Accordingly, despite the publication of a supplement in 1984, the appearance of a second edition is now decidedly overdue.

My thanks go to my wife, Philippa Watson, and to all those colleagues of the Legal Service of the European Commission and others who provided invaluable help and assistance, such as René Barents, Eric White, Richard Condon and Nicholas Pumfrey. My special gratitude is reserved for Marina Thielemans-Gatti, who typed the lion's share of the manuscript, and Ingrid Sejhrouchni who typed the rest (other than Chapter 3, which was all that I could manage with my very limited typing ability).

Responsibility for the views expressed in this book is mine alone. The law is stated as at 1 August 1988.

PETER OLIVER

Brussels, August 1988

CHAPTER I

Introduction

At the very heart of the EEC lies the customs union. As testimony to this the fathers of the Treaty chose to set out the provisions relating to it in Title I of the Treaty, immediately after the eight introductory articles. Likewise, Article 3 which lists eleven 'activities' of the EEC, begins with the 'elimination, as between Member States, of customs duties and of quantitative restrictions on the import and export of goods, and of all other measures having equivalent effect', followed by 'the establishment of a common customs tariff and of a common commercial policy towards third countries'.

The purpose of this book is to examine only a part of Title I, namely Articles 30 to 36, which in principle prohibit quantitative restrictions and measures of equivalent effect on imports and exports between Member States. Briefly stated, quantitative restrictions are non-tariff quotas or total bans on trade, while the concept of measures of equivalent effect covers a multitude of other trade restrictions not falling under any other chapter of the Treaty of Rome. It cannot be sufficiently emphasised that this concept is not limited to technical customs matters but covers such questions as intellectual property, price controls and indications of origin. However, this prohibition on quantitative restrictions and measures of equivalent effect is subject to a number of exceptions, which will also be examined. In addition, this book will briefly consider the powers of the Community to pass legislation to eliminate technical barriers to trade. On the other hand, trade between the EEC and third countries falls outside the scope of this work.

First, Articles 30 to 36 must be put in their context, both in historical terms and in terms of their place in the European Community as a whole. To understand the historical context of these provisions one must glance at two quite separate organisations, the GATT and the OEEC.

The General Agreement on Tariffs and Trade[1] was concluded by 23 countries in October 1947 and came into force 'provisionally' in January 1948. Its object was and is to guard against protectionism in international trade. It was conceived as part of a much grander plan, the establishment of an International Trade Organisation which never

---

[1] See generally Jackson, *World Trade and the Law of GATT* (1969); Dam, *The GATT, Law and International Economic Organisation* (1970); McGovern *International Trade Regulation*, 2nd ed. (1986).

1

saw the light of day as it was blocked by the United States. Yet with the aid of a number of changes, the GATT has been able to operate on its own without its intended institutional base. While the GATT provides that tariffs are only to be reduced, it requires the outright abolition of quantitative restrictions: Article XI, entitled 'General Elimination of Quantitative Restrictions', provides in paragraph 1 that 'no prohibitions or restrictions other than duties, taxes or other charges, whether made effective through quotas, import or export licences or other measures, shall be instituted or maintained' between contracting parties.[2] The subsequent paragraphs and articles contain a number of exceptions to this rule, the most important of which is the balance of payments exception in Article XII. This permits a contracting party to adopt import restrictions necessary

'(i) to forestall the imminent threat of, or to stop a serious decline in its monetary reserves, or
(ii) in the case of a contracting party with very low monetary reserves, to achieve a reasonable rate of increase in its reserves'.

Without using the term 'measures of equivalent effect to quantitative restrictions', the GATT does in fact contain certain rules relating to such measures. These are to be found not only in Article XI already mentioned but also in Article III which states, *inter alia*, that measures on the sale, transport, distribution or use of products 'should not be applied to imported or domestic products so as to afford protection to domestic production'.

In practice these provisions have not been notably successful in reducing non-tariff barriers in international trade, but that is perhaps not surprising given that the parties to the agreement are a large number of States from all corners of the globe and are at varying stages of economic development. These parties now number over 80. In any case, although Member States of the European Community are parties to the GATT, they are no longer bound by it as between themselves.[3] Naturally, though, the Community must still observe the GATT in relations with third countries.[4]

---

[2] This is the provision of the GATT that was in point in the judgment of the European Court of Justice in the *International Fruit Case*, see n.4 below.

[3] See *EEC Commission* v. *Italy* and *Nederlandse Spoorwegen* cases and other sources cited in n.4 below.

[4] On the relationship between the GATT and the EEC see generally Case 10/61 *EEC Commission* v. *Italy* [1962] E.C.R. 1, [1962] C.M.L.R. 187 ('in matters governed by the EEC Treaty, that Treaty takes precedence over agreements concluded between Member States before its entry into force, including agreements made within the framework of GATT'); Cases 21–24/72 *International Fruit Company* v. *Produktschap voor Groenten en Fruit* [1972] E.C.R. 1219, [1975] 2 C.M.LR. 1; Case 9/73 *Schlüter* v. *Hauptzollamt Lörrach* [1973] E.C.R. 1135 and Case 38/75 *Nederlandse Spoorwegen* v. *Inspecteur der Invoerrechten* [1975] E.C.R. 1439, [1976] 1 C.M.L.R. 167; Case 112/80 *Dürbeck* v. *Hauptzollamt Frankfurt am Main-Flughafen* [1981] E.C.R. 1095, [1982] 3 C.M.L.R. 314; Case 245/81 *Edeka* v. *Germany* [1982] E.C.R. 2745; Case 266/81 *SIOT* v. *Italian Minister of Finance* [1983] E.C.R. 731, [1984] 2 C.M.L.R. 231; Case 193/85 *Cooperative Co-Frutta* v. *Amministrazione delle Finanze dello Stato* (judgment of 7 May 1987); casenotes by Ehlermann and Forman [1973] C.M.L.Rev. 336, Rideau [1973] C.D.E. 465 and Nicolaysen [1974] EuR 51; Bourgeois 'De GATT-Overeenkomst en het EEG-Verdrag']1974] S.E.W. 408; Petersmann 'Application of GATT by the Court of Justice of the European Communities' [1983] C.M.L.Rev. 397; (eds.) Hilf and Petersmann *GATT und Europäische Gemeinschaft* (1986).

2

The Organisation for European Economic Co-operation (OEEC)[5] was set up by a Convention signed shortly after the GATT, in April 1948. It was primarily intended to administer the aid provided under the Marshall Plan for the post-war economic reconstruction of Western Europe. Accordingly it included all non-communist European States other than Finland, with the Federal Republic of Germany and Spain not becoming members until 1949 and 1959 respectively. In addition, the United States and Canada became associate members in 1959 and Yugoslavia took part in certain activities of the Organisation as from 1957. Since the abolition of barriers to trade was seen as being intimately linked to Europe's economic recovery, the Council of the OEEC called on its members as from 1949 to make a series of fixed reductions of their import quotas, subject to certain escape clauses. This culminated in a decision of January 1955 to raise the basic minimum level of liberalisation to 90 per cent. of the value of imports, which decision is referred to in Articles 31 and 33(6) of the Treaty of Rome. By the end of 1956 overall liberalisation was over 85 per cent., so that much had been done to pave the way for the entry into force of the Treaty of Rome. Subsequently, in 1961, the Organisation was transformed into the Organisation for Economic Co-operation and Development (OECD) including the United States, Canada, Australia, New Zealand and Japan among its members.

The immediate forerunner of the EEC is the European Coal and Steel Community (ECSC), set up by the Treaty of Paris of 1951. On 1 January 1958 the ECSC was joined by the European Economic Community itself, established by the Treaty of Rome signed in March of the previous year, and by the European Atomic Energy Community (Euratom) set up by another Treaty of Rome of the same date. Each of these three Communities continues to exist as a separate legal entity functioning according to its own rules, but they are now run by the same institutions—the Commission, the Council of Ministers, the Parliament and the Court of Justice. In reality the EEC is by far the most important of the three Communities. This book is therefore confined to the EEC.[6] Thus throughout this book the term 'Treaty of Rome' will be used to designate the Treaty establishing the EEC, and not the Euratom Treaty.

Returning, then, to the Treaty of Rome itself, it is necessary to give a brief outline of its principal provisions so that Articles 30 to 36 can be seen in the context of the Treaty as a whole. As was stated at the beginning, one of the fundamental aims of the Treaty was to establish a customs union between the parties to it. According to a widely received definition, a customs union, in contrast to a free trade area, does not merely involve liberalisation of trade between the parties; it also entails the establishment of essentially uniform rules for goods

[5] See generally Palmer and Lambert, *European Unity—A Survey of the European Organisations* (1968).
[6] But see Chap. 2, n.1.

coming from third countries. Acceptance of this definition is to be found both in an opinion of the Permanent Court of International Justice of 1931[7] and in Article XXIV of the GATT. The terms of the Treaty of Rome are in line with this definition. Accordingly, the Treaty contains provisions for the establishment of a common customs tariff (Articles 18 to 29) and further provides for a common commercial policy with respect to trade with third countries (Article 113). Likewise, Article 9 stipulates that the provisions on the free movement of goods apply not only to products originating in Member States but also to goods originating in third countries but in free circulation in the Community. This means, in essence, that goods from third countries are assimilated to Community goods for this purpose when they have undergone all the appropriate import formalities and any customs duties payable have been levied.[8]

The Treaty provisions on the free movement of goods fall into two distinct sections—and a bit. Articles 12 to 17 lay down total prohibitions on customs duties and charges of equivalent effect between Member States, which fall outside the scope of this book. As already stated, Articles 30 to 36 cover quantitative restrictions and measures of equivalent effect on imports and exports between Member States. In addition Article 37 relates to trade restrictions linked to or forming part of State monopolies. However, it is far from clear to what extent Article 37 is independent of the other provisions on the free movement of goods, a matter to which Chapter XI of this book is devoted.

Nevertheless, the free movement of goods is only one of the 'four freedoms' existing between Member States within the Community. The others are the free movement of persons, covering both employed workers on the one hand (Article 48 to 51) and the establishment of self-employed persons and undertakings on the other (Articles 52 to 58); the free movement of services (Articles 59 to 66) and the free movement of capital (Articles 67 to 73), which is as yet the least advanced of the four.

Furthermore, Articles 92 to 94 of the Treaty govern aids granted by Member States. Article 92(1) states in effect that such aids are 'incompatible with the common market' in so far as they affect trade between Member States. However, by way of exception to this, Article 92(2) states that certain rather narrow categories of aid, such as compensation for natural disasters, 'shall be considered compatible with the Common Market'. Also the subsequent provisions lay down the conditions and procedures according to which the Commission or the Council may exempt other aids from the rule in Article 92(1). Next, Article 95 prohibits internal taxation which discriminates against

---

[7] On the 'customs system between Germany and Austria' Permanent Court of International Justice, the Compendium of Consultative Decrees, Directives and Opinions, Series A–B, no. 41, p.51.

[8] See paras. 2.12 et seq.

identical or competing imported products in favour of domestic products.

The Treaty also provides for a common agricultural policy (Articles 38 to 47) and a common transport policy (Articles 74 to 84). In addition, Articles 85 and 86 prohibit certain types of restrictive agreements and practices and the Commission is empowered to take action against undertakings infringing these prohibitions, if necessary by means of fines. More important for the purposes of this book are Articles 100 and 100A which relate to harmonisation and which are considered at length in Chapter XII of this book.

These provisions did not all take immediate effect when the Treaty came into force on 1 January 1958. Article 8 provides for a 12-year transitional period consisting of three four-year stages. Some Articles of the Treaty are expressed to take effect during this transitional period; this is the case with Article 34 prohibiting quantitative restrictions and measures of equivalent effect on exports, which took effect at the end of the first stage of the transitional period. Other Articles of the Treaty, such as Article 30 prohibiting the same measures on imports, were not expressed to take effect until the end of the transitional period. However, the Treaty also foresaw the possibility of accelerating certain measures and use was made of this. Furthermore, as the reader will be aware, Denmark, Ireland and the United Kingdom did not join the EEC until 1 January 1973. Their Act of Accession set out transitional measures, although certain provisions of the Treaty of Rome took effect at once. Greece acceded to the EEC on 1 January 1981 but also benefited from a similar system of transitional measures.[9] Finally, Spain and Portugal became members of the Community on 1 January 1986 and the transitional measures relating to their accession are still in force.[10] The whole question of the dates at which Articles 30 to 36 have taken and will take effect under the Treaty of Rome and the Acts of Accession will be discussed in greater detail in Chapters V and VI below.

Finally, the Single European Act which came into force on 1 July 1987 has effected some major amendments to the Treaty of Rome. In so far as is relevant, these are considered in Chapter XIII.

---

[9] See Treaty of Accession [1979] O.J. L291.
[10] See Treaty of Accession [1985] O.J. L302.

CHAPTER II

Scope: Subject matter

2.01 This is the first of three chapters dealing with the scope of the Treaty provisions on the free movement of goods between Member States, and more particularly Articles 30 to 36. It is the purpose of this chapter to examine first the concept of goods and then the transactions which benefit from these provisions. Consequently, the first part of this chapter is devoted to the definition of the term 'goods', while the second part is concerned with the concept of goods 'in free circulation' in the Member States. In the third section we shall see that the nationality of the owner of goods is irrelevant for the purposes of the rules on the free movement of goods. Lastly, in the fourth section we shall consider which transactions are governed by the Treaty provisions on the free movement of goods, and in particular the relationship between these rules and those relating to the other three freedoms enshrined in the Treaty—the free movement of workers, services and capital.

As already mentioned in Chapter I, the ECSC and Euratom Treaties fall outside the scope of this book. Article 232 EEC states that the provisions of the EEC Treaty shall not 'affect' the provisions of the ECSC, nor shall they 'derogate' from those of the Euratom Treaty. Therefore Articles 30 to 36 EEC do not apply to these Treaties. Consequently, 'coal' and 'steel' as defined by Annex I to the ECSC Treaty, and 'goods subject to the nuclear common market', as defined by Annex IV to the Euratom Treaty, will not be considered here.[1]

It should also be pointed out that the structure of Title I of the Treaty requires that 'goods' have the same meaning for purposes of Articles 12 to 17 (customs duties and taxes of equivalent effect) as for Articles 30 to 36 (quantitative restrictions and measures of equivalent effect). This is why some cases on Articles 12 to 17 will be discussed in this chapter, although those provisions fall outside the scope of this book.

---

[1] Arts. 4(a) ECSC and 93 Euratom prohibit quantitative restrictions on imports or exports of the products to which they apply respectively. Measures of equivalent effect are not expressly prohibited in those Treaties, although they are perhaps prohibited impliedly. On the ECSC Treaty see generally Cases 9 and 12/60 *Vloeberghs* v. *High Authority* [1961] E.C.R. 197, 36/83 *Mabanaft* v. *Hauptzollamt Emmerich* [1984] E.C.R. 2497 and 45/84R *EISA* v. *E.C. Commission* [1984] E.C.R. 1759.

I. THE MEANING OF 'GOODS'

2.02 The first point to notice is that, whereas in certain cases such as Article 9(1), the Treaty uses the term 'goods', in others such as Articles 9(2) and 10(1) the expression 'products' has been preferred. However, although a similar distinction is to be found in the French, Italian and Dutch[2] texts, this appears to owe more to a desire to ring the changes than to convey any difference of meaning[3]—indeed the German text uses the word *Waren* throughout.[4] Consequently, it is clear that the term 'goods' covers 'agricultural products' within the meaning of Article 38 of the Treaty, that is products listed in Annex II thereto.[5]

Furthermore, neither Article 30 nor Article 34—laying down the prohibition on quantitative restrictions respectively on imports and on exports—uses the terms 'goods' or 'products'. Instead they refer respectively to 'imports' and 'exports'. There can be little doubt that by this is meant imports and exports of 'goods'—an interpretation which is confirmed by the reference in Article 36 to 'restrictions on imports, exports or goods in transit'.

2.03 Nowhere in the Treaty is the concept of 'goods' defined. However, the Court of Justice has stated that

> 'by goods, within the meaning of [Article 9 of the Treaty], there must be understood products which can be valued in money and which are capable, as such, of forming the subject of commercial transactions.'

This definition was laid down in Case 7/68 *EEC Commission* v. *Italy*[6] in which the Italian Government, brought before the Court for failing to lift its duty on exports of articles of artistic, historic, archæological or ethnographic nature in accordance with Article 16, claimed that such articles did not constitute 'goods'. This submission was rejected by the Court, since art treasures fell within its definition of goods. Had the Court reached the opposite conclusion it would have deprived of all meaning the exception clause in Article 36 covering restrictions justified on the grounds of 'the protection of national treasures possessing artistic, historic or archæological value'.[7] As already pointed out, 'goods' must have the same meaning under Articles 30 to 36 as under Articles 12 to 17.

2.04 Quite naturally, in *EEC Commission* v. *Italy* the Court defined goods as products having commercial value. Yet refuse, if anything, has a negative value: people are paid to remove it. An

---

[2] The French text use *marchandises* and *produits*, the Italian *merci* and *prodotti* and the Dutch *goederen* and *produkten*.
[3] Campbell, *Common Market Law* (1969), Vol. 2, para. 2014.
[4] Likewise Danish only uses *varer*.
[5] See generally Chap. X.
[6] [1968] E.C.R. 423, [1969] C.M.L.R. 1.
[7] See paras. 8.59 *et seq.* below.

interesting case on this point arose in the United States in the following circumstances: in 1973 New Jersey passed a law prohibiting, with a few narrow exceptions, the importation of solid or liquid waste which originated or was collected outside the territorial limits of the State. Large cities in other States, and in particular Philadelphia and New York had been disposing of much of their refuse in certain privately-owned sites in New Jersey. The United States Supreme Court held the law unconstitutional in that it discriminated against refuse from other States.[8] If a similar case arose in the Community, it is submitted that refuse must be treated as goods even though it only has 'negative' value.[9]

2.05 Some further light was shed on the meaning of 'goods' in the *Sacchi*[10] case. Criminal proceedings had been brought against the operator of a private television station for allegedly infringing the Italian State monopoly over television broadcasting. One question put to the court was whether the principle of the free movement of goods applied to this activity.[11] In this connection it should be pointed out that the first paragraph of Article 60 states that 'services shall be considered "services" within the meaning of this Treaty where they are normally provided for remuneration, *in so far as they are not governed by the provisions relating to the freedom of movement for goods*, capital and persons'.[12] Thus the rules on the free movement of services and those on the free movement of goods cannot apply to the same aspect of a given measure.

The Court replied in the following terms:

> 'In the absence of express provision to the contrary in the Treaty, a television signal must, by reason of its nature, be regarded as provision of services.
>
> Although it is not ruled out that services normally provided for remuneration may come under the provisions relating to goods, such is however the case, as appears from Article 60, only in so far as they are governed by such provisions.
>
> It follows that the transmission of television signals, including those in the nature of advertisements, comes, as such, within the rules of the Treaty relating to services.

---

[8] *Philadelphia* v. *New Jersey* 437 U.S. 617, 98 S.Ct. 2531 (1978). For a comparison between the rules on the free movement of goods under the Treaty of Rome and under the American Constitution see Slot, *Technical and administrative obstacles to trade in the EEC* (1975); Roth, *Freier Warenverkehr und staatliche Regelungsgewalt in einem Gemeinsamen Markt* (1976); Kommers and Waelbroek, 'Legal Integration and the Free Movement of Goods: The American and European Experience' in *Integration through Law*, Vol. I, book 3.

[9] This conclusion is supported by the reference to waste and scrap in Art. 4(2)(i) of Reg. 802/68 on the definition of the origin of goods—see para. 2.10 below. However that regulation does not purport to define 'goods'.

[10] Case 155/73 [1974] E.C.R. 409, [1974] 2 C.M.L.R. 177. See March Hunnings [1975] *Journal of Business Law* 72.

[11] Other questions concerned the interpretation of various provisions including Arts. 37, 86 and 90. With respect to Art. 37 see para. 11.03 below.

[12] The italics are those of the author.

On the other hand, trade in material sound recordings, films, apparatus and other products used for the diffusion of television signals are subject to the rules relating to freedom of movement for goods'.[13]

Confirmation of this ruling is to be found in *Procureur du Roi* v. *Debauve*.[14] A number of individuals and undertakings engaged in the diffusion of cable television had been prosecuted before the Belgian courts for infringing the prohibition on television advertising in Belgium. Asked by the Liège court to rule whether this prohibition contravened the Treaty provisions on the freedom to provide services, the Court began by stating that:

'Before examining those questions the Court recalls that it has already ruled in its judgment of 30 April 1974 (Case 155/73 *Sacchi* [1974] E.C.R. 490), that the broadcasting of television signals, including those in the nature of advertisements, comes, as such, within the rules of the Treaty relating to services. There is no reason to treat the transmission of such signals by cable television any differently'.[15]

March Hunnings[16] criticises the Court's ruling on this point in both *Sacchi* and *Debauve*. In his view both types of broadcasting are movements of goods:

'We are faced in reality with two different forms of transportation, the difference being that between sending a photographic print or matrix from the *Financial Times* in London to its second printing plant in Frankfurt by post or special messenger and sending it by wireless or teleprinter or fax. The end result is exactly the same: the physical object in London has been transported into the hands of the recipient in Frankfurt.'

2.06 In *R.* v. *Thompson, Johnson and Woodiwiss*[17] the Court was called upon to distinguish the concept of goods from those of capital and current payments. Articles 67 to 73 of the Treaty govern the free movement of capital between Member States 'to the extent necessary to ensure the proper functioning of the common market'[18] without defining what is meant by 'capital'. However, the Council has adopted directives for the implementation of Article 67[19] and,

---

[13] Paras. 6 and 7 of the judgment.

[14] Case 52/79 [1980] E.C.R. 833, [1981] 2 C.M.L.R. 362; Bennett [1980] E.L.Rev. 224.

[15] Para. 8 of the judgment.

[16] [1980] C.M.L.Rev. 564.

[17] Case 7/78 [1978] E.C.R. 2247, [1979] 1 C.M.L.R. 47; Prout [1979] E.L.Rev. 187.

[18] By reason of this qualification the effect of the Treaty provisions on free movement of capital is more limited than that of the other three freedoms—goods, persons and services. Furthermore, the principle of the free movement of capital is subject to a wide variety of exceptions contained, for instance, in Arts. 68(3), 70(2) and 73. See generally van Ballegooijen, 'Free Movement of Capital in the European Economic Community' [1976] 2 *Legal Issues of European Integration 1*; Seidel, 'Escape Clauses in European Community Law' [1978] C.M.L.Rev. 283; Mègret and Sarmet in *Le droit de la Communauté économique européenne* (1971) Vol. 3; Kiemel in Groeben, Boeckh, Thiesing, Ehlermann, *Kommentar zum EWG-Vertrag* (1983) Vol. 1, 704; Campbell, *op. cit.* n.3 above, Vol. 3, 797; Oliver, 'Free Movement of Capital between Member States: Article 67(1) EEC and the Implementing Directives' [1984] E.L.Rev. 401.

[19] Dir. of 11 May 1960 ([1960] O.J. Spec.Ed. 921) amended by Dir. 62/21 of 18 December 1962 ([1963] O.J. Spec.Ed. 62). Since the judgment in *Thompson* further amendments have been effected by Dirs. 85/583 ([1985] O.J. L372/39) and 86/566 ([1986] O.J. L332/22).

although these directives do not purport to give a definition of 'capital' either, they incorporate a list of capital movements. Current payments on the other hand are governed by Article 106, which requires Member States to 'authorise, in the currency of the Member State in which the creditor or the beneficiary resides, any payments connected with the movement of goods, services or capital' to the extent that such movement has been liberalised pursuant to the Treaty.[20] Such payments are not further defined in the Treaty either.

In *Thompson* the three defendants were charged before the English courts with importing Krugerrands and exporting silver alloy coins between April and June 1975 contrary to various provisions of English law. The coins fell into three categories:

(i) Krugerrands (which were legal tender only in South Africa),
(ii) British silver alloy coins minted before 1947 which were still legal tender,
(iii) British silver alloy half-crowns minted before 1947 which, although no longer legal tender, could be exchanged at the Bank of England and were protected from destruction other than by the State on the grounds that the State enjoyed a right akin to a property right in them.

In each case the commodity value of the coins far exceeded their face value. When this case came before it on appeal by the defendants, the Court of Appeal referred four questions under Article 177 to ascertain whether the import and export restrictions were compatible with Community law. It sought to do so essentially by asking whether the coins were 'capital' within the meaning of Articles 67 to 73, and in any case whether these restrictions were justified by Article 36.

The difficulty posed by these questions is underlined by the fact that the first directive implementing Article 67[21] includes imports and exports of gold and 'means of payment of every kind' in the list of capital movements, while the Common Customs Tariff[22] mentions coins which are not collectors' pieces (heading number 72–01), as well as coins which are collectors' pieces (heading number 99–05), and banknotes (heading number 49–07).

2.07 Many of the intervenors before the Court deduced from this that the decision as to which Treaty provisions to apply depended not on the nature of the items, but on the purpose for which they

---

[20] Börner, 'Rechtsfragen des Zahlungs- und Kapitalverkehrs in der EWG'. [1966] EuR 97; Zuleeg in Groeben, *etc.*, n.18 above, Vol. I at 1815; Mègret, 1976, n.18 above; see also paras. 6.29 and 7.29.

[21] Dir. of 11 May 1960, n.19 above.

[22] The Common Customs Tariff is brought up to date annually. For 1987 see Regs. 3618/86 ([1986] O.J. L345). For 1988, see Reg. 2658/87 ([1987] O.J. L256/1) instituting the Combined Nomenclature.

were imported—though as to the exact criterion to be applied there were distinct differences between those intervenors.

However, the Court appears to have concentrated rather on the nature of the articles, since it ruled as follows:

> 'The aim of Article 106 is to ensure that the necessary monetary transfers may be made for the liberalisation of movements of capital and for the free movement of goods, services and persons.
>
> It must be inferred from this that under the system of the Treaty means of payment are not to be regarded as goods falling within the purview of Articles 30 to 37 of the Treaty.
>
> Silver alloy coins which are legal tender in a Member State are, by their very nature, to be regarded as means of payment and it follows that their transfer does not fall within the provisions of Articles 30 to 37 of the Treaty.
>
> Although doubts may be entertained on the question whether Krugerrands are to be regarded as means of legal payment it can nevertheless be noted that on the money markets of those Member States which permit dealings in these coins they are treated as being equivalent to currency.
>
> Their transfer must consequently be designated as a monetary transfer which does not fall within the provisions of the said Articles 30 to 37.
>
> Having regard to the abovementioned considerations it is unnecessary to deal with the question under what circumstances the transfer of these two categories of coins might possibly be designated either as a movement of capital or as a current payment.
>
> Question 1(c) refers to silver alloy coins of a Member State, which have been legal tender in that State and which, although no longer legal tender, are protected as coinage from destruction.
>
> Such coins cannot be regarded as means of payment within the meaning stated above, with the result that they can be designated as goods falling within the system of Articles 30 to 37 of the Treaty.'

Thus it held that the coins in categories (i) and (ii) were not goods, whereas those in category (iii) were goods.[23]

In an area that is already beset with conceptual difficulties, it is perhaps unfortunate that the Court chose to refer to concepts which it did not define. Presumably the notion of 'means of payment' is wider than that of legal tender, but how wide is it? Is 'means of legal payment' the same as 'means of payment'? And what is meant by being 'treated as being equivalent to currency'?

The only clear proposition that can be distilled from this judgment is that coins which are still legal tender in a Member State are not 'goods'. One might also deduce from the passage relating to Krugerrands that coins which are legal tender in a third country are not 'goods' either.

Moreover, it would seem that the ruling in *Thompson* would apply equally to banknotes. This view is perhaps supported by *Casati*[24] where banknotes denominated in Deutschmarks were also

---

[23] As to the third category, see para. 8.30 below.
[24] Case 203/80 [1981] E.C.R. 2595, [1982] 1 C.M.L.R. 365.

in effect held to constitute 'means of payment' for the purpose of the Directive implementing Article 67.[25]

2.08 We can summarise the Court's case law on the meaning of 'goods' as follows:

> 'Goods' means 'products which can be valued in money and which are capable, as such, of forming the subject of commercial transactions'. Neither television broadcasts nor 'means of payment' are 'goods.'

II. GOODS 'ORIGINATING IN THE MEMBER STATES' AND GOODS FROM THIRD COUNTRIES IN 'FREE CIRCULATION' IN THE COMMUNITY

2.09 Article 9(2) of the Treaty stipulates that the provisions on the free movement of goods, including Articles 30 to 36, apply to 'products originating in Member States and to products coming from third countries which are in free circulation in Member States.[26] Each of these two concepts will be examined in turn.

As to the territorial extent of the Member States for this purpose, the reader is referred to Chapter III of this book.

A. Goods originating in the Member States

2.10 This concept is nowhere defined in the Treaty. However, assistance is to be derived from Regulation 802/68[27] defining the concept of the origin of goods. Article 1 of this Regulation states that the definition it lays down shall apply for the purposes of:

> '(a) the uniform application of the Common Customs Tariff, of quantitative restrictions, and of all other measures adopted, in relation to the importation of goods, by the Community or by Member States;

---

[25] The sequel is of some interest. Naturally, on the basis of the Court of Justice's ruling the Court of Appeal dismissed the defendants' appeal. However, events did not turn out very well either for a German company called AGOSI (Allgemeine Gold- und Silberscheidean-stalt), which claimed to be the owner of the Krugerrands and to have been induced to part with them to Thompson and Johnson by fraud on the part of these two. AGOSI therefore brought an action before the English courts against the British Customs and Excise Commissioners seeking a declaration that they were entitled to the return of these Krugerrands, which the Commissioners had confiscated. AGOSI claimed, *inter alia*, that the Krugerrands were not 'goods' for the purposes of the Customs and Excise Act 1952, s.44, which provided that: 'Where . . . any imported goods are concealed or packed in any manner appearing to be intended to deceive an officer, those goods shall be liable to forfeiture'. On an analysis of customs legislation since 1833 the Court of Appeal found, however, that 'goods' must be construed as including gold and silver bullion and coin, and therefore Krugerrands. On this and other grounds AGOSI's action failed: *Allgemeine Gold- und Silberscheideanstalt* v. *Customs and Excise Commissioners* [1980] 2 W.L.R. 555, [1980] 1 C.M.L.R. 488. Nevertheless it does not appear that the Court of Appeal's judgment conflicts in any way with that of the Court of Justice in *Thompson*.

[26] Matters relating to quantitative restrictions and measures of equivalent effect in direct trade between the Community and third countries fall outside this book.

[27] [1968] J.O. L148/1 as amended.

(b) the uniform application of all measures adopted, in relation to the exportation of goods, by the Community or by Member States;

(c) the preparation and issue of certificates of origin.'

The concept of origin is defined principally in Articles 4 and 5 of the Regulation. Article 4 provides as follows:

'1. Goods wholly obtained or produced in one country shall be considered as originating in that country.

2. The expression "goods wholly obtained or produced in one country" means:

(a) mineral products extracted within its territory;

(b) vegetable products harvested therein;

(c) live animals born and raised therein;

(d) products derived from live animals raised therein;

(e) products of hunting or fishing carried on therein;

(f) products of sea-fishing and other products taken from the sea by vessels registered or recorded in that country and flying its flag;

(g) goods obtained on board factory ships from the products referred to in (f) originating in that country, if such factory ships are registered or recorded in that country and flying its flag;

(h) products taken from the sea-bed or beneath the sea-bed outside territorial waters, if that country has, for the purposes of exploitation, exclusive rights to such soil or subsoil;

(i) waste and scrap products derived from manufacturing operations and used articles, if they were collected therein and are only fit for the recovery of raw materials;

(j) goods which are produced therein exclusively from goods referred to in subparagraphs (a) to (i) or from their derivatives, at any stage of production.'

Article 5 provides:

'A product in the production of which two or more countries were concerned shall be regarded as originating in the country in which the last substantial process or operation that is economically justified was performed, having been carried out in an undertaking equipped for the purpose, and resulting in the manufacture of a new product or representing an important stage of manufacture.'

By virtue of Article 3 these provisions do not apply to the petroleum products listed in Annex I to the Regulation. Furthermore, special rules have been adopted in relation to particular products.[28] The picture is further complicated by the fact that a large number of agreements concluded by the Community both with developing and developed countries contain special rules of origin.[29]

2.11 Notwithstanding what has already been said, it should not be thought that all goods originating in Member States are necessarily in free circulation in the Community. Thus goods produced in the

---

[28] On rules of origin see generally Forrester, 'EEC Customs law: Rules of Origin and Preferential Duty Treatment' [1980] E.L.Rev. 167 and 257.

[29] For instance, the agreements with the EFTA countries, *e.g.* Austria ([1972] J.O. L300/3, 38, as amended), with certain non-EFTA Mediterranean countries (*e.g.* Cyprus [1977] O.J. L339/19, as amended), and with the African, Caribbean and Pacific countries (Protocol 1 to Lomé III [1986] O.J. L86/98 and [1986] O.J. L292/52).

Community under inward processing relief arrangements provided for by Council Regulation 1999/85[30] are not in free circulation; if they are put into free circulation, those arrangements are discharged (Article 18(2)(e)). Also, once goods having Community origin have been exported from the Community in the normal way[31] they cease to be in free circulation in the Community.[32]

B. Goods from third countries in free circulation in the Community

2.12   As regards this second category of goods benefiting from free movement within the Community according to Article 9(2), Article 10(1) of the Treaty stipulates that:

> 'Products coming from a third country shall be considered to be in free circulation in a Member State if the import formalities have been complied with and any customs duties or charges having equivalent effect which are payable have been levied in that Member State, and if they have not benefited from a total or partial drawback of such duties or charges.'

Various commentators have suggested that these conditions are fulfilled if the customs duties payable have merely been determined, whether or not they have been paid.[33] This is in fact permitted by Council Directive 79/695[34] which harmonises procedures for the release of goods into free circulation. Article 13(1) of that Directive provides that:

> 'the customs authority may release the goods for free circulation only when import duties have been paid or guaranteed or payment of them has been deferred under the conditions laid down in Directive 78/453.'

Article 2(1) of Council Directive 78/453[35] on the deferred payment of import and export duties provides:

> 'Subject to the applicant giving appropriate security, the form of which shall be specified by the competent authorities of the Member States, they shall . . . grant him deferment of the import duties . . . for which he is liable . . .'

Article 20 of Commission Directive 82/57,[36] which implements Directive 79/695, goes one step further. This provision enables customs authorities to release goods into free circulation pending the outcome of checks which they have undertaken with a view to assessing the amount of import duties. No distortion of trade can

---

[30] [1985] O.J. L188/1.
[31] The procedures are laid down by Council Dir. 81/177 ([1981] O.J. L83/40) implemented by Commission Dir. 82/347 ([1982] O.J. L156/1).
[32] However, Council Reg. 754/76 ([1976] O.J. L89/1) as amended permits such goods to be returned to the Community in certain circumstances without payment of customs duties.
[33] Waelbroeck in *Le droit de la Communauté économique europénne* (1970) Vol. I, 43; Ehlermann, n.18 above.
[34] [1979] O.J. L205/19. The dir. is based on Art. 100. The Member States were not bound to implement it until 1 July 1982 (Art. 27 as amended by Dir. 81/853 ([1981] O.J. L319/1)). The same applies to the Commission's implementing directive, Dir. 82/57 ([1982] O.J. L28/38), subsequently amended by Dir. 83/371 ([1983] O.J. L204/63).
[35] [1978] O.J. L146/19.
[36] See n.34 above.

result, since security must have been lodged and the customs authorities will have in their possession all the information necessary to assess the amount of the duties. Consequently, it is submitted that Article 20 is in no way at variance with Article 10(1) of the Treaty, a succinct provision which in any case does not purport to provide in detail for every hypothetical situation.

2.13   The term 'drawback' in Article 10(1) means a repayment or reduction of the import duties payable. Where Community legislation has provided a suspension or reduction of all goods of a particular description and origin, the full amount of the duty is not payable at all. Consequently, in those circumstances no drawback has been granted. Similarly, where for any reason sums paid to the customs authorities exceed the amount lawfully due and the excess is repaid to the importer,[37] no drawback is granted.

Indeed, it is arguable that the final limb of Article 10(1) relates only to drawbacks granted by the Member States. The Member States have long since lost the power to grant drawbacks except when they have been specifically empowered to do so by Community legislation. It would follow on this view that the final limb of Article 10(1) has ceased to have effect. Whether or not that is so, it seems clear that goods continue to be in free circulation even if the import duties on them have been repaid or remitted on equitable grounds under Article 13 of Council Regulation 1430/79.[38]

2.14   What if there has been fraud or error? Where the goods have never been cleared through customs at all, then presumably they are not in free circulation even if they have been mistakenly treated as being so. On the other hand, where the appropriate customs formalities have been completed but the amount of duties has been incorrectly assessed, it would seem that the goods are in free circulation but the unpaid sums are still due. They may be recovered by the customs authorities in accordance with Council Regulation 1697/79[39] on the post clearance recovery of import duties. At all events, as in all customs cases the utmost importance will be attached to the certificates issued in respect of the goods.

2.15   As required by Article 10(2), first sub-paragraph, the Commission adopted a number of measures on the methods of administrative co-operation for applying this provision.[40] As required by the second sub-paragraph of Article 10(2) the Commission also laid down

---

[37] Art. 2 of Council Reg. 1430/79 on the repayment or remission of import or export duties ([1979] O.J. L175/1) as last amended by Council Reg. 3799/86 ([1986] O.J. L352/19).
[38] See n.37 above.
[39] [1979] O.J. L197/1, as amended.
[40] See in particular the decs. of 5 December 1960 ([1960] O.J. Spec.Ed. 29/61), 17 July 1962 ([1962] O.J. Spec.Ed. 2140/62), 64/503 ([1964] O.J. Spec.Ed. 2293/64), 70/41 ([1970] O.J. Spec.Ed. L13/13), 71/14 ([1971] O.J. Spec.Ed. L6/35).

provisions applicable, as regards trade between Member States, to goods originating in another Member State in whose manufacture products have been used on which the exporting Member State has not levied the appropriate customs duties or charges of equivalent effect or which have benefited from a total or partial drawback of such duties or charges.[41] However, these measures have all ceased to have effect and have been superseded by Community customs legislation adopted on the basis of other provisions.[42]

2.16   Once goods have been put into free circulation in the Community, what is the consequence of their having that status? The assimilation of goods from third countries put into free circulation in a Member State to goods originating in the Community was categorically underlined by the Court in *Donckerwolcke* v. *Procureur de la République*[43] in the following terms:

> 'It appears from Article 9 that, as regards free circulation of goods within the Community, products entitled to "free circulation" are definitively and wholly assimilated to products originating in Member States.
>
>   The result of this assimilation is that the provisions of Article 30 concerning the elimination of quantitative restrictions and all measures having equivalent effect are applicable without distinction to products originating in the Community and to those which were put into free circulation in any one of the Member States, irrespective of the actual origin of the products'.[44]

A particularly clear illustration of this principle is to be found in Case 288/83 *E.C. Commission* v. *Ireland*[45] where it was held that the defendant State had infringed Article 30 by imposing an import licensing system for potatoes originating in Cyprus but in free circulation in the United Kingdom.

2.17   However, this principle does not apply to all matters, as the Court emphasised in the *EMI Records* v. *CBS*[46] cases. There, the facts were as follows: until 1917 one undertaking had held the 'Columbia' trade mark for records both in the United States and in Europe. That year saw the first of a series of transactions which resulted in CBS holding the trade mark in the United States and EMI owning it in all the Member States of the Community. EMI brought proceedings against CBS in the United Kingdom, Denmark and West Germany, giving rise to three parallel references. The Court held that Article 30 had no bearing on this question, since

---

[41] See, in particular, dec. of 16 December 1958 ([1958] J.O. 614) dec. of 28 June 1960 ([1960] J.O. 933), Dec. 63/637 ([1963] J.O. 2782), Dec. 68/284 ([1968] J.O. L167/10).
[42] *E.g.* Council Reg. 1999/85 (n.30 above); also Council Regs. 222/77 and 223/77 ([1977] O.J. L38), as amended, on the Community transit procedure.
[43] Case 41/76 [1976] E.C.R. 1921 at 1933; [1977] 2 C.M.L.R. 535 at 550.
[44] For the application of that principle in the *Donckerwolcke* case see para. 9.35 below.
[45] [1985] E.C.R. 1761, [1985] 3 C.M.L.R. 152; see Usher 'The Single Market and Goods imported from Third Countries' [1986] Y.E.L. 159 at 179.
[46] Case 51/75 [1976] E.C.R. 811, [1976] 2 C.M.L.R. 235; Case 86/75 [1976] E.C.R. 871, [1976] 2 C.M.L.R. 235; Case 96/75 [1976] E.C.R. 913, [1976] 2 C.M.L.R. 235; see para. 8.129 below.

no movement of goods between Member States was involved. It rejected the defendants' reliance on the principle of the assimilation of third country goods in free circulation in the Member States, in the following terms:

> 'Since [Articles 9(2) and 10(1)] only refer to the effects of compliance with customs formalities and paying customs duties and charges having equivalent effect, they cannot be interpreted as meaning that it would be sufficient for products bearing a mark applied in a third country and imported into the Community to comply with the customs formalities in the first Member State where they were imported in order to enable them to be marketed in the Common Market as a whole in contravention of the rules relating to the protection of the mark.'[47]

It is submitted that Advocate General Warner's rather drier response to this particular argument of the defendants is more accurate:

> 'The argument of the defendants is, as I understand it, that once records made in America and bearing the mark Columbia have been cleared through customs in a Member State, they are, provided they have not benefited from a drawback, to be assimilated to records originating in a Member State. So they are. But I do not see how this assists the defendants. If they were to manufacture similar records in a Member State, they would not thereby render themselves entitled to market them in infringement of EMI Records Limited's registered marks, either in that Member State or in any other.'[48]

Nevertheless the Court's ruling on this point is of interest as it may eventually build on it, perhaps in the context of technical standards.[49]

2.18   Also, certain provisions create exceptions to the rule that goods originating in third countries are to be treated as Community goods once the appropriate customs formalities have been completed. The following account does not include transitional provisions[50]:

> (i) The most important of these is Article 115 of the Treaty which applies where the execution of national commercial policy measures is threatened by 'deflection of trade' or where 'differences between such measures [of national commercial policy] lead to economic difficulties in one or more of the Member States'. In such circumstances, the Commission 'shall authorise Member States to take the necessary protective measures, the conditions and details of which it shall determine'.

This provision is considered at length in Chapter IX of this book.[51] Suffice it to say here that, although this provision is intended to become gradually redundant as purely national measures of commercial policy are replaced by the common commercial policy based on uniform principles in accordance with Article 113 EEC,

---

[47] Paras. 16, 16 and 9 of the respective judgments.
[48] At 860.
[49] See para. 6.60 below.
[50] *E.g.* Arts. 109–119 of the first Act of Accession, since lapsed.
[51] Para. 9.21 *et seq.*

recourse to this exception has continued unabated in the last few years.

2.19   (ii) A further exception is contained in the Protocol on German Internal Trade[52] annexed to the EEC Treaty, Article 1 of this Protocol provides as follows:

> 'Since trade between the German authorities subject to the Basic Law for the Federal Republic of Germany and the German territories in which the Basic Law does not apply is a part of German internal trade, the application of this Treaty in Germany requires no change in the treatment currently accorded this trade.'

This has been taken to mean that the Community may not impose or lift restrictions on trade between the two Germanies,[53] whether in the form of tariff or non-tariff barriers.

However, the important provision for present purposes is in Article 3 of the Protocol, which reads:

> 'Each Member State may take appropriate measures to prevent any difficulties arising for it from trade between another Member State and the German territories in which the Basic Law for the Federal Republic of Germany does not apply.'

It seems clear that goods imported from the German Democratic Republic under the Protocol are in principle in free circulation[54] so that Article 3 constitutes an exception to Article 9 EEC. It is clear from its wording that this exception can be applied even before difficulties in trade actually exist, to prevent such difficulties arising.[55] Arguably, national measures under Article 3 do not require the approval of the Commission and a Member State taking such measures is not even required to inform the Commission. On the other hand, in accordance with general principles of Community law, it may be assumed that measures will not be 'appropriate' if they are more restrictive than is necessary to achieve their legitimate purpose.[56]

2.20   (iii) Another exception is contained in the Protocol to the EEC Treaty on goods originating in and coming from

---

[52] Tomuschat, 'Rechtsfragen zum Handelspolitischen Arrangement zwischen der EWG und den sich um dem Beitritt bewerbenden Staaten' [1969] EuR 287; Zuleeg 'Grundvertrag und EWG-Protokoll über den innerdeutschen Handel' [1973] EuR 209; Ehlermann, Kupper, Lambrecht, Ollig, *Handelspartner DDR—Innerdeutsche Wirtschaftsbeziehungen* (1975); Cases 14/74 *Norddeutsches Vieh- und Fleischkontor* v. *Hauptzollamt Hamburg-Jonas* [1974] E.C.R. 899, 23/79 *Geflügelschlachterei Freystadt* v. *Hauptzollamt Hamburg-Jonas* [1979] E.C.R. 2789 and 314/85 *Foto-Frost* v. *Hauptzollamt Lübeck-Ost* [1988] 3 C.M.L.R. 57; written questions 283/79 ([1980] O.J. C105/1) and 672/84 ([1985] O.J. C19/8).

[53] Ehlermann, *op. cit.* n.52 above, at 245. However, it would appear that Community legislation harmonising the conditions under which goods may be sold in the Community (see Chap. XII) can apply to imports from the GDR into the Federal Republic. The same would appear to apply to veterinary legislation.

[54] Ehlermann, *op. cit.* n.52 at 250.

[55] Ehlermann, *op. cit.* n.52 at 250.

[56] See para. 9.01.

certain countries and enjoying special treatment when imported into a Member State. This Protocol provides in Article 1 that the application of the EEC Treaty

> 'shall not require any alteration in the customs treatment applicable, at the time of the entry into force of this Treaty, to imports: (a) into the Benelux countries of goods originating in and coming from . . . the Netherlands Antilles . . .'

The other countries and territories in the list all have traditional ties with the Netherlands, France or Italy as the case may be. Article 2 of the Protocol stipulates that

> 'goods imported into a Member State and benefiting from the treatment referred to above shall not be considered to be in free circulation in that State within the meaning of Article 10 of this Treaty when re-exported to another Member State.'

This Protocol is probably obsolete. Certainly it no longer applies to the Netherlands Antilles or Surinam.[57] In addition, many of the third countries in question such as Morocco and Tunisia have now concluded agreements with the Community. At least as far as goods covered by such agreements are concerned the Protocol would appear to have been superseded or suspended.[58]

2.21   (iv) A further exception is contained in the Protocol to the first Act of Accession on the import of New Zealand butter and cheese into the United Kingdom. Article 1(4) of that Protocol provides that the butter and cheese imported into the United Kingdom in accordance with that Protocol 'may not become the subject of intra-Community trade'. With regard to cheese the arrangements laid down by the Protocol lapsed on 31 December 1977 (Article 5(3)). On the other hand, the Council has exercised its powers under Article 5(2) to extend the arrangements for butter imports beyond that date.[59]

2.22   (v) Lastly, an exception is contained in Article 4(2)(a) of the Protocol on the Canary Islands and Ceuta and Melilla which is annexed to the Act of Accession of Spain and Portugal.[60] As explained below,[61] according to Article 1 goods originating in those territories are in essence assimilated to goods from third countries. Article 4(2)(a) stipulates that bananas originating in the Canaries shall be exempt from customs duties when 'released for free circulation'

---

[57] See paras. 3.02 and 3.03 below and the notes thereto.
[58] In Case 26/69 *EEC Commission* v. *France* [1970] E.C.R. 565, [1970] C.M.L.R. 444, which concerned this Protocol, the Court more or less tacitly accepted that such agreements could have this effect.
[59] See now Reg. 2335/86 ([1986] O.J. L203/7).
[60] [1985] O.J. L302/400.
[61] Para. 3.03.

in the rest of Spain (other than Ceuta and Melilla). It then goes on to provide that 'bananas imported under the abovementioned arrangements may not be deemed to be in free circulation in the said part of Spain within the meaning of Article 10 of the EEC Treaty when they are reconsigned to another Member State.[62]

III. THE NATIONALITY OF THE OWNER

2.23 It is only the status of the goods and not the nationality of their owner which is the determining factor for the application of the Treaty provisions on the free movement of goods. This has been emphasised by the Court in relation to the prohibition on charges of equivalent effect in Article 12:

> '. . . The Treaty prohibits any pecuniary charge on imports and exports between Member States, irrespective of the nationality of the traders who might be placed at a disadvantage by such measures. Thus, in applying these provisions, there is no justification for a distinction to be made according to whether the measures in question adversely affect certain Member States and their nationals, or all the citizens of the Community, or only the nationals of the Member State which was responsible for the measures in question': *Sociaalfonds voor Diamantarbeiders* v. *Brachfeld*.[63]

This statement also holds good for Articles 30 to 36.

In highly exceptional circumstances it may be otherwise when the owner of the goods is a national of a third state enjoying less than cordial relations with one or more Member States. It might then be possible for the Member States to have recourse to Article 224 to prohibit imports or exports in view of such tense relations.[64]

IV. THE TRANSACTIONS COVERED

2.24 The first two parts of this chapter considered what items benefit from the Treaty provisions governing the free movement of goods between Member States and in particular Articles 30 to 36. This section is concerned with the relationship between these provisions and those relating to the other three freedoms enshrined in the Treaty—the free movement of workers (Articles 48 *et seq.*), the freedom of establishment (Articles 52–58), the free provision of services (Articles 59–66) and the free movement of capital (Articles 67–73). Lastly, we shall examine whether goods moving between Member States for non-economic purposes enjoy the benefit of the provisions on the free movement of goods.

[62] As to Canary pineapples, see Art. 7 of Council Reg. 1391/87 concerning certain adjustments to the arrangements applied to the Canary Islands ([1987] O.J. L133/5).
[63] Cases 2–3/69 [1969] E.C.R. 211, [1969] C.M.L.R. 335, paras. 24–26 of the judgment; see generally Oliver 'Non-EEC nationals and the Treaty of Rome' [1985] Y.E.L. 57.
[64] Para. 9.56.

2.25 First, however, it is helpful to set out certain movements which clearly fall under the provisions on the free movement of goods. As the reader will be aware, the classic case involves goods passing from one Member State to another to be sold in the second State.[65]

The same applies where the goods merely transit through the second Member State to be sold in another Member State or even outside the Community. This can be deduced from the fact that transit is simply a particular type of importation and of exportation, but it is also expressly stated in Article 36, which begins: 'The provisions of Articles 30 to 34 shall not preclude prohibitions or restrictions on imports, exports or goods in transit . . .'

Equally, the Treaty provisions on the free movement of goods surely apply where an individual resident in one Member State seeks to import into it goods he has bought in another Member State. This point was made by Advocate General Warner in *R. v. Henn and Darby*[66]:

> 'There is trade between Member States [for the purposes of Articles 30 to 36] when an individual imports into a Member State for his own use goods that he has bought in another Member State.'

Similarly, the Commission has formally expressed the view that 'the provisions of the EEC Treaty relating to the free movement of goods clearly also apply to goods and catalogues sent by mail order firms from one Member State to another'.[67]

2.26 Again, the same applies when goods are imported from one Member State to another, where they were produced or where they have already been put on the market. In other words, the provisions on the free movement of goods apply to re-imports. This emerges clearly from *Deutsche Grammophon* v. *Metro*[68] where it was held to be contrary to Article 30 to exercise rights akin to copyright to prevent the reimportation by a parallel importer of records manufactured in Germany; the records had been reimported with a view to undercutting prices imposed by the manufacturer by means of a retail price maintenance scheme. However, in the specific circumstances of *Leclerc* v. *Au Blé Vert*,[69] which concerned resale price maintenance for books, the Court ruled that Article 30 could not be invoked with respect to goods 'exported for the sole purpose of reimportation in order to circumvent legislation of the type at

---

[65] As to transactions contrived to speculate in currency or to export capital from a Member State, see paras. 6.29, 7.29 and 8.21 below.

[66] Case 34/79 [1979] E.C.R. 3795, [1980] 1 C.M.L.R. 346.

[67] Written question 1079/84 ([1985] O.J. L62/38). Also, in Case 50/85 *Schloh* v. *Auto Contrôle Technique* [1987] 1 C.M.L.R. 450, Art. 30 was held to apply where goods had been imported by an individual for his own use. However, the Court did not expressly address this question.

[68] Case 78/70 [1971] E.C.R. 487, [1971] C.M.L.R. 631.

[69] Case 229/83 [1985] E.C.R. 1, [1985] 2 C.M.L.R. 296; see para. 7.75 below.

issue'. As has been pointed out,[70] it is not easy to reconcile the two cases: the only apparent difference between them is that in *Deutsche Grammophon* the resale price maintenance was imposed by the manufacturer, whereas in *Leclerc* it was imposed by the State.

2.27   Having thus outlined the principal movements of goods to which Articles 30 to 36 apply, the relationship between these provisions and Articles 59 to 66 on the free provision of services may now be considered. The only stipulation in the Treaty as to this relationship is to the effect that the provisions on services only apply when those on goods do not: Article 60.[71]

2.28   One area in which this question has arisen is advertising. The Court has already delivered the following rulings with relation to advertising:

On the one hand, the Court has held in the *Sacchi*[72] and *Debauve*[73] cases considered earlier in this chapter that prohibitions or restrictions on television advertising fell to be considered under Articles 59 to 66.

On the other hand, Article 2(3)(m) of Commission Directive 70/50[74] lists as measures of equivalent effect within the meaning of Article 30 those measures which 'prohibit or limit publicity in respect of imported products only, or totally or partially confine publicity to domestic products only'. In keeping with this, in Case 152/78 *E.C. Commission* v. *France*,[75] the Commission maintained that certain French provisions restricting the advertising of alcoholic drinks contravened Article 30 in that they fell more heavily on imported drinks than on French drinks although such a distinction was not justified on health grounds. Without adverting to Article 59, the Court stated:

> 'As a preliminary point it should be observed that there is no dispute between the parties on whether a restriction on freedom of advertising for certain products may constitute a measure having an effect equivalent to a quantitative restriction within the meaning of Article 30 of the Treaty. Although such a restriction does not directly affect imports it is however capable of restricting their volume owing to the fact that it affects the marketing prospects for the imported products. The issue in point is therefore whether the prohibitions and restrictions on advertising laid down by the French legislation place a handicap on the importation of alcoholic products from other Member States'.[76]

It is submitted that there is no contradiction here: in the *Sacchi* and *Debauve* cases the restriction was more closely connected with

---

[70] Hornsby 'Public and Private Resale Price Maintenance Systems in the Publishing Sector: the Need for Equal Treatment in European Law' [1985] E.L.R. 381 at 394.
[71] Para. 2.05 above.
[72] See n.10 above.
[73] See n.14 above.
[74] [1970] O.J. L13/29, see para. 6.03 below.
[75] [1980] E.C.R. 2299, [1981] 2 C.M.L.R. 743.
[76] Para. 11 of the judgment.

services, while in *E.C. Commission* v. *France* it was more closely connected with goods.

2.29 In two recent cases the Court held that the manufacture of goods does not constitute the provision of services within the meaning of Article 59. The first of these, *E.C. Commission* v. *France*,[77] related to a tax benefit granted under French law to newspaper publishers in relation to printing expenses on condition that their publications were printed in France. The Commission claimed that this condition infringed Article 30. France argued *inter alia* that Article 30 was not the relevant provision and that instead one must look to the Treaty provisions on services, since printing was a service. The Court dismissed this argument on the grounds that printing 'leads directly to the manufacture of a physical article'. Also, it referred to the provisions in Article 60 of the Treaty that 'services shall be considered to be "services" within the meaning of this Treaty where they are normally provided for remuneration, in so far as they are not covered by the provisions relating to freedom of movement for goods, capital and persons'. In the result this ruling is welcome, since the restriction on imports was the predominant aspect of the measure.[78] Yet a restriction on printers established in other Member States carrying out work *in France* would surely fall under Article 59.

The Court applied the same test in *Cinéthèque* v. *Fédération Nationale des Cinémas Français*.[79] That case concerned French legislation providing that, once the French authorities had authorised a particular film to be shown in the cinemas, no videocassettes of that film could be sold or hired for private showing within one year. The case concerned two separate films. The copyright owner of each film had granted a licence to produce and issue videocassettes before the expiry of the one-year period. In each case the licensee undertook to exploit his licence, which covered France together with certain other States both inside and outside the Community, to maximum commercial advantage. The copyright owners and the licensees contended that the legislation concerned infringed Articles 30, 34 and 59. The questions posed by the national Court referred expressly to all three provisions. The Court held that Article 59 was not in point. When the licensee exploited the licence, he was not providing 'services' to the copyright owner; instead he was producing goods. Moreover, the Court referred once again to the rule enshrined

---

[77] Case 18/84 [1985] E.C.R. 1339, [1986] 1 C.M.L.R. 605.

[78] *Contra* Marenco 'La Giurisprudenza comunitaria sulle mesure di effetto equivalente a una restrizione quantitativa 1984–1986' [1988] *Foro Padano IV*, 166 who is concerned at the consequent of this ruling for the common transport policy.

[79] Cases 60 and 61/84 [1985] E.C.R. 2605, [1986] 1 C.M.L.R. 365. Marenco, *op. cit.*, agrees with this ruling.

in Article 60 that the Treaty provisions on services are subsidiary to those on goods.[80]

As already suggested, it is surely right that when a Member State imposes a restriction on the manufacture of goods elsewhere in the Community, that measure constitutes an obstacle to imports and thus falls under Article 30. On the other hand, when a Member State imposes restrictions on persons coming from other Member States to manufacture goods on its own territory, then Article 30 is not relevant. Article 59 is then the applicable provision.[81]

2.30 Another area of difficulty concerns import restrictions on goods such as tools required for the performance of a service under Article 59. In this connection Title III, Part B of the Council's General Programme for the abolition of restrictions on the freedom to provide services lists among the restrictions to be eliminated by that programme 'any prohibition of, or hindrance to, the movement of the item to be supplied in the course of the service or of the materials comprising such item or of the tools, machinery, equipment and other means to be employed in the provision of the service.[82] However, as Graf[83] points out, the opening words of Title III expressly state that this is subject to the Treaty provisions on the free movement of goods. Furthermore, when it adopted the General Programme, the Council made a declaration in which it recognised that customs duties on such goods could not be regarded as restrictions on services. Following this, the Commission addressed a recommendation to the Member States inviting them to abolish such duties, without prejudice to the obligations resulting from Articles 12 and 14 of the Treaty.[84]

The Council has adopted two Directives implementing this programme which concern the film industry and which provide for the abolition of certain import restrictions on films: Directives 63/607[85] and 65/264.[86] These Directives are expressed to be based·on the EEC Treaty as a whole, and 'in particular Article 63(2) thereof'.

It is submitted, therefore, that neither the Commission nor the Council has committed itself on this issue. Nor has the Court ever been called upon to rule on it. Nevertheless, given the Court's insistence on the residual nature of the Articles on services as stipulated in Article 60, it seems likely that it would hold that

---

[80] The Court did not consider the restriction on the *hire* of videocassettes. This, it is submitted, fell under Art. 59.

[81] Or Art. 52, as the case may be, but not Art. 34.

[82] [1962] O.J. Spec.Ed. 3; Ehlermann in Groeben, Boeckh, Thiesing, n.18 above, Vol. I at 265.

[83] *Der Begriff 'Maßnahmen gleicher Wirkung wie mengenmässige Einfuhrbeschränkungen' im EWG-Vertrag* (1972) 88.

[84] Rec. of 8 November 1962 ([1962] J.O. 2767/62). See also Rec. 64/412 ([1964] J.O. 1814/64) on the customs treatment of teaching materials.

[85] [1963] O.J. Spec.Ed. 2661/13.

[86] [1965] O.J. Spec.Ed. 1437/65.

restrictions on the temporary import of tools of trade fall under Article 30.

2.31 A new dimension was added to the problem of the relationship between the Treaty Articles on goods and those on services by the judgment in *Luisi and Carbone*.[87] It was held there that under Article 59 a person is entitled to cross from one Member State to another for the purpose of receiving a service. It was further held that a tourist was a recipient of services, as were persons travelling for the purposes of business, education or medical care. Whether restrictions on goods bought by tourists or other recipients of services fall under Articles 30 to 36 or Article 59 is not yet established. Nevertheless, in the light of Article 60 it would appear that Articles 30 to 36 apply.

2.32 In any case, it may be that the distinction between goods and services will not always be of great practical importance: it appears from the Court's judgments in *Debauve* and in *Coditel* v. *Ciné Vog*,[88] and more particularly from Advocate General Warner's conclusions in those cases, that the result of applying Article 59 to a given case will often be the same as that of applying Articles 30 to 36.[89] However, only nationals of Member States can rely on Article 59 *et seq.*, whereas for the application of the Treaty provisions on the free movement of goods the nationality of the owner is irrelevant.[90] Again, where Community legislation is concerned, the difference might be of some consequence in the past: Article 63 (services) only requires a qualified majority in the Council after the first stage of the transitional period, whereas Article 100 (which had to be used in the case of industrial goods for want of any more specific provision) requires a unanimous vote. On the other hand, legislation relating to agricultural goods could always be based on Article 43 which requires a qualified majority. In any case, the situation as regards industrial goods has now been altered by the introduction of Article 100A.[91]

2.33 In determining the demarcation line between the free movement of goods and the free movement of workers, the same

[87] Cases 286/82 and 26/83 [1984] E.C.R. 377, [1985] 3 C.M.L.R. 52. See Van der Woude and Mead 'Free Movement of the Tourist in EEC Law' [1988] C.M.L.Rev. 117.

[88] Case 62/79 [1980] E.C.R. 881, [1981] 2 C.M.L.R. 362.

[89] Everling 'Sur la jurisprudence recente de la Cour de justice en matière de libre prestation de services rendus dans d'autres Etat membres' [1984] C.D.E. 3. Also, the Court has in effect applied Art. 36 by analogy to services: para. 8.119 below, and Case 352/85 *Bond van Adverteerders* v. *Netherlands* (judgment of 26 April 1988).

[90] Para. 2.23 above.

[91] See para. 13.06 below.

considerations should apply[92]: the test should be whether the goods or the workers aspect is predominant in the transaction concerned.

In practice, conflict between these two sets of provisions will rarely arise. Examples are:

—restrictions on the import or export between Member States of a worker's tools of trade, and

—restrictions on the transfer of an individual's personal effects for the purpose of settling in and taking up employment in another Member State.

2.34 The considerations set out in the previous paragraph apply equally to the relationship between Articles 30 and 52.

There is little danger of a clash between Article 34 and Article 52 given the Court's narrow construction of the former provision.[93]

2.35 The dividing line between the scope of the provisions on goods and those on capital is particularly difficult to draw. We saw in paragraph 2.06 that one and the same article—gold coins—is variously described as goods and as capital by different Community instruments. As already pointed out, some of the parties intervening before the Court in *Thompson*[94] concluded from this that in determining whether to apply the rules on goods or capital one must look to the purpose of the transfer. The Court held that coins which were a 'means of legal payment' were not 'goods' (though it did not decide whether such coins were capital under Article 67 or current payments under Article 106). Thus, it did not take into account the purpose for which the coins were transferred, but it did not exclude the relevance of this factor. It is still probable that the same physical objects may be considered as 'goods' when their export is counterbalanced by a transfer of equivalent value to the exporting Member State, and 'capital' when there is no such transfer.[95]

Naturally this whole question is of less practical importance if 'capital' only covers financial capital movements[96]—and not jewellery, furs or pictures or other objects of value.[97]

---

[92] The similarity between Arts. 48 (workers) and 59 (services) has been stressed by the Court, notably in Case 36/74 *Walrave v. Union Cycliste Internationale* [1974] E.C.R. 1405, [1975] 1 C.M.L.R. 320.

[93] Para. 6.66 below.

[94] See n.17 above.

[95] See Prout, n.17 above.

[96] For this view, see van Ballegooijen, n.18 above; *contra* Everling in Wohlfarth-Everling-Glaesner-Sprung *Die Europäische Wirtschaft, Kommentar zum Vertrag* (1960), 203. In Case 65/79 *Chatain* [1980] E.C.R. 1345, [1981] 3 C.M.L.R. 418, the French customs authorities considered that the purchase price paid for pharmaceuticals by the French subsidiary of Sandoz to its parent company in Switzerland had been artificially inflated in order to export capital to Switzerland. However, since this case involved imports from a third country, quite different provisions of Community law were in point so that it provides no assistance here.

[97] One quite different aspect of the relationship between goods and capital deserves a brief mention here. In *Thompson* the Commission claimed that where movements of capital were effected by the transfer of physical assets, such assets did not constitute capital for all purposes; thus they were still subject to customs formalities. The Court did not allude to this important point, but in any case it would appear to have no bearing on the application of Arts. 30 to 36.

2.36 This issue arose in *E.C. Commission* v. *Italy*.[98] In that case the Commission claimed that Italian legislation requiring deposits to be lodged with respect to the advance payments for imports infringed Article 30 and the Directives implementing Article 67.[99] These Directives require movements of capital listed in Part A of Annex I thereto to be liberalised, and this list includes the 'granting and repayment of short- and medium-term credits related to commercial transactions'. Both Advocate General Slynn and the Court found that the Italian measures infringed Article 30. However, the Advocate General took the view that in so far as the Commission relied on the capital Directives its case should be dismissed. He gave two reasons for this view: firstly, the national measures were essentially concerned with payments connected with the free movement of goods and not capital; secondly, advance payments of goods could not be regarded as credit for the purposes of the Directives.

On the other hand, the Court held that, as the measures infringed Article 30, there was no need to consider whether they also fell foul of the Directives. The relationship between Articles 30 and 67 was thus left open.

Thus this case did not clarify this issue.

2.37 As already mentioned, it was held in *Luisi and Carbone* that tourists are recipients of services. Yet there remains a residual category of persons not covered by that judgment whose status is still unclear: for example, persons wishing to go to another Member State so as to take part in a political demonstration there.[100]

One's immediate reaction might be to say that if a person cannot enter a Member State, then his goods should not be able to do so either.

However, the contrary view was put most forcefully by Advocate General Warner in *Henn and Darby*.[101] The case involved the compatibility with Article 30 of the prohibition contained in section 42 of the (British) Customs Consolidation Act 1876 on importing indecent or obscene articles. In its observations before the Court the United Kingdom suggested that Article 30 does not apply to import restrictions in so far as they affect only private individuals. The Advocate General rejected this submission, although the word

[98] Case 95/81 [1982] E.C.R. 2187.
[99] See n.19 above.
[100] See generally Rec. 68/289 ([1968] J.O. L167/16), Reg. 1544/69 ([1969] J.O. L191/1) as amended, Reg. 1818/75 ([1975] O.J. L185/3) as amended; written question 289/79 on identity checks at the Community's internal frontiers ([1980] O.J. C116/1); Commission Proposal of 31 July 1979 for a Council Directive on a right of residence for nationals of Member States in the territory of another Member State ([1979] O.J. C207/14), as amended; the A.G. in Case 118/75 *Watson and Belmann* [1976] E.C.R. 1185 at 1204, [1976] 2 C.M.L.R. 552 at 559; Hartley *EEC Immigration Law* (1978), p.96, Wyatt [1976] E.L.Rev. 558.
[101] See n.66 above.

'trade' appears in a number of Articles in Title I, such as Articles 9 and 36:

> 'No-one . . . would suggest that, because the word "trade" is occasionally used in Articles 12 to 17, relating to the elimination of customs duties between Member States, private individuals moving their possessions from one Member State to another may still be subjected to customs duties, or that, because that word is occasionally used in Articles 18 to 29, relating to the Common Customs Tariff, private individuals who bring their possessions into the Community from outside it are subject, not to the Common Customs Tariff, but to the erstwhile tariffs of Member States. By a parity of reasoning, Article 30, which is the leading Article on the elimination of quantitative restrictions between Member States, and which does not itself use the word "trade", cannot be interpreted as limited to transactions by or between traders'.[102]

Although the Court found that a measure could not constitute arbitrary discrimination within the meaning of Article 36 when there was no lawful trade in the goods at issue within the Member State concerned, that cannot be taken as a ruling on the point under consideration here.

The force of the Advocate General's reasoning—and, in particular, the analogy with the Common Customs Tariff—is considerable. It may well be that the free movement of goods is so central to the structure of the Treaty that all movements of goods between Member States are caught by its provisions except those covered by other parts of the Treaty—such as Articles 59 and 67.[103]

2.38   In conclusion, while the concept of 'goods' is reasonably clear, it is far from certain how the Treaty provisions on the free movement of goods relate to those concerning the other three freedoms enshrined in the Treaty.

---

[102] At p.3827.
[103] Dir. 69/196 ([1969] O.J. Spec.Ed. 232), which covers the harmonisation of exemptions from turnover tax and excise duty on travellers' personal luggage having no commercial character, is of no assistance. It is expressed to be based on the entire Treaty and 'in particular Art. 99 thereof'. This art. falls within the Chapter of the Treaty on tax provisions and is not linked to any of the four freedoms in particular.

CHAPTER III

Scope: Territory

3.01 For those with a taste for the obscure a consideration of the territorial application of the Treaty of Rome may afford a spree of intellectual satisfaction, involving as it does a glance at many a far-flung corner of the globe, both in Europe and beyond. Added to this is the fact that different parts of the Treaty have different territorial application, so that territories such as the Isle of Man are subject to some but not all of the provisions of the Treaty.[1] The question here, then, is to define the area to which Articles 30 to 36 apply, both as regards the benefit they confer and the burden they impose. In other words, what is the area in which Articles 30 to 36 must be observed? There is a rebuttable presumption that this coincides with the area from which goods must be taken as originating in the Community to enjoy the benefit of these provisions.

3.02 Before considering this question mention should be made of Part IV of the Treaty entitled 'Association of the Overseas Countries and Territories' and running from Articles 131 to 136. These Articles apply to territories listed in Annex IV to the Treaty as amended,[2] which include such non-European territories as the Falkland Islands, the Netherlands Antilles and the French overseas territories (such as French Polynesia and the Wallis and Futuna Islands).[3] In fact, a number of territories appearing on the list have since attained independence so that Articles 131 to 136 no longer apply to them— even though none of them has been removed from the list. The Court ruled to this effect in *Lensing* v. *Hauptzollamt Berlin-Packhof*,[4] which concerned the former French colony of Guinea. Although Guinea remained on the list of OCTs, it had in fact become independent in 1958. Since it had never concluded any association agreement with the Community, the Court held that imports from that country were no longer exempt from customs

---

[1] See generally, Groux '"Territorialité" et Droit Communautaire' [1987] R.T.D.E. 5. For the application of Arts. 48 *et seq.* see Hartley *EEC Immigration Law* 293 (1978).
[2] By Art. 1 of the Convention of 13 November 1962 ([1964] J.O. 2414), which adds the Netherlands Antilles to this list, and Art. 24(2) of the first Act of Accession.
[3] The first Act of Accession added a sub-paragraph to Article 227(3) which reads 'This Treaty shall not apply to those overseas countries and territories having special relations with the United Kingdom of Great Britain and Northern Ireland which are not included in [Annex IV to this Treaty]'. Thus Hong Kong falls wholly outside the scope of the Treaty, including Part IV.
[4] Case 147/73 [1973] E.C.R. 1543.

duties. At all events, these 'overseas countries and territories' are not in the Community at all, as the opening words of Article 131 show clearly: 'The Member States agree to associate with the Community the non-European countries and territories which . . .' Therefore, in the absence of any reference thereto in Articles 131 to 136, Articles 30 to 36 do not apply to the OCTs.[5]

3.03 The territorial scope of the Treaty is governed first and foremost by Article 227. The effects of this provision with respect to Articles 30 to 36 can be summarised as follows:

(a) Belgium, Greece,[6] the Republic of Ireland, Luxembourg and Italy are included in their entirety for all purposes. Similarly, the whole territory of Portugal, including the Azores and Madeira, has been within the Community for all purposes since 1 January 1986 by virtue of Article 24 of the Act of Accession of Spain and Portugal.[7]

(b) The Treaty applies to Denmark, excluding the Faroe Islands. By virtue of Article 227(5)(a) the Danish Government was entitled to make a declaration, at any time up to and including 31 December 1975, to the effect that the Treaty applied to these islands. No such declaration was ever made, so that the Faroes are outside the Community.

The Treaty originally applied to Greenland as from Denmark's accession to the Community. However, by a special Treaty[8] this state of affairs was altered so that it now has the status of an OCT. It is therefore governed by Articles 131 to 136, subject however to certain exceptions contained in the Protocol to the new Treaty. The latter came into force on 1 February 1985.

(c) The Treaty also applies to the whole of the European territory of France. In addition, Article 227(2) provides that the rules on the free movement of goods apply to the French overseas departments, of which there are now four: Guadeloupe, Martinique, Réunion and French Guyana.[9] These are to be

[5] However, special arrangements, modelled on those applicable under the Third Lomé Convention, have been made under Art. 136 in relation to quantitative restrictions and measures of equivalent effect in trade between the Community and the OCTs: Council Dec. 86/283 ([1986] O.J. L175/1).
[6] See the Joint Declaration on Mount Athos annexed to the Act of Accession of Greece [1979] O.J. L291/186.
[7] [1985] O.J. L302. Art. 377 shows clearly that the Azores and Madeira are within the Community. Macao is not in the Community, nor is it an OCT: see the agreement on textiles concluded between that territory and the Community ([1986] O.J. L293/185).
[8] [1985] O.J. L29/1; see Lefaucheux 'Le nouveau régime de relations entre le Groenland et la Communauté Economique Européenne' [1985] R.M.C. 81, Weiss 'Greenland's Withdrawal from the European Communities' [1985] E.L.Rev. 173.
[9] See generally Case 148/77 *Hansen* v. *HZA Flensburg* [1978] E.C.R. 1787, [1979] 1 C.M.L.R. 604, where the Court delivered an almost revolutionary judgment on the application of Art. 95 to the French overseas departments; see also written question 1839/84 ([1985] O.J. C263/1).

distinguished from the French overseas *territories* which are OCTs.

More puzzlingly, Article 227(2) still purports to apply certain parts of the Treaty, including that relating to the free movement of goods, to Algeria.[10] The reason for this is that, when the Treaty was signed, Algeria was part of French territory. Yet common sense suggests that, that country having become independent on 1 July 1962, it is outside the scope of the Treaty. To this end one might call in aid the Court's ruling in *Lensing*, already mentioned.

(d) The Treaty applies to the entire territory of the Federal Republic of Germany. By a 'Declaration on the application of the Treaties to Berlin' made at the time of signing the Treaty, the Government of that State reserved the right to declare when depositing its instruments of ratification, that the Treaty applied to *Land* Berlin (West Berlin).[11] Such a declaration was in fact made so that the Treaty applies to West Berlin. Although inter-German trade is the subject of the special Protocol discussed in the previous chapter,[12] the German Democratic Republic is nevertheless outside the scope of the Treaty.

(e) According to Dutch constitutional law the Kingdom of the Netherlands extends beyond the European territory of the Netherlands to cover the overseas territories. Although Article 227(1) states without more that the Treaty applies to the Kingdom of the Netherlands, this is qualified by a special Protocol signed on the same day as the Treaty of Rome.[13] This Protocol entitled the Dutch Government, 'by way of derogation from Article 227', to ratify the Treaty on behalf of the Kingdom in Europe and Netherlands New Guinea. In fact, only the European part of the Kingdom became part of the Community and Netherlands New Guinea became an OCT. Subsequently the Netherlands Antilles and Surinam also became OCTs.[14]

---

[10] This curious question is examined in depth by Tavernier 'Aspects juridiques des relations économiques entre la CEE et l'Algérie' [1972] R.T.D.E. 1; see also Waelbroeck in *Le droit de la CEE* (1970) Vol. 1, 146.

[11] See Huette 'Berlin and the European Communities' [1983] Y.E.L. 1.

[12] See para. 2.19 above. The Court has held that 'the dispensation thus granted does not have the result of making the German Democratic Republic part of the Community, but only that a special system applies to it as a territory which is not part of the Community': Case 14/74 *Norddeutsches Vieh- und Fleischkontor* v. *HZA Hamburg-Jonas* [1974] E.C.R. 899.

[13] Protocol on the application of the Treaty establishing the EEC to the non-European parts of the Netherlands.

[14] As to the Netherlands Antilles see n.2 above. On 14 August 1962 the Netherlands extended ratification to Surinam which became an OCT although it was never formally included in Annex IV. However, Surinam has become an independent State and is therefore no longer an OCT. The same applies to Netherlands New Guinea, which has become part of Indonesia.

(f) By virtue of Articles 24 and 25 of the Act of Accession of Spain and Portugal the Treaty applies to the whole territory of Spain, subject to certain derogations relating to the Canary Islands and the North African enclaves of Ceuta and Melilla. These derogations, which are set out in Article 25 itself and in the Protocol concerning those territories, are of startling complexity. Suffice it to say here that according to Article 1 of the Protocol goods originating in the Canaries or in Ceuta or Melilla shall not be deemed 'when released for free circulation in the customs territory of the Community, to be goods fulfilling the conditions of Articles 9 and 10 of the EEC Treaty'. The same is expressed to apply to products coming from those Spanish territories but originating in third countries. In short, according to the Protocol Articles 30 to 36 of the Treaty do not apply to exports from these territories to the rest of the Community.

As regards goods coming from the rest of the Community to the Canaries, Ceuta and Melilla, it is unclear whether these may be subject to quantitative restrictions or measures of equivalent effect. The draftsmen of the Act of Accession and the Protocol appear to have overlooked the matter.

(g) In addition to Great Britain and Northern Ireland the Treaty also applies to various dependent territories of the United Kingdom. Article 227(4) states that 'the provisions of this Treaty shall apply to the European territories for whose external relations a Member State is responsible'. Plainly this covers Gibraltar.[15] Yet it is by no means certain that Articles 30 to 36 apply to trade between Gibraltar and the rest of the Community.

The only exception provided for in the Treaties with respect to this territory is to be found in Article 28 of the first Act of Accession, which states that:

> 'Acts of the institutions of the Community relating to the products in Annex II to the EEC Treaty and the products subject, on importation into the Community, to specific rules as a result of the implementation of the common agricultural policy, as well as the acts on the harmonis- ation of legislation of Member States concerning turnover taxes shall not apply to Gibraltar unless the Council, acting unanimously on a proposal from the Commission, provides otherwise.'

Since the provisions on the free movement of goods are not excluded by this Article, one might think that they apply to Gibraltar. Indeed this may hold good even for agricultural products since Article 28, it might be thought, does not provide otherwise.

Yet the opposite view is undoubtedly supported by the practice of the Council and the Commission which has been

---

[15] See written questions 1823/84 ([1985] O.J. C341/1) and 655/85 ([1985] O.J. C341/8).

to assimilate Gibraltar to a third country for the purposes of trade in all goods. Thus in Council Regulation 288/82[16] on common rules for imports, which forms part of the common commercial policy based on Article 113 of the Treaty, Gibraltar is listed among the third countries and territories concerned. Similarly, according to Council Regulation 2151/84[17] on the customs territory of the Community Gibraltar is not within the Community's customs territory. Moreover, in answer to a written question[18] the Commission has stated:

> 'On the basis of the 1972 Act of Accession, and in particular the exclusion of Gibraltar from the customs territory, the provisions of the EEC Treaty concerning the free movement of goods within the Community do not apply to Gibraltar and the territory is treated as a "third country" for the purposes of measures under the common commercial policy directly involving the import or export of goods. These arrangements, which were not covered by the negotiations on Spain's accession, are not affected by Spain's membership . . .'

This view appears to be based on the assumption that, in view of Gibraltar's special status, the authors of the 1972 Act of Accession must be taken to have intended to exclude Gibraltar from the territorial scope of the Community for the purposes of trade in goods.

Furthermore, Article 227(5)(c) provides that notwithstanding anything in paragraphs 1 to 4 of that Article 'This Treaty shall apply to the Channel Islands and the Isle of Man only to the extent necessary to ensure the implementation of the arrangements for those islands' set out in the Act of Accession. These islands are covered by a special Protocol to the Act of Accession, Article 1(1) of which begins: 'The Community rules on customs matters and quantitative restrictions, in particular those of the Act of Accession, shall apply to the Channel Islands and the Isle of Man under the same conditions as they apply to the United Kingdom'. Article 1(2) in effect states that the same rules apply to agricultural products. Although only quantitative restrictions and not measures of equivalent effect are expressly mentioned in this provision, it is probable that this wording is sufficient to cover both types of measure.[19] The latter view is borne out by the Commission's answer to a written question in which it declared that 'In accordance with Protocol 3 of the Accession Treaty, the Community rules allowing free movement of goods apply in

---

[16] [1982] O.J. L35/1.
[17] [1984] O.J. L197/1.
[18] Written question 1823/84 (see n.15 above).
[19] Ehlermann in Groeben, Boeckh, Thiesing *Kommentar zum EWG-Vertrag* (1974) Vol. I, 276. See para. 5.12 below.

trade between the Isle of Man and other Member States'.[20] In view of the subject-matter of the question the Commission's statement appears to extend to measures of equivalent effect. Furthermore, in answer to other written questions the Commission has declared that under the Protocol the Channel Islands and the Isle of Man are 'included in the customs union'.[21]

On the other hand, the Treaty does not apply to the Sovereign Base Areas of the United Kingdom in Cyprus: Article 227(5)(b).

(h) As already pointed out, Article 227(4) stipulates that: 'The provisions of this Treaty shall apply to the European territories for whose external relations a Member State is responsible'. It is unclear whether Monaco and San Marino fall within this provision.[22] In answer to a written question,[23] the Commission has stated that as Monaco has not signed the Treaty of Rome, it did not form part of the EEC; it went on to state, however, that the provisions on the free movement of goods in the Community apply to goods originating in Monaco by virtue of Council Regulation 2151/84 on the customs territory of the Community.

It seems clear that Andorra is not covered by Article 227(4) and is therefore outside the Community for all purposes. At all events, this is the view of the Member States, as is shown by a joint declaration on future trade arrangements with Andorra appended to the Act of Accession of Spain and Portugal.[24] According to that declaration 'an arrangement governing trade relations between the Community and Andorra' is to be 'finalised within a period of two years of the date of entry into force of the Act of Accession'. That undertaking has not yet been implemented.

3.04 What of the sea and the sea-bed?[25] Article 227 provides that the Treaty applies to the Member States without referring to their respective territories, although the concept of territory does appear

---

[20] Written question 409/80 ([1980] O.J. C217). On the Channel Islands and the Isle of Man, see generally Simmonds 'The British Islands and the Community' [1968–69] C.M.L.Rev. 153 and [1970] C.M.L.Rev. 454. On Protocol 3 and the Isle of Man, see Case 32/79 *E.C. Commission* v. *United Kingdom* [1980] E.C.R. 2043, [1981] 1 C.M.L.R. 219 on fisheries, where, however, the Court avoided the issue.

[21] Written questions 2116/84 ([1985] O.J. C168/25) and 1408/85 ([1986] O.J. C48/15).

[22] See Bathurst in *Legal Problems of an Enlarged European Community* (1972) 162; Smit and Herzog *Law of the European Economic Community* para. 6–210; Campbell *Common Market Law* Vol. III para. 8–5; Thiesing in Groeben, Boeckh, Thiesing, Ehlermann *Kommentar zum EWG-Vertrag* (1983) Vol. II, 107.

[23] Written question 1215/80 ([1980] O.J. C335/10).

[24] [1985] O.J. L302/488.

[25] See generally Brouir 'Le réglement du Conseil de la CEE de 1970 sur les pêcheries' [1973] C.D.E. 20; Koers 'The external authority of the EEC in regard to marine fisheries' [1977] C.M.L.Rev. 269. Groux, *op. cit.,* at p.19.

in Articles 48 to 52 covering the free movement of workers and the right of establishment respectively. Article 84(2) empowers the Council to extend the common transport policy to sea and air transport. The Court has held[26] that this provision does not prevent the 'general rules of the Treaty' such as Articles 48 to 51 from applying to sea transport even in the absence of a specific decision by the Council.

Although the Treaty contains no provision dealing specifically with sea fishing, its provisions on agriculture (Articles 39 to 46) provide an appropriate basis for a common fisheries policy and legislation on sea fishing has therefore been based on these provisions. Furthermore, Articles 100 to 103 of the first Act of Accession are devoted to this matter. The Court has also had occasion to consider it in a series of cases brought before it.[27] In the present context the first of these cases, *Kramer,* is the most important because one of the questions put to the Court was whether fishing quotas not fixed under Community auspices infringed Article 30. The Court found that such quotas were compatible with Article 30 on the grounds that, despite restricting 'production' in the short term, they ensured supplies in the long term.[28] In so doing the Court made no allusion to the geographical scope of Article 30, but there can be no doubt from the judgment that it applies to the resources of the sea: in answer to another question the Court held that the Community has power to 'take any measures for the conservation of the biological resources of the sea', even as regards the high seas.

It appears that Articles 30 to 36 apply to fish and other products caught on the high seas by a vessel lawfully flying the flag of a Member State as is shown by Regulation 802/68[29] defining the concept of origin of goods. By virtue of Article 4(2)(f) thereof 'products of sea-fishing and other products taken from the sea by vessels registered or recorded in [a] country and flying its flag' are taken to originate in that country.[30]

Moreover, it is submitted that Articles 30 to 36 also apply to resources extracted from that part of the sea-bed over which Member

---

[26] Case 167/73 *E.C. Commission* v. *France* [1974] E.C.R. 359, [1974] 2 C.M.L.R. 216.

[27] In particular see Cases 3, 4 and 5/76 *Kramer* [1976] E.C.R. 1279, [1976] 2 C.M.L.R. 440, noted by Wyatt [1977] E.L.Rev. 41; Case 61/77 *E.C. Commission* v. *Ireland* [1977] E.C.R. 937, [1978] 2 C.M.L.R. 466; Case 88/77 *Minister for Fisheries* v. *Schonenberg* [1978] E.C.R. 473, [1978] 2 C.M.L.R. 519; Cases 185–204/78 *van Dam* [1979] E.C.R. 2345, [1980] 1 C.M.L.R. 350; Case 141/78 *France* v. *U.K.* [1979] E.C.R. 2923, [1980] 1 C.M.L.R. 6.

[28] See para. 7.86 below.

[29] [1968] J.O. L148/1. See Case 100/84, *E.C. Commission* v. *U.K.* (joint fishing operations) [1985] E.C.R. 1170, [1985] 2 C.M.L.R. 199, and para. 2.10 above.

[30] As regards the application of Community VAT legislation to the high seas, see Cases 168/84 *Berkholz* v. *Finanzamt Hamburg-Mitte-Altstadt* [1985] E.C.R. 2251, [1985] 3 C.M.L.R. 667, and 283/84 *Trans Tirreno Express* v. *Ufficio Provinciale IVA* [1986] E.C.R. 231, [1986] 2 C.M.L.R 100.

States exercise sovereign rights.[31] According to Article 4(2)(h) of Regulation 802/68 products are considered to originate in a country where they have been 'taken from the sea-bed or beneath the sea-bed outside territorial waters, if that country has, for the purposes of exploitation, exclusive rights to such soil or sub-soil'.

3.05 As will be explained below,[32] Articles 30 and 34 apply only to goods passing between Member States; goods moving within a Member State are not caught by these provisions. Consequently, when fish caught by a British ship are landed in the United Kingdom these Articles do not apply. Similarly, for these purposes a European territory which falls within Article 227(4) of the Treaty must surely be deemed to form part of the Member State which is responsible for its external relations. Accordingly, Articles 30 and 34 do not cover movements of goods between the territory and the Member State.

3.06 Finally, mention should be made of Council Regulation 2151/84[33] on the customs territory of the Community. Like its predecessor, Council Regulation 1496/68,[34] this Regulation is based on Article 235. The 1984 Regulation itself has been amended to take account of Greenland's departure from the Community[35] and the accession of Spain and Portugal.[36] The following features of Regulation 2151/84 as amended are worthy of note:

— according to Article 4 'the provisions of this Regulation shall be without prejudice to . . . (b) the arrangements applicable to Saint-Pierre-et-Miquelon'. This particular provision is designed to take account of the successive changes in status of this French dependency. After being an overseas department for a short period, it has now re-acquired its original status of OCT;

— the Canaries, Ceuta and Melilla are outside the Community's customs territory. On this point the Regulation merely incorporates the express stipulation to this effect in Article 1(2) of the Protocol to the Act of Accession relating to these territories;

— the Regulation provides that the Channel Islands and the Isle of Man are within the Community's customs territory. However, it says nothing about Gibraltar which is therefore outside that territory;

---

[31] See the Commission memorandum of 18 September 1970 SEC(70)3095 Final, reprinted in C.C.H. C.M.R., para. 9625. In Case 8/79 *Filby* v. *Insurance Office* the National Insurance Commissioner referred a number of questions requiring the Court to rule on the application of the Community legislation on social security for migrant workers to the continental shelf. However, the British Government amended its legislation and the case was struck out.

[32] Para. 6.74 below.

[33] See n.17 above.

[34] [1968] J.O. L238/1.

[35] Council Reg. 319/85 ([1985] O.J. L34/32).

[36] Act of Accession ([1985] O.J. L302/153).

— pursuant to certain treaties concluded in the 19th century, the Austrian territories of Jungholz and Mittelberg are included, although plainly they are not in the Community;

— conversely, certain German and Italian territories such as Heligoland and the commune of Livigno are excluded, although they are clearly within the Community;

— Monaco and San Marino are included although they are probably not in the Community; in contrast, Andorra is not included;

— Article 1(2) provides:

> 'The following shall be included in the customs territory of the Community:
> (a) the territorial sea of the coastal Member States and their internal waters;
> (b) the airspace of each Member State.'

On the latter point, Regulation 2151/84 differs markedly from Regulation 1496/68 which it replaced. Article 4 of the earlier Regulation stipulated that 'this Regulation shall not affect the customs system applicable to the continental shelf or that applicable to the waters and foreshores situated between the coast or shore and the limit of territorial waters'.

However, Article 1(2) of the new Regulation does not refer to the continental shelf. In the absence of any other provision on the point, the continental shelf is therefore outside the customs territory as defined by the Regulation. According to the preamble this is simply because 'in the current situation there is no reason to integrate the continental shelf adjacent to the territories of the Member States into the customs territory of the Community'.

The precise effect of Regulation 2151/84 on the territorial scope of Articles 30 to 36 is a vexed question. On the one hand, the Regulation manifestly seeks to define the customs boundary of the Community for the purposes of the common customs tariff. The Treaty provisions on the free movement of goods clearly cannot extend to goods crossing that boundary. On the other hand, it is questionable whether a mere Regulation can determine the scope of provisions of the Treaty. Indeed, it appears from Article 3 that the Regulation has a more modest aim, namely to delimit the area in which the 'customs rules of the Community' apply. Accordingly, the better view is that there is a *rebuttable* presumption that the customs territory of the Community as defined in the Regulation is identical with the area to which Articles 30 to 36 apply.

CHAPTER IV

Scope: Persons bound

4.01 The question to be examined in this chapter is what persons or bodies are bound by Articles 30 to 36. This question arises with respect to the Member States, the Community institutions and, finally, private parties (individuals or non-State bodies). Each of these will be examined in turn. Since Articles 30 to 36 must in this respect be construed in the same way as Articles 12 to 17 prohibiting customs duties and taxes of equivalent effect, some of the cases discussed in this chapter relate to the latter set of provisions.

I. MEMBER STATES

4.02 The very terms of these Articles show beyond doubt that they cover State measures. Thus the first paragraph of Article 31 reads: 'Member States shall refrain from introducing between themselves any new quantitative restrictions or measures having equivalent effect'. Similarly the first paragraph of Article 32 stipulates that 'in their trade with one another Member States shall refrain from making more restrictive the quotas and measures having equivalent effect existing at the date of entry into force of this Treaty'. Further clear references to the fact that State measures are concerned are to be found in Articles 33, 34 and 35.

4.03 What is meant by the 'State' in this context? This concept is to be interpreted widely to cover the public authorities of a Member State in general.[1] This embraces not only central government but also regional and local government[2]: it is irrelevant to the Community whether discrimination against a product from another Member State emanates from the federal, the provincial or the parish authorities, so long as that discrimination exists.[3] Thus the Commission has recently sought interim measures against Ireland with respect to a clause inserted in an invitation to tender issued by the town of

---

[1] Béraud 'Les mesures d'effect équivalent au sens des articles 30 et suivants du Traité de Rome' [1968] R.T.D.E. 265 at 278.

[2] Graff, *Der Begriff, 'Maßnahmen gleicher Wirkung wie mengenmässige Einfuhrbeschränkungen in dem EWG-Vertrag'* (1972) 125 et seq.

[3] Dir. 70/32 of the Commission ([1970] J.O. L13/1) describes as measures of equivalent effect provisions which discriminate against the purchase of imported goods by the State or local authorities. However, it does not state expressly whether it covers *measures emanating* from local authorities.

Dundalk, which was alleged to infringe Article 30. In his Order[4] the President of the Court stated:

'Since that clause was inserted in the specifications by Dundalk Urban District Council, a body subject to the authority of the Minister for the Environment and for whose acts Ireland is responsible, the barrier to intra-Community trade to which it *prima facie* gives rise is imputable to Ireland.'

4.04 Likewise, Articles 30 to 36 apply not only to measures of the executive, but also of the legislature or of the judiciary. This has now been made clear by the Court in *Dansk Supermarked* v. *Imerco*[5] where it held that:

'Articles 30 and 36 of the EEC Treaty must be interpreted to mean that the judicial authorities of a Member State may not prohibit, on the basis of a copyright or of a trade mark, the marketing on the territory of that State of a product to which one of those rights applies. . . .'

In addition, it is generally accepted[6] that an action can be brought under Article 169 against a Member State with respect to judicial acts. However, this is not to say that a single decision by a national court will necessarily render a Member State liable to a declaration under Article 169, at least where an appeal lies against that decision.

In this connection the following statement by Advocate General Warner in *R.* v. *Bouchereau* deserves mention:

'It is obvious . . . that a Member State cannot be held to have failed to fulfil an obligation under the Treaty simply because one of its courts has reached a wrong decision. Judicial error, whether due to the misapprehension of facts or to misapprehension of the law, is not a breach of the Treaty. In the judicial sphere, Article 169 could only come into play in the event of a court of a Member State deliberately ignoring or disregarding Community law.'[7]

4.05 Moreover, there exists in the Community a myriad of different types of public undertakings, semi-public bodies and 'quangos' (quasi-autonomous national governmental organisations), fulfilling a host of different functions and roles, ranging from the social and cultural to the commercial and industrial. Little clear indication exists as to which acts of such bodies are to be attributed to the State for the present purposes. What is more, an already confused picture is complicated by the existence of Article 37 (which relates specifically to State monopolies of a commercial character and which is the subject of Chapter XI of this book), of Article 90 on public

---

[4] Case 45/87R *E.C. Commission* v. *Ireland* [1987] 2 C.M.L.R. 563.
[5] Case 58/80 [1981] E.C.R. 181, [1981] 3 C.M.L.R. 590. See also Case 434/85 *Allen and Hanbury's Ltd.* v. *Generics* [1988] 1 C.M.L.R. 701 at para. 25.
[6] Written question 100/67 ([1967] J.O. 270/3); written question 349/69 ([1970] J.O. C20/3). In Cases 77/69 *E.C. Commission* v. *Belgium* [1970] E.C.R. 237, [1974] 1 C.M.L.R. 203, and 8/70 *E.C. Commission* v. *Italy* [1970] E.C.R. 961 the Court held that: 'The obligations arising from the Treaty devolve upon States as such and the liability of a Member State under Art. 169 arises whatever the agency of the State whose action or inaction is the cause of the failure to fulfil its obligations, even in the case of a constitutionally independent institution'.
[7] Case 30/77 [1977] E.C.R. 1999 at 2020, [1977] 2 C.M.L.R. 800 at 810.

undertakings and other undertakings on which the Member States confer special rights,[8] and of Article 222.[9] None of these provisions is particularly straightforward.

However, where a Member State uses such a body as a medium for the execution of a measure, then that measure plainly emanates from the State, regardless of the precise status of the body concerned. This is what occurred in *E.C. Commission* v. *Ireland*.[10] That case concerned the 'Buy Irish' campaign, which was launched by the Irish Government but implemented by the Irish Goods Council. Although that organisation took the form of a private company, it had been set up by the Government, members of its Management Committee were appointed by a Minister and it was predominantly financed by the State. Thus the Court had no difficulty in finding that the campaign had been 'introduced' by the Irish Government and 'prosecuted with its assistance' and was thus attributable to that Government.[11]

Similarly, when the power to pass binding acts of a legislative or administrative nature is delegated by the State to a public or private body, those acts would seem to be attributable to the State for the purposes of Articles 30 to 36.[12]

One might also have thought that, whenever an act of a private person has been approved by the public authorities as required by law, then that act is attributable to the State. Thus in *Haug-Adrion* v. *Frankfurter Versicherungs-AG*[13] the Commission advanced the view that insurance conditions drawn up by private insurance companies but formally approved by public authorities were attributable to the State. Yet this argument fell on deaf ears. Without deciding the point the Advocate General inclined to the contrary view, while the Court decided the case on other grounds.

4.06 The Commission has advocated a broader approach to the general problem of deciding what acts are attributable to the State. In its answer to Written Question 862/83 it stated that:

---

[8] See para. 9.03 below.

[9] See para. 9.52 below.

[10] Case 249/81 [1982] E.C.R. 4005, [1983] 2 C.M.L.R. 104; see paras. 6.05, 6.25 and 7.25 below.

[11] See also generally Case 290/83 *E.C. Commission* v. *France* (Crédit Agricole) [1985] E.C.R. 439, [1986] 2 C.M.L.R. 546, at para. 15.

[12] See Béraud, n.1 above; see also Case 190/73 *Van Haaster* [1974] E.C.R. 1123, [1974] 2 C.M.L.R. 521, where the defendant in the main case was charged before the Dutch courts with infringing a provision of a binding regulation adopted by the Produktschap voor Siergewassen, an organisation of producers of ornamental plants; the Court held this provision to be a measure of equivalent effect to a quantitative restriction. However, the Court did not refer expressly to the question in point here. Also, after its adoption by the Produktschap, the regulation received the approval of the Minister of Agriculture. A similar ruling with respect to a levy imposed by the same body was delivered in Case 51/74 *Van der Hulst's Zonen* v. *Produktschap voor Siergewassen* [1975] E.C.R. 79, [1975] 1 C.M.L.R. 236.

[13] Case 251/83 [1984] E.C.R. 4277, [1985] 3 C.M.L.R. 266, noted by Marenco 'La giurisprudenza communitaria sulle misure di effetto equivalente a una restrizione quantitativa' [1984–1986] *Il Foro Padano* 1988 IV, p.166.

'as regards the problem of standards, it should be pointed out that they are very often drawn up by private bodies and, as such, are not binding. If, however, such standards have been made *de jure* or *de facto* obligatory by the State authorities, their compatibility with the provisions of the Treaty and with the provisions relating to the free movement of goods (in particular Articles 30 to 36) would have to be reviewed.'[14]

That approach is closely reflected in Council Directive 83/189[15] laying down a procedure for the provision of information in the field of technical standards and regulations, discussed at length in Chapter XII. The Court has yet to rule on the validity of this criterion.

4.07 Finally, if a restriction on trade between Member States is provided for by a State measure, it is of no consequence that an individual or other private party must apply to the authorities to obtain the benefit of that restriction.[16] This is because the measure still flows from the State.

It will be clear from the above that State measures do not necessarily have to be binding to fall foul of Articles 30 to 36. This point is discussed at greater length at paragraph 6.10 below.

II. THE COMMUNITY INSTITUTIONS[17]

4.08 Can Community legislation validly prohibit or restrict trade between Member States? Alternatively, can such legislation authorise Member States to take such action?

The concept of harmonisation of national rules by the Community (whether under Article 100 or any other Article of the Treaty such as Article 43 on the common agricultural policy) presuppposes the power to adopt standards with which products from all the Member States must comply. This will involve the submission of certain goods to particular conditions, such as labelling or packaging requirements, and will sometimes entail the complete prohibition of goods falling within certain categories. While a standard laid down in some but not all Member States may restrict interstate trade, it will cease to do so once it is introduced throughout the Community: all Member States will then apply the same standard so that goods from one Member State can be imported and sold in all the others. In such a case no problem arises as to the compatibility of the

---

[14] [1983] O.J. C315/15.

[15] [1983] O.J. L109/8, see para. 12.12 below.

[16] Matthies 'Herkunftsangaben und Europäisches Gemeinschaftsrecht' in *Festschrift für Schiedermair* (1976) 395.

[17] See Mertens de Wilmars, 'De heffingen van gelijke werking als de douanerechten' in *Liber Amicorum J. van Houtte* at 697; Matthies 'Die Verfassung des Gemeinsamen Marktes' in *Das Europa der Zweiten Generation, Gedächtnisschrift* (1981), Vol. I, 115; Oliver, 'La législation communautaire et sa conformité avec la libre circulation des marchandises' [1979] C.D.E. 245.

Community legislation with the Treaty provisions on the free movement of goods.

Nevertheless it may happen that the Community institutions decide to subject movements of certain goods between Member States to certain taxes or procedures or even to prohibit them altogether.

4.09 The starting point for the consideration of this type of case must be the Court's statement in *Ramel* v. *Receveur des Douanes*[18] to the effect that:

> 'the extensive powers, in particular of a sectoral or regional nature, granted to the Community institutions in the conduct of the Common Agricultural Policy must, in any event as from the end of the transitional period, be exercised from the perspective of the unity of the market to the exclusion of any measure comprising the abolition between Member States of customs duties and quantitative restrictions or charges or measures having equivalent effect'.

The case had arisen out of the 'wine war' between France and Italy, which flared up at the end of 1975. Article 31(1) of Regulation 816/70[19] laying down additional provisions for the common market organisation in wine prohibited charges of equivalent effect to customs duties in the internal trade of the Community, subject to one exception not material here. However, Article 31(2) stated that:

> 'by way of derogation from the provisions of paragraph 1, so long as all the administrative mechanisms necessary for the management of the market in wine are not in application . . . producer Member States shall be authorised in order to avoid disturbances on their markets to take measures that may limit imports from another Member State.'

In 1975 there was an exceptional influx of Italian wine into the French market owing to a particularly good harvest as well as to successive devaluations of the lira. With a view to limiting that influx the French Government levied a charge on certain Italian wines in September of that year. The Commission brought an action under Article 169 against France for failure to comply with its Treaty obligations, but discontinued it when the French measure was repealed with effect from 1 April 1976.

However, the plaintiffs in the main proceedings had been required to pay the charges at issue on various consignments of wine from Italy and now sought to recover those sums in actions against the French customs authorities. The Tribunal d'Instance of Bourg-en-Bresse, before which these actions were brought, accordingly asked the Court of Justice whether Article 31(2) of the Regulation was compatible with the Treaty and, if so, whether it continued to be applicable.

---

[18] Cases 80–81/77 [1978] E.C.R. 927.
[19] [1970] O.J. Spec.Ed. (I) 234.

The Court began by considering Article 38(2) of the Treaty, which reads:

'Save as otherwise provided in Articles 39 to 46, the rules laid down for the establishment of the common market shall apply to agricultural products.'

The Court found nothing in Articles 39 to 46—the provisions of the Treaty dealing with agriculture—which either expressly or by necessary implication provided for or authorised the introduction of charges of equivalent effect to customs duties in intra-Community trade at the end of the transitional period.[20]

After making the statement already quoted, the Court therefore concluded that:

'Article 31(2) of Regulation 816/70 in so far as it authorises producer Member States to prescribe and levy, in intra-Community trade in the products covered by the organisation of the market which that regulation sets up, charges having an effect equivalent to customs duties, is incompable with Article 13, in particular paragraph (2) thereof, and with Articles 38 to 46 of the Treaty and is consequently invalid.'

4.10 The case concerned taxes but it is expressly stated in the passage first quoted here that the same result will apply to quantitative restrictions and measures of equivalent effect. Indeed, this is also clear from a *dictum* in *Rivoira*.[21] There the Court was called upon to interpret Regulation 2513/69[22] on the co-ordination and standardisation of the treatment accorded by each Member State to imports of fruit and vegetables from non-member countries, and Regulation 1524/70[23] implementing the Agreement between Spain and the EEC of 1970. It held that the power conferred by those Regulations on Member States to impose quantitative restrictions on Spanish grapes over a certain period was limited to direct imports from third countries, on a proper reading of Article 1 of Regulation 2513/69. It added that:

'the said Article 1 could not have covered the application by a Member State of restrictions on the importation of products in free circulation within the Community from other Member States, because such an ambit would have constituted a derogation from the fundamental rules of the Treaty on the free movement of goods.'[24]

4.11 The same principle applies where tariff or non-tariff quotas on imports from third countries are allocated between Member States, as the Court stated unequivocally in *E.C. Commission* v. *E.C. Council*[25] (rum quotas). To implement Protocol No. 5 to the Second Lomé Convention the Council adopted a regulation in

---

[20] A similar approach to the interpretation of Art. 38(2) has been used by the Court in Cases 90–91/63 *EEC Commission* v. *Belgium and Luxembourg* [1964] E.C.R. 625, [1965] C.M.L.R. 58 and Case 48/74 *Charmasson* v. *Minister of Economic Affairs* [1974] E.C.R. 1383, [1975] 2 C.M.L.R. 208 discussed at para. 10.02 below.

[21] Case 179/78 [1979] E.C.R. 1147, [1979] 3 C.M.L.R. 456.

[22] [1970] J.O. L318/6.

[23] O.J. Spec.Ed. Second Series I External Relations (1), 269.

[24] See also the A.G. in Case 34/78 *Yoshida* v. *Kamer van Koophandel* [1979] E.C.R. 115 at 147, [1979] 2 C.M.L.R. 747 at 752.

[25] Case 218/82 [1983] E.C.R. 4063, [1984] 2 C.M.L.R. 350.

relation to each annual tariff quota of rum and related products from the ACP States. For 1982/1983 it adopted Regulation 1699/82,[26] Article 4(2) of which provided that:

> 'The United Kingdom shall take the steps necessary to ensure that the quantities imported from the ACP States under the conditions laid down in Articles 1 and 2 are restricted to those meeting its domestic consumption requirements.'

The Commission sought the annulment of this provision on the grounds that it required the United Kingdom to restrict exports in contravention of Article 34 EEC. In its defence the Council argued, *inter alia*, that the provision did not have this meaning but merely required the United Kingdom to refrain from importing quantities exceeding its domestic needs. To this end, it relied on the French version of Article 4(2), which was more favourable to this interpretation than the English version.

The Advocate General found for the Commission. In her view both versions of Article 4(2) constituted export restrictions. She also pointed out that the United Kingdom had in fact adopted legislation making re-exports of ACP rum economically prohibitive. The Court took the opposite view. Confirming *Ramel*, it held that:

> 'If, as the Commission maintains, that provision did contain a prohibition on exportation from the United Kingdom to the other Member States it would indeed be contrary to the Treaty provisions on the free movement of goods; while, therefore, as the Court has confirmed, division of a global tariff quota into national quotas may, in certain circumstances, be compatible with the Treaty, that is subject to the express condition that it does not hinder the free movement of the goods forming part of the quota after they have been admitted to free circulation in the territory of one of the Member States.'

In line with its earlier ruling in *Gaston Schul* v. *Inspecteur der Invoerrechten*,[27] it then stated that, when the meaning of a provision of secondary Community law is in doubt, preference must be given to the interpretation rendering that provision compatible with the Treaty. It therefore found for the Council, while upholding the basic principle relied on by the Commission.

A particularly clear illustration of the same principle is to be found in *Migliorini*[28] which also concerned the allocation of a tariff quota between Member States. The Italian authorities had brought criminal proceedings against the defendants for re-exporting to Germany quantities of frozen beef imported into Italy from Czechoslovakia as part of Italy's portion of a Community quota for that product. The Italian authorities regarded the very action of re-exporting the beef as smuggling. In answer to a question posed pursuant to Article 177 the Court held that the Council Regulation opening the quota and allocating it between Member States did not 'authorise the Member States to adopt measures intended to prevent, restrict or affect the re-exportation of goods which have been

---

[26] [1982] O.J. L189/1.
[27] Case 15/81 [1982] E.C.R. 1409, [1982] 3 C.M.L.R. 229.
[28] Case 199/84 [1985] E.C.R. 3317.

properly imported under that quota and which are consequently in free circulation in a Member State.'

It follows from *E.C. Commission* v. *E.C. Council* and *Migliorini* that where a Community quota is divided between Member States, that division only affects direct imports from the third countries concerned. Once the goods have been put into free circulation in the Community they may move freely between the Member States like any other product.[29]

4.12 In two cases the Court, while adhering strictly to these principles, has held Community legislation imposing limited restriction on trade between Member States to be lawful: *REWE-Zentrale* v. *Direktor der Landwirtschaftskammer Rheinland*[30] and *Denkavit Nederland* v. *Hoofdproduktschap voor Akkerbouwprodukten*.[31] In *REWE-Zentrale* it was argued for the first time that a directive fell foul of Article 30. The instrument in question was Council Directive 77/93[32] on protective measures against the introduction into the Member States of harmful organisms of plants or plant products, which is based on Articles 43 and 100. On a reference for a preliminary ruling the plaintiffs in the main case contended that the Directive was incompatible with Article 30 in so far as it permitted an importing Member State to subject as many as one-third of all consignments of plants and plant products to phytosanitary controls. This was said to be excessive since under the Directive the exporting Member State was required to carry out systematic checks.[33]

The Court stressed once again that the Community institutions were bound to observe the principle of the free movement of goods, which was one of the fundamental principles of the common market. Nevertheless, it found that they enjoyed a measure of discretion in exercising their powers under Articles 43 and 100, which had not been exceeded with respect to the Directive. In reaching this conclusion the Court had regard to the specific problems of phytosanitary protection. It also found that under the Treaty provisions referred to harmonisation may be effected in stages and national obstacles to trade abolished gradually. This necessarily implies that the contested provision may in time cease to be valid. Indeed, Advocate General Slynn, who took the same view as the Court, said as much.

In its preliminary ruling in *Denkavit Nederland* the Court likewise dismissed arguments to the effect that Commission Regulation 1725/79[34] on aid for processed skimmed milk was contrary to Article

---

[29] However, as to the application of Art. 115 EEC in such circumstances, see para. 9.40 *et seq.* below.

[30] Case 37/83 [1984] E.C.R. 1229, [1985] 2 C.M.L.R. 586.

[31] Case 15/83 [1984] E.C.R. 2171.

[32] [1977] O.J. L26/20.

[33] See para. 8.58 below.

[34] [1979] O.J. L199/1.

34. It followed from Articles 6 and 7 of that Regulation that in the case of exports proof that the conditions for the grant of aid had been met must be furnished by Community T5 documents (or by the Benelux 5 document in the case of Benelux exports). On the other hand, where the finished product was put on the market in the Member State of production, proof was to be furnished according to the method laid down by the Member State, provided that that method ensured adequate guarantees of compliance with the conditions concerned. This disparity resulted in the aid being paid later with respect to exports than with respect to goods put on the national market. Denkavit therefore contended that these provisions were contrary, *inter alia,* to Article 34 and a largely identical provision contained in Article 22(1) of Council Regulation 804/68[35] on the common organisation of the market in milk and milk products.

Following the Advocate General, a three-judge Chamber of the Court held the Regulation to be compatible with all the provisions and principles of Community law relied on by Denkavit. In relation to Article 34 it held that the documents of proof required in each case, though not identical, were equivalent. Moreover, the later payment of aid for exports was held to be inevitable: the transmission of documents between the authorities of different Member States was bound to take longer than the forwarding of documents within a single Member State. It is also significant that elsewhere in its judgment, in a passage concerned with the principle of proportionality, the Court pointed to the particular dangers of fraud as regards exports. For instance, the risk of paying aid twice with respect to the same goods might be greater where exports were concerned.

4.13   It is established, then, that the Community institutions must have regard to the principle of the free movement of goods in framing their legislation. However, certain judgments of the Court indicate that in this matter the Community institutions enjoy a greater measure of freedom than the Member States.

The first of these, *REWE-Zentral* v. *HZA Kehl,*[36] was one of a series of three cases[37] decided on the same day, all of which concerned the validity of Regulation 974/71[38] establishing the system of monetary compensatory amounts.[39] Of these only the REWE case concerned interstate trade and thus raised the question of the compatibility of these levies with Articles 9, 12 and 13 of the Treaty prohibiting charges of equivalent effect to customs duties. In answer to a

---

[35] [1968] O.J. Spec.Ed. (I) 176, subsequently amended.
[36] Case 10/73 [1973] E.C.R. 1175.
[37] The other two cases were Cases 5/73 *Balkan-Import-Export* v. *HZA Berlin-Packhof* [1973] E.C.R. 1091 and Case 9/73 *Carl Schlüter* v. *HZA Lörrach* [1973] E.C.R. 1135.
[38] [1971] O.J. L106/1.
[39] This is the mechanism informally known as 'green currencies'. See Gilsdorf 'The system of Monetary Compensation from a Legal Standpoint' [1980] E.L.Rev. 341 and 433.

question raised by a national court under Article 177, the Court
ruled that:

> 'Although the compensatory amounts do constitute a partitioning of the
> market, here they have a corrective influence on the variations in fluctuating
> exchange rates which, in a system of market organisation for agricultural
> products based on uniform prices, might cause disturbances in trade in these
> products.
> Diversion of trade caused solely by the monetary situation can be considered
> more damaging to the common interest, bearing in mind the aims of the
> common agricultural policy, than the disadvantages for the measures in dispute.
> Consequently these compensatory amounts are conducive to the maintenance
> of a normal flow of trade under the exceptional circumstances created tempora-
> rily by the monetary situation.
> They are also intended to prevent the disruption in the Member State
> concerned of the intervention system set up under Community regulations.
> Furthermore, these are not levies introduced by some Member States
> unilaterally, but Community measures which, bearing in mind the exceptional
> circumstances of the time, are permissible within the framework of the common
> agricultural policy.
> Thus, the Council, by adopting them, did not contravene the provisions
> referred to by the national court.'

4.14 In the second case, *Bauhuis* v. *Netherlands*,[40] the Court was
confronted with a rather different type of tax, although it was also
confined to agricultural products. In accordance with the provisions
of the Dutch law relating to livestock, the plaintiff in the main
action was required to pay fees for public health inspection, *inter
alia*, on exports of pigs, 'bovine animals' and horses. Directive
64/432[41] required the exporting Member State to carry out certain
veterinary and public health inspections of pigs and 'bovine animals'
without stating whether a charge might be levied for such inspections. The object of the Directive was to shift supervision to the
exporting Member State so as to avoid the need for multiple
inspections at subsequent frontiers, and thereby to facilitate intra-
Community trade. The Directive does not apply to horses.

In an action before it in which the plaintiff contested the compatibility of these charges with Community law, the Arrondissements-
rechtbank of The Hague asked the Court of Justice to decide
whether charges of this kind constituted charges of equivalent effect
to customs duties on exports contrary to Article 16 of the Treaty.

The Court had already held[42] that, even when an inspection is
justified under Article 36 on human or animal health grounds, any
sum charged for that inspection constitutes a prohibited charge of
equivalent effect to a customs duty if it is levied according to criteria
not comparable with those employed in fixing charges on similar
domestic products. Consequently, in *Bauhuis* the Court held that

---

[40] Case 46/76 [1977] E.C.R. 5.
[41] [1964] O.J. Spec.Ed. 164.
[42] Case 29/72 *Marimex* v. *Italian Finance Administration* [1972] E.C.R. 1309, [1973]
C.M.L.R. 486.

the charges for the inspection of horses were contrary to Article 16, such inspections not being provided for by Community legislation.

Yet the Court adopted a radically different approach to the other charges, since they related to inspections which:

> 'are not[43] laid down unilaterally by each Member State but have been made obligatory and uniform in the case of all the products in question whichever the exporting Member State or the Member State of destination may be.
>
> On the other hand they are not prescribed by each Member State in order to protect some interest of its own but by the Council in the general interest of the Community.
>
> They cannot therefore be regarded as unilateral measures which hinder trade but rather as operations intended to promote the free movement of goods, in particular by rendering ineffective the obstacles to this free movement which might be created by the measures for veterinary and public health inspections adopted pursuant to Article 36.
>
> In these circumstances fees charged for veterinary and public health inspections, which are prescribed by a Community provision, which are uniform and are required to be carried out before despatch within the exporting country do not constitute charges having an effect equivalent to customs duties on exports, provided that they do not exceed the actual cost of the inspection for which they are charged.'[44]

4.15   A ruling which must undoubtedly rest on its special facts was that in *Kind* v. *E.C. Commission and Council*.[45] That case concerned the validity of Article 9(3) of Council Regulation 1837/80 on the common organisation of the markets in 'sheepmeat' and 'goatmeat'[46] which imposed a clawback on exports of mutton and lamb from the United Kingdom to other Member States. The clawback was equal to the amount of the variable slaughter premium granted by the United Kingdom by virtue of the Regulation, no such premium being granted in the other Member States. The regulations in question were part of the common market organisation for those products, which was not established until October 1980. The plaintiffs brought an action for compensation under Article 215 EEC, arguing, *inter alia*, that the clawback constituted a charge of equivalent effect contrary to Articles 9, 12, 13 and 16.

The Court rejected that argument. It first pointed out that the contested provisions were transitional in nature, being designed to bring about a gradual convergence in the markets in mutton and lamb in the Member States; that convergence was intended to be

---

[43] Unfortunately the word 'not' appears to be missing in the English text, but the other language versions indicate that it should be there.

[44] For criticisms of this ruling see Barents 'Charges of Equivalent Effect to Customs Duties' [1978] C.M.L.Rev. 415 and Kohler, *Abgaben zollgleicher Wirkung im Recht der Europäischen Gemeinschaften* (1978). It should also be pointed out that in Case 89/76 *E.C. Commission v. Netherlands* [1977] E.C.R. 1355, [1978] 3 C.M.L.R. 630 the Court reached a similar conclusion with respect to fees charged for the phytosanitary inspection of plant exports provided for not by Community legislation, but by an international convention to which all the Member States were party.

[45] Case 106/81 [1982] E.C.R. 2885, noted by Lenaerts [1983] C.M.L.Rev. 839.

[46] [1980] O.J. L183/1, subsequently amended.

complete by April 1984, as was stated in the regulations themselves. In a crucial passage it then stated:

> 'within the framework of a regulation, namely Regulation No. 1837/80, the provisions of which, according to Article 34 thereof, are to be reviewed before 1 April 1984, the charge on exports provided for by Article 9(3) of that regulation is inseparable in principle from the intervention system which is made up of payment of the variable slaughter premium in Community regions where buying-in is not practised by the intervention agencies. Therefore, the charge does not constitute, as the applicant maintains, a charge having an effect equivalent to a customs duty but is in reality intended to offset exactly the effects of the slaughter premium, thereby enabling products from the Member States or regions in which the premium is paid to be exported to other Member States without disturbing their markets. If there were no claw-back, offers emanating from a Member State which applies the slaughter premium might be made on markets in other Member States at prices appreciably lower than those obtaining in the latter and might bring, through a fall in prices, the intervention measures which the Community would thus in fact be called upon to finance for a second time, albeit perhaps in another form.'

This ruling seems questionable: the clawback was designed to offset a disparity caused by the fact that the premium was granted in the United Kingdom alone; this disparity, which was sanctioned by Regulation 1837/80, was surely irreconcileable with the fundamental principle that Community law is to be applied uniformly in all the Member States. Moreover, it is hard to see how the supposedly temporary nature of this state of affairs could render the clawback lawful.

At all events, the Court to some extent qualified this ruling in *United Kingdom* v. *E.C. Commission*,[47] the sequel to *Kind*. It was held there that the Commission had exceeded its powers under Regulation 1837/80 by imposing a clawback on exports from the United Kingdom of animals and products for which the slaughter premium had not been and could not be granted. In so doing the Court cited *Ramel* and referred to the provision in Article 43(3)(b) that a common market organisation must ensure 'conditions for trade within the Community similar to those existing in a national market'. It also noted that, although the disparities in the common market organisation concerned were supposedly transitional in nature, they had still not been removed. It added:

> 'The incomplete state of such a common organisation of the market, which is due in particular to the fact that a particular support measure is reserved for producers of a specific region and is liable to improve their competitive position, may call for corrective measures to restore equality between producers in all regions so far as their competitive position is concerned. Such measures, in so far as they constitute obstacles to the free movement of goods to which any common organisation of the market must aspire, are necessarily of an exceptional nature and therefore their scope must be strictly limited to their specific objective in the context of bringing about market conditions which come closest to those of an internal market.'

---

[47] Case 61/86 [1988] 2 C.M.L.R. 98; see also Case 162/86 *The Queen* v. *Intervention Board for Agricultural Produce ex parte Livestock Sales Transport* [1988] 2 C.M.L.R. 186.

Accordingly it does not appear to be beyond the realms of possibility that the Court might one day lose its patience with the Council's failure to abolish the disparities in the current, 'transitional' common market organisation for 'sheepmeat' and 'goatmeat' and find that the considerations underlying its ruling in *Kind* have ceased to apply.

4.16 Leaving aside the controversial judgment in *Kind* one may tentatively conclude that Community legislation restricting trade between Member States is lawful if it satisfies the following cumulative conditions:

(i) It must be uniform throughout the Member States. This must, however, be subject to the rule that objectively different situations require different treatment.[48] Otherwise the validity of the Community's regional policy would be in serious doubt.

(ii) It must be adopted 'in the general interest of the Community'. It is not clear quite what is meant by this, but in *REWE-Zentral* v. *Bundesmonopolverwaltung für Branntwein*[49] (the 'Cassis de Dijon' case), discussed at length in Chapter VI of this book, the Court found that national measures constituting obstacles to interstate trade must be accepted in so far as those provisions may be recognised as being necessary in order to satisfy mandatory requirements relating in particular to the effectiveness of fiscal supervision, the protection of public health, the fairness of commercial transactions and the defence of the consumer. The concept of general interest for the purposes of Community legislation must be at least as wide as that obtaining for national measures. At all events, the provisions of Articles 2 and 3 of the Treaty will serve as a general guide to the concept of general interest for these purposes.

(iii) It must be 'intended to promote the free movement of goods' although in itself it is restrictive of trade between Member States. This requirement may in fact merge with (ii) above. In many cases, it is something of a misnomer to describe such measures as restrictive of interstate trade, because they are in fact less restrictive than the measures which would be necessary in their absence. Such is the case, for example, with the public health inspections at issue in *Bauhuis*: in the absence of the export inspections laid down by the Directive, the Member States would in practice have been obliged to carry out checks on imports, which would be justified under Article 36 of the Treaty but which would constitute a greater restriction on trade.

---

[48] Case 13/63 *EEC Commission* v. *Italy* [1963] E.C.R. 165, [1963] C.M.L.R. 289.
[49] Case 120/78 [1979] E.C.R. 649, [1979] 3 C.M.L.R. 494.

(iv) The restrictive effects of the Community measure must not be greater than is necessary to attain the legitimate end in view. The Court has held in other contexts that, since the principle of the free movement of goods is a fundamental principle of the Treaty, exceptions to it may only be allowed in so far as they are necessary.[50]

4.17 It is probable, though, that the burden of proof is different in the case of Community legislation than in the case of national measures. While there is a presumption that national measures creating restrictions on interstate trade are unjustified,[51] the opposite should apply to Community legislation. Indeed as already pointed out, an apparent obstacle to interstate trade contained in Community legislation will often turn out not to be an obstacle at all by comparison with the situation which would have existed in its absence.

4.18 In any case, it can be concluded that the Community institutions are bound to have regard in adopting legislation to the principle of the free movement of goods. Having established this, the question arises whether these institutions are bound by Articles 9 to 17 and 30 to 36 EEC themselves or rather by rules which are analogous to them. No clear indication can be found in the Treaty itself. Although in some instances it states simply that the restrictions in question are prohibited 'between Member States' (as in Articles 9(1), 30 and 34(1)), in others the obligations in point are expressed to be addressed to the Member States (as in Article 31, which states that 'Member States shall refrain from introducing . . .'). Little if any conclusion can be drawn from the existence of these two forms of words.

In *Ramel*[52] it was held that the Community provision concerned was contrary to Article 13 itself, but according to Matthies[53] this was merely because the provision did not itself impose an import duty but merely permitted the Member States to do so. He firmly takes the view that the Community legislator is bound by the *principle* of the free movement of goods, and not by Articles 9 to 17 or 30 to 36 as such. In his view, the free movement of goods is a fundamental principle of Community law to be observed by the Community institutions in the performance of their tasks, much in the same way as the principles of non-discrimination and of proportionality. This view appears to be supported by *REWE-Zentrale*[54] in which the Court stated:

[50] With respect to Art. 36, see Case 104/75 *de Peijper* [1976] E.C.R. 613, [1976] 2 C.M.L.R. 271 discussed at para. 8.10 below; see also para. 9.01 below.
[51] See para. 8.03 below.
[52] See n.18 above.
[53] See n.16 above.
[54] See n.30 above.

'although it is true, as the Commission emphasised in its observations, that Articles 30 to 36 of the Treaty apply primarily to unilateral measures adopted by the Member States, the Community institutions themselves must also have due regard to freedom of trade within the Community, which is a fundamental principle of the common market.'

4.19 Whatever attitude one adopts to this particular problem, it seems clear that the Court has plotted a middle course: while setting bounds to the freedom enjoyed by the Community institutions in this regard, it has ensured that this freedom is greater than that permitted to the Member States in view of the special tasks which the Community is called upon to perform. In addition, the Community institutions possess special powers under exception or escape clauses such as Articles 103, 108 and 115 of the EEC. These are discussed in Chapter IX below.

III. PRIVATE PARTIES

4.20 There remains the difficult question as to whether private parties—individuals and non-State bodies—are bound by the provisions of Articles 30 to 36.[55] Frequently, restrictions on interstate trade resulting from the action of private parties will fall under Articles 85 and 86 of the Treaty relating to competition.[56] But these provisions only apply in the case of agreements between undertakings (Article 85) or action taken by one undertaking acting alone where that undertaking has a dominant position (Article 86). Other restrictions on imports and exports due to the actions of private parties fall outside Articles 85 and 86. Let us take two examples:

— an insurance company without any dominant position refuses to insure imported cars, without being party to any agreement to that effect;

— a dockers' union takes industrial action with the specific aim of preventing imports (it is generally considered that trade unions fall outside the scope of the concept of 'undertakings' in Articles 85 and 86).

In each case it will be assumed that no Member State has in any way supported the action in question.[57]

4.21 Clearly such behaviour is contrary to the spirit of the Treaty but is it unlawful? Put in more technical terms, do Articles 30 and

---

[55] See van Gerven 'The Recent Case Law of the Court of Justice concerning Arts. 30 and 36 of the EEC Treaty' [1977] C.M.L.Rev. 5; Matthies, *op. cit.* n.16 above; VerLoren van Themaat 'De artikelen 30–36 van het EEG-Verdrag' [1980] *RM Themis* 4–5 378; Barents 'New Developments in Measures Having Equivalent Effect' [1981] C.M.L.Rev. 271, at 275; Gormley *Prohibiting Restriction on Trade within the EEC* (1985) at 258–262.

[56] As to the relationship between Arts. 30 to 36 on the one hand and Arts. 85 and 86 on the other see paras. 6.30 and 6.31 below.

[57] Any action encouraged by the State, even in a non-binding form, constitutes a State measure for this purpose: para. 6.07 below.

34 have 'horizontal effect'? Perhaps surprisingly, the Court has not yet been called upon to decide the point. On the other hand, in Written Question 909/79 the Commission was asked whether industrial action which prevents goods from crossing national frontiers was contrary to the letter of the Treaty. The Commission replied[58] in the following somewhat non-committal terms:

> '. . . the Commission agrees that, although the type of action described by the Honourable Member does not contravene Article 30 of the EEC Treaty, it could under certain circumstances disrupt trade within the Community.'

4.22 Proponents of the view that such action is contrary to Article 30 would rely on the following arguments:

First, they would rely on the Court's case law[59] stating that the exercise of industrial property rights to exclude imports from other Member States can in certain circumstances be contrary to Article 30. They would rely in particular on certain passages in these judgments suggesting that such exercise is to be regarded as the act of the private party concerned. An example is the following passage in *Deutsche Grammophon* v. *Metro*[60]:

> '. . . the essential purpose of the Treaty, which is to unite national markets into a single market . . . could not be attained if, under the various legal systems of the Member States, nationals of those States were able to partition the market and bring about arbitrary discrimination or disguised restrictions on trade between Member States'.

Similarly, in *Dansk Supermarked*[61] the Court stated that:

> '. . . it is impossible in any circumstances for agreements between individuals to derogate from the mandatory provisions of the Treaty on the free movement of goods.'

4.23 Secondly, they would advert to the Court's decision in *Walrave* v. *Union Cycliste Internationale*.[62] That case concerned alleged discrimination on the grounds of nationality within a private sporting organisation. One of the points which arose for decision was whether a private body was bound by Article 48 of the Treaty on the free movement of workers and Article 59 on the free provision of services. The Court ruled as follows:

> 'Articles 7, 48, and 59 have in common the prohibition, in their respective spheres of application, of any discrimination on grounds of nationality.
>
> Prohibition of such discrimination does not only apply to the action of public authorities but extends likewise to rules of any other nature aimed at regulating in a collective manner gainful employment and the provision of services . . .

---

[58] [1980] O.J. C156/10.
[59] See paras. 8.94 *et seq.* below.
[60] Case 78/70 [1971] E.C.R. 487 at 500, [1971] C.M.L.R. 631 at 657.
[61] See n.5 above.
[62] Case 36/74 [1974] E.C.R. 1405, [1975] 1 C.M.L.R. 320.

It follows that the provisions of Articles 7, 48 and 59 of the Treaty may be taken into account by the national court in judging the validity or the effects of a provision inserted in the rules of a sporting organisation'.[63]

This ruling was subsequently confirmed in *Donà* v. *Mantero*.[64]

4.24 This case law is particularly interesting in that the structure of Articles 59 to 66 on services is in one sense analogous to those relating to goods. While Article 59 simply states that 'restrictions on freedom to provide services within the Community shall be progressively abolished during the transitional period in respect of nationals of Member States', the third paragraph of Article 60 as well as Articles 62 and 64 are expressed to be addressed to the Member States (as is Article 62, which states that 'Member States shall not introduce any new restrictions . . .').[65] In *Walrave* the Court addressed itself to this question in the following terms:

> 'Although the third paragraph of Article 60, and Articles 62 and 64 specifically relate, as regards the provision of services to the abolition of measures by the State, this fact does not defeat the general nature of the terms of Article 59, which makes no distinction between the source of the restrictions to be abolished'.

4.25 The third argument is based on *Defrenne* v. *Sabena*.[66] That case concerned the interpretation of Article 119 of the Treaty, the first paragraph of which reads:

> 'Each Member State shall during the first stage ensure and subsequently maintain the application of the principle that men and women should receive equal pay for equal work.'

In reply to a preliminary question the Court ruled that Article 119 prohibited discrimination in pay between men and women, whether by private or by public organisations. The following passages of the judgment are particularly illustrative in the present context:

> 'It is also impossible to put forward arguments based on the fact that Article 119 only refers expressly to "Member States".
>
> Indeed, as the Court has already found in other contexts, the fact that certain provisions of the Treaty are formally addressed to the Member States does not prevent rights from being conferred at the same time on any individual who has an interest in the performance of the duties thus laid down. . . .
>
> . . . in its reference to "Member States", Article 119 is alluding to those States in the exercise of all those of their functions which may usefully contribute to the implementation of the principle of equal pay. . . .
>
> Therefore, the reference to "Member States" in Article 119 cannot be interpreted as excluding the intervention of the courts in direct application of the Treaty'.[67]

---

[63] At 1418–1419.
[64] Case 13/76 [1976] E.C.R. 1333, [1976] 2 C.M.L.R. 578.
[65] See para. 4.18 above.
[66] Case 43/75 [1976] E.C.R. 455, [1976] 2 C.M.L.R. 98.
[67] At 475.

In other words, the judiciary is one of the organs of the Member States and is bound by Article 119 in the same way as the other organs of the States.

4.26 The first argument[68] should, it is submitted, be rejected: the exercise of industrial rights by a private person merely constitutes reliance on measures adopted by the Member States; without legislation, patent, trade mark and copyright protection would simply not exist.[69] It is true however, that the second and third arguments have considerable force.

Arguably, the question has now been settled by the judgment in *Van de Haar*[70] in which the Court was called upon to compare Articles 30 and 85. The Court replied that, whereas Article 85 'belongs to the rules on competition which are addressed to undertakings and associations of undertakings and which are intended to maintain effective competition in the common market', Article 30 'belongs to the rules which seek to ensure the free movement of goods and, to that end to eliminate measures taken by Member States . . .' Gormley[71] may well be right in his view that, even if the Court was not directly addressing the question whether the acts of private parties may infringe Article 30, the contention that they may do so is weakened by this ruling.

4.27 Be that as it may, it cannot yet be completely ruled out that Articles 30 to 36 or, more probably, certain analogous principles[72] can bind private parties in certain circumstances. However, it is not clear how wide this rule is, if it exists at all:

(a) first, it would be extremely cumbersome if most acts caught by Article 85 or 86 simultaneously contravened Articles 30 to 36 (or analogous principles);

(b) measures attributable to the State discriminating against imported goods in public supply contracts are contrary to Article 30[73]; yet it would clearly be far-fetched to hold that a private person with no dominant position and acting alone would fall foul of Article 30 (or an analogous principle) if he chose not to purchase imported goods.[74]

---

[68] See para. 4.22 above.
[69] See the passage from *Dansk Supermarked* quoted in paragraph 4.04 above; A.G. Warner in Cases 55 and 57/80 *Musik-Vertrieb Membran* v. *GEMA* [1981] E.C.R. 147 at 174–5, [1981] 2 C.M.L.R. 44 at 56–57; and Daniele 'Réflexions d'ensemble sur la notion de mesures ayant un effet équivalent à des restrictions quantitatives' [1984] R.M.C. 477 at 479. *Contra* Waelbroeck, 'Les rapports entre les règles sur la libre circulation des marchandises et les règles de concurrence applicables aux entreprises de la CEE' in *Liber Amicorum Pierre Pescatore* (1987) 781.
[70] Cases 177 and 178/82 [1984] E.C.R. 1797, [1985] 2 C.M.L.R. 566.
[71] *Op. cit.* at 261.
[72] For this view see Matthies, *op cit.*, n.17 above.
[73] See paras. 7.23 *et seq.* below.
[74] Matthies, *op. cit.* n.17 above.

4.28   At all events, it is submitted, the acts of private parties not attributable to the State cannot give rise to infringement proceedings under Article 169 of the Treaty. Such actions can only be brought against the Member States and not against private parties; and there is no reason to suppose that a Member State can be held responsible in this way for the act of a private person which that Member State has neither required nor in any way incited.[75] It is true that, when asked about violent action taken by individuals to obstruct lorries carrying imports into a Member State, the Commission has stated[76] that 'under Community law Member States' Governments are required to take the necessary steps to prevent such action'. Nevertheless, this type of situation might be regarded as *sui generis* and in any case the Commission did not specify whether such an obligation was imposed on Member States by Article 5, Article 30 or some other provision.

Finally, it should be emphasised that the other chapters of this book in principle concern only those measures which are attributable to the Member States. Measures attributable to the Community institutions or to private parties are only referred to incidentally.

---

[75] Wägenbaur in Groeben, Boeckh, Thiesing, Ehlermann *Kommentar zum EWG-Vertrag* (1983) Vol. I at 246. Lecrenier appears to suggest otherwise ('Les articles 30 et suivants CEE et les procédures de contrôle prévues par la directive 83/189 CEE' [1985] R.M.C. 6 at 18 *et seq.*). Yet this view is surely based on a misreading of Case 104/75 *De Peijper* [1976] E.C.R. 613 at 637, [1976] 2 C.M.L.R. 271 at 305–306 where it was held that Member States are under a duty to take positive steps to reduce to a minimum restrictions which they themselves have imposed (see generally para. 6.20 below). Thus, it was held that the Dutch authorities could not allow their legislation on the importation of pharmaceuticals to be exploited by manufacturers so as to thwart parallel imports. She has overlooked the fact that the legislation emanated from the Dutch State, not from manufacturers.

[76] Answer to Written questions 591/83 and 614/83 ([1983] O.J. C323/14).

CHAPTER V

Quantitative restrictions

Quantitative restrictions on imports and exports are prohibited by Articles 30 and 34 respectively, unless they are justified under Article 36.

This chapter is divided into three sections covering respectively the timetable for the abolition of these restrictions, the direct applicability of the prohibition, and the definition of the concept of quantitative restrictions. Article 36 is not considered in this chapter, since it is the subject of Chapter VIII.

I. THE TIMETABLE

5.01 With respect to imports, the basic prohibition on quantitative restrictions is to be found in Article 30, which provides:

> 'Quantitative restrictions and measures having equivalent effect shall, without prejudice to the following provisions, be prohibited between Member States.'

The timetable for the abolition of these measures is governed by the subsequent provisions. Articles 31 and 32 EEC lay down a 'standstill' rule as from the date of entry into force of the Treaty of Rome. The former provision states that Member States shall refrain from introducing new quantitative restrictions as between themselves, whereas the first paragraph of Article 32 prohibits Member States from making existing quotas more restrictive. The second paragraph of Article 32 declares that quotas shall be abolished by the end of the transitional period, 31 December 1969, at the latest and Article 33 sets out the system for their progressive abolition during this period. Article 35 states that the abolition of quantitative restrictions may be effected more rapidly than is provided for in Article 33, and indeed by Article 3 of Council Decision 66/532 of 26 July 1966[1] such restrictions were to be abolished immediately. In accordance with Article 191 of the Treaty, that provision took effect when the decision was notified to the Member States.

However, Article 3 of that decision expressly excludes agricultural products from its scope. All the regulations establishing common

---

[1] [1966] J.O. 165. This was preceded by two earlier acceleration decisions: those of 12 May 1960 (J.O. 12.9.1960) and 15 May 1962 (J.O. 28.5.1962).

market organisations[2] for agricultural products during the transitional period prohibited quantitative restrictions with respect to those products from the date of their entry into force. For agricultural products not yet subject to a common market organisation the prohibition took effect at the end of the transitional period.[3]

Article 34 EEC prohibits quantitative restrictions on exports as from the end of the first stage of the transitional period, namely 31 December 1961. The better view is that the prohibition applied to agricultural products as from the same date.[4] Although Article 34 does not expressly require Member States to refrain from introducing new restrictions on exports during the first stage of the transitional period, such an obligation can be deduced from its general structure.[5]

5.02 The first Act of Accession provides for the abolition of quantitative restrictions on imports and exports between the old and the new Member States as from its entry into force on 1 January 1973: Article 42. However, the prohibition took effect one month later for agricultural products subject to a common market organisation at the date of accession: Articles 60(1) and 151. For other agricultural products quantitative restrictions have been prohibited since 1 January 1978.[6] In addition, Article 43 entitled Member States to retain restrictions on exports of waste and scrap metal of iron and steel for a two-year period, except Denmark and the Republic of Ireland, which were granted periods of three and five years respectively. Finally two Protocols to the Act of Accession laid down exceptions for the Republic of Ireland. Protocol 6 set out a timetable for the abolition of Irish import quotas of stockings, brushes and brooms, superphosphate and certain vehicle parts, which exception expired on 1 July 1975. It also authorised the retention until 1 July 1975 of quantitative restrictions on exports from that State of certain hides and skins, certain types of woods and certain metals. Protocol 7 entitled the Irish Government to maintain until 1 January 1985 its quota system applicable to the assembly and import of motor vehicles applied in accordance with the Motor Vehicles (Registration of Importers) Act 1968.

5.03 The Act of Accession of Greece[7] likewise provides for the immediate abolition of quantitative restrictions on imports or exports between the Nine and Greece as from the date of accession, namely

---

[2] For the meaning of this term see para. 10.01 below.
[3] See para. 10.02 below.
[4] See para. 10.04 below.
[5] This can be deduced in particular from the fact that Art. 34(2) requires Member States to abolish, by the end of the first stage of the transitional period, export restrictions 'which are in existence when this Treaty enters into force', see Waelbroeck in *Le Droit de la Communauté Economique Européenne* (1970), Vol. 1, 113; Wägenbaur in Groeben, Boeckh, Thiesing, Ehlermann *Kommentar zum EWG-Vertrag* (1983), Vol. 1, 279.
[6] See para. 10.05 below.
[7] [1979] O.J. L291.

1 January 1981: Article 35. This applied also to agricultural products covered by a common organisation of the market: Article 65(1). On the other hand, Annex III to the Act lists a number of industrial products for which Greece could gradually reduce quantitative restrictions and abolish them on 31 December 1985 by virtue of Article 36 of the Act. Also, as in the first Act of Accession, there is a special provision for export restrictions on waste and scrap metal of iron or steel falling within heading no. 73.03: Article 37 provides that such arrangements could be maintained for a period of two years from 1 January 1981, in so far as they were not more restrictive than those applied to exports to third countries.[8] Finally, Article 65(2) provides that:

> 'in respect of products not covered, on the date of accession, by a common organisation of the market, the provisions of Title II concerning the progressive abolition of charges having equivalent effect to customs duties and of quantitative restrictions and measures having equivalent effect shall not apply to those charges, restrictions and measures if they form part of a national market organisation on the date of accession. This provision shall only apply until the common organisation of the market for these products is implemented and not later than 31 December 1985 and to the extent strictly necessary to ensure the maintenance of the national organisation.'

The better view is that both Greece and the other Member States could rely on this provision.[9]

5.04 Spain and Portugal acceded to the Community on 1 January 1986. By virtue of Article 42 of the Act of Accession[10] quantitative restrictions on imports and exports between the Ten and Spain were to be abolished on 1 January 1986. In addition, fruit and vegetables are subject to a special regime (Articles 136 *et seq*.). Transitional exceptions are contained in Articles 43, 45 and 46. Furthermore Article 49 and Protocol 9 to the Act require Spain to 'control' exports to the Ten of certain textile goods under prescribed conditions until 31 December 1989.

In trade between Spain and the Ten in agricultural products covered by a common market organisation quantitative restrictions on imports and exports were to be abolished by 1 March 1986, by virtue of Article 76(1). That rule is itself subject to an exception contained in Articles 81 to 85, which provides for a 'supplementary trade mechanism'[11] for a series of products until 31 December 1995. Agricultural products not subject to a common market organisation are governed by Article 76(2). The language of that provision is

---

[8] It appears from other language texts that the reference to import restrictions in the English text of Art. 37 is erroneous and that the Art. is intended to cover *export* restrictions.
[9] See paras. 10.05 and 10.06 below.
[10] [1985] O.J. L302, see generally Didier and Grisay 'Adhésion de l'Espagne et du Portugal: régime douanier des échanges de produits industriels' [1987] C.D.E. 255.
[11] In Case 119/86 *Spain* v. *E.C. Council and Commission* (judgment of 20 October 1987) it was held to be lawful for the defendants to impose a system of certificates and deposits as part of the supplementary trade mechanism.

almost identical to that of Article 65(2) of the Greek Act of Accession, except that it applies expressly to measures forming part of a national market organisation in Spain or in another Member State. The exception created by Article 76(2) is to lapse on 31 December 1995.

Similarly, Article 202 provides that quantitative restrictions on imports and exports between Portugal and the Ten were to be abolished on 1 January 1986. Transitional exceptions are contained in Articles 203 and 207 (read with Protocol 18). In addition, Article 206 and Protocol 17 require Portugal to 'control' exports of certain textile products until 31 December 1988 to the Ten and until 31 December 1989 to Spain.

As regards trade between Portugal and the Ten in agricultural products covered by a market organisation, Articles 244(1) and 249 to 252 are similar to the provisions already discussed in relation to Spain (Articles 76(1) and 81 to 86). However, for the agricultural products caught by Article 259 a different set of provisions, contained notably in Articles 269 to 279, applies.

Agricultural products not covered by a common market organisation are governed by Article 244(2) which corresponds to Article 76(2) relating to Spain, although there are anomalous differences in wording between the two paragraphs.

Trade between Spain and Portugal is governed by other provisions again. Article 54 states that the Kingdom of Spain shall apply Articles 30 to 53 of the Act in its trade with the Portuguese Republic, 'subject to the conditions set out in Protocol 3'. Likewise, Article 214 provides that 'the Portuguese Republic shall apply Articles 189 to 213 in its trade with the Kingdom of Spain, subject to the conditions set out in Protocol 3'. None of these provisions covers agricultural products. Articles 88 and 256 require the Council to adopt the arrangements applicable to trade in such goods between the two countries. In addition, a joint declaration on the arrangements applicable to trade in agricultural products between Spain and Portugal is annexed to the Act of Accession. This declaration states: 'In their mutual trade in agricultural products, each of the new Member States shall apply in principle with respect to the other the provisions and transitional mechanisms provided for in the Act of Accesssion under the arrangements applicable to their respective trade with the Community as at present constituted. . .' The declaration then goes on to qualify this statement of principle with respect to certain products. The Council has implemented Articles 88 and 256 by Regulation 3792/85,[12] which is expressed to take account of the joint declaration.

5.05 It follows from what has been said in the previous paragraphs that no transitional exemption from the prohibition on quantitative

---

[12] [1985] O.J. L367/7.

restrictions on imports or exports between Member States has applied since the end of 1985 apart from those contained in the Act of Accession of Spain and Portugal.

Article 226 of the Treaty of Rome, which empowered the Commission to authorise any of the original six Member States in serious economic difficulties to adopt safeguard measures during their transitional period is referred to briefly in Chapter IX, as are the analogous provisions in the successive Acts of Accession.[13] Also, permanent exceptions to the prohibition on quantitative restrictions are discussed in Chapters VIII and IX.

II. DIRECT EFFECT

5.06 In *Salgoil* v. *Italian Ministry for Foreign Trade*[14] an Italian court asked the Court of Justice to 'determine whether the provisions of Article 30 *et seq.* of the Treaty, especially Article 31, also produce effects on the relationship between a Member State and its nationals'. Since this question was posed during the transitional period, the Court saw no need to decide the question in relation to Article 30 itself, but only in relation to Articles 31 to 33.

In this connection the Court found that the initial paragraphs of Articles 31 and 32—the contents of which were discussed at the beginning of this chapter—did produce 'direct effects on the legal relationships between Member States and those subject to their jurisdiction'.[15] On the other hand, the second paragraph of Article 32 and Article 33, both of which concerned the gradual elimination of existing quotas, did not produce such effects.

5.07 Not until 1977 did the Court decide this point with respect to Article 30 itself, in *Iannelli* v. *Meroni*.[16] It did so in the following terms:

> 'The prohibition of quantitative restrictions and measures having equivalent effect laid down in Article 30 of the Treaty is mandatory and explicit and its implementation does not require any subsequent intervention of the Member States or Community institutions.
>
> The prohibition therefore has direct effect and creates individual rights which national courts must protect; this occurred at the end of the transitional period at the latest, that is to say on 1 January 1970 as the provisions of the second paragraph of Article 32 of the Treaty indicate.'

Likewise in *Pigs Marketing Board* v. *Redmond*[17] the Court held that Articles 30 and 34 were 'directly applicable and that as such

---

[13] Chapter 9, fn. 3.
[14] Case 13/68 [1968] E.C.R. 453, [1969] C.M.L.R. 181.
[15] In the case of Art. 31 the Court held that such efforts were delayed for a period of up to six months, by virtue of the second paragraph of that Art.
[16] Case 74/76 [1977] E.C.R. 557, [1977] 2 C.M.L.R. 688.
[17] Case 83/78 [1978] E.C.R. 2347, [1979] 1 C.M.L.R. 177.

they confer on individuals rights which the courts of Member States must protect'.

It is clear that these pronouncements apply equally to quantitative restrictions and to measures of equivalent effect.

III. THE DEFINITION OF QUANTITATIVE RESTRICTIONS

5.08 The Court of Justice has held that 'the prohibition on quantitative restrictions covers measures which amount to a total or partial restraint of, according to the circumstances, imports, exports or goods in transit': *Geddo v. Ente Nazionale Risi.*[18] In that case it was clear beyond all doubt that the national measure at issue did not fall within that definition.

However, this matter was raised subsequently with respect to section 42 of the Customs Consolidation Act 1876 prohibiting the importation into the United Kingdom of indecent or obscene articles. The case in question was *R. v. Henn and Darby*[19] in which the defendants had been convicted before the English courts of contravening this section.

When it was contended before it that this provision was contrary to Article 30, the Court of Appeal[20] rejected this argument, *inter alia*, on the grounds that the term 'quantitative restrictions' connoted restrictions 'concerned with quantity' and not total prohibitions. This ruling caused some surprise in that one of the principal aims of the Treaty of Rome was to guard against protectionism between the Member States—an aim which would be completely undermined if the Court of Appeal's interpretation were followed. More concretely, the Court of Appeal's judgment was contrary to the ruling of the Court of Justice in the *Geddo* case and failed to take account of the opening words of Article 36:

'The provisions of Articles 30 to 34 shall not preclude *prohibitions*[21] or restrictions on imports, exports or goods in transit justified on grounds of public morality. . . .'

The defendants then appealed to the House of Lords, which made its first reference ever to the Court of Justice on this and other points arising out of the case. It was not contended by any party before the Court of Justice that the Court of Appeal's interpretation had been correct and it was virtually a foregone conclusion that the Court would hold, as indeed it did, that a prohibition on imports of pornographic articles fell under Article 30. Nevertheless it is interesting to note that although the reference only contemplated

---

[18] Case 2/73 [1973] E.C.R. 865 at 879, [1974] 1 C.M.L.R. 13 at 42.
[19] Case 34/79 [1979] E.C.R. 3795, [1980] 1 C.M.L.R. 246, see paras. 8.08 and 8.26 *et seq.* below.
[20] [1978] 1 W.L.R. 1031.
[21] The italics are those of the author.

the possibility that the prohibition was a measure of equivalent effect, both the Advocate General and the Court specifically found that it was a quantitative restriction pure and simple.

5.09 Thus the concept of quantitative restrictions covers not only 'quotas', which term appears in Articles 32 and 33, but also absolute prohibitions on imports or exports, as the case may be. This is so whatever the nature of the imports or exports, be they reimports or goods in transit,[22] or re-exports.[23] Furthermore, a quantitative restriction may be based on legislation or merely be an administrative practice.[24] On the other hand, the Articles in question only cover non-tariff quotas; under these, import or export bans are imposed once the ceiling has been reached. Tariff quotas (under which customs duties are imposed on goods exceeding the ceiling laid down) infringe Articles 12 *et seq.* if they are imposed between Member States.

5.10 Nevertheless, the exact dividing line between quantitative restrictions and measures of equivalent effect is not yet fully clear. For instance, the requirement of import or export licences has been held to constitute a measure of equivalent effect.[25] Yet such a requirement amounts to a prohibition on import or export without the requisite licence.[26] The same applies with respect to the obligation to produce sanitary or veterinary certificates for imports or exports.[27]

The distinction might perhaps be made in the following manner:
— when an import or export prohibition relates to the goods themselves (*i.e.* their size, weight, composition, presentation, *etc.* . . . .), then it constitutes a quantitative restriction[28];
— when the prohibition relates to factors extraneous to the goods themselves (*e.g.* the failure to obtain an import or export licence, or to produce a certificate), then it constitutes a measure of equivalent effect.

5.11 On this view an import prohibition designed to protect industrial property rights constitutes a quantitative restriction rather than a measure of equivalent effect.[29] On this view also the national

---

[22] See paras. 2.25 and 2.26 above.

[23] See para. 6.64 below.

[24] See paras. 6.10 and 6.11 below.

[25] See para. 7.03 below.

[26] Case 194/85 *E.C. Commission* v. *Greece* (bananas) (judgment of 25 February 1988) was concerned with an import licensing system under which licences were always or almost always refused. The Court found it unnecessary to decide whether this system constituted a quantitative restriction or a measure of equivalent effect.

[27] See para. 7.04 below.

[28] It is submitted that this applies even to an import prohibition coupled with a prohibition on sale within the Member State concerned. On the other hand, a prohibition on sale in itself constitutes a measure of equivalent effect: para. 7.52 below. See generally Ehlermann in Groeben, Boeckh, Thiesing *Kommentar zum EWG-Vertrag* (1974), at 253–354.

[29] As to justification, see para. 8.94 *et seq.* below.

provision at issue in Case 153/78 *E.C. Commission* v. *Germany*[30] would be considered a quantitative restriction. That case arose out of proceedings brought under Article 169 of the Treaty with respect to a German provision prohibiting the importation of meat products processed in a country other than the one in which the original animals were slaughtered. In ruling that this measure was contrary to Article 30, the Court did not decide whether it was a quantitative restriction or a measure of equivalent effect, as it was not necessary to decide this.[31]

5.12 In any case, it would seem that the distinction between quantitative restrictions and measures of equivalent effect is only material with respect to the transitional periods laid down by the Treaty of Rome and the Acts of Accession, in the following manner:

— whereas quantitative restrictions were to be abolished as between the original Member States in 1966,[32] this did not occur for measures of equivalent effect until 1 January 1970[33];

— the first Act of Accession provided for the immediate abolition of quantitative restrictions,[34] while measures of equivalent effect were subject to a two-year period of grace[35];

— Article 36 of the Act of Accession of Greece[36] entitled that country to retain quantitative restrictions on certain industrial products for a certain period, without creating a corresponding exception with respect to measures of equivalent effect.

However, it should be recalled[37] that Protocol 3 to the first Act of Accession on the Channel Islands and the Isle of Man begins:

'The Community rules on customs matters and quantitative restrictions, in particular those of the Act of Accession, shall apply to the Channel Islands and the Isle of Man under the same conditions as they apply to the United Kingdom.'

Although measures of equivalent effect are not expressly mentioned, it is probable that this Protocol covers such measures[38]—particularly

---

[30] [1979] E.C.R. 2555, [1980] 1 C.M.L.R. 198.

[31] In many other cases concerning measures which might properly be described as quantitative restrictions the Court has ruled instead that those measures constituted measures of equivalent effect or has simply stated without more that they were contrary to Art. 30; see *e.g.* Cases 40/82 *E.C. Commission* v. *United Kingdom* (Newcastle disease) [1982] E.C.R. 2793, [1982] 3 C.M.L.R. 497 and [1984] E.C.R. 283, 74/82 *E.C. Commission* v. *Ireland* [1984] E.C.R. 317, 59/82, *Schutzverband gegen Unwesen in der Wirtschaft* v. *Weinvertriebs* [1983] E.C.R. 1217, [1984] 1 C.M.L.R. 319 and 261/85 *E.C. Commission* v. *United Kingdom* (pasteurised milk) [1988] 2 C.M.L.R. 11. As to exports see Case 172/82 *Syndicat National des Fabricants Raffineurs d'Huile de Graissage* v. *Inter-Huiles* [1983] E.C.R. 555, [1983] 3 C.M.L.R. 485. In none of these cases has anything turned on the distinction between quantitative restrictions and measures of equivalent effect.

[32] See para. 5.01 above.

[33] See para. 6.02 below.

[34] See para. 5.02 above.

[35] See para. 6.07 Below.

[36] See para. 5.03 above.

[37] See para. 3.03 above.

[38] See para. 3.03 above.

in the light of the Court's ruling in *Iannelli* v. *Meroni* which suggests that 'quotas' in Article 32 covers measures of equivalent effect.[39]

Unless otherwise stated, the rules discussed in this book apply in the same way to quantitative restrictions as to measures of equivalent effect. In particular, the prohibition on quantitative restrictions is subject to the exception clauses discussed in Chapters VIII and XI.

[39] See the passage quoted at 5.07 above.

CHAPTER VI

Measures of equivalent effect: General

6.01 Article 30 provides that: 'Quantitative restrictions on imports and all measures having equivalent effect shall . . . be prohibited between Member States.' Article 34 is couched in the same terms, except that it applies to restrictions on exports.

As will be seen, the concept of measures of equivalent effect to quantitative restrictions differs from that of quantitative restrictions themselves in that it is considerably wider and more complex. Indeed the definition of this concept forms the crux of this book. For this reason this chapter contains more sections than Chapter V. These are: the timetable for the abolition of measures of equivalent effect, the definition of measures of equivalent effect on imports, the definition of such measures relating to exports, *de facto* harmonisation, and finally, 'purely national' restrictions. The direct applicability of the prohibition of measures of equivalent effect on imports and exports has already been dealt with in paragraph 5.06 above.

The compatibility of specific national measures with Articles 30 and 34 will be considered in Chapter VII.

Finally, in determining whether a particular measure falls under Article 30 or Article 34, it is imperative to proceed in two stages. The first question to ask is: does this measure restrict imports (or exports) so as to be caught by Article 30 (or Article 34)? If so, then the second question arises, namely: is the measure nevertheless justified in Community law and thus lawful? Justification is considered in Chapter VIII.

I. THE TIMETABLE

6.02 The reader is referred to paragraphs 5.01 to 5.05 above which cover the timetable for the abolition of quantitative restrictions, since the rules are broadly the same.

As between the original Member States the only difference in the timetable of abolition of quantitative restrictions and measures of equivalent effect is that Decision 66/532[1] only applied to quantitative restrictions.

---

[1] [1966] J.O. 165.

Consequently the prohibition on measures of equivalent effect on imports did not take effect until the end of the transitional period[2]— except as regards products already covered by a common market organisation or by a Directive based on Article 33(7). That paragraph provides:

'The Commission shall issue directives establishing the procedure and timetable in accordance with which the Member States shall abolish, as between themselves, any measures in existence when this Treaty enters into force which have an effect equivalent to quotas.'

This provision did not apply to exports.

6.03 It is clear from the context, and in particular the second paragraph of Article 32, that Article 33(7) lapsed at the end of the transitional period. During that period the Commission adopted five directives on the basis of this provision:

— Directive 64/486[3] requiring the Federal Republic of Germany progressively to abolish its import restrictions on potatoes; this Directive was exceptional in that it was addressed to one Member State only, the others being addressed to all the Member States;

— Directive 66/682[4] requiring the Member States to abolish, save for certain listed products, measures by which the importation of a product is made conditional on the exportation or purchase or sale of a domestic product;

— Directive 66/683[5] requiring the Member States to abolish, other than for certain products listed in the annex to the Directive, measures which partially or totally prohibit the use of an imported product; or subject the entitlement to a benefit, other than an aid within the meaning of Article 92 of the Treaty, to the total or partial use of a national product;

— Directive 70/32[6] requiring the Member States to abolish legislative provisions and put an end to administrative practices discriminating against the supply of imported goods to public authorities;

— Directive 70/50[7] was by far the most important of the five Directives; it was not limited to any particular type of measure like the other Directives, but set out a lengthy list of measures

---

[2] By some quirk of drafting the Treaty does not actually state that measures of equivalent effect on imports were to be abolished at the end of the transitional period. The second para. of Art. 32 stipulates that 'quotas shall be abolished by the end of the transitional period at the latest.' It appears that the term 'quotas' must be stretched beyond its natural meaning to include measures of equivalent effect; this appears to be the approach adopted by the Court in Case 74/76 *Iannelli* v. *Meroni* [1977] E.C.R. 557, [1977] 2 C.M.L.R. 688, see para. 5.06 above. In any case, there cannot be a shadow of a doubt that the prohibition on measures of equivalent effect on imports did take effect at the end of the transitional period: see *e.g.* the *Iannelli* case.

[3] [1964] J.O. 2253.
[4] [1966] J.O. 3745.
[5] [1966] J.O. 3748.
[6] [1970] J.O. L13/1, para. 7.23 below.
[7] [1970] J.O. L13/29. See Annex I to this Book.

which it required the Member States to abolish as being measures of equivalent effect; it also set out the Commission's general thinking at that time as to the scope and meaning of this concept; it will be described in greater detail during the course of this chapter.

6.04   During the transitional period these Directives may well have been directly effective[8] and thus capable of being relied on by individuals before the national courts. However, at the end of the transitional period Article 30 itself acquired direct effect,[9] so that this function of these Directives has been superseded. Also, any clauses in the Directives exempting particular products or measures lapsed at the end of the transitional period.

In addition, Article 33(7) empowers the Commission to issue Directives relating only to measures 'in existence when this Treaty enters into force.'[10] However, it would be anomalous if different criteria were to apply as regards measures adopted after the Treaty came into force. Moreover, in Case 12/74 *E.C. Commission* v. *Germany*,[11] the Court cited Directive 70/50 with approval with respect to a German statute of 1971, although it did not refer to this particular issue.

Moreover, while the Court has often quoted and followed Directive 70/50, it has also, as we shall see later,[12] implicitly rejected certain aspects of it, in particular its approach to 'indistinctly applicable' measures.

6.05   The Court has been invited to rule on the effect of Directive 70/50 in two cases. Firstly, in *E.C. Commission* v. *Ireland* ('Buy Irish')[13] the Court declined to rule on the challenge to the Directive mounted by the defendant. In Ireland's view Article 33(7), on which the Directive was based, only empowered the Commission to lay down procedures and timetables for the abolition of measures of equivalent effect without defining that concept. The Commission countered this with the argument that the power to give a non-exhaustive definition of the concept of measures of equivalent effect must have been impliedly conferred on it by Article 33(7). Since that concept was not defined in the Treaty, great uncertainty would have ensued if the Commission had laid down procedures and timetables without defining it. Advocate General Capotorti endorsed the view put forward by the Irish Government that the Directive was *ultra*

---

[8] See generally Case 33/70 *SACE* v. *Italian Ministry of Finance* [1970] E.C.R. 1213, [1971] C.M.L.R. 123.

[9] Para. 5.06 above.

[10] See Graf *Der Begriff 'Maßnahmen gleicher Wirkung wie mengenmässige Einfuhrbeschränkungen' im EWG-Vertrag* (1972), 25.

[11] [1975] E.C.R. 181 at 193, [1975] 1 C.M.L.R. 340 at 364 *et seq.* See para. 7.35 below.

[12] See paras. 6.48 and 7.03 below.

[13] [1982] E.C.R. 4005, [1983] 2 C.M.L.R. 104.

vires. Secondly, in *E.C. Commission* v. *Italy*,[14] the Commission relied on Article 2(3)(b) of Directive 70/50 but the defendant advanced an argument based on the wording of that provision to show that it was not applicable. On this point the Court ruled:

> 'With regard to the applicability of the criteria in Directive 70/50, it must be pointed out, as can be seen from the terms of Article 2(3) of that directive, that the measures having equivalent effect listed therein are advanced by way of example. Moreover, Directive 70/50 must be read in the light of Article 30 of the Treaty and it may not be relied upon as a means of defeating the objective set out in that Article, an objective which it itself is also intended to achieve. The Italian Republic's argument based on Directive 70/50 must therefore be rejected.'

6.06 In summary, while in legal theory these directives may have been directly effective since their adoption, as a matter of practice they have been relegated in importance since the end of the transitional period, when Article 30 itself acquired direct effect. Since then the Court has delivered a considerable body of case law on the concept of measures of equivalent effect under Article 30. This case law has largely superseded the Directives so that *in practice* they merely serve as non-binding guidelines to the interpretation of Article 30[15]—is so far as they have not been implicitly set aside by the case law of the Court. This perhaps explains why the Court declined to rule on the validity of Directive 70/50 in the *Buy Irish* case.

6.07 Under the first Act of Accession, measures of equivalent effect to quantitative restrictions on imports and exports were to be abolished by 1 January 1975 by virtue of Article 42(2) of that Act. The exceptions to that rule are those set out above at paragraph 5.02.

Centrafarm v. *Sterling Drug Inc.*[16] and *Centrafarm* v. *Winthrop*[17] concerned the use of patents and trade marks respectively to prevent imports into a Member State of goods put on to the market of another Member State by the patentee and trade mark holder or with his consent. In each case the Court held that such use was contrary to Article 30 without being justified under Article 36. The Court then turned to the interpretation of Article 42 of the Act of Accession: since these cases concerned imports from the United Kingdom and the Netherlands and the reference to the Court of Justice occurred in

---

[14] Case 103/84 (subsidies for the purchase of national vehicles) [1986] E.C.R. 1759, [1987] 2 C.M.L.R. 825.

[15] Matthies, 'Herkunftsangaben und Europäisches Gemeinschaftsrecht' in *Festschrift für Schiedermair* (1976), 397, Mestmäcker, *Die Vereinbarkeit von Preisregelungen und dem Arzneimittelmarkt mit dem Recht der Europäischen Wirtschaftsgemeinschaft* (1980) 29; for the view that Dir. 70/50 is binding see Sabiani, 'L'incidence du droit de la Communauté économique européenne sur la réglementation française de prix' [1975] R.T.D.E. 496, Winkel 'Die Vereinbarkeit staatlicher Preislenkungsmaßnahmen mit dem EWG-Vertrag' [1976] NJW 2050; see generally the A.G. in Case 12/74 *E.C. Commission* v. *Germany* [1975] E.C.R. 181 at 208, [1975] 1 C.M.L.R. 340 at 343.

[16] Case 15/74 [1974] E.C.R. 1147, [1974] 2 C.M.L.R. 480.

[17] Case 16/74 [1974] E.C.R. 1183, [1974] 2 C.M.L.R. 480.

1974, the national court asked in effect whether the prohibition could be invoked with respect to such imports before 1975.

On this point the Court replied:

> 'In the context, [Article 42(2)] can refer only to those measures having an effect equivalent to quantitative restrictions which, as between the original Member States, had to be abolished at the end of the transitional period, pursuant to Articles 30 and 32 to 35 of the EEC Treaty.
>
> It therefore appears that Article 42 of the Act of Accession has no effect upon prohibitions on importation arising from national legislation concerning industrial and commercial property.
>
> It follows that Article 42 of the Act of Accession cannot be invoked to prevent importation into the Netherlands, even before 1 January 1975, of goods put on to the market in the United Kingdom under the conditions set out above by the patentee or with his consent.'

This reasoning is apparently based on two premises. The first is that Article 36 is to be treated quite separately from Article 30; yet how could this be so? The second is that measures of equivalent effect, which are *prima facie* covered by Article 36 but on closer examination are not so covered, are to be abolished earlier than their brethren measures of equivalent effect which correspond to none of the heads of justification under Article 36; why? The Advocate General took the opposite view[18] from the Court on this point.

6.08   The provisions of the Greek Act of Accession already set out in paragraph 5.03 above also apply to measures of equivalent effect. The exception is Article 36 of that Act, which sets out a timetable for the gradual elimination of quantitative restrictions on products listed in Annex III thereto but which does not apply to measures of equivalent effect. In addition, Article 38 gave Greece a three-year period starting on 1 January 1981 to eliminate its import deposits and cash payments in force in Greece on 31 December 1980. Finally, by Article 39 the 8 per cent. general preference applied in Greece on public contracts was to be progressively eliminated over a five-year period starting on 1 January 1981.

6.09   As regards the Act of Accession of Spain and Portugal the reader is referred generally to paragraph 5.04 above. By virtue of Article 42 measures of equivalent effect on imports and exports between Spain and the Ten were to be abolished on 1 January 1986. A transitional exception in favour of Spain is contained in Article 44. Moreover, Article 47 provides for a highly important exception relating to certain patents. This exception, which is of indefinite duration, is discussed in Chapter VIII.[19]

The timetable for the abolition of measures of equivalent effect in trade in agricultural products between Spain and the Ten is that described in paragraph 5.04.

---

[18] At p.1178.
[19] Para. 8.113.

Measures of equivalent effect on imports and exports between Portugal and the Ten were to be abolished on 1 January 1986 by virtue of Article 202. Transitional exceptions in favour of Portugal are contained in Articles 204 and 205. An exception of indefinite duration in relation to certain patents is laid down by Article 209; it is in the same terms *mutatis mutandis* as that contained in Article 47 with respect to Spain.

As regards to trade between Spain and Portugal the relevant provisions are those discussed in the last part of paragraph 5.04.

II. THE MEANING OF 'MEASURES'

6.10 The Commission has consistently taken the view that even non-binding acts may be caught by Article 30 or 34. This is shown by the preamble to Directive 70/50 where it stated:

> 'Whereas for the purpose of Article 30 *et seq.* "measures" means laws, regulations, administrative provisions, administrative practices, and all instruments issuing from a public authority, including recommendations;
>
> Whereas for the purposes of this Directive "administrative practices" means any standard and regularly followed procedure of a public authority; whereas "recommendations" means any instruments issuing from a public authority which, while not legally binding on the addressees thereof, cause them to pursue a certain conduct . . .'

In the *Buy Irish* case[20] the Court to a considerable extent endorsed the Commission's view that non-binding measures could constitute measures of equivalent effect. The Irish authorities had orchestrated an extensive campaign for the promotion of Irish goods within Ireland. The campaign was aimed at all categories of purchaser, be they individual consumers, industrial or commercial undertakings or State bodies. The Commission considered that taken as a whole these measures infringed Article 30. The Irish Government argued, *inter alia*, that they were not 'measures' at all since they were not binding and that they therefore fell outside Article 30 altogether.

The Court rejected this defence. It held that the campaign reflected the Irish Government's 'considered intention to substitute domestic products for imported products on the Irish market and thereby to check the flow of imports from other Member States'. The campaign amounted

> 'to the establishment of a national practice, introduced by the Irish Government and prosecuted with its assistance, the potential effect of which on imports from other Member States is comparable to that resulting from goverment measures of a binding nature.
>
> Such practice cannot escape the prohibition laid down by Article 30 of the Treaty solely because it is not based on decisions which are binding upon undertakings. Even measures adopted by the government of a Member State which do not have binding effect may be capable of influencing the conduct of

---

[20] See n.13 above.

traders and consumers in that State and thus of frustrating the aims of the Community as set out in Article 2 and enlarged upon in Article 3 of the Treaty.

That is the case where, as in this instance, such a restrictive practice represents the implementation of a programme defined by the government which affects the national economy as a whole and which is intended to check the flow of trade between Member States by encouraging the purchase of domestic products, by means of an advertising campaign on a national scale and the organisation of special procedures applicable solely to domestic products and where those activities are attributable as a whole to the government and are pursued in an organised fashion throughout the national territory.'

In this passage the Court did not go so far as to state that all non-binding measures emanating from the authorities of a Member State may fall under Articles 30. Perhaps the reason for this was a desire to exclude ephemeral acts such as casual remarks by ministers but they can probably not be described as acts of the Member States in any case. This ruling does not lay down any general criterion for distinguishing between acts constituting 'measures' and mere ephemeral acts.

6.11   The same tendency can be discerned in the Court's ruling in *E.C. Commission* v. *France* (postal franking machines).[21] That case concerned a British company, which had sought without success to have its franking machines approved by the defendant's authorities, although its machines were in lawful use in a considerable number of other countries throughout the world. The Commission put before the Court a history of lengthy delays and repeated rejections of the company's applications by the defendant's authorities. The Commission did not contend that the relevant French legislation was in any way unlawful, but only its application in practice.

The Court ruled as follows:

'The fact that a law or regulation such as that requiring prior approval for the marketing of postal franking machines conforms in formal terms to Article 30 of the EEC Treaty is not sufficient to discharge a Member State of its obligations under that provision. Under the cloak of a general provision permitting the approval of machines imported from other Member States, the administration might very well adopt a systematically unfavourable attitude towards imported machines, either by allowing considerable delay in replying to applications for approval or in carrying out the examination procedure, or by refusing approval on the grounds of various alleged technical faults for which no detailed explanations are given or which prove to be inaccurate . . .

It must however be noted that for an administrative practice to constitute a measure prohibited under Article 30 that practice must show a certain degree of consistency and generality. That generality must be assessed differently according to whether the market concerned is one on which there are numerous traders or whether it is a market, such as that in postal franking machines, on which only a few undertakings are active. In the latter case, a national administration's treatment of a single undertaking may constitute a measure incompatible with Article 30.'

---

[21] Case 21/84 [1985] E.C.R. 1356, noted by Gormley [1985] E.L.Rev. 449.

While it is clearly right to exclude purely ephemeral acts, the criterion laid down here seems excessively narrow: taken at its face value it would appear to leave the door open to abuse by Member States in sectors served by a large number of traders. Why should the lawfulness of an unjustified restriction depend on the number of competitors on the market? Moreover, the test propounded by the Court opens a Pandora's box of conceptual difficulties: 'few', 'numerous', 'traders' and 'market'[22] may all have to be defined.

6.12 Other types of non-legislative acts may also constitute 'measures' for this purpose.[23] Thus, the financing of a scheme or project or the grant of a loan by public authorities may constitute a 'measure'—for example the grant of a loan to public officials for the purchase of cars on condition that they buy national cars.[24] Furthermore, a Treaty concluded by a Member State can also be a 'measure'.[25]

6.13 A legislative measure kept on the statute book will be a 'measure' even if it is not applied or has not entered into force; this is not least because it will cause confusion and might deter potential importers.[26] Conversely, a legislative measure, which has not yet been formally adopted, will constitute a measure if it is applied in practice. What is more, importers may be deterred from importing certain goods if they know that their sale is soon to be prohibited by the Member State in question. Thus, even if it were not applied, a draft legislative measure might contravene Articles 30 to 34, at least if it were used by a Member State to deter potential importers from importing goods which do not conform to the draft measure.[27]

---

[22] One is reminded of the difficulties encountered in defining the relevant market under Art. 86.

[23] Para. 17 of the judgment of 11 December 1985 in Case 192/84 *E.C. Commission* v. *Greece* (credit for agricultural machinery) [1985] E.C.R. 3967, [1988] 1 C.M.L.R. 420 suggests that any act of a Member State which creates an 'ambiguous and uncertain situation' to the detriment of imports may fall under Art. 30; see also the A.G. in Case 173/83 *E.C. Commission* v. *France* (waste oils) [1985] E.C.R. 491 at 495.

[24] See Case 192/84 (n.23 above) where a State ban on credit for imported farm machinery was held contrary to Art. 30 but see para. 6.22 *et seq.* below.

[25] See, however, Art. 234 discussed at para. 9.61 *et seq.* below.

[26] See the A.G. in Case 68/76 *E.C. Commission* v. *France* [1977] E.C.R. 515 at 541, [1977] 2 C.M.L.R. 161 at 175 and n.23 above.

[27] In its Communication on the *Cassis de Dijon* case discussed below (para. 6.42), the Commission stated that:

'to forestall later difficulties, the Commission will be informing Member States of potential objections, under the terms of Community law, to provisions they may be considering introducing which come to the attention of the Commission.'

This does not mean that any instrument is capable of infringing Art. 30, even when that instrument is in draft form. Presumably, it is designed primarily to show that the Commission reserves the right to point out to a Member State that a draft which that State is considering adopting would, if adopted, infringe Art. 30.

See also Dec. 83/189 ([1983] O.J. L109/8) laying down a procedure for the provision of information in the field of technical standards and regulations discussed at para. 12.12 below.

6.14   As has been explained earlier in this book,[28] measures falling under Article 30 or 34 may emanate not only from central government but also from regional or local government. They may also emanate from the executive, the legislature or the judiciary.[29]

6.15   A measure is not rendered compatible with Articles 30 and 34 simply because a procedure is provided under national law for obtaining an exemption. Thus in *International Fruit Company* v. *Produktschap voor Groenten en Fruit*[30] the Court held that a 'national measure, which requires, *even purely as a formality*,[31] import or export licences or any other similar procedure' was precluded by Articles 30 and 34. Also, in *Openbaar Ministerie* v. *Van Tiggele*,[32] having held that a particular system of minimum prices was contrary to Article 30, the Court continued:

> 'This is the conclusion which must be drawn even though the competent authority is empowered to grant exemptions from the fixed minimum price and though this power is freely applied to imported products, since the requirement that importers and traders must comply with the administrative formalities inherent in such a system may in itself constitute a measure having an effect equivalent to a quantitative restriction.'

This was confirmed in *Fietje*.[33]

6.16   Also, unlike Articles 85 and 86 relating to competition Articles 30 and 34 are subject to no *de minimis* rule: *Van de Haar*.[34] As Barents[35] points out this rule may be justified on the grounds that *State* interventions on the market may be said to have an appreciable effect by their very nature.

III. MEASURES OF EQUIVALENT EFFECT ON IMPORTS

A. General

6.17   Quantitative restrictions always take effect at the borders of the Member State which imposes them. Measures of equivalent effect may do so, but need not. Some classic examples of measures of equivalent effect may be cited from Directive 70/50 already referred to:

> 'measures which: . . .
>   (f) lower the value of an imported product, in particular by causing a reduction in its intrinsic value, or increase its costs;
>   . . .

---

[28] Para. 4.03 above.
[29] Para. 4.04 above.
[30] Cases 51–54/71 [1971] E.C.R. 1107, see para. 7.03 below.
[31] The italics are those of the author.
[32] Case 82/77 [1978] E.C.R. 25, [1978] 2 C.M.L.R. 528; see, however, para. 8.14 below.
[33] Case 27/80 [1980] E.C.R. 3839, [1981] 3 C.M.L.R. 722.
[34] Cases 177–178/82 [1984] E.C.R. 1797, [1985] 2 C.M.L.R. 566, confirmed in Cases 269/83 *E.C. Commission* v. *France* (periodicals) [1985] E.C.R. 837, [1985] 2 C.M.L.R. 399, and 103/84, n.14 above.
[35] 'Measures of Equivalent Effect: Some Recent Developments' [1981] C.M.L.Rev. 271 at 287.

(h) . . . subject imported products to conditions which are different from those laid down for domestic products and more difficult to satisfy;

. . .

(j) subject imported products only to conditions, in respect, in particular of shape, size, weight, composition, presentation, identification or putting up, or subject imported products to conditions which are different from those for domestic products and more difficult to satisfy;

(k) hinder the purchase by private individuals of imported products only, or encourage, require or give preference to the purchase of domestic products only;

. . .'

6.18 That the concept of measures of equivalent effect is indeed a wide one is confirmed by the classic definition of such measures set out in *Procureur du Roi* v. *Dassonville*:

'All trading rules enacted by Member States, which are capable of hindering, directly or indirectly, actually or potentially, intra-Community trade are to be considered as measures having an effect equivalent to quantitative restrictions.'[36]

Time and again this definition has been repeated in the Court's case law, though with minor variations: for instance, the term 'trading rules' does not always appear; and the Court sometimes speaks of obstacles 'to imports between Member States' rather than to 'intra-Community trade'.[37] At all events, it is clear from this formula that one must look to the *effects* of a measure and not to its aims in deciding whether it falls under Article 30.[38] Furthermore, it is not necessary to show that a measure actually restricts imports, but only that it *potentially* does so.

It follows that it is inappropriate to consider statistical evidence as to the volume of imports of products subject to the national measure in question; even if imports have actually increased since the measure was introduced, they might have increased more in the absence of such a measure.[39] These are obviously factors of fundamental importance in the interpretation of Article 30.

6.19 What is more, Article 30 does not only cover restrictions on imports pure and simple, but also restrictions on:

(a) re-imports[40]; or

(b) goods in transit[41]; or

(c) indirect imports[42]; or

---

[36] Case 8/74 [1974] E.C.R. 837 at 852, [1974] 2 C.M.L.R. 436 and 453.

[37] *E.g.* 'a direct or indirect, real or potential hindrance to imports between Member States,' Case 4/75 *Rewe-Zentralfinanz* v. *Landwirtschaftskammer* [1975] E.C.R. 843 at 858, [1977] 1 C.M.L.R. 599 at 618; see also Case 104/75 *De Peijper* [1976] E.C.R. 613 at 635, [1976] 2 C.M.L.R. 271 at 304.

[38] The intention of the author of a measure may be evidence, however, that it is not justified under Art. 36; see para. 8.12 below. But see also para. 8.130.

[39] See paras. 22 and 25 of the *Buy Irish* judgment (n.13 above).

[40] Para. 2.26 above.

[41] Para. 2.25 above.

[42] Para. 7.04 *et seq.* below.

(d) parallel imports. This was spelt out by the Court in *De Peijper*[43] where it held that 'rules or practices which result in imports being channelled in such a way that only certain traders can effect these imports, whereas others are prevented from doing so' are measures of equivalent effect under Article 30; or

(e) imports of raw materials or semi-finished products, even where the finished product is subject to no restrictions. This emerges clearly from the recitals to Directive 70/50,[44] which state that measures of equivalent effect can apply 'at any marketing stage.' It emerges also from the Court's judgment in *Eggers* v. *Freie Hansestadt Bremen*[45]; or

(f) conversely, imports of the finished product when the raw material is subject to no restrictions: *Campus Oil* v. *Minister for Industry and Energy.*[46]

6.20   In addition, it is clear that to comply with Article 30 Member States must not only refrain from imposing restrictions on imports. In some cases Article 30 imposes an obligation on Member States to take positive steps to reduce, so far as possible, restrictions which they themselves have imposed.[47] Thus, they are required to provide reasonable customs facilities,[48] for instance in keeping customs posts open during reasonable hours and in providing adequate staff and equipment to carry out veterinary and public health checks with due speed. Similarly, in *De Peijper*[49] the Court ruled that Member States were under an active duty to co-operate with one another so as to ensure that registration formalities with respect to parallel imports of pharmaceuticals be reduced to the minimum; and in *Denkavit Futtermittel* v. *Minister of Agriculture*[50] it found a similar duty to co-operate with respect to veterinary checks on animal feed.

6.21   On the other hand, the prohibition on measures of equivalent effect like that on quantitative restrictions is subject to the specific exception contained in Article 36, which is examined in detail in Chapter VIII.

---

[43] N.37 above; see also Case 154/85R and 154/85 *E.C. Commission* v. *Italy* (parallel imports of vehicles), respectively [1985] E.C.R. 1753, [1986] 2 C.M.L.R. 159 and judgment of 17 June 1987.
[44] See n.7 above.
[45] Case 13/78 [1978] E.C.R. 1935, [1979] 1 C.M.L.R. 562.
[46] Case 72/83 [1984] E.C.R. 2727, [1984] 3 C.M.L.R. 544, para. 16 of the judgment; see para. 7.22 below.
[47] For this view see Schiller 'Gewährt Art. 30 des EWG-Vertrages dem Gemeinschaftsbürger neben einem subjectiven Abwehrrecht auch ein subjectives Leistungsrecht?' [1980] RIW/AWD 569.
[48] Para. 7.15 below.
[49] N.37 above.
[50] Case 251/78 [1979] E.C.R. 3369, [1980] 3 C.M.L.R. 513.

6.22   What is more, the concept of measures of equivalent effect is not so wide as to cover restrictions on movements of goods falling under other provisions of the Treaty. This was clearly stated by the Court in *Iannelli* v. *Meroni*,[51] in the following terms:

> 'However wide the field of application of Article 30 may be, it nevertheless does not include obstacles to trade covered by other provisions of the Treaty.
> In fact, since the legal consequences of the application or of a possible infringement of these various provisions have to be determined having regard to their particular purpose in the context of all the objectives of the Treaty, they may be of a different kind and this implies that their respective fields of application must be distinguished, except in those cases which may fall simultaneously within the field of application of two or more provisions of Community law.'

Consequently, the following fall outside the scope of Article 30:
— customs duties and charges of equivalent effect (Articles 9 to 16)
— aids (Articles 92 to 94)
— internal taxation (Articles 95 to 99).
However, it may be otherwise as regards restrictions on current payments (Article 106).

Each of these will be examined in turn, after which the relationship between Article 30 and Articles 85 and 86 will be considered.

On the other hand, the relationship between Articles 30 and 37 is discussed in Chapter XI and that between Articles 30 and 100 in Chapter XII so that there is no need to consider them at this juncture. Likewise, the relationship between Article 30 and the Treaty provisions relating to the free movement of persons, services and capital has been covered in Chapter II.

6.23   In *Iannelli* the Court held that customs duties and charges of equivalent effect within the meaning of Articles 9 to 16 EEC do not fall under Article 30. This ruling was confirmed in *Kortmann*,[52] in which a parallel importer of pharmaceutical products claimed that costs incurred in registering these products as required under Dutch law were contrary to Article 30, on the grounds that the registration was superfluous as the 'official' importer had already effected such registration. The Court held that such costs fell to be examined under Articles 9 to 13 and 95 and not under Article 30.

This is not to say, however, that every measure requiring importers or persons selling imported goods to pay a sum of money falls automatically outside Article 30. We shall see in the next chapter that the obligation to pay a deposit when importing goods[53] is caught by Article 30, as are certain types of fines.[54] Furthermore, in *Musik-Vertrieb Membran* v. *GEMA*[55] the Court classified copyright royalties as measures of equivalent effect rather than taxes of equivalent effect

---

[51] Case 74/76 [1977] E.C.R. 557, [1977] 2 C.M.L.R. 688.
[52] Case 32/80 [1981] E.C.R. 251, [1982] 3 C.M.L.R. 46.
[53] Para. 7.29 below.
[54] Para. 7.10 below.
[55] Cases 55/80 and 57/80, [1981] E.C.R. 147, [1981] 2 C.M.L.R 44, para. 8.118 below.

on the grounds that they were really damages paid for the infringement of copyright. Similarly, in *Orlandi* v. *Minister of Foreign Trade*,[56] Advocate General Slynn took the view that an obligation to pay an import deposit which could be forfeited to the State in certain circumstances contravened Article 30 and not Articles 9 to 13. The Court declined to interpret Articles 9, 10 and 13 as requested by the national court. However, since it also considered the measure concerned to violate Article 30, it impliedly endorsed the Advocate General's view that it did not constitute a charge of equivalent effect.

6.24   In the *Iannelli* case the Court also considered the relationship between Article 30 and Articles 92 to 94 relating to State aids.[57] Those provisions stipulate that such aids are in principle incompatible with the common market, but lay down a number of exceptions to that rule[58] and give the Commission a wide discretion to accept a State aid in derogation of this principle. Consequently, the Court held that this principle of incompatibility did not have direct effect, whereas Article 30 did have such effect. In the light of this the Court ruled that:

> 'The effect of an interpretation of Article 30 which is so wide as to treat an aid as such within the meaning of Article 92 as being similar to a quantitative restriction referred to in Article 30 would be to alter the scope of Articles 92 and 93 of the Treaty and to interfere with the system adopted in the Treaty for the division of powers by means of the procedure for keeping aids under constant review as described in Article 93.'

Yet the Court at once proceeded to qualify this ruling as follows:

> 'Nevertheless the position is different if it is possible when a system of aid is being analysed to separate those conditions or factors which, even though they form part of this system, may be regarded as not being necessary for the attainment of its object or for its proper functioning.
>
> In the latter case there are no reasons based on the division of powers under Articles 92 and 93 which permit the conclusion to be drawn that, if other provisions of the Treaty which have direct effect are infringed, those provisions may not be invoked before national courts simply because the factor in question is an aspect of aid.'

It might have been preferable for the Court to follow the Advocate General and rule that the principle that an aid could not fall under Article 30 was unqualified: as Dashwood had pointed out,[59] the test which the Court laid down lacks clarity and may prove very hard to

---

[56] Cases 206, 207, 209 and 210/80 [1982] E.C.R. 2147 at 2171; para. 7.29 below.

[57] See also Case 82/77, n.32 above. Some guidance is perhaps also to be derived from Case 73/79 *E.C. Commission* v. *Italy* [1980] E.C.R. 1533, [1982] 1 C.M.L.R. 1, although that case concerns the relationship between Arts. 92–93 and 95; see Gilmour 'The Enforcement of Community Law by the Commission in the Context of State Aids: the Relationship between Articles 93 and 169 and the Choice of Remedies' [1981] C.M.L.Rev. 63.

[58] Thus, it would seem that an aid may fall outside Art. 92(1) altogether on the grounds that it is too insignificant to 'affect trade between Member States'; Cases 296 and 318/82 *Netherlands* v. *E.C. Commission* [1985] E.C.R. 817, [1985] 3 C.M.L.R. 380 and Case 248/84 *Germany* v. *E.C. Commission* (judgment of 14 October 1987). In contrast, Arts. 30 and 34 are not subject to any *de minimis* rule: para. 6.16.

[59] [1977] E.L.Rev. 376; *contra* Schramme 'Rapport entre les mesures d'effet équivalent à des restrictions quantitatives et les aides nationales' [1985] R.T.D.E. 487.

apply. This is perhaps borne out by the Court's attempt to apply its severability test to the case in hand: it ruled that Article 30 would apply to that aspect of an

> 'arrangement whereby aid is granted to traders who obtain supplies of imported products through a State agency but is withheld when the products are imported direct, if this distinction is not clearly necessary for attainment of the objective of the said aid or for its proper functioning.'

6.25 The approach followed by the Court in *E.C. Commission* v. *Ireland* ('Buy Irish')[60] differs sharply from this, although there is no direct conflict between the two judgments.

In its defence, Ireland had argued that the campaign was to be judged on the basis of Articles 92 and 93 and not Article 30. The Court gave this argument short shrift: 'The fact that a substantial part of the campaign is financed by the Irish Government and that Articles 92 and 93 of the Treaty may be applicable to financing of that kind does not mean that the campaign itself may escape the prohibitions laid down in Article 30.' The Court also went on to observe that 'in any case, if the Irish Government considered that such financing amounted to aid within the meaning of Articles 92 and 93 it ought to have notified the aid to the Commission in accordance with Article 93(3).'

6.26 The problem arose once again in *E.C. Commission* v. *France* (tax benefit for newspapers).[61] That case concerned legislation granting a tax advantage to newspaper publishers on condition that the publications were printed in France. Once again the Commission brought proceedings for the breach of Article 30 and the defendant Member State maintained that the relevant provision was in fact Article 92. Once again this argument was dismissed. The Court began by pointing out, as it had done in the *Buy Irish* case, that the scheme had never been notified to the Commission. Secondly, it ruled that 'Articles 92 and 94 cannot, as is clear from a long line of cases decided by the Court, be used to frustrate the rules of the Treaty on the free movement of goods or the rules on the repeal of discriminatory tax provisions. According to those cases, provisions relating to the free movement of goods, the repeal of discriminatory tax provisions and aid have a common objective, namely to ensure the free movement of goods between Member States under normal conditions of competition.' It concluded from this that 'the mere fact that a national measure may possibly be defined as an aid within the meaning of Article 92 is therefore not an adequate reason for exempting it from the prohibition contained in Article 30,' and went on to find for the Commission.

---

[60] Case 249/81, see n.13 above.
[61] Case 18/84 [1986] 1 C.M.L.R. 605; para. 2.29 above.

Essentially the same reasoning was applied in *E.C. Commission* v. *Italy*,[62] where State subsidies for the purchase of national vehicles were held to contravene Article 30.

6.27   It is not unfair to say that the law on the relationship between Articles 30 and 92 is now in a considerable state of uncertainty. Yet this is an inherently vexed issue which does not permit of any easy answer. At all events, it is notable that in the last two cases mentioned (*France* and *Italy*) the contested measure was severable from the aid itself: in *France* the Commission did not object to the tax advantage, but to the condition attached to it; and in *Italy* also the Commission's sole objection was to the condition of origin attached to the subsidy. Thus even on the *Iannelli* test, both of the measures in issue in those two cases would fall under Article 30. The *Buy Irish* case was different in that there the publicity campaign in favour of Irish goods was not a condition or an element of any broader measure.

Also, in these three infringement proceedings the Court was no doubt influenced by the unattractive nature of the defence concerned: by arguing that the measures concerned fell outside Article 30 because they constituted aids within the meaning of Article 92, when they had failed to notify them, the Member States were seeking to profit by their own wrong. No such considerations were present in *Iannelli*.

Accordingly, Flynn[63] and Marenco[64] may well be right in suggesting that *Iannelli* has not been reversed.[65]

6.28   As regards internal taxation, in *Fink-Frucht* v. *Hauptzollamt München*,[66] one of its earlier cases on Article 30, the Court held that one and the same national provision could not fall to be considered under Article 30 and Article 95. This was subsequently confirmed in *Iannelli*. Furthermore, in *Bergandi* v. *Directeur Général des Impôts*[67] it was held that restriction of a fiscal nature was to be considered under Article 95 alone and not under Article 30.

What is more, in a dictum in Case 159/78 *E.C. Commission* v. *Italy*[68] the Court held that:

> 'frontier controls remain justified . . . in so far as they are necessary . . . for the levying of internal taxation within the meaning of Article 95 of the Treaty when the crossing of the frontier may legitimately be assimilated to the situation which, in the case of domestic goods, gives rise to the levying of the tax . . .'

---

[62] N.14 above.

[63] [1987] E.L.Rev. 131 (casenote).

[64] 'La giurisprudenza comunitaria sulle misure di effetto equivalente a una restrizione quantitativa (1984–1986)' [1988] *Il Foro Padano* IV, 166.

[65] The present author's conclusion that *Iannelli* has been reversed ('A Review of the Case Law of the Court of Justice on Articles 30 to 36 EEC in 1985' [1986] C.M.L.Rev. 325 at 334) now seems somewhat rash. In any case, he never intended to suggest that every State aid relating to goods falls under Art. 30.

[66] Case 27/67 [1968] E.C.R. 223, [1968] C.M.L.R. 228.

[67] Case 252/86 (judgment of 3 March 1988).

[68] [1980] E.C.R. 3247, [1980] 3 C.M.L.R. 446, see paras. 7.85 and 8.67 *et seq.*

6.29 Article 106(1) obliges the Member States to 'authorise, in the currency of the Member State in which the creditor or the beneficiary resides, any payments connected with the movement of goods, services or capital' as and when those movements themselves are liberalised.[69] In the first edition of this book it was suggested that a restriction on payment cannot be caught by Articles 30 and 106 simultaneously. However, since then the Court has held[70] that a requirement to lodge deposits for the payment of imports is contrary to Article 30. Accordingly, unless Article 106(1) is too narrow to apply to such a measure, the view expressed in the first edition must be revised.[71] If that is so, then this must be one of the exceptional cases which according to *Iannelli* 'may fall within the field of application of two more provisions of Community law.'[72]

6.30 It is appropriate at this stage to turn to the relationship between Articles 30 and 34 on the one hand and Articles 85 and 86 on the other. We saw in an earlier chapter[73] how in principle Articles 30 and 34 covered State measures whereas Articles 85 and 86 cover the agreements and practices of private undertakings. Indeed, Verloren van Themaat,[74] Matthies[75] and Barents[76] have focused on the similarities between the two sets of provisions: both prohibit restrictions on imports (or exports, as the case may be), subject to a justification clause (Articles 36 and 85(3)). Yet there are notable differences. As the Court pointed out in *Van de Haar*,[77] Articles 30 and 85 pursue quite different aims from one another and, while the latter is subject to a *de minimis* rule, the former is not. Consequently, although a comparison between the two sets of provisions will yield results of great practical importance, the reader well versed in competition law should not be lulled into thinking that the principles he knows can quite simply be applied unaltered to State measures under Articles 30 to 36.

6.31 Can the two sets of provisions apply to one and the same set of circumstances? The ruling in *GB-Inno* v. *ATAB*[78] appears to suggest

---

[69] See generally para. 2.07 above.

[70] Case 95/81 *E.C. Commission* v. *Italy* [1982] E.C.R. 2187, paras. 7.29 and 8.21 below; see also Case 124/85 *E.C. Commission* v. *Greece* (meat) [1988] 2 C.M.L.R. 518.

[71] This view is possibly supported by para. 25 of the judgment in Case 308/86 *Lambert* (judgment of 14 July 1988). Para. 29 of the Opinion in Case 240/86 *E.C. Commission* v. *Greece* (cereals) (judgment of 24 March 1988) is perhaps of no immediate assistance.

[72] See the closing words of the passage quoted in para. 6.22 above.

[73] Paras. 4.20 *et seq.* above.

[74] 'Zum Verhältnis zwischen Artikel 30 und Artikel 85 EWG-Vertrag,' *Festschrift für Gunther*, (1976), 373, 'De artikelen 30–36 van het EWG-Vertrag' [1980] *R.M. Themis* 4/5, 378 at 399.

[75] 'Die Verantwortung der Mitgliedstaaten für den freien Warenverkehr im Gemeinsamen Markt' in *Festschrift für Ipsen* (1977), 669 at 672 *et seq.*

[76] See n.35 above.

[77] See n.34 above.

[78] Case 13/77 [1977] E.C.R. 2115, [1978] 1 C.M.L.R. 283; see also the A.G. in Case 82/77, n.32 above, at 47, and Case 5/79 *Buys* [1979] E.C.R. 3203, [1980] 2 C.M.L.R. 99.

that a national measure may simultaneously be caught by Article 30 (or Article 34) and Article 86, read with Articles 3(f) and 5.

It seems clear that the same would apply to national measures facilitating the conclusion of agreements contrary to Article 85, especially as the Court also held in that judgment that 'Member States may not enact measures enabling private undertakings to escape from the constraints imposed by Articles 85 to 94 of the Treaty.' In addition, if Articles 30 and 34 cover measures facilitating agreements or abuses by undertakings contrary to Articles 85 and 86, then *a fortiori* Articles 30 and 34 must apply to measures requiring such agreements or abuses. At all events, it is now plain that a State measure will only fall foul of Articles 3(f), 5 and 85 read together if it requires undertakings to enter into agreements or concerted practices; the imposition of trade restrictions in another form will not fall foul of these provisions.[79]

B. 'Indistinctly applicable' measures under Articles 30 and 36

6.32   Two questions are of central importance to this book:
— to what extent does Article 30 cover measures applying in the same way to domestic and imported goods ('indistinctly applicable' measures)?
— what is the relationship between Articles 30 and 36 to the extent that Article 30 does cover such measures?

6.33   The Commission encountered the problem of 'indistinctly applicable' measures at a very early stage. The first case concerned fertilisers.[80] By a Belgian Royal Decree of 1961 only ammonium nitrate containing at least 22 per cent. nitrogen could be sold in Belgium, be it domestically produced or imported ammonium nitrate. The normal nitrogen content in the Community was 20·5 per cent. This meant that producers of ammonium nitrate in other Member States were faced with the choice of making a special production for Belgium or stopping exports to that country. The Belgian authorities were unable to show any convincing reason for this measure and it was clear that it was designed to protect Belgian producers. The Commission prevailed upon the Belgian authorities to repeal the measure by a Royal Decree of 1962.

6.34   Perhaps more telling to the non-scientist was the French blanket case. A French Ministerial Decree of 1968 provided that only blankets of particular sizes could be sold in France. It was no accident that the decreed sizes were those already applied by French producers. This

---

[79] See *e.g.* Cases 5/79 *Buys*, n.78 above; *Van de Haar* (n.34 above) (noted by Marenco [1984] R.T.D.E. 527) and 231/83 *Leclerc* [1985] E.C.R. 315, [1985] 2 C.M.L.R. 524; also generally Case 229/83 *Leclerc* v. *Au Blé Vert* [1985] E.C.R. 1, [1985] 2 C.M.L.R. 286, and D. Waelbroeck, 'Application des règles de concurrence du Traité de Rome à l'autorité publique' [1987] R.M.C. 25 and M. Waelbroeck 'Les rapports entre les règles sur la libre circulation des marchandises et les règles de concurrence applicables aux entreprises dans la CEE' in *Liber Amicorum Pierre Pescatore* (1987) at 781.
[80] Written question 118/66 ([1966] J.O. 901 at 903).

meant that blanket manufacturers in other Member States were obliged to stop exporting to France or to have a special production for the French market with all the resulting expense, whereas French manufacturers continued to produce as before. The French Government was unable to show that the measure was justified on any grounds known to Community law, since its object was clearly to protect French manufacturers. The French authorities therefore bowed to pressure from the Commission and repealed the Decree. This case shows with the utmost clarity how an 'indistinctly applicable' measure can be blatantly protectionist in its effects.

6.35   In the light of these cases, the Commission set out a twofold definition of measures of equivalent effect under Article 30 in its Directive 70/50[81]:

— overtly discriminatory ('distinctly applicable') measures: those which apply to imported products only and make importation more costly or more difficult, and those which impose on imported products a condition differing from that required for domestic products and more difficult to satisfy (Article 2 of the Directive);

— 'indistinctly applicable' measures: those which are equally applicable to domestic and to imported products; these were lawful unless their restrictive effect exceeded the effects intrinsic to trade rules. This would be the case in particular where the restrictive effects on the free movement of goods were out of proportion to their purpose or where the same objective could be achieved by other means less restrictive of trade (Article 3).

Thus while overtly discriminatory measures were automatically considered to be measures of equivalent effect, there was a presumption that 'indistinctly applicable' measures were compatible with Article 30.

The Directive is expressed to apply without prejudice to Article 36: Article 5(2).

6.36   In the early days, the views of legal authors as to the concept of measures of equivalent effect could be divided into three categories[82]:

— the narrow definition (Seidel, Graf, Marx, to a certain extent also Meier);

---

[81] Para. 6.03 above; prior to this Dir., the Commission also gave indications of its views in its answers to written question 118/66, n.80 above; written question 64/67 ([1967] J.O. 169/11) and written question 185/67 ([1968] J.O. C5/5).

[82] The views of the authors listed here have evolved over the years in accordance with changing events, in particular the Court's case law. For summaries of the various views see Ehlermann in Groeben, Boeckh, Thiesing, *Kommentar zum EWG-Vertrag* (1974), Vol. I, 263, Waelbroeck, *Les réglementations nationales de prix et le droit communautaire* (1975), 23 *et seq.*; Meij and Winter, 'Measures having an effect equivalent to quantitative restrictions' [1976] C.M.L.Rev. 79; van Gerven, 'The Recent Case Law of the Court of Justice concerning Articles 30 and 36 of the EEC Treaty' [1977] C.M.L.Rev. 5; Ehlermann, 'Das Verbot der Maßnahmen gleicher Wirkung in der Rechtsprechung des Gerichtshofes' in *Festschrift für Ipsen* (1977), 579; Veelken, 'Maßnahmen gleicher Wirkung wie mengenmässige Beschränkungen' [1977] EuR 311; VerLoren van Themaat, 'De artikelen 30–36 van het EEG-Verdrag', *op. cit.* n.74 above.

— the wide definition (VerLoren van Themaat, Waelbroeck);
— the intermediate approach, some of whose proponents support Directive 70/50 (Béraud, Donâ-Viscardini), while others criticise that Directive (Ulmer, Steindorff).

6.37   According to the narrow view only 'distinctly applicable' measures[83] fell to be considered as measures of equivalent effect under Article 30. Seidel,[84] the first author to take this approach, relied on an analogy with quotas. Graf[85] reached this conclusion on the basis of a comparison between the four freedoms, while Marx[86] based his theory on an analysis of Article 100. Meier's[87] initial approach was particularly restrictive: according to him, only those measures that operated at the frontier were measures of equivalent effect. Measures operating at a later stage and in particular at the point of sale, fell outside Article 30 altogether in his view.

The overwhelming disadvantage of this school of thought was that it would lead to Article 30 being circumvented simply by careful drafting of national legislation. In any case, it has become untenable since *Dassonville*.[88]

6.38   According to VerLoren van Themaat[89] and Waelbroeck,[90] the proponents of the wide definition, Article 30 did not only apply to measures discriminating against imports. In their view, all measures restricting inter-State trade were prohibited by Article 30, unless they were justified under Article 36 or were governed by other provisions of the Treaty. In support of this view, they pointed to the wide formulation of Article 30, which makes no mention of discrimination. Meij and Winter,[91] who adhered to this theory in a qualified form, also criticised Article 3 of Directive 70/50 on the grounds that it purports to deprive Article 36 of its proper scope by using the test of justification to decide whether a measure fell under Article 30 in the first place.[92]

---

[83] See para. 6.32 above.
[84] 'Der EWG-rechtliche Begriff der "Maßnahmen gleicher Wirkung wie eine mengenmässige Beschränkung"' [1976] N.J.W. 2081.
[85] *Op. cit.* n.10 above.
[86] *Funktion und Grenzen der Rechtsangleichung nach Art. 100 EWG-Vertrag* (1976) in particular at 84 *et seq.*
[87] In Ehle and Meier *EWG-Warenverkehr* (1971), 158 *et seq.*
[88] N.36 above.
[89] 'Bevat art. 30 van het EEG-Verdrag slechts een non-diskriminatie-beginsel ten aanzien van invoerbeperkingen' 15 S.E.W. 632; see also his comments on Dirs. 70/32 and 70/50 in (1970) 18 S.E.W. 258.
[90] *Le droit de la Communauté économique européenne* (1970) Vol. I, 102.
[91] *Op. cit.* n.82 above.
[92] See para. 7.41 below; by a parity of reasoning Art. 5(2) of Dir. 70/50, in so far as it provides that the Dir. applies without prejudice to Art. 36 EEC, is meaningless as far as 'indistinctly applicable' measures are concerned.

On the other hand, the effect of this wide definition of measures of equivalent effect was to overstretch Article 36, which only applies to measures pursuing goals of a non-economic nature.[93] In consequence, Waelbroeck[94] added the rider that to come under Article 30 a measure must have a direct causal effect on imports or on the marketing or use of an imported product so that economic policy measures affecting such matters as interest rates and incomes[95] fall outside Article 30. However, as has been pointed out,[96] the test of directness is no easier to apply than that of discrimination. Nor does it accord with the *Dassonville*[97] formula according to which measures capable of hindering intra-Community trade 'directly or indirectly, actually or potentially' constitute measures of equivalent effect. Similarly, Meij and Winter sought to overcome the same difficulty by putting forward the view that the concept of measures of equivalent effect only covered 'trading rules.' However, as they themselves admitted, it is not clear what is meant by 'trading rules'.[98]

6.39 The intermediate approach has been followed by those authors[99] who advocate the definition laid down by Directive 70/50. A second form of intermediate approach was adopted by Steindorff[100] who stated that the concept of measures of equivalent effect only applied to discriminatory measures but, unlike the proponents of the narrow definition, he considered that discrimination in this context covered not only discrimination of form but also discrimination of substance. This meant that one must look behind a measure which is not discriminatory 'on its face' to see whether it is discriminatory in practice. Unfortunately the practical difficulties of applying such a test are very considerable[101] since it may involve consideration of complicated statistical data. What is more, on this test a measure may constantly oscillate between being discriminatory and not being discriminatory.[102]

This prompted Ulmer[103] to suggest yet another intermediate position. He criticised the test of discrimination, claiming that it was often hard to determine what was meant by this concept, and thus to apply the

---

[93] See para. 8.19 below.
[94] *Op. cit.* n.82 above, at p.19 *et seq.*
[95] See para. 7.89 below.
[96] Van Gerven, *op. cit.* n.82 above, at p.9.
[97] See para. 6.18 above.
[98] In addition, the Court does not always use the term 'trading rules'; see para. 6.18 above.
[99] Béraud, 'Les mesures d'effet équivalent au sens des articles 30 et suivants du Traité de Rome' [1968] R.T.D.E. 265; Dona, 'Les mesures d'effet équivalent à des restrictions quantitatives' [1973] R.M.C. 224; Mattera, 'Libre circulation des marchandises et articles 30 à 36 du Traité CEE' [1976] R.M.C. 500.
[100] In *Dienstfreiheit und Versicherungsaufsicht im Gemeinsamen Markt* (1971), 79 at 82.
[101] Peter Ulmer 'Zum Verbot mittelbarer Einfuhrbeschränkungen im EWG-Vertrag' [1973] G.R.U.R. Int. 502 at 507.
[102] With respect to one category of measures, namely certain price controls, the Court does appear to apply the test of discrimination of substance: para. 7.65 *et seq.* below. The result is that it is extremely difficult to determine whether a given maximum price control is compatible with Art. 30 or not; para. 7.81 below.
[103] *Op. cit.* n.101 above.

test. He gave as an example the requirement that goods of a certain kind, domestic and imported, bear an indication of origin likely to reduce the attraction of the imported product for consumers. Furthermore, the test could not be applied at all to measures concerning products for which no national production exists. His solution was to suggest that the test set out in Article 3 of the Directive was to be applied to *all* measures, whether discriminatory or not.

6.40 Ulmer's view may have influenced the Advocate General and the Court in the leading case of *REWE-Zentral* v. *Bundesmonopolverwaltung für Branntwein*[104] (commonly called the *'Cassis de Dijon'* case). The plaintiffs, who sought to import the French blackcurrant-based drink known as 'Cassis de Dijon', contested the validity of a provision of German law requiring spirits to have a minimum alcohol content. Cassis de Dijon, which in France has a content of between 15 per cent. and 20 per cent., fell into the category of products required to have 25 per cent. under the German provision. The German court referred two questions on the compatibility of such a measure with Articles 30 and 37[105] respectively.

Advocate General Capotorti's conclusions are of particular interest since, it is submitted, they throw light on certain aspects of the Court's judgment. He rejected the presumption contained in Directive 70/50 that 'indistinctly applicable' measures were compatible with Article 30. In his view this presumption was based on an 'attitude of prudence' which ceased to be justified after the end of the transitional period. On the other hand, he considered that consumer protection, though it did not expressly figure in the heads of justification in Article 36, did in fact fall under that provision. Applying both Article 36 EEC and Article 3 of the Directive, he found that a minimum alcohol requirement constituted an unjustified restriction on imports contrary to Article 30.

6.41 The Court's starting point was that 'in the absence of common rules relating to the production and marketing of alcohol' it is for

---

[104] Case 120/78 [1979] E.C.R. 649, [1979] 3 C.M.L.R. 494; case notes, *inter alia*, by Millarg [1979] EuR 420; Deringer and Sedemund [1979] N.J.W. 1079; Oliver [1980] C.M.L.Rev. 109; Wyatt [1981] E.L.Rev. 185; see also Meier, 'Zur Kombination von nationalen Lebensmittel-Begriffsbestimmungen und Vorschriften zum Schutz des Verbrauchers gegen Irreführungen als Rechtfertigungsgründe nach Art. 36 EWGV' [1980] W.R.P. 59; Meier, 'Kennzeichnung statt Verkehrsbote—Die Rechtsprechung als Schrittmacher des Lebensmittelrechts' *Schriftenreihe des Bundes für Lebensmittelrecht und Lebensmittelkunde* (1980) 94 Heft 47; Dashwood 'Cassis de Dijon: A major step in the liberalization of trade' [1981] 9 E.I.P.R. 268; Capelli 'Les malentendus provoqués par l'arrêt sur le "Cassis de Dijon"' [1981] R.M.C. 421; Masclet, 'Les articles 30, 36 et 100 du Traité CEE à la lumière de l'arrêt "Cassis de Dijon"' [1980] R.T.D.E. 64; Mattera, 'L'arrêt "Cassis de Dijon": une nouvelle approche pour la réalisation et le bon fonctionnement du marché intérieur' [1980] R.M.C. 505; VerLoren van Themaat, *op. cit.* n.82 above; Barents, *op. cit.* n.35 above.

[105] As regards Art. 37, see para. 11.12 below.

the Member States to regulate these matters on their own territory.[106]
Thereupon the Court stated that:

> 'Obstacles to movement within the Community resulting from disparities
> between the national laws relating to the marketing of the products in question
> must be accepted in so far as those provisions may be recognised as being
> necessary in order to satisfy mandatory requirements relating in particular to
> the effectiveness of fiscal supervision, the protection of public health, the
> fairness of commercial transactions and the defence of the consumer.'

It is clear from the words 'in particular' that the 'mandatory
requirements' listed are merely examples. The list given in the
judgment is therefore not exhaustive.[107]

The Court then proceeded to reject the German Government's
arguments to the effect that the restriction in question was justified
on the grounds of public health and consumer protection. In
particular, as regards consumer protection, it held that a reasonable
labelling requirement would constitute an adequate guarantee for
the consumer so that the imposition of a minimum alcohol requirement for drinks intended for human consumption constituted a
measure of equivalent effect contrary to Article 30, if it applied to
the importation of alcoholic beverages lawfully produced and
marketed in another Member State.

6.42 This ruling is clearly a landmark in the Court's case law on
Article 30, especially as it has now been confirmed in a series of
subsequent judgments.[108] To underline the importance of this ruling
the Commission took the unusual step of issuing a Communication[109]
setting out the consequences flowing from it.

On the other hand it would be wrong to describe *Cassis de Dijon*
as a 'revolutionary' judgment. Rather it has brought together in a
new form strands that were to be found in various earlier cases.[110]

6.43 At all events, the first case to confirm *Cassis* was *Gilli and
Andres*.[111] Since then, the ruling in *Cassis* has been reiterated and
applied on countless occasions, notable recent examples including
E.C. Commission v. *Germany* (beer)[112] and *E.C. Commission* v.

---

[106] On this part of the judgment see paras. 10.08 and 12.24 below.

[107] See para. 8.93 *et seq.* below.

[108] See para. 7.52 *et seq.* below.

[109] [1980] O.J. C256/2. See Annex I to this book. Barents, *op. cit.*, n.35 above, criticises
this Communication, notably on the grounds of lack of clarity. Moreover, he objects to the
fact that the Communication does not state whether the approach set out in Dir. 70/50 is
henceforth to be abandoned by the Commission. Judge Touffait in 'Les entraves techniques
à la libre circulation des marchandises' (*Recueil Dalloz-Sirey* 1982, Chronique 37) is also
critical of the Communication; see Chap. XII, n.54. For a less critical view see Gormley
[1981] E.L.Rev. 454.

[110] Case 13/77, n.78 above, see para. 7.71 below; Case 82/77, n.32 above, see para. 7.73
below.

[111] Case 788/79 [1980] E.C.R. 2071 at 2078, [1981] 1 C.M.L.R. 146 at 154.

[112] Case 178/84 [1988] 1 C.M.L.R. 780, para. 7.46 below.

France (substitute milk powder).[113] The latter case is particularly
striking since the measure held to be unlawful there could not in
any sense be regarded as protecting a typical national product: the
sale of substitute milk powder was not permitted in any form or
under any designation; the situation was therefore wholly different
from that in *Cassis de Dijon* since the measure contested in that
case required imports to be brought into line with German products,
thereby putting the latter at an advantage; and while the avowed
aim of the ban on substitute milk powder was to protect the dairy
sector, milk could scarcely be regarded as a typically French product
especially as substitutes are normally produced in other Member
States with a sizeable dairy industry.

Another particularly important ruling following *Cassis* was
Cinéthèque v. *Fédération Nationale des Cinémas Français*.[114] That
case concerned a prohibition on the sale or rental of video cassettes
of any film within one year of that film being authorised for showing
in the cinema. The Advocate General there took the view that, since
that measure was 'indistinctly applicable' and not 'protectionist', it
fell outside Article 30. The Court took the opposite view. It accepted
that the measure did 'not have the purpose of regulating trade
patterns' and its effect was 'not to favour national production as
against the production of other Member States, but to encourage
cinematographic production as such'. Yet it found that despite this
the measure fell foul of Article 30 unless it was justified.[115]

However, given the vast body of cases concerning indistinctly
applicable measures decided since *Cassis,* it is scarcely surprising to
find a small number of judgments which diverge from it. In this
connection, the two groups discussed in the next two paragraphs
should be noted.

6.44   *Oebel*[116] concerned *inter alia* a prohibition on the delivery of
bread during the night. One of the reasons given by the Court for
holding this restriction to be compatible with Article 30 was that it
applied 'to the same extent to all producers, wherever they are
established.' Similarly, the defendant in *Blesgen*[117] had been charged
with holding in stock on premises adjoining his hotel spirits with a
view to selling them in that hotel, contrary to Belgian law; spirits
were defined under that legislation as drinks with an alcoholic
strength exceeding 22 degrees at a temperature of 15 degrees centi-
grade. The defendant's plea that such a law infringed Article 30 was
rejected primarily on the grounds that 'the restrictions placed on
the sale of the spirits in question make no distinction whatsoever

---

[113] Case 216/84 (judgment of 23 February 1988), para. 7.58 below.
[114] Cases 60 and 61/84 [1985] E.C.R. 2605, [1986] 1 C.M.L.R. 365.
[115] Admittedly, the Court then took the unprecedented and questionable step of holding
the measure to be justified without saying on what grounds: para. 8.23 below.
[116] Case 155/80 [1981] E.C.R. 3147, para. 7.62 below.
[117] Case 75/81 [1982] E.C.R. 1211, [1983] 1 C.M.L.R. 431, para. 7.87 below.

based on their nature or origin. Such a legislative measure has therefore in fact no connection with the importation of the products and for that reason is not of such a nature as to impede trade between Member States.' More recently, in *Directeur Général des Impôts* v. *Forest*[118] nationally imposed flour-milling quotas were held to fall outside Article 30, when the quotas applied in the same way to imported and to domestic wheat.

These statements are completely at variance with *Cassis de Dijon* since there a measure applying in the same way to domestic goods and to imports was held to contravene Article 30. Moreover, the Advocate General in *Cinéthèque* cited *Oebel* and *Blesgen* in support of his conclusion which, as we have seen, was wholly rejected by the Court.

Quite apart from this, the defendant in *Oebel* was not in any event entitled to rely on Article 30 because he was producing bread within Germany.[119] Although the Court did not refer to this point, it was no doubt influenced by it. Equally, there is no evidence in the report in *Forest* that the defendant had been milling imported wheat.

Finally, the passage quoted above from *Blesgen* is generally understood to mean that Article 30 is subject to a rule of remoteness.[120] On this view, there must come a point at which the effect of a measure on imports is so tenuous that that measure falls outside Article 30.

6.45 Secondly, in two cases in which 'indistinctly applicable' measures were held to infringe Article 30 the Court stressed that the measures had protective effects: *E.C. Commission* v. *Italy* (cider vinegar)[121] and *Prantl*.[122] Yet the Court has never found a measure to be lawful because it lacks protective effects. Indeed, *Cinéthèque* and *E.C. Commission* v. *France* (substitute milk powder) are authority to the contrary.

6.46 In the light of this case law it is submitted that the test of whether a measure constitutes a measure of equivalent effect is not whether it discriminates against imports, but whether it *restricts* imports.[123] This approach is entirely in keeping with the definition of measures of equivalent effect laid down in *Dassonville*[124]:

---

[118] Case 148/85 [1988] 2 C.M.L.R. 577.
[119] Para. 6.74 below.
[120] Dashwood 'The Cassis de Dijon line authority' in *In Memoriam J.D.B. Mitchel* (1983) 145 at 152; Gormley *Prohibiting Restrictions on Trade within the EEC* (1985) at 252, see also para. 7.90 below. It is submitted, however, that the measure in issue in *Blesgen* was not too remote to fall under Art. 30: see para. 7.87 below.
[121] Case 193/80 [1981] E.C.R. 3019 at 3034.
[122] Case 16/83 [1984] E.C.R. 1299 at 1327, [1985] 2 C.M.L.R. 238 at 255.
[123] Gormley, *op. cit.* n.120 above, at pp.262–263.
[124] Para. 6.18 above.

'all trading rules enacted by Member States, which are capable of hindering, directly or indirectly, actually or potentially, intra-Community trade.'

Yet discrimination continues to be relevant in two ways. First, a measure discriminating against imports constitutes *per se* an actual or potential, direct or indirect restriction on them. Secondly, with certain categories of measures of equivalent effect, discrimination is an inherent element. Examples are discrimination in the award of public supply contracts or measures inciting the purchase of national products. In these cases, discrimination is the very essence of the measure, and if it were removed, there would be no restriction on imports left. For these reasons, the continued mention of discrimination in some of the Court's judgments on Article 30 is quite consistent with *Cassis de Dijon*.[125]

Also, the rule that Article 30 embraces all restrictions on imports not covered by other Treaty provisions is perhaps subject to 2 exceptions:

(i) it would appear that as regards certain price controls discrimination is the determining criterion[126];

(ii) it may be that the effect of certain measures on imports is so remote or so tenuous that those measures are not caught by Article 30 at all.[127] If so, then it is on those grounds that 'indistinctly applicable' legislation on shop opening hours is compatible with Article 30.[128] However, such a rule could apply only to extreme cases.

6.47   In 1984 Marenco[129] mounted a rearguard attack on the view that non-discriminatory measures may be caught by Article 30. In his view discrimination is the very essence of measures of equivalent effect, although he defines discrimination fairly widely to cover 'indistinctly applicable' measures which require manufacturers of other Member States to institute a special production for exports to the offending State. By this means he seeks to bring the *Cassis de Dijon* line of cases within his theory. His article is long and cogently argued so that it would be quite impossible to attempt to refute each of his arguments here. However, it should be said that even at that time the following objections could be levelled against his theory:

— he claims that Articles 30 and 34 must be based on the same principles contending that Article 30 must be brought into line with Article 34; yet this view is surely untenable[130];

---

[125] Gormley, *op. cit.* n.120 above, at 264–265.
[126] Para. 7.65 below.
[127] N.120 above. See also Case 69/88, *Krantz* v. *Netherlands* (pending).
[128] Para. 7.90 below.
[129] 'Pour une interprétation traditionnelle de la notion de mesure d'effect équivalent à une restriction quantitative' [1984] C.D.E. 291.
[130] Para. 6.63 below. Gormley, *op. cit.* n.120 above, at p.265.

— he relies heavily on *Oebel* and *Blesgen* although they are at variance with the overwhelming body of cases; only in those two judgments has the Court found measures to fall outside Article 30 on the grounds that they were not discriminatory; in other cases the Court has referred to the non-discriminatory nature of measures, but in relation to justification.[131]

In the meantime, the Court has delivered its judgments in *Cinéthèque* and in *E.C. Commission* v. *France* (substitute milk products) so that there is surely no room left for Marenco's theory. Since both were judgments of the full Court, the ruling of the five-judge Chamber in *Forest* appears to be of little avail to supporters of Marenco's theory.

On the other hand, Marenco may well be right in suggesting that certain measures are too remote from imports to fall within Article 30, one example being indistinctly applicable legislation limiting shopping hours.[132] Yet it is submitted that such a rule of remoteness can only apply in extreme cases.

6.48   Be that as it may, another feature of *Cassis de Dijon* is that, following the Advocate General, the Court appears to have reversed the presumption of legality contained in Article 3 of Directive 70/50; consequently the burden of proof is now borne by the party seeking to show that a measure restricting trade is justified. This is shown by the wording of the Court's judgment in *Gilli and Andres*, the first to confirm *Cassis de Dijon*. There the Court held that

'it is only where rules, which apply without discrimination to both domestic and imported products, may be justified as necessary in order to satisfy imperative requirements . . . that they may constitute an exception to the requirements arising under Article 30.'

Yet the mere fact that Directive 70/50 has been implicitly overruled to this extent does not mean that it ceases to have any value.[133]

6.49   One question left open by *Cassis de Dijon* was the relationship between the 'mandatory requirements' laid down by that judgment and Article 36. That provision is not mentioned at all in the *Cassis de Dijon* judgment. Two schools of thought have evolved on this matter:

(i) According to the first view, the dichotomy between 'distinctly applicable' and 'indistinctly applicable' measures lives on so that,

---

[131] Gormley, *op. cit.* at 264–265.

[132] This consideration has led Waelbroeck in 'Mesures d'effet équivalent, discrimination formelle et matérielle dans la jurisprudence de la Cour de Justice' in *Liber Amicorum Frédéric Dumon* and Defalque 'Le concept de discrimination en matière de libre circulation des marchandises' [1987] C.D.E. 471 to follow Marenco's theory, albeit in a much attenuated form.

[133] Paras. 6.05 and 6.06 above.

— 'distinctly applicable' measures may only be justified on the grounds expressly set out in Article 36, whereas

— 'indistinctly applicable' measures may be justified *in addition* under the mandatory requirements.

This means that the question whether an 'indistinctly applicable' measure is necessary to satisfy a 'mandatory requirement' is to be weighed up *within* Article 30. Only if an 'indistinctly applicable' measure is found to be unjustified according to this test does it fall to be considered as a measure of equivalent effect at all.

On this view, moreover—and this perhaps is the crucial point—'indistinctly applicable' measures are granted more favourable treatment in that the 'mandatory requirements' apply to them alone.

6.50   (ii) According to the second view, the 'mandatory requirements' are regarded as being subsumed under Article 36, either on the grounds that they fall under the heading of public policy[134] or that they constitute additions to the list of grounds of justification set out in Article 36.[135] On this view, *all* measures whether 'distinctly' or 'indistinctly' applicable' are subject to the same twofold test:

— does this measure actually or potentially, directly or indirectly restrict imports so as to fall under Article 30?

— if so, is it justified under Article 36 as extended by the 'mandatory requirements'[136]?

6.51   In support of the first theory, it should be said that the Court has repeatedly held that Article 36 must be interpreted narrowly since it constitutes an exception to a fundamental principle of Community law.[137]

Yet the following points, which were made in support of the other theory in the first edition of this book, still hold good[138]:

(i) This theory avoids the undue harshness resulting from the first theory with respect to 'distinctly applicable' measures *necessary* on, for instance, consumer protection grounds. According to the first theory, even though they are necessary, such measures are contrary to Article 30. According to the second theory, such measures are considered to fall under Article 30, but they may be justified under Article 36.

---

[134] Meier, *op. cit.* n.104 above.

[135] Masclet, *op. cit.* n.104 above, at p.264.

[136] A logical and consistent application of this theory would mean that quantitative restrictions would also be subject to the exceptions contained in 'mandatory requirements'.

[137] Para. 8.01 below.

[138] It was also contended that the first theory would create confusion because public health, which was mentioned in *Cassis de Dijon* as being a mandatory requirement, is also listed in Art. 36. However, this problem appears to have been solved because it has been the consistent practice of the Court to treat public health within Art. 36 and not as a 'mandatory requirement'.

(ii) It is submitted that the 'mandatory requirements' have the same properties as the grounds of justification in Article 36. Thus, for instance, the Member State bears the burden of proof that its measure is justified as with Article 36.[139] Also, as the Court expressly stated in *Cassis* in the passage quoted above, a measure will only be justified by a 'mandatory requirement' if it is necessary to attain that end—just as with Article 36.[140] Again, it is submitted that the 'mandatory requirements' cannot justify a national measure where Community legislation containing sufficient guarantees with respect to those requirements has come into force, just as with Article 36.[141]

(iii) The first theory keeps in being the dichotomy between 'distinctly' and 'indistinctly applicable' measures and this dichotomy gives rise to great difficulty.

6.52 The Court has so far been able to overcome the problem referred to in point (i) by means of the unsatisfactory device described below. That is not to say, however, that that problem has been solved.

As to point (ii) it has lost none of its force. Since the Court has now accepted that consumer protection may justify restrictions otherwise prohibited by Article 30, does it make sense to approach it differently from, say, plant health merely because in 1957 consumer protection did not yet arouse much passion?

Point (iii) remains as poignant as ever. Suffice it to quote two examples from the recent case law of the Court. *Prantl*[142] concerned a German statutory provision to the effect that only wines from certain specified regions of Germany could be marketed in bottles of a particular shape. This measure was held by the Court to be 'indistinctly applicable.' Yet under this provision the sale of all imported wine in bottles of the shape concerned was prohibited, whereas some German wines could be lawfully sold in such bottles. Also, in *Leclerc* v. *Au Blé Vert*[143] a resale price maintenance scheme whereby the price was fixed by the manufacturer in the case of imports was held to be 'distinctly applicable'. Yet the Court had ruled to the opposite effect in *GB-Inno* v. *ATAB*.[144]

6.53 It was not until its ruling in Case 113/80 *E.C. Commission* v. *Ireland*[145] that the Court ruled on the issue referred to in

---

[139] Para. 6.48 above and para. 8.03 below.
[140] Para. 8.10 below.
[141] Para. 8.15 below. In *Cassis de Dijon*, the 'mandatory requirements' were held only to apply 'in the absence of common rules' (see para. 6.41 above).
[142] N.122 above.
[143] Case 229/83 [1985] E.C.R. 1, [1985] 2 C.M.L.R. 286, noted by Kuyper [1985] C.M.L.Rev. 787; see para. 7.76 below.
[144] N.78 above.
[145] [1982] E.C.R. 1625, [1982] 1 C.M.L.R. 706; see Judge Touffait *op. cit.* n.109 above.

paragraphs 6.49 and 6.50. That case arose out of proceedings brought by the Commission under Article 169 of the Treaty with respect to two Irish Orders requiring certain metal objects to bear an origin marking. The Orders only applied to imported goods and were thus 'distinctly applicable.' The Irish Government contended that these measures were justified on the grounds of consumer protection, a 'mandatory requirement'. Thus the question whether the 'mandatory requirements' applied to 'distinctly applicable' measures was squarely posed. The Court ruled in the following terms:

> 'The orders concerned in the present case are not measures which are applicable to domestic products and to imported products without distinction but rather a set of rules which apply only to imported products and are therefore discriminatory in nature, with the result that the measures in issue are not covered by the decisions cited above which relate exclusively to provisions that regulate in a uniform manner the marketing of domestic products and imported products.'

Yet the Court then proceeded to rule that it is 'necessary to consider whether the contested measures are indeed discriminatory or whether they constitute discrimination in appearance only.' The Court then examined the measures to see if they were justified on consumer protection grounds (and found they were not). This appears to go back on the passage of this judgment just quoted. The idea that a 'distinctly applicable' measure may be justified on the grounds of consumer protection has been put out by the door and let in through the window!

Despite its apparent lack of logic this reasoning has been applied by the Court in a number of subsequent judgments.[146] Consequently, to maintain the view expressed in the first edition of this book that the 'mandatory requirements' fall within Article 36 might be equated by some to sparring with windmills. Yet the fact remains that in following this approach the Court always appears to reach the same result as it would have done by applying Article 36. This is why Chapter VIII of this book considers Article 36 and the 'mandatory requirements' together.

6.54   Nevertheless, there is one exceptional case in which the Court might have reached a different conclusion on the basis of Article 36, namely *Leclerc* v. *Au Blé Vert*.[147] As mentioned earlier, this case concerned a resale price maintenance scheme which was held to be 'distinctly applicable.' However, it went on to hold that as regards re-imports the scheme was 'indistinctly applicable.' Yet the Court then refused altogether to consider whether the scheme was justified

---

[146] *E.g.* Cases 177/83 *Kohl* v. *Ringelhan* [1984] E.C.R. 3651, [1985] 3 C.M.L.R. 340, and 207/83 *E.C. Commission* v. *United Kingdom* (indications of origin) [1985] E.C.R. 1201, [1985] 2 C.M.L.R. 259. This case law has moreover been referred to with approval by: Judge Touffait, *op. cit.*, VerLoren van Themaat 'La libre circulation des marchandises après l'arrêt "Cassis de Dijon"' [1982] C.D.E. 123 and Gormley, *op. cit.* at p.57.

[147] N.143 above.

on the grounds of consumer protection (a 'mandatory requirement') stating that the legislation 'discouraged the marketing of imported products'! This has compounded the confusion.

C. The principle of equivalence

6.55   In the penultimate ground of its judgment in *Cassis de Dijon* the Court ruled that:

> 'There is . . . no valid reason why, provided that they have been lawfully produced and marketed in one of the Member States, alcoholic beverages should not be introduced into any other Member State; the sale of such products may be subject to a legal prohibition on the marketing of beverages with an alcohol content lower than the limit set by national rules.'

Consequently, in the operative part of its judgment, the Court ruled that a measure of the kind in question was contrary to Article 30 'where the importation of alcoholic beverages lawfully produced and marketed in another Member State is concerned.'[148]

Although the Court did not spell out the principle of equivalence expressly in *Cassis de Dijon,* it did so in its subsequent ruling in *Fietje.*[149] There, the Court held in effect that the obligation to declare the nature of goods on their label was, in principle, justified on consumer protection grounds. However, it added that:

> 'There is no longer any need for such protection if the details given on the original label of the imported product have as their content information on the nature of the product and that content includes at least the same information and is just as capable of being understood by the consumers in the importing State as the description prescribed by the rules of that State . . .'

The Court also made the point very clearly in *E.C. Commission v. France* (woodworking machines)[150] when it held that a Member State:

> '. . . is not entitled to prevent the marketing of a product originating in another Member State which provides a level of protection of the health and life of humans equivalent to that which the national rules are intended to ensure or establish. It is therefore contrary to the principle of proportionality for national rules to require such imported products to comply strictly and exactly with the provisions or technical requirements laid down for products manufactured in the Member States in question when those imported products afford users the same level of protection.'[151]

6.56   The Commission attached particular importance to the passage quoted from *Cassis de Dijon* in its Communication[152] on that case. It drew the conclusion that this passage was of general application, asserting that:

---

[148] Case 788/79, n.111 above and Case 130/80 *Kelderman* [1981] E.C.R. 527.

[149] N.33 above.

[150] Case 188/84 [1986] E.C.R. 419.

[151] See also the passage quoted at para. 7.24 below from the Order of 13 March 1987 in Case 45/87R *E.C. Commission* v. *Ireland* (Dundalk Water Supply) [1987] 2 C.M.L.R. 563.

[152] N.109 above.

'*Any product*[153] imported from another Member State must in principle be admitted to the territory of the importing Member State if it has been lawfully produced, that is, conforms to rules and processes of manufacture that are customarily and traditionally accepted in the exporting country, and is marketed in the territory of the latter . . .

The principles decided by the Court imply that a Member State may not in principle prohibit the sale in its territory of a product lawfully produced according to technical or quality requirements which differ from those imposed on its domestic products. Where a product 'suitably and satisfactorily' fulfills the legitimate objective of a Member State's own rules (public safety, protection of the consumer or the environment, *etc.*) the importing country cánnot justify prohibiting its sale in its territory by claiming that the way it fulfils the objective is different from that imposed on domestic products.'[153]

6.57   This calls for a number of comments:

(i) The judgments do not define what is meant by lawful marketing in the Member State of production. Nor does the Commission's Communication. Presumably it will be enough if, on production, the goods are lawfully sold for export. There would appear to be no need for an initial sale entirely within the producing Member State before the goods are sold for export.[154]

6.58   (ii) As the Commission pointed out in its Communication, even if a product is lawfully produced and marketed in a Member State, it may not be sold within another Member State which has higher standards than the Member State of production—provided always that those higher standards are justified as being necessary to satisfy mandatory requirements. Thus if the optimal standard for a given product is 100 and the importing Member State requires 80, then it may justifiably prohibit the sale of goods conforming to the standard of only 70 imposed by the producing Member State. The same applies *a fortiori* if the producing Member State imposes no minimum standards at all. But, as already explained,[155] there is always a rebuttable presumption that the higher standard is not necessary.

On the other hand if two Member States both require a standard of 80 but lay down different means of reaching that result, then each must permit the sale of the other's product. That is what we have called the principle of equivalence.

It will not always be clear whether two standards are

---

[153] The emphasis is that of the author.
[154] According to Gormley, *op. cit.* at p.48, the requirement is in truth that the goods must be lawfully produced *or* marketed in the exporting Member State.
[155] Para. 6.48 above.

in fact equivalent. Member States are under a duty to take active steps[156] to establish whether this is so.

6.59 (iii) What is important in this context is not whether the producing Member State imposes a standard equivalent to that of the importing Member State. What matters rather is whether the product in question *in fact* meets a standard equivalent to that of the importing Member State—assuming that the product was lawfully produced in the Member State of production. This is illustrated by *Fietje* which in essence concerned the compatibility with Articles 30 to 36 of the obligation to indicate the denomination 'liqueur' on goods of a particular kind. The Court found that such a requirement fell foul of Article 30 if the goods *in fact* bore a label containing information of equivalent value to the consumer. The Court did not state that it was necessary to look into the legislation of the producing Member State to consider whether it required such labelling.

6.60 Does the mention in *Cassis de Dijon* of goods lawfully produced and marketed *in a Member State* mean that the principle of equivalence does not apply to goods originating in a third State but in free circulation in the Community[157]? It is submitted that it does not mean this: the wording of the judgment is determined by the fact that in the case itself the goods in question did originate in a Member State.

Let us take the following example: a product is manufactured in a third country and is then put in free circulation in Member State A, whereupon it is imported into Member State B.[158] The following solution is tentatively proposed:

(a) the principle of equivalence has no bearing within Member State A. For the question whether Member State A can prevent the product being put into free circulation, Article 30 is not relevant at all. As regards a prohibition on sale, it is submitted that the principle of equivalence does not apply either and it is therefore not enough that the product presents guarantees equivalent to the norms laid down by Member State A; the product must conform to those norms themselves.

---

[156] Paras. 6.20 above and 12.24 below.

[157] Some language versions of the initial cyclostyled text of the judgment in Case 788/79 *Gilli* (see n.111 above) stated that it was enough that goods were lawfully marketed in a Member State. However, a corrigendum was then published adding the requirement of lawful *production* in a Member State thus bringing it into line with *Cassis*. The remarks of Meier on this aspect of the *Gilli* judgment in [1981] EuR 43 at 46 concern the unamended version of the judgment.

[158] This is quite different from the case where restrictions are imposed on direct imports into the Community, a subject which falls outside the scope of this book.

(b) when the goods are then imported from Member State A to Member State B, there will of course be no problem if they actually meet the standards laid down by Member State B. But, in any case, if the goods comply with the norms of Member State A, then they are assimilated to goods originating in Member State A for this purpose in accordance with Article 9(2) of the Treaty.[158a]

6.61 What are the practical consequences for the non-specialist of the principle of equivalence? Potentially these are enormous. Mattera[159] sees this ruling as a step away from the faceless world of Euro-bread, Euro-beer and Euro-toys. Instead, local specialities from every Member State can in principle be bought and sold in their traditional form all over the Community. This gives the consumer a wide range of products to choose from.

On the other hand, this ruling has been criticised on the grounds that it will result in a lowering of standards.[159a] Yet, as has just been explained, the effect of the ruling is that a Member State may prohibit the sale of goods complying with a lower standard than its own, provided the higher standard is justified. Thus, for instance, it cannot seriously be argued that the judgment in *Gilli*—in which the Court held that the prohibition in a Member State on the sale of cider vinegar was contrary to Article 30—resulted in any lowering of standards. The Court's case law shows that the Court consistently upholds measures which are genuinely justified on, say, consumer protection grounds.[160]

6.62 Finally, there is some danger that with respect to the prevention of unfair trading the test of lawful marketing and production in another Member State will be supplanted, at least in part, by the requirement that the importing Member State must have regard to 'the fair and traditional practices observed in the various Member States.' This new criterion is discussed in paragraphs 8.86 and 8.89 below.

IV. MEASURES OF EQUIVALENT EFFECT ON EXPORTS

6.63 Before examining the concept of measures of equivalent effect falling under Article 34, it is as well to consider why Member States impose restrictions on exports at all. A Member State will normally

---

[158a] See para. 2.16. above.

[159] *Op. cit.* n.104 above at p.50.

[159a] Seidel 'Die Sogenannte Cassis-de-Dijon Rechtsprechung des Europäischen Gerichtshofes und der Schutz von Herkunftsangaben in der Europäischen Gemeinschaft' [1984] G.R.U.R. Int. 80.

[160] See paras. 8.70 *et seq.* below, see Judge Everling 'Die Cassis de Dijon Rechtsprechung des EuGH und ihre Auswirkungen auf die Ernährungswirtschaft', Heft 10, *Schriftenreihe des Bundes für Lebensmittelrecht und Lebensmittelkunde* (1987).

be moved to take such action by one or more of the following motives[161]:
— a desire to ensure supplies;
— the protection of jobs in processing industries (in this case the export restriction will cover the raw material or component part, but not the finished product);
— the prevention of parallel exports (so that manufacturers established in the Member State in question will be able to obtain higher profits in their export trade);
— the maintenance of the quality of exports;
— the preservation of works of art for the nation.[162]

6.64 The timetable for the abolition of such measures is that set out in paragraphs 5.01 to 5.05 and 6.07 and 6.09 above: Article 33(7) and the Directives[163] adopted under it apply only to measures of equivalent effect on imports.

Sections II and III(A) of this chapter apply *mutatis mutandis* to Article 34. In so far as discrimination is relevant, it is discrimination against goods intended for export in favour of goods intended for the domestic market. This applies whether these goods were produced in the Member State in question or are merely in free circulation there; it is clear that the prohibition in Article 34 applies to re-exports.[164] Like measures of equivalent effect on imports, such measures relating to exports may take effect at the border but do not necessarily do so. Classic examples are: export licences[165]; measures which lower the value of a product intended for export or increase its cost; and measures which discourage the sale of products for export. Once again, a measure will not fall under Article 34 if it is caught by another prohibition in the Treaty, such as Article 16, 92 or 95.

6.65 As we have seen,[166] a measure restricting imports will fall under Article 30, even if it applies to domestic and imported products in the same way. The fundamental question concerning Article 34 is: can measures fall within the concept of measures of equivalent effect under Article 34, even if they apply in the same way to exports and to goods intended for the domestic market? In other words, does a measure restricting exports fall under Article 34 even if it does not discriminate against exports? At first sight, there would appear to be no obstacle to Article 34 covering this type of measure, especially as the *Dassonville*[167] formula does not

---

[161] As to the relevance of the object of the measure, see para. 6.68 and n.176 below.
[162] Measures adopted for the latter motive will often be justified under Art. 36: see paras. 8.59 *et seq.* below.
[163] Para. 6.02 *et seq.* above.
[164] Restrictions on re-exports may infringe both Art. 30 and Art. 34.
[165] Para. 7.92 *et seq.* below.
[166] Para. 6.40 *et seq.* above.
[167] Para. 6.18 above.

purport to be limited to measures of equivalent effect on imports.[168] Nevertheless, on closer examination the problem becomes more complex.

In this context it is necessary to distinguish between
— restrictions on production; and
— restrictions on sale.
These will be taken in turn.

6.66   In *Groenveld* v. *Produktschap voor Vee en Vlees*[169] which concerned a prohibition on producing horse meat, the Court held that Article 34 'concerns national measures which have as their specific object or effect the restriction of patterns of exports and thereby the establishment of a difference between the domestic trade of a Member State and its export trade in such a way as to provide a particular advantage for national production or for the domestic market of the State in question at the expense of the production or of the trade of other Member States.' This was the first case concerning the compatibility with Article 34 of a restriction on the production of goods not covered by an agricultural organisation of the market.[170] Yet this ruling was delivered by a Chamber of the Court and constituted such a radical break from the previous case law on Articles 30 and 34 that there was reason to think that it would not be followed by the full Court.[171]

6.67   Nevertheless, VerLoren van Themaat[172] has expressed the view that this ruling is correct. In his view Article 34 only applies to restrictions imposed on exports alone or falling more heavily on exports than on goods put on the national market: in other words, he takes the view that Article 34 only covers 'distinctly applicable' measures.[173] It is indeed true that if all restrictions on production were held to fall under Article 34, that provision would be very wide indeed. For instance, legislation imposing the requirement to obtain planning permission before building a factory would fall under Article 34, as would legislation relating to health and safety at work. Such measures would then be incompatible with the Treaty unless it could be shown that they were justified.

---

[168] The *Dassonville* formula was incorporated (though in rather an oblique way) in para. 16 of the judgment in Case 53/76 *Procureur de la République* v. *Bouhelier* [1977] E.C.R. 197 at 205, [1977] 1 C.M.L.R. 436 at 444; that judgment concerned Art. 34.

[169] Case 15/79 [1979] E.C.R. 3409, [1981] 1 C.M.L.R. 207.

[170] See paras. 7.86 and 10.15.

[171] See also para. 7.96 below.

[172] *Op. cit.* n.82 above.

[173] He points out (*op. cit.* at 391) that on the basis of *Groenveld* the U.K. and the Netherlands would be entitled to restrict production of North Sea oil and gas respectively without falling foul of Art. 34—provided that such restrictions applied in the same way to products intended for the domestic market and for export.

VerLoren van Themaat deduces from Article 52 that Article 34 cannot be so wide. Article 52 relates to the right of establishment and provides in particular that

> 'freedom of establishment shall include the right to take up and pursue activities as self-employed persons and to set up and manage undertakings . . . under the conditions laid down for its own nationals by the law of the country where such establishment is effected . . .'

That provision thus appears to be a prohibition on discrimination rather than on restrictions on the freedom of establishment. VerLoren van Themaat takes the view that Article 52 would be undermined if all restrictions on establishment simultaneously fell under Article 34. He therefore regards such a wide definition of measures of equivalent effect under Article 34 as contrary to the 'system of the Treaty.' This leads him to the conclusion that the *Groenveld* judgment is of general significance, since it avoids this potential conflict between Articles 34 and 52.

6.68 Against this background, the *Groenveld* formula was reiterated by the full Court in *Oebel*[174] with respect to a prohibition on baking at night. However, in so doing the Court omitted the final words of that formula ('at the expense of the production or of the trade of other Member States') which in any case appeared highly anomalous. The shortened formula appears in virtually all the subsequent cases[175] on Article 34. Under these circumstances, the shortened formula requires dissection here. For a measure to constitute a measure of equivalent effect under Article 34, it appears to lay down two cumulative conditions:

— the measure must have as its specific object[176] or effect the restriction of patterns of export; and

— it must discriminate in favour of goods intended for the domestic market against exports so as to favour national production[177] or the domestic market of the State in question.

This would be a very onerous burden of proof to discharge. For instance, on this test a measure applying in the same way to goods intended for the national market and for export will fall outside Article 34 altogether even if it restricts exports and its sole object

---

[174] N.116 above.

[175] *E.g.* Cases 141–143/81 *Holdijk* [1982] E.C.R. 1299, [1983] 2 C.M.L.R. 635, para. 11 of the judgment; 172/82 *Syndicat National des Fabricants Raffineurs d'Huile de Graissage* v. *Inter-Huiles* [1983] E.C.R. 555, [1983] 3 C.M.L.R. 485, para. 12 of the judgment; 237/82 *Jongeneel Kaas* v. *Netherlands* [1984] E.C.R. 43, [1985] 2 C.M.L.R. 53, para. 22 of the judgment. However, the *Groenveld* formula is recited in full at para. 25 of the judgment in Case 15/83 *Denkavit Nederland* v. *Hoofdproduktschap voor Akkerbouwprodukten* [1984] E.C.R. 2171.

[176] Until *Groenveld* it had been thought that the object of a measure was always irrelevant in determining whether it fell under Art. 30 or 34: para. 6.18 above.

[177] It is not entirely clear how a restriction on exports could favour national production, unless it be national production of finished products where the restriction applies to the raw material or component parts.

is to restrict exports without there being any objective justification for this. Thus the prohibition contained in Article 34 could often be circumvented simply by careful drafting of national legislation. Read literally this ruling would have the effect of excluding from the scope of Article 34 all but the most flagrant measures such as export licences.

6.69 In fact, any measure which discriminates against exports must *per se* have as its specific object or effect to restrict patterns of exports. Consequently, it is preferable not to construe the formula as containing two separate and cumulative conditions. Perhaps the test itself is contained in the first part of the formula: to constitute a measure of equivalent effect under Article 34 a measure must have as its specific object or effect to restrict patterns of exports. On this view, the second limb is merely a gloss on the first and simply gives an example of a measure having as its specific object or effect the restoration of patterns of exports. Furthermore, the Court has now expressly stated that it is contrary to Article 34 to require certificates of equality for exports only[178]—as indeed it must be if Article 34 is not to be largely deprived of its meaning. This indicates that the second limb of the *Groenveld* test is to be interpreted loosely. In any event the *Groenveld* formula may need further refinement if improper restrictions on exports are not to slip through the net of Community law.

6.70 So much for restrictions on production. What of restrictions on sale? The *Groenveld* formula purports to apply to all restrictions on export whether they apply at the stage of production or of sale. Yet it is interesting to note that *Groenveld* itself concerned a restriction on production, as did that aspect of *Oebel* to which the Court applied that formula (namely the prohibition on night baking). In *Oebel* itself, as regards the prohibition on night delivery of bread—a restriction on sale—the Court applied the same test for Articles 30 and 34.[179]

Indeed, there appears to be no reason why *Cassis de Dijon* cannot be applied *mutatis mutandis* to Article 34 as regards restrictions on sale. This category of measures comprises provisions of the type at issue in *Cassis de Dijon* itself: measures prohibiting the sale of certain products; or relating to the presentation of products. Frequently, national measures of this kind do not apply to sales for export. Nevertheless, to the extent that such measures do cover sales for export, there appears to be no real reason why *Cassis de Dijon*

---

[178] *Jongeneel Kaas* (n.175 above) confirming *Bouhelier* (n.168 above) a case decided before *Groenveld*. In *Jongeneel* the Court also implied (in para. 22 of the judgment) that quality standards which apply only to exports or which are more stringent for exports, are contrary to Art. 34; see similarly para. 11 of the judgment in *Holdijk* (n.175 above).

[179] See para. 7.62 below.

should not apply to them; in other words, in the absence of justification such restrictions may be contrary to Article 34 even though they apply in the same way to exports and to goods put on the national market.

Gormley[180] has pointed out that in *Syndicat National des Fabricants Raffineurs d'Huile de Graissage* v. *Inter-Huiles*[181] a three-judge Chamber of the Court applied the *Groenveld* formula to a restriction on sale. However, that case concerned in truth a quantitative restriction and not a measure of equivalent effect. On any view the *Groenveld* formula does not relate to quantitative restrictions, so that it was not really in point in *Inter-Huiles*. That is perhaps implicitly recognised by a subsequent judgment[182] of the full Court relating to the same subject matter as *Inter-Huiles* in which the *Groenveld* formula was not recited.

6.71 Lastly, do the 'mandatory requirements' laid down in *Cassis de Dijon*[183] apply to measures of equivalent effect on exports? There is every reason to suppose that they do. In his observations in *Groenveld* and *Oebel*, Advocate General Capotorti propounded the view that the 'mandatory requirements' did apply to export restrictions.[184] Moreover, the Court in *Oebel* more or less implied this to be so.[185]

Nonetheless it is difficult to see how the Court can find room for the 'mandatory requirements' to apply to export restrictions if it continues to rule that:

— the 'mandatory requirements' do not apply to 'distinctly applicable' measures[186]; and

— the concept of measures of equivalent effect under Article 34 only covers measures discriminating against exports ('distinctly applicable' measures).

V. DE FACTO HARMONISATION

6.72 We saw in an earlier part of this chapter[187] how the Court held in the *Cassis de Dijon* case that, in the absence of a mandatory requirement, a Member State is bound to admit goods lawfully produced and marketed in another Member State. If all the Member States impose precisely the same technical standard for a particular

---

[180] *Op cit.*, n.120 above, at 110; note also this author's interesting theory that the *Groenveld* formula is derived from American case law (at 102).

[181] N.175 above.

[182] Case 173/83 *E.C. Commission* v. *France* [1985] E.C.R. 491 (para. 8 of judgment).

[183] Para. 6.40 *et seq.* above.

[184] However, he took the view that *Cassis de Dijon* could quite generally be applied *mutatis mutandis* to Art. 34 so that 'indistinctly applicable' measures fell under that provision. As we have seen, the Court held otherwise in *Groenveld* and *Oebel*.

[185] Para. 8.92 below.

[186] Para. 6.53 above.

[187] Paras. 6.55 *et seq.* above.

product, then goods not complying with that standard cannot be lawfully produced or marketed in any Member State of the Community. There will then be no restriction on imports or exports between Member States so that neither Article 30 nor Article 34 will be infringed. It is submitted then that, as regards technical standards, *de facto* harmonisation is compatible with Articles 30 to 36.[188] To hold otherwise would be to interpret Articles 30 to 36 as guaranteeing access to the market or, in other words, creating a fundamental right to sell goods commercially.[189] This goes considerably further than the mere prohibition on unnecessary restrictions on inter-State trade.

To take one example, should all Member States require a particular drink to have an alcoholic content of at least 15 per cent., there will be no infringement of Articles 30 to 34, simply because there will be no restrictions on imports or exports between Member States. This will be so whether or not Member States have acted in concert. It will be otherwise, however, if one single Member State imposes a different minimum alcohol requirement or none at all: trade between that State and the others will then be restricted. This shows that *de facto* harmonisation is no lasting substitute for Community legislation.

6.73 However, it must not be overlooked that as a general rule if all Member States enact the same restriction they will all be infringing Article 30. Thus, for instance, if they all subject imports of a certain product to unnecessary import controls, then they are all committing an infringement. Only technical standards cease to constitute import restrictions once they are adopted by all the Member States.

VI. 'PURELY NATIONAL' MEASURES

6.74 Do Articles 30 and 34 prohibit restrictive national measures relating to goods which affect neither imports nor exports? Similarly, can a domestic producer supplying only the domestic market invoke either of these provisions against a measure on the grounds that the measure also restricts imports or exports? For example:

— can a producer of goods in a Member State invoke Article 30 or 34 against a restriction on sale in that Member State in respect of goods put on the national market?
— can an importer of goods originating in England, Scotland or Wales rely on Article 30 with respect to a restriction on importing those goods to Northern Ireland?

---

[188] In a rather different context, Case 89/76 *E.C. Commission* v. *Netherlands* [1977] E.C.R. 1355, [1978] 3 C.M.L.R. 630, which concerned phytosanitary controls on exports, shows that the Court attaches importance to *de facto* harmonisation.

[189] See Schiller, *op. cit.* n.47 above; this theory is also discussed by Grabitz 'Das Recht auf Zugang zum Markt nach dem EWG-Vertrag' *Festschrift für Ipsen* (1977), 645. The cases discussed below show that the scope of Arts. 30 and 34 is more limited than this.

As will be seen, the result for national goods must be the same whether the measure complained of applies only to national goods or applies also to goods from other Member States.

6.75 In the first edition of this book it was contended that 'purely national' measures are not caught by these provisions at all. The reasoning ran as follows: Article 30 prohibits 'quantitative restrictions on imports and all measures having equivalent effect' while Article 34 prohibits the same measures with respect to exports. Thus, it can be deduced from the wording of these provisions that a measure applying neither to imports nor to exports but applying only to domestic goods put on the national market falls outside Articles 30 and 34 altogether. In a series of cases the Court has now ruled that this reasoning is correct.

The matter first arose directly in *Waterkeyn*.[190] This constituted the sequel to *E.C. Commission* v. *France*[191] where the Court had held in the operative part of its judgment that 'by subjecting advertising in respect of alcoholic beverages to discriminatory rules and thereby maintaining obstacles to the freedom of intra-Community trade, the French Republic has failed to fulfil its obligations under Article 30 of the EEC Treaty.' It had reached this conclusion notwithstanding the fact that a minority of French-produced alcoholic drinks was subject to the more severe restrictions on categories of drink which were typically imported. The principal question which arose in *Waterkeyn* was whether the Court had ruled the legislation to be contrary to Article 30 only in so far as it applied to imports or whether its ruling also extended to domestically produced drinks. In answer to a request for a preliminary ruling the Court held that its earlier ruling was limited to imports. It is clear from the wording of the judgment that the result flows from the nature of Article 30 itself rather than merely from the terms of the earlier judgment.

6.76 This was confirmed in *Oosthoek's Uitgeversmaatschappij*,[192] which related to Dutch legislation prohibiting the promotion of sales by means of free gifts, subject to certain immaterial exceptions. The defendants in the main case were prosecuted for seeking to induce the public to buy their encyclopædias in this way. Some of these encyclopædias had been produced in Belgium, while others had been produced in the Netherlands. As regards the second category, the Court simply held that

'the application of the Netherlands legislation to the sale in the Netherlands of encyclopædias produced in that country is in no way linked to the

---

[190] Cases 314–316/81 and 83/82 [1982] E.C.R. 4337, [1983] 2 C.M.L.R. 145.
[191] Case 152/78 [1980] E.C.R. 2299, [1981] 2 C.M.L.R. 743.
[192] Case 286/81 [1982] E.C.R. 4575, [1983] 3 C.M.L.R. 428.

importation or exportation of goods and does not therefore fall within the scope of Articles 30 and 34 of the EEC Treaty.'

6.77 As regards Article 30, the position is stated most clearly of all in *Cognet*.[193] The defendant had been charged with selling books at a 20 per cent. discount contrary to French law. Following the Court's ruling in *Leclerc* v. *Au Blé Vert*[194] that law had been amended so as to provide for an exemption for all books imported from another Member State where they had been marketed. This exemption extended to books published in France and exported and then re-imported into France. The accused therefore maintained that the law discriminated against French books put directly on the French market and was therefore contrary to Community law. The Court rejected this view. As to Article 30 it held:

'. . . Article 30 of the EEC Treaty does not forbid such a difference of treatment. The purpose of that provision is to eliminate obstacles to the importation of goods and not to ensure that goods of national origin always enjoy the same treatment as imported or reimported goods. The absence of restrictions as regards the selling price of reimported books does not prejudice the sale of such books. A difference in treatment between goods which is not capable of restricting imports or of prejudicing the marketing of imported or reimported goods does not fall within the prohibition contained in Article 30.'[195]

6.78 One objection can be levelled against the view that 'purely national' measures fall outside Articles 30 and 34: the concept of the domestic products of a Member State must be defined. Yet there appears to be no reason for not applying by analogy the principles laid down in the Community Regulations on origin.[196]

6.79 Lastly, a common market organisation may widen the prohibitions contained in Articles 30 and 34[197] so as to prohibit even 'purely national' measures.

VII. CONCLUSION

6.80 It is submitted then that with certain exceptions the concept of measures of equivalent effect under Article 30 embraces all restrictions on imports not covered by other provisions of the Treaty—even if they do not discriminate against imports.[198]

On the other hand, as regards restrictions on production, the concept of measures of equivalent effect under Article 34 is considerably narrower. It remains to be seen whether the same applies to

---

[193] Case 355/85 [1987] 3 C.M.L.R. 942; Grelon 'La loi Lang sur le prix du livre et la discrimination à rebours' [1987] R.T.D.E. 405.
[194] Case 229/83 [1985] E.C.R. 2, [1985] 2 C.M.L.R. 286.
[195] See also Case 98/86 *Mathot* [1988] 1 C.M.L.R. 411.
[196] See para. 2.10 above.
[197] Para. 10.14 below.
[198] See para. 6.46 above.

other types of export restrictions, although there is no reason why it should do so.

Once it has been established that a particular measure falls under Article 30 or 34, then it must be considered whether that measure is justified under Article 36 or the 'mandatory requirements.' A distinction must always be made between the question whether a measure constitutes a restriction on imports and whether it is justified. Thus determining whether a measure is compatible with Article 30 or 34 is a two-stage process. At all events, it is submitted that the grounds of justification should be the same whether a measure falls under Article 30 or Article 34 and whether it is 'distinctly applicable' or 'indistinctly applicable'.

CHAPTER VII

Measures of Equivalent Effect: II

7.01 In the previous chapter we considered the general principles relating to measures of equivalent effect. The purpose of the present chapter is to consider specific measures with a view to establishing whether or not they constitute measures of equivalent effect under Article 30 or 34 as the case may be. Articles 30 and 34 will be examined in turn. Naturally we shall leave out of account those measures which fall to be considered under other provisions of the Treaty.[1]

As we saw in the previous chapter, the compatibility of a national measure with Article 30 or 34 must be tested in two stages, by asking two fundamental questions:
— Does this measure constitute a measure of equivalent effect falling under Article 30 or Article 34?
— If so, is it justified under Article 36 or the 'mandatory requirements'?

This chapter is concerned with the first of these two questions, while the second is dealt with in the following chapter. However, it has not been found possible to avoid mentioning Article 36 altogether.

7.02 Lastly, it should be pointed out that a large number of the Court's rulings discussed here concern agricultural products falling under a common market organisation.[2] As will be explained later in this book,[3] it is not clear whether rulings of this kind are in fact interpretations of the common market organisation in question rather than of Articles 30 and 34. This means that it is uncertain whether such rulings apply to all products.

I. MEASURES OF EQUIVALENT EFFECT UNDER ARTICLE 30

Import licences

7.03 The obligation to obtain an import licence or permit from the importing Member State before importing goods is a clear

---

[1] Para. 6.22 *et seq.* above.
[2] On the meaning of this concept of common market organisations, see para. 10.01 below.
[3] Paras. 10.11 *et seq.* below.

example of a measure of equivalent effect. In one of the first cases on Article 30 to come before it, *International Fruit Company* v. *Produktschap voor Groenten en Fruit*,[4] the Court decided that this held good even where licences were granted automatically and the Member State concerned did not purport to reserve the right to withhold a licence. It did so in the following terms:

> 'Apart from the exceptions for which provision is made by Community law itself [Articles 30 and 34(1)] preclude the application to intra-Community trade of a national provision which requires, even purely as a formality, import or export licences or any other similar procedure.'

The reason clearly is that even automatic licences can give rise to delay and abuse on the part of the importing Member State. The effect of this ruling was implicitly to strike down Article 2(2) of Commission Directive 70/50[5] in so far as that provision suggests that a mere formality is compatible with Article 30.

This ruling has been repeated in a number of subsequent cases, notably *Donckerwolcke* v. *Procureur de la République*,[6] which show that such measures constitute measures of equivalent effect rather than quantitative restrictions.[7]

The obligation to produce certain certificates

7.04 We are concerned here with the requirement that an importer produce certain types of certificate on importation, whether furnished by the authorities of an exporting Member State or by any other public or private body outside the importing Member State. This is to be distinguished from the case of import licences granted by the importing Member State itself, which was discussed in the previous section.

The first major case on Article 30, *Procureur du Roi* v. *Dassonville*,[8] was concerned with this type of measure. That case concerned a Belgian Royal Decree of 1934 prohibiting the importation into Belgium of spirits bearing a designation of origin officially recognised by the Belgian Government without an official document certifying their entitlement to such designation. The designation of origin 'Scotch Whisky' had been duly adopted by the Belgian Government. In 1970 (before Britain joined the Community) the defendants in the main case were parallel importers who had imported into Belgium various quantities of Scotch whisky from France, where they were in free circulation. They were charged with forging the official certificates of authenticity. In a reference for a preliminary ruling

---

[4] Cases 51–54/71 [1971] E.C.R. 1107.
[5] [1970] O.J. Spec.Ed. L13/29; see paras. 6.03 *et seq.* above.
[6] Case 41/76 [1976] E.C.R. 1921, [1977] 2 C.M.L.R. 535; the following cases concern export licences: Case 53/76 *Bouhelier* [1977] E.C.R. 197, [1977] 1 C.M.L.R. 436, Case 68/76 *E.C. Commission* v. *France* [1977] E.C.R. 515, [1977] 2 C.M.L.R. 161.
[7] As to justification see paras. 8.38, 8.56 and 8.57 below.
[8] Case 8/74 [1974] E.C.R. 837, [1974] 2 C.M.L.R. 436, noted by Joliet [1975] M.L.R. 200 and Wellinghausen [1975] EuR 322.

the Brussels court asked the Court of Justice, *inter alia*, whether measures of this kind were compatible with Article 30. In its reference the Brussels court pointed out that the effect of the Belgian provisions was to make imports of whisky from France impossible, since France did not require such certificates of authenticity.

The Court replied as follows:

'All trading rules enacted by Member States which are capable of hindering, directly or indirectly, actually or potentially, intra-Community trade are to be considered as measures having an effect equivalent to quantitative restrictions.

In the absence of a Community system guaranteeing for consumers the authenticity of a product's designation of origin, if a Member State takes measures to prevent unfair practices in this connection, it is however subject to the condition that these measures should be reasonable and that the means of proof required should not act as a hindrance to trade between Member States and should, in consequence, be accessible to all Community nationals.

Even without having to examine whether or not such measures are covered by Article 36, they must not, in any case, by virtue of the principle expressed in the second sentence of that Article, constitute a means of arbitrary discrimination or a disguised restriction on trade between Member States.

That may be the case with formalities, required by a Member State for the purpose of proving the origin of a product, which only direct importers are really in a position to satisfy without facing serious difficulties.

Consequently, the requirement by a Member State of a certificate of authenticity which is less easily obtainable by importers of an authentic product which has been put into free circulation in a regular manner in another Member State than by importers of the same product coming directly from the country of origin constitutes a measure having an effect equivalent to a quantitative restriction as prohibited by the Treaty.'

7.05   It is clear from this passage that Article 30 prohibits not only restrictions on imports as such, but also measures discriminating in favour of direct imports against indirect imports. As already explained, the facts in *Dassonville* arose before Britain had acceded to the Community, so that it is manifest that this principle applies even where the country of origin is not a Member State.

7.06   Indeed, the wording of this passage suggests that the requirement that imports be accompanied by a certificate of authenticity is not in itself a measure of equivalent effect. The wording suggests, rather, that this requirement only constituted a measure of equivalent effect because the certificates were harder to obtain for indirect imports than for goods coming directly from the country of origin. However, this is merely due to the fact that *Dassonville* was the first major judgment of the Court on Article 30 and the Court's case law has evolved considerably since then. That the obligation to produce a certificate on importation in itself constitutes a measure of equivalent effect is shown by later cases. In particular, in *Denkavit*

Futtermittel v. *Minister für Ernährung*[9] concerning imports of animal feed the Court held that

> 'the concept of a measure having an effect equivalent to a quantitative restriction . . . applies to the obligation to produce a certificate to the effect that the imported feeding-stuffs have undergone specified treatment in the exporting country.'

It is submitted, then, that any requirement to produce a document on importation[10] constitutes a measure of equivalent effect under Article 30. This applies whatever the nature of the document, be it a certificate of authenticity, or origin,[11] or a sanitary, veterinary or phytosanitary certificate. However, this is perhaps subject to the proviso that import controls fall outside Article 30 in so far as they are inherent in the customs procedure.[12] Again, inasmuch as such requirements do fall under Article 30, they will frequently be justified under Article 36 particularly on health grounds—although it is not clear that certificates of origin could ever be justified,[13] except possibly for the limited category of products for which origin may be essential.[14]

7.07   An element of confusion has, however, been caused by the Court's ruling in *E.C. Commission* v. *Belgium*[15] (sometimes known as *'Dassonville II'*). Since imports of Scotch whisky into Belgium were still subject to the restriction at issue in the first *Dassonville* case—except for certain 'liberalising measures' introduced as a matter of practice—the Commission brought proceedings under Article 169 of the Treaty against Belgium for infringement of Article 30. Yet the Court rejected the Commission's action.

The Court held that the test to be applied was: do these measures create for the indirect importer 'difficulties in obtaining certificates which are unreasonable in relation to those which that State imposes on a direct importer'? It went on to rule as follows:

> 'The Commission has not satisfactorily refuted the argument of the Belgian Government that those liberalising measures have contributed to an appreciable improvement in the position in relation to direct importers or traders wishing to import spirits bearing a protected designation of origin into Belgium from another Member State where they are in free circulation, but has confined itself to stating that in spite of the said measures the system of control adopted

---

[9] Case 251/78 [1979] E.C.R. 3369, [1980] 3 C.M.L.R. 513; see also Case 53/76, n.6 above, as regards exports.

[10] Similar restrictions operating at a later stage *e.g.* sale also constitute measures of equivalent effect: para. 7.52 below.

[11] Case 154/85 *E.C. Commission* v. *Italy* (parallel imports of vehicles) (judgment of 17 June 1987) related *inter alia* to certificates of origin. However, the Commission apparently did not impugn this requirement and the judgment is unclear on the point. Nor is any assistance to be derived from the interim Order of the President in that case [1985] E.C.R. 1753, [1986] 2 C.M.L.R. 159.

[12] Para. 7.85 below.

[13] Para. 9.48 below.

[14] Paras. 7.38 and 7.48 *et seq.* below.

[15] Case 2/78 [1979] E.C.R. 1761, [1980] 1 C.M.L.R. 216.

by the Belgian Government still involves the importer of those products into Belgium in more difficulties than would result from the system of sealing and labelling which it advocates.

That fact relied on by the Commission nevertheless cannot in itself constitute a failure by the Kingdom of Belgium to fulfil its obligations under Article 30 of the Treaty.

It is clear from those considerations that, even if the system for checking the authenticity of products bearing a designation of origin as applied by the Belgian Government involves the importer of those products into Belgium in more difficulties than would result from a system of sealing and labelling, that fact cannot in itself constitute a failure by the Kingdom of Belgium to fulfil its obligations under Article 30 of the Treaty.

For those reasons the action must be dismissed.'

7.08   This ruling appears to be irreconcilable with the rest of the Court's case law on Article 30 for two reasons:

Firstly, the first question to be asked in each case is, it is submitted, whether the measure in question restricts imports. In this connection it is not enough to consider whether the measure puts the direct importer in a more favourable position than the indirect importer. Otherwise a separate category of measures is created to which this (less stringent) test is applied—and how is this category to be circumscribed? In laying down this 'direct/indirect importer' test the Court was presumably influenced by the wording of the first *Dassonville* judgment,[16] yet it cannot be deduced from that earlier judgment that this is necessarily the test to be applied. What is more, the 'direct/indirect importer' test runs counter to the rest of the case law on Article 30.

Secondly, as will be seen in the following chapter,[17] it is a golden rule that a measure cannot be justified under Article 36 if it is unnecessarily restrictive on imports having regard to the purpose to be achieved. Yet by declining to have regard to the system of sealing and labelling advocated by the Commission, the Court in effect refused to apply this well established principle in *E.C. Commission* v. *Belgium*.

Import inspections

7.09   The obligation to submit imports or exports to veterinary, sanitary, phytosanitary and other similar inspections on imports or exports constitutes a measure of equivalent effect within the meaning of Articles 30 and 34 respectively. This was established with respect to phytosanitary controls on apple imports (designed to track down the formidable San José scale insect) in *Rewe-Zentralfinanz* v. *Landwirtschaftskammer*[18] and with respect to veterinary and public health inspections on veal imports in *Simmenthal* v. *Minister for*

---

[16] See the last para. of the passage of *Dassonville* quoted at para. 7.04 above.
[17] Para. 8.10.
[18] Case 4/75 [1975] E.C.R. 843, [1977] 1 C.M.L.R 599.

Finance.[19] Frequently such inspections will be justified under Article 36 on the grounds of the protection of the health and life of humans, animals or plants, as the case may be.[20] It is also probable that frontier controls inherent in the customs procedure fall outside Article 30 altogether.[21]

A most important step in the simplification and reduction of inspections was taken by the Council in adopting Directive 83/643[22] on the facilitation of physical inspections and administrative formalities in respect of the carriage of goods between Member States, which is based on Articles 43, 75, 84 and 100 of the Treaty. By virtue of Article 1, this Directive applies to all movements of goods between Member States and to all goods, other than ships and aircraft used as means of transport. Article 2 provides that:

> 'Member States shall take the necessary measures to ensure that in the course of any carriage operation the various inspections and formalities are carried out with the minimum of delay necessary and:
> — as far as possible, in one place,
> — with the inspection being carried out by means of spot checks, except in duly justified circumstances.'

Furthermore, the first paragraph of Article 9 reads as follows:

> 'Where, in exceptional and justified cases, a Member State intends to introduce a new inspection or formality, it shall inform the Commission thereof.'

This being merely a requirement to inform the Commission, it would appear to lack direct effect.[23]

Certain sanctions or fines

7.10   There are three ways in which fines or other sanctions imposed for an offence under national law with respect to imported goods may fall under Article 30:

(i)   it is clear that a sanction attached to a restriction on imports will be contrary to Article 30 if the restriction itself is: *Procureur de la République* v. *Rivoira.*[24]

(ii) It is also evident that criminal penalties discriminating against imported goods are contrary to Article 30: *Cayrol* v. *Rivoira.*[25] This may occur where national law either lays down no such penalties with respect to domestic goods or lays down lighter penalties with respect to domestic goods.

---

[19] Case 35/76 [1976] E.C.R. 1871, [1977] 2 C.M.L.R. 1; see also the following cases—Case 251/78, n.9 above; Case 132/80 *United Foods and Van den Abeele* v. *Belgian State* [1981] E.C.R. 995, [1982] 1 C.M.L.R. 273; Case 42/82 *E.C. Commission* v. *France*, [1983] E.C.R. 1013, [1984] 1 C.M.L.R. 160 (see also Case 42/82R [1982] E.C.R. 841).

[20] See paras. 8.39 *et seq.* and 8.58 below.

[21] Para. 7.85 below.

[22] [1983] O.J. L359/8, amended by Dir. 87/53 ([1987] O.J. L24/33).

[23] Case 174/84 *Bulk Oil* v. *Sun International* [1986] E.C.R. 559, [1986] 2 C.M.L.R. 732.

[24] Case 179/78 [1979] E.C.R. 1147, [1979] 3 C.M.L.R. 456, para. 14 of judgment; for the facts, see para. 9.37 below.

[25] Case 52/77 [1977] E.C.R. 2261, [1978] 2 C.M.L.R. 253, para. 5 of judgment; for the facts, see para. 9.36 below.

(iii) Lastly there is a measure of equivalent effect under Article 30 when a Member State imposes a penalty for a customs irregularity, if that penalty is disproportionately high in view of the fact that the Member State is not entitled to prohibit the importation of the goods in question.

7.11   This last point was established in *Donckerwolcke* v. *Procureur de la République*[26] and in *Cayrol* v. *Rivoira.* In each case criminal proceedings had been brought against persons who had imported goods into France and falsely declared them to originate in a Member State. In each case, however, although the goods were in free circulation in the Community, they had in fact originated in a third country. The object of the reference was to ascertain whether the requirement of a declaration of origin imposed by the French authorities, and connected measures, were contrary to Article 30. As regards penalties the Court held:

> 'The fact that the importer did not comply with the obligation to declare the real origin of the goods cannot give rise to the application of penalties which are disproportionate taking account of the purely administrative nature of the contravention . . .
> In general terms any administrative or penal measure which goes beyond what is strictly necessary for the purposes of enabling the importing Member State to obtain reasonably complete and accurate information on the movement of goods falling within specific measures of commercial policy[27] must be regarded as a measure having an effect equivalent to a quantitative restriction prohibited by the Treaty.'

7.12   It is submitted that this principle must apply equally to penalties imposed for the contravention of other customs requirements imposed by the Member States. The principle does not apply, however, where the Member State is entitled to prohibit or restrict the importation of the goods in question, since in such a case the offence is not 'purely administrative': this was made clear in *Procureur de la République* v. *Rivoira* where the Court held that criminal penalties 'cannot be applied without regard being had to the fact that the present case did not concern prohibited imports.' As will be explained in the next two chapters of this book, the reasons why a Member State may be entitled to restrict or prohibit imports are manifold: for instance, the restrictions may be justified under Article 36 or the Member State may have obtained an authorisation under Article 115 to prohibit the importation of the goods. Thus, to take but one example, if an importer evades a compulsory sanitary or veterinary control justified by Article 36, that is not an offence of a 'purely administrative nature'—even, it is submitted, if the goods

---

[26] N.6 above, discussed at para. 9.35 below; see generally Case 65/79 *Procureur de la République* v. *Chatain* [1980] E.C.R. 1345, [1981] 3 C.M.L.R. 418.
[27] The phrase 'specific measures of commercial policy' would appear to be a reference to Art. 115; see paras. 7.14 and 9.33 below.

in fact presented no danger to health and so would have had to be admitted after the sanitary or veterinary control had been carried out.

When the offence is of a 'purely administrative' nature, what types of penalty are excessive? In *Donckerwolcke* and *Cayrol* the Court gave two examples: firstly, seizure of the goods, and, secondly, any pecuniary penalty fixed according to the value of the goods.

It is hard to imagine how any penalties falling under Article 30 could be justified under Article 36.

Certain obligatory declarations of origin

7.13   In certain circumstances the requirement that the importer make a declaration of origin at the time of importation is contrary to Article 30. This was laid down in the *Donckerwolcke* judgment already discussed where the Court held that:

> 'The requirement by the importing Member State of the indication of the country of origin on the customs declaration document for products in free circulation . . . does not in itself constitute a measure of equivalent effect . . . if the goods in question are covered by measures of commercial policy adopted by that State in conformity with the Treaty.
>
> Such a requirement would, however, fall under the prohibition contained in Article 30 of the Treaty if the importer were required to declare, with regard to origin, something other than what he knows or may reasonably be expected to know . . .'

This was confirmed in *Cayrol* v. *Rivoira* and *Procureur de la République* v. *Rivoira*, both of which have also been discussed.

It is clear, then, that the obligation to make a declaration of origin constitutes a measure of equivalent effect under Article 30 where it applies to an importer who does not know and cannot reasonably be expected to know the origin of the goods.

7.14   Furthermore, the reference to 'measures of commercial policy adopted by that State in conformity with the Treaty' is a reference to Article 115 with which *Donckerwolcke* was also concerned.[28] It is not entirely clear from the wording of the judgment whether, quite apart from the limitation explained in the preceding paragraph, declarations of origin may be required:

(i) only where the Commission has authorised the adoption of exceptional measures under Article 115 (in which case Article 30 is ousted in any case);

(ii) also where the Member State is intending to apply to the Commission for authorisation to adopt exceptional measures under Article 115; or

(iii) under any circumstances.

---

[28] Para. 9.35 below.

From the general wording of the judgment it would appear that the first of these three interpretations is unduly restrictive.

In any case, where an obligation to make a declaration of origin constitutes a measure of equivalent effect, it is hard to envisage how it could ever be justified under Article 36.[29]

Unreasonably limited customs facilities

7.15 It seems clear that Member States may not unduly restrict the operating hours of customs posts (*e.g.* open them only on Mondays). Nor may they unduly limit the points of entry (as would be the case, for instance, if Britain were to require all imported apples to be landed in Glasgow and nowhere else). In either case, the Member State would be infringing Article 30.[30]

On the other hand, it would probably be going too far to require that all points of entry into each Member State remain open for all products 24 hours a day, since this would involve very considerable costs. What is more, certain categories of products require specialised personnel to carry out technical checks such as veterinary or sanitary controls. It is submitted, therefore, that in so far as restrictions on customs facilities are 'reasonable' they are compatible with Article 30—whether one considers that they fall outside Article 30 altogether as being restrictions inherent in the customs clearance procedure,[31] or that they are justified under Article 36.[32] Whichever of these two theories is adopted it will not be an easy task to determine what restrictions are 'reasonable,' especially as this must vary from case to case.

7.16 Only in one case, *United Foods and Van den Abeele* v. *Belgian State*,[33] has the Court been called upon to rule on a measure of this kind and even there the ruling on this particular point does not deal with this problem at any length. The national court asked the Court of Justice whether various aspects of a systematic and obligatory sanitary control on fish at the border were compatible with the Treaty. One of the questions posed was whether it was compatible with Article 30 for the national authorities to limit the number of points and the hours at which such sanitary controls were carried out, thus possibly limiting the customs posts and the hours for importing fish. The Court replied as follows:

---

[29] See also n.11 above.
[30] Para. 6.20 above; see also Ehlermann in Groeben, Boeckh, Thiesing *Kommentar zum EWG-Vertrag* (1974) Vol. I, 257.
[31] Para. 7.85 below.
[32] Para. 8.11 below.
[33] Case 132/80; see n.19 above. In Case 107/81 *E.C. Commission* v. *Italy*, the Commission claimed that Italy had infringed Art. 30 by unduly restricting the number of customs posts through which certain steel products could be imported. (The products in question fell under the EEC Treaty.) However, Italy withdrew the measure complained of and the Commission's action was accordingly struck out.

'If, with regard to the determination by the customs authority of the premises where control is to be carried out as well as of days and times of their opening, it appears that the effect of these measures is to hinder imports they would be justified only on condition that they could be shown to satisfy objective requirements appearing to the organisation of the public health service.'

7.17 However, Council Directive 83/643[34] has gone some way towards clarifying this issue. Article 5(1) provides:

'1. Member States shall see to it that:
(a) where the volume of traffic so warrants, frontier posts are open, except when traffic is prohibited, so that:
— frontiers can be crossed 24 hours a day, with the corresponding inspections and formalities, in the case of goods placed under a customs transit procedure, their means of transport and vehicles travelling unladen, save where frontier inspection is necessary to prevent the spread of disease,
— inspections and formalities relating to the movement of means of transport and goods which are not being carried under a customs transit procedure may be performed from Monday to Friday during an uninterrupted period of at least 10 hours and on Saturday during an uninterrupted period of at least six hours, unless those days are public holidays;
(b) as regards vehicles and goods transported by air, the hours referred to in the second indent of subparagraph (a) are adapted in such a way as to meet actual needs and for that purpose may be split in accordance with the flow of traffic;
(c) transshipments which, under existing regulations, customs services allow to be carried out without their immediate supervision can be effected at any time in such a way as to meet actual needs.'

It will be noted that the operation of this provision is subject to the condition that the 'volume of traffic so warrants.' It is also subject to certain exceptions of which the most important is contained in Article 5(4) as amended:

'For the frontier posts and customs services referred to in paragraph 1, and under the conditions laid down by Member States, the competent authorities of the Member States shall provide, if specifically requested during business hours and for sound reasons, for inspections and formalities to be carried out, as an exception, outside business hours, on condition that, where relevant, payment be made for services so rendered.'

Obligatory advance warning to customs

7.18 Also in *United Foods*[35] the Court was asked whether it was compatible with Article 30 to require an importer of fish to inform the customs authorities in writing at least 24 hours beforehand of the date and hour and point of importation and of the nature, quantity and provenance of the goods. In view of the extraordinarily onerous nature of these measures, the Court's ruling on this matter is perhaps rather cursory:

---

[34] N.22 above.
[35] N.19 above.

117

'The requirement that notice must be given in writing setting forth all the details prescribed under the legislation at issue at least 24 hours before importation appears to be incompatible with the speed of transactions and of transportation in this field, given the perishable nature of the goods in question.'

It is submitted that any obligation to give an advance warning of an importation to customs authorities is a measure of equivalent effect contrary to Article 30, even if the goods are not of a perishable nature. Only with respect to imports of a highly unusual nature or in other exceptional circumstances will such a requirement be justified.

7.19   Article 5(2) of Directive 83/643 provides:

'Where general compliance with the periods referred to in paragraph 1(a), second indent, and (b) poses problems for veterinary services, Member States shall see to it that, with at least 12 hours' notice from the carrier, a veterinary expert is available during those periods: in the case of the transport of live animals, however, this notice may be increased to 18 hours.'[36]

Undue customs delays

7.20   The subjection of imports to unreasonable delays in customs clearance or other unreasonable delays in import formalities will contravene Article 30. Thus in *E.C. Commission* v. *France*[37] France was held to have infringed Article 30 by delaying the customs clearance of various consignments of Italian wine on the grounds that the accompanying documents required by the Community wine regulations were not in order. In the first place some irregularities in the customs documents were of a minor nature. The Court cited, apparently by way of example, the failure to fill in the documents in typescript or in block capitals, although the entries were legible; and the failure to complete the documents, even though they contained all the information required. In these cases there had been a failure to comply with the Community legislation, but that did not justify objections being made to a document by the customs authorities.

On the other hand, the Court found that there had also been cases of substantial irregularities occurring: the documents had failed to give certain information required or were illegible. Even with respect to such documents the Court found that the French authorities had acted unlawfully in holding up imports since they had not taken steps to settle the irregularities as was specifically required by the Community wine regulations. Furthermore, they had suddenly and without warning gone back on a gentleman's agreement of several years' standing with the Italian authorities according to which

---

[36] This is the corrected version, the corrigendum being at [1987] O.J. L46/55. Para. 1 is set out in para. 7.17 above.

[37] See n.19 above and paras. 8.09 and 8.39 below.

irregularities in documents accompanying wine imports were waived. Since this ruling relates to the Community wine regulations as well as to Article 30, it is difficult to extrapolate general principles from it. Nevertheless it would seem to be authority for the proposition that minor irregularities in customs documents will not justify a refusal by the authorities of a Member State to clear imports through customs. It is also probable that the provision in the Community wine regulations requiring the customs authorities concerned to 'regularise' any irregularities in the documents is in fact the expression of a general requirement on Member States to do so, which is part of their duty to co-operate with one another so as to facilitate trade.

7.21 At all events, such a duty of co-operation is now partly enshrined in Directive 83/643. Article 6 as amended provides that:

> 'Member States shall take the measures necessary to ensure that waiting time caused by the various inspections and formalities does not exceed the time required for their proper completion. To that end, they shall organise the business hours of the departments which are to carry out inspections and formalities, the staff available and the practical arrangements for processing goods and documents associated with the carrying out of the inspections and formalities in such a way as to reduce waiting time in the flow of traffic to a minimum.'

Measures restricting the use of imported products or requiring the use of domestic products

7.22 Directive 66/683,[38] based on Article 33(7), required Member States to abolish measures which

(a) partially or totally prohibited the use of an imported product;
(b) required the partial or total use of a domestic product;
(c) subjected the entitlement to a benefit, other than an aid within the meaning of Article 92 of the Treaty, to the total or partial use of a national product.[39]

In addition, Article 2(3)(k) of Directive 70/50 defines as measures of equivalent effect those measures which 'require . . . the purchase of domestic products only.'

A provision of this kind was at issue in *Peureux* v. *Directeur des Services Fiscaux*.[40] The plaintiffs wished to distil some oranges steeped in alcohol, which they had imported from Italy, where they were in free circulation. The defendant contested their right to do this on the basis of a provision in the *Code Général des Impôts* stating that: 'distillation of all imported raw material with the exception of fresh fruit other than apples, pears or grapes shall be prohibited.' On a reference from a French court under Article 177,

---

[38] [1966] J.O. 3748, para. 6.03 above.
[39] Dir. 66/683 itself exempted certain products from its operation, but those exemptions ceased to have effect at the end of the transitional period; para. 6.04 above.
[40] Case 119/78 [1979] E.C.R. 975, [1980] 3 C.M.L.R. 337.

the Court found that such a measure constituted a measure of equivalent effect contrary to Article 30.

Also in *Campus Oil* v. *Minister for Industry and Energy*[41] the requirement that importers of petroleum products purchase a specific proportion of their supplies from the one remaining national oil refinery was held to constitute a measure of equivalent effect.

Discrimination in public supply contracts

7.23   Any measure by which public authorities discriminate against imported goods in the award of public supply contracts is a measure of equivalent effect contrary to Article 30. Such measures were the subject of Commission Directive 70/32[42] based on Article 33(7) of the Treaty. That Directive prohibited measures relating to the supply of goods to the State, regional or local authorities and other legal persons governed by public law, (a) which totally or partially prohibited the use of an imported product; or (b) which required the total or partial use of domestic products or granted domestic products a preference other than an aid under Article 92; or (c) made the supply of imported products more difficult or onerous. Foremost among such measures—though not specifically mentioned in the Directive—are those by which the public authorities of a Member State award a contract to a tenderer offering goods manufactured within that State, thus discriminating against another tenderer offering imported goods at more favourable terms.[43] Such infringements of Article 30 by the Member States are rife, but difficult to prove.

7.24   The only ruling to date on this type of measure is to be found in the Order of the President in *E.C. Commission* v. *Ireland*.[44] This case concerned a contract to be concluded by Dundalk Urban District Council for the construction of a water main. The invitation to tender stipulated that all asbestos cement pressure pipes must be certified as complying with the relevant Irish standard. In fact, only one manufacturer had obtained such approval for its pipes and this was an Irish company. Consequently a tender for pipes manufactured in Spain was not considered. The Commission, which maintained that this was contrary *inter alia* to Article 30, sought an interim order to ensure that no contract was concluded for the work pending either final judgment or a settlement between the Commission and Ireland. In a key passage of his Order the President stated:

---

[41] Case 72/83 [1984] E.C.R. 2727, [1984] 3 C.M.L.R. 544; see paras. 8.16, 8.20 and 8.33 below.

[42] [1970] J.O. L13/1, para. 6.03 above; Turpin, 'Public contracts in the EEC' [1972] C.M.L.Rev. 411.

[43] The concept of a 'measure' for the purposes of Art. 30 is a wide one: para. 6.10 *et seq.* above.

[44] Case 45/87R, Order of 13 March 1987, [1987] 2 C.M.L.R. 563.

'Although it would seem normal that in a public works contract such as that at issue the materials to be used may be required to comply with a certain technical standard, even a national standard, in order to ensure that they are appropriate and safe, such a technical standard cannot, without creating *prima facie* a barrier to trade which is contrary to Article 30 of the EEC Treaty, have the effect of excluding, without so much as an examination, any tender based on another technical standard recognised in another Member State as providing equivalent guarantees of safety, performance and reliability.'

However, the application for interim measures was rejected on the grounds that:

'In this case the objective of the public works contract in question, namely to secure water supplies for the inhabitants of the Dundalk area by 1990 at the latest, and the aggravation of the existing health and safety hazards for them if the award of the contract at issue is delayed tilt the balance of interests in favour of the defendant. It should be stressed that a quite different assessment might be arrived at in the case of other public works contracts serving different purposes where a delay in the award of the contract would not expose a population to such health and safety hazards.'

The case also concerned Community legislation passed so as to facilitate supervision of the prohibition of discrimination in the field of public supply contracts. That legislation will be considered in Chapter XII.[45]

Incitement to purchase domestic products

7.25   Article 2(3)(k) of Directive 70/50 defines as measures of equivalent effect, *inter alia*, those measures which '. . . encourage . . . or give preference to the purchase of domestic products only.[46]

The *locus classicus* on this type of measure is *E.C. Commission* v. *Ireland* ('Buy Irish').[47] This case concerned a campaign run by the Irish Government and designed to encourage all classes of purchaser within Ireland, be they end consumers, industrialists or State bodies, to buy Irish goods in preference to imported goods. This campaign took a variety of forms, the main one being a wide-ranging advertising campaign in which purchasers were asked to give preference to goods bearing the Guaranteed Irish symbol. Other forms of promotion were also used such as the compilation and distribution to industrialists at trade fairs and elsewhere of catalogues of producers of particular types of product. There was also a Sell Irish campaign mounted with the aim of persuading shops to stock and sell Irish goods in preference to imported goods. There was no real doubt that the campaign was attributable to the State.[48] Accordingly, the

---

[45] Para. 12.28 *et seq.* below.

[46] On the other hand, measures by which a Member State promotes the sale or advertises its own products *outside* its own territory are in themselves entirely compatible with Art. 30. Such measures in no way restrict trade between Member States. On the contrary, they promote exports. (This does not mean that all methods of promoting exports are open to the Member States: see, *e.g.* Arts. 92 *et seq.* EEC.)

[47] Case 249/81 [1982] E.C.R. 4005, [1983] 2 C.M.L.R. 104; paras. 6.10 and 6.25 above.

[48] Para. 4.05 above.

Court upheld the Commission's contention that the campaign taken as a whole infringed Article 30. In so doing the Court stressed the distinction between the 'Buy Irish' campaign and

> 'advertising by private or public undertakings or by a group of undertakings, to encourage people to buy goods produced by these undertakings. Regardless of the means used to implement it, the campaign is a reflection of the Irish Government's considered intention to substitute domestic products for imported products on the Irish market and thereby to check the flow of imports from other Member States.'

7.26 Light was shed on the scope and meaning of the 'Buy Irish' judgment by the ruling in *Apple and Pear Development Council* v. *Lewis*.[49] The plaintiff body was set up by statutory instrument with the principal function of promoting apples and pears in England and Wales. This included advertising on television (with the use of such slogans as 'Polish up your English') and in the press and in stores. It concentrated to a considerable extent on varieties grown in England and Wales such as Cox and Bramley apples and Conference pears. The Court held that Article 30 did not prevent a body such as the Development Council

> 'from drawing attention, in its publicity, to the specific qualities of fruit produced within the Member State in question or from organising campaigns to promote the sale of certain varieties, mentioning their particular properties, even if those varieties are typical of national production; on the other hand, it would be contrary to Article 30 of the Treaty for such a body to engage in publicity intended to discourage the purchase of products from other Member States or to disparage those products in the eyes of consumers, or to advise consumers to purchase domestic products solely by reason of their national origin.'

7.27 In view of the importance of this matter, the Commission has published[50] 'guidelines for Member States' involvement in promotion of agricultural and fisheries products.' It is not possible to reproduce these guidelines in this book, but the following passages are worthy of note:

> 'Identification of the producing country by word or symbol may be made providing that a reasonable balance between references, on the one hand to the qualities and varieties of the product and, on the other hand, its national origin is kept. The references to national origin should be subsidiary to the main message put over to consumers by the campaign and not constitute the principal reason why consumers are being advised to buy the product.'
> 'References to quality control should only be made where the product is subjected to a genuine and objective system of control of its qualities.'

No such guidelines exist for industrial products.

---

[49] Case 222/82 [1983] E.C.R. 4083, [1984] 3 C.M.L.R. 733. This case was also decided on the basis of Council Reg. 1035/72 establishing the common market organisation for fruit and vegetables. However, there is no reason to believe that the Court would have reached a different result had it decided the case on the basis of Art. 30 alone or had the products concerned not been subject to a common market organisation.
[50] [1986] O.J. C272/4.

The obligation to appoint a representative in the importing Member State

7.28 Article 2(3)(g) of Directive 70/50 defines as measures of equivalent effect under Article 30 those measures which 'make access of imported products to the domestic market conditional upon having an agent or representative in the territory of the importing Member State.' *E.C. Commission* v. *Belgium*[51] concerned legislation making the sale of certain pesticides and phyto-pharmaceutical products in Belgium subject to authorisation from the Belgian Government. It was further provided that such authorisation could only be obtained by a person established in Belgium who had responsibility for the marketing of one of those products as producer, importer, proprietor or concessionnaire. Only the latter provision was impugned by the Commission. The Court held that the obligation to appoint a representative within the importing Member State fell within Article 30 and was not justified under Article 36.[52] This ruling was subsequently confirmed in *E.C. Commission* v. *Germany*[53] which related to pharmaceuticals.

Conditions of payment, obligatory deposits and guarantees and restrictions on credit

7.29 Article 2(3) of Directive 70/50 defines as measures of equivalent effect measures which

'(h) lay down conditions of payment in respect of imported products only
     . . .;
 (i) require, for imports only, the giving of guarantees or making of payments on account.'

The term 'guarantees' is clearly used to cover deposits.[54]

The view that the obligation to pay an import deposit constitutes a measure of equivalent effect has now been upheld in *E.C. Commission* v. *Italy*.[55] That case involved Italian legislation making advance payments for imports subject to the lodging of a deposit which would be forfeited to the State if the goods were not imported within the period prescribed. The Court held that:

'although the measures in question were enacted for the purpose of preventing currency speculation, they do not constitute specific rules for the attainment of that objective but general rules dealing with the intra-Community transactions as a whole where payment is made in advance. In fact, in so far as the Italian Government extends its rules to cover payments made by letters of credit and similar documents, the financial method usually employed for

---

[51] Case 155/82 [1983] E.C.R. 531, [1983] 2 C.M.L.R. 556.
[52] Para. 8.50 below.
[53] Case 247/81 [1984] E.C.R. 1111, [1985] 1 C.M.L.R. 640.
[54] See also Art. 38 of the Act of Accession of Greece and Case 58/83 *E.C. Commission* v. *Greece* (payments for imports in cash) [1984] E.C.R. 2027, [1986] 1 C.M.L.R. 673.
[55] Case 95/81 [1982] E.C.R. 2187, incorporated by reference in Cases 206, 207, 209 and 210/80 *Orlandi* v. *Ministry of Foreign Trade* [1982] E.C.R. 2147; see casenote Oliver [1982] C.D.E. 42 and paras. 6.29 above and 8.21 below.

imports of goods in certain commercial sectors, it is dealing with a means of payment normally employed in international trade. The measures in question thus affect not only speculative operations but normal commercial transactions, and since their effect is to render imports more difficult or burdensome than internal transactions, they produce restrictive effects on the free movement of goods. For these reasons and in so far as they produce these effects, the measures at issue are contrary to Article 30.'

This passage implies that means of payment not normally employed in international trade may be subject to certain restrictions. Perhaps therefore Member States may place certain restrictions on the payment for large consignments of goods in cash.[56] In another passage of the same judgment the Court stated that

'the Member States remain free to employ all means of ensuring that payments made abroad relate exclusively to genuine transactions, subject always to the condition that such means do not hinder the freedom of intra-Community trade as defined in the Treaty.'

It follows that a Member State is entitled to prohibit transactions set up as devices to conceal currency speculation provided that genuine imports are not restricted. Indeed, Advocate General Sir Gordon Slynn said as much.[57]

Yet what is meant by 'genuine transactions'? This term, which is taken from Article 5 of the first Capital Directive[58] must be construed broadly, since exceptions to fundamental principles of Community law are always to be defined as narrowly as possible. It is therefore submitted that a genuine transaction probably occurs whenever goods are actually imported—unless for instance, they are subsequently smuggled out of the importing Member State. In addition, there may be perfectly valid reasons why a proposed importation cannot go ahead; in such a case a transaction must also be regarded as genuine.[59]

7.30   Similarly, restrictions on credit for imported goods constitute measures of equivalent effect. Thus *E.C. Commission* v. *Greece*[60] concerned a circular which required the main credit institution in Greek agriculture to refrain from granting loans for the purchase of certain agricultural machinery, in the absence of a certificate from the Ministry stating that such machinery was not manufactured in Greece. This measure was held to contravene Article 30.

Certain advertising restrictions

7.31   Article 2(3)(m) of Directive 70/50 defines as measures of equivalent effect on imports measures which 'prohibit or limit

---

[56] See Case 203/80 *Casati* [1981] E.C.R. 2595, [1982] 1 C.M.L.R. 365.
[57] At p.2209.
[58] Dir. of 4 May 1960 ([1960] O.J. Spec.Ed. 921), as amended; see para. 2.06 above.
[59] See also para. 8.21 below.
[60] Case 192/84 [1985] E.C.R. 3967, [1988] 1 C.M.L.R. 420.

publicity in respect of imported products only, or totally or partially confine publicity to domestic products only.'

In Case 152/78 *E.C. Commission* v. *France*[61] the Commission brought infringement proceedings against a French measure setting out four different groups of alcoholic drinks and laying down different degrees of restriction for each group. For two of these groups there was no advertising restriction, for a third limited advertising was allowed and for the fourth no advertising was permitted at all. Although at first sight there was nothing discriminatory about these rules, the groups were so defined that drinks of a kind normally imported were subject to greater restrictions than drinks normally produced in France which had similar properties and therefore presented a similar health risk. For example, rum and products distilled from wine, cider or fruit were subject to no restriction, whereas similar products with a cereal base such as whisky could not be advertised at all. The Court held that even though some French products were subject to restrictions, this legislation put imported products at a disadvantage and thus fell under Article 30. Nor was it justified under Article 36, precisely because it constituted arbitrary discrimination.

Restrictions on sales promotion

7.32   In *Oosthoek's Uitgeversmaatschappij*[62] a ban on the promotion of sales by means of free gifts was held to constitute a measure of equivalent effect contrary to Article 30 in the absence of justification.[63] The ban applied in the same way to domestic and imported goods.

Restrictions or requirements on stocking goods

7.33   Article 2(3)(n) of Commission Directive 70/50 defines as measures of equivalent effect under Article 30 measures which

'prohibit, limit or require stocking in respect of imported goods only; totally or partially confine the use of stocking facilities to domestic products only, or make the stocking of imported products subject to conditions which are different from those required for domestic products and more difficult to satisfy.'

There is as yet no other authority on *restrictions* on stocking goods.[64] On the other hand, *Eggers* v. *Freie Hansestadt Bremen*[65] concerned a measure *requiring* goods to be stocked. There the Court in effect

---

[61] [1980] E.C.R. 2299, [1981] 2 C.M.L.R. 743; para. 2.28 above.
[62] Case 286/81 [1982] E.C.R. 4575, [1983] 3 C.M.L.R. 428.
[63] See para. 8.78 below.
[64] However, see Case 75/81 *Blesgen* v. *Belgium* [1982] E.C.R. 1211, [1983] 1 C.M.L.R. 431, para. 7.87.
[65] Case 13/78 [1978] E.C.R. 1935, [1979] 1 C.M.L.R. 562.

held to be contrary to Article 30 a German measure providing that wine-based spirits could only bear certain designations of quality if they were stored for at least six months on German territory. This case will be discussed more fully below.[66]

Reference back to the law of the exporting Member State

7.34   Article 2(3)(p) of Directive 70/50 defines as measures of equivalent effect measures which 'prescribe that imported products are to conform, totally or partially, to rules other than those of the importing country.' The Court has now had occasion to rule on such a measure, in *Schutzverband gegen Unwesen in der Wirtschaft v. Weinvertriebs*.[67] That case concerned a provision of German law prohibiting the importation of wine-based drinks unless they conformed to the requirements of the State of production and they could be sold there for human consumption in an unaltered state. According to Italian law vermouth sold in Italy was to have an alcohol content of at least 16 per cent. It followed that Italian-made vermouth could only be imported into Germany if it met that requirement. Yet there were two anomalies: the Italian regulation did not apply to vermouth produced in Italy and exported; and German law did not lay down any minimum alcohol requirement for German-made vermouth. In view of the latter anomaly the measure was thus blatantly discriminatory. The Court therefore held that it constituted a measure of equivalent effect which could not be justified on consumer protection grounds since it was distinctly applicable.[68]

The abusive reservation of designations of origin or quality or of generic terms

7.35   Article 2(3)(s) of Directive 70/50 defines as measures of equivalent effect contrary to Article 30 measures 'which confine names which are not indicative of origin or source to domestic products only.' The French text reads: '*qui . . . réservent aux seuls produits nationaux des dénominations ne constituant pas des appellations d'origine ou des indications de provenance.*' The terms *appellations d'origine* and *indications de provenance* are terms of art in French law,[69] but there is no equivalent term in English law.

---

[66] Para. 7.40 below.
[67] Case 59/82 [1983] E.C.R. 1217, [1984] 1 C.M.L.R. 319.
[68] See para. 6.53 above.
[69] For a comparative study of the law of several western countries, see *Protection of Geographical Denominations of Goods and Services*, ed. Cohen Jehoram (1980).

Case 12/74 *E.C. Commission* v. *Germany*[70] concerned measures of this type. A German statute provided that in addition to other conditions the appellation *Sekt* could only be used to describe a German sparkling wine or sparkling foreign wine if German was an official language throughout the whole of the country of production.[71] What is more, the appellation *Prädikatssekt* could only describe a *Sekt* containing at least 60 per cent. of German grapes. Again, the appellation *Weinbrand* was reserved to a certain type of German spirits and for similar foreign products if German was the official language throughout the whole of the country of production. On the other hand, sparkling wines and spirits produced in countries in which German is not such an official language were, in principle, compelled to use less prestigious appellations.

The Commission contended that the appellations *Sekt, Prädikatssekt* and *Weinbrand* were generic terms which the German authorities had attempted to transform into indirect indications of origin, at the same time requiring imported products to bear less attractive appellations. It therefore brought proceedings against the Federal Republic for infringement of Article 30 and, as regards sparkling wine, of the equivalent provision contained in Regulation 816/70 establishing the common market organisation in wine.[72] The Court found for the Commission. After citing Article 2(3)(s) of the Directive[73] it held:

> 'To the extent to which [appellations of origin and indirect indications of origin] are protected by law they must satisfy the objectives of such protection, in particular the need to ensure not only that the interests of the producers concerned are safeguarded against unfair competition, but also that consumers are protected against information which may mislead them.
>
> These appellations only fulfil their specific purpose if the product which they describe does in fact possess qualities and characteristics which are due to the fact that it originated in a specific geographical area.
>
> As regards indications of origin in particular, the geographical area of origin of a product must confer on it a specific quality and specific characteristics of such a nature as to distinguish it from all other products.'

With reference to the appellations *Sekt* and *Weinbrand* the Court continued:

> 'An area of origin which is defined on the basis either of the extent of national territory or a linguistic criterion cannot constitute a geographical area within the meaning referred to above, capable of justifying an indication of

---

[70] [1975] E.C.R. 181, [1975] 1 C.M.L.R. 340 noted by March Hunnings [1975] J.L. 171, Wyatt [1975] M.L.R. 679, Marenco [1975] *Dir. Int. Scamb.* 358; see Mattera 'L'indication d'origine sur les produits et les règles de la libre circulation des marchandises à l'intérieur de la Communauté' [1975] *Dir. Int. Scamb.* 208; Matthies 'Herkunftsangaben und Europäisches Gemeinschaftsrecht' in *Festschrift für Schiedermair* (1976); also Beier 'Das Schutzbedürfnis für Herkunftsangaben und Ursprungsbezeichnungen im Gemeinsamen Markt' [1977] G.R.U.R. Int. 1 and (in English) Cohen Jehoram, *op. cit.* n.69 above, at 183.
[71] This 'language clause' was apparently designed to cover Austrian *Sekt* and *Weinbrand*: A.G. Warner [1975] E.C.R. at 204, [1975] 1 C.M.L.R. 340 at 346.
[72] [1970] J.O. L99.
[73] See para. 6.04 above.

origin,[74] particularly as the products in question may be produced from grapes of indetermined origin.

In this instance, it is not disputed that the area of origin referred to by the legislation on wine products does not show homogeneous natural features which distinguish it in contrast to adjacent areas, as the natural characteristics of the basic products used in the manufacture of the product in question do not necessarily correspond to the line of the national frontier.'

7.36 The Court went on to reject the argument to the effect that the products covered by the appellations *Sekt* and *Weinbrand* were different from all other products by virtue of their process of production:

'In the case of wine products, the natural features of the area of origin, such as the grape from which these products are obtained, play an important role in determining their quality and their characteristics.

Although the method of production used for such products may play some part in determining these characteristics, it is not alone decisive, independently of the quality of the grape used, in determining its origin.

Moreover, the method of production of a wine product constitutes a criterion which is all the less capable of being by itself sufficient [when] it is not linked with the use of a specific type of grape [so that] the method in question may be employed in other geographical areas.'

The wording of this part of the judgment implies that it applies only to 'wine products.'

7.37 Nor would the Court accept opinion polls put in evidence by the German Government, which data were intended to show that the German consumer took the terms *Sekt* and *Weinbrand* to refer to German products only. This was not only because such data were inherently unreliable, but also because:

'the protection accorded by the indication of origin is only justifiable if the product concerned actually possesses characteristics which are capable of distinguishing it from the point of view of its geographical origin [so that] in the absence of such a condition this protection cannot be justified on the basis of the opinion of consumers such as may result from polls carried out on the basis of statistical criteria.'

7.38 As regards the term *Prädikatssekt* the Court ruled that:

'as the legislation on wine products does not define the grapes which must be used in the production of *Prädikatssekt* with reference to their specific character but only on the basis of their national origin, the minimum percentage required does not necessarily imply that the product in question is actually of a special quality in comparison with *Sekt* and thus warrants the protection accorded to it.'

Lastly, the measures in question were not protected by Article 36 because they were caught by the second sentence of that provision. The Court therefore concluded that the measures in question were contrary to Article 30 and, as regards sparkling wine, to Regulation 816/70.

---

[74] See, however, the A.G. at p.207.

7.39   Beier has written a detailed critique[75] of this judgment. He agrees with the Court that the reservation of the national measures in question constituted measures of equivalent effect within the meaning of Article 30 without being justified under Article 36. Yet he would reach this conclusion by a different route: in his opinion the terms *Sekt* and *Weinbrand* are not designations of origin or indications of origin at all, but purely generic names (like 'potatoes' or 'gloves'); seen in this light, the reservation of these terms to national products and the resulting use of less appealing terms for imported products could not possibly be justified under Article 36. On the other hand, the Court began by taking these terms as direct appellations of origin and then, finding that they were not justified, held that they were not appellations of origin after all. Had the Court followed the approach which he suggests, this unduly complicated and circuitous reasoning would have been avoided. By this method, the Court would have avoided a number of pronouncements which Beier proceeds to criticise. He singles out for particular criticism the Court's statement that designations of origin and indications of origin 'only fulfil their specific purpose if the product which they describe does in fact possess specific qualities and characteristics which are due to the fact that it originated in a specific geographical area.' He asks whether such highly reputed appellations as 'Brussels lace' and 'Munich beer' can only be protected if it is shown that these products possess specific qualities or characteristics. In particular, he asks, to protect the term 'Munich beer' would it be necessary to show that the same product could not be produced outside Munich by reason of the special qualities of Munich water?[76]

7.40   Another case involving this kind of measure was *Eggers* v. *Freie Hansestadt Bremen*.[77] This concerned the compatibility with Article 30 of a German statutory provision according to which spirits from wine could be designated as *Qualitätsbranntwein aus Wein* (high quality spirits made from wine) or as *Weinbrand* (brandy) only if:

— at least 85 per cent. of the alcoholic content was derived from home-produced wine distillate; and

— the whole of the wine distillate used had been kept for at least six months in oaken casks in the factory where the distillate produced on national territory had been manufactured.

After citing Article 2(3)(s) of Directive 70/50 the Court held:

'In order to be effective the prohibition on the reserving of certain designations (other than those indicative of origin or source), and in particular designations of quality, for domestic products only must extend to measures which distinguish between domestic products according to whether or not the

[75] *Op. cit.* n.70 above.
[76] See also Marenco, *op. cit.* n.70.
[77] N.65 above.

raw materials or the semi-finished products from which they are manufactured have been produced or treated on national territory and which reserve for goods derived from semi-finished products, treated on national territory, special designations such as to give them an advantage in the opinion of the traders or consumers concerned.

In fact in a market which, as far as possible, must present the features of a single market, entitlement to a designation of quality for a product can—except in the case of the rules applicable to registered designations of origin and indications of origin—only depend upon the intrinsic objective characteristics governing the quality of the product compared with a similar product of inferior quality and not on the geographical locality where a particular production stage took place.

It follows from all the foregoing considerations that a national measure which makes the right to use a designation of quality for a domestic product subject to the condition that the semi-finished product from which it was manufactured was either produced or treated on national territory and refuses to allow the use of that designation simply because the semi-finished product was imported from another Member State, is a measure having an effect equivalent to a quantitative restriction.

The fact that the use of that designation of quality is optional does not mean that it ceases to be an unjustified obstacle to trade if the use of that designation promotes or is likely to promote the marketing of the product concerned as compared with products which do not benefit from its use.'

7.41 The wording of these two judgments and particularly that in *E.C. Commission* v. *Germany* does not readily accord with the theory that in deciding whether a measure is compatible with Articles 30 and 36 it is necessary to decide

(1) whether the measure constitutes a restriction on imports and if so,

(2) whether the measure is justified under Article 36.

The Court's approach in *E.C. Commission* v. *Germany* was to consider the question of justification before considering Article 36—which meant that consideration of Article 36 was superfluous. As Meij and Winter[78] put it, 'the *Sekt* case demonstrates that Article 36 is emptied of its substance and its meaning if no distinction is made between the problem of the qualification of State rules as measures of equivalent effect (Article 30) and the question under what circumstances Member States may continue to apply such measures (Article 36)'. However, in their *results* these judgments are compatible with the following analysis:

— the reservation to national products only of any designation which is attractive to the consumer constitutes a measure of equivalent effect;

— such reservation is only justified under Article 36 if on an objective view the designation can only be taken to describe national products.

---

[78] 'Measures Having Equivalent Effect to Quantitative Restrictions' [1976] C.M.L.Rev. 79 at 103.

7.42 It should also be pointed out that, while these two cases concern measures by which a Member State reserves a designation for its own products, an infringement of Article 30 could also occur in the following manner: Member State A reserves the right to use a particular designation within its territory to the products of Member State B, whereas in reality the products of other Member States should also be entitled to the use of that designation. Such a restriction would not be justified under Article 36, since it would constitute arbitrary discrimination.[79]

7.43 In Case 193/80 *E.C. Commission* v. *Italy*[80] the Court was concerned *inter alia* with a national measure prohibiting the use of the term 'vinegar' (*aceto*) in Italy for vinegar other than wine vinegar.[81] The effect of this measure, which was clearly designed to protect Italian wine producers, was to make all vinegar other than wine vinegar virtually unsaleable in that country. Nevertheless, it is important to note that, unlike the measures at issue in the *E.C. Commission* v. *Germany* and *Eggers* cases, this particular measure applied in the same way to domestic products and to imports. The Italian Government sought to show that, for the Italian consumer, the term *aceto* had come to refer only to wine vinegar to the exclusion of all other vinegars. However, the Court found, by reference to the definition given in the relevant heading of the Common Customs Tariff, that the term was in fact a generic one, covering various different types of vinegar. The Court held that, where a generic term such as this refers to a number of different varieties of product, the reservation of that term to one of those varieties only constitutes a measure of equivalent effect contrary to Article 30.

On the other hand, the Court recognised that the Italian consumer might have become conditioned by the contested measure to think of *aceto* as covering only wine vinegar. The Italian Government could therefore adopt other, less restrictive measures to protect the consumer, such as a requirement that the precise nature of the product be set out on a label affixed to the product. But the Court stressed that such a requirement would have to apply in the same way to all varieties of vinegar, including wine vinegar.[82]

7.44 A particularly important case was *Prantl*,[83] which concerned a German measure reserving the right to market wines in bottles of a particular shape known as *Bocksbeutel* to wines from particular

---

[79] Para. 8.05 below.
[80] [1981] E.C.R. 3019.
[81] As to the prohibition on the sale of vinegar other than wine vinegar, see para. 7.53 below.
[82] See also Case 281/83 *E.C. Commission* v. *Italy* (failure to implement the ruling in Case 193/80) [1985] E.C.R. 3397, [1987] 1 C.M.L.R. 865, and para. 8.73 below.
[83] Case 16/83 [1984] E.C.R. 1299, [1985] 2 C.M.L.R. 238.

regions of Germany. Although the Court accepted that the shape of the bottle constituted an indirect indication of geographical origin it held that it was contrary to Article 30 to prohibit the sale in Germany of wine from the Italian Tyrol in such bottles, when this accorded with the 'fair and traditional' usage of that region. The case is discussed more fully in Chapter VIII.[84]

7.45 *Miro*[85] was in a sense the sequel to *Cassis de Dijon*. Whereas the earlier case concerned a complete ban on the sale of certain drinks containing less than the stipulated minimum alcohol content, *Miro* concerned a measure linking the right to use a generic name to the respect of a minimum alcohol requirement. Under Dutch law the use of the name 'jenever' (gin) was permitted only for products with an alcohol content of at least 35 per cent. The defendants imported from Belgium quantities of gin with an alcohol content of only 30 per cent., gin of this type having been produced in Belgium for many years. No minimum alcohol content for gin was prescribed in Belgian law at the relevant time. The defendants were charged with possessing with a view to sale bottles with labels bearing the word 'jenever,' even though those labels also stated that the alcohol content was 30 per cent. The Court found this to be a restriction on imports which, not being justified,[86] was contrary to Article 30.

7.46 *E.C. Commission* v. *Germany* (beer)[87] was in many ways similar to *E.C. Commission* v. *Italy* (vinegar). The Court found there that it was contrary to Article 30 for the defendant to restrict the use of the designation 'beer' to products made from a prescribed range of raw materials. Once again, the contested restriction applied in the same way to imported goods as to domestic production, but such raw materials as rice and maize which are frequently used for manufacturing beer in other Member States were precluded. The defendant had argued that the *Italian vinegar* case should be distinguished on the grounds that the measure in issue in that case had made it impossible for Member States with no vines to sell domestically-produced vinegar in Italy, whereas all Member States could produce barley (a permitted raw material) and could therefore comply with the German rules. As Advocate General Slynn pointed out, this difference was of no consequence whatever.

The Court held that the contested restriction was not justified on consumer protection grounds, at least when such raw materials as rice and maize, frequently used for the manufacture of beer in other Member States, were precluded. The Court gave two grounds for

---

[84] See para. 8.86 below.
[85] Case 182/84 [1985] E.C.R. 3731, [1986] 3 C.M.L.R. 545.
[86] See paras. 8.82 and 8.88 below.
[87] Case 178/84 [1988] 1 C.M.L.R. 780, noted by Rabe [1987] EuR 253, and see Brouwer 'Free Movement of Foodstuffs and Quality Requirements; Has the Commission got it wrong?' [1988] C.M.L.Rev. 237; see paras. 8.72 and 8.79 below.

this finding. Firstly, the Member State must not crystallise given consumer habits so as to consolidate an advantage acquired by national industries concerned to comply with them. Secondly, 'beer' was a generic term in the other Member States and in Community law (as shown by common customs tariff heading 22.03). Even in German legislation—indeed in other provisions of the very statute in issue—the word 'beer' was used to denote certain drinks not conforming to the German requirements. Thus the Court rejected the defendant Government's rather surprising argument to the effect that 'beer' was not a generic term.

7.47 Finally, *SMANOR*[88] was concerned with French legislation prohibiting the use of the term 'yoghourt' for deep-frozen yoghourt, even in conjunction with another word indicating that the product was deep-frozen; under French law this product could only be sold as 'deep-frozen fermented milk'. Such legislation was held to be contrary to Article 30 where the labelling made it clear that the product was deep-frozen, unless its characteristics were not those which a consumer would be led to expect from the use of the denomination 'yoghourt'. The Codex Alimentarius adopted by the FAO and the World Health Organisation showed that the principal characteristic of products sold as 'yoghourt' was that they contained large quantities of living lacto-bacillae. Thus the measure was contrary to Article 30 unless the deep-frozen product was substantially different from fresh yoghourt, notably as regards the numbers of such bacillae. This was a matter for the national court to decide.

Obligatory origin marking

7.48 A measure requiring the origin of goods to be marked on them constitutes a measure of equivalent effect.[89] On the other hand, it is clear that it is perfectly lawful for traders to indicate the origin of their goods of their own accord should they so wish.

The first case on this type of measure to be decided by the Court of Justice was Case 113/80 *E.C. Commission* v. *Ireland*.[90] This case concerned two Irish statutory instruments prohibiting the importation into and sale in the Republic of Ireland of certain categories of metal articles bearing certain motifs unless they were marked with a word or words indicating that they were manufactured outside the Republic. The list of articles included not only jewellery but also such objects as buckles, dress-combs and key-rings. The motifs ranged from those with specifically Irish associations to

---

[88] Case 298/87 (judgment of 14 July 1988).
[89] Written question 197/69 ([1969] J.O. C151/2), Written question 721/80 ([1980] O.J. C283/20), Written question 880/79 ([1980] O.J. C86/14), Written question 1116/79 ([1980] O.J. C82/21), Written question 1409/80 ([1981] O.J. C60/41), Written question 1634/80 ([1981] O.J. C78/21), Mattera, *op. cit.*, n.70 above.
[90] [1981] E.C.R. 1625, [1982] 1 C.M.L.R. 706.

thatched cottages. There was no corresponding origin marking requirement with respect to such goods manufactured within the Republic of Ireland. Consequently, the measures in question were 'distinctly applicable'.[91]

The Commission brought infringement proceedings against Ireland with respect to these measures. It claimed that the obligation to mark the origin on goods was only justified if this was necessary to avoid the purchaser being misled as to the true origin of a product bearing a false or misleading indication. It pointed out that it will be more important for the purchaser to know whether a product is or is not of a particular origin where such origin implies a certain quality, basic materials or process of manufacture or a particular place in the folklore or tradition of the region in question.[92]

The Commission claimed that the metal articles covered by the Irish measures did not fall within these conditions and thus the measures were not justified on the grounds of consumer protection, the prevention of unfair competition or any other grounds. The Commission added that even if the statutory instruments had applied in the same way to Irish goods, they would still not have been justified.

7.49   While finding for the Commission in the case before it, the Court did not find it necessary to rule on all those points. Having noted that most of the products in question were souvenirs, it ruled that:

> 'The essential characteristic of the souvenirs in question is that they constitute a pictorial reminder of the place visited, which does not by itself mean that a souvenir, as defined in the [Irish] Orders, must necessarily be manufactured in the country of origin.
>
> . . . it is important to note that the interests of consumers and fair trading would be adequately safeguarded if it were left to domestic manufacturers to take appropriate steps such as affixing, if they so wished, their mark of origin to their own products or packaging.'

Consequently, it held that the measures at issue infringed Article 30.

7.50   Unlike the Irish case, Case 207/83 *E.C. Commission* v. *United Kingdom*[93] concerned a measure which purported to apply in the same way to imports and to domestic products. The measure related to four categories of goods, namely clothing and textiles, domestic electrical appliances, footwear and cutlery. Subject to certain exceptions, it prohibited the retail sale of such goods unless they were marked with or accompanied by an indication of origin.

---

[91] Paras. 6.32 and 6.53 above.
[92] Certain types of alcoholic drinks fall within this head: Reg. 355/79 ([1979] O.J. L54/99) requires that certain categories of wine bear an indication of origin.
[93] Case 207/83 [1985] E.C.R. 1201, [1985] 2 C.M.L.R. 259.

Unlike the Advocate General, the Court found that this legislation constituted a measure of equivalent effect. Firstly, the Court pointed out that, although its requirements could be satisfied by indicating the origin on a notice accompanying the goods, evidence showed that in practice retailers insisted that the origin of the goods should be marked on the goods themselves by the manufacturer. Secondly, 'it has to be recognised that the purpose of indications of origin or origin marking is to enable consumers to distinguish between domestic and imported products and that this enables them to assert any prejudices which they may have against foreign products. As the Court has had the occasion to emphasise in various contexts, the Treaty, by establishing a common market and progressively approximating the economic policies of the Member States, seeks to unite national markets in a single market having the characteristics of a domestic market. Within such a market, the origin marking requirement not only makes the marketing in a Member State of goods produced in other Member States in the sectors in question more difficult; it also has the effect of slowing down economic interpenetration in the Community by handicapping the sale of goods produced as a result of a division of labour between Member States.'

In view of these considerations, the Court concluded that the contested provisions were liable to 'have the effect of increasing the production costs of imported goods and making it more difficult to sell them on the United Kingdom market.'

The Court then went on to reject the United Kingdom's defence based on consumer protection. 'The requirements relating to the indication of origin of goods are applicable without distinction to domestic and imported products only in form because, by their very nature, they are intended to enable the consumer to distinguish between those categories of products, which may thus prompt him to give his preference to national products.'[94]

The Court held in addition that:

> 'the fact that United Kingdom consumers associate a product's quality with its national origin does not appear to have been a consideration which prompted the United Kingdom Government when it suggested to the Commission that, as far as the Member States of the Community were concerned, it was prepared to accept the indication "Made in the European Community". Besides, if the national origin of goods brings certain qualities to the minds of consumers, it is in manufacturers' interests to indicate it themselves on the goods or on their packaging and it is not necessary to compel them to do so. In that case, the protection of consumers is sufficiently guaranteed by rules which enable the use of false indications of origin to be prohibited. Such rules are not called in question by the EEC Treaty.'

The Court did not specify whether there are exceptional circumstances in which a Member State can go beyond merely prohibiting

---

[94] See para. 6.53 below.

false (or misleading) indications of origin and require an indication of origin.[95]

Certain rules of procedure and evidence

7.51 It was established in *Procureur Général* v. *Arnaud*[96] that a rule of procedure can constitute an infringement of Article 30. The reference arose out of a series of prosecutions of French wine traders for illegal enrichment ('over-alcoholisation') of certain quantities of red wine. The French Code du Vin creates a rebuttable presumption of over-alcoholisation of wine if the proportion of alcohol to reduced extract is in excess of a certain figure. The Cour d'Appel of Bordeaux asked, *inter alia*, whether this presumption was compatible with the Regulations setting up a common market organisation in wine, which included a provision prohibiting quantitative restrictions and measures of equivalent effect.

The Court replied that a rebuttable presumption of this kind was compatible with Article 30 unless its application could put at a disadvantage wines from other Member States as where, for example, the presumption was harder to rebut in the case of wines from other Member States.[97] There is every reason to suppose that the same ruling would apply to industrial products and to agricultural products not covered by a common market organisation. Presumably also this ruling would be applicable to any rule of judicial procedure.[98]

The prohibition on the sale of goods

7.52 It has always been clear that a prohibition on sale applying to imported goods only was a measure of equivalent effect under Article 30. Thus Article 2(3) of Directive 70/50 defines as measures of equivalent effect measures which

'(j) . . . subject imported products to conditions which are different from those of domestic products and more difficult to satisfy;
(k) hinder the purchase by private individuals of imported products only . . .'

Thus a prohibition on selling imported goods covered by industrial property rights constitutes a measure of equivalent effect within the meaning of Article 30 although it might be justified under Article 36.[99]

---

[95] See para. 8.76 below.
[96] Cases 89/74, 18–19/75 [1975] E.C.R. 1023, [1975] 2 C.M.L.R. 490; see also Cases 10–14/75 *Lahaille* [1975] E.C.R. 1053.
[97] See also Case 202/82 *E.C. Commission* v. *France* (pasta) [1984] E.C.R. 933, [1985] 2 C.M.L.R. 185.
[98] See Case 22/80 *Boussac* v. *Gerstenmeier* [1980] E.C.R. 3427, [1982] 1 C.M.L.R. 202 on the compatibility of a rule of procedure with Art. 7 EEC.
[99] See para. 8.94 *et seq.* below.

However, the *Cassis de Dijon* judgment[100] showed that all measures including 'indistinctly applicable measures' prohibiting the sale of a product containing particular ingredients are measures of equivalent effect under Article 30—though they will frequently be justified under Article 36. As the reader will be aware, the Court held in that case that the imposition of a minimum alcohol requirement with respect to drinks was contrary to Article 30.[101] That judgment has been considered at length in the previous chapter and requires no further comment here.

7.53   The Court had occasion to build on that judgment in *Gilli and Andres*.[102] An Italian Decree prohibited the sale in Italy of all vinegar, be it Italian or imported, other than wine vinegar. Since such vinegar constitutes no health hazard, it was clear that the sole object of the Decree was to protect Italian wine products. The defendants were charged before the Italian courts with contravening the Decree by selling quantities of cider vinegar imported from Germany, whereupon a reference for a preliminary ruling was made asking the Court whether this Decree was compatible with Article 30. As the Court pointed out, it was undisputed that cider vinegar was harmless to health and that the vinegar at issue in the main proceeding was provided with a sufficiently clear label indicating that it was cider vinegar, thus avoiding any possibility of the consumer's confusing it with wine vinegar. It continued:

> 'Thus there is no factor justifying any restrictions on the importation of the product in question from the point of view either of the protection of public health or of the fairness of commercial transactions or of the defence of the consumer . . .
>
> It appears therefore that a unilateral requirement, imposed by the rules of a Member State, prohibiting the putting on the market of vinegars not produced from the acetic fermentation of wine constitutes an obstacle to trade which is incompatible with the provisions of Article 30 of the Treaty.'

This judgment was confirmed, albeit in somewhat modified terms, in Case 193/80 *E.C. Commission* v. *Italy*.[103]

7.54   Next, the case of *Officier van Justitie* v. *Koninklijke Kaas-fabriek Eyssen*[104] concerned a prohibition on the use of a preservative called nisin in processed cheese sold in the Netherlands. In criminal proceedings brought against a manufacturer for having in stock with

---

[100] Case 120/78 [1979] E.C.R. 649, [1979] 3 C.M.L.R. 494, para. 6.40 above.

[101] As to minimum alcohol requirements, see also *Miro*, n.85 above.

[102] Case 788/79 [1980] E.C.R. 2071, [1981] 1 C.M.L.R. 146, noted by Meier [1981] EuR 43.

[103] See n.80 above. See also para. 6.45 above. In *Gilli and Andres* the Court had said that the prohibition on the sale of all vinegar other than wine vinegar was contrary to Art. 30. But in Case 193/80, the Court limited its judgment to the prohibition on the sale of other agricultural vinegars. This was simply because, in its letter of formal notice opening the infringement proceedings, the Commission had expressly excluded synthetic vinegar from the scope of those proceedings.

[104] Case 53/80 [1981] E.C.R. 409, [1982] 2 C.M.L.R. 20.

a view to sale quantities of such cheese containing nisin, the national court asked the Court in effect whether the measure at issue was justified under Article 36. After pointing out that other Member States permitted the use of nisin either without limit or subject to certain maximum limits, the Court stated:

> 'In view of this disparity of rules it cannot be disputed that the prohibition by certain Member States of the marketing on their territory of processed cheese containing added nisin is of such a nature as to affect imports of that product from other Member States where, conversely, the addition of nisin is wholly or partially permitted and that it for that reason constitutes a measure having an effect equivalent to a quantitative restriction.'

The Court found, however, that the measure in question was justified on grounds of public health under Article 36.[105]

7.55   The reference in *Kelderman*[106] concerned the Dutch Broodbes-luit, which stipulated that all bread sold in the Netherlands must contain a proportion of dry matter falling within fixed bands. The defendants were charged with selling in the Netherlands brioches from France containing a quantity of dry matter falling outside the permitted limits. Since the Court found that the measure of the kind in question was not necessary to fulfil any mandatory require-ment such as the protection of public health or consumer protection, it held that it was contrary to Article 30.

7.56   In *Frans-Nederlandse Maatschappij voor Biologische Produc-ten*,[107] the Court was asked whether a prohibition on the sale of plant protection products without prior Government approval was compatible with Article 30 in so far as it applied to a product imported from another Member State where it had received such approval. Once again, the national legislation applied in the same way to domestic products and to imports. However, it is significant that the justification advanced by the Member State for the measure, namely public health, is one of the grounds of justification set out in Article 36. Consequently, the Court framed its judgment in terms of Articles 30 and 36 taken together, even though the question put by the national court mentioned Article 30 alone. At all events, it is clear from the judgment that a measure of this kind will be contrary to Article 30 in certain circumstances discussed more fully in paragraph 8.46 below.

7.57   In *Industrie Diensten Groep* v. *Beele*,[108] the Court found that the prohibition on the sale of imported or domestically produced goods constituting a slavish imitation of other goods already on the national market of the Member State concerned was in principle a

---

[105] Para. 8.43 below.
[106] Case 130/80 [1981] E.C.R. 527.
[107] Case 272/80, [1981] E.C.R. 3277, [1982] 2 C.M.L.R. 497.
[108] Case 6/81, [1982] E.C.R. 707, [1982] 3 C.M.L.R. 102.

measure of equivalent effect under Article 30. The Court went on to find, however, that such a prohibition was, under certain circumstances set out in the next chapter,[109] justified on the grounds of consumer protection and the prevention of unfair competition.

7.58   Other measures in this category which have been held to infringe Article 30, subject to their being justified, include:
  — a ban on the sale of beer exceeding the nationally prescribed acidity level[110]:
  — a ban on the sale of beer made from ingredients other than barley, malt and hops[111];
  — a ban on the sale of substitute milk powder (*i.e.* 'coffee whitener' not based on milk products)[112];
  — a prohibition on the sale of pasta made wholly or partly from soft wheat.[113]

Requirements as to the presentation of products

7.59   Article 2(3)(j) of Directive 70/50 defines as measures of equivalent effect under Article 30 measures which 'subject imported products only to conditions, in respect in particular of shape, size, weight, composition, presentation, identification or putting up . . .' It follows from the *Cassis de Dijon* ruling[114] that all obstacles to the sale of imported goods constitute measures of equivalent effect under Article 30, subject to the application of Article 36.

An 'indistinctly applicable' measure relating to the presentation of goods fell to be considered in *Fietje*.[115] The defendant was charged with marketing in the Netherlands an apple-based drink containing 25 per cent. alcohol which did not bear the legend 'liqueur' as required by the Dutch Likeurbesluit. The Court held that the measure was contrary to Article 30 in certain circumstances discussed more fully in the following chapter of this book.[116]

7.60   Similar measures which have been held contrary to Article 30, subject to their being justified, include:
  — an 'indistinctly applicable' ban on the sale of silver-plated articles without the requisite hallmarks[117];

---

[109] See para. 8.85 below.
[110] Case 94/82 *De Kikvorsch* [1983] E.C.R. 947, [1984] 2 C.M.L.R. 323.
[111] Case 176/84 *E.C. Commission* v. *Greece* [1988] 1 C.M.L.R. 813.
[112] Case 216/84 *E.C. Commission* v. *France* (judgment of 23 February 1988).
[113] Cases 407/85 *Drei Glocken* v. *USL* and 90/86 *Zoni* (judgments of 14 July 1988).
[114] N.100 above.
[115] Case 27/80 [1980] E.C.R. 3839, [1981] 3 C.M.L.R. 722.
[116] Para. 8.74 below.
[117] Case 220/81 *Robertson* [1982] E.C.R. 2349, [1983] 1 C.M.L.R. 556; para. 8.75 below.

— an 'indistinctly applicable' requirement that margarine be sold in cubic packaging so as to distinguish it from butter[118];
— a ban on the sale of *pétillant de raisin* (a drink with a 3 per cent. alcohol content) in bottles of a type associated with champagne.[119]

Measures requiring unnecessary translations

7.61 In *Fietje*[120] it was held that a Member State may not require labelling to be in its language where the information contained on the original label in another language is equally comprehensive to consumers in that State. This principle no doubt extends to other information relating to consumer goods.

Indeed, the same principle surely applies to documents directed not at consumers, but at officials of the importing State. Thus the Commission has stated[121] that a French official circular requiring all customs documents to be in French was contrary to Article 30. Perhaps the same applies to documents required for the type approval of products. Yet, there are undoubtedly cases in which such a requirement may be justified, albeit that no criterion for assessing such justification appears to be readily available. In relation to customs documents the Commission has stated[122] that 'a translation of such documents can only be demanded in cases where there are serious doubts about what they contain or they are not understood at all,' but this is a subjective test not susceptible to proof.

Restrictions on the delivery of goods

7.62 The case of *Oebel*[123] primarily concerned a German measure prohibiting the baking of bread during the night. This measure in itself had no bearing on imports. However, it was supplemented by an ancillary measure prohibiting the *delivery* of bread during the night. This prohibition on delivery, which applied in the same way to imports and to domestic products, was considered by the Germany authorities to be necesary for the enforcement of the prohibition on night baking. On a reference from a German court, the Court of Justice was in effect asked to rule, *inter alia,* whether a prohibition on night delivery of this kind was compatible with Articles 30 and 34. The Advocate General took the view that such a measure did constitute a measure of equivalent effect although it might in certain

---

[118] Case 261/81 *Rau* v. *De Smedt* [1982] E.C.R. 3961, [1983] 2 C.M.L.R. 496; para. 8.72 below.
[119] Case 179/85 [1988] 1 C.M.L.R. 135, para. 8.89 below.
[120] See n.115 above.
[121] Written questions 1744/82 ([1983] O.J. C92/20), 2126/82 ([1983] O.J. C141/9), 2319/83 ([1983] O.J. C232/5) and 1032/83 ([1983] O.J. C359/11).
[122] Written question 1032/83 (see n.121 above).
[123] Case 155/80 [1981] E.C.R. 1993, [1983] 1 C.M.L.R. 390.

circumstances be justified. The Court, taking a radically different view, ruled that such a measure was compatible with these provisions, on the following grounds:

It so happened that the German legislation at issue prohibited night deliveries to individual consumers and to points of retail sale, but did not apply to deliveries to depots or middle-men. The Court considered that, in view of this and because the prohibition applied 'to the same extent for all producers, wherever they are established,' there was no restriction on imports or exports between Member States, so that such legislation was compatible with Articles 30 and 34.

There would seem to be something of a *non sequitur* in this reasoning: surely a prohibition on delivering goods to individual consumers and to points of retail sale during the night does constitute an actual or potential, direct or indirect hindrance to interstate trade? Indeed it is hard to reconcile this ruling with the general principles laid down by the Court with respect to Articles 30 to 36.

Black lists for pharmaceuticals

7.63   *Duphar* v. *Netherlands*[124] was one of the most difficult cases on Article 30 which the Court has ever had to decide. It concerned a list of pharmaceutical products drawn up by the Dutch authorities which did not qualify for reimbursement out of the State social security fund in view of their allegedly excessive cost. Each of these excluded products could, it was said, be replaced by another product which was equally effective and less costly. Under the scheme national products and imports were treated in the same way. The plaintiffs were pharmaceutical companies which claimed that the scheme was contrary *inter alia* to Article 30.

Plainly such a scheme may actually or potentially, directly or indirectly impede imports. Yet its object was to reduce State spending. While this objective is wholly unobjectionable in itself, it is of a purely economic nature and thus cannot be justified under Article 36.[125]

Advocate General Mancini considered that the contested measure constituted a measure of equivalent effect under Article 30, since it discouraged the purchase of the products concerned so as to cause a fall in imports. However, in his view the scheme was justified on public health grounds under Article 36. He conceded that its immediate aim was to reduce public expenditure but stressed that its ultimate purpose was to protect public health. He regarded it as contradictory and hypocritical to acknowledge the importance of the protection of public health, while at the same time denying the Member States the means for ensuring proper health care. It might

---

[124] Case 238/82 [1984] E.C.R. 523, [1985] 1 C.M.L.R. 256.
[125] See para. 8.19 below; see also para. 8.11 below.

be that the measure in issue in the main case was disproportionately restrictive having regard to the end to be achieved, but that was for the national court to determine. At the same time he wholly rejected the Commission's suggestion that the improvement of the financial management of a public sickness insurance scheme be regarded as a 'mandatory requirement' justifying measures applying to imports and domestic goods in the same way under the terms of *Cassis de Dijon*.[126] If this were to be accepted as justification, then it was only a short step to extending that to all terms of public or social expenditure.

The Court also found that such a scheme might in certain circumstances be lawful but reached that result by a different route. It began by stressing that in other Member States only those pharmaceuticals on the official list qualified for reimbursement, all other products being excluded. In the Netherlands, on the other hand, the converse applied: all products were subject to reimbursement except those specifically excluded. Next, it rejected the Dutch Government's argument to the effect that this provision could be equated with that of a private body purchasing goods on the market. Despite this, the Court acknowledged that 'social security institutions are substituted for consumers as regards responsibility for the payment of medical expenses.' Accordingly, even though it might restrict imports, such legislation was held to fall outside Article 30 if certain conditions were satisfied. These conditions were as follows: the exclusionary lists must be drawn up in accordance with objective criteria without reference to the origin of the products (*e.g.* the existence on the market of other, less expensive products having the same therapeutic effect or the fact that a product may be purchased without a prescription); they must be verifiable by any importer; and it must be possible to amend the lists whenever compliance with the specific criteria so required.

On the other hand, the Court held that, if these conditions were not met, then the measure was caught by Article 30 and was not justified under Article 36. That provision could not 'justify a measure whose primary objective is budgetary in as much as it is intended to reduce the operating costs of a sickness insurance scheme.'

While the Court's judgment will have been widely welcomed in its result, the reasoning is questionable, as it cannot readily be squared with the *Dassonville* formula. However, the Advocate General's view that such a scheme can be justified on public health grounds also seems less than satisfactory, since it would appear to stretch that ground of justification beyond its normal meaning.

At all events, the terms of the judgment are scarcely capable of being applied to other cases. The ruling is based on the idea that,

---

[126] N.100 above.

in choosing between two competing products, the State was in effect exercising the function of a consumer.

7.64 The Commission has published a Communication[127] devoted *inter alia* to 'measures taken by Member States relating to . . . the reimbursement of medicinal products.' While it is impossible to reproduce the relevant section of that Communication in full here, the following passages are worthy of note:

> 'The definition of groups or categories of products which are approved or ineligible for reimbursement must be based on objective, general criteria of a therapeutic nature. When therapeutic classes are defined, for reimbursement purposes, they may not therefore be reduced to a single product or single active substance, which by the approval of one class would allow the reimbursement of a particular product and, by the prohibition of another class, would prevent another product having an equivalent therapeutic effect from being reimbursed.'

> 'The Commission regards the following as incompatible with the principles set out above:
> — the exclusion from reimbursement, for one or more therapeutic classes, of proprietary products only, regardless of price, or the approval for reimbursement of unbranded products only, regardless of price,
> — the exclusive approval for reimbursement, for each therapeutic class or for all therapeutic classes, of a predetermined number of medicinal products.'

The Commission also contains various statements as to the procedures to be followed by Member States in this regard. In particular, when they receive an application for the approval of a medicinal product for reimbursement, Member States are, it is said, required to act within a reasonable period and this may in no case exceed 120 days.

In addition, the Commission has now submitted to the Council a draft Directive[128] on the matter.

Certain price controls

7.65 The term 'price controls' is used here to cover the following types of measure: price freezes, minimum[129] and maximum prices, minimum and maximum profit margins and resale price maintenance. Countless variants and combinations of these types of measure are imposed by the different Member States with respect to various products.[130] All the Member States impose price controls of some kind on some products, most frequently highly sensitive products such as pharmaceuticals. It is thus of the greatest practical importance

---

[127] [1986] O.J. C310/7.

[128] [1987] O.J. C17/6.

[129] As regards minimum prices for agricultural products during the transitional period, see Art. 44 EEC.

[130] See Westphal and Jürgensen 'The effects of national price controls in the European Economic Community' *Commission of the E.C., Studies Collection, Competition—Approximation of Legislation* Series No. 9 (1970).

to determine to what extent State price controls are compatible with Article 30.[131]

Furthermore, price controls generally form an integral part of the economic policies of the Member States. The Treaty has in principle left intact the right of each Member State to take the economic policy measures it deems necessary; this emerges in particular from Articles 103(1), 104 and 145.[132] This explains why the Court has trodden more warily with regard to price controls than with regard to other types of measure falling under Article 30. It would have been rash indeed to have held that all price controls automatically constituted measures of equivalent effect.

7.66 At all events the Commission in Article 2(3) of Directive 70/50 defined as measures of equivalent effect measures which:

'(a) lay down, for imported products only, minimum or maximum prices below or above which imports are prohibited, reduced or made subject to conditions liable to hinder importation; or

(b) lay down less favourable prices for imported products than for domestic products; or

(c) fix profit margins or any other price components for imported products only or fix these differently for domestic products and for imported products, to the detriment of the latter; or

(d) preclude any increase in the price of the imported product corresponding to the supplementary costs and charges inherent in importation; or

(e) fix the prices of products solely on the basis of the cost price or the quality of domestic products at such a level as to create a hindrance to importation.'

7.67 This has now been supplemented by a body of case law of the Court, much of which concerns products not subject to a common market organisation.[133]

The Court's case law[134] on the compatibility of national price controls with the common market organisations themselves—and in

---

[131] Waelbroeck, *Les réglementations nationales de prix et le droit communautaire* (1975); Sabiani, 'L'incidence du droit de la Communauté Economique Européenne sur la réglementation française des prix' [1975] R.T.D.E. 470 and 633; Winkel, 'Die Vereinbarkeit staatlicher Preislenkungsmaßnahmen mit dem EWG-Vertrag' [1976] N.J.W. 2048; Matthies, 'Die Verantwortung der Mitgliedstaaten für den freien Warenverkehr im Gemeinsamen Markt' in *Festschrift für Ipsen* (1977); Mestmäcker, *Vereinbarkeit von Preisregelungen auf dem Arzneimittelmarkt mit dem Recht der Europäischen Wirtschaftsgemeinschaft* (1980) (summary in English); Capelli, *Controllo dei Prezzi e Normativa Comunitaria* (1981). Galmot and Biancarelli 'Les réglementations nationales en matière de prix au regard du droit communautaire' [1985] R.T.D.E. 269.
[132] See also para. 7.89 below.
[133] See paras. 10.09 *et seq.* below.
[134] Case 31/74 *Galli* [1975] E.C.R. 47, [1975] 1 C.M.L.R. 211, noted by VerLoren van Themaat [1973] C.M.L.Rev. 422; Case 154/77 *Dechmann* [1978] E.C.R. 1573, [1979] 2 C.M.L.R. 1; Case 223/78 *Grosoli* [1979] E.C.R. 2621; Case 10/79 *Toffoli* [1979] E.C.R. 3301; Cases 95–96/79 *Kefer and Delmelle* [1980] E.C.R. 103; Case 216/86 *Antonini* (judgment of 1 July 1987); Berardis 'The common organisation of agricultural markets and national price regulations' [1980] C.M.L.Rev. 539; Colinet and Maresceau, 'Interprétation et application du droit communautaire dans le domaine des réglementations des prix des produits agricoles de l'arrêt Dechmann à l'arrêt Kefer-Delmelle' [1980] C.D.E. 507.

particular the provisions of those organisations relating to price formation—fall outside the scope of this book.

7.68   The first cases in which the Court ruled on the compatibility of price controls with Article 30 were the two parallel cases of *Tasca*[135] and *SADAM* v. *Comitato Interministeriale dei Prezzi*,[136] both involving maximum prices for sugar fixed by the Italian authorities. In each case the national court asked whether such maximum prices were compatible with Article 30 and with Regulation 1009/67.[137] As regard Article 30 the Court replied in each case:

> 'Article 30 of the Treaty prohibits in trade between Member States all measures having an effect equivalent to quantitative restrictions and this prohibition is repeated in Article 35 of Regulation No. 1009/67 as regards the market in sugar. For the purposes of this prohibition it is sufficient that the measures in question are likely to constitute an obstacle, directly or indirectly, actually or potentially, to imports between Member States. Although a maximum price applicable without distinction to domestic and imported products does not in itself constitute a measure having an effect equivalent to a quantitative restriction, it may have such an effect, however, when it is fixed at a level such that the sale of imported products becomes, if not impossible, more difficult than that of domestic products. A maximum price, in any event in so far as it applies to imported products, constitutes therefore a measure having an effect equivalent to a quantitative restriction, especially when it is fixed at such a low level that, having regard to the general situation of imported products compared to that of domestic products, dealers wishing to import the products in question into the Member State concerned can do so only at a loss.'

7.69   It would appear[138] that the measures which the Court describes in this passage as applying in the same way to imports and to domestic products (and thus 'indistinctly applicable') in fact fall under Article 2(3)(d) and (e) of Directive 70/50 since the objection to these measures is that they fail to take account of the special position of imports. Yet Article 2(3) of Directive 70/50 covers 'distinctly applicable' measures only. This shows how precarious is the distinction between 'distinctly applicable' and 'indistinctly applicable' measures.

More curious is the fact that the passage quoted from the *Tasca* and *SADAM* judgments appears to contradict itself. On the one hand the Court states that a maximum price applying to domestic products and to imports in the same way does not in itself constitute a measure of equivalent effect, but only does so when it makes the sale of imported products more difficult than that of domestic products. On the other hand, in the following sentence the Court holds that a maximum price does constitute a measure of equivalent

---

[135] Case 65/75 [1976] E.C.R. 291, [1977] 2 C.M.L.R. 183, noted by Waelbroeck [1977] C.M.L.Rev. 94.
[136] Cases 88–90/75 [1976] E.C.R. 323, [1977] 2 C.M.L.R. 183, noted by Waelbroeck, *op. cit.* n.135 above.
[137] [1967] O.J. Spec.Ed. 304.
[138] Winkel, *op. cit.* n.131 above, at p.2051.

effect 'especially when . . .' There appears to be no way of reconciling these two statements. However, as will be seen below, subsequent judgments such as *GB-Inno* v. *ATAB,* and *Danis* follow the former line: maximum prices applying in the same way to domestic products and to imports do not in themselves constitute measures of equivalent effect.

7.70   The Court also held in *SADAM* that a Member State could not rely on Article 103[139] to justify a maximum consumer price contrary to Article 30. There is every reason to think that this ruling applies to all products, even those not covered by a common market organisation; and that it applies to all price controls. On this view Article 103 can never be relied on to justify a price control falling under Article 30.

7.71   This brings us to *GB-Inno* v. *ATAB*[140] itself. By Belgian law, excise duty on Belgian or imported manufactured tobacco was to be calculated on the basis of the price appearing on the tax label; furthermore this price, freely chosen by the manufacturer or the importer as the case may be, was the compulsory selling price to the consumer. This measure was therefore at once broadly equivalent to a *minimum* and a *maximum* price control. In an action in which it was accused of selling below this price, GB-Inno, a major Belgian supermarket chain, claimed that this system was contrary to a number of provisions of Community law, including Article 30. The national court asked four questions, the third of which concerned the compatibility of such a measure with Article 30.

Before the answers to those questions, the Court's judgment contains a section entitled 'general observations.' In this section the Court pointed out that the prohibition on selling cigarettes *above* the price used for calculating the tax was essential to make the tax workable.[141] This could not be said of the prohibition on selling below this price, which was designed rather to protect small retailers against destructive competition from supermarkets. It also noted that while in theory there was nothing to prevent a retailer from determining his own price by obtaining tobacco products with appropriate labels, this required the co-operation of the manufacturer or importer and of the Belgian tax authorities and this co-operation might be difficult to obtain.

In answer to the third question the Court held:

> 'Although a maximum price applicable without distinction to domestic and imported products does not in itself constitute a measure having an effect equivalent to a quantitative restriction, it may have such an effect, however,

---

[139] See paras. 9.04 *et seq.* below.
[140] Case 13/77 [1977] E.C.R. 2115, [1978] 1 C.M.L.R. 283; see Koppensteiner, 'Vertikale Preisbindung durch Gesetz als Maßnahme gleicher Wirkung wie eine mengenmässige Einfuhrbeschränkung' [1977] AWD/RIW 518.
[141] See para. 8.67 below.

when it is fixed at such a level that the sale of imported products becomes, if not impossible, more difficult than that of domestic products.

On the other hand, a system whereby the prices are freely chosen by the manufacturer or the importer as the case may be and imposed on the consumer by a national legislative measure, and whereby no distinction is made between domestic products and imported products, generally has exclusively internal effects.

However, the possibility cannot be excluded that in certain cases such a system may be capable of affecting intra-Community trade.'

The Court therefore concluded that, even taking into account the inherent barriers to trade due to differences in the tax systems of the Member States, it was possible that such a system might hinder, directly or indirectly, actually or potentially, imports between Member States. This was for the national court to assess.[142]

7.72   The Court subsequently extended this case law to *price freezes* in *Openbaar Ministerie* v. *Danis*.[143] The defendants in the main case were traders in animal feedstuffs accused of increasing their prices without notifying the Belgian Minister of Economic Affairs as required by a Belgian Ministerial Order. That Order provided that all price increases were to be notified to the Minister at least two months before they took effect and that the Minister could extend this period. The Belgian court consequently asked the Court of Justice whether such a measure was compatible with Article 30.

After repeating the *Dassonville* formula the Court stated:

'National rules of this kind, even if they are confined to requiring the producer or importer to "notify" proposed price increases before they are applied, have the effect of a price freeze, since the prices quoted by the producer prior to his notification are, in fact, "frozen" for at least the duration of the waiting period.

Whilst rules imposing a price freeze which are applicable equally to national products and to imported products do not amount in themselves to a measure having an effect equivalent to a quantitative restriction, they may in fact produce such an effect when prices are at such a level that the marketing of imported products becomes either impossible or more difficult than the marketing of national products. That is especially the case where national rules, while preventing the increased prices of imported products from being passed on in sale prices, freeze prices at a level so low that—taking into account the general situation of imported products in relation to that of national products—traders wishing to import the products in question into the Member State concerned can do so only at a loss, or, having regard to the level at which prices for national products are frozen, are impelled to give preference to the latter products.'

Although the Court was only asked to rule on the compatibility of such measures with Article 30, it then went on to rule on their compatibility with the common market organisation in cereals.

---

[142] See also Cases 177–178/82 *Van de Haar* [1984] E.C.R. 1797, [1985] 2 C.M.L.R. 566.

[143] Cases 16–20/79 [1979] E.C.R. 3327, [1980] 3 C.M.L.R. 492, noted by Waelbroeck [1981] *Revue Critique de Jurisprudence Belge* 12. See also Case 5/79 *Buys* [1979] E.C.R. 3203, [1980] 2 C.M.L.R. 493.

7.73 Lastly, the Court has also had occasion to rule on the compatibility with Article 30 of *minimum prices* and *minimum profit margins,* in *van Tiggele.*[144] There the defendant was charged before a Dutch court with having sold spirits below minimum prices fixed by the Dutch authorities. Different rules applied to three different types of spirit:

(a) for 'new hollands gin' and *vieux* the retail price must be the manufacturer's catalogue price per unit (if any) plus 0.60 Fl. per unit and VAT, the total of which must in no case be lower than 11.25 Fl. per litre;

(b) for 'old hollands gin' the minimum retail price was fixed at 11.25 Fl. per litre;

(c) for other spirits, the minimum retail price was the actual purchase price plus VAT.

These are products not covered by a common organisation of the market.

The Court replied to the question put by the Dutch court as follows:

> 'Whilst national price-control rules applicable without distinction to domestic products and imported products cannot in general [hinder, directly or indirectly, actually or potentially imports between Member States], they may do so in specific cases.
>
> Thus imports may be impeded in particular when a national authority fixes prices or profit margins at such a level that imported products are placed at a disadvantage in relation to identical domestic products either because they cannot profitably be marketed in the conditions laid down or because the competitive advantage conferred by lower cost prices is cancelled out . . .'

Applying this test, the Court found, firstly, that a prohibition on retail sales below the purchase price paid by the retailer 'cannot produce effects detrimental to the marketing of imported products alone' and therefore did not infringe Article 30. Secondly, the fixing of a minimum profit margin at a specific amount rather than as a percentage of the cost price, is 'likewise incapable of producing an adverse effect on imported products which may be cheaper as in the present case where the amount of the profit margin constitutes a relatively significant part of the final retail price'. Thirdly, as regards *minimum prices* the Court took the view that:

> 'this is not so in the case of a minimum price fixed at a specific amount which, although applicable without distinction to domestic products and imported products, is capable of having an adverse effect on the marketing of the latter in so far as it prevents their lower cost price from being reflected in the retail selling price.'

7.74 The law relating to *fixed profit margins* was clarified by the judgment in *E.C. Commission* v. *Italy.*[145] Although that case was decided on the basis of Article 37 alone, it drew on and applied

---

[144] Case 82/77 [1978] E.C.R. 25, [1978] 2 C.M.L.R. 528.
[145] Case 78/82 [1983] E.C.R. 1955.

earlier case law relating to Article 30; accordingly, there is every reason to believe that the Court's ruling would have been the same had it been based on Article 30. Italy had a State monopoly in the production and distribution of tobacco products. The right to carry out retail sales of these products was limited to tobacconists approved by the tax authorities, of whom there were admittedly some 80,000. The Commission claimed that the provision of Italian law whereby these retailers always took 8 per cent. of the retail value of their sales infringed Article 37, even though the price was freely determined by the manufacturer. In its view the effect of this provision was to put Italian products, by definition manufactured by the State monopoly, at an advantage over imports.

After rehearsing the principles laid down in *Tasca, van Tiggele* and *Danis,* the Court stated:

> 'In the present case, the rules in dispute do not affect the freedom of producers to fix the retail price of their products. Competition may be freely pursued in the essential field of retail prices. Foreign producers of tobacco products are free either to take advantage of more competitive production costs or to pass on higher production costs in their entirety. It is not contested that the uniform margin represents an adequate remuneration to tobacconists for the retailing of tobacco products, whether they be imported or domestic products.

Consequently the action was dismissed.

As already mentioned, in *Van Tiggele* the Court had held that '. . . the fixing of the minimum profit at a specific amount, and not as a percentage of the cost price, applicable without distinction to domestic products and imported products is . . . incapable of producing an adverse effect on imported products which may be cheaper, as in the present case where the amount of the profit margin constitutes a relatively significant part of the final retail price.' Taking the two cases together, one might be tempted to think that all kinds of measures restricting profit margins fall outside Article 30—were it not for the ruling in *Roelstraete* discussed below.

7.75 *Roussel* v. *Netherlands*[146] concerned *maximum prices.* This case arose against the background of considerably higher prices for pharmaceuticals in the Netherlands than in certain other Member States where they were kept artificially low by State price controls. This meant that companies manufacturing pharmaceuticals in the low price Member States were able to make substantial profits on their sales in the Netherlands. This was resented by the Dutch Government because 80 per cent. of the pharmaceuticals purchased in the Netherlands were imported and it bore the lion's share of the cost through its sickness insurance scheme. Until June 1982 it fixed maximum profit margins annually by reference to the prices charged in the preceding year. That system applied to domestic and imported products in the same way. In June 1982 it adopted a new

---

[146] Case 181/82 [1983] E.C.R. 3849; [1985] 1 C.M.L.R. 834.

system of price controls with the avowed aim of reducing the profits made on imported pharmaceuticals from the low price Member States. The new legislation laid down maximum profits margins for imported pharmaceuticals calculated on the basis of the factory gate price of each product in the Member State of production, though such factors as transport costs and VAT were also taken into account. On the other hand, the old legislation continued to apply to pharmaceuticals produced in the Netherlands. The result of this legislative change was that the maximum prices for Dutch pharmaceuticals remained unchanged whereas imports were now to be sold at drastically reduced prices. A number of pharmaceutical companies brought an action against the Dutch Government claiming that the new legislation infringed Article 30, whereupon the national court requested the Court of Justice to rule on the point.

The Court held without more that such legislation was contrary to Article 30. There was a presumption that price controls applying to imports and domestic goods in the same way did not constitute a measure of equivalent effect. However, that presumption did not apply here because this legislation applied to imports in a different way and put them at a disadvantage.[147] Although factory gate prices were the starting point of the calculation in both cases, in the low price Member States factory gate prices were kept artificially low as a result of pressure from the governments concerned whereas in the Netherlands there was no such pressure. The Court did not advert to the problem of justification at all. However, it did briefly remark that Member States were entitled to take measures to reduce inflation and to limit increases in the cost of pharmaceuticals provided that imports were not put at a disadvantage.[148]

7.76   *Leclerc* v. *Au Blé Vert*[149] concerned *resale price maintenance* for books. The French law in issue, generally known as the *loi Lang,* required publishers to fix the retail price at which retailers were obliged to sell, subject to the possibility of granting discounts of no more than 5 per cent. of that price. The price of imported books was to be fixed by the importer instead, the principal distributor being deemed to be the importer. Where books published in France were imported, the retail price was to be no lower than that fixed by the publisher. The provision in question applied to all books intended for retail sale in France, whatever their origin. The law contained a number of exceptions, none of which were relevant to the proceedings.

---

[147] For another price control which was more onerous as regards imports see Cases 80 and 159/85 *Nederlandse Bakkerij Stichting* v. *Edah* [1988] 2 C.M.L.R. 113.

[148] Another discriminatory maximum price régime for pharmaceuticals was held to be contrary to Art. 30 in Case 56/87 *E.C. Commission* v. *Italy* (judgment of 9 June 1988).

[149] Case 229/83 [1985] E.C.R. 1, [1985] 2 C.M.L.R. 524, noted by Kuyper [1985] C.M.L.Rev. 787.

Leclerc was a chain of supermarket stores which had been prohibited by injunction from selling at more than 5 per cent. below the fixed retail price.

Although the French legislation also banned sales at prices higher than that fixed by the publisher or importer, this was not in issue.

As to Articles 30 to 36, the Court began by rejecting the French Government's contention that the legislation treated imported and domestically-produced books in the same way. The law transferred the responsibility for fixing retail prices to the principal distributor who was at a different stage of the commercial process from the publisher. This made it impossible for any other importer of the same book to charge the retail price in France that he considered adequate in the light of the cost price in the State in which it was published. Such a provision therefore created separate rules for imported books which were liable to impede trade between Member States. Accordingly, it constituted a measure of equivalent effect.

This analysis is in direct contrast to that in *GB-Inno*.[150] That case also concerned resale price maintenance with the price of the domestic product being determined by the manufacturer and the price of the imported product by the importer. The Court ruled that the prohibition on selling above the price on the tax label freely chosen by the manufacturer or importer made no distinction between domestic and imported products. It can surely not be logically suggested that such a régime is 'indistinctly applicable' in so far as it prohibits retail sales above the price chosen by the manufacturer or importer, but 'distinctly applicable' in so far as it prevents the retailer from selling below that price. This demonstrates once again how frail is the differentiation between 'distinctly applicable' and 'indistinctly applicable' measures.

At all events, as regards re-imports of goods published in France the Court held that 'a provision requiring such books to be sold at the retail price fixed by the publisher does not make a distinction between domestic and imported books.'[151]

The Court then went on to rule that the measures could not be justified on consumer protection grounds since this was a mandatory requirement and could not therefore justify measures of the kind in issue, in effect because they were distinctly applicable.[152] The Court did not stop to explain why this should be so as regards re-imports, given that it had just held the measure to be indistinctly applicable with respect to them.

Thus the measure was held to contravene Article 30 in so far as it affected both imports and re-imports. However, it found that it was otherwise 'where it is established that the books in question

---

[150] Para. 7.71 above.
[151] See, however, para. 2.26 above.
[152] See para. 6.53 above.

were exported for the sole purpose of re-importation in order to circumvent legislation of the type at issue.'[153]

The question which arises in the aftermath of *Leclerc* is this: can a Member State (State A) lawfully extend its resale price maintenance legislation to imports by requiring the retail price fixed by the manufacturer in the exporting Member State (State B) to be observed? This puts him on the same footing as the manufacturer in the importing Member State (State A) and thus appears at first sight to be an attractive solution. Yet it is by no means free of difficulty since it prevents parellel importers from taking advantage of the lower prices that might be available in State B.[154]

7.77 In *Cullet* v. *Leclerc*[155] which related to petrol, the Court expanded on its ruling in *van Tiggele* on *minimum prices*. Put shortly, minimum prices for petrol were held to contravene Article 30 when they were fixed on the basis of national ex-refinery prices only, thereby depriving imported products of any competitive advantage. This ruling can scarcely be said to break new ground.

7.78 *Maximum profit margins* were considered by the Court for the first time in relation to Article 30 in *Roelstraete*.[156] The case related to pork, beef and veal and indeed the Court was primarily concerned with the common market organisations for those products.[157] As regards Article 30, it was held to be contrary to that provision for a Member State to fix a gross profit margin at a single amount applicable both to the domestic product and to imports, without making any allowance for the costs of importation. In such circumstances the net profit of a retailer who has imported his products from other Member States is reduced by an amount corresponding to the import costs and is therefore lower than the profit which he can make by buying his products on the national market. Such a system discourages imports.[158]

This judgment is to be contrasted with the Court's rulings on other types of fixed profit margins in *van Tiggele* and *E.C. Commission* v. *Italy*.[159]

7.79 It is submitted that the main principles laid down in this series of cases may be summarised as follows:

(a) a maximum price or price freeze applicable without distinction

---

[153] Para. 2.26 above.
[154] As to parallel imports, see generally para. 6.19 above.
[155] Case 231/83 [1985] E.C.R. 315, [1985] 2 C.M.L.R. 524.
[156] Case 116/84 [1985] E.C.R. 1705, [1986] 3 C.M.L.R. 562.
[157] The judgment was in part a clarification of the earlier ruling in *Kefer and Delmelle* (n.134 above) which did not mention Art. 30.
[158] See also Case 188/86 *Lefevre* (judgment of 2 July 1987).
[159] See para. 7.74 above.

to domestic and imported products does not necessarily constitute a measure of equivalent effect.

(b) However, such measures do constitute measures of equivalent effect when prices are fixed or frozen at such a level that the marketing of imported products becomes either impossible or more difficult than the marketing of national products. This is particularly the case when prices are fixed at a level so low that—taking into account the general situation of imported products in relation to that of national products—traders wishing to import the products in question can only do so at a loss.

(c) A prohibition on retail sales at a loss does not constitute a measure of equivalent effect.

(d) The fixing of a minimum profit margin at a specific amount rather than as a percentage of the cost price does not constitute a measure of equivalent effect either. The same applies to a fixed retail profit margin which is a proportion of the retail price freely determined by the manufacturer at least when it constitutes adequate remuneration for the retailers.

(e) In contrast, a maximum gross profit margin which is fixed at a single amount applicable both to domestic products and to imports and which fails to make allowances for the costs of importation is caught by Article 30.

(f) A minimum price fixed at a specific amount which, although applicable without distinction to domestic and imported products, can restrict imports by preventing their lower cost price from being reflected in the retail selling price, is a measure of equivalent effect.

(g) Resale price maintenance probably falls within Article 30 whenever the retail price of imported goods is fixed by the importer.

7.80   The Commission has now published a Communication[160] on price controls for medical products. This Communication consists largely of a summary of the case law, but it also contains some fresh points of note. Thus, the section entitled 'Determination of Prices' begins:

> 'The general principles to be observed here are grouped around two main aspects: realistic prices and transparency of prices. Each product must be able to have its own price, calculated on the basis of its real cost using a transparent method of calculation.'

Another noteworthy passage is set out in the next paragraph.

7.81   The most important undecided questions are the following:
Firstly, what is meant by the 'general situation of imported products compared to that of domestic products' which, the Court

---

[160] See n.127 above.

153

has repeatedly said, must be considered in judging whether a maximum price is set too low? According to Mestmäcker[161] one must look at the market prices of the product in question in other Member States, add to them the costs of exporting and deduct the costs spared by exporting. This means that transport costs must be considered. The same applies to currency fluctuations. It follows that, since currencies can fluctuate considerably from day to day, a given price control can suddenly cease to be compatible with Article 30—or just as suddenly become compatible with Article 30.[162]

In the Communication referred to in the preceding paragraph the Commission appears to have gone further, saying:

> 'If, when new products are placed on the market, Member States can justify asking firms for information to enable them to assess the components of the prices that such firms propose to charge, they must then allow pharmaceutical firms to take account of the various elements making up the cost of the products (research, raw materials, processing, advertising, transport, expenses and charges inherent in importing, *etc.*).'

The same calculations must be made in deciding whether a particular minimum price restriction is such as to cancel out the competitive advantage of imports.

7.82   Secondly, are price controls contrary to Article 30 only if they discriminate against imports? This may be the case with regard to maximum prices, since the Court has repeatedly held that they only constitute measures of equivalent effect if they are fixed at a level such that the sale of imported products becomes, if not impossible, then more difficult than that of domestic products. Thus for such price controls the criterion to be applied would seem to be whether the measures in question constitute discrimination in substance. If this is so, then maximum price controls constitute an exception to the principle formulated earlier in this book[163] according to which the concept of measures of equivalent effect under Article 30 extends to all restrictions on imports and does not merely cover discriminatory measures.

However, Mestmäcker[164] takes the view that maximum prices restricting imports do fall under Article 30 even if they do not discriminate against imports, at least in some cases. For example, he considers that a measure requiring both domestic products and imports to be sold at a loss would be caught by Article 30.

It is possible that a more stringent test is to be applied to minimum price controls, since by their very nature they are apt to prevent cheap imports.[165]

---

[161] *Op. cit.* n.131 above, at p.53.
[162] It could perhaps be argued that the uncertainty created for potential importers would in itself make such a price control a measure of equivalent effect.
[163] Para. 6.46 above.
[164] *Op. cit.* n.131 above, at pp.52–53.
[165] VerLoren van Themaat 'De artikelen 30–36 van het EEG-verdrag' [1980] R.M. Themis 4/5, 378 at 386.

In any case, it is not yet clear whether the test to be applied to price controls is that of discrimination against imports or that of the restriction of imports.

7.83   Thirdly, can price controls ever be justified under Article 36 on the mandatory requirements? It is submitted that they can only very rarely be so justified even though the grounds of justification have been extended.[166] This is because Article 36 is 'directed to eventualities of a non-economic kind'.[167] *Campus Oil*[168] was an exceptional case, where the price at which petroleum products had to be purchased was in effect incidental to the purchasing obligation; in these circumstances the Court took the view that it might be justified if certain conditions were fulfilled.

7.84   On the other hand, there can be no doubt that the Community has power to adopt legislation on prices and indeed in *Centrafarm* v. *Sterling Drug*,[169] the Court held that 'it is part of the Community authorities' task to eliminate factors likely to distort competition between Member States, in particular by the harmonisation of national measures for the control of prices . . .'

What is the correct legal basis in the Treaty for such measures?[170] Waelbroeck[171] takes the view that Article 103(2) EEC[172] relating to 'conjunctural' policy constitutes the basis for Community price controls. On the other hand, he considers that Article 100[173] of the Treaty—the classic basis for harmonisation—would only permit the harmonisation of national price measures and not their substitution by Community price controls. Harmonisation under Article 100, he argues, would leave the national price structures substantially intact and thus serve no practical purpose.

The Commission has set out its position on this question in answer to Written Question No. 185/80.[174] As regards Article 100, the Commission said that this provision empowered the Community 'to bring national laws and regulations into line where they directly affect the establishment or functioning of the common market'. The Commission added that Article 103(2) and (3) conferred on the Community the power to take action with respect to short-term economic policy in this regard and in particular with respect to inflation. However, it stated that 'so far . . . the Community has not considered it necessary to act under Articles 103 . . . or 100

---

[166] Paras. 6.41 *et seq.* above. On Art. 103, see para. 7.70 above.
[167] Para. 8.19 below.
[168] N.41 above, see para. 8.33 below.
[169] Case 15/74 [1974] E.C.R. 1147 at 1164; [1974] 2 C.M.L.R. 480 at 505.
[170] See generally Lambotte 'Le programme communautaire de lutte contre la hausse des prix' [1974] C.D.E. 515 and [1975] C.D.E. 371.
[171] *Op. cit.* n.131 above, p.57 *et seq.*
[172] Paras. 9.04 and 12.04.
[173] Para. 12.02 below.
[174] [1980] O.J. C316/1.

with a view to influencing prices or approximating national pricing laws, either in individual sectors or in general'.

II. MEASURES FALLING OUTSIDE ARTICLE 30

7.85 In addition to the cases already mentioned, the following types of measure have been held to be compatible with Article 30 (without falling under any other provision of the Treaty):

(i) Article 2(3)(r) of Directive 70/50 in effect excludes from the definition of measures of equivalent effect such import controls as are 'inherent in the customs clearance procedure.' This raises the fundamental question of what controls are 'inherent' in the customs clearance procedure.

At all events, in Case 159/78 *E.C. Commission* v. *Italy*[175] the Court embroidered on that provision, in the following terms:

> 'As regards intra-Community trade, since all customs duties on imports and exports and all charges having equivalent effect and all quantitative restrictions on imports and exports and measures having equivalent effect had to be abolished pursuant to Title I of the Treaty, by the end of the transitional period at the latest, it should be emphasised that customs controls properly so-called have lost their *raison d'être* as regards such trade. Frontier controls remain justified only in so far as they are necessary either for the implementation of the exceptions to free movement referred to in Article 36 of the Treaty; as for the levying of internal taxation, within the meaning of Article 95 of the Treaty when the crossing of the frontier may legitimately be assimilated to the situation which, in the case of domestic goods, gives rise to the levying of the tax, as for transit controls; as finally where they are essential in order to obtain reasonably complete and accurate information on movement of goods within the Community. These residuary controls must nevertheless be reduced as far as possible so that trade between Member States can take place in conditions as close as possible to those prevalent on a domestic market.'

The express mention of Article 36 at the beginning of the list may indicate that the rest of the list is an interpretation of Article 30 and not of Article 36. In other words, it appears to confirm the implication in Article 2(3)(r) of the Directive that such formalities fall outside Article 30 altogether rather than being justified under Article 36. The reference to the compilation of 'reasonably complete and adequate information on movement of goods within the Community' perhaps covers the ruling in *Donckerwolcke*[176] to the effect that an importer may be required to state the origin of goods on the customs documents when he knows such origin or can reasonably be expected to know it.

Applying the general statement to the facts, the Court dismissed the Commission's claim that certain provisions of the Italian Customs Code infringed Articles 30 and 34 because they required the owner of the goods either to clear them through customs himself or to appoint a professional customs agent, so that clearance by a

---

[175] [1979] E.C.R. 3247, [1980] 3 C.M.L.R. 446.
[176] Paras. 7.13 *et seq.* above.

non-professional agent was almost impossible. The Italian Government stated that by a legal fiction any person was deemed to be the owner for this purpose if he had possession of the goods when they entered or left the customs territory and acted in his own name and bore liability jointly with the owner. Accepting this assertion, the Court found that there was no infringement of Article 30 or 34.

7.86   (ii) In *Kramer*[177] the Court was asked to rule on the compatibility of fishing conservation quotas with Articles 30 and 34 and the common market organisation for fish.[178] The Court replied as follows:

> 'National regulations such as those forming the subject-matter of the present proceedings on the one hand and the prohibition laid down in Article 30 *et seq.* of the Treaty on the other hand relate to different stages of the economic process, that is to say, to production and to marketing respectively.
>
> The answer to the question whether a measure limiting agricultural production impedes trade between Member States depends on the global system established by the basic Community rules in the sector concerned and on the objectives of those rules. In this connection, the nature and the circumstances of "production" of the product in question, fish in the present case, should also be taken into consideration. Measures for the conservation of the resources of the sea through fixing catch quotas and limiting the fishing effort, whilst restricting "production" in the short term, are aimed precisely at preventing such "production" from being marked by a fall which would seriously jeopardise supplies to customers. Therefore, the fact that such measures have the effect, for a short time, of reducing the quantities that the States concerned are able to exchange between themselves cannot lead to these measures being classified among those prohibited by the Treaty, the decisive factor being that in the long term these measures are necessary to ensure a steady, optimum yield for fishing.'

While this ruling is obviously of the utmost importance to the fisheries sector, it may well not apply to any other products.

7.87   (iii) The ruling in *Blesgen* v. *Belgium*[179] is highly controversial.

The case concerned a Belgian statute which prohibited the sale or offer for sale in a public place of spirits for consumption there. For these purposes, 'public places' included bars, hotels and restaurants, while 'spirits' meant any drink with an alcohol content of over 22 degrees. As an ancillary measure, the same law also banned the storage of spirits in bars, hotels and restaurants and in adjoining places. Belgium has a small production of spirits, but most spirits consumed in Belgium are imported. On the other hand, Belgium's production and consumption of beer—which falls well below 22 degrees of alcohol—is considerable. But wine and vermouth, not

---

[177] Cases 3, 4 and 6/76 [1976] E.C.R. 1279, [1976] 2 C.M.L.R. 440.
[178] See paras. 10.09 *et seq.* below.
[179] N.64 above, noted by Waelbroeck [1983] C.D.E. 241.

typically Belgian products, also have an alcohol content below 22 degrees.

The defendant, who ran an hotel, was convicted of keeping quantities of spirits in premises adjoining his hotel. He appealed to the Belgian Cour de Cassation which asked the Court of Justice whether legislation of this kind constituted a measure of equivalent effect under Article 30 and, if so, whether it was justified on public health grounds under Article 36.

Applying the theory put forward earlier[180] one would have little difficulty in reaching the conclusion that the legislation concerned constituted a measure of equivalent effect under Article 30, even though it applied to Belgian spirits and imported spirits in exactly the same way. Indeed, this was the conclusion reached by most of the parties which intervened before the Court.

On the other hand, the question whether the measures were justified was considerably more difficult. There was no doubt whatsoever that they were originally designed to reduce alcoholism and thus to protect public health (and indeed public morality). Yet there was also evidence to suggest that they did not in fact reduce the consumption of alcohol. Moreover, it was clear that this law was highly beneficial to Belgian breweries.

Both the Advocate General and the Court simply side-stepped this difficult question of justification by holding that the legislation did not constitute a measure of equivalent effect in the first place. In a somewhat personal interpretation of the case law, the Advocate General claimed that that concept only covered *de jure* or *de facto* discrimination against imports. In support of this view, he cited *inter alia* the *Groenveld* formula[181] which had hitherto been thought to apply only to export restrictions under Article 34. Throughout his opinion, the Advocate General was in effect attempting to put the clock back to before *Cassis de Dijon* while at the same time claiming to be consistent with that judgment.

The Court proceeded to follow him. Referring to Article 3 of Commission Directive 70/50,[182] it held that national measures affecting the marketing of products fell under Article 30 even if they applied to imports and domestic products in the same way, provided that their restrictive effect on the free movement of goods exceeded the effects intrinsic to trade rules. The Court continued:

> 'That is not however the case with a legislative provision concerning only the sale of strong spirits for consumption on the premises in all places open to the public and not concerning other forms of marketing the same drinks. It is to be observed in addition that the restrictions placed on the sale of the spirits in question make no distinction whatsoever based on their nature or origin. Such a legislative measure has therefore in fact no connection with the

---

[180] Para. 6.46 above.
[181] Paras. 6.66 *et seq.* above.
[182] Para. 6.03 above.

importation of the products and for that reason is not of such a nature as to impede trade between Member States.'

It is difficult to reconcile this ruling with *Cassis de Dijon* and the plethora of cases that have followed it. However, as mentioned earlier,[183] this ruling may be taken as indicating the possible existence of a rule of remoteness which would bring outside the scope of Article 30 all measures having only the most tenuous effect on imports. Even so, it is submitted that the measure in issue in *Blesgen* did not fall within that category since any prohibition on the sale of spirits for consumption in public seems bound to have a real effect on imports.

7.88   (iv) *Directeur Général des Impôts* v. *Forest*[184] concerned a system of flour-milling quotas under which each mill held certain quotas. The Court's ruling in relation to Article 30 was in the following terms:

'It must be pointed out that even though a restriction on the quantities of wheat which may be milled may prevent millers from buying wheat, millers are free to buy imported wheat to cover part or all of their requirements. It therefore appears that such a system of quotas at the level of flour production in fact has no effect on wheat imports and is not likely to impede trade between Member States.

It follows that such legislation cannot be regarded as a measure having equivalent effect to a quantitative restriction on imports for the purposes of Article 30 of the EEC Treaty.'

7.89   (v) A deflationary economic policy consisting of keeping interest rates and the national currency high and/or an incomes policy is designed to slow down the economy as a whole and thus one of its effects will be to reduce imports. Yet it is submitted that such measures probably do not fall under Article 30. This is probably because under the Treaty the primary responsibility for economic policy rests with the Member States.[185] This emerges particularly from Article 104: 'Each Member State shall pursue the economic policy needed to ensure the equilibrium of its overall balance of payments and to maintain confidence in its currency, while taking care to ensure a high level of employment and a stable level of prices.' Nevertheless, Member States are to regard 'conjunctural policy' and exchange rates as a matter of common concern (Articles 103(1) and 107(1)[186] respectively); and indeed they are required to co-ordinate their economic policies (Articles 6(1), 102A and 145).

---

[183] Para. 6.46 above.
[184] Case 148/85 [1988] 2 C.M.L.R. 577.
[185] See generally Mégret in *Le droit de la Communauté Economique Européenne* (1976) Vol. 6.
[186] On Art. 107 see paras. 9.14 *et seq.*

In spite of this, Member States must conduct their economic policies within the bounds permitted by Community law. Thus in Case 6/69 *E.C. Commission* v. *France*[187] the defendant State was held to have infringed Article 92 by granting a preferential rediscount rate for exports. Again the Court has held that a Member State could not rely on Article 103 to justify a measure falling under Article 30.[188] On the other hand, the measures being discussed here are an inherent part of economic policy and it is hard to see how they could fall outside the bounds permitted by Community law. Perhaps the Court had this type of measure in mind when it ruled in *GB-Inno* v. *ATAB*[189] that the concept of measures of equivalent effect did not cover measures which 'are *per se* permitted as being the visible or hidden expression of powers retained by the Member States.'

7.90   (vi) Clearly, any measure not restricting imports is compatible with Article 30. As mentioned in paragraph 7.87, some measures may perhaps be regarded as having such a tenuous effect on imports that they fall outside Article 30 altogether; (this should not however be confused with the *de minimis* rule which does not apply to Article 30).[190] It is perhaps on these grounds that one might say that legislation limiting shop opening hours is compatible with that provision. This perhaps depends on whether there is any reliable evidence to show whether or not people buy less because shop opening hours are limited. The Commission has already expressed the view[191] that such legislation does not normally affect inter-State trade.[192]

III. MEASURES OF EQUIVALENT EFFECT UNDER ARTICLE 34

7.91   As we saw in the previous chapter,[193] many of the principles applying to measures of equivalent effect on imports under Article 30 apply *mutatis mutandis* to measures of equivalent effect on exports under Article 34. In so far as discrimination is relevant under Article 34 it is discrimination in favour of goods intended for the national market against goods intended for export.

---

[187] [1969] E.C.R. 523, [1970] C.M.L.R. 43.
[188] Para. 7.70 above.
[189] N.140 above, at p.2147.
[190] Para. 6.16 above.
[191] Written question 226/84 ([1984] O.J. C232/13).
[192] As to restrictions on Sunday trading, see Cases 118/88 *Suffolk C.D.C.* v. *Notcutts*, 134/88 *Linsey* v. *Payless D.I.Y.*, 145/88 *Torfaen B.C.* v. *B. & Q. plc* and 166/88 *Wakefield* v. *B. & Q.* (all pending).
[193] Paras. 6.64 *et seq.* above.

Some of the cases on Article 34 have been dealt with earlier in this chapter[194] and there is consequently no need to repeat them. Furthermore, the cases on export restrictions which are interpretations of common market organisations rather than Article 34 are dealt with in Chapter X.[195]

Export licences and certificates

7.92 This type of measure arose for consideration in Case 68/76 *E.C. Commission* v. *France*.[196] As a result of the sharp drop in potato production in Europe in 1975, the French Government subjected exports of potatoes to the production of an export certificate endorsed by a Government body bearing the acronym FORMA. Citing its ruling in the *International Fruit Company* case[197] the Court held that:

> 'even if in connection with intra-Community trade the FORMA granted its endorsement without delay and for all quantities requested and even if the object of the measures was merely to ascertain the intentions of the exporters, it must be held to be a measure having an effect equivalent to a quantitative restriciton on imports.'

7.93 The measure at issue in *Procureur de la République* v. *Bouhelier*[198] was somewhat more complex. Exporters of particular categories of watches were required either to obtain an export licence or to obtain a certificate attesting that the watches were of a given quality. No such requirements were laid down for watches sold within France. The certificates were issued by a technical body recognised by the French Government, known as Cetehor.

The Court held that the obligation to obtain an export licence was contrary to Article 34, as was the obligation to obtain a certificate of quality. What is more, the latter obligation could not be justified since it constituted arbitrary discrimination.[199]

7.94 In *Jongeneel Kaas* v. *Netherlands*[200] the Court stated that a national rule requiring producers to place on cheese a control stamp attesting compliance with national rules on quality was compatible with Article 34, provided that the requirement applied in the same way to domestic production marketed in the Member State concerned and to goods intended for export. The same held good for inspections and inspection documents. On the other hand, to require inspection documents for exports only was contrary to

---

[194] Para. 7.62 and 7.86 above.
[195] Paras. 10.13 *et seq.* below; see also para. 8.69 below.
[196] N.6 above.
[197] N.4 above.
[198] N.6 above.
[199] Para. 8.05 below.
[200] Case 237/82 [1984] E.C.R. 483, [1985] 2 C.M.L.R. 53; see paras. 10.14 *et seq.* below, noted by Waelbroeck [1985] C.M.L.Rev. 109.

Article 34. In support of the latter proposition the Court cited its earlier judgment in *Bouhelier*.

This provides welcome confirmation that *Bouhelier* is still good law after *Groenveld* v. *Produktschaap voor Vee en Vlees*,[201] as indeed it would have to be if Article 34 were not to be deprived of its meaning.[202]

Discriminatory conditions of insurance

7.95   *Haug-Adrion* v. *Frankfurter Versicherungs-AG*[203] was a somewhat unusual case. The plaintiff bought a car in Germany and exported it to Belgium where he lived. For this purpose he obtained insurance coverage for third-party liability from the defendants under conditions approved by the public authorities. Under these conditions companies were permitted not to grant a no-claims bonus for cars fitted with customs plates (*i.e.* cars intended for export). The defendant took advantage of this possibility. The plaintiff claimed that the relevant condition discriminated against exports and thus fell foul of Article 34.

The Court rejected this view. After rehearsing the *Groenveld* formula it held:

> 'National rules such as those in question in the main proceedings do not fall within that category; they merely authorise insurance companies to take into account in their tariff conditions particular circumstances in which vehicles are used which increase or diminish the insurance risk, such as, for example, the use of vehicles registered under customs plates.
>
> Quite apart from the fact that the enactment of such rules in a Member State in no way prohibits insurers in that State from granting a bonus in respect of vehicles registered under customs plates, there is nothing to suggest that a tariff condition such as that at issue in the main proceedings, covered by such rules, gives any advantage whatever to national products or to the domestic market of the Member State concerned.'

One might have thought that the granting of less favourable terms for exports, when officially approved by the State, was indeed a restriction on exports contrary to Article 34 even after *Groenveld*.

Restrictions on production

7.96   The first case to come before the Court concerning the compatibility with Article 34 of a restriction on the production of goods not covered by a common market organisation[204] was *Groenveld* itself.[205] On a reference under Article 177 the Court was asked

---

[201] Case 15/79 [1979] E.C.R. 3409, [1981] 1 C.M.L.R. 207, para. 6.66 above.
[202] For a further case on export documents, see Case 15/83 *Denkavit Nederland* v. *Hoofdproduktschap voor Akkerbouwprodukten* [1984] E.C.R. 2171, para. 4.12 above.
[203] Case 251/83 [1984] E.C.R. 4277, [1985] 3 C.M.L.R. 266, para. 4.05 above.
[204] For cases on products covered by such organisations see paras. 7.86 above and 10.09 *et seq.* below.
[205] N.201 above.

to rule on the compatibility with Article 34 of a Dutch measure prohibiting a manufacturer of processed meat products from having in stock and processing horsemeat. The plaintiffs wished to begin the manufacture of horsemeat sausages and consequently sought a determination by the courts as to the validity of this measure. The unusual aspects of the Dutch regulation were that:

— butchers dealing in horsemeat were entitled to manufacture horsemeat sausages provided they sold them directly to consumers and not to middlemen;

— the import and export of horsemeat sausages were not in themselves prohibited so that traders could import them, either from Member States or third countries, and re-export them either to Member States or third countries.

The defendant body stated that it had adopted these rules in view of the strong aversion felt in the United Kingdom, the United States and the Federal Republic of Germany to the consumption of horsemeat by human beings. The mere fact that British consumers might think that Dutch exports of processed meat might contain horsemeat would seriously harm Dutch exports. Furthermore, the defendant claimed that it was practically impossible to detect the presence of horsemeat in processed meat products, and this is why it found it necessary to prohibit manufacturers of such products from having in stock or processing horsemeat.

The Court was swayed by these arguments. It held that Article 34

'concerns national measures which have as their specific object or effect the restriction of patterns of exports and thereby the establishment of a difference in treatment between the domestic trade of a Member State and its export trade in such a way as to provide a particular advantage for national production or for the domestic market of the State in question at the expense of the production or of the trade of other Member States. This is not so in the case of a prohibition like that in question which is applied objectively to the production of goods of a certain kind without drawing a distinction depending on whether such goods are intended for the national market or for export.

The foregoing appreciation is not affected by the circumstance that the regulation in question has as its objective *inter alia* the safeguarding of the reputation of the national production of meat products in certain export markets within the Community and in non-member countries where there are obstacles of a psychological or legislative nature to the consumption of horsemeat where the same prohibition is applied identically to the product in the domestic market of the State in question. The objective nature of that prohibition is not modified by the fact that the regulation in force in the Netherlands permits the retail sale of horsemeat by butchers. In fact that concession at the level of local trade does not have the effect of bringing about a prohibition at the level of industrial manufacture of the same product regardless of its destination.'

The Court concluded that a prohibition of the kind in question was compatible with Article 34.

Yet it is submitted that there are two inconsistencies in this argument: first, the Dutch rules with respect to the domestic market allowed butchers to manufacture processed horsemeat and sell it to consumers so that the rules did not in fact discriminate against exports; secondly, the Court overlooked the fact that the effect desired by the Produtkschap could have been achieved by adequate labelling requirements, and that the prohibition was excessive for this reason. It is submitted therefore that the Court should have followed the Advocate General who found that such a measure was contrary to Article 34.

Consequently the result arrived at in the judgment, which was delivered by a Chamber of the Court, should be treated with the greatest caution.

7.97   Nevertheless, the test laid down in the first paragraph quoted above from the *Groenveld* judgment was expressly confirmed by the full Court in *Oebel*.[206] Applying this criterion, the Court found that a prohibition on night baking applying in the same way to goods intended for the domestic market and to goods intended for export was not a measure of equivalent effect within the meaning of Article 34.

Similarly, the Court ruled in *Holdijk*[207] that national legislation laying down minimum standards for enclosures for fattening calves, which does not make any distinction as to whether the animals or their meat are intended for the national market or for exports, is compatible with Article 34. Likewise, in *Jongeneel Kaas*,[208] minimum standards for cheese which made no distinction as to whether the cheese was intended for the domestic market or for export, were also held to be compatible with Article 34.

IV. CONCLUSION

7.98   This is clearly a remarkable body of case law. The Court has plotted a bold course ever since its ruling in *International Fruit* that an import licensing system constituted a measure of equivalent effect even if licences were granted automatically on demand.[209]

Nevertheless, in view of the large numbers of cases relating to Article 30, there are inevitably certain differences of approach. In particular, some judgments[210] tend to blur the distinction between the existence of a restriction and the justification for it, while most do not. Yet apart from a few difficult cases,[211] all the judgments can in their result be reconciled with the view that except as regards certain types of price control[212] the concept of measures of equivalent

---

[206] See n.123 above.
[207] Cases 141–143/81 [1982] E.C.R. 1299, [1983] 2 C.M.L.R. 635.
[208] N.200 above.
[209] See para. 7.03 above.
[210] See *e.g.* para. 7.41 above.
[211] See in particular paras. 7.07 and 7.87.
[212] See para. 7.82 above.

effect under Article 30 generally embraces all restrictions on imports not covered by any other provision in the Treaty and regardless of whether such restrictions discriminate against imports. On the other hand, as regards measures of equivalent effect under Article 34 the basic principles do not yet appear to have been fully worked out.

CHAPTER VIII

The main exception: Article 36 EEC and the 'mandatory requirements'

8.01 Article 36[1] of the EEC Treaty reads:

> 'The provisions of Articles 30 to 34 shall not preclude prohibitions or restrictions on imports, exports or goods in transit justified on grounds of public morality, public policy or public security; the protection of health and life of humans, animals or plants; the protection of national treasures possessing artistic, historic or archaeological value; or the protection of industrial and commercial property. Such prohibitions or restrictions shall not, however, constitute a means of arbitrary discrimination or a disguised restriction on trade between Member States.'[2]

The wording of this provision shows that it applies both to quantitative restrictions and to measures of equivalent effect. Furthermore, it covers the latter whether they are 'distinctly' or 'indistinctly applicable.'[3] Moreover, it is also clear from the wording of Article 36 that it merely entitles the Member States to exercise certain powers subject to certain limits: it does not oblige them to exercise those powers.

As the Court held in *Bauhuis* v. *Netherlands,*[4] Article 36 'constitutes a derogation from the basic rule that all obstacles to the free movement of goods between Member States shall be eliminated and must be interpreted strictly'. As explained in paragraph 9.01 below, it shares this trait with the other exceptions to the prohibition on restrictions on the free movement of goods between Member States.

---

[1] See generally Ehlermann 'Die Bedeutung des Artikels 36 EWGV für die Freiheit des Warenverkehrs' [1973] EuR 1 and materials cited in nn.81, 103, 119 and 131 to Chap. VI.
[2] This provision is clearly modelled on the considerably lengthier Art. XX of GATT which begins: 'Subject to the requirement that such measures are not applied in a manner which would constitute a means of arbitrary or unjustifiable discrimination between countries where the same conditions prevail, or a disguised restriction on international trade, nothing in this Agreement shall be construed to prevent the adoption or enforcement by any contracting party of measures: (a) necessary to protect public morals; (b) necessary to protect human, animal or plant life or health . . . etc.' However, the exceptions allowed by the two Arts. are not all identical: in particular, Art. XX includes a number of specific exceptions such as restrictions on the import or export of gold or silver and restrictions on the products of prison labour, which are not to be found in Art. 36 EEC.
[3] For this terminology, see para. 6.32 above.
[4] Case 46/76 [1977] E.C.R. 5.

8.02 As has already been mentioned at some length in Chapter VI,[5] the Court in *Cassis de Dijon*[6] and subsequent cases has recognised a series of 'mandatory requirements' in addition to the grounds of justification in Article 36: the 'mandatory requirements' recognised so far are the effectiveness of fiscal supervision, consumer protection, the prevention of unfair competition, the improvement of working conditions and, it would seem, the protection of the environment; but the list is not closed. The Court insists that these 'mandatory requirements' fall under Article 30 and not Article 36; and it also purports to follow a different approach when deciding whether a given measure is justified under a 'mandatory requirement' from that which it follows in relation to Article 36. Yet the two approaches appear to lead to the same result in each case. Accordingly, it is appropriate to deal with Article 36 and the 'mandatory requirements' in one and the same chapter.

8.03 The Court has held that a national authority relying on Article 36 bears the burden of proving that contentious measures are justified under that provision: *Denkavit Futtermittel* v. *Minister of Agriculture*.[7] It is submitted that this ruling cannot be limited to national authorities, so that any party seeking to rely on Article 36 bears the burden of proof. Indeed, it is submitted that the Court made the same point in relation to the 'mandatory requirements' in *Gilli and Andres*[8] when it held:

> 'It is only where national rules . . . may be justified as being necessary in order to satisfy imperative requirements relating in particular to the protection of public health, the fairness of commercial transactions and the defence of the consumer that they may constitute an exception to the requirements arising under Article 30.'

8.04 Having made these preliminary points we can now turn to the essence of Article 36. This is that to be justified under that exception a national provision:

— must fall within one of the grounds of justification set out in the first sentence or within one of the other 'mandatory requirements'; and

— must not constitute arbitrary discrimination nor a disguised restriction on trade between Member States and must be justified.

Although it is rather artificial to separate the two conditions, it is necessary to do so here. It is appropriate to deal with the second condition before the first.

---

[5] Para. 6.40 *et seq.* above.
[6] Case 120/78 *Rewe-Zentral* v. *Bundesmonopolverwaltung für Branntwein* [1979] E.C.R. 649, [1979] 3 C.M.L.R. 494.
[7] Case 251/78 [1979] E.C.R. 3369, [1980] 3 C.M.L.R. 513.
[8] Case 788/79 [1980] E.C.R. 2071, [1981] 1 C.M.L.R. 146; para. 6.43 above.

I. PROPORTIONALITY AND NON-DISCRIMINATION

'Arbitrary discrimination'

8.05   It is generally considered that the word 'arbitrary' is super-fluous in Article 36.[9] Its use is no doubt due to the fact that the term 'arbitrary discrimination' appears in Article XX of GATT, on which Article 36 is modelled. Such discrimination can take the following forms:

— the most obvious is discrimination against imports in favour of domestic products, either by applying a restriction to imported products only or by applying a greater restriction with respect to imported products. An example is Case 152/78 *E.C. Commission* v. *France*[10] where advertising restrictions on alcoholic drinks were framed in such a way as to fall more heavily on imports. The Court held that, even though in principle advertising restrictions on alcoholic drinks would be justified under Article 36 on public health grounds, the particular measures in question were not so justified because they constituted arbitrary discrimination—even though some domestically produced drinks were caught by the heavier restrictions[11];

— conversely, a restriction falling solely or more heavily on exports to the exclusion of products intended for the domestic market also constitutes arbitrary discrimination. Thus in *Bouhelier*[12] the requirement to obtain certificates of quality for exports of watches was held to constitute arbitrary discrimination, since no corresponding obligation existed as regards watches intended for the domestic market[13];

— *Dassonville*[14] shows that discrimination between imports coming directly from the State of production and indirect imports will constitute arbitrary discrimination.[15] The *Dassonville* case itself shows that this holds good even where the goods were produced outside the Community: at the material time the United Kingdom had not yet acceded to the Community;

— it can be deduced from the *De Peijper*[16] case discussed below that discrimination against parallel imports will also constitute arbitrary discrimination;

---

[9] Ehlermann in Groeben, Boeckh, Thiesing, *Kommentar zum EWG-Vertrag* (1974) 293–294; see, however, Graf, *Der Begriff 'Maßnahmen gleicher Wirkung wie mengenmässige Einfuhrbeschränkungen' in dem EWG-Vertrag* (1972) 106 *et seq.*

[10] [1980] E.C.R. 2299, [1981] 2 C.M.L.R. 743; see para. 7.31 above.

[11] Similarly, see Case 121/85 *Conegate* v. *H.M. Customs and Excise* [1986] 1 C.M.L.R. 739, para. 8.29 below.

[12] Case 53/76 [1977] E.C.R. 197, [1977] 1 C.M.L.R. 436.

[13] It is true that Art. 36 was not expressly mentioned, but the mere use of the words 'arbitrary discrimination' in the judgment can be taken as an implied reference to that provision.

[14] Case 8/74 [1974] E.C.R. 837, [1974] 2 C.M.L.R. 436.

[15] See paras. 7.04 *et seq.* above.

[16] Case 104/75 [1976] E.C.R. 613, [1976] 2 C.M.L.R. 271.

— finally, where Member State A discriminates in favour of goods coming from or originating in Member State B as against those coming from or originating in Member State C, that is also arbitrary discrimination.

8.06   However, there will be no arbitrary discrimination in any of these cases if the difference of treatment is objectively justified. Thus in a quite different context in *Italy* v. *EEC Commission*[17] the Court defined the principle of non-discrimination under the Treaty as follows: 'The different treatment of non-comparable situations does not lead automatically to the conclusion that there is discrimination. An appearance of discrimination in form may therefore correspond in fact to an absence of discrimination in substance. Discrimination in substance would consist in treating either similar situations differently or different situations identically.'

Also, in *Rewe-Zentralfinanz* v. *Landwirtschaftskammer*[18] the Court was asked, *inter alia*, whether the obligation to submit imports of apples to phytosanitary controls constituted arbitrary discrimination under Article 36, when no corresponding requirement existed with respect to domestically produced apples. The Court replied that:

'The different treatment of imported and domestic products, based on the need to prevent the spread of the harmful organism could not, however, be regarded as arbitrary discrimination if effective measures are taken in order to prevent the distribution of contaminated domestic products and if there is reason to believe, in particular on the basis of previous experience, that there is a risk of the harmful organism's spreading if no inspection is held on importation.'

8.07   On a different but related point the Court held in *Procureur du Roi* v. *Debauve*[19] that 'differences, which are due to natural phenomena, cannot be described as "discrimination" within the meaning of the Treaty; the latter regards only differences in treatment arising from human activity.' Although this case concerned services rather than goods, it is submitted that this particular part of the judgment is of general application. The case involved the prosecution of a number of individuals and undertakings engaged in the diffusion in Belgium of cable television from other Member States for infringing the prohibition on television advertising in Belgium. One of the questions referred by the Belgian court under Article 177 was whether a prohibition of this kind constituted 'discrimination based on the geographical locality of the foreign broadcasting station which would be able to transmit advertisements only within its natural receiving zone [inside Belgian territory], as these zones may, because

---

[17] Case 13/63 [1963] E.C.R. 165, [1963] C.M.L.R. 289; the case concerned Art. 226 (see Chap. IX, n.4).
[18] Case 4/75 [1975] E.C.R. 843, [1977] 1 C.M.L.R. 599.
[19] Case 52/79, [1980] E.C.R. 881, [1981] 2 C.M.L.R. 362; see para. 2.05 above.

of the differences in density of population, be of very different interest from the advertising point of view.' The point of this question was that even if the prohibition on television advertising in Belgium covered re-transmission by cable television of broadcasts of other Member States, nevertheless broadcasting networks in neighbouring countries could not avoid reaching certain frontier districts of Belgium. The Court, however, reached the conclusion that this would not constitute discrimination.

8.08   What if the laws of some of the constituent parts of a Member State are less restrictive than the measures applying to imports into the entire territory of that Member State? This was essentially one of the issues in *R. v. Henn and Darby*,[20] which concerned the offence of importing 'indecent or obscene articles' into the United Kingdom. That offence covered certain categories of article which might lawfully be sold in some, but not all, constituent parts of the United Kingdom. On this point the Court held that:

> 'the fact that certain differences exist between the laws enforced in the different constituent parts of a Member State does not thereby prevent that State from applying a unitary concept in regard to prohibitions on imports imposed on grounds of public morality, on trade with other Member States.'

Later passages of the judgment could perhaps be taken as implied acceptance by the Court of the Advocate General's view[21] that 'where the Member State concerned is so constituted that there are variations in the laws of different parts of it, that in my opinion is a factor—it may be an important factor—to be taken into account in applying the test' of whether more restrictive treatment of imports is reasonable. This judgment will be more closely examined under the heading 'public morality' below.

'Disguised restriction'

8.09   It has been suggested[22] that Article 36 would have much the same meaning even if this expression were not there. Yet in *Henn and Darby*[23] the Court stated that the second sentence of Article 36 'is designed to prevent restrictions on trade based on the grounds mentioned in the first sentence of Article 36 from being diverted from their proper purpose.'[24] This may presumably be taken as an interpretation of the words 'disguised restriction.'

The Court built on this ruling in *E.C. Commission v. United Kingdom*.[25] This case concerned a ban on imports into the United

---

[20] Case 34/79 [1979] E.C.R. 3795, [1980] 1 C.M.L.R. 246, noted by Faull [1980] C.D.E. 446; Weiler [1981] M.L.R. 91, Catchpole and Barav [1980] *Leg. Issues Eur. Int.* 1. The Court's judgment was applied by the House of Lords at [1980] 2 W..L.R. 633.
[21] At 3831 (E.C.R.), 265 (C.M.L.R.).
[22] Ehlermann, *op. cit.* 294.
[23] N.20 above.
[24] With respect to trade marks, see para. 8.115 *et seq.*
[25] Case 40/82 [1982] E.C.R. 2793, [1982] 3 C.M.L.R. 497.

Kingdom of poultry products, eggs and egg products from those Member States (including France) which did not have a policy of slaughtering flocks infected with Newcastle disease. The United Kingdom sought to justify this ban on animal health grounds. However, the Court found that its real purpose was to protect domestic production. It deduced this from a number of facts. First of all, for some months prior to the introduction of the ban the British Government had been subject to pressure from domestic poultry producers to block imports. This was well documented in the British press. Secondly the ban was announced on 27 August 1981 and came into effect on 1 September 1981. It was thus introduced so hastily that the Commission and the Member States were neither consulted nor even informed in good time. This timing also had the effect of excluding French Christmas turkeys from the British market for the 1981 season. Thirdly, when France sought to comply with the new British requirements, the United Kingdom refused to take cognizance of it, adding a further requirement which France did not meet. The Court concluded that the import ban constituted a disguised restriction on imports.

The view that a measure is not justified under Article 36 if it is enacted for protectionist reasons would clearly lead to questionable results. It would mean that, even where a measure was in itself undoubtedly justified under Article 36, it could nevertheless be held to fall outside the protection of that Article on the grounds that the Member State concerned had acted out of the wrong motives. Not only would this create considerable legal uncertainty, but it would also have the undesirable result that measures would be unlawful even though they were justified in themselves. However, the Court avoided this pitfall: it held in effect that, since the import ban constituted a disguised restriction on trade between Member States, the presumption that it was not justified under Article 36 was increased. It thus left room for a finding that the ban was justified on animal health grounds although it constituted a disguised restriction on trade between Member States. In the event it found that the ban was not so justified.

There is some difficulty in reconciling this reasoning with the language of Article 36 which suggests that, if a measure is caught by the second sentence, it cannot be justified. Thus it appears preferable to regard protectionist motives as *evidence* that a measure is not justified. This appears to be the approach following by the Court in *E.C. Commission* v. *France* ('Italian wine').[26]

'Justified'

8.10 According to the rule of proportionality a measure may not restrict trade between Member States more than is necessary to

---

[26] Case 42/82 [1983] E.C.R. 1013, [1984] 1 C.M.L.R. 160, para. 8.39 below.

achieve its legitimate object. This was clearly set out by the Court in *De Peijper*[27] as follows:

> 'It emerges from Article 36 that national rules or practices which do restrict imports of pharmaceutical products or are capable of doing so are only compatible with the Treaty to the extent to which they are necessary for the effective protection of health and life of humans.
>
> National rules or practices do not fall within the exception specified in Article 36 if the health and life of humans can [be] as effectively protected by measures which do not restrict intra-Community trade so much.'

The Court made the same point in a different way in *Eggers* v. *Freie Hansestadt Bremen*[28] when it held:

> 'Article 36 is an exception to the fundamental principle of the free movement of goods and must, therefore, be interpreted in such a way that its scope is not extended any further than is *necessary*[29] for the protection of those interests which it is intended to secure.'

It is submitted that the Court was making the same point once again in *Cassis de Dijon*[30] when it held: 'Obstacles to movement within the Community . . . must be accepted in so far as those provisions may be recognised as being necessary in order to satisfy mandatory requirements.'

8.11   Moreover, the Court also held in the *De Peijper* case that:

> 'Article 36 cannot be relied on to justify rules or practices which, even though they are beneficial, contain restrictions which are explained primarily by concern to lighten the administration's burden or reduce public expenditure, unless, in the absence of the said rules or practices, this burden or expenditure clearly would exceed the limits of what can reasonably be required.'[31]

8.12   In paragraph 8.09 it was suggested that, where the Member State is proved to have acted out of protectionist motives, that is *evidence* that the measure concerned is not justified. The ruling in *E.C. Commission* v. *France* ('Italian wine')[32] appears to constitute authority for this proposition.

Quite apart from statements made by the authorities of the Member State concerned, the following have been taken by the Court to show the existence of protectionist motives[33]: pressure from domestic producers to restrict imports; the sudden introduction

---

[27] See n.16 above.

[28] Case 13/78 [1978] E.C.R. 1935, [1979] 1 C.M.L.R. 562; para. 7.40 above.

[29] The italics are those of the author.

[30] See n.6 above.

[31] See also para. 8.35 below. At first sight this statement would appear to mean that the avoidance of undue expenditure is itself a ground of justification under Art. 36. On closer examination, however, it would seem that it is an interpretation of 'justified.' This means that the avoidance of undue expenditure can only justify a restriction on trade when it is linked to a ground of justification, in this case public health. For this view see Ehlermann 'Das Verbot der Maßnahmen gleicher Wirkung in der Rechtsprechung des Gerichtshofes' in *Festschrift für Ipsen* (1977), 579 at 590–591.

[32] Case 42/82, n.26 above.

[33] See Cases 40/82, n.25 above, and 42/82, n.26 above.

of a measure without consultation of the Commission or the other Member States; and inconsistent or erratic action.

8.13   A further principle of Article 36 is that it cannot be used by a Member State to impose its own standards or morals on other Member States. This point was made—perhaps even overstated—by the Advocate General in *Dassonville*[34] when he said that on the basis of this provision Member States may derogate from the prohibition on quantitative restrictions and measures of equivalent effect 'only for the purpose of the protection of their own interests and not for the protection of the interests of other States.'

However, this principle is clearly subject to limitations, as is shown by *Bauhuis* v. *Netherlands*.[35] One of the questions which arose there was whether, even in the absence of Community legislation, exporting Member States could carry out veterinary and public health controls on animals for the benefit of the importing Member State. The Court held that such a practice was compatible with Article 36. This was subsequently confirmed in Case 89/76 *E.C. Commission* v. *Netherlands*[36] concerning phytosanitary inspections on plants. Moreover, it is submitted that a Member State is entitled to prohibit trade in animals or plants threatened with extinction even if they are not indigenous to that Member State.[37]

8.14   Next, what if imports are subject to restrictions justified under Article 36 but the public authorities are empowered to relax the restrictions in individual cases?

In *Denkavit Futtermittel*[38] the Court ruled as follows:

'Article 36 of the Treaty cannot be interpreted as meaning that it forbids in principle a national authority, which has imposed by a general rule veterinary and public health restrictions on imports . . ., from providing that it will be possible to derogate therefrom by individual measures left to the discretion of the administration if such derogations assist the simplification of the restrictions imposed by the general rules and if this power of derogation does not[39] give rise to arbitrary discrimination between traders of different Member States.

Nevertheless it does not automatically follow that each of the conditions to which the national authority subjects the grant of authorisation itself complies with what is permitted by Article 36. It is in each case for the national courts . . . to determine whether these conditions are necessary to attain the objective which Article 36 allows to be sought. . . .'

This approach was later confirmed by the Court in *Fietje*.[40] There it held:

---

[34] N.14 above at 860.
[35] See n.4 above.
[36] [1977] E.C.R. 1355, [1978] 3 C.M.L.R. 630.
[37] Wägenbaur in Groeben, Boeckh, Thiesing, Ehlermann *Kommentar zum EWG-Vertrag* (1983) Vol. I at 291.
[38] See n.7 above.
[39] The word 'not' is missing from the English text but it is clear from the sense and from other language texts that it should be there.
[40] Case 27/80, [1980] E.C.R. 3839, [1981] 3 C.M.L.R. 722.

'in the case of a measure justified on grounds recognised by the Treaty, the Treaty does not forbid in principle provision being made for the possibility of granting derogations therefrom by individual decisions left to the discretion of the administration. However, exceptions must not lead to the favouring of domestic products because this would constitute arbitrary discrimination against or a disguised restriction on products imported from other Member States.'

On the other hand, said the Court in *Denkavit Futtermittel,* if the individual dispensation 'only made possible a relaxation of a general supervisory system which went beyond what Article 36 permits it would be necessary to consider it on its own merits in the light of the exceptions permitted by Article 36. . . . '[41]

8.15 Lastly, as regards the relationship between Article 36 and Community legislation, the Court held in *Simmenthal* v. *Italian Minister of Finance*[42] that:

'Article 36 is not designed to reserve certain matters to the exclusive jurisdiction of Member States but permits national laws to derogate from the principle of the free movement of goods to the extent to which such derogation is and continues to be justified for the attainment of the objectives referred to in that Article.'

The question referred by the national court was whether systematic veterinary and public health checks on meat imports into Italy from another Member State were compatible with Articles 30 and 36. The Court found that certain Community Directives harmonising health checks in the exporting Member State rendered systematic import checks unnecessary so that they were no longer justified under Article 36.

In the subsequent cases of *Tedeschi* v. *Denkavit,*[43] *Ratti,*[44] and *Denkavit Futtermittel* v. *Minister of Agriculture*[45] the Court repeated the passage quoted above, adding:

'Where, in application of Article 100 of the Treaty, Community directives provide for the harmonisation of the measures necessary to ensure the protection of animal and human health and establish Community procedures to check that they are observed, recourse to Article 36 is no longer justified and the appropriate checks must be carried out and the measures of protection adopted within the framework outlined by the harmonising directive.'[46]

8.16 This is not to say that every Directive provides exhaustive guarantees such as to oust the application of Article 36.[47] It is a

---

[41] See also Case 82/77 *Van Tiggele* [1978] E.C.R. 25, [1978] 2 C.M.L.R. 528; para. 7.72 above.

[42] Case 35/76 [1976] E.C.R. 1871, [1977] 2 C.M.L.R. 1.

[43] Case 5/77 [1977] E.C.R. 1555, [1978] 1 C.M.L.R. 1.

[44] Case 148/78 [1979] E.C.R. 1629, [1980] 1 C.M.L.R. 96.

[45] See n.7 above.

[46] This passage is in fact taken from the *Tedeschi* case; there are insignificant textual differences between the three judgments; see also Case 28/84 *E.C. Commission* v. *Germany* (compound feedingstuffs) [1985] E.C.R. 3097.

[47] Even a Reg. setting up a common organisation of the market may fail to oust Art. 36 in the absence of express wording: written question 468/80 ([1980] O.J., C302/3) concerning a ban on growing hemp. However, this will only occur in highly exceptional circumstances.

question of the wording of each Directive whether the guarantees it provides are exhaustive. Thus in the *Rewe-Zentralfinanz*[48] case concerning phytosanitary controls on apple imports to check for San José Scale insects, the Court found that recourse could still be had by Member States to Article 36 in spite of the existence of a Directive[49] on the control of that very insect; this was because that Directive expressly authorised the Member States to adopt such stricter provisions as might be necessary.[50]

In this context the ruling in *Campus Oil* v. *Minister for Industry and Energy*[51] is of some concern. This case concerned a requirement that importers of petroleum products into Ireland purchase a specified proportion of their supplies from the one remaining Irish refinery. Ireland maintained that it was necessary to keep the refinery in operation so as to guarantee supplies, particularly in the event of a crisis. Yet the Community had adopted legislation[52] designed to meet this very problem, and this required Member States *inter alia* to maintain minimum stocks of petroleum products of at least 90 days' average consumption. While acknowledging that this legislation provided 'certain guarantees' in this regard to a Member State with no or virtually no crude oil of its own, the Court considered that it did not afford 'an unconditional assurance that supplies will in any event be maintained at least at a level sufficient to meet its minimum needs'; it therefore found that this legislation did not preclude a Member State from relying on Article 36. Read literally this ruling appears alarming: as Currall[53] has pointed out, it is difficult to imagine that any measure can give an unconditional assurance that the interest in question will be protected in all circumstances. Indeed, the 'unconditional assurance' test is at variance with the Court's case law on Article 36, which requires the Member States to admit imports affording less than absolute guarantees with regard to health and safety.

8.17 On the other hand, directives cannot extend the powers enjoyed by the Member States under Article 36. This was held in *De Peijper*,[54] which was concerned with the formalities laid down by the Dutch authorities for giving approval to pharmaceutical products imported from other Member States. Having ruled that

[48] See n.18 above. See also Case 73/84 *Denkavit Futtermittel* v. *Land Nordrhein-Westfalen* [1985] E.C.R. 103, [1986] 2 C.M.L.R. 482.
[49] Dir. 69/466 ([1969] J.O. L323/5).
[50] See also *e.g.* Case 406/85 *Gofette* (judgment of 11 June 1987).
[51] Case 72/83 [1984] E.C.R. 2727, [1984] 3 C.M.L.R. 544; see para. 8.20.
[52] Council Dir. 68/414 ([1968] II O.J. Spec.Ed. 586) as amended by Council Dir. 72/425 ([1972] J.O. L291/154); Council Dir. 73/238 ([1973] O.J. L228/1); and Council Dir. 77/186 ([1977] O.J. L61/23) and 77/706 ([1977] O.J. L292/9).
[53] 'Some Aspects of the Relation between Articles 30–36 and Article 100 of the EEC Treaty, with a closer look at optimal harmonisation' [1984] Y.E.L. 169 at 189; see also Gormley *Prohibiting Restrictions on Trade within the EEC* (1985) at 137–138.
[54] See n.16 above.

formalities of this kind might constitute measures of equivalent effect the Court went on to consider the contention of the British, Danish and Dutch Governments that such measures were necessary to comply with the Council Directives on the approximation of national provisions relating to proprietary medicinal products.[55] The Court rejected this contention on the grounds that 'the sole aim of these directives is to harmonise national provisions in this field; they do not and cannot aim at extending the very considerable powers left to Member States in the field of public health by Article 36.' This is merely a particular manifestation of the general rule discussed earlier in this book to the effect that Community legislation may not create undue barriers to trade between Member States.[56]

II. THE GROUNDS OF JUSTIFICATION

8.18   As explained at the beginning of this chapter, it is intended to cover here the 'mandatory requirements' set out in the *Cassis de Dijon* case[57]: the 'effectiveness of fiscal supervision' (*i.e.* the prevention of tax evasion), the 'fairness of commercial transactions' (*i.e.* the prevention of unfair competition) and consumer protection. The protection of the environment and the improvement of working conditions will also be discussed.

It is submitted that these requirements are in practice treated by the Court in the same way as the grounds of justification set out in Article 36.[58] For reasons of convenience these points will be considered before industrial and commercial property.

8.19   It must be borne in mind, however, that in Case 7/61 *EEC Commission* v. *Italy*,[59] the first case on Article 36, the Court held that Article 36 is directed to eventualities of a non-domestic kind. The importance of this rule cannot be sufficiently stressed: if it were otherwise, a coach and horses would be driven through the very principle of the free movement of goods. Thus it is by no means surprising to find the Court re-affirming this rule on numerous occasions recently.[60] It follows that such objects as the promotion of employment or investment, curbing inflation and controlling the balance of payments fall outside Article 36. Similarly in *Sandoz*[61] the Court held that it could not under any circumstances be justified under Article 36 for the authorities of a Member State to refuse to

---

[55] Dir. 65/65 ([1965] O.J. Spec.Ed. 20); Dirs. 75/318 and 75/319 ([1975] O.J. L147/13).
[56] Para. 4.08 *et seq.*
[57] See n.6 above.
[58] Paras. 6.40 *et seq.* above.
[59] [1961] E.C.R. 317, [1962] C.M.L.R. 39.
[60] *E.g.* Cases 95/81 *E.C. Commission* v. *Italy* (import deposits) [1982] E.C.R. 2187; 288/83 *E.C. Commission* v. *Ireland* (Cyprus potatoes) [1985] E.C.R. 1761, [1985] 3 C.M.L.R. 152; for a difficult case see, however, Case 238/82 *Duphar* v. *Netherlands* [1984] E.C.R. 523, [1985] 1 C.M.L.R. 256, see para. 7.62 above.
[61] Case 174/82 [1983] E.C.R. 2445, [1984] 3 C.M.L.R. 43.

authorise the sale of a product on the ground that there was no demand for it.

The same rules must apply to the mandatory requirements if the principle of the free movement of goods is not to be undermined.

8.20 In *Campus Oil*[62] Ireland argued that the requirement that importers of petroleum products purchase a specified proportion of their needs from the one remaining Irish refinery was justified for the purpose of ensuring essential supplies, particularly in the event of a crisis, although Ireland has no crude oil of its own. At the same time, this requirement plainly served to keep the refinery in operation and was thus of economic benefit to Ireland. The two aims were indissociable. After confirming that 'Article 36 refers to matters of a non-economic nature', the Court went on:

> 'However, in the light of the seriousness of the consequences that an interruption in supplies of petroleum products may have for a country's existence, the aim of ensuring a minimum supply of petroleum products at all times is to be regarded as transcending purely economic considerations and thus as capable of constituting an objective covered by the concept of public security.'

This may apply whenever a measure is based equally on economic grounds and on grounds which are admissible under Article 36 or the 'mandatory requirements.' However, when the economic purpose is predominant the measure cannot be justified.[63]

8.21 The Court has, it is true, accepted that a Member State may take limited measures to prevent imports being used to speculate in currency or to export capital which it is not required to liberalise. In *E.C. Commission* v. *Italy*[64] the defendant argued that legislation making the advance payment for imports subject to the lodging of a deposit was justified for preventing currency speculation. Although the Court dismissed this argument, it accepted that 'the Member States remain free to employ all means of ensuring that payments made abroad relate exclusively to genuine transactions, subject always to the condition that such means do not hinder the freedom of intra-Community trade as defined in the Treaty.' This raises the question of the definition of genuine transactions', a point discussed earlier in this book.[65] The Court appeared to go further in *E.C. Commission* v. *Greece*,[66] where the defendant maintained that a ban on the import of certain cuts of meat was justified to prevent unlawful exports of capital. This argument was dismissed on the

---

[62] See n.51 above. See also Case 118/86 *Nertsvoederfabriek Nederland* (judgment of 6 October 1987).
[63] In any case, the existence of an economic incentive for the Member State to adopt the measure will be evidence that it is not justified: para. 8.09 above.
[64] Case 95/81, n.60 above.
[65] Para. 7.29 above.
[66] Case 124/85 [1988] 2 C.M.L.R. 518.

grounds that 'measures which, as in this case, impede intra-Community trade more than is necessary cannot come within the scope of the power which the Member States continue to have with regard to the control of transfers of foreign currency.' Unlike the judgment in *E.C. Commission* v. *Italy,* this passage, if read literally, necessarily implies that limited restrictions on genuine imports may be justified for these purposes.

However, even if that is so, it should not be thought that this is an exception to the principle that measures falling under Article 30 or Article 34 cannot be justified on purely economic grounds. Rather, if it exists at all, this exception must flow from the Community provisions on the free movement of capital. Indeed the passage just quoted from *E.C. Commission* v. *Italy* is based on Article 5 of the first capital Directive.[67]

8.22 The first four grounds of justification are similar to the exceptions to the free movement of workers, the freedom of establishment and the free provision of services as regards public policy, public security and public health (Articles 48(3), 56(1) and 66 respectively).[68] It is probable that the same meaning should be given to those terms in Article 36 as in the equivalent Articles, yet this is not necessarily so. Certain disparities will be due to the inherent differences between movements of goods on the one hand and persons and services on the other. Other differences may be due to the fact that the list of grounds in Article 36 is more detailed so that the term 'public policy' can be interpreted more narrowly.

8.23 *Cinéthèque* v. *Fédération Nationale des Cinémas Français*[69] is probably the only case in which the Court has held a restriction falling under Article 30 or Article 34 to be justified without specifying the grounds of justification. The case concerned national legislation providing that, within one year of the authorisation to show a film, no video cassettes of that film could be sold or hired for private showing unless either: (a) a dispensation had been granted by the competent authorities; or (b) the film was not being shown at all in the cinemas during that period. Production of video cassettes in France during the one-year period was not forbidden, nor was there any ban on imports. The alleged aim of this legislation was

---

[67] Dir. of 11 May 1960 ([1960] O.J. Spec.Ed. 921), as amended; see para. 2.06 above.

[68] On workers see in particular Dir. 64/221 ([1964] J.O. 850) Case 41/74 *Van Duyn* v. *Home Office* [1974] E.C.R. 1337, [1975] 1 C.M.L.R. 1; Case 30/77 *R.* v. *Bouchereau* [1977] E.C.R. 1999, [1977] 2 C.M.L.R. 800; Wooldridge, 'Free Movement of EEC Nationals: "The limitation based on public policy and public security"' [1977] E.L.Rev. 190, Evans, 'Ordre Public, Public Policy and the United Kingdom Immigration Law' [1978] E.L.Rev. 370; Hartley, *EEC Immigration Law* (1978), Chap. 5; on services see in particular Dir. 64/221 already referred to and Case 52/79 *Procureur du Roi* v. *Debauve* [1980] E.C.R. 881, [1981] 2 C.M.L.R. 362; Case 62/79 *Coditel* v. *Ciné Vog Films* [1980] E.C.R. 883, [1981] 2 C.M.L.R. 362.

[69] Cases 60 and 61/84 [1985] E.C.R. 2605, [1986] 1 C.M.L.R. 365.

to protect the film industry, although it was clearly also highly beneficial to cinema owners. The Court found that such legislation was contrary to Article 30 unless it was justified. As to justification it said simply this:

'. . . a national system which, in order to encourage the creation of cinematographic works irrespective of their origin, gives priority, for a limited initial period, to the distribution of such works through the cinema, is so justified.'

This case was undoubtedly one of considerable difficulty.[70] Yet the practice of ruling a restriction to be justified, without specifying under what head of Article 36 or under what 'mandatory requirement' it falls, is scarcely conducive to legal certainty and is therefore to be regretted.

8.24 On another point, in *E.C. Commission* v. *France*[71] the defendant Member State argued that its ban on the sale of substitute milk powder was justified in view of the Community's vast surpluses of milk and milk powder: to allow substitutes would, it claimed, undermine the common agricultural policy. The Court gave this argument short shrift, stating that, even if national measures bolstered a common policy, they could not run counter to one of the fundamental principles of the Community such as the free movement of goods unless they were justified on grounds recognised in Community law.[72]

8.25 Finally, can the European Convention on Human Rights be used as a guide to the interpretation of Article 36 and the meaning of the 'mandatory requirements'? One would have thought that it could. While the Court has fallen short of ruling that the Convention binds the Community as such or is part of Community law as such, it has asserted[73] that it provides guidelines for the Court when laying down those fundamental rules which are part of Community law. Furthermore the judgment in *Rutili* v. *Minister for the Interior*[74] strongly suggests that Article 48(3) is to be read in the light of the Convention; this is of particular relevance since, as mentioned in paragraph 8.22, Article 48(3) is analogous to Article 36. Consequently, it is by no means surprising to find Advocate General Warner referring to a judgment of the European Court of Human Rights for assistance in interpreting the public morality exception in Article 36 in *Henn and Darby*.[75]

---

[70] See para. 8.93 below.
[71] Case 216/84 (judgment of 23 February 1988).
[72] See also Cases 407/85 *Drei Glocken* v. *USL* and 90/86 *Zoni* (judgments of 14 July 1988) (prohibition on the sale of pasta made wholly or partly from soft wheat contrary to Article 30).
[73] *E.g.* Cases 4/73 *Nold* v. *Commission* [1974] E.C.R. 491 at 507, [1974] 2 C.M.L.R. 338, 44/79 *Hauer* v. *Land Rheinland-Pfalz* [1979] E.C.R. 3727 at 3745, [1980] 3 C.M.L.R. 42 and 63/83 *R.* v. *Kirk* [1984] E.C.R. 2689 at 2718, [1984] 3 C.M.L.R. 522 at 538.
[74] Case 36/75 [1975] E.C.R. 1205.
[75] N.20 above.

Advocate General Slynn expressed the same view in *Cinéthèque*[76] where the plaintiffs had contended that the contested provision was in breach of the principle of the freedom of expression enshrined in Article 10 of the Convention and therefore incompatible with Community law. However, the Court saw no merit whatsoever in the plaintiff's argument based on the Convention, dismissing it with a single phrase in the following terms:

> 'Although it is true that it is the duty of this Court to ensure observance of fundamental rights in the field of Community law, it has no power to examine the compatibility with the European Convention of national legislation which concerns, as in this case, an area which falls within the jurisdiction of the national legislators.'[77]

In this case one cannot but agree with the Court that little assistance was in fact to be derived from Article 10 of the Convention; this was simply because in view of the dearth of relevant pronouncements of the European Commission and European Court of Human Rights it was a highly vexed question whether national legislation of the kind in question was compatible with this provision. Surely in these circumstances it would have been fruitless for the Court first to have decided the meaning of Article 10 as an 'incidental question' and then to use its finding as an aid to interpretation of the Treaty of Rome.

Yet the Court's apparent absolute refusal to have regard to the Convention at all is not easy to reconcile with the earlier cases referred to, notably *Rutili*.

Public morality

8.26 The first judgment[78] of the Court of Justice on public morality under Article 36 is *Henn and Darby*.[79] At its simplest the Court's decision in this case means that a Member State may rely on this provision to prohibit imports of pornographic material when there is no lawful trade in such goods within its territory. Yet on closer examination it proves more complex.

The facts were that the defendants were convicted of importing into the United Kingdom a lorry-load of pornographic films and magazines originating in Denmark, contrary to section 42 of the Customs Consolidation Act 1876. The object of the reference was

---

[76] See n.69 above.

[77] At 2627.

[78] See however, written question 375/77 ([1977] O.J. C265/8): the Commission took the view that a Member State, which bans cruelty in the rearing and slaughtering of poultry (*e.g.* a ban on battery rearing), may *not* ban imports from other Member States applying less stringent rules. In particular, such an import ban would not be justified on the grounds of public morality, since 'any affront to public morals . . . would occur solely in the country where the cruel treatment takes place and can be witnessed by the local population, and not in the importing country.' This view may perhaps be regarded as unduly restrictive, if it is indeed correct that a Member State is entitled to prohibit trade in animals or plants threatened with extinction even if they are not indigenous to that Member State. (See para. 8.13 above.)

[79] See n.20 above.

primarily to ascertain whether this provision was compatible with Articles 30 and 36.[80]

As to whether such a measure was justified on the grounds of public morality within the meaning of Article 36, the Court ruled:

> 'In principle, it is for each Member State to determine in accordance with its own scale of values and in the form selected by it the requirements of public morality in its territory. In any event, it cannot be disputed that the statutory provisions applied by the United Kingdom in regard to the importation of articles having an indecent or obscene character come within the powers reserved to the Member States by the first sentence of Article 36.'

The use of the words 'in principle' indicates that the Member States may only exercise their discretion within the boundaries of a Community-wide concept of public morality. This is much the same as the Court's rulings on the concept of public policy in Article 48(3) in *Van Duyn* v. *Home Office* and *R.* v. *Bouchereau*[81]:

> 'the concept of public policy in the context of the Community and where, in particular, it is used as a justification for derogating from the fundamental principle of freedom of movement for workers, must be interpreted strictly, so that its scope cannot be determined unilaterally by each Member State without being subject to control by the institutions of the Community. Nevertheless the particular circumstances justifying recourse to the concept of public policy may vary from one country to another, and it is therefore necessary in this matter to allow the competent national authorities an area of discretion within the limits imposed by the Treaty.'[82]

As will be clear from the passage quoted above, in *Henn and Darby* the Court did not seek to define the boundaries of the concept of public morality.

8.27 So much for the general principle. However, the picture in *Henn and Darby* itself was complicated by the fact that section 42 of the Customs Consolidation Act 1876 was more restrictive than the laws applying within the United Kingdom in three respects:

— in no part of the United Kingdom was it a criminal offence merely to possess pornographic material otherwise than with a view to sale, yet such possession at a point of entry into the United Kingdom contravened section 42;

— whereas section 42 prohibited the importation of indecent and obscene articles (standard A), in England and Wales only the sale of 'obscene' material was prohibited, while 'indecent' material could be sold (standard B); thus articles which were merely 'indecent' without being so offensive as to be considered 'obscene' could be sold within England and Wales but could not be imported into any part of the United Kingdom;

— again as far as articles sold within England and Wales were concerned, the Obscene Publications Acts 1959 and 1964

---

[80] See also paras. 5.08 above and 9.61 below.
[81] See n.68 above.
[82] The parallel with the *Van Duyn* and *Bouchereau* cases was made by the A.G. in *Henn and Darby* at p.3828 (E.C.R.).

excepted from the provisions of those Acts obscene articles when their publication was, despite their obscenity, 'justified as being for the public good on the ground that it is in the interests of science, literature, art or learning, or of other objects of general concern.' No equivalent defence existed under the Customs Consolidation Act.

The object of the fifth and sixth questions posed by the House of Lords was in effect to ascertain whether the import prohibition could be justified under Article 36. The Court held that such a prohibition was to justified, in the following terms:

'[The second sentence of Article 36] is designed to prevent restrictions on trade based on the grounds mentioned in the first sentence of Article 36 from being diverted from their proper purpose and used in such a way as either to create discrimination in respect of goods originating in other Member States or indirectly to protect certain national products. That is not the purport of a prohibition such as that in force in the United Kingdom, on the importation of articles which are of an indecent or obscene character. Whatever may be the differences between the laws on this subject in force in the different constituent parts of the United Kingdom, and notwithstanding the fact that they contain certain exceptions of limited scope, these laws, taken as a whole, have as their purpose the prohibition, or at least, the restraining, of the manufacture and marketing of publications or articles of an indecent or obscene character. In these circumstances it is permissible to conclude, on a comprehensive view, that there is no lawful trade in such goods in the United Kingdom. A prohibition on imports which may in certain respects be more strict than some of the laws applied within the United Kingdom cannot therefore be regarded as amounting to a measure designed to give indirect protection to some national product or aimed at creating arbitrary discrimination between goods of this type depending on whether they are produced within the national territory or another Member State.'

8.28 The statement that there was no lawful trade in indecent or obscene articles within the United Kingdom lies at the core of this argument, but is factually incorrect: in most parts of the United Kingdom there was in fact lawful trade in articles which were indecent but not obscene and in obscene articles justified 'for the public good.'

The approach followed by the Advocate General appears to be more in keeping both with the facts and with the previous case law of the Court. In his view the test must in each case be whether any element of discrimination inherent in the prohibition or restriction on imports under consideration is in all the circumstances proportionate to its legitimate purpose. To prevent, to guard against or to reduce the likelihood of breaches of the domestic laws of the Member State concerned was a legitimate purpose. The Advocate General pointed out that in the present case there was probably no discrimination since (1) the articles appeared so obscene and unmeritorious that it was probably a criminal offence to sell them in any part of the United Kingdom, and (2) it is clear that a man who imports in bulk does so with a view to sale. Yet in so far as there was discrimination there might well be arbitrary discrimination under Article 36:

> 'I doubt if the application of that test [of proportionality] would justify the prohibition of the importation into the United Kingdom of a book that was lawfully on sale in English bookshops. Clearly it would be unreasonable and disproportionate to forbid the importation of such a book just because of the risk that it might be . . . put on sale in Scotland or the Isle of Man. Those very same risks flow from the publication of the book in England.'

8.29 Light has now been shed on the judgment in *Henn and Darby* by the ruling in *Conegate* v. *H.M. Customs and Excise*.[83] Conegate had attempted to import from Germany various consignments of 'inflatable dolls which were clearly of a sexual nature and other erotic articles.' These were seized by the United Kingdom customs authorities as being 'indecent and obscene' articles whose importation was prohibited under section 42 of the Customs Consolidation Act 1878, the provision which had also been in issue in the earlier case. There was no absolute ban on the manufacture and sale of such articles within the United Kingdom, although there was a total ban on their sale in the Isle of Man. In England and Wales they were only subject to three lesser restrictions: they could not be sent through the post; they could not be displayed in public; and in areas where local authorities had chosen to subject sex shops to licences, they could only be sold in licensed sex shops, and in any event only to persons of 18 years of age or over. The situation in Northern Ireland was broadly similar. As for Scotland, there was a dispute between the parties as to whether such goods could be freely sold there.

The Court held that a Member State could not rely on the public morality exception in Article 36 in order to prohibit the importation of goods from other Member States when its legislation contained no prohibition on the manufacture or marketing of the same goods on its territory. It continued:

> 'However, the question whether or not such a prohibition exists in a State comprised of different constituent parts which have their own internal legislation can be resolved only by taking into consideration all the relevant legislation. Although it is not necessary, for the purposes of the application of the abovementioned rule, that the manufacture and marketing of the products whose importation has been prohibited should be prohibited in the territory of all the constituent parts, it must at least be possible to conclude from the applicable rules, taken as a whole, that their purpose is, in substance, to prohibit the manufacture and marketing of those products.'

On the basis of the three limited restrictions in force in England and Wales, the Court therefore in effect concluded that the goods could be lawfully marketed within the United Kingdom so that their importation could not be prohibited. Although the Court did not expressly say so, it may be deduced from the judgment that in

---

[83] N.11 above.

such circumstances the import ban constituted arbitrary discrimination within the meaning of the last sentence of Article 36.

Public Policy

8.30 Public policy being of a more general nature than the other grounds of justification in Article 36, it presumably only comes into play when the other grounds are not in point. This can be deduced from *Campus Oil*[84] where the Court without giving reasons held that public security, and not public policy, was the applicable head of justification.[85]

With respect to the public policy exception to the free movement of workers the Court held in *Bouchereau*[86] that 'recourse by a national authority to the concept of public policy presupposes . . . the existence . . . of a genuine and sufficiently serious threat to the requirements of public policy affecting one of the fundamental interests of society'.[87]

An echo of that ruling is to be found in *R. v. Thompson, Johnson and Woodiwiss*.[88] As we saw in an earlier chapter,[89] that case concerned a prohibition on the import and export of certain coins into and out of the United Kingdom. We also saw how the Court found that only one of the three categories of coin in issue was to be regarded as goods under Community law: the British silver alloy half-crowns minted before 1947 which, although no longer legal tender, could be exchanged at the Bank of England and were protected from destruction other than by the State. In its fourth and final question the Court of Appeal (Criminal Division) asked, *inter alia*, whether the prohibition on the export of such coins was justified on the grounds of public policy under Article 36. In its submissions to the Court the United Kingdom Government put forward three reasons for the prohibition on the export of these coins:

  (i) to ensure that there was no shortage of current coins for use by the public;
 (ii) to ensure that any profit resulting from any increase in the value of the silver content of the coins would accrue to the United Kingdom, since it had minted them;
(iii) to prevent the destruction of United Kingdom coins occurring outside its jurisdiction, it being a criminal offence to destroy coins of the realm within the United Kingdom.

The Court was clearly swayed by these arguments, since it ruled:

---

[84] N.51 above; see ground 33 of the judgment and A.G. Slynn at p.2764 (E.C.R.).
[85] Case note by Mortelmans [1984] C.M.L.Rev. 687 at 705.
[86] N.68 above.
[87] 'Public policy' does not necessarily have the same meaning under Art. 36: see para. 8.22 above.
[88] Case 7/78 [1978] E.C.R. 2247, [1979] 1 C.M.L.R. 47.
[89] See paras. 2.06 and 2.07.

'It is for the Member States to mint their own coinage and to protect it from destruction.

A ban on exporting such coins with a view to preventing their being melted down or destroyed in another Member State is justified on grounds of public policy within the meaning of Article 36 of the Treaty, because it stems from the need to protect the right to mint coinage which is traditionally regarded as involving the fundamental interests of the State.'

It has been objected[90] that this is a retreat from the Court's earlier ruling that Article 36 does not justify measures of economic protection.[91] Yet it is submitted that that objection is ill-founded, since the judgment is in fact based on the assertion that the State enjoyed a right akin to a property right in the coins. The protection of a property right is a very different matter from the protection of the economy as a whole. In any case, the earlier ruling has since been reaffirmed on a number of occasions.[92]

8.31 Public policy (as well as public security) was relied on by France in *Cullet* v. *Leclerc*.[93] It claimed that the contested price controls on petroleum products were necessary to avert unrest on the part of retailers. This argument was rejected by Advocate General VerLoren van Themaat in the following forthright terms:

'. . . the acceptance of civil disturbances as justification for encroachments upon the free movement of goods would, as is apparent from experiences of the last year, . . . have unacceptably drastic consequences. If road-blocks and other effective weapons of interest groups which feel threatened by the importation and sale at competitive prices of certain cheap products or services, or by immigrant workers or foreign businesses, were accepted as justification, the existence of the four fundamental freedoms of the Treaty could no longer be relied upon. Private interest groups would then, in the place of the Treaty and Community . . . institutions, determine the scope of those freedoms. In such cases, the concept of public policy requires, rather, effective action on the part of the authorities to deal with such disturbances.'

The Court refrained from ruling on the general issue raised, but remarked cryptically:

'. . . the French Government has not shown that it would be unable, using the means at its disposal, to deal with the consequences which an amendment of the rules in question in accordance with the principles set out above would have upon public order and security.'

Probably, then, none of the grounds of Article 36 covers this type of eventuality. However, in extreme circumstances Article 224 may be applied,[94] but *Cullet* did not concern such circumstances.

Public security
8.32 This limb of Article 36 covers in particular security matters normally associated with the police, such as crime detection and

---

[90] Wyatt [1981] E.L.Rev. 483.
[91] See para. 8.19 above.
[92] See para. 8.19 above.
[93] Case 231/83 [1985] E.C.R. 305, [1985] 2 C.M.L.R. 524.
[94] Ehlermann, *op. cit.* n.9 above, at 291; para. 9.56 *et seq.* below.

prevention and the regulation of traffic. In so far as trade in arms, munitions and war material is concerned, the more general provisions of Article 223 apply.[95] Again, in the event of sedition, war or threat of war, Member States are granted sweeping powers to disregard the Treaty by Article 224.[96] That would presumably be the appropriate provision to apply in the event of civil disturbances caused by economic difficulties (*e.g.* unrest of consumers in the case of price increases, of producers in the case of falling prices, or workers in the case of redundancies).[97]

8.33   Public security was in issue in *Campus Oil*.[98] Advocate General Slynn expressed the view that the maintenance of essential oil supplies fell within 'public security,' since it was vital to the stability and cohesion of the life of the modern State. 'Public security' in Article 36 was not limited to external military security which largely fell to be dealt with under Articles 223 to 225; nor was it limited to the maintenance of law and order within the State, although it might include this.

The Advocate General pointed out that the Irish court had so far made only a few of the necessary findings of fact. Accordingly, he implied that the Court should confine itself to giving guidance to the Irish court as to the considerations to be taken into account in deciding whether the contested measure was in fact justified on public security grounds. He thereafter kept within the limits which he had set himself. In particular, he refrained from deciding whether any restrictions under Article 30 were justified to maintain in operation a refinery such as Whitegate. He concluded that the Court should rule along the lines that

> 'such legislation will be justified under Article 36 on the grounds of public security, and thereby not precluded by Article 30, if it is necessary, other than on economic grounds, to maintain essential services and supplies. It will not be necessary for this purpose where the requisite oil supplies can be ensured by other means which are less restrictive of imports, such as the keeping of stocks.'

The Court held that the maintenance of essential oil supplies was covered by the public security exception, since not only a country's economy but 'above all its institutions, its essential public services and the survival of its inhabitants' depended upon it. However, the Court did not give any general indication as to the meaning of 'public security' in Article 36 or its relationship with Articles 223 to 225.

Unlike the Advocate General, the Court apparently did not regard the absence of crucial findings of fact by the referring court as any form of constraint. It therefore proceeded to rule that it was justified

---

[95] See para. 9.53 below.
[96] See para. 9.56 below.
[97] Ehlermann, *op. cit.* n.9 above, at 291, and see para. 8.31 above.
[98] N.51 above.

on public security grounds for a Member State with no crude oil of its own to keep a refinery in operation, a point which the Advocate General had left open. The submission had been put forward by the plaintiffs and the Commission that a refinery would be of no assistance in a crisis since no crude oil would be available. That argument was dismissed. Instead, the Court was swayed by the argument that 'the fact of having refinery capacity in its territory enables the State concerned to enter into long-term contracts with the oil-producing countries for the supply of crude oil to its refinery which offer a better guarantee of supplies in the event of a crisis.' The Court's ruling on this point virtually determined the outcome of the case.

Having regard to the principle of proportionality, the Court went on to hold that compulsory sales were only justified if the refinery's output could not be freely disposed of at competitive prices. Even then, the quantities of petroleum products covered by such a system must not exceed the minimum supply requirements without which the public security of the State concerned would be affected; nor must they exceed the level of production necessary to keep the refinery's production capacity available in the event of a crisis and to enable it to continue to refine at all times the crude oil covered by long-term contracts concluded by the State. These were matters for the national judge to determine.

As to the price, the Court held that, if compulsory sales were justified, this could be fixed by the competent minister on the basis of the costs incurred in the operation of the refinery. This matter is arguably purely economic. Never before has the Court held any form of price control to be justified under Article 36. Yet in *Campus Oil* the price was inextricably bound up with the compulsory purchasing requirement.

This judgment, which might be regarded as a serious blow for the prospects of creating a common energy policy, has not gone uncriticised.[99]

The protection of human health and life

8.34 It seems scarcely necessary to repeat here the Court's ruling in *De Peijper*[100] that 'national rules or practices do not fall within

---

[99] Thus Gormley, *Prohibiting restrictions of trade within the EEC; the theory and application of Articles 30 to 36 of the EEC Treaty* (1985) at 139, has pointed to the excessively vague nature of the expression 'essential public services' which the Court failed to define and Marenco 'La giurisprudenza comunitaria sulle misure di effetto equivalente a una restrizione quantitativa (1984–1986)' [1988] *Il Foro Padano* IV, 166 has questioned whether the maintenance of a refinery in Ireland was necessary to refine oil covered by long-term contracts; in his view, Ireland could ensure supplies equally well by having such oil refined in refineries not situated on Irish soil. Both authors have expressed surprise at the Court giving its blessing under Art. 36 to such an apparently protectionist measure (Gormley at 139).
[100] See n.16 above.

the exception specified in Article 36 if the health and life of humans can [be] as effectively protected by measures which do not restrict intra-Community trade so much.' This is of course the rule of proportionality which applies to Article 36 generally[101] and indeed to all exceptions to the principle of the free movement of goods.[102] It follows that a Member State:

> '. . . is not entitled to prevent the marketing of a product originating in another Member State which provides a level of protection of the health and life of humans equivalent to that which the national rules are intended to ensure or establish. It is therefore contrary to the principle of proportionality for national rules to require such imported products to comply strictly and exactly with the provisions or technical requirements laid down for products manufactured in the Member State in question when those imported products afford users the same level of protection.'[103]

However, in *De Peijper* the Court also ruled that the 'health and the life of humans rank first among the property or interests protected by Article 36 and it is for the Member States, within the limits imposed by the Treaty, to decide what degree of protection they intend to assure, and in particular how strict the checks to be carried out are to be.' Consequently, a Member State may take steps to guard against a risk of this kind, however slight, so long as that risk is genuine. For instance, if a disease is liable to claim one life in the entire population of a Member State over a 20-year period, then that Member State is entitled to adopt stringent controls against it—provided always that those controls are not more restrictive of trade between the Member States than is necessary to prevent anyone catching the disease.

When considering public health it should be borne in mind that there is a large body of relevant Community legislation; when it provides exhaustive guarantees, such legislation ousts Article 36 in accordance with the rule discussed earlier in this chapter.[104]

8.35 The *De Peijper* case itself arose out of criminal proceedings brought before the Dutch court against a parallel importer accused of contravening Dutch public health legislation by supplying pharmacies in the Netherlands with pharmaceutical products imported from the United Kingdom without the consent of the Dutch authorities, and with failing to have in his possession certain documents connected with these products. Having ruled in effect that measures restricting parallel imports were measures of equivalent effect within the meaning of Article 30, the Court went on to consider the compatibility of rules of the kind in question with Article 36. In

[101] Para. 8.10 below.
[102] Para. 9.01 below.
[103] Case 188/84 *E.C. Commission* v. *France* (woodworking machines) [1985] E.C.R. 419; see generally para. 6.55 *et seq.* above.
[104] See para. 8.15 above.

this connection, the Court held in the operative part of its judgment that:

> 'Given a factual situation such as that described in the first question national rules or practices which make possible for a manufacturer of the pharmaceutical product in question and his duly appointed representatives, simply by refusing to produce the documents relating to the medicinal preparation in general or to a specific batch of that preparation, to enjoy a monopoly of the importing and marketing of the product must be regarded as being unnecessarily restrictive and cannot therefore come within the exceptions specified in Article 36 of the Treaty, unless it is clearly proved that any other rules or practices would obviously be beyond the means which can reasonably be expected of an administration operating in a normal manner.'

In the grounds of its judgment the Court did in fact suggest two methods by which such restrictions might be lessened: Member States might compel the manufacturer or his duly appointed representative to deliver up the necessary information, and 'simple co-operation between the authorities of the Member States would enable them to obtain on a reciprocal basis the documents necessary for checking certain largely standardised and widely distributed products.' The Court continued:

> 'Taking into account all these possible ways of obtaining information the national public health authorities must consider whether the effective protection of health and life of humans justifies a presumption of the non-conformity of an imported batch with the description of the medicinal preparation, or whether on the contrary it would not be sufficient to lay down a presumption of conformity with the result that, in appropriate cases, it would be for the administration to rebut this presumption.'

What if there are minor differences in composition between the 'official' and the parallel imports? This was in effect the second question put by the national court, which indicated that the differences might be so minor that it was likely that they were deliberately created by the manufacturer with a view to preventing parallel imports. The Court replied in the following terms:

> 'It is only if the information or documents to be produced by the manufacturer or his duly appointed importer show that there are several variants of the medicinal preparation and that the differences between these variants have a therapeutic effect that there would be any justification for treating the variants as different medicinal preparations, for the purpose of authorising the relevant documents, it being understood that the answer to the first question remains valid as regards each of the authorisation procedures which have become necessary.'

8.36   At this juncture it is appropriate to break down the case law into categories according to the nature of the measures concerned. However, these categories are by no means watertight and indeed the judgments contain many express references to cases considered in other categories.

(i) *Retreatment in the importing Member State*

8.37 *E.C. Commission* v. *United Kingdom*[105] was concerned *inter alia* with the requirement that imported ultra-heat treated milk undergo the heat treatment process a second time in the United Kingdom. This was tantamount to a total ban on imports, since it rendered them economically prohibitive. Although there were disparities between the laws of the Member States regarding such heat treatment, the Court found that in fact these disparities were limited. Moreover, the Court referred to other technical factors which ensured that UHT milk produced in the various Member States was of similar quality as regards health. Accordingly, it sufficed to require imported UHT milk to meet such conditions as were absolutely necessary and this could be evidenced by certificates issued by the exporting Member State. While this case turned in part on the technical data concerned, it is hard to imagine such a retreatment requirement ever being justified.

(ii) *Import licences*

8.38 The accidents of litigation have determined that the cases concerning the justification of import licences have related to animal health, not human health. Yet there is every reason to believe that those cases, which are discussed in paragraphs 8.56 and 8.57 below, apply *mutatis mutandis* to human health. On that view, whether a scheme whereby a separate licence must be issued for each consignment is justified cannot be judged according to any general rules, but must be decided on a case-by-case basis. Such a state of affairs scarcely satisfies the principle of legal certainty. What is more, one might have thought that such a system of specific import licences would by its very nature be unduly restrictive and thus unjustified.

(iii) *Import controls and inspections*

8.39 It is probable that, in the absence of a reasonable suspicion in relation to a specific consignment, an importing Member State may not duplicate checks relating to a particular disease or harmful substance carried out by the exporting Member State and evidenced by the appropriate certificates, except by way of spot or random checks. While this proposition has yet to be elevated by the Court to the status of a general rule, there will surely be few circumstances, if any, in which it does not apply.

The early cases[106] were all references for a preliminary ruling and the Court left it to the national judges to decide whether a sufficient degree of co-operation existed between the Member States to create

---

[105] Case 124/81 [1983] E.C.R. 203, [1983] 2 C.M.L.R. 1, noted by Wainwright [1983] C.M.L.Rev. 365.

[106] *E.g. De Peijper*, para. 8.35 above, *Denkavit*, n.7 above.

a presumption that health certificates issued by the exporting State were accurate. The ruling in *E.C. Commission* v. *United Kingdom*[107] constituted an important step forward because there for the first time the Court was able to find as a fact that 'in the case of UHT milk the conditions are satisfied for there to be a presumption of accuracy in favour of the statements contained in such documents.' This precluded the defendant from carrying out controls on imports other than 'by means of samples.'

Similarly, one of the measures impugned by the Commission in *E.C. Commission* v. *France*[108] was the excessively frequent analysis by the French authorities of imports of Italian wine. The frequency of these analyses varied from time to time but there were periods when as many as three out of four consignments were analysed. Yet on the French Government's own admission it was sufficient to examine 10 per cent. of all consignments. Furthermore the percentage of consignments of Italian wine analysed was considerably higher than that of loads of French wine transported within France. The third reason give by the Court for holding the frequency of the analyses to be unjustified was as follows:

> 'It is an established fact that checks are also carried out by the Italian authorities in order to ensure that wine produced in Italy complies with the Community rules and that consumers and the health and life of humans are protected. The French authorities were under a duty to take into account the existence of those checks carried out in the country of origin of the wine. Adulteration or irregularities discovered in particular cases prior to the period in question certainly cannot justify a general suspicion in relation to all imports of Italian wine or the carrying out of systematic analyses when no similar practice exists in relation to French wine.'

8.40 If the Court has so far fought shy of ruling that the Member State is never entitled systematically to duplicate all checks carried out by the exporting Member State, the Council has been bolder. Article 3(1) of Council Directive 84/643[109] on the facilitation of physical inspections and administrative formalities in respect of the carriage of goods between Member States provides, in so far as is relevant:

> 'For the purposes of implementing this Directive and without prejudice to the possibility of carrying out spot checks, the importing Member States or the Member States through which the goods are passing in transit shall recognise the inspections carried out and the documents drawn up by the competent authorities of another Member State which show that the goods comply with the requirements of the Member State of import or transit.'

By virtue of Article 1, this Directive applies to all movements of goods between Member States and to all goods, other than ships and aircraft, used as means of transport. Moreover, it is based on

---

[107] N.105 above; see also Case 261/85 *E.C. Commission* v. *United Kingdom* (pasteurised milk) [1988] 2 C.M.L.R. 11.
[108] N.26 above.
[109] [1983] O.J. L359/8, see paras. 7.09, 7.17, 1.19 and 7.21 above.

Articles 43 and 100 of the Treaty (as well as Articles 73 and 84) so that Article 3(1) would appear to cover public health checks. It is difficult to know what meaning to ascribe to the words 'for the purposes of implementing this Directive'; they may well be otiose.

8.41 On a related point, in *E.C. Commission* v. *France* the Court went on to hold that, in the absence of reasonable suspicion of fraud or irregularity, the importing Member State was not justified in detaining consignments of wine until the analysis was complete. The reasons given by the Court for this ruling were that it was not always the practice of the French authorities to detain French wine during the analysis of a sample; and that the Community provisions on wine enabled a consignment to be located once the results of the analysis were known. These reasons are peculiar to that case so that it would not necessarily be possible to apply this part of the judgment to other products.

(iv) *Certificates*

8.42 It will be apparent from the preceding paragraphs that the requirement that imports be covered by health certificates issued in the exporting Member State will be justified—provided that the importing Member State is entitled to prescribe the health standards to which the certificates relate.

(v) *Additives and vitamins*

8.43 The first case on additives was *Officier van Justitie* v. *Koninklijke Kaasfabriek Eyssen*.[110] The case arose out of a prosecution before the Dutch courts of a Dutch company manufacturing processed cheese both for the home market and for export. The defendant was charged with having in stock with a view to sale quantities of cheese containing a preservative known as nisin. Dutch Regulations forbade the use of nisin in processed cheese sold on the home market, although they laid down an exemption with respect to exports. Reliable studies showed that nisin was not necessarily harmful in itself, but only became harmful when consumed in excessive quantities. However, it had not yet been established what the acceptable daily intake was. In view of this, a number of Member States permitted the use of nisin up to certain specified limits, and the United Kingdom and France even permitted its use without limit. Nevertheless, the Court held that the ban imposed by the Dutch authorities was justified on public health grounds. In reaching this conclusion the Court cited the fact that the acceptable daily intake had not yet been established, that such intake depended not only on one particular product but on the entire dietary habits of an individual, and that such habits varied from one Member State

---

[110] Case 53/80 [1981] E.C.R. 409, [1982] 2 C.M.L.R. 20.

to another. Given such varying dietary habits, the specific exemption with respect to exports did not render the measure in issue arbitrarily discriminatory.[111]

However, the Court avoided ruling on whether the system of 'positive lists' is justified under Article 36. This is the system applied throughout the Western world, whereby additives are presumed to be harmful until the contrary is proved; unless an additive figures on the list of permitted additives established by legislation, its use is unlawful. Nisin did not figure on the positive list laid down by Dutch legislation. At first sight, the system of positive lists runs counter to the rebuttable presumption that a restriction is not justified under Article 36.[112] The German Government therefore seized this opportunity to invite the Court to rule that the system of positive lists was justified under Article 36, since there was no other scientific method of determining whether additives were harmless. As the Advocate General pointed out, however, it was not necessary to decide this point in the case.

8.44 In a series of subsequent cases culminating in *E.C. Commission v. Germany* (beer),[113] the Commission has built on this ruling, while at the same time addressing itself to the problem of positive lists. That case concerned a blanket prohibition imposed by Germany on all additives in beer, including those approved for use in beer by other Member States. The Court reaffirmed that, in so far as scientific opinion is uncertain and in the absence of harmonisation, it is for the Member States to decide what degree of health protection they intend to achieve.

The Member States are entitled to make the sale of foodstuffs containing additives subject to an authorisation procedure for each additive, it being understood that authorisations are granted *erga omnes* for use in particular foodstuffs or in all foodstuffs or for other specific uses. However, where goods containing an additive approved in another Member State are exported from that State, the importing Member State is bound to do the following:

(i) it must authorise the use of that additive, if (a) international scientific data (particularly those compiled by scientific committees operating under the auspices of the Community and the FAO) showed it to be harmless to individuals with the

---

[111] Meier has nevertheless suggested ([1983] RIW 864) that the existence of such an exemption for exports is *evidence* that such a restriction is not justified.

[112] See para. 8.03 above.

[113] Case 178/84 [1988] 1 C.M.L.R. 780, noted by Rabe [1987] EuR 253; see also Cases 174/82 *Sandoz* (n.61 above), 227/82 *Van Bennekom* [1983] E.C.R. 3883, 247/84 *Motte* [1985] E.C.R. 3887, 304/84 *Muller* (judgment of 6 May 1986) and 176/84 *E.C. Commission* v. *Greece* (beer) [1988] 1 C.M.L.R. 813.

dietary habits of its population and (b) if it meets a genuine technical or other need;[114]

(ii) it must make readily available to companies an administrative procedure for seeking a general authorisation for the use of particular additives, which procedure can be concluded within a reasonable time. (As to this procedure, it may be assumed that, although the Court did not repeat it, the following statement in *Sandoz*[115] is still good law: 'although the national authorities may, in so far as they do not have it themselves, ask the importer to produce the information in his possession relating to the composition of the product and the technical or nutritional reasons for adding vitamins, they must themselves assess, in the light of all the relevant information, whether authorisation must be granted pursuant to Community law.' It follows from this passage that the Member State is under a positive duty to take active steps to establish whether the additive is harmful.);

(iii) it must ensure that an action may be brought before the courts with respect to a refusal to grant an authorisation.[116] The Court stressed that in such proceedings the Member State bears the burden of showing that the restriction is indeed justified under Article 36 on public health grounds.

8.45   In the same case, the Court went on to rule that Germany had not satisfied these conditions and that the contested legislation was thus not justified. It had simply imposed a blanket prohibition on the use of all the additives in beer authorised in other Member States, without regard to the dietary habits of its population. What is more, it had not provided for any procedure whereby companies could obtain approval for particular additives. The fact that some of the additives concerned were permitted in Germany for all or nearly all other drinks was also evidence that the ban was unjustified.

The Court also rejected the defendant's interpretation of the concept of technical need. Germany had argued that there was no technical need for the additives concerned since German beer was manufactured without them. Instead, the Court held, the question

---

[114] In *Sandoz,* which concerned added vitamins, the Court held that a nutritional need would also suffice, while in *Motte* and *Muller* it implied that an economic need would suffice. The judgment in *Motte* also suggests that, as regards flavouring or colouring matters, an organoleptic or psychological need will qualify.

[115] N.61 above, see also Case 272/80 *Frans-Nederlandse Maatschappij voor Biologische Producten* [1981] E.C.R. 3277, [1982] 2 C.M.L.R. 497, para. 8.46 below.

[116] It is not clear how this differs from the general duty on Member States to make judicial remedies available for the enforcement of directly applicable Community rights: see *e.g.* Cases 33/76 *Rewe-Zentralfinanz* v. *Landwirtschaftskammer für das Saarland* [1976] E.C.R. 1989, [1977] 1 C.M.L.R. 533 and 45/76 *Comet* v. *Produktschap voor Siergewassen* [1976] E.C.R. 2043, [1977] 1 C.M.L.R. 533, Barav 'La répétition de l'indû dans la jurisprudence de la Cour de Justice des Communautés européennes' [1981] C.D.E. 507, Hubeau 'La répétition de l'indû en droit communautaire' [1981] R.T.D.E. 442, Oliver 'Enforcing Community Rights in the English Courts' [1987] M.L.R. 881.

whether a technical need for a particular additive existed had to be determined in the light of the following factors: the raw materials actually used; the views of the authorities of the Member State where the product was legally produced and marketed; and the results of international scientific research.

The ruling in the *beer* case contrasts with that in *Motte*[117] which concerned certain colouring agents used in potted lumpfish roe imported into Belgium. Those colorants were authorised for use in lumpfish roe in Germany, from where the product had been exported, and they were authorised in Belgium for use in other foodstuffs; however, the Belgian authorities had not authorised their use in lumpfish roe. An administrative procedure existed whereby traders could seek official approval for the use of the additives concerned in the product, but no such application had ever been made. In these circumstances, the Court held that the contested restriction was justified, rejecting the Commission's arguments to the contrary.

(vi) *Prohibited pesticides*

8.46 *Frans-Nederlandse Maatschappij voor Biologische Producten*[118] concerned a fungicide used for disinfecting sugar vats. This product had not been approved in the Netherlands, but it had been imported from France where it had been approved after scientific tests similar to those which the Dutch authorities would have carried out. As to the lawfulness of an importing Member State prohibiting sales of a product in such circumstances the Court ruled as follows:

> 'It follows from Article 30 in conjunction with Article 36 of the Treaty that a Member State is not prohibited from requiring plant protection products to be subject to prior approval, even if those products have already been approved in another Member State. The authorities of the importing State are however not entitled unnecessarily to require technical or chemical analyses or laboratory tests when the same analyses or tests have already been carried out in another Member State and the results are available to those authorities or may at their request be placed at their disposal.'

The crucial question is clearly what is meant by 'unnecessarily.'

8.47 Thereafter, in *Heijn*[119] the Court was asked to rule on the lawfulness of a national measure prescribing a maximum permitted level of residue of a particular pesticide on apples. The Court held that Member States must take account of the fact that pesticides are substances which are both necessary to agriculture and dangerous to health. They could regulate the presence of residues of pesticides on foodstuffs in a way which could vary from one country to another according to the climate, the normal diet of the population and its state of health. The Court did however enter the proviso that the

---

[117] See n.113 above.
[118] See n.115 above.
[119] Case 94/83 [1984] E.C.R. 3263, discussed in written question 1581/84 ([1985] O.J. C176/4).

authorities of the importing Member State were 'obliged to review the prescribed maximum level if it appears to them that the reasons which led to its being fixed have changed, for example, as a result of the discovery of a new use for such and such a pesticide.'

This ruling was confirmed in *Mirepoix*,[120] although the Court did add that a review would also be necessary in the event of further information becoming available through scientific research. This case concerned a total ban on the treatment of onions with a particular pesticide, whereas *Heijn* had merely concerned a permitted maximum level of residues. The Commission therefore invited the Court to distinguish *Heijn* on these grounds, but the Court declined.

Plainly, according to these judgments the Member States enjoy greater freedom to prohibit or restrict the use of particular pesticides than they do in relation to additives and vitamins according to the judgments relating to those products. Yet it seems likely that *Heijn* and *Mirepoix* have been superseded, at least in part, by the latter body of case law and in particular the *Beer* case. For instance, there appears to be no reason why Member States should not be required to make available an administrative procedure for the authorisation of particular pesticides. In any case, whether or not *Heijn* and *Mirepoix* are still good law, an effective judicial remedy must be available to contest a Member State's refusal to approve a particular product.[121]

(vii) *Maximum levels of bacteria*

8.48   *Melkunie*[122] related to a national measure fixing the maximum permissible level of active non-pathogenic micro-organisms in milk. As one would expect, the Court held that it was justified on health grounds for Member States to impose restrictions of this kind. More significant is its ruling that Member States may fix the maximum level sufficiently low to take account of (a) the needs of particularly sensitive consumers and (b) the fact that after purchase consumers may store the product in less than ideal conditions.

The Court made no mention whatever of any obligation on Member States to review their maximum permitted levels in particular circumstances. Nevertheless, the Court's case law on additives and vitamins is surely applicable here now.

(viii) *The prohibition of harmless foodstuffs*

8.49   The sale of a particular category of foodstuffs may not be prohibited solely because it is of limited nutritional value. This was established in *E.C. Commission* v. *France* (substitute milk powder)[123] where the Court also pointed out that apart from substitute milk powder there were many products having little nutritional value on

---

[120] Case 54/85 [1986] E.C.R. 1067, [1987] 2 C.M.L.R. 44.
[121] See n.116 above.
[122] Case 97/83 [1984] E.C.R. 2367, [1986] 2 C.M.L.R. 318.
[123] See n. 71 above.

the market and these were not subject to any restriction on sale in the defendant Member State.

(ix) *The obligation to appoint a representative in the importing Member State*

8.50 *E.C. Commission v. Belgium*[124] concerned a provision that approval for the sale of certain pesticides and phyto-pharmaceutical products in Belgium could only be granted to a person established there with responsibility for the sale of the product concerned as producer, importer, proprietor or concessionnaire. It was common ground between the parties that some or all of the products concerned were toxic. The Commission nevertheless contested the Belgian Government's view that the requirement that the person concerned be established in Belgium was justified on public health grounds. The Court upheld the Commission's view.

Firstly, the Belgian Government argued that it was necessary for a person responsible for the product concerned to be established on Belgian territory for the proper completion of the approval formalities, the enforcement of the rules on labelling, the verification of the conformity of the product marketed with the product approved and the availability of information in the event of an accident or a complaint. The Court took the view that these matters could be fully satisified by appropriate administrative measures taken when the application was examined and the approval granted, without its being necessary to require the establishment of a representative on the national territory.

The Belgian Government claimed, secondly, that it was necessary to ensure that a person was present on national territory to be prosecuted for any contravention of public health legislation. The Court held that, while criminal sanctions may have a deterrent effect, that effect was not increased by the requirement concerned. The Court thus appears to have accepted the view expressed by Advocate General Rozès that responsible persons in other Member States could equally well be prosecuted by the Belgian authorities.

This ruling was confirmed in *E.C. Commission* v. *Germany* (pharmaceuticals)[125] where the Court added that 'the possibility that the authorisation might be suspended or revoked is an incentive to the manufacturers and the person responsible for placing products on the market to comply with the rules in force.'

(x) *Type approval for machines used at work*

8.51 In *E.C. Commission* v. *France*[126] the Court ruled that the French safety requirements for woodworking machines were justified on public health grounds, although they were stricter than those prevailing

---

[124] Case 155/82 [1983] E.C.R. 531, [1983] 2 C.M.L.R. 566, para. 7.28 above.
[125] Case 247/81 [1984] E.C.R. 1111, [1985] 1 C.M.L.R. 640.
[126] N. 103 above.

in other Member States. The French legislation was based on the idea that the users of machines must be protected from their own mistakes and that the machine must be so designed as to limit the user's intervention to the absolute minimum. In other Member States, the predominant approach to the problem was different. In Germany in particular the basic principle was that the worker should receive thorough and continuing training so as to be capable of responding correctly if a machine does not function properly.

The Court stated that it was 'contrary to the principle of proportionality for national rules to require such imported products to comply strictly and exactly with the provisions or technical requirements laid down for products manufactured in the Member State in question when those imported products afford users the same level of protection.' However, it found that the Commission had failed to prove that imported woodworking machines did in fact protect users equally well; the German approach to accident prevention had not been shown to be as satisfactory as the French approach. The Commission had put in statistics showing that the machines manufactured according to the specifications of other Member States did not cause more accidents than machines made to French standards. Nevertheless, in the Court's view such statistics could not establish by themselves that the French approach did not provide greater protection to users since they left out of account other factors such as 'the extensive training of users'.[127]

One can deduce from this that a Member State is not required to grant type approval for dangerous machines which can only be used safely after extensive training, if machines meeting the specifications laid down by that State do not require such training. Yet the Court cannot be taken to have given its blessing to national rules which exploit users' habits so as to give an advantage to domestic manufacturers.[128]

The Court also held that it was lawful for the defendant to require applicants for type approval to transport their machines to France for testing.

(xi) *Roadworthiness tests*

8.52 *Schloh* v. *Auto Contrôle Technique*[129] concerned the requirement that imported cars undergo a roadworthiness test prior to their registration, the cars concerned not being of a category covered by any relevant Community Directive. The Court held that such a requirement was not justified on health grounds in respect of unused cars covered by a certificate of conformity to the vehicle types approved in the importing Member States. In contrast, it found that it was

---

[127] As regards Arts. 30 to 36, the Court displays no great love of statistics; see also para. 7.37 above.

[128] See Case 178/84 (paras. 7.46 and 7.58 above).

[129] Case 50/85 [1987] 1 C.M.L.R. 450, on car registration; see also Case 406/85 *Gofette and Gilliard* (judgment of 11 June 1987).

justified on these grounds as regards used cars, provided that cars originating in the importing Member State were treated in the same way.

(xii) *Miscellaneous*

8.53 There are many other cases in which the Court has found a restriction not to be justified on public health grounds. Examples[130] are:
— a minimum alcohol requirement: *Cassis de Dijon*;[131]
— a prohibition on the importation of meat-based products manufactured in one Member State from animals slaughtered in another Member State: *E.C. Commission v Germany*;[132]
— a prohibition on the importation and sale of vinegar other than wine vinegar: *Gilli and Andres*;[133]
— a prohibition on the sale of bread containing more than a certain quantity of dry matter: *Kelderman*.[134]

Animals and plants

8.54 The principles relating to the health and life of animals[135] and plants[136] are the same as those relating to human life and health—with the obvious and fundamental difference that the human health and life is more important. In a case[137] concerning national legislation prescribing the conditions and minimum size of enclosures for fattening calves the Court has held that this matter is covered by Article 36; it follows that the 'protection of the health and life of animals' extends to animal welfare. The term 'plants' must be taken to cover plants and trees and their produce generally. As already mentioned,[138] a Member State may protect animals or plants threatened with extinction although they are not indigenous to its territory. It should also be pointed out that there is a body of Community legislation relating to animal and plant health.

8.55 A ban on the importation of poultrymeat, poultry products and most eggs and egg products from all countries which did not prohibit vaccination against Newcastle disease (a poultry disease) was held not

[130] See also Case 35/76 *Simmenthal*, n. 42 above, Case 46/76 *Bauhuis*, n.4 above; Case 152/78 *E.C. Commission* v. *France*, n. 10 above.
[131] N. 6 above.
[132] Case 153/78 [1979] E.C.R. 2555, [1980] 1 C.M.L.R. 198, para. 5.11 above.
[133] See n. 8 above.
[134] Case 130/80, [1981] E.C.R. 527.
[135] See *e.g.* Case 35/76 *Simmenthal*, n. 42 above; Case 46/76 *Bauhuis*, n. 4 above, Case 251/78 *Denkavit Futtermittel*, n. 7 above.
[136] See Case 4/75 *Rewe-Zentralfinanz*, n. 18 above; Case 89/76 *E.C. Commission* v. *Netherlands* n. 36 above.
[137] Cases 141–143/81 *Holdijk* [1982] E.C.R. 1299 at 1314; [1983] 2 C.M.L.R. 635 at 650.
[138] See para. 8.13 above.

to be justified in *E.C. Commission* v. *United Kingdom*[139] and *E.C. Commission* v. *Ireland*.[140] For several decades Ireland and Northern Ireland had had a policy of prohibiting such vaccination coupled with a requirement to slaughter any infected flocks. All imports from countries which permitted vaccination were banned. The thinking behind this policy was that vaccination might mask the disease, so that vacinated birds might in fact be infected by field virus. Quite suddenly, in August 1981 Great Britain switched to this system with effect from 1 September 1981. This meant that without warning all Member States other than Denmark and Ireland were deprived of the possibility of exporting the products concerned to Great Britain. In particular, this change had the effect of excluding French turkey products from the lucrative Christmas market in Great Britain.

As regards Great Britain the Court had no difficulty in finding that the ban was not justified, especially in view of various factors indicating that the true purpose of the switch to a non-vaccination policy was to protect domestic production, notably from French imports.[141]

The question was more complex in relation to Ireland and Northern Ireland, since these factors were not present and they had particularly good records with respect to Newcastle disease. The Court nevertheless found that even there the ban was unjustified. This was in the first place because internationally accepted statistics showed a steady reduction in outbreaks within the Community in recent years so that the incidence of the disease had become rather limited. Under these circumstances the risk of flocks being infected by field virus, which had entered vaccinated birds and remained active in the carcases of those birds, was extremely slight. That risk could not justify a complete ban on imports from countries which permitted vaccination. Moreover the 'prohibition of imports of carcases and poultrymeat is in any event out of proportion to the aim pursued where those imports come from a country in which no outbreak of Newcastle disease has been detected over a number of years and where, moreover, it is established that the carcases and meat in question are of unvaccinated birds.'

The rulings concerning Ireland and Northern Ireland are particularly significant in view of their particularly good record and of the long-standing nature of the import ban. They indicate that in the absence of specific grounds of suspicion a blanket prohibition of this kind will rarely, if ever, be justified.

8.56   The question whether import licences could be justified on animal health grounds first arose in *E.C. Commission* v. *United Kingdom* ('UHT milk and cream').[142] The defendant maintained that

---

[139] Case 40/82 [1982] E.C.R. 2793, [1982] 3 C.M.L.R. 497 (Great Britain) and [1984] E.C.R. 283.
[140] Case 74/82 [1984] E.C.R. 317.
[141] See para. 8.09 above.
[142] N. 105 above.

a system of individual import licences applying to each consignment of ultra-heat treated milk or cream was justified, notably because these products might be imported before an outbreak of foot-and-mouth disease in the exporting region had become known; in such cases it was essential to be able to trace a consignment and destroy it, and this could only be done by means of specific import licences. The Commission contested this view. It regarded import licences as creating uncertainty for importers and a risk of delay without constituting a real health guarantee for the importing Member State. A less restrictive solution which was also more satisfactory from the health point of view was the requirement that imports of the products concerned be accompanied by a certificate made out by a veterinary surgeon officially approved by the exporting Member State showing that the requisite health standards were met—provided of course that these health standards were themselves justified. It was for this reason that a system of health certificates issued by the exporting Member State was laid down in the Community's own veterinary Directives. The Commission therefore considered that import licences were more restrictive than was necessary to protect animal health and were therefore not justified. However, it did not rule out that there might be other cases in which an import licensing system was justified.

The Advocate General gave only qualified approval to the Commission's position. He found that import licences were justified provided that they were issued immediately and automatically, subject to production on importation of certificates attesting to UHT treatment in the exporting country, and provided that no more stringent requirements were imposed as regards those certificates than applied to the UHT treatment of milk produced within the United Kingdom.

On the other hand the Court endorsed the Commission's position, in the following terms:

> 'Even though the United Kingdom maintained at the hearing that current administrative practice permits licences to be issued promptly and automatically, a system requiring the issue of an administrative authorisation necessarily involves the exercise of a certain degree of discretion and creates legal uncertainty for traders. It results in an impediment to intra-Community trade which, in the present case, could be eliminated without prejudice to the effectiveness of the protection of animal health and without increasing the administrative or financial burden imposed by the pursuit of that objective. That result could be achieved if the United Kingdom authorities abandoned the practice of issuing licences and confined themselves to obtaining the information which is of use to them, for example, by means of declarations signed by the importers, accompanied if necessary by the appropriate certificate'.

However, the Court made it clear that its ruling was confined to the present case.

8.57 In the two cases discussed in paragraph 8.55[143] the Court confirmed that the question whether specific import licences could be

---

[143] Nn. 139 and 140 above.

justified on animal health grounds was indeed to be decided on a case by case basis. The criterion to be applied was 'the relationship between, on the one hand, the inconvenience caused by the administrative and financial burdens imposed under such a system and, on the other hand, the dangers and risks for animal health resulting from the imports in question.' Applying this criterion the Court found that specific import licences for certain poultry and egg products were justified on animal health grounds in relation to Ireland and Northern Ireland, but not as regards Great Britain. The reason given was the exceptionally high health standards of Irish and Northern Irish flocks over recent years, which were not matched by flocks in Great Britain. Regrettably the Court refrained once again from giving any general indication as to when import licences will be justified. Lawyers will therefore not find it easy to advise their clients on the circumstances in which import licences will be justified on animal health grounds.

Be that as it may, it is submitted that the less restrictive requirement that imports be accompanied by veterinary certificates should suffice in nearly every case.

Lastly, it should be noted that in the Newcastle disease cases the Commission expressly excluded 'open general licences' from the scope of its application. By this it meant licences which (i) are published and open to all importers (ii) require no further authorisation from the authorities of the importing Member State, and (iii) are subject to no other condition. The Commission's position is possibly vindicated by the ruling in *Denkavit Futtermittel* v. *Land Nordrhein-Westfalen*[144] where a licence to import an unlimited amount of feedingstuffs was held to be justified when it was subject only to the requirement to produce a copy of that licence with each consignment together with a veterinary certificate from the exporting Member State, which was valid for one year, to the effect that the goods had undergone a specified process.

8.58 Finally, there remains the problem of import controls. As already mentioned,[145] subject perhaps to very limited exceptions, in the absence of a reasonable suspicion in relation to a specific consignment an importing Member State may not duplicate controls carried out to protect human health by the exporting Member State, although the importing State may make random checks or spot checks. This must apply *a fortiori* to animal or plant health checks.

Nevertheless, in *REWE-Zentrale* v. *Direktor der Landwirtschafts-kammer Rheinland*[146] the Court rejected the argument that Council Directive 77/93 on protective measures against the introduction into the Member States of harmful organisms of plants or plant products contravened Article 30 in that it permitted an importing Member State

---

[144] N. 48 above.
[145] See para. 8.39 *et seq.* above.
[146] Case 37/83 [1984] E.C.R. 1229, [1985] 2 C.M.L.R. 586.

to subject as many as one third of all consignments of plants and plant products to phytosanitary controls. The Court found that the Community institutions had not exceeded the discretionary power conferred by Articles 43 and 100 on which the Directive was based, since harmonisation could properly be effected in stages and national obstacles to trade be abolished gradually. This necessarily implies that the contested provision may in time cease to be valid. Indeed, Advocate General Slynn, who took the same view as the Court, said as much.

The protection of national treasures possessing artistic, historic or archaeological value

8.59   Normally this head of justification[147] will be relied on to justify restrictions on exports; indeed, it will rarely, if ever, be invoked to prevent imports. So it is that the only case concerning this ground of justification to come before the Court of Justice, Case 7/68 *EEC Commission* v. *Italy*,[148] involved an export restriction on art treasures. However, as already explained,[149] that restriction took the form of an export tax and the Court held that Article 36 could not be relied on to justify a tax. In view of this neither the Court nor the Advocate General found it necessary to interpret this limb of Article 36.

8.60   The following questions arise in this connection:

(a) What is meant by a 'treasure'? Clearly the use of this term indicates that the work must be of special importance.[150] If an item satisfies this standard on historical or archaeological grounds then it need have no artistic merit.

If not, then it must be decided whether it is of sufficient artistic merit to be described as an artistic treasure. This is a type of decision which a court is not well equipped to make, so that it must inevitably rely to a considerable extent on expert evidence. When the expert witnesses agree, this matter will be relatively straightforward[151] but it will be an almost intractable problem in the face of contradictory evidence.

---

[147] See generally Mattera 'Cultura e libera scambio dei beni artistici all'interno della Communita' [1976] Dir. Scambi Int. 12; 'Community action in the cultural sector' E.C. Bull. Supp. 6/77.

[148] [1968] E.C.R. 423, [1969] C.M.L.R. 1.

[149] Para. 2.03 above.

[150] It is true that there is some difference between the French and English language versions on the one hand and certain other versions on the other. The latter do not speak of 'treasures' but only of 'artistic heritage.'

[151] In the English case of *Re Pinion* [1965] 2 W.L.R. 919 the Court of Appeal was in the rather unusual position of having to rule on the artistic merit of certain objects, but was spared the difficulty of contradictory evidence as to merit. There a testator had directed that his studio and its contents be endowed as a museum. On the basis of undivided expert evidence the Court of Appeal found that the material in question was merely a 'mass of junk' so that the bequest did not constitute a valid charitable trust. (One of the experts expressed his surprise that 'so voracious a collector should not by hazard have picked up even one meritorious object'.)

As Mattera points out,[152] it is only in exceptional circumstances that works by contemporary artists will satisfy this test, while Wägenbaur[153] inclines to the view that they can never do so.

8.61 (b) Does the use of the term 'national treasures' exclude objects of artistic, historical or archaeological value only to a *region* of a Member State? At a time of growing interest in regional culture, it does not seem plausible to exclude such objects from the protection of Article 36. It seems fitting to apply the maxim that the greater includes the lesser: the reference to national treasures must be taken to include regional treasures.

8.62 (c) Does this limb of Article 36 only cover objects which are products of the civilisation or culture of the Member State concerned? Where an item is a historical or archaeological treasure without being an artistic treasure, then it would seem that a Member State can only retain it if it has such value to that Member State. On this view, the Netherlands could not prevent the exportation of an item of historical or archaeological importance only to Italy (a Member State) or Peru (a third country).

8.63 However, the situation may possibly be different where artistic treasures are concerned; if so, the United Kingdom may prevent the export to another Member State of a Titian or a Ming vase. On this reading 'national treasures' is taken to refer to art treasures belonging to the nation and not to treasures of national art. In favour of this view one might rely on the practical consideration that once Member States are required to let such works of art out of their clutches, then they may often disappear from the Community altogether; the cultural loss would then be borne by the entire Community. Ranged against this practical view is the formidable argument that Article 36, as an exception to a fundamental rule of the Treaty, must be interpreted restrictively.[154]

8.64 Clearly the question whether Member States may prevent the export of artistic treasures produced by other cultures is of considerable practical importance. Suffice it to mention an article in *The Times*[155] concerning a difference of opinion between the British authorities and the Rijksmuseum of Amsterdam over a silver plaque of the 'Adoration of the Shepherds' dated 1617 by Paul van Vianen, considered one of the greatest Dutch silversmiths. The Rijksmuseum had agreed to buy the plaque and when the British authorities withheld an art export

---

[152] See n. 147 above.
[153] *Op. cit.* at 296.
[154] Gormley (*op. cit.* at 183) considers that the narrower interpretation would frustrate the purpose of this ground of justification.
[155] *The Times*, 8 October 1980.

licence, it apparently claimed that this was contrary to Article 36 on the grounds that the work of art was Dutch and not British. This case posed the problem in a most poignant way because the work was a product of the culture of the very country to which it would have been exported.

8.65 Be that as it may, whether we are concerned with artistic, historical or archaeological treasures, it is submitted that the test must be whether the treasures have a place in the history, civilisation or culture of the Member State concerned: the Community rules for determining the origin of goods, which have been discussed earlier in this book,[156] can be of little assistance here. For instance, a treaty or other document may have a central place in Belgian history even though it was signed outside Belgium (on non-Belgian paper). Likewise, a work by Turner is a part of British culture, even if it was painted in Italy.

Applying this test, it can happen that more than one Member State has a claim to a particular work. This may occur in particular where an artist settled outside his home country or where territory has changed hands.

8.66 In the light of these considerations it is tentatively suggested that the following approach should be adopted in deciding whether a particular Member State may retain a given object on the grounds of its artistic, historical or archaeological value:

— first, is the object of such historical or archaeological value to *this* Member State or any of its regions as to qualify as a 'treasure'? If so, then the Member State is entitled to retain it without more, regardless of whether it has any artistic value. If not, then:
— can the object be described as an *artistic* treasure? If not, then it falls outside this limb of Article 36. If it is an artistic treasure, then:
— is it a product of the civilisation or culture of *this* Member State? If so, then it may be retained under this part of Article 36. If not, then one has to decide the point of principle whether the Member State concerned may retain the object nevertheless.

The effectiveness of fiscal supervision

8.67 This is the first of the three 'mandatory requirements' added by the Court in the *Cassis de Dijon*[157] case. This term, which is something of a newcomer to the English language, is intended to cover the prevention and detection of tax evasion.

---

[156] Para. 2.10.
[157] N. 6 above.

It is probable that the mention of the effectiveness of fiscal supervision is a reference to the earlier case of *GB-Inno* v. *ATAB*.[158] That case arose out of the prosecution of a Belgian supermarket chain, GB-Inno, for selling cigarettes below the price appearing on the tax label, contrary to Belgian law. The Belgian Cour de Cassation asked the Court of Justice whether this provision was compatible with, *inter alia*, Article 30. In what amounted to an *obiter dictum* the Court stated:

> 'In a system in which, as in Belgium, the basis of assessment to excise duty and to VAT is the retail selling price, a prohibition on selling tobacco products at a price higher than the retail selling price appearing on the tax label constitutes an essential fiscal guarantee, designed to prevent producers and importers from undervaluing their products at the time of paying the taxes.'

8.68 The Court had occasion to consider this ground of justification once again in *Carciati*.[159] The facts were that one Mr. Fink, a German national, had entrusted a car registered in Germany to the defendant for him to use in Italy on his frequent business visits. Since the defendant was resident in Italy, he was charged with having in his possession and using within the Italian customs territory a car registered abroad in infringement of the provisions governing temporary importation. The Italian court therefore referred to the Court of Justice the question whether the Italian provisions governing the matter were compatible with 'the Community rules in relation to the free movement of goods'. The Italian provisions were essentially dictated by the New York Customs Convention of 1954, to which all Member States were party, and by Community VAT directives. In the light of this, the Court held that:

> 'Member States retain broad powers to take action in respect of temporary importation, specifically for the purpose of preventing tax frauds. It follows that if the measures adopted to that end are not excessive, they are compatible with the principle of the free movement of goods.
>
> As regards the prohibition imposed by a Member State on persons resident in its territory on the use of vehicles imported temporarily tax-free, it is an effective way of preventing tax frauds and ensuring that taxes are paid in the country of destination of the goods.'

Although neither the reference nor the judgment refers to Articles 30 to 36, they refer generally to the Treaty provisions on the free movement of goods so that they are of relevance here.

8.69 The facts of *Abbink*[160] were quite different. The defendant in the main case was primarily resident in the Netherlands, but he was also resident in Saarbrücken in Germany, where he worked for the wholesale florist's owned by his son. Every week he went back and

---

[158] Case 13/77 [1977] E.C.R. 2115, [1978] 1 C.M.L.R. 283. Para. 7.70 above.
[159] Case 823/79 [1980] E.C.R. 2773, [1981] 2 C.M.L.R. 193; see also Case 159/78 *E.C. Commission* v. *Italy* (customs agents) [1979] E.C.R. 3247, [1980] 3 C.M.L.R. 446, discussed at para. 7.84 above.
[160] Case 134/83 [1984] E.C.R. 4097, [1986] 1 C.M.L.R. 579.

forth between the two places, buying flowers on the Dutch market and exporting them to Saarbrücken. One day when he was on his way back to Germany he was questioned by the Dutch police about his use of a company car with a German registration plate. Since he was resident in the Netherlands, this led to his being charged with driving a foreign-registered car there without paying Dutch tax on it.

After the material facts arose, the Council passed Directive 83/182[161] on tax exemptions within the Community for certain means of transport temporarily imported into one Member State from another. That Directive has relaxed the restrictions concerned to some extent. However, it does not apply to vehicles intended for transporting goods. Thus, even if it had been in force at the material time, it would have been of no avail to the defendant.

At all events the court at Arnhem made a reference for a preliminary ruling asking whether such a measure was compatible with the Treaty provisions on the free movement of goods, even where the car was driven without any intention of evading tax. It was clear that the question as worded could only be answered in the negative. Unfortunately the Dutch court did not ask any question about the fact that the vehicle was being used by the defendant in the course of his employment exporting goods to another Member State, where his employers were established.

In its submissions the Commission stressed that measures of this kind caused very considerable problems to frontier workers who have no intention of evading tax.[162] It illustrated this by reference to various complaints which it had received from such persons. In extreme cases the prohibition on a person driving a temporarily imported vehicle in the Member State in which he resides led to such persons having to give up their jobs altogether. For instance, a person cannot deliver goods to his own Member State in a foreign-registered lorry. The Commission took the view that in circumstances such as those in *Abbink* the prohibition in question was contrary to Article 34, since it was more restrictive than necessary to prevent tax evasion.

The Advocate General went some way with the Commission. In his view *Carciati* was not the last word on the matter. However, he rejected the broad view advocated by the Commission. He concentrated instead on the fact that the product concerned, namely flowers, is an agricultural product governed by a common market organisation. His conclusion was that in relation to such a product a measure of this kind was contrary to Article 38(2) read with Article 34 when it could be proved that the vehicle was being used for exporting the goods concerned. Yet it is submitted with respect that nothing should turn on the fact that the goods concerned were agricultural goods covered by a common market organisation; this fact does not appear to have any bearing on the measure concerned.

---

[161] [1983] O.J. L105/59.
[162] See also its answer to written question 22/82 ([1982] O.J. C262/1).

The five-judge Chamber of the Court decided the case purely on the narrow wording of the question, without giving any guidance on the wider problem. Citing *Carciati*, it held that the prohibition on residents of a Member State driving within that State cars which had been temporarily imported there and thus had not been subject to VAT there was compatible with the Treaty provisions on the free movement of goods, even where the persons concerned did not intend to evade tax.

An opportunity for the Court to rule on this major obstacle to the free movement of goods was thus lost.[163]

Consumer protection[164]

8.70   In Case 12/74 *E.C. Commission* v. *Germany*[165] the Court held that:

> 'To the extent to which [registered designations of origin and indirect indications of origin] are protected by law they must satisfy the objectives of such protection, in particular the need to ensure not only that the interests of the producers concerned are safeguarded, but also that consumers are protected against information which may mislead them'.[166]

This appears to mean that a measure may be justified on the grounds both of consumer protection and of the prevention of unfair competition, but not on one of these grounds alone. As Beier[167] has pointed out, this view is open to the most severe doubt. At all events, it seems clear from the subsequent case law generally and in particular *Cassis de Dijon*,[168] which appears to treat consumer protection and the prevention of unfair competition as two wholly separate 'mandatory requirements', that the Court has gone back on this statement in *E.C. Commission* v. *Germany*.

Nevertheless, the two grounds of justification are so closely interlinked that, to gain a complete picture of this area of the law, the reader would be well advised to peruse paragraphs 8.81 to 8.90 below.

8.71   It goes virtually without saying that a ban on false or misleading *labelling* is justified on consumer protection grounds. Thus, in

---

[163] But see the important judgments in Cases 249/84 *Ministère Public* v. *Profant* [1985] E.C.R. 3237, [1986] 2 C.M.L.R. 378, and 127/86 *Ledoux* (judgment of 6 July 1988), neither of which concerned goods.

[164] See the 1982 FIDE Report on 'Consumer Protection and the Common Market' and Brouwer 'Free Movement of Foodstuffs and Quality Requirements: Has the Commission got it Wrong?' [1988] C.M.L.Rev. 237.

[165] [1975] E.C.R. 181, [1975] 1 C.M.L.R. 340, para. 7.35 above. See the caveat about this case at para. 7.33 above.

[166] It is true that part of the judgment purports to be an interpretation of Art. 30 rather than Art. 36.

[167] 'Das Schutzbedürfnis für Herkunftsangaben und Ursprungsbezeichnungen im Gemeinsamen Markt' [1977] G.R.U.R. Int. 1, which appeared in English as 'The Need for Protection of Indications of Source and Appellations of Origin in the Common Market' in *Protection of Geographic Denominations of Goods and Services* ed. Cohen Jehoram (1980), 183 *eq seq*.

[168] See n. 6 above.

De Kikvorsch[169] the Court was concerned with a provision of Dutch law which made it an offence to state the specific strength of the original wort of beer on the packaging. The Dutch Government maintained that this prohibition was necessary to prevent the consumer confusing that information with the alcohol content, which was required to be stated on the packaging. The Court held that, if this was so, the prohibition was justified on consumer protection grounds.

By the same token, it emerges clearly from the judgment in *E.C. Commission* v. *United Kingdom*[170] that the Member States may prohibit false or misleading indications of origin.

8.72 What might be termed the 'golden rule' is the principle that the sale of a product should never be prohibited when the consumer will be sufficiently protected by adequate labelling requirements.[171] Thus in *Cassis de Dijon* itself the Court ruled that one cannot 'regard the mandatory fixing of minimum alcohol contents as being an essential guarantee of the fairness of commercial transactions, since it is a simple matter to ensure that suitable information is conveyed to the purchaser requiring the display of an indication . . . of the alcohol content on the packaging of products.' Similarly in *Gilli and Andres*,[172] where the defendants had been prosecuted for importing apple vinegar contrary to Italian law, the Court held that the national prohibition in question was not justified on the grounds of consumer protection because 'the receptacles containing [the] vinegar are provided with a sufficiently clear label indicating that it is in fact apple vinegar, thus avoiding any possibility of the consumers confusing it with wine vinegar.' Likewise, in *Rau* v. *De Smedt*[173] the requirement that margarine be sold in cubic packaging to distinguish it from butter was held to be unjustified, since adequate labelling would suffice.

The same principle has been held to be applicable to products such as beer which are not necessarily sold to the consumer in packaged form: the requisite labelling can perfectly well appear on the barrel or tap, if draft beer is consumed at the point of sale.[174] Yet in *E.C. Commission* v. *France* (substitute milk products)[175] the Court recognised that there were difficulties about giving detailed information to consumers about foodstuffs consumed in restaurants. However, it held that, since detailed information was not given about other products consumed in restaurants, it would not be justified to single out substitute milk products and impose specific requirements of this kind

---

[169] Case 94/82 [1983] E.C.R. 947, [1984] 2 C.M.L.R. 323.
[170] Case 207/83 [1985] E.C.R. 1201, [1985] 2 C.M.L.R. 259, para. 7.49 above.
[171] On labelling, see generally Dir. 79/112 on the approximation of the laws of the Member States relating to the labelling, presentation and advertising of foodstuffs for sale to the ultimate consumer ([1979] O.J. L33/1), subsequently amended.
[172] See n. 8 above, see also Case 130/80, n. 134 above.
[173] Case 261/81 [1982] E.C.R. 3961, [1983] 2 C.M.L.R. 496.
[174] Case 178/84, n. 113 above.
[175] N. 71 above.

in relation to them. On the other hand, in *Drei Glocken* v. *USL* and *Zoni*,[176] the Court appeared to suggest that Italy would be entitled to require restaurants to inform customers that their pasta was based on soft wheat.

8.73   In the same way, in Case 193/80 *E.C. Commission* v. Italy[177] the Court held that, while it was contrary to Article 30 to reserve the use of the term 'vinegar' (*aceto*) to wine vinegar, it would be justified to require the exact nature of the product to be set out on a label affixed to that product. But the Court stated that such a labelling requirement would only be justified if it applied to wine vinegar in the same way as to other types of vinegar. It is significant that on this point the Court did not follow the Advocate General's approach: he took the view that Italy was justified in prohibiting the use of the word *aceto* used alone as a description of vinegar not derived from wine, but that it was unjustified in prohibiting the use of that word coupled with another word or words indicating that the product is derived from a substance other than wine, such as cider or malt. The Court was clearly at pains to ensure that the same treatment should be accorded to wine vinegar (the 'typically Italian' product) and other types of vinegar.[178]

8.74   It should by no means be thought, however, that all labelling requirements are necessarily justified, as is shown by *Fietje*.[179] The defendant in the main case was a trader, who had sold in the Netherlands an alcoholic drink imported from West Germany bearing the label in German *Berentzen Appel–Aus Apfel mit Weizen-korn 25 vol. %*. He was prosecuted for not indicating the word *likeur* or *liqueur* on the bottles as required by Dutch law; drinks with a specified alcohol and sugar content were required to bear this indication. In reply to a reference by the Dutch court as to the compatibility of such a measure with Article 30, the Court ruled:

> 'If national rules relating to a given product include the obligation to use a description that is sufficiently precise to inform the purchaser of the nature of the product and to enable it to be distinguished from products with which it might be confused, it may well be necessary, in order to give consumers effective protection, to extend this obligation to imported products also, even in such a way as to make necessary the alteration of the original labels of some of these products . . .
>   However, there is no longer any need for such protection if the details given on the original label of the imported product have as their content information on the nature of the product and that content includes at least the same information, and is just as capable of being understood by consumers in the

---

[176] See n. 72 above.

[177] [1981] E.C.R. 3019; see also Case 281/83 *E.C. Commission* v. *Italy* [1985] E.C.R. 3397, [1987] 1 C.M.L.R. 865.

[178] Synthetic vinegars, however, fell outside the scope of this ruling; see Chapter VII, n. 102.

[179] N. 40 above.

importing State, as the description prescribed by the rules of that State. In the context of Article 177 of the EEC Treaty, the making of the findings of fact necessary in order to establish whether there is such equivalence is a matter for the national court.'

It emerges from this passage that a Member State will not always be justified in requiring all labelling to be in its own language: if the particular words appearing on the label are just as comprehensible to the consumer of that Member State as the equivalent words in his own language, then the requirement is not justified.[180]

8.75 The same approach was followed in *Robertson*[181] which concerned a process analogous to labelling, namely hallmarking. The Belgian provision in question required silver-plated articles to bear hallmarks of a particular type. Although Belgium was the only Member State to require silver-plated ware to be hallmarked, the Court found such a requirement to be justified. However, this was subject to the qualification that:

'. . . there is no longer the need for such protection where articles of that kind are imported from another Member State in which they have been lawfully marketed, if they are already hallmarked in accordance with the legislation of that State, on condition however that the indications provided by the hallmarks prescribed by that State, in whatever form, contain information which includes indications equivalent to those provided by the hallmarks prescribed by the Member State of importation and intelligible to consumers of that State.

It is for the national court to make the findings of fact needed for the purposes of determining whether or not such equivalence exists.'

It has been suggested[182] that in the light of this passage the importing Member State may require the article to bear relevant information in the form of a hallmark rather than any other form.

8.76 Whether it will ever be justified to require the origin of goods to be marked on them or displayed on an accompanying notice is a question that was not clearly decided in *E.C. Commission* v. *United Kingdom*,[183] as mentioned earlier in this book.[184] The Court held there that a Member State could lawfully prohibit 'false indications of origin,' a term which was presumably intended to embrace misleading indications of origin. However, this leaves open the question whether certain limited categories of goods hold themselves out by their very nature or appearance as having a particular origin.

8.77 As mentioned in Chapter VII,[185] the abusive reservation of appellations of origin or generic names is not justified on consumer

---

[180] See para. 7.60 above.
[181] Case 220/81 [1982] E.C.R. 2349, [1983] 1 C.M.L.R. 556.
[182] Case note by D. Waelbroeck [1983] C.D.E. 241.
[183] See n. 170 above.
[184] Para. 7.50 above.
[185] Paras. 7.35 *et seq.*; see also paras. 8.86 *et seq.* below.

protection grounds. The same applies to designations of quality.[186] It is irrelevant that the use of such appellations, names or designations is optional.[187] In contrast, in *Industrie Diensten Groep* v. *Beele*,[188] the Court in effect held that the prohibition on passing off was justified on consumer protection grounds; but, since that case is primarily concerned with the prevention of unfair competition it is discussed more fully in paragraph 8.85 below.

8.78 On another point, it was held in *Oosthoek's Uitgeversmaatschappij*[189] that:

> 'the offering of free gifts as a means of sales promotion may mislead consumers as to the real prices of certain products and distort the conditions on which genuine competition is based. Legislation which restricts or even prohibits such commercial practices for that reason is therefore capable of contributing to consumer protection and fair trading.'

8.79 When deciding whether a practice is liable to confuse the consumer, what yardstick is to be used: the understanding of the average consumer of the importing State, or that of the average Community consumer? The Court's case law is unclear on this point, and indeed the answer may vary according to the type of practice concerned.

Thus, on the one hand in *Fietje* the Court stated unequivocally that, as regards a label in another Community language, one must have regard to the linguistic ability of the average consumer of the *importing* State. Indeed, it could scarcely be otherwise: any attempt to apply a Community wide criterion in determining whether a Dutchman can understand a particular label in German would surely be doomed to failure. It is submitted that the same would generally apply to cases which turn on the associations evoked by particular words in the language of the importing State.[190] The statement in *Robertson* that the same test applies to hallmarks is perhaps less easy to explain.

On the other hand, in a series of cases the Court has held that adequate labelling would afford sufficient protection to the consumer.[191] In each of these cases the Court has not considered the ability of consumers in the State concerned to understand clear labels in their own language, but has—rightly, it is submitted,—assumed that consumers throughout the Community are alike in this respect. Furthermore, in *E.C. Commission* v. *Germany* (beer)[192] the Court stated that Member

---

[186] Case 13/78, n. 28 above.
[187] *Ibid.*
[188] Case 6/81 [1982] E.C.R. 707, [1982] 3 C.M.L.R. 102.
[189] Case 286/81 [1982] E.C.R. 4575, [1983] 3 C.M.L.R. 428.
[190] See, however, para. 7.37 above. Also, in Case 298/87 *SMANOR* (judgment of 14 July 1988) the Court determined the meaning of the word 'yoghourt' to the French consumer on the basis of the Codex Alimentarius adopted by the FAO and the World Health Organisation; see para. 7.47 above. Yet this term is particularly international in nature.
[191] See para. 8.72 above.
[192] N. 113 above and para. 7.46 above.

States may not crystallise the habits of consumers so as to consolidate an advantage acquired by national industries concerned to comply with them; thus it was not justified to prohibit the sale as 'beer' of a product containing rice and beer merely because this was traditionally prohibited in Germany.

There is no inherent contradiction between these two lines of case law. Certain matters, particularly those connected with a particular language, are inherently related to the understanding of consumers in a particular Member State, while others are not. By its very nature, the Court is inherently less well equipped than a national court to rule on cases falling within the former category.

8.80 In conclusion, it should not be overlooked that the charge has been levelled against the judgment in *Cassis de Dijon* and the subsequent cases that they have resulted in a lowering of quality standards.[192a] However, this is not necessarily so.[193] The Court has held that certain particular restrictions (*e.g.* a minimum alcohol requirement, a prohibition on the sale of cider vinegar and a prohibition on the sale of bread containing a certain proportion of dry matter)[194] were not justified on consumer protection grounds or any other grounds. Moreover, in each case the products concerned were traditional products of another Member State. But the Court has not ruled that a Member State may *never* prohibit the sale of a product on quality grounds, as distinct from health grounds. Nevertheless, it is arguable that it will always be a sufficient guarantee for the consumer to ban the sale of low quality products under a given designation rather than to ban them altogether. For example, on this view there is no necessity to prohibit the sale of 'orange juice' containing only 2 per cent. orange, since it is enough to ban its sale under that name.

The prevention of unfair competition

8.81 The term 'prevention of unfair competition' is used here as being more appropriate than the expression 'the fairness of commercial transactions' used in the *Cassis de Dijon*[195] case. Indeed the term 'unfair competition' was used in *E.C. Commission* v. *Germany*.[196] Perhaps the best guidance on the meaning of this concept can be drawn from Article 10*bis* inserted into the Paris Convention for the Protection of Industrial Property of 1883.[197] This provision reads as follows:

> '(1) The countries of the Union are bound to assure the nationals of such countries effective protection against unfair competition;

[192a] See para. 6.61 above.
[193] Para. 6.61 above.
[194] See paras. 7.54 *et seq.* above.
[195] N. 6 above.
[196] N. 165 above.
[197] In principle the Treaty of Rome prevails over the Convention as between Member States: see paras. 9.61 *et seq.* below. Consequently, the Paris Convention only gives guidance on this matter, rather than being binding.

(2)   Any act of competition contrary to honest practices in industrial or commercial matters constitutes an act of unfair competition;

(3)   The following in particular shall be prohibited:

1.   all acts of such a nature as to create confusion by any means whatever with the establishment, the goods, or the industrial or commercial activities, of a competitor;

2.   false allegations in the course of trade of such a nature as to discredit the establishment, the goods, or the industrial or commercial activities, of a competitor;

3.   indications or allegations the use of which in the course of trade is liable to mislead the public as to the nature, the manufacturing process, the characteristics, the suitability for their purpose, or the quantity, of the goods.'[198]

The concept of unfair competition therefore broadly corresponds to practices actionable in English law for passing off or slander of title.[199]

8.82   On the other hand, it would seem that where a Member State prohibits the sale of goods having a particular content or presentation so as to prevent them from benefiting from some advantageous provision of its own law, then this ground of justification is not in point. The ruling in *Miro*[200] appears to be authority for this proposition. In that case the Dutch Government sought to justify its prohibition on the use of the name *jenever* for drinks with an alcohol content of less than 35 per cent. on the grounds *inter alia* that such a product would attract a lower rate of tax and excise duties. This would, it submitted, confer an unfair price avantage on such products. The Court dismissed this argument on the grounds that:

'Such differences in taxes and excise duties charged under national legislation are part of the objective conditions of competition of which every trader may freely take advantage, provided that purchasers are given information so that they can freely make their choice on the basis of the quality and price of the products.'

This wording suggests that the same principle might perhaps apply where the legislation conferring the advantage is not that of the importing Member State.[201]

8.83   As already pointed out,[202] the Court in effect stated in *E.C. Commission* v. *Germany*[203] that a measure might only be justified on the grounds of unfair competition if it was simultaneously justified on the grounds of consumer protection; the Court appears to have retreated from that unduly restrictive position. Yet the fact remains that the ground of the prevention of unfair competition is so often

---

[198]   See Bodenhausen's Guide to the Paris Convention (1968).

[199]   For a comparative study, see Ulmer's series of volumes entitled *La répression de la concurrence déloyale dans les Etats membres de la Communauté économique européenne* (1967).

[200]   Case 182/84 [1985] E.C.R. 3731, [1986] 3 C.M.L.R. 545.

[201]   A.G. Slynn rejected the argument on other grounds, namely that it was entirely economic (see para. 8.19 above).

[202]   Para. 8.70 above.

[203]   N. 165 above.

closely linked to that of consumer protection as to stand or fall with it; if there is no danger of the consumer being misled, then frequently other procedures will not be subject to unfair competition.[204]

8.84 However, in *Dansk Supermarked* v. *Imerco*[205] the question of unfair competition did arise independently of consumer protection. The facts were that Imerco, a syndicate of Danish ironmongers, had a dinner service made in the United Kingdom to celebrate its 50th anniversary. Each item of the service was decorated with pictures of Danish royal castles and bore Imerco's name and a legend referring to its 50th anniversary. The exclusive right to sell this service was reserved to the members of the syndicate. It was agreed between Imerco and the British manufacturer that 'seconds'—which amounted to about 20 per cent. of production because of the criteria chosen— could be sold on the British market, but should on no accout be exported to Denmark or to other Scandinavian countries. However, Dansk Supermarked acquired some such 'seconds' on the British market and proceeded to sell them in Denmark, whereupon Imerco brought an action against it before the Danish courts. The action reach the Supreme Court of Denmark which put a question to the Court for a preliminary ruling asking in effect whether it was compatible with Article 36 to prevent such importers on the grounds of copyright protection, trade mark protection or the prevention of unfair competition.

The Court replied with respect to unfair competition as follows:

'In order to reply to that question it must first of all be remarked that Community law does not in principle have the effect of preventing the application in a Member State to goods imported from other Member States of the provisions on marketing in force in the State of importation. It follows that the marketing of imported goods may be prohibited if the conditions on which they are sold constitute an infringement of the marketing usages considered proper and fair in the Member State of importation.

It must nevertheless be emphasised, as the Court of Justice has stressed in another context in its judgment of 25 November 1971 (Case 22/71 *Béguelin* [1971] E.C.R. 949, [1972] C.M.L.R. 81), that the actual fact of the importation of goods which have been lawfully marketed in another Member State cannot be considered as an improper or unfair act since that description may be attached only to offer or exposure for sale on the basis of circumstances distinct from the importation itself . . .

The second part of the reply to the question submitted must thus be that Article 30 of the Treaty must be interpreted as meaning:

That the importation into a Member State of goods lawfully marketed in another Member State cannot as such be classified as an improper or unfair commercial practice, without prejudice however to the possible application of legislation of the State of importation against such practices on the ground of the circumstances or methods of offering such goods for sale as distinct from the actual fact of importation. . . .'

---

[204] *E.g.* Case 12/74, n. 165 above; Case 120/78, n. 6 above.
[205] Case 58/80 [1981] E.C.R. 181, [1981] 3 C.M.L.R. 590 noted by Dyckjaes-Hansen [1982] 3 E.I.P.R. 85.

This last proviso appears to relate to a point made by the Advocate General: he took the view that, although in principle sales of 'seconds' could not be prevented on the grounds of unfair competition, it would be otherwise if they held themselves out to the consumer as being of first quality.

8.85   The prevention of unfair competition was also in point in *Industrie Diensten Groep* v. *Beele*.[206] There, the appellants in the main case had imported certain cable conduits into the Netherlands for a number of years. The Dutch patent had now expired and the respondents had begun to market in the Netherlands other cable conduits imported from Germany, which bore a striking resemblance to those imported by the appellants. The appellants alleged before the Dutch courts that the respondents' goods constituted slavish imitation of their own, and thus sought an injunction preventing the respondents from marketing their products in the Netherlands. In English law, this would have amounted to an action for passing off. In its reference for a preliminary ruling, the Dutch court asked the Court of Justice in essence whether it would be contrary to Articles 30 to 36 to grant such an injunction, stating that the similarity between the two products was greater than necessary.

Citing Article 10*bis* of the Paris Convention, the Court replied that it was justified on the grounds of the prevention of unfair competition and on consumer protection grounds to prohibit the sale of imported goods which were, 'for no compelling reason practically identical to the products imitated' and caused unnecessary confusion. On the latter point, the Court stressed that 'the judgment of the national court shows that the question whether or not such imitation is necessary was considered not only from the technical point of view, but also from the economic and commercial point of view.'

8.86   The ruling in *Prantl*[207] is one of the most important delivered by the Court in relation to the free movement of goods in the last few years.

It concerned a German statutory provision to the effect that only wines from certain specified regions of Germany could be marketed in bottles of a particular shape known as *Bocksbeutel*. According to a tradition going back several centuries, wine from these regions was sold in these bottles of a squat and bulbous shape. The overwhelming majority of these wines are white. It so happened that red wine produced in the Italian Tyrol had been marketed, both in that region and elsewhere, in bottles of an almost identical shape for at least a century. The defendant in the main case was charged with selling or holding for sale quantities of red Italian wine in such bottles in contravention of the provision of German law referred to. The German

---

[206] See n. 188 above.
[207] Case 16/83 [1984] E.C.R. 1299, [1985] 1 C.M.L.R. 688, see para. 7.44 above.

court requested the Court to deliver a preliminary ruling on whether such a provision was compatible with Articles 30 and 36 when applied to imports.

The Court found that such a measure could not be justified as preventing unfair competition (or on consumer protection grounds). Such grounds could not justify the prohibition on the sale of imported wines in bottles of a certain shape so as to protect an indirect designation of geographical origin without regard to the 'fair and traditional practices observed in the various Member States.' The offending Italian bottles, which were identical or virtually identical to the *Bocksbeutel,* met that test since they were traditionally used in certain regions of Italy. (This 'fair and traditional' test, which gives rise to some concern, will be discussed further in paragraph 8.89 below.)

Moreover, the Court went on to hold that there was no danger of the consumer's being misled, since the Community legislation on the labelling of quality wines was 'particularly comprehensive' and thus ensured that such confusion was avoided.[208]

8.87   This case points to a crucial distinction between rights constituting industrial and commercial property and those protected merely by the rules on the prevention of unfair competition. The Court described the *Bocksbeutel* bottle as an indirect indication of geographical origin; it was contended by the German Government that as such it was to be regarded as industrial and commercial property within the meaning of Article 36 and that the importation of similar bottles could therefore be precluded. The Court dismissed this argument in the following terms:

> 'In this regard it need merely be observed, without its being necessary to resolve these questions of law raised by that argument, that producers who traditionally use a bottle of a specific shape may not in any event successfully rely upon an industrial or commercial property right in order to prevent imports of wines originating in another Member State which have been bottled in identical or similar bottles in accordance with a fair and traditional practice in that State.'

This ruling is to be contrasted with that in *Terrapin* v. *Terranova,*[209] in which precisely the opposite conclusion was reached in relation to trade marks and trade names. This leads one inevitably to one of two alternative conclusions: either indirect indications of geographical origin do not constitute industrial and commercial property; or the concept of industrial and commercial property is broad enough to embrace weaker rights such as this which afford less protection than the better recognised forms of industrial and commercial property. The former view is preferable, if only to avoid semantic confusion.[210]

---

[208] See generally para. 8.72 above.
[209] Case 119/75 [1976] E.C.R. 1039, [1976] 2 C.M.L.R. 482, para. 8.132 below.
[210] See also para. 8.90 below.

8.88   The prevention of unfair competition also arose in *Miro*.[211] Under Dutch law 'gin' was defined as a drink with an alcohol content of at least 35 per cent. It was prohibited to use the name *jenever* or other related designations for products with a lower alcohol content. The defendants imported from Belgium quantities of gin with an alcohol content of 30 per cent. Such gin had been produced in Belgium for many years. At the material time Belgium imposed no alcohol requirement for this product. The alcohol content was clearly indicated on the label, but the name *jenever* was also used. The defendants, who were charged with the offence of possessing stocks of bottles so labelled with a view to sale, claimed that the relevant provisions of Dutch law infringed Article 30.

Referring *inter alia* to *Prantl* the Advocate General reached the conclusion that the measure was not justified. However, he expressly left open the question as to what would be the position of gin containing a mere 15 per cent. alcohol, a point which had been raised by the Dutch Government.

The Court also found on the basis of *Prantl* that the measure was not justified, subject to the condition that 'the purchaser is provided with proper information.' In reaching this conclusion, the Court more or less directly applied the 'fair and traditional' test first laid down in *Prantl*. It did not rule on the hypothetical problem of gin having a far lower alcohol content.

8.89   As already mentioned, the 'fair and traditional' test is the source of some concern. The time-honoured criterion laid down in *Cassis de Dijon* is that the goods must have been 'lawfully produced and marketed in another Member State.[212] This criterion is more satisfactory than the 'fair and traditional' test on two counts. First of all, it is far more conducive to legal certainty: whether marketing and production are lawful is a question of law, while 'fair' and 'traditional' are largely subjective terms.[213] Secondly, the requirement of 'traditional' usage will prevent imports of new products—scarcely a desirable result. What is more, it is surely undesirable that the two tests should coexist alongside each other.

In these circumstances the judgment in *E.C. Commission* v. *Germany*[214] is of particular interest. *Pétillant de raisin* is a product which has been made in France since 1956 from partially fermented grape juice and has always been marketed in bottles similar in shape to that of the traditional champagne-type bottle with a wired mushroom shaped stopper; its alcoholic strength does not exceed 3 per cent. Under German legislation its sale in such bottles was prohibited. This

---

[211] N. 200 above. Consumer protection was not, however, in point since the referring court has found that the label gave rise to no confusion. In a sense, that court thereby pre-empted discussion on the central issue raised by the case.

[212] Para. 6.45 *et seq.* above.

[213] Brouwer, *op. cit.*, n. 164 above, at 253.

[214] Case 179/85 [1988] 1 C.M.L.R. 135.

was anomalous because under the legislation the use of such bottles was not in fact reserved for champagne and sparkling wines: cider and certain sparkling drinks made from fruit juice could also be sold in bottles of this kind.

Advocate General Slynn considered that the restriction was not justified, since the labelling was sufficient. As to the 'fair and traditional' test he had this to say:

'. . . whereas the "fair and traditional usage" test may be appropriate in a case like *Prantl* where the question of indirect designation of origin arose, it does not seem to me that it has to be established in every case. If it did, the development and marketing of new products would be stifled. The appropriate test in a case like the present is in my view stated in *Cassis de Dijon*—whether the product was "lawfully produced and marketed" in one Member State. If it is, it may be marketed in another Member State subject to mandatory requirements of the kind indicated in *Cassis de Dijon* and subject to the provisions of Article 36 of the Treaty. I should in any event accept that the sale of a product for thirty years in a particular container was capable of amounting to a fair and traditional usage.'

The Court also found that the labelling sufficed. It continued:

'As regards the Federal Government's arguments concerning fair trading, it must be borne in mind, as is clear from the documents and oral arguments submitted to the Court, that:

(i) since production began in 1956, *pétillant de raisin* has been lawfully and continuously marketed in France and other Member States in its original presentation consisting of the traditional champagne-type bottle with its traditional stopper. It cannot therefore be maintained that such a presentation is used on the German market for unfair trading purposes or to exploit the good name of other products.

(ii) in any event, the traditional champagne-type bottle with its traditional stopper has been used for a long time in the Member States to bottle not only champagne and sparkling wine but also a number of other beverages such as cider or drinks made from fruit juice without conferring on their manufacturers an exclusive right to use that type of presentation and without affecting fair trading;

(iii) the German legislation itself allows the traditional champagne-type bottle to be used to bottle not only sparkling wines but also sparkling drinks made from fruit or berries.

Therefore, the marketing of *pétillant de raisin* on the German market in the bottle in which it has been continuously and lawfully marketed since it came onto the market 30 years ago must be regarded as satisfying the requirements arising from the need to have regard on all sides for the fair and traditional practices observed in the various Member States, and it is not necessary to consider whether the presentation in question is technically or economically necessary for the producer.'

This ruling has watered down the test of 'fair and traditional' usage to a considerable extent. It remains to be seen whether this test is to continue and, if so, what its function is to be.

8.90 Another interesting, albeit unrelated, case was *Kohl* v. *Ringelhan & Rennett*,[215] which concerned the right to use the 'distinctive sign' consisting of the letters 'r + r' in white against a contrasting background. That sign had been used by the German firm Ringelhan &

---

[215] Case 177/83 [1984] E.C.R. 3651, [1985] 3 C.M.L.R. 340.

Rennett, which had set up the defendant company as its subsidiary in France in 1971 and had gone bankrupt in 1982. The defendant company had been taken over by a third party. The plaintiff was a competing company which brought an action before the German courts claiming that the defendant was not entitled to use the distinctive sign in Germany without indicating that it no longer had any economic or legal connection with its former parent. The plaintiff relied on the German law of unfair competition. The national court made a reference for a preliminary ruling on this matter, on the basis that the use of the distinctive sign by the defendant was lawful in France.

The Court began by pointing out that the plaintiff company did not itself claim the right to use the distinctive sign in question. It merely contended that the use of this sign by the defendant gave a misleading impression to the public that its products emanated from, or were connected with, the bankrupt company. This was why industrial and commercial property was not directly raised in the case: even if the right to use the sign constituted industrial and commercial property, the plaintiff was unable to rely on it.

Next, the Court went on to consider whether the measure at issue was 'indistinctly applicable.' It found that it was not. The reason for prohibiting the use of the sign was that it misled the public into thinking that the goods were of German origin, when in fact they were imported from France. Thus there was discrimination against imported goods. Accordingly, the measure could not be justified on grounds of the prevention of unfair competition (or consumer protection).[216]

Like *Prantl*, this case illustrates the difference between industrial and commercial property on the one hand and rights protected merely by the rules relating to the prevention of unfair competition on the other.

The protection of the environment

8.91   It appears that the protection of the environment is also a ground of justification either under Article 36 or as a 'mandatory requirement.' The Commission took this view in its answer to Written Question 1285/77[217] on a Danish measure prohibiting the use of one way (non-reusable) bottles. In its answer the Commission stated that 'there is no doubt that environmental protection can be regarded as a matter of general concern which may justifiably be accorded priority over the free movement of goods.[218] It repeated this view in its

---

[216] See para. 6.53 above.
[217] [1979] O.J. C214/5.
[218] See also the A.G. in Cases, 3, 4 and 6/76 *Kramer* [1976] E.C.R. 1279 at 1325, [1976] 2 C.M.L.R. 440.

Communication on the *Cassis de Dijon* case.[219] Two judgments[220] of the Court can probably be taken to confirm this view.

Frequently, measures justified on environmental grounds will be justified on the grounds of the protection of the health and life of human beings, animals or plants. However, this will not always be so.

The improvement of working conditions

8.92 Health and safety at work fall under the heading of public health in Article 36. It would appear, though, that the improvement of working conditions constitutes a 'mandatory requirement' even in the absence of any health considerations. This emerges from *Oebel*,[221] which concerned national legislation prohibiting the baking of bread at night. The Advocate General found that such a measure was justified on the grounds that it served to improve working conditions. In so doing he referred to Article 117 of the Treaty, which begins: 'Members States agree upon the need to promote improved working conditions and an improved standard of living for workers. . . .'

Although the Court found that a measure of this kind fell outside Articles 30 and 34 altogether, it indirectly confirmed the Advocate General's finding on this point, by stating that the prohibition on night baking was a legitimate economic and social policy decision aimed at improving working conditions in a manifestly sensitive sector and thus compatible with the objects of general interest recognised by the Treaty.

Article 117 was not referred to by the Court. What is more, the Court's observations on this point were confined to the promotion of improved working conditions. The promotion of an improved standard of living for workers, also mentioned in Article 117, is not mentioned in the judgment. It is submitted that this is simply because the promotion of an improved standard of living is a goal of a purely economic nature and therefore cannot justify restrictions on imports and exports.[222]

Other possible grounds

8.93 As has already been pointed out earlier in this book,[223] the 'mandatory requirements' set out in *Cassis de Dijon* do not purport to be exhaustive. It follows that further grounds could be added to the list of grounds of justification contained in Article 36. It should be borne in mind, however, that Article 36 is 'directed to eventualities

---

[219] [1980] O.J. C256/2, see para. 6.42 above.
[220] Cases 240/83 *Procureur de la République* v. *ADBHU* [1985] E.C.R. 532 (paras. 13 and 15 of judgment) and 54/85 *Mirepoix* [1986] E.C.R. 1067, [1987] 2 C.M.L.R. 44.
[221] Case 155/80 [1981] E.C.R. 1993, [1983] 1 C.M.L.R. 390.
[222] As to the 'working environment,' see now also Art. 118A inserted into the Treaty by the Single European Act ([1987] O.J. L169/1), discussed at para. 13.23 below.
[223] Para. 6.41 above.

of a non-economic kind', and the same must apply to the mandatory requirements, if the principle of the free movement of goods is not to be undermined.[224]

It is perhaps for the latter reason that the Court has so far declined to decide whether the protection of culture constitutes a 'mandatory requirement' capable of justifying restrictions on imports or exports. The problem is most delicate. On the one hand, the protection of culture is obviously a worthy objective which should have its place in Community law and which is by no means fully covered by the exception in Article 36 relating to 'the protection of national treasures possessing artistic, historic or archaeological value.' On the other hand, to bring whole sectors of commercial activity virtually outside Article 30 on the grounds that they involve the production of 'cultural' goods would be unthinkable. Moreover, 'culture' is notoriously difficult to define: to classify all books (let alone all films!) as 'culture' would be manifestly absurd. Both in *Leclerc* v. *Au Blé Vert*[225] and in *Cinéthèque*[226] the Court was able to avoid grasping this particular nettle.[227]

Industrial and commercial property

8.94   The most important types of industrial and commercial property are patents,[228] trade marks,[229] and copyright[230] with plant breeder's rights[231] being of lesser importance. In the terminology of the legal systems of some Member States copyright is not regarded as 'industrial and commercial property' but rather as 'intellectual or

---

[224] Para. 8.19 above; see also para. 8.24 above.

[225] Case 229/83 [1985] E.C.R. 5, [1985] 2 C.M.L.R. 286.

[226] N. 69 above; without taking a position as to the protection of culture, the A.G. (at p. 2613) found that, if the measure was necessary for the maintenance of the film industry and the supply of films to the consumer, that was legitimate.

[227] As it did in relation to services in Case 352/85 *Bond van Adverteerders* v. *Netherlands* (judgment of 26 April 1988).

[228] As with trade marks and copyright, the literature is vast; see, *e.g.* Johannes, *Gewerblicher Rechtsschutz und Urheberrecht im Europäischen Gemeinschaftsrecht* (1973); *Industrial property and copyright in European Community Law* (1976); Demaret, *Patents, Territorial Restrictions and EEC Law* (1978); Guy and Leigh, *The EEC and Intellectual Property* (1981).

[229] See *e.g.* Ullrich, 'Libre circulation des marchandises et droit des marques' [1975] R.T.D.E. 395; von Bar, *Territorialität des Warenzeichens und Erschöpfung des Verbreitungsrechts im Gemeinsamen Markt* (1977); Hefermehl, Ipsen, Schluep, Sieben, *Nationaler Markenschütz und freier Warenverkehr in der Europäischen Gemeinschaft* (1979); Johannes, *op. cit.* n. 228 above; Guy and Leigh, *op. cit.* n. 228 above; Evans 'Trade Marks and Consumer Interests in EEC Law' [1983] I.C.L 241.

[230] See, *e.g.* Dietz, *Das Urheberrecht in der Europäischen Gemeinschaft* (1978); *Copyright Law in the European Community* (1978); Johannes, *op. cit.* n. 228 above; Guy and Leigh, *op. cit.* n. 228 above; Hoffman, 'Copyright and the Treaty of Rome, Recent Developments: an overview' [1981] 9 E.I.P.R. 254; Reischl 'La Protection de la Propriété Industrielle et Commerciale et le Droit d'Auteur dans le marché Commun' [1982] C.D.E. 3; Harris 'Community Law and Intellectual Property; Recent Cases in the Court of Justice' [1982] C.M.L.Rev. 61; Joliet and Delsaux 'Le droit d'auteur dans la jurisprudence de la Cour de Justice des Communautés Européennes' [1985] C.D.E. 381.

[231] In Case 258/78 *Nungesser* v. *E.C. Commission* [1982] E.C.R. 2015, [1983] 1 C.M.L.R. 278 these were held to constitute industrial and commerical property (para. 35 of the judgment).

artistic property' so that there was some doubt whether copyright fell under this heading of Article 36. However, this doubt was finally dispelled by the judgment of the Court in *Membran* v. *GEMA*[232] in ruling that this expression in Article 36 'includes the protection conferred by copyright, especially when exploited commercially in the form of licences capable of affecting distribution in the various Member States of goods incorporating the protected literary or artistic work.' Design copyright has also been held to constitute 'industrial and commercial property' for the purposes of Article 36.[233]

In addition, other types of rights are perhaps to be included within the concept of industrial and commercial property under Article 36.[234] However, as indicated in paragraph 8.87, it now seems probable that appellations and indications of origin do not fall within this ground of justification and are to be subsumed instead under the joint headings of consumer protection and unfair competition. At all events, it would seem wrong that any consequences should turn on whether or not particular rights or interests fall under the heading of industrial and commercial property rather than any other heading. What matters rather is how far such rights or interests may be permitted, on their proper construction, to restrict trade between Member States.

8.95 The Community law relating to industrial and commercial property can be divided into three aspects:
  (i) Articles 30 to 36
  (ii) Articles 85 and 86; and
  (iii) harmonisation and co-ordination.
Clearly, only the first of these falls squarely within the scope of this book. However one cannot avoid a brief mention of the second and third aspects.

8.96 It is appropriate to begin with the measures adopted by the Community and under Community auspices to harmonise and co-ordinate industrial and commercial property law.

As regards patents, the Community Patent Convention[235] was signed by the Member States in Luxembourg in 1975. The C.P.C. interlocks with the international patent system created by the European Patent Convention signed at Munich in 1973, which covers a wider range of West European States and which entered into force in 1977. Nevertheless the C.P.C. is expressed to be subject to the

---

[232] Cases 55 and 57/80 [1981] E.C.R. 147, [1981] 2 C.M.L.R. 44, noted by Alexander [1981] C.M.L.Rev. 422.

[233] Case 144/81 *Keurkoop* v. *Nancy Kean Gifts* [1982] E.C.R. 2853, [1983] 2 C.M.L.R. 47, discussed by Bonet 'Propriétés intellectuelles' [1984] R.T.D.E. at 316.

[234] See Harris, 'The Application of Article 36 to Intellectual Property' [1976] 1 E.L.Rev. 515.

[235] [1976] O.J. L17; see Cornish, 'The European Patent Conventions' [1976] J.B.L. 112; McClellan, 'La Convention sur le brevet communautaire' [1978] C.D.E. 202; Singer, *Das Neue Europäische Patentsystem* [1979].

Treaty of Rome: Article 93. By virtue of Article 5 of the Convention, the Court of Justice is to have jurisdiction in respect of it. Its essential object is to enable an applicant to obtain a single patent applying throughout the Community without prejudice to the right of the Member States to grant national patents. In addition, it contains a small number of provisions harmonising aspects of national patent laws. In the present context Articles 32 and 81 of the C.P.C. are of particular importance and will be mentioned again below. It should be noted, however, that the C.P.C. has not been ratified by all the Member States and has consequently not entered into force. Despite this the Court appears to be willing to use the C.P.C. as a guide to the interpretation of Community provisions which are in force.[236]

With respect to trade marks the Commission has now formally proposed two draft instruments[237] to be adopted by the Council. These consist respectively of a proposal for a first Council Directive to approximate the laws of the Member States relating to trade marks, which proposal is based on Article 100 of the Treaty[238]; and a proposal for a Council Regulation based on Article 235 of the Treaty[239] setting up a Community trade mark system operating alongside those of the Member States.

Work has also begun in the Commission on harmonising copyright laws.[240]

8.97 It is now appropriate to turn briefly to Articles 85 and 86. The Court has held repeatedly[241] that the exercise of an industrial property right[242] may fall foul of Article 85 when it constitutes 'the subject, the means or the result of a restrictive practice'. Moreover, it has held[243] that the exercise of an industrial property right will not in itself constitute an abuse of a dominant position under Article

---

[236] Case 288/82 *Duijnstee* v. *Goderbauer* [1983] E.C.R. 3663, [1985] 1 C.M.L.R. 765 (para. 27); see also Case 19/84 *Pharmon* v. *Hoechst* [1985] E.C.R. 2281, [1985] 3 C.M.L.R. 775.

[237] [1980] O.J. C351/1 (the draft Directive) and 5 (the draft Regulation) amended in [1985] O.J. C351/4 and [1984] O.J. C230/1 respectively. Supplement 5/80 to the Bulletin contains an art. by art. commentary on these draft provisions. See also Morcom, 'The legitimacy of a European Trade Mark System' [1980] E.I.P.R. 359, Armitage, 'The CTM: Comments on the Latest Drafts of the Proposed EEC Regulation and Directive' [1981] E.I.P.R. 72; Schwartz, 'Das Markenrecht in der Europäischen Gemeinschaft—Eine Zwischenbilanz' [1981] G.R.U.R. Int. 1; Gormley, 'The Commission's proposals on trade marks' [1981] E.L.Rev. 385 and 463; Morcom, 'The future of Trade Marks in the EEC' [1982] J.B.L. 70.

[238] Para. 12.01 below.

[239] Para. 12.05 below.

[240] Written question 792/80 ([1980] O.J. C269/28); see Report of a meeting held by the Commission on the duration of copyright protection [1980] E.I.P.R. D310; Davies, 'Harmonisation of copyright legislations in the European Communities' [1981] E.I.P.R. 67.

[241] *E.g.* Case 40/70 *Sirena* v. *Eda* [1971] E.C.R. 69, [1971] C.M.L.R. 260; Case 51/75 *EMI Records* v. *CBS United Kingdom* [1976] E.C.R. 811, [1976] 2 C.M.L.R. 235.

[242] The term 'industrial property' is used here for convenience instead of 'industrial and commercial property.'

[243] *E.g.* Case 40/70, n. 241 above.

86. For that provision to be infringed three elements must be present: the undertaking must have a dominant position within the Common Market or a substantial part of it; the exercise of the industrial property right must be an improper exploitation thereof; and that improper exploitation must be liable to affect trade between Member States.

A considerable body of Commission Decisions and other instruments has been established on the compatibility of the exercise of industrial property rights with Articles 85 and 86.[244] Moreover, the first cases[245] on industrial and commercial property to come before the Court related to Articles 85 and 86, not least because the prohibitions in Article 30 on quantitative restrictions on imports and measures of equivalent effect did not come into effect until 1968 and 1970 respectively.[246] Although Article 36 had come to be relied on by the Court as an aid to the interpretation of Articles 85 and 86,[247] it was not until the Court's landmark decision in *Deutsche Grammophon* v. *Metro*[248] that the Court applied Articles 30 to 36 to industrial property rights quite independently of the Treaty provisions on competition. Accordingly, since Articles 85 and 86 fall outside the scope of this book, we can begin with the *Deutsche Grammophon* case.

8.98 The case law on the compatibility with Articles 30 to 36 of the exercise of industrial property rights can be summarised in the following rules:

Rule 1: The Court has repeatedly held that, although the Treaty does not affect the existence of industrial and commercial property rights recognised by the legislation of a Member State, the *exercise* of those rights may nevertheless fall foul of Article 30 or Article 34. This must be taken to mean that the exercise of such rights may infringe those Articles even if the relevant national legislation on the acquisition, transfer or extinction of such rights is lawful. Such legislation will itself only rarely be contrary to Article 30 or Article 34.

Rule 2: Subject to certain exceptions, the exclusive right guaranteed by national legislation on industrial and commercial property is exhausted when a product has been lawfully distributed on the market of a Member State by the owner of the right or with his consent. Thereafter the owner of the right may not oppose the importation of the product into any other Member State, nor may

---

[244] See, *e.g.* Bellamy and Child, *Common Market Law of Competition* 3rd. ed. (1987).
[245] Cases 56 and 58/64 *Consten and Grundig* v. *EEC Commission* [1966] E.C.R. 299, [1966] C.M.L.R. 418; Case 24/67 *Parke, Davis* v. *Centrafarm* [1968] E.C.R. 55, [1968] C.M.L.R. 47; Case 40/70, n. 241 above.
[246] Paras. 5.01 *et seq.* and 6.02 *et seq.* above.
[247] Case 40/70, n. 241 above.
[248] Case 78/70 [1971] E.C.R. 487, [1971] C.M.L.R. 631.

he oppose its re-importation into the Member State where it was first marketed.

Rule 3: A trade mark right may not be relied on with a view to prohibiting the marketing in a Member State of goods lawfully produced in another Member State under an identical trade mark having the same origin.

Rule 4: Where the same person holds a particular industrial property right in all the Member States, another person holding that right with respect to a third country may not manufacture or market his goods within the Community in reliance on that right—even when there is a common origin.

Rule 5: Subject to Rules 2 and 3 above (and to the application of Articles 85 and 86) the holder of an industrial property right may rely on that right to prohibit the importation or sale of goods from other Member States. However, such rights may not be exercised in such a way as to constitute arbitrary discrimination or a disguised restriction on trade between Member States.

Each of these rules will now be examined in turn.

Rule 1

8.99   The rule that the Treaty does not affect the existence of industrial and commercial property rights, which is set out in nearly all the cases on industrial and commercial property, appears to be derived from Article 222 which stipulates that: 'This Treaty shall in no way prejudice the rules in Member States governing the system of property ownership'.[249] The effect of this rule is simply that industrial property rights remain unaffected by the Treaty except that they may not be used to prohibit or restrict imports in the circumstances set out in the following rules and may not be used in such a way as to fall foul of Articles 85 and 86.

A clear illustration of this rule is to be found in *Keurkoop* v. *Nancy Kean Gifts*,[250] the first case in which a party challenged the method by which industrial and commercial property is acquired rather than its extension to imports from other Member States. Nancy Kean Gifts had registered the design of a handbag manufactu- red in Taiwan under the Uniform Benelux Law on Designs even though it was not the author of the design and was not acting with the consent of the author. This was wholly compatible with the Uniform Law which simply provided that in such a case the author of the design could apply within five years to have the registration set aside in favour of himself. It was not open to any other person to contest the registration on the grounds that the person who had obtained it was neither the author nor acting with the author's consent. Keurkoop then began importing the handbag in question

---

[249] This provision was in issue in the first cases on industrial property, see n. 245 above; see also para. 9.52 below.
[250] See n. 233 above.

into the Netherlands, whereupon Nancy Kean Gifts brought an action against it before the Dutch courts. In its first question referred under Article 177 the Dutch court in effect asked whether such liberal provisions as to registration were justified under Article 36.

The Court replied that 'in the present state of Community law and in the absence of Community standardisation or of a harmonisation of laws the determination of the conditions and procedures under which protection is granted is a matter of national rules and, in this instance, for the common legislation established under a regional union between Belgium, Luxembourg and the Netherlands referred to in Article 233 of the Treaty.' Consequently a provision of the kind in question was held to be compatible with Article 30.

8.100 *Nancy Kean* has now been confirmed in *Thetford Corporation* v. *Fiamma SpA.*[251] The plaintiffs there, who owned United Kingdom patents for portable lavatories granted under the Patents Act 1949, sought to prevent the defendants from importing such lavatories from Italy. This invention had appeared in patent specifications filed more than 50 years previously, but the Patents Act expressly stipulated that this constituted no bar to the valid grant of a patent. In these circumstances the defendants maintained that such a patent lacked the novelty or inventive step necessary for it to be covered by Article 36.

Like Advocate General Mischo, the Court dismissed the defendants' argument on the basis of *Nancy Kean*. Also rejected was the suggestion that *Nancy Kean* was to be distinguished on the grounds that patent law had been subject to a higher degree of harmonisation than design copyright law. The Court pointed out that there was as yet no Community harmonisation of patent law, and found no relevant provisions in any international convention.

Moreover, it went on to re-affirm this by ruling that the '50-year rule' did not constitute a disguised restriction on trade between Member States, since it 'aimed to make it possible to give a reward, in the form of the grant of a patent, even in cases in which an "old" invention was "rediscovered". In such cases the United Kingdom legislation was designed to prevent the existence of a former patent specification which had never been utilised or published from constituting a ground for revoking a patent which had been validly issued.'

8.101 Nevertheless, the rulings in *Nancy Kean* and *Thetford* cannot be taken to mean that every conceivable restriction on the acquisition of industrial and commercial property is necessarily justified under Article 36. For instance, were a Member State to limit the protection

---

[251] Case 35/87 (judgment of 30 June 1988).

afforded by an industrial property right to products manufactured within its territory, that would surely be unjustified. Again, it would presumably be unjustified for a Member State to stipulate that a right may only be registered by a person with a place of business or representation in its territory.[252] What is more, the passage quoted above from *Thetford* suggests that, had the invention been published or utilised in the United Kingdom or any other Member State, the Court would have held the exception in Article 36 to be inapplicable. (The filing of a patent application does not constitute publication.)

Logically, the same principles must apply to national provisions governing the transfer or extinction of industrial property rights. For instance, it could scarcely be lawful for a Member State to confiscate patents exploited solely by imports so as to ensure that they are exploited instead by production within its territory.[253]

8.102   The view expressed in the previous paragraph is borne out by the opening sub-paragraph of Protocol 8 to the Act of Accession of Spain and Portugal,[254] which provides:

> 'The Kingdom of Spain shall upon accession adjust its patent law so as to make it compatible with the principles of the free movement of goods and with the level of protection of industrial property attained in the Community, in particular in the fields of contractual licensing rules, of exclusive compulsory licensing, of the compulsory exploitation of a patent and also the patent of importation.'

Similarly, the first sub-paragraph of Protocol 19[255] reads:

> 'The Portuguese Republic undertakes, upon accession, to adjust its patent law so as to make it compatible with the principles of the free movement of goods and with the level of protection of industrial property attained in the Community. In particular, the Portuguese Republic shall repeal, on accession, the provisions of Article 8 of Decree No. 27/84 of 18 January 1984, under which the holder of a patent granted in Portugal must, in order to enjoy the exclusive rights conferred by that patent, manufacture on Portuguese territory the patented product or the product obtained by using a patented process.'

8.103   The Court has now taken its first step along this path in *Allen and Hanbury's* v. *Generics (U.K.).*[256] This case did not concern the acquisition, transfer or extinction of patents or other primary industrial property rights, but related to patent *licences*. Under English law a patent can be endorsed with the words 'licences of right' and this entitles any person to a licence at a fee to be agreed with the patent-holder or, failing that, to be fixed by the Comptroller-General of Patents. Such endorsement may be

---

[252] See para 7.28 above.
[253] See para. 8.130 below. At least in certain circumstances, such an act of confiscation could conceivably infringe Articles 52, 106(3) (read with Annex III which specifically refers to patents designs, trade marks and inventions) and 221.
[254] [1985] O.J. L302/424.
[255] [1985] O.J. L302/458.
[256] Case 434/85 [1988] 1 C.M.L.R. 701.

requested by the patent-holder or it may in certain circumstances be imposed on him. In addition, the (English) Patents Act 1977 provided that the term of patents was henceforth to be 20 years, whereas it had previously been 16 years. Under the Act existing patents which still had a certain time to run could be extended for a further 4 years to bring them into line with the new 20-year term. However, during that 4-year period such patents were deemed to be endorsed with the words 'licences of right.'

Allen and Hanbury's were the proprietor of the patent granted in 1967 for the drug 'salbutamol.' That patent would normally have expired in September 1983, but was extended until September 1987 by virtue of the Patents Act 1977. In November 1983 Generics sought to agree a licence with Allen and Hanbury's to import salbutamol from Italy to the United Kingdom, but negotiations broke down. Generics then applied to the Comptroller-General of Patents to settle the terms of a licence. However, before the Comptroller-General had reached a decision, Generics informed Allen and Hanbury's in writing of its intention to begin importing the product from Italy where it could not be patented and was marketed without Allen and Hanbury's consent. Allen and Hanbury's thereupon sought an injunction against Generics and the case ultimately reached the House of Lords which referred a series of questions for a preliminary ruling.[257]

By its first question the House of Lords asked in effect whether section 46(3)(c) of the Patents Act 1977 was compatible with Articles 30 to 36. Under that provision an injunction cannot be granted for the infringement of a patent by production within the United Kingdom where the patent is endorsed with the words 'licences of right' and the defendant agrees to take such a licence on terms to be settled by agreement with the patent-holder or, in default of agreement, by the Comptroller-General of Patents; but an injunction can be granted against such a defendant who infringes the patent by importation into the United Kingdom.

The Court held that such a prohibition on imports could only be justified under Article 36 if 'that prohibition is necessary in order to ensure that the proprietor of such a patent has, *vis-à-vis* importers, the same rights as he enjoys against producers who manufacturer the product in the national territory, that is to say the right to a fair return from his patent.' Since the Court found that such a prohibition was not necessary for this purpose it concluded that it was not justified.

By the second question the House of Lords asked in essence whether Articles 30 and 36 prohibited public authorities from imposing on a licensee terms preventing the importation from other Member States of a product covered by a patent endorsed 'licences

---

[257] For a fuller account of the English law and the facts see the judgment of the House of Lords [1986] R.P.C. 203.

of right' if those authorities could not refuse to grant a licence for the manufacture of the product within the territory of the Member State concerned and for the sale of that product there. The Court replied that, since precisely the same considerations applied as in relation to the first question, Articles 30 and 36 did indeed prohibit such a practice.

Thirdly, the House of Lords asked whether the answers to the first and second questions were affected by the fact that the article in question was a pharmaceutical product imported from a Member State where such products were not patentable. The Court replied that, since the patent-holder would obtain a fair return by way of fees under the English licences of right, this factor was of no relevance.

8.104 The interesting point about *Allen and Hanbury's* is that licences of right are close to compulsory licences: although the two are granted for different reasons, their effects are broadly the same. It would seem to follow that a Member State may not grant compulsory licences for the manufacture of goods on its territory, while refusing to grant them for imports from other Member States.

Yet there appears to be a more fundamental problem in relation to compulsory licences. The principal ground on which these are granted is that the patent has not been sufficiently worked in the Member State concerned. This is clearly reflected in English law in section 48 of the Patents Act 1977, paragraph (3)(b) (ii) of which even lists among the grounds for the grant of a compulsory licence the fact 'that a demand for the product in the United Kingdom . . . is being met to a substantial extent by importation.' However, one would have thought that, in deciding whether to grant a compulsory licence, the authorities of a Member State are bound by Articles 30 and 36 to have regard to production in the Community as a whole.

On this view[258] such authorities may not grant a compulsory licence where the needs of that Member State are being met by imports from other Member States (although there is nothing to prevent such licences being granted on quite different grounds).

Indeed this appears to be the effect of Article 82 read with Article 47 of the Community Patent Convention (which is admittedly not yet in force). Article 47 provides:

> 'A compulsory licence may not be granted in respect of a Community patent on the ground of lack or insufficiency of exploitation if the product covered by the patent, which is manufactured in a Contracting State, is put on the market in the territory of any other Contracting State, for which such a licence is requested, in sufficient quantity to satisfy needs in the territory of that other Contracting State. This provision shall not apply to compulsory licences granted in the public interest.'

---

[258] Demaret 'Industrial Property Rights, Compulsory Licences and the Free Movement of Goods under Community Law' [1987] I.I.C. 161, 'Patent und Urheberrechtsschutz, Zwangslizenzen und freier Warenverkehr im Gemeinschaftsrecht' [1987] G.R.U.R. Int. 1.

Article 82 provides:

> 'Article 47 shall apply *mutatis mutandis* to the grant of compulsory licences for lack or insufficiency of exploitation of a national patent.'

Admittedly one must not overlook the ambiguous final sentence of Article 47, nor Article 89(1) which entitles Member States to ratify the Convention subject to a reservation regarding Articles 47 and 82.

At all events, a compulsory licence granted to stem imports from other Member States is not so far removed from the Portuguese measure referred to in the provision of Protocol 19 to the Act of Accession quoted in paragraph 8.102.[259]

Rule 2: The exhaustion of rights principle

8.105 This rule was first laid down in *Deutsche Grammophon* v. *Metro.* The facts were that Deutsche Grammophon had manufactured certain records in Germany, which it had sold to its subsidiary Polydor in Paris and which then came into the hands of Metro. Deutsche Grammophon sought an injunction against Metro to prevent it from selling these records in Germany in breach of the protection granted by German law to manufacturers of sound recordings, which protection is akin to copyright. The Hamburg court requested the Court of Justice to rule, *inter alia*, on whether the application of such a national law to exclude goods in these circumstances was contrary to Articles 5 and 85(1) of the Treaty. Article 5(2) imposes on the Member States a general obligation to 'abstain from any measure which could jeopardise the attainment of the objectives of this Treaty.'

The Court held that if the exercise of an industrial property right was not the subject, the means or the result of an agreement so as to fall under Article 85, its compatibility with the provisions of the Treaty on the free movement of goods must be examined and in particular Article 36. It continued:

> 'On the assumption that those provisions may be relevant to a right related to copyright, it is nevertheless clear from that Article that, although the Treaty does not affect the existence of rights recognised by the legislation of a Member State with regard to industrial and commercial property, the exercise of such rights may nevertheless fall within the prohibitions laid down by the Treaty. Although it permits prohibitions or restrictions on the free movement of products, which are justified for the purpose of protecting industrial and commercial property, Article 36 only admits derogations from that freedom to the extent to which they are justified for the purpose of safeguarding rights which constitute the specific subject-matter of such property.
>
> If a right related to copyright is relied upon to prevent the marketing in a Member State of products distributed by the holder of the right or with his consent on the territory of another Member State on the sole ground that such distribution did not take place on the national territory, such a prohibition

---

[259] *Pharmon* v. *Hoechst* (n. 236 above) related to compulsory licences but is not relevant since it concerned exports; see para. 8.109 below.

which would legitimise [*sic*] the isolation of national markets, would be repugnant to the essential purpose of the Treaty, which is to unite national markets into a single market.'

8.106 It has been made clear that an industrial property right will be exhausted in this way even if the products were not covered by any such industrial property right under the law of the Member State where the goods were distributed by the holder of the right in the importing Member State or with his consent. This was laid down in *Merck* v. *Stephar*.[260] There Merck held the patent in the Netherlands for a certain pharmaceutical product, which it also put on the market in Italy. That product was not covered by any patent in Italy, because at the time when it was first sold there pharmaceutical products could not be patented under Italian law. Although that particular provision of Italian law was held unconstitutional in 1978, the product in question no longer fulfilled the requirement of novelty under Italian law so that it still could not be patented. At all events, Stephar acquired quantities of this product on the market and resold them in the Netherlands. The question that arose for decision was whether Merck could use its Dutch patent to prevent such imports.

On a reference from a Dutch court, the Court of Justice held in effect that a patent could not be used in this way since it had been exhausted when the goods were put on the Italian market. If the holder of a patent in a product chose to market it in a Member State where it was not patentable, then he must bear the consequences.

8.107 There can be little doubt that Merck could have prevented the imports if the goods had been put on the Italian market by a third party without Merck's consent, at least if that third party had no economic connections of any kind with Merck.[261]

On a different point it would appear that, since the Court reached this solution in a case where patent protection never was available in the Member State of first distribution, then *a fortiori* the same solution must apply when the patent has lapsed in that Member State for whatever reason (*e.g.* expiry of maximum protection period, failure to pay a renewal fee, etc.). In addition the ruling in Merck would appear to be applicable not only to patents but to other forms of industrial property as well.

At this stage, it is appropriate to consider the application of the exhaustion of rights principle to patents, trade marks, copyright and plant breeders' rights in turn.

---

[260] Case 187/80 [1981] E.C.R. 2063, [1981] 3 C.M.L.R. 463, noted by Handoll [1982] 1 E.I.P.R. 26; compare Case 24/67, n. 245.

[261] Indeed, in Case 15/74 the Court implied this: see the passage quoted at para. 8.108 below. As to 'economic connections' see para. 8.111 below.

A. PATENTS

8.108   The first case in which the exhaustion of rights principle was applied to patents was *Centrafarm* v. *Sterling Drug*.[262] This case arose against the background of widely divergent prices for pharmaceuticals on the Dutch and British markets: these were some 50 per cent. higher in the Netherlands than in Britain. Centrafarm therefore bought in Britain and resold in the Netherlands quantities of a certain drug bearing the trade mark 'Negram.' The patents for this product in both these countries were held by an American company, Sterling Drug Inc., which had granted a licence to its respective subsidiary in each country. The goods had been put on the British market in the normal way by susidiaries of Sterling Drug Inc. A reference was made by the Dutch court hearing an action by Sterling Drug to prevent the parallel import. In that reference the Court of Justice was asked in particular to rule on whether it was compatible with Articles 30 to 36 to exercise the patent to prevent such imports.

In its reply the Court first reiterated its established distinction between the existence and the exercise of industrial property rights, and then continued:

> 'Inasmuch as it provides an exception to one of the fundamental principles of the common market, Article 36 in fact only admits of derogations from the free movement of goods where such derogations are justified for the purpose of safeguarding rights which constitute the specific subject-matter of this property.
>
> In relation to patents, the specific subject-matter of the industrial property is the guarantee that the patentee, to reward the creative effort of the inventor, has the exclusive right to use an invention with a view to manufacturing industrial products and putting them into circulation for the first time, either directly or by grant of licences to third parties, as well as to oppose infringements. . . .
>
> Whereas an obstacle to the free movement of goods . . . may be justified on the grounds of protection of industrial property where such protection is invoked against a product coming from a Member State where it is not patentable and has been manufactured by third parties without the consent of the patentee and in cases where there exist patents, the original proprietors of which are legally and economically independent, a derogation from the principle of the free movement of goods is not, however, justified where the product has been put on to the market in a legal manner, by the patentee himself or with his consent, in the Member State from which it has been imported, in particular in the case of a proprietor of parallel patents.'[263]

Thus the Court held in effect that Articles 30 to 36 did not permit the use of patents to prevent the sale of an imported product in a case such as that before the Dutch court.[264]

---

[262] Case 15/74 [1974] E.C.R. 1147, [1974] 2 C.M.L.R. 480, noted by van Nieuwenhoven Helbach [1976] C.M.L.Rev. 37. For a national measure which apparently flouts the principles laid down in that case, see written question 1257/81 ([1982] O.J. C53/5).

[263] In contrast, in *Allen and Hanbury's* (n. 256 above) it was held that, when a patent is endorsed 'licences of right,' the proprietor merely has a right to a fair return from his patent.

[264] The Court also held that the existence of price differences or health considerations did not justify the use of a patent to prevent imports in this way. As regards public health measures, the Court said that these 'must be such as may properly be adopted in the field of health control; and must not constitute a misuse of the rules concerning industrial and commercial property.'

In addition, in answer to a specific question on the point, the Court ruled that it was irrelevant whether or not the patentee and the licensees belonged to the same concern:

> 'the factor which above all else characterises a restriction of trade between Member States is the territorial protection granted to a patentee in one Member State against importation of the product which has been marketed in another Member State by the patentee himself or with his consent.'

8.109 The ruling in *Pharmon* v. *Hoechst*[265] concerned goods produced under compulsory patent licences. Hoechst owned a patent in the Netherlands and the United Kingdom in respect of a process for manufacturing medicine known as frusemide. In 1972, DDSA Pharmaceuticals Ltd. obtained from the United Kingdom Patent Office a compulsory licence to exploit this invention in the United Kingdom on the basis of section 41 of the Patents Act 1949, which was then in force. By virtue of this provision the Comptroller-General of Patents was required to grant to any applicant a compulsory licence over any patent for foodstuffs, medicines or surgical instruments unless it appeared to him that there were good reasons for refusing the application. The purpose of this provision was to ensure that such products could be obtained at the lowest possible price consistent with the patentee deriving a reasonable advantage from his patent rights. The licence in question could not be assigned, nor was it exclusive. Although a prohibition on exportation was attached to this licence, DDSA disregarded it and sold a large consignment of its frusemide tablets to Pharmon, a Dutch company. It would seem that Hoechst had never received royalties in respect of this consignment, as it should have done. Pharmon intended to market these tablets in the Netherlands, but Hoechst obtained an injunction to restrain it from doing so.

Ultimately these proceedings reached the Hoge Raad which referred three questions for a preliminary ruling. By its first question it asked generally whether it was compatible with the Treaty provisions on the free movement of goods for a patent holder to exercise his rights under the legislation of a Member State to prevent supplies of a product being put into circulation, when those supplies had been manufactured in another Member State by a compulsory licensee under a parallel patent owned by the same patent holder in that Member State.

Rarely has a party been so isolated before the Court as Pharmon: it was alone in contending that a patent holder could not use his patent to prevent such imports. It claimed that the nature of the compulsory licence was not appreciably different from that of a licence freely granted, in view of the procedural rules concerning

---

[265] N. 236 above, noted by White [1986] C.M.L.Rev. 719 and see Demaret, *op. cit.*

the grant of compulsory licences, the legal protection afforded to the patent holder and the fact that he receives reasonable compensation. Moreover, it argued that the decision of the national authorities to grant the licence was deemed to replace the patent holder's consent so that the exhaustion of rights principle applied. In support of its case it cited a number of judgments concerning this principle, notably *Merck* v. *Stephar*. That case, it contended, shows that a person who takes out a patent in a Member State accepts the whole body of the law of that Member State, including that relating to compulsory patents.[266]

Hoechst, on the other hand, was supported by the Commission and all six intervening Member States. To counter Pharmon's arguments it was contended first of all that the nature of a compulsory licence is different from that of a licence freely granted, in particular because there are no negotiations between the licensor and the licensee. Also, it was argued that the objectives of the two sorts of licence are different: a licence freely granted is a regular means of exploiting a patent, but a compulsory licence is intended to meet the special needs of a Member State. Next, it was claimed that, when a compulsory licence is granted, the patent holder does not consent directly or indirectly. Article 81(3) of the Community Patent Convention, discussed below, was also relied on. Finally, Hoechst and the six Member States—but apparently not the Commission—maintained that, in accordance with the principle of the territoriality of the acts of the public authorities of a Member State, a compulsory licence cannot confer on its holder rights in the territories of the other Member States. There was a danger that an unscrupulous Member State might grant compulsory licences with a view to enabling its industry to capture the market of other Member States.

In the light of these considerations, Advocate General Mancini reached the conclusion that in principle it was compatible with Articles 30 to 36 for a patent holder to exercise his rights under the law of a Member State to prevent the importation and sale of products produced under a compulsory licence. However, he put in the following proviso: it would be otherwise in his view where the patent holder had expressly or impliedly consented to the grant of the compulsory licence, whether before or after the product was marketed. This proviso was necessary because there might be links between the patent holder and the compulsory licensee. For instance, the compulsory licensee might be a subsidiary of the patent holder. He regarded *Merck* v. *Stephar* as authority for the proposition that consent was of the essence in each case.

After setting out the facts and arguments the Court merely stated:

---

[266] It also relied on Case 192/73 *Van Zuylen Frères* v. *Hag* [1974] E.C.R. 731, [1974] 2 C.M.L.R. 127, see para. 8.125 below; as to the CPC, it referred to Art. 93, see para. 8.112 below.

'It is necessary to point out that where, as in this instance, the competent authorities of a Member State grant a third party a compulsory licence which allows him to carry out manufacturing and marketing operations which the patentee would normally have the right to prevent, the patentee cannot be deemed to have consented to the operation of that third party. Such a measure deprives the patent proprietor of his right to determine freely the conditions under which he markets his products.

As the Court held most recently in its judgment of 14 July 1981 (*Merck* v. *Stephar* cited above), the substance of a patent right lies essentially in according the inventor an exclusive right for first placing the product on the market so as to allow him to obtain the reward for his creative effort. It is therefore necessary to allow the patent proprietor to prevent the importation and marketing of products manufactured under a compulsory licence in order to protect the substance of his exclusive rights under his patent.'

Regrettably, the Court did not put in the same proviso as the Advocate General. Nevertheless, it is conceivable that, if a case were to arise in which economic links existed between a patent holder and a compulsory licensee, the Court might depart from *Pharmon*.

By its second question the national court asked if it made any difference whether the compulsory licence was expressed to be subject to a prohibition on exportation. The third question asked whether it was relevant whether a patent holder was entitled to royalties for products produced under the compulsory license and whether he had actually received such royalties. All those who put in observations regarded these matters as irrelevant, as did the Advocate General. The Court endorsed this view, without giving any reasons.[267]

8.110   This case law has been given legislative form in the Community Patent Convention (which, as already mentioned, has not yet come into force). Article 32 governs the exhaustion of rights under Community patents. More relevant in the present context is Article 81, which closely mirrors Article 32 but which governs the exhaustion of rights conferred by national patents. Article 81(1) provides:

'The rights conferred by a national patent in a Contracting State shall not extend to acts concerning a product covered by that patent which are done within the territory of that Contracting State after that product has been put on the market in any Contracting State by the proprietor of the patent or with his express consent, unless there are grounds which, under Community law, would justify the extension to such acts of the rights conferred by the patent.'

It is not entirely clear what is meant by 'express' consent. At all events, the requirement that the consent be 'express' is apparently designed to avoid any claim that a patent holder had tacitly consented to a product being put on the market by a third party in a Member State where no patent protection existed.[268]

---

[267] As to whether this ruling reverses *Hag* and (as regards compulsory licences) *Membran* (n. 232 above), see para. 8.129 and n.280 below respectively.

[268] McClellan, *op. cit.* n.235 above, at 215.

Nor is the scope of the last half-sentence ('unless there are grounds') clear.[269]

8.111 Article 81(2) stipulates that:

'Paragraph 1 shall also apply with regard to a product put on the market by the proprietor of a national patent, granted for the same invention in another Contracting State, who has economic connections with the proprietor of the patent referred to in paragraph 1. For the purpose of this paragraph, two persons shall be deemed to have economic connections where one of them is in a position to exert a decisive influence on the other, directly or indirectly, with regard to the exploitation of a patent, or where a third party is in a position to exercise such an influence on both persons.'

This means that the principle of exhaustion set out in Article 81(1) shall apply to prevent a patent holder in one Member State from exercising his patent rights to prevent imports of patented goods put on the market in another Member State by another patent holder, provided that 'economic connections' exist between the two patent owners.[270]

8.112 Lastly, Article 81(3) states that:

'The preceding paragraphs shall not apply in the case of a product put on the market under a compulsory licence.'

Article 81(3) simply provides that the exhaustion principle shall not apply with respect to compulsory licences *under the conditions set out in Article 81(1) and (2)*. It never purported to oust the exhaustion principle altogether with respect to compulsory licences, since by virtue of Article 93 the Treaty of Rome takes precedence over the Community Patent Convention. At all events, as already mentioned, the Court has now resolved this problem in *Pharmon* v. *Hoechst*.

8.113 Finally, an exception to the rule in *Merck* v. *Stephar* is contained in Article 47 of the Act of Accession[271] of Spain and Portugal, which is in the following terms:

'1. Notwithstanding Article 42, the holder, or his beneficiary, of a patent for a chemical or pharmaceutical product or a product relating to plant health, filed in a Member State at a time when a product patent could not be obtained in Spain for that product may rely upon the rights granted by that patent in order to prevent the import and marketing of that product in the present Member State or States where that product enjoys patent protection even if that product was put on the market in Spain for the first time by him or with his consent.
2. This right may be invoked for the products referred to in paragraph 1 until the end of the third year after Spain has made these products patentable.'

---

[269] See generally the A.G. in Case 187/80, n.260 above.
[270] This provision does not contemplate the application of the doctrine of common origin; see paras. 8.125 *et seq.* below.
[271] [1985] O.J. L302/1; as to Art. 42, see paras. 5.04 and 6.09 above.

Article 204 of the Act, which relates to Portugal, is in the same terms *mutatis mutandis*.

B. TRADE MARKS

8.114   *Centrafarm* v. *Winthrop*[272] arose out of the same facts as the *Sterling Drug* case. The only difference was that while *Sterling Drug* concerned the patent, *Winthrop* concerned the trade mark 'Negram.' These trade marks were owned outright by the subsidiaries of the Sterling Drug group in Britain and the Netherlands respectively, rather than being owned by the American patent company and licensed to the local subsidiary as in the case of the patents. The question referred by the national court was analogous to that in *Sterling Drug*.

The Court's ruling was also along the same lines as in *Sterling Drug*. It defined the specific subject-matter of trade marks as:

> 'the guarantee that the owner of the trade mark has the exclusive right to use that trade mark, for the purpose of putting products protected by the trade mark into circulation for the first time, and is therefore intended to protect him against competitors wishing to take advantage of the status and reputation of the trade mark by selling products illegally bearing that trade mark.'[273]

The Court's conclusion was on the same lines as in the patent case: it was incompatible with the Treaty provisions on the free movement of goods to exercise a trade mark in one Member State to prohibit the sale there of a product which one has marketed oneself under that trade mark in another Member State or which has been so marketed with one's consent.[274]

8.115   The judgment in *Winthrop* has been developed by that in *Hoffmann-La Roche* v. *Centrafarm*.[275] There *Centrafarm* had acquired Valium tablets on the British market, where they had been marketed by Hoffmann-La Roche. It then repacked them for the German market, affixed the plaintiffs' trade mark to the new packages, and put them on the German market. The Hoffmann-La

---

[272] Case 16/74 [1974] E.C.R. 1183, [1974] 2 C.M.L.R. 480, noted by van Nieuwenhoven Helbach, *op. cit.* n.262 above.

[273] It has been pointed out that the mention of competitors would appear to rule out the use of trade marks to prevent the importation or sale of completely dissimilar goods from other Member States; Cohen Jehoram in the [1982] FIDE Report on 'The Elimination of Non-Tariff Barriers with Particular Reference to Industrial Property Rights including Copyright' at 8.7. However, in *Sterling Drug* (and the other decided cases) the Court was not concerned with this issue so that it is quite possible that the Court might allow the use of trade marks to exclude dissimilar goods.

[274] The Court also made the points already discussed with respect to patents in n.264 above. However, it did not allude to the fact that the goods had not been put on the market by Winthrop BV, but by another subsidiary of the Sterling Drug group. Nor did Winthrop BV gives its express consent. However, in view of the fact that Winthrop BV was part of the same group as the company that put the goods on the market, tacit assent can be deemed to have been given.

[275] Case 102/77 [1978] E.C.R. 1139, [1978] 3 C.M.L.R. 217; noted van Empel [1979] C.M.L.Rev. 251, Alexander [1979] C.D.E. 75, Röttiger [1980] E.I.P.R. 322; the exhaustion principle was also reaffirmed with respect to trade marks in Case 58/80, n.205 above.

Roche group owned this particular mark both in Britain and in Germany. The question posed by the German court was in essence whether it was compatible with the Treaty for the plaintiffs to rely on their German trade mark to prevent Centrafarm effecting parallel imports under these conditions.

The Court first repeated its definition of the specific subject-matter of trade marks already laid in *Winthrop*. It continued:

> 'In order to answer the question whether that exclusive right involves the right to prevent the trade mark being affixed by a third person after the product has been repackaged, regard must be had to the essential function of the trade mark, which is to guarantee the identity of the origin of the trade marked product to the consumer or ultimate user, by enabling him without any possibility of confusion to distinguish that product from products which have another origin. This guarantee of origin means that the consumer or ultimate user can be certain that a trade marked product which is sold to him has not been subject at a previous stage of marketing to interference by a third person, without the authorisation of the proprietor of the trade mark, such as to affect the original condition of the product. The right attributed to the proprietor of preventing any use of the trade mark which is likely to impair the guarantee of origin so understood is therefore part of the specific subject-matter of the trade mark right.
>
> It is accordingly justified under the first sentence of Article 36 to recognise that the proprietor of a trade mark is entitled to prevent an importer of a trade marked product, following repackaging of that product, from affixing the trade mark to the new packaging without the authorisation of the proprietor.'

The Court added, however, that the prevention of marketing repackaged products constitutes a disguised restriction on trade between Member States within the meaning of the second sentence of Article 36 where:

— it is established that the use of the trade mark right by the proprietor, having regard to the marketing system which he has adopted, will contribute to the artificial partitioning of the markets between Member States; and

— it is shown that the repacking cannot adversely affect the original condition of the product; and

— the proprietor of the mark receives prior notice of the marketing of the repackaged product; and

— it is stated on the new packaging by whom the product has been repackaged.

In this connection, the Court expressly stated that 'it is irrelevant in answering the legal question raised . . . that the question referred by the national court is exclusively concerned with medical products.'

8.116 Similar problems were raised in *Centrafarm* v. *American Home Products Corporation*.[276] American Home Products (AHPC) owned the trade mark 'Serenid D' for the United Kingdom, which

---

[276] Case 3/78 [1978] E.C.R. 1823, [1979] 1 C.M.L.R. 326, noted by van Empel, Alexander, Röttiger, *op. cit.* n.275.

mark covered a particular pharmaceutical product. It also owned the trade mark 'Seresta' in the Benelux countries for a product which had the same therapeutic properties as 'Serenid D' but presented certain minor differences such as a difference of taste. Centrafarm acquired quantities of this product on the British market, where it had been marketed by the AHPC group. It then removed the 'Serenid D' mark, affixed the 'Seresta' mark instead and placed this product on the Dutch market. The question referred by the Dutch court was once again whether under the Treaty the trade mark holder could prevent such parallel imports.

The Court once again repeated its definition of the specific subject-matter of a trade mark and added that the essential function of the trade mark is to guarantee the identity of the origin of the trade marked product to the consumer or ultimate user. It concluded that:

> 'This guarantee of origin means that only the proprietor may confer an identity upon the product by affixing the mark. The guarantee of origin would in fact be jeopardised if it were permissible for a third party to affix the mark to the product, even to an original product . . . The right granted to the proprietor to prohibit any unauthorised affixing of his mark to his product accordingly comes with the specific subject-matter of the trade mark.'

The Court then considered whether the exercise of this right may constitute a disguised restriction on trade between Member States within the meaning of Article 36:

> 'In this connection it should be observed that it may be lawful for the manufacturer of a product to use in different Member States different marks for the same product.
>
> Nevertheless it is possible for such a practice to be followed by the proprietor of the marks as part of a system of marketing intended to partition the markets artificially.
>
> In such a case the prohibition by the proprietor of the unauthorised affixing of the mark by a third party constitutes a disguised restriction on trade for the purposes of the abovementioned provision.
>
> It is for the national court to settle in each particular case whether the proprietor has followed the practice of using different marks for the same product for the purpose of partitioning the markets.'

As Advocate General Capotorti put it,[277] a company which sells an identical product under different trade marks in different Member States must provide an 'appropriate objective justification' for doing so.

8.117 Further refinements were added by *Pfizer* v. *Eurim-Pharm*.[278] Eurim-Pharm was a parallel importer, which had imported into Germany quantities of an antibiotic called Vibramycin, which had been produced and marketed in Britain by the British subsidiary of Pfizer. The trade marks 'Vibramycin' and 'Pfizer' for Germany were

---

[277] At p.1850.
[278] Case 1/81 [1981] E.C.R. 2913, [1982] 1 C.M.L.R. 406, noted by Handoll [1982] 3 E.I.P.R. 83.

owned by Pfizer. It is the practice in Germany for doctors to prescribe packets of 8, 16 or 40 tablets, whereas in Britain they were sold in packets of 10 and 50. Consequently, to take account of German usage it was necessary for Eurim-Pharm to repack the tablets. However, it was possible for them to do this without tampering with or touching the tablets, because they were contained in blister-packs of five. So Eurim-Pharm simply removed the blister-packs from their original packets and put them inside new packets. These new packets contained a window through which could be seen a label bearing the words 'Vibramycin' and 'Pfizer.' The outer packing also stated that the tablets had been produced by Pfizer Ltd. of Great Britain and that they had been repacked and imported by Eurim-Pharm. Also, Eurim-Pharm had obviously done its home-work on the case law of the Court, because it took the trouble to inform Pfizer of what it was doing.

In the resulting action for trade mark infringement, the German court in its first question asked the Court of Justice whether a trade mark could be relied on to prevent such imports. The Court replied as follows:

> 'Article 36 of the Treaty must be interpreted as meaning that the proprietor of a trade mark right may not rely on that right in order to prevent an importer from marketing a pharmaceutical product manufactured in another Member State by the subsidiary of the proprietor and bearing the latter's trade mark with his consent, where the importer, in repackaging the product, confined himself to replacing the external wrapping without touching the internal packaging and made the trade mark, affixed by the manufacturer to the internal packaging, visible through the new external wrapping, at the same time clearly indicating on the external wrapping that the product was manufactured by the subsidiary of the proprietor and repackaged by the importer.'

In its second question, the national court asked whether, for the purpose of establishing that there is a disguised restriction on trade between Member States within the meaning of Article 36, it was necessary to prove an intention on the part of the trade mark owner to partition the common market or whether it was sufficient to prove that he exercised his trade mark rights in such a way that the common market was in fact partitioned. In other words, was the test a subjective or an objective one?

This question was obviously posed in the light of the *American Home Products* judgment, where the Court had concentrated on the subjective element, namely the trade mark owner's intention. Following the Commission, the Advocate General took the view that it was only in the special circumstances of the *American Home Products* case, where one person owned a different trade mark in each Member State concerned for the same product, that the test was a subjective one. If it were otherwise, 'on the basis of the objective criterion adopted in the judgment in *Hoffmann–La Roche* v. *Centrafarm*, the proprietor of the parallel trade marks would ultimately find himself, in the light of Community law, in a position where he could never lawfully exercise his right. To avoid this excessively restrictive result, the Court took the view that in such circumstances it is not appropriate to speak of a disguised restriction on intra-Community trade except where the practice, adopted by or under the direction of the same proprietor, of using different trade marks for the same product in the various Member States is indicative of a plan to partition the markets.' However, in other cases the correct test was, according to the Advocate General, an objective one.

The Court ruled that, in view of its answer to the first question, it need not reply to the second question.

C. COPYRIGHT

8.118   The first judgment relating to the exhaustion of copyright was the *Deutsche Grammophon* case already discussed. That judgment was developed in *Musik-Vertrieb Membran* v. *GEMA*.[279] That case concerned sound recordings put on the British market and imported into Germany. GEMA, the German copyright protection society, acting on behalf of the copyright owners, brought two actions before the German courts against importers of these sound recordings. It sought the difference between the royalty fees of 6·25 per cent. already paid in Britain in accordance with the Copyright Act 1956, and the 8 per cent. due under German law. The question which arose was whether the principle of exhaustion operated to prevent GEMA recovering that difference.

The Court held that in view of the principle of exhaustion a party was indeed barred from recovering the difference between the two rates of copyright. It pointed out that a copyright owner was free to decide in which Member State to put his work on the market, and in so doing must be aware of the different rates of royalties. It rejected GEMA's argument that under the Copyright Act 1956 a compulsory licence was available in the United Kingdom to any manufacturer prepared to pay the royalty of 6·25 per cent. to the copyright owner.[280]

8.119   *GEMA* is the first case in which the Court expressly ruled that copyright falls under the concept of industrial and commercial property in Article 36.[281] In *Deutsche Grammophon* the Court avoided a decision on the point and consequently avoided defining

---

[279] See n.232 and para. 6.23 above. This judgment in effect confirms the judgment of the Brussels Court of Appeal in *Time Limit* v. *SABAM* [1979] 2 C.M.L.R. 578; see also Case 58/80 n.205 above.

[280] It is questionable whether this judgment still stands in relation to compulsory licences, since the Court in *Pharmon* v. *Hoechst* (n.236 above) reached the opposite conclusion as regards compulsory patent licences (without referring to *Membran*). The two judgments may, however, be reconciled in that *Membran* concerned copyright, whereas *Pharmon* concerned patents.

[281] See para. 8.94 above.

the specific subject-matter of copyright. In *GEMA* the Court did not in terms rule on the specific subject-matter of copyright either. However, it is interesting to note what the Court said in rejecting an argument put forward by the French Government. That argument was to the effect that the exhaustion principle did not apply to copyright because the purpose of copyright was to enable an author to claim authorship of the work and to object to any distortion, mutilation or other alteration thereof, or any other action in relation to that work which would be prejudicial to his honour or reputation. The Court refuted this argument in the following terms:

'It is true that copyright comprises moral rights of the kind indicated by the French Government. However, it also comprises other rights, notably the right to exploit commercially the marketing of the protected work, particularly in the form of licences granted in return for payment of royalties.'

It was on this basis that the Court concluded that the principle of exhaustion applied to copyright.

8.120 *Coditel* v. *Ciné Vog*[282] concerned not the free movement of goods but the free provision of services under Article 59 of the Treaty. That case concerned the film rights for the film *Le Boucher*. In 1969 the owners of the film rights assigned those rights with respect to Belgium to Ciné Vog, stipulating that the film was not to be shown on television in Belgium until 40 months after the first performance in that country. The owners then assigned the rights to broadcast the film in the Federal Republic of Germany to the German television broadcasting station. The Belgian cable television companies, Coditel, picked up directly on their aerial the film *Le Boucher* broadcast on German television in January 1971 and retransmitted it directly in Belgium. Ciné Vog then brought an action for infringement before the Belgian courts.

On a reference under Article 177 the Court found in effect that Ciné Vog's copyright had been infringed.

'A cinematographic film belongs to the category of literary and artistic works made available to the public by performances which may be infinitely repeated. In this respect the problems involved in the observance of copyright in relation to the requirements of the Treaty are not the same as those which arise in connection with literary and artistic works, the placing of which at the disposal of the public is inseparable from the circulation of the material form of the works, as in the case of books or records.'

Consequently, it held that 'the right of the copyright owner and his assigns to require fees for any showing of a film is part of the essential function of copyright in this type of literary and artistic work.' It would appear that the term 'essential function' is equivalent to that of 'specific subject-matter.'

---

[282] Case 62/79 [1980] E.C.R. 833, [1981] 2 C.M.L.R. 362, noted by Harris [1980] E.I.P.R. 163, see also the sequel Case 262/81 *Coditel* v. *Ciné-Vog* [1982] E.C.R. 3381, [1983] 1 C.M.L.R. 49, which concerned Art. 85.

The Court continued:

'Whilst Article 59 of the Treaty prohibits restrictions upon freedom to provide services, it does not thereby encompass limits upon the exercise of certain economic activities which have their origin in the application of national legislation for the protection of intellectual property, save where such application constitutes a means of arbitrary discrimination or a disguised restriction on trade between Member States. Such would be the case if that application enabled parties to an assignment of copyright to create artificial barriers to trade between Member States.'

There can be no doubt that, although this case concerned Article 59, the terminology used has been borrowed from Article 36. At all events, the Court found that the mere fact that the geographical limit of a particular assignment of performing rights coincided with national frontiers did not constitute either arbitrary discrimination or a disguised restriction on trade between Member States.

The Court concluded that:

'The exclusive assignee of the performing right in a film for the whole of a Member State may therefore rely upon his right against cable television diffusion companies which have transmitted that film on their diffusion network having received it from a television broadcasting station established in another Member State, without thereby infringing Community law.'

In the light of the subsequent ruling in *Musik-Vertrieb Membran* v. *GEMA* it may be that the ratio of *Coditel* is that the specific subject-matter of performing rights is different from that of other types of copyright.

8.121 The latter view appears to be borne out by the judgment in another difficult case, *Basset* v. *SACEM*.[283] Mr. Basset was the owner of a French discothèque who had failed to pay the agreed royalties to the French copyright society, SACEM. French law differs from that of most other Member States in that fees due for the communication of a sound recording to the public are divided into two: in addition to the royalty relating to the performing right, a 'supplementary reproduction royalty' is payable; to a French lawyer this term indicates that the 'supplement' is of the same nature as the classic copyright royalty due when the recordings are marketed, although as will be seen this is in fact questionable. In any case, the sum of the two fees is not necessarily any higher than the single amount due in other Member States. In a reference for a preliminary ruling the Court was asked whether it was compatible with Articles 30 and 36 to charge the 'supplement' in respect of sound recordings manufactured and marketed in another Member State where it was unknown.

After pointing out that the French law concerned applied to

---

[283] Case 402/85 [1987] 3 C.M.L.R. 173.

imported goods in the same way as to domestic goods, the Court held:

> '. . . disregarding the concepts used by French legislation and practice, the supplementary mechanical reproduction fee may thus be analysed as constituting part of the payment for an author's rights over the public performance of a recorded musical work. Moreover, the amount of that royalty, like that of the performance fee strictly so called, is calculated on the basis of the discothèque's turnover and not the number of records bought or played.
>
> It follows that, even if the charging of the fee in question were to be capable of having a restrictive effect on imports, it does not constitute a measure having equivalent effect prohibited under Article 30 of the Treaty inasmuch as it must be regarded as a normal exploitation of copyright and does not constitute a means of arbitrary discrimination or a disguised restriction on trade between Member States for the purposes of Article 36 of the Treaty.'

One unusual feature of this ruling is that the charging of the 'supplement' was held to fall outside Article 30 altogether rather than to be justified under Article 36. This is possibly due to the fact referred to by the Court that this fee was calculated on the basis of discothèque's turnover and not of the number of records bought or played.

Yet the fact remains that this judgment seems to suggest that the principle of exhaustion does not apply in the same way to performing rights (to which the Court in effect assimilated the 'supplement') as to classic copyright. In this regard the contrast with the ruling in *Musik-Vertrieb Membran* v. *GEMA* is particularly striking.

8.122 This view now appears to be confirmed by *Warner Bros* v. *Christiansen*.[284] True, that case concerned not performing rights, but lending rights for video cassettes which entitle their holder to a fee each time a video cassette is commercially rented. Yet the two rights are akin to one another in that royalties are not paid once and for all when the goods are marketed, but continue to be due for each and every transaction.

Video lending rights are provided for by Danish legislation, but are as yet unknown in the United Kingdom. Warner Bros. owned the British copyright in the film *Never say never again* which it had made in the United Kingdom. It ceded its video lending rights in Denmark to Metronome, the second plaintiff. Mr. Christiansen, who owned a video rental business in Copenhagen, bought a cassette of the film in London and imported it into Denmark where he intended to rent it out. The plaintiffs sought an injunction from the Danish courts to prevent him from doing so. The Danish appeal court asked the Court to rule in effect whether Articles 30 to 36 permitted the owner of the video lending right to withhold his consent to the rental of cassettes in such circumstances.

The Court first held that the restriction on the rental of cassettes indirectly affected imports and thus fell under Article 30.

However, the Court went on to rule that in the circumstances in

---

[284] Case 158/86 (judgment of 17 May 1988).

question the measure was justified, thereby rejecting the Advocate General's views to the contrary based on *Musik-Vertrieb Membran* v. *GEMA*. The Court began by pointing out that the Danish legislation applied in the same way whether the video cassettes were produced in Denmark or imported. Next, it stated that classic copyright did not give film makers remuneration in respect of the rental of video cassettes which was proportionate to the number of rentals or granted them a sufficient share in the rental market. Accordingly, video lending rights constituted industrial and commercial property within the meaning of Article 36. Finally, the Court rejected the analogy with *Musik-Vertrieb Membran* on the basis that the video lending right would be undermined if the owner was unable to exercise his right to authorise rentals of video cassettes marketed with his consent in another Member State where no lending rights existed.

Although this is not set out in terms in the final passage of its judgment, the Court appears to have distinguished *Musik-Vertrieb Membran* on the grounds that video lending rights by their very nature apply to continuing transactions whereas classic copyright does not. Yet, if this is so, why should it be at all relevant whether video lending rights exist in the Member State where the video cassettes were first marketed?

On the other hand, it is surely contrary to the principle of proportionality to entitle the holder of the video lending rights to prohibit rentals of video cassettes, where it would suffice to protect the specific subject-matter of those rights for him to be entitled to the fees (if necessary at nationally imposed rates).[285] The right to prohibit certain transactions altogether properly attaches to classic copyright except where it is exhausted. Since the Court ruled expressly that the owners of the lending right may lawfully prohibit rentals, there is a distinct danger that they will divide up the common market in video cassettes. The principle of exhaustion of classic copyright would thus be wholly undermined in this sector. Furthermore, for the reasons already mentioned the same would presumably apply to goods which are the subject of performing rights.

No doubt these issues will be clarified by future case law.

D. PLANT BREEDERS' RIGHTS

8.123   The ruling in *Nungesser*[286] would appear to be indirect authority for the view that plant breeders' rights are subject to the exhaustion of rights principle just like other forms of industrial property, although the case concerned Article 85. The applicant undertakings sought the annulment of a Commission Decision finding that certain contracts relating to plant breeders' rights in hybrid maize seeds infringed Article 85. They argued, *inter alia*,

---

[285] See, however, para. 8.135 below.
[286] N.231 above.

that territorial protection was necessary with respect to such rights for two reasons: firstly, cultivation of the seeds depended on climatic conditions and on the nature of the soil so that the seeds had to be adapted to the particular conditions of the country where they were to be used; secondly hybrid seeds, once developed, were liable to become genetically unstable and must therefore be reproduced under the control of the breeder or his licensee. For these reasons plant breeders' rights were said to be different from other forms of industrial and commercial property. The Court gave short shrift to that contention:

> 'That line of argument fails to take into account, however, that many products capable of forming the subject-matter of a trade mark or a patent, in particular certain food or pharmaceutical products, are in a similar situation. Although the reasons put forward by the applicants are based on correct findings of fact, they are not sufficient to justify a special system for breeders' rights in relation to other industrial or commercial property rights.'

E. COMMENT

8.124 Some authors[287] have criticised the Court's case law on the exhaustion of rights principle, claiming that the real concern of the Court has been the free movement of goods and that the Court has attached little importance to the protection of industrial property rights. These authors maintain that in defining the specific subject-matter of the various industrial property rights the Court has failed to have regard to the varying purposes of these rights in the different Member States. Indeed it is even suggested that the definition has been drafted precisely with a view to reaching the desired result.

These criticisms appear unduly harsh. While opinions may of course differ as to the rights and wrongs of various aspects of this case law, the exhaustion of rights principle itself—which is wholly judge-made law—is surely to be welcomed as a remarkable compromise between two conflicting interests, namely the free movement of goods and the protection of nationally based industrial property rights. In this context Rule 5 below must not be overlooked.

Rule 3: The common origin principle

8.125 This rule was spelt out in *Van Zuylen Frères* v. *Hag*.[288] The facts were that at the beginning of this century Hag AG, a German company, acquired trade marks in the name 'Hag' for coffee in a number of countries. As regards Belgium and Luxembourg it became the holder of these rights in 1908. Between the two World Wars Hag created a Belgian subsidiary and transferred to it its trade mark rights for Belgium and Luxembourg. In 1944 the Belgian authorities

---

[287] Cohen Jehoram *op. cit.* n.273 above; Cornish in the same FIDE Report; Gotzen 'Gewerbliche Schutzrechte und Urheberrecht in der Rechtsprechung des Europäischen Gerichtshofs zu Art. 30–36 des EWG-Vertrags' [1984] G.R.U.R. Int. 146.

[288] See n.266 above and casenotes by Alexander [1974] C.M.L.Rev. 387, Jacobs [1975] I.C.L.Q. 643.

sequestered the shares of Hag Belgium as enemy property and subsequently sold them to the Van Oevelen family. Later, Hag Belgium assigned its trade marks for Belgium and Luxembourg to Van Zuylen Frères, the distributors of their coffee. The result was that the German 'Hag' trade mark on the one hand and the Belgian and Luxembourg 'Hag' trade mark on the other, although of common origin, were now held by two totally unconnected parties, Hag AG and Van Zuylen. When the German company began marketing its products under the name 'Hag' in Luxembourg, Van Zuylen commenced infringement proceedings before the Tribunal d'Arrondissement of Luxembourg. In a reference under Article 177 that court asked in effect whether the exclusion of goods from a Member State in such circumstances was contrary *inter alia* to Articles 30 and 36. In its reference the referring court stated that 'no legal, financial, technical or economic link' existed between the parties.

The Court's answer was as follows:

> 'The exercise of a trade mark tends to contribute to the partitioning of the markets and thus to affect the free movement of goods between Member States, all the more so since—unlike other rights of industrial and commercial property—it is not subject to limitations in point of time.
>
> Accordingly, one cannot allow the holder of a trade mark to rely upon the exclusiveness of a trade mark right, which may be a consequence of the territorial limitation of national legislations—with a view to prohibiting the marketing in a Member State of goods legally produced in another Member State under an identical trade mark having the same origin . . .
>
> While in such a market the indication of origin of a product covered by a trade mark is useful, information to consumers on this point may be ensured by means other than such as would affect the free movement of goods.'

In its subsequent judgment in *Terrapin* v. *Terranova*[289] the Court sought to provide further justification for this ruling by stating that in a case such as this 'the basic function of the trade mark to guarantee to consumers that the product has the same origin is already undermined by the sub-division of the original right.'

8.126 In its second question the national court asked whether the same would be the case if the marketing of the product covered by the trade mark were effected not by the holder of the trade mark in that Member State but by a third party, who had duly acquired the goods in that Member State. The Court replied that 'if the holder of a trade mark in one Member State may himself market the product covered by the trade mark in another Member State, then this also applies to a third party who has duly acquired this product in the first State.'

8.127 It is clear from the Court's answer to the first question that a person acquiring a trade mark in one Member State may sell goods

---

[289] N.209 above.

under that mark throughout the Community. Moreover, it will be remembered that the Belgian and Luxembourg marks had been confiscated from the German company by the public authorities. It follows that the common origin principle applies not only where a trade mark has been split up by voluntary assignment, but also where it has been split up by an act of the public authorities contrary to the will of the trade mark holders.[290]

8.128 It is the latter aspect of the *Hag* case that has attracted very considerable criticism.[291] Indeed, Leigh and Guy go as far as to say that 'one is hard pressed to think of any objective justification for the Court's decision in the *Hag* case, at least as regards its answer to the first question referred to it'.[292] The most important criticisms are:

Firstly, that the *Hag* ruling seems inconsistent with the ruling in *Centrafarm* v. *Winthrop* to the effect that the specific subject-matter of a trade mark is 'the guarantee that the owner of the trade mark has the exclusive right to use that trade mark, for the purpose of putting products protected by the trade mark into circulation for the first time.' Under *Hag*, that 'exclusive' right must now be shared between Van Zuylen and Hag. (True, the Advocate General pointed out[293] that the German company had taken the trouble to mark the origin of its product on the package, and suggested that such labelling could be made obligatory. Yet this surely does not meet this objection, since the purpose of the trade mark itself is to identify the goods with a particular manufacturer, as the Court itself recognised when defining the specific subject-matter of trade marks.[294])

Secondly, it is not clear why the historical fact that two trade marks have a common origin should affect their exercise today, when there are no continuing links between the parties. It is hard to see why the result should be any different from that in *Terrapin* v. *Terranova* discussed below.

8.129 In any case, although the Court had not had the opportunity to hear a second case raising the question of common origin, it did expressly confirm that principle in the *Terrapin* case in what amounts to an *obiter dictum*.

On the other hand, the ruling in *Pharmon* v. *Hoechst*[295] could be regarded as reversing that in *Hag* especially as the issuance of

---

[290] In *Terrapin* the Court expressly affirmed that the common origin principle applied when a trade mark had been divided 'as a result of public constraint.'
[291] *E.g.* Cornish, *op. cit.* at 9.10; van Gerven and Gotzen *ibid.*, at 1.16; Gotzen, *op. cit.* (n.287 above) at 149.
[292] *Op. cit.* n.228 above, at 122.
[293] At p. 754.
[294] Para. 8.114 above.
[295] N.236 above.

compulsory licences is a milder form of expropriation than outright confiscation. At the very least, *Pharmon* must be taken to mean that the doctrine of common origin does not apply to patents. Yet it is notable that, although *Hag* was relied on by the plaintiff in *Pharmon*, the Court did not refer to it.

8.130 Even if *Hag* is reversed, it seems hard to imagine that a Member State could lawfully confiscate industrial property rights (with or without the other assets of the company concerned) *with a view to* restricting imports.[296] The purpose of the sequestration in *Hag* was different, as it must be understood against the background of the political events of the time; in any case, it occurred well before the Treaty of Rome came into force. This appears to be an exceptional case where one must have particular regard to the motives of a Member State in assessing the compatibility of a measure in Articles 30 and 36.[297]

Rule 4

8.131 At this stage it will come as no surprise to the reader to learn that Articles 30 to 36 only apply to restrictions on trade between Member States. This simple principle is the basis of the Court's ruling in the *EMI Records* v. *CBS* cases.[298] Those cases concerned the 'Columbia' trade mark which until 1917 had belonged to the same undertaking both in Europe and the United States. However, by a series of transactions that trade mark had become vested in CBS as regards the United States and in the EMI group as regards every single Member State of the EEC. When CBS sought to import records into the EEC bearing the Columbia trade mark, EMI commenced infringement proceedings before the British, German and Danish courts. Each of the three courts in question proceeded to make a reference under Article 177 asking in particular whether the sale of such goods could lawfully be prevented.

After pointing out that Article 30 only prohibited quantitative restrictions and measures of equivalent effect between Member States, the Court found that 'the exercise of a trade mark right in order to prevent the marketing of products coming from a third country under an identical mark . . . does not affect the free movement of goods between Member States and thus does not come under the prohibitions set out in Article 30 *et seq.* of the Treaty.' The Court added that it was not necessary to examine whether there was a common origin between the two Columbia trade marks, 'since

---

[296] See para. 8.99 *et seq.* above.
[297] See paras. 6.18, 8.09 and 8.12 above.
[298] Case 51/75, n.241 above; Case 86/75 [1976] E.C.R. 871, [1976] 2 C.M.L.R. 235; Case 96/75 [1976] E.C.R. 913, [1976] 2 C.M.L.R. 235. The ruling in each of the three cases is virtually identical. See casenotes by Laddie [1976] E.L.Rev. 499, Alexander [1976] C.D.E. 431.

that question is relevant only in relation to considering whether within the Community there are opportunities for partitioning the market.'[299]

The Court also held that Articles 30 to 36 did not entitle the holder of the trade mark in a third country to manufacture and market his products within the Community either himself or through his subsidiaries established in the Community. As the Court pointed out, if it were otherwise a coach and horses would be driven through the protection of industrial and commercial property established by Article 36.

8.132 The essential point in these cases was that EMI held the Columbia trade mark with respect to all the Member States. Had there been one Member State in which CBS had held the mark, the the common origin principle laid down in *Van Zuylen Frères* v. *Hag* would have applied. Consequently, CBS could have distributed its Columbia records from that Member State to all the others.

Rule 5

8.133 This rule emerges from *Terrapin* v. *Terranova*. Terranova was a German company manufacturing dry plaster and other building materials in the Federal Republic under the 'Terranova' trade mark. Terrapin was a British company manufacturing prefabricated houses in Britain under the trade mark 'Terrapin' and exporting them to Germany under that mark. The trade marks were duly registered in Germany and the United Kingdom respectively and could be lawfully used there. There was no connection between the two companies or the two trade marks. An action was brought before the German courts in which the German company objected to the use of the 'Terrapin' mark in Germany. The case reached the Bundesgerichtshof which took the view that a risk of confusion existed so that the sale of the imported goods under the 'Terrapin' mark constituted an infringement under German law. It duly made a reference under Article 177 asking whether Articles 30 to 36 prohibited an import ban on such goods in these circumstances.

After rehearsing the general principles already discussed here, the Court ruled as follows:

> 'On the other hand in the present state of Community law an industrial or commercial property right legally acquired in a Member State may legally be used to prevent under the first sentence of Article 36 of the Treaty the import of products marketed under a name giving rise to confusion where the rights in question have been acquired by different and independent proprietors under different national laws. If in such a case the principle of the free movement of goods were to prevail over the protection given by the respective national laws, the specific objective of industrial and commercial property rights would be undermined. In the particular situation the requirements of the free

---

[299] See also para. 2.17 above. The Court also held that there was no trade agreement on which CBS could rely.

movement of goods and the safeguarding of industrial and commercial property rights must be so reconciled that protection is ensured for the legitimate use of the rights conferred by national laws, coming within the prohibition on imports 'justified' within the meaning of Article 36 of the Treaty, but denied on the other hand in respect of any improper exercise of the same rights of such a nature as to maintain or effect artificial partitions within the common market.'

This last sentence is perhaps a reference back to an earlier passage in the judgment where the Court said that industrial property rights may not be exercised in such a way as to constitute arbitrary discrimination or a disguised restriction on trade between Member States. In particular, it held that a trade mark owner must exercise his rights with the same strictness whatever the national origin of the infringer.

8.134 *Terrapin* v. *Terranova* concerned trade marks and trade names, but there is every reason to think that the principles laid down in that judgment apply by analogy to other forms of industrial property.[300] Indeed, the Court ruled to the same effect in *Nancy Kean*[301] which concerned design copyright. As the Court pointed out in the passage quoted here, if industrial property rights could not be relied on to prevent imports even in the absence of any exhaustion, common origin, restrictive agreement between the parties or discriminatory exercise, then such rights would in general be undermined.[302]

8.135 Finally, in *Thetford* it was contended on behalf of the defendants that, even if a patent-holder was entitled under Article 36 to take action with respect to imports, the proper remedy was an order for the payment of a reasonable royalty or other monetary award; the grant of an injunction prohibiting imports was, they maintained, contrary to the principle of proportionality. However, having regard to the specific subject-matter of patents, the Court held that the grant of such an injunction was perfectly lawful.

The same must apply to most other categories of industrial property. However, as already suggested,[303] the specific subject-matter of video lending rights is such that their owner should be entitled merely to obtain a reasonable royalty, not to prohibit imports.

---

[300] See Guy and Leigh, *op. cit.* n.228 above, at 158.
[301] N.233 above.
[302] The rule in *Terrapin* v. *Terranova* does not apply to rights protected merely by the rules on the prevention of unfair competition; see para. 8.87 above.
[303] See para. 8.122 above.

CHAPTER IX

Other exception clauses[1]

9.01 No small degree of academic effort, and, one suspects, intellectual excitement, has been expended in the search for a satisafactory definition of the closely related concepts of 'exception clauses' and 'escape clauses' in the Treaty of Rome. No attempt will be made here to join this search. The term 'exception clause' is merely used in this chapter as a convenient overall concept to cover provisions in the Treaty which permit measures to be taken which would otherwise fall foul of Articles 30 to 34. Such Treaty provisions are of various kinds: some vest the powers in question in the Member States as of right, while others require the adoption of a Decision or other binding act by the Commission or, in some cases, the Council. This act will normally take the form of an authorisation to the Member State in question to take a particular measure. Again, some exception clauses such as Articles 36 and 223 may only be invoked on non-economic grounds, while others such as Articles 108 and 109 may be relied on only in cases of economic difficulty. However, all these provisions share one common trait: since they constitute an exception to a fundamental principle of the Treaty, namely the free movement of goods, measures taken pursuant to them may be no more restrictive than is necessary to realise the legitimate object in view.[2]

9.02 Article 36, which is by far the most important exception clause in relation to Articles 30 to 34, has already been discussed at length in the previous chapter. It therefore requires no further examination here.

Nor is it intended to consider here the exceptions (other than Article 115) to the rule that on being put into free circulation goods

---

[1] See generally Gori, *Les clauses de sauvegarde des traités CECA et CEE* (1967); Opperman, 'Schutzklauseln in der Endphase des gemeinsamen Marktes' [1969] EuR 231; Müller-Heidelberg, *Schutzklauseln im Europäischen Gemeinschaftsrecht* (1970); Lejeune, *Un droit des temps de crise: les clauses de sauvegarde de la CEE* (1975); Mégret, *Le droit de la Communauté économique européenne* (1976), Vol. 6; Groeben, Boeckh Thiesing, Ehlermann, *Kommentar zum EWG Vertrag* 3rd ed. (1983).

[2] This rule of proportionality is expressly laid down in Arts. 109(1), 115(3) and 226(3) but applies to all exception clauses; see in particular Müller-Heidelberg, *op. cit.* at 114; Lejeune, *op. cit.* at 305 and paras 9.33 *et seq.* below; with respect to Art. 36 see Case 104/75 *de Peijper* [1976] E.C.R. 613, [1976] 2 C.M.L.R. 271 and para. 8.01 above; with respect to Art. 226 (n.3 below), see Cases 73–74/63 *Handelsvereniging Rotterdam* v. *Minister van Landbouw* [1964] E.C.R. 1, [1964] C.M.L.R. 198.

from third countries are assimilated to goods of Community origin; these exceptions have already been discussed at length in paragraphs 2.19 to 2.22 of this book.

Article 46 will be considered at paragraph 10.08 below, since it relates only to agricultural produce. Lastly, it is not proposed to examine here the exception clauses which only apply during the various transitional periods.[3]

This leaves the following Articles of the Treaty to be considered in turn in this chapter: Articles 90, 103, 104, 107–109, 115, 222–225, 233 and 234. Articles 90, 104, and 222 do not according to the Court's case law constitute exceptions to Articles 30 to 34. They have been included nevertheless for the purpose of discussing the rulings concerned.

ARTICLE 90

9.03   The first two paragraphs of Article 90 provide:

'1. In the case of public undertakings and undertakings to which Member States grant special or exclusive rights, Member States shall neither enact nor maintain in force any measure contrary to the rules contained in this Treaty, in particular to those rules provided for in Article 7 and Articles 85 to 94.

2. Undertakings entrusted with the operation of services of general economic interest or having the character of a revenue-producing monopoly shall be subject to the rules contained in this Treaty, in particular to the rules on competition, in so far as the application of such rules does not obstruct the performance, in law or in fact, of the particular tasks assigned to them. The development of trade must not be affected to such an extent as would be contrary to the interests of the Community.'

The third and final paragraph is not in point here.

9.04   These provisions are highly complex and give rise to considerable difficulties of interpretation.[4] Yet it is now clear that neither paragraph can constitute an exception to Article 30 or 34.

In *Pigs Marketing Board* v. *Redmond*[5] the Court was concerned with Article 90(1). It noted that that paragraph expressly provides

---

[3] Art. 226 EEC empowered the Commission to authorise a Member State in serious economic difficulties to take exceptional measures *during the transitional period*; see Case 13/63 *Italy* v. *EEC Commission* [1963] E.C.R. 165, [1963] C.M.L.R. 289, Cases 73–74/63 (n. 2 above) and 37/70 *Rewe-Zentrale* v. *Hauptzollamt Emmerich* [1971] E.C.R. 23, [1971] C.M.L.R. 238. Broadly similar provisions are to be found in Art. 135 of the first Act of Accession, 130 of the Act of Accession of Greece ([1979] O.J. L291) and 379 of the Act of Accession of Spain and Portugal ([1985] O.J. L302) respectively. On Art. 130 of the Act of Accession of Greece see Cases 258/81 *Metallurgiki Halyps* v. *E.C. Commission* [1982] E.C.R. 4261, 114/83 *Kerisnel* v. *E.C. Commission* [1984] E.C.R. 2589, [1985] 2 C.M.L.R. 767, 289/83 *GAARM* v. *E.C. Commission* [1984] E.C.R. 4295, [1986] 3 C.M.L.R. 15 and 11/82 *Piraiki-Patraiki* v. *E.C. Commission* [1985] E.C.R. 227, [1985] 2 C.M.L.R. 4.

[4] See *e.g.* Page 'Member States, Public Undertakings and Article 90' [1982] E.L.Rev. 19, Hochbaum in Groeben, Boeckh, Thiesing, Ehlermann, *op. cit.* (n.1 above), Vol. I at 1527.

[5] Case 83/78 [1978] E.C.R. 2347 at 2369, [1979] 1 C.M.L.R. 177 at 201; see also generally Case 13/77 *GB Inno* v. *ATAB* [1977] E.C.R. 2115, [1978] 1 C.M.L.R. 283.

that as regards the undertakings in question the Member States 'shall neither enact nor maintain in force any measure contrary to the rules contained in this Treaty'. From this it concluded that this paragraph did not exempt such undertakings from the Treaty provisions on the free movement of goods.

In *Campus Oil* v. *Ministry for Industry*[6] the Greek Government argued that Article 30 did not apply because the Irish oil refinery which the Irish Government sought to protect by means of the contested measures was caught by Article 90(2). The Court rejected this suggestion in the following terms:

> 'Article 90(2) is intended to define more precisely the limits within which, in particular, undertakings entrusted with the operation of services of general economic interest are to be subject to the rules contained in the Treaty. Article 90(2) does not, however, exempt a Member State which has entrusted such an operation to an undertaking from the prohibition on adopting, in favour of that undertaking and with a view to protecting its activity, measures that restrict imports from other Member States contrary to Article 30 of the Treaty.'

This would appear to mean that Article 90(2) can never constitute an exception to Article 30; it must follow from this that the same is true of Article 34. Although the Court gave no grounds for this pronouncement, it will be welcomed by those who value legal certainty. In view of the extraordinarily vague and ambiguous wording of Article 90(2) and its lack of direct applicability,[7] much confusion would have ensued had the Court's ruling on the point gone the other way.

ARTICLE 103

9.04   Article 103 provides:

> '1. Member States shall regard their conjunctural policies as a matter of common concern. They shall consult each other and the Commission on the measures to be taken in the light of the prevailing circumstances.
> 2. Without prejudice to any other procedures provided for in this Treaty, the Council may, acting unanimously on a proposal from the Commission, decide upon the measures appropriate to the situation.
> 3. Acting by a qualified majority on a proposal from the Commission, the Council shall, where required, issue any directives needed to give effect to the measures decided upon under paragraph 2.
> 4. The procedures provided for in this Article shall also apply if any difficulty should arise in the supply of certain products.'

The authors of the English version of the Treaty appear to have donated a new word to the language: the English reader who does not recall meeting the word 'conjunctural' will be gratified to learn that this predicament is shared by the *Shorter Oxford English Dictionary*. Yet it is clear from the meaning of the term in other Community languages that it is intended to mean 'relating to short-term economic policy'. No definition of 'conjunctural policy' is to

---

[6] Case 72/83, [1984] E.C.R. 2727, [1984] 3 C.M.L.R. 544.
[7] Case 10/71 *Ministère Public* v. *Müller-Hein* [1971] E.C.R. 723.

be found in the Treaty, however. For such a definition one must turn to the following statement in the Advocate General's conclusions in *Balkan* v. *HZA Berlin-Packhof*[8]: 'one is able to think in terms of conjunctural policy when the whole course of the economic process is guided by reference to short-term goals (in which connection one also has to consider goals of general economic policy—*e.g.* stable price levels, a high rate of employment, controlling the balance of payments, optimum economic growth).'

9.05 Is Article 103(4) to be read in the light of the preceding paragraphs and therefore limited to conjunctural policy? In Ehlermann's view[9] it is not so limited. This means that it allows for measures intended to combat difficulties of supply, which only affect the products in question and not the economy as a whole. Another—quite separate—question is whether in addition to shortages of supply Article 103(4) also covers cases of excess supply. Opinions are divided on this point.[10]

9.06 In *SADAM* v. *Comitato Interministeriale dei Prezzi*,[11] the Court held that a Member State could not rely on Article 103 to justify a measure falling under Article 30. Although that case concerned an agricultural product subject to a common organisation of the market, there is every reason to think that this ruling is of general application. It follows that Article 103 does not create an exception to Article 30 on which Member States can rely.

9.07 On the other hand, it has now become clear that Article 103 grants the Council considerable freedom to adopt exceptional measures. The leading case here is the *Balkan* case already referred to which concerned the validity of the system of monetary compensatory amounts.[12] At the time of the events giving rise to the litigation Regulation 974/71,[13] which established this system, was based on Article 103. One of the questions referred by the German court hearing the case was whether the Regulation was invalid by virtue of its basis. In fact, shortly before the reference was made, Articles 28, 43 and 235 of the Treaty were substituted as its legal bases by Regulation 2746/72,[14] but that did not deprive the question of its

---

[8] Case 5/73 [1973] E.C.R. 109 at 122. This case is based on the same facts as Case 10/73 *Rewe-Zentral* v. *Hauptzollamt Kehl* [1973] E.C.R. 1175. See para. 4.13 above.
[9] In Groeben, Boeckh, Thiesing *Kommentar zum EWG Vertrag* 2nd ed. (1974) Vol. I, 1354.
[10] For the view that Art. 103(4) applies to gluts see Gori, *op. cit.* 179, Müller-Heidelberg *op. cit.* 293; *contra* Ehlermann, *op. cit.* 1354, Zuleeg in Groeben, Boeckh, Thiesing, Ehlermann, *op. cit.* (n.1 above), Vol. I at 1800.
[11] Cases 88–90/75 [1976] E.C.R. 323, [1977] 2 C.M.L.R. 183, see paras. 7.67 *et seq.* above.
[12] This is the mechanism informally known as the 'green currencies'. See Gilsdorf, 'The System of Monetary Compensation from a Legal Standpoint' [1980] E.L.Rev. 341 and 433.
[13] [1971] J.O. L106/1.
[14] [1972] J.O. L291/148.

purpose. The Court held that the agricultural provisions of the Treaty conferred power on the Community institutions to take short-term economic policy measures in the agricultural sector. On the other hand, Article 103 did not 'relate to those areas already subject to common rules, as is the organisation of agricultural markets'. In spite of this, the Court went on to rule that owing to the time needed to give effect to the procedures laid down in Articles 40 and 43, the Council was justified in making interim use of the powers conferred on it by Article 103 of the Treaty. In support of this conclusion the Court cited 'the suddenness of the events with which the Council was faced, the urgency of the measures to be adopted, the seriousness of the situation and the fact that these measures were adopted in an area intimately connected with the monetary policies of Member States'.

The Court also rejected the plaintiff's submission that only directives and decisions could be passed on the basis of Article 103, not regulations. It held, on the contrary, that the second paragraph of that Article confers on the Council 'the powers necessary to adopt, in principle, any conjunctural measures which may appear to be needed in order to safeguard the objectives of the Treaty'. From this it is clear that this provision is not to be interpreted narrowly. What is more, the phrase 'measures appropriate to the situation' in Article 103(2) meant that the Council could choose the type of act most suitable to the circumstances.

9.08 It is clear, then, that the powers conferred on the Community institutions by Article 103 are extensive. Thus:

(a) the *Balkan* ruling seems to imply that Article 103 may be used as the basis for measures of a general and permanent nature[15]:

(b) by holding that Article 103 was inappropriate merely because it does not relate to 'areas already subject to common rules', this judgment implies that a similar measure could be adopted under Article 103 if it fell within an area not yet subject to common rules;

(c) it is clear that even within those wide boundaries the Council enjoys a considerable margin of discretion; this was stated by the Court in two judgments which are of no further concern in the present context, *Compagnie d'Approvisionnement* v. *E.C. Commission*[16] and *Merkur* v. *E.C. Commission*.[17]

9.09 Article 103 does not constitute an express exception to the general rules of the Treaty. Nevertheless, it is generally agreed that in certain circumstances measures of conjunctural policy or supply

---

[15] Mégret, *op. cit.* 4.
[16] Cases 9 and 4/71 [1972] E.C.R. 391, [1973] C.M.L.R. 529.
[17] Case 43/72 [1973] E.C.R. 1055.

policy based on Article 103 may create restrictions on inter-State trade.[18] This is clearly subject to the general requirement already discussed to the effect that such measures may not be more restrictive than is necessary to attain the legitimate object in view. It has also been suggested that exceptional measures based on Article 103 may only be of a temporary nature.[19] On the other hand, it would appear to follow from the broad wording of Article 103 ('measures appropriate to the situation') that the exceptional measures may be taken under it not only when a crisis actually occurs but also when there is an imminent threat of a crisis. At all events, the Commission and the Council appear to have arrived at an early stage at the conclusion that measures based on Article 103 could restrict inter-State trade in a way which would otherwise be contrary to Articles 30 to 34: by Decision 63/689,[20] the Council on the proposal of the Commission authorised Belgium to restrict exports of pork and live pigs for a fixed period, in view of the serious shortage of these products; such a restriction would normally have fallen foul of Article 34, if imposed by a Member State.

9.10 Still in force today is the elaborate system set up by the Council on the basis of Article 103 with respect to exports between Member States of crude oil and petroleum products.[21] Decision 77/186,[22] as amended by Decision 79/879,[23] provides that where difficulties arise in the supply of these products in one or more Member States, the Commission may make intra-Community trade in some of them subject to a system of licences to be granted automatically by the exporting Member State. These licences are to be granted without delay and free of administrative charges in respect of any quantity requested and for a minimum period of 15 working days and a maximum period of one month. By virtue of Article 2 of the Decision, whenever a shortfall in the supply of crude oil and/or petroleum products, whether actual or imminent, creates an abnormal increase in trade in petroleum products between Member States, the Commission may, at the request of a Member State, authorise that Member State to suspend the issue of export licences or cut short the period of validity of existing licences or, if necessary, to revoke them. By virtue of Article 3, the same applies where the supply of the products in a Member State is endangered or may

---

[18] Gori, *op. cit.* 178–179; Müller-Heidelberg, *op. cit.* 295; Mégret, *op. cit.* Vol. 6, 5; Ehlermann, *op. cit.* 1351–1352.

[19] Lejeune, *op. cit.* 247; Mégret, *op. cit.* Vol. 6, 5.

[20] [1963] J.O. 3108.

[21] On the Community's oil policy generally see Evans, 'The Development of a Community Policy on Oil' [1980] C.M.L.Rev. 371, Forrester and Syngellakis, 'Developments in EEC energy policy from 1977' [1980] E.L.Rev. 402; see also Case *77/77 BP* v. *E.C. Commission* [1978] E.C.R. 1513, [1978] 3 C.M.L.R. 174.

[22] [1977] O.J. L61/23 supplemented by Commission Dec. 78/890 [1978] O.J. L311/13. See *Campus Oil*, n.6 above.

[23] [1979] O.J. L270/58.

reasonably be expected to be so. In either case, the Council may meet within 48 hours to amend or repeal the Commission's authorisation. Article 4 empowers a Member State, in the event of a sudden crisis in that Member State, when any delay would be gravely prejudicial to its economy, to suspend the issue of export licences for 10 days, after consulting the Commission and informing the other Member States. Article 4(a) also empowers a Member State faced with such a crisis to suspend for 10 days the validity of licences already granted. In either case the Council may decide on further appropriate measures. Lastly, Article 5 provides for the early amendment or repeal of exceptional measures, should they prove no longer necessary.

9.11 It is also worth noting a dictum of the Court in *B.P.* v. *E.C. Commission*,[24] an action for the annulment of a Commission Decision finding that the companies concerned had abused a dominant position contrary to Article 86 by various practices during the acute oil shortage in the Netherlands of 1973–1974. In this dictum the Court in effect stated that Article 103 was a legal basis for Community legislation imposing rationing in times of crisis. Indeed, it expressed its regret at the absence of any such rules; this in its view amounted to a serious failure to act which revealed 'a neglect of the principle of Community solidarity which is one of the foundations of the Community'.

9.12 It is clear, then, that various measures already adopted under Article 103 have created restrictions on intra-Community trade. Yet it should be pointed out that such measures only constitute a minority of the measures based on Article 103, some of which concern such matters as the temporary suspension of customs duties on certain goods[25] or the co-ordination of the conjunctural policies of Member States.[26] What is more, it would seem that as regards matters falling within its purview, Article 103 can be used as a legal basis for Community harmonising legislation—at least of a short-term nature—which in no way restricts the free movement of goods between Member States.[27]

Be that as it may, there seems little room for doubt that Article 103 is the appropriate basis for Community measures restricting exports between Member States of goods in short supply, at least if they are of brief duration. In this respect it goes beyond the bounds within which the Community legislator must normally keep.[28] It is not clear what other types of measures derogating from

[24] N.21 above.
[25] *E.g.* Dec. 64/530 ([1964] J.O. 2389), Dec. 65/266 ([1965] J.O. 1462), Reg. 2101/76 ([1976] O.J. L235/17).
[26] *E.g.* Dec. of 9 March 1960 ([1960] J.O. 764), Dec. 75/785 ([1975] O.J. L330/50).
[27] See para. 12.04 below.
[28] See paras. 4.08 *et seq.* above.

the free movement of goods Article 103 permits. Yet unlike some of the other provisions discussed in this chapter, it will only permit absolute import bans in extreme cases, if at all.[29]

ARTICLE 104

9.13   This provision reads as follows:

> 'Each Member State shall pursue the economic policy needed to ensure the equilibrium of its overall balance of payments and to maintain confidence in its currency, while taking care to ensure a high level of employment and a stable level of prices.'

In *E.C. Commission* v. *Italy*[30] (advance payments for imports), which concerned Article 30, the Court said:

> '. . . Article 104 merely sets out the general objectives of the economic policy which the Member States may pursue, regard being had to their membership of the Community. It accordingly may not be invoked in order to derogate from the other provisions of the Treaty.'

ARTICLE 107

9.14   Article 107 provides:

> '1. Each Member State shall treat its policy with regard to rates of exchange as a matter of common concern.
> 2. If a Member State makes an alteration in its rate of exchange which is inconsistent with the objectives set out in Article 104 and which seriously distorts conditions of competition, the Commission may, after consulting the Monetary Committee, authorise other Member States to take for a strictly limited period the necessary measures, the conditions and details of which it shall determine, in order to counter the consequences of such alteration.'

9.15   Three conditions must be satisfied before an authorisation under Article 107(2) can be granted by the Commission:

— The Member State must alter its exchange rate. In certain circumstances the maintenance of a particular rate of exchange may run counter to Article 104, but such a state of affairs cannot fall under Article 107(2). On the other hand, the condition is satisfied if the Member State allows its currency to float or introduces a multiple exchange rate.[31]

— The alteration must be inconsistent with the objectives set out in Article 104.

---

[29] In particular, even if Art. 103(4) does cover gluts (n.10 above), it could presumably not be used to create import bans between Member States: while this would divide up the Community market, it is hard to envisage any resulting gain to the Community as a whole; such measures would thus fail to meet the requirement of proportionality (n.2 above). On the other hand, it is submitted that Art. 103 might well be an appropriate basis for the imposition of production quotas or similar measures.

[30] Case 95/81 [1982] E.C.R. 2187.

[31] Carreau, 'La Communauté économique européenne face aux problèmes monétaires' [1971] R.T.D.E. 589; Ehlermann, *op. cit.* 1397; Zuleeg, *op. cit.* 1844.

— The alteration must seriously distort conditions of competition; an alteration in an exchange rate can be incompatible with Article 104 by being excessively high or excessively low, but it would appear that only a devaluation can fall under Article 107(2) because only this can seriously distort conditions of competition.[32]

9.16 On no account may a Member State rely on this exception without prior authorisation from the Commission. This the Commission may grant either on its own initiative or at the request of a Member State. In the latter case, the Commission may not simply act as a rubber stamp but must actively exercise its discretion, since it is the guardian of the Treaty.[33] By whatever method the procedure has been initiated, the Commission cannot grant an authorisation without first consulting the Monetary Committee provided for in Article 105(2); this consists of two members appointed by each Member State and two members appointed by the Commission. Should the Commission decide to authorise exceptional action by a Member State, no provision is made for the council to overturn or alter the Commission's decision.

The exceptional measures which may be taken under this Article include quantitative restrictions and measures of equivalent effect[34]— provided always that less restrictive measures would be inadequate.[35] Whatever the nature of the measures, Article 107 expressly states that they must be strictly limited in time.

It would appear that the exemption clause contained in Article 107(2) has never been applied.

ARTICLE 108

9.17 By virtue of Article 108(3) the Commission may authorise a Member State to 'take protective measures, the conditions and details of which the Commission shall determine'.[36] However, this is only the culmination of an elaborate procedure set in train

'where a Member State is in difficulties or is seriously threatened with difficulties as regards its balance of payments either as a result of an overall disequilibrium in its balance of payments, or as a result of an overall disequilibrium in its balance of payments or as a result of the type of currency at its disposal, and where such difficulties are liable in particular to jeopardise the functioning of the common market or the progressive implementation of the common commcercial policy.'

---

[32] Ehlermann, *op. cit.* 1397.
[33] See paras. 9.33 *et seq.* below.
[34] Ehlermann, *op. cit.* 1398.
[35] See n.2 above.
[36] Clearly a Member State may not unilaterally resort to exceptional measures under this provision: *EEC Commission* v. *Italy* (import deposits), n.30 above.

It is widely accepted that the term 'balance of payments difficulties' may cover difficulties arising out of a balance of payments surplus, and is not confined to cases of deficit.[37] As is clear from its express words, Article 108 may be applied before such difficulties arise; it is enough that there is a serious threat of them arising.

9.18 The procedure is divided into three stages. At the first stage the Commission examines the monetary position of the Member State in question and then makes recommendations as to the action which that State should take. Should this prove to be insufficient the procedure moves on to the second stage, that of 'mutual assistance' consisting of directives or decisions adopted by the Council by a qualified majority on a proposal put forward by the Commission after consulting the Monetary Committee.[38] The Article sets out a non-exhaustive list of forms which the mutual assistance may take, including in particular the granting of credits by other Member States. Only if 'the mutual assistance recommended by the Commission is not granted by the Council or if the mutual assistance granted and the measures taken are insufficient' may the Commission authorise the Member State in difficulty to take exceptional measures. Indeed, according to Ehlermann,[39] if these conditions are fulfilled, the Commission is bound to grant such an authorisation, since Article 108(3) states that the Commission 'shall authorise . . .' However, the Commission is required actively to exercise its discretion in this matter and not act merely as a rubber stamp.[40] Such an authorisation, which, it would seem, must be granted by a decision within the meaning of Article 189,[41] may be revoked or altered by the Council acting by a qualified majority: Article 108(3), second paragraph.

9.19 The exceptional measures which the Commission may authorise under Article 108(3) include quantitative restrictions and measures of equivalent effect,[42] provided always that such draconian measures are necessary to counteract the balance of payments difficulties in question.[43] Accordingly, by Decision 68/301[44] adopted under Article 108(3) the Commission authorised France to restrict imports of cars and certain other products, in order to overcome the economic difficulties encountered by France in the wake of the

---

[37] Ehlermann, *op. cit.* 1404–1405; Mégret, *op. cit.* 33; Zuleeg, *op. cit.* 1865; as to exceptional measures taken by Germany to counteract its balance of payments surplus, though without any authorisation under Art. 108(3), see Case 27/74 *Demag* v. *Finanzamt Duisburg* [1974] E.C.R. 1037 and particularly A.G. Reischl at 1057.

[38] See para. 9.16 above as to the composition of the Monetary Committee.

[39] Ehlermann, *op. cit.* 1412.

[40] See para. 9.33 below.

[41] A.G. Reischl in *Demag*, n.37 above, at 1057.

[42] Ehlermann, *op. cit.* 1412.

[43] See n.2 above.

[44] [1968] J.O. L178/15.

political unrest of May 1968. Another example is Decision 74/287,[45] by which the Commission authorised Italy to subject imports to the lodging with the Bank of Italy of a six-month interest-free loan amounting to not more than 50 per cent. of the value of the goods.

A particularly striking example of the use of Article 108(3) is Decision 85/594[46] which authorised Greece to require interest-free deposits to be lodged for the importation of certain goods; the list of goods concerned takes up 28 pages of the Official Journal.

ARTICLE 109

9.20 Where a Member State suffers a sudden crisis in its balance of payments and mutual assistance is not granted immediately by the Council under Article 108(2), then Article 109 empowers it to take the necessary protective measures itself. As the two Articles are part of one and the same procedure, they must be construed analogously. This means that protective measures adopted under Article 109 may include quantitative restrictions and measures of equivalent effect.[47] Article 109(1) states that 'such measures must cause the least possible disturbance in the functioning of the common market and must not be wider in scope than is strictly necessary to remedy the sudden difficulties which have arisen'. However, this is merely the expression of a general principle common to all exception clauses in the Treaty.[48]

9.21 It is clear, then, that Article 109 empowers Member States unilaterally to take exceptional measures striking at the very core of the Community on purely economic grounds. For this reason it is subject to important guarantees:
  (i) Although the balance of payments difficulties must be of the same kind as those in Article 108, they must fulfil three additional conditions:
      1. They must be in the nature of a crisis;
      2. This crisis must actually have occurred; and
      3. It must be sudden.
      Furthermore, Article 109 cannot be applied if mutual assistance under Article 108(2) is forthcoming.
  (ii) The unilateral measures are merely to act as a stop-gap until the crisis is dealt with by the Community. This is why Article 109(2) provides that 'the Commission and the other Member States shall be informed of such protective measures not later than when they enter into force'. This was the provision which the Court had occasion to interpret in Cases 6 and

---

[45] [1974] O.J. L152/18.
[46] [1985] O.J. L375/9.
[47] Ehlermann, *op. cit.* 1417.
[48] See n.2 above.

11/69 *E.C. Commission* v. *France*.[49] The background to this
case is the economic crisis which arose in France in 1968. By
Decision 68/301 of 23 July 1968 based on Article 108(3)[50] the
Commission authorised France to take various protective
measures, including the fixing of a rediscount rate for exports
more favourable than the general rate. However, that Decision
stipulated that as from 1 November 1968 the difference
between the two rates was not to exceed 1·5 points. When
France exceeded that limit, the Commission brought infringement proceedings against it. In ruling that France had in fact
committed an infringement, the Court rejected, *inter alia*,
France's defence that the failure to respect the conditions
attached to the Commission's decision was covered by Article
109 in view of a fresh monetary crisis which had arisen in the
autumn of 1968.[51] The Court held that to rely on this provision
a Member State must inform the Commission and the other
Member States of its protective measures in accordance with
Article 109(2) and in so doing must make express reference
to Article 109. Since France had not done this, it could not
rely on Article 109.

9.22   The second sentence of Article 109(2) provides:

'The Commission may recommend to the Council the granting of mutual
assistance under Article 108.'

Article 109(3) provides:

'After the Commission has delivered an opinion and the Monetary Committee
has been consulted, the Council may, acting by a qualified majority, decide
that the State concerned shall amend, suspend or abolish the protective
measures referred to above.'

At first sight it might appear from these provisions that the Commission and the Council may stand back and refrain from all intervention, but the Court has held in effect that it is incumbent on them
to intervene at the earliest possible moment.[52] This is natural in view
of the sweeping powers which Member States enjoy by virtue of
Article 109.

It is not necessary in this context to explore all the procedural
permutations which may occur.[53] Suffice it to point out the following
possible trains of events:

— the Council may consider that there are no balance of payments
    difficulties such as to render Article 108 or 109 applicable, in
    which case it must require the Member State concerned to

---

[49] [1969] E.C.R. 523, [1970] C.M.L.R. 43.
[50] See n.44 above.
[51] France had in fact relied on Art. 109 in June and July 1968 before Dec. 68/301 was
taken, but that was not in question before the Court.
[52] Cases 6 and 11/69, see n.49 above.
[53] For these, see in particular Lejeune, *op. cit.* 155; Zuleeg, *op. cit.* 1877.

abolish its unilateral measures or at least amend them so that
they no longer constitute exceptional measures;
— the Commission may recommend mutual assistance under
  Article 108(2) to the Council; if the Council proceeds to adopt
  that recommendation, then Article 109 ceases to be applicable
  and Article 108 takes over;
— if the Commission recommends mutual assistance but the
  Council does not grant it or the mutual assistance granted
  proves insufficient, then the Commission may authorise exceptional measures under Article 108(3); once again, Article 109
  ceases to have effect.

ARTICLE 115[54]

9.23   Article 115 provides as follows:

> 'In order to ensure that the execution of measures of commercial policy taken
> in accordance with this Treaty by any Member State is not obstructed by
> deflection of trade, or where differences between such measures lead to
> economic difficulties in one or more of the Member States, the Commission
> shall recommend the methods for the requisite co-operation between Member
> States. Failing this, the Commission shall authorise Member States to take the
> necessary protective measures, the conditions and details of which it shall
> determine.
>
> In case of urgency during the transitional period, Member States may
> themselves take the necessary measures and shall notify them to the other
> Member States and to the Commission, which may decide that the States
> concerned shall amend or abolish such measures.
>
> In the selection of such measures, priority shall be given to those which
> cause the least disturbance to the functioning of the Common Market and
> which take into account the need to expedite, as far as possible, the introduction
> of the common customs tariff.'

After Article 36, this is in practice the most important exception to
Articles 30 and 34. It can only be applied with respect to goods
originating in third countries in free circulation in the Community.[55]
This can be deduced from the case law on Article 115 discussed
below according to which it constitutes a major exception to the
rule laid down in Article 9 of the Treaty that such goods are
assimilated to goods originating in the Community.[56] In particular,

---

[54] Opperman, 'La clause de sauvegarde de l'Article 115 du Traité de la CEE' [1965] R.M.C.
376; Lejeune, *op. cit.* 189; Mégret, *op. cit.* n.1 above, 384; Börner in *Schutzmaßnahmen im
Gemeinsamen Markt* (1976), 67; Weber, 'Die Bedeutung des Art. 115 EWGV für die Freiheit
des Warenverkehrs' [1979] EuR 29; Lux, 'Ausschluß von der Gemeinschaftshandlung bei
Umwegeinfuhren (Art. 115 EWGV)' [1979] EuR 359; Kretschmer, 'Beschränkungen des
innergemeinschaftlichen Warenverkehrs nach der Kommissionsentscheidung 80/47 ᴵEWG'
[1981] EuR 63; Vogelzang, 'Two Aspects of Article 115 EEC Treaty' [1981] C.M.L.R. 169;
Kretschmer in Groeben, Boeckh, Thiesing, Ehlermann, *op. cit.* n.1 above, Vol. I, 1965.
[55] Art. 115 does not apply to goods from third countries not yet in free circulation in the
Community—even if such goods have already transited through one or more Member States.
In any case, such goods falls outside the scope of this book.
[56] Para. 2.12 *et seq.* above.

in *Donckerwolke* v. *Procureur de la République*[57] the Court stated that:

> 'Article 115 allows difficulties [due to differences in commercial policy capable of bringing about deflections of trade or of causing economic difficulties in certain Member States] to be avoided by giving to the Commission the power to authorise Member States to take protective measures particularly in the form of derogation from the principle of free circulation within the Community of products which originated in third countries and which were put into free circulation in one of the Member States.'

Indeed it can be described as the major exception to this rule.

9.24 From its wording it is quite clear that Article 115 continues to apply after the end of the transitional period. However, it can only apply where national measures of commercial policy have not been supplanted by Community measures. Nevertheless, the establishment of the common commercial policy is not yet complete, and in view of the grave economic situation Article 115 has continued to be applied frequently in recent years, particularly with regard to textiles. This is clearly shown by the following table:

	Number of requests to the Commission by Member States (figures in brackets concern textiles)	Number of requests granted by the Commission
1982	241 (156)	174
1983	253 (176)	188
1984	215 (155)	165
1985	211 (143)	176

9.25 Community measures supplanting national commercial policy measures will most often be based on Article 113 governing the common commercial policy on trade with third countries,[58] though they may be based on other provisions of the Treaty such as Article 43 concerning the common agricultural policy. In either case such measures may take the form of autonomous Community legislation or of agreements with third States. These measures relate only to direct trade with third countries and do not cover goods in free circulation in the Community, whether they originate in the Community or in third countries. Thus they fall outside the scope of this book.

Suffice it to say therefore that the systems provided for by these measures and the roles of Member States under them are varied and

---

[57] Case 41/76 [1976] E.C.R. 1921 at 1937, [1977] 2 C.M.L.R. 535 at 551.

[58] On the common commercial policy see in particular Mégret, *op. cit.* 365; Pescatore 'External Relations in the Case Law of the Court of Justice of the European Communities' [1979] C.M.L.Rev. 615; Ernst and Beseler in Groeben, Boeckh, Thiesing, Ehlermann, *op. cit.* Vol. I, 1981.

complex.[59] At which point the threshold is crossed beyond which Article 115 cannot be applied is unclear. According to the judgment in the two *Tezi Textiel*[60] cases Article 115 can be applied to bolster quotas divided out between Member States by the Community, provided that the disparities in conditions of importation into different Member States are due in part to purely national measures. Yet as the Advocate General said in that case, this will encourage the Council to perpetuate the use of Article 115.

At all events, the test to be applied in each case is whether *this* product originating in *this* country is subject to Community measures of commercial policy such as to oust Article 115.

9.26 Before examining the relevant case law and legislation, an overall description of the nature of Article 115 is required. The following will be discussed in turn: the circumstances in which the provision may be applied, the procedure to be followed, the exceptional measures which may be taken and the application of Article 115 to exports.

9.27 The circumstances in which Article 115 may be applied appear to be twofold:
   (a) Where exceptional measures are necessary to 'ensure that the execution of measures of commercial policy taken in accordance with this Treaty by any Member State is not obstructed by deflection of trade'. The typical situation envisaged here is this: there are as yet no Community rules creating or banning quantitative restrictions on the import of wooden toys from Ruritania (a third country). Italy has imposed a quota or other commercial policy measure on wooden toys coming from Ruritania. However, this measure is being undermined because such toys are being put into free circulation in France and then imported into Italy from France. Once the toys are put into free circulation in the Community they are assimilated to Community goods, so that the Italian Government cannot prevent its quota from being undermined in this way without resorting to Article 115.

According to various authors,[61] deflection of trade may also occur by the phenomenon of substitution. Here the Ruritanian toys are

---

[59] See in particular Reg. 1765/82 on common rules for imports from State-trading countries ([1982] O.J. L195/1) which prohibits Member States from imposing quantitative restrictions on particular goods originating in particular East block countries, subject, however, to various safeguard clauses. Reg. 288/82 ([1982] O.J. L35) as amended lays down a similar prohibition with respect to particular goods originating in virtually all other countries, again subject to the application of various safeguard clauses. Neither instrument concerns measures of equivalent effect. See Kretschmer, *op. cit.* (Groeben, Boeckh, *etc.*) at 1969.

[60] Cases 59/84 *Tezi Textiel* v. *E.C. Commission* [1986] E.C.R. 887, [1987] 3 C.M.L.R. 64 and 242/84 *Tezi Textiel* v. *Ministry of Economic Affairs* [1986] E.C.R. 933, [1987] 3 C.M.L.R. 64.

[61] Opperman, *op. cit.* 381; Lejeune, *op. cit.* 194; Börner, *op. cit.* 73.

absorbed in the French market (or the market of another Member State), thereby enabling French wooden toys to come on to the Italian market in their stead. Yet, even if these authors are correct in their view that this constitutes a deflection of trade, how can Article 115 be applied? It has already been explained that this provision can only be used against goods originating in third countries and not against goods originating in the Community.

No deflection of trade will occur where the toys have acquired Community origin in France. They will have done this if they have undergone there a 'substantial process or operation that is economically justified . . ., having been carried out in an undertaking equipped for the purpose, and resulting in the manufacture of a new product or representing an important stage of manufacture' by virtue of Article 5 of Regulation 802/68 on the concept of origin of goods.[62] As already explained, Article 115 can have no application to goods originating in the Community.

It has also been suggested[63] that even under this limb of Article 115 disparities must exist between the relevant commercial policy measures of the Member States. It is true that in its answer to Written Question 772/78[64] the Commission stated that the existence of such disparities was a necessary condition for the application of Article 115. Yet it may be that Article 115 could be applied in the following hypothetical situation: France and Italy have an identical quota for toys originating in Ruritania (to return to the first example above); both quotas have been exhausted but most of the toys put into free circulation make their way to Italy. Indeed the toys may have been imported through France with the very intention of evading the Italian quota. There is no disparity between the national measures, but it is submitted that a deflection of trade may have occurred nevertheless.

It appears that a mere danger of deflection of trade would suffice to bring Article 115 into play.[65] Naturally this would have to be a real danger, not merely a fanciful one.

Lastly, the national measure of commercial policy to be protected must have been taken 'in accordance with this Treaty'. This, it is submitted, merely means that the measures must be compatible with Community law.

9.28   (b) Where 'differences between such measures [of national commercial policy] lead to economic difficulties in one or more of the Member States'. It is hard to give any precise definition of 'economic difficulties' in this context,

---

[62] [1968] J.O. L148/1; see para. 2.10 above.
[63] Lux, *op. cit.* 362.
[64] [1979] O.J. C45/21.
[65] Mégret, *op. cit.* 386; the A.G. in Case 62/70 *Bock* v. *E.C. Commission* [1971] E.C.R. 897 at 916, [1972] C.M.L.R. 160.

but it must be borne in mind that Article 115 constitutes an exception to one of the fundamental rules of the Treaty, so that it cannot be invoked lightly. There must also be a causal connection between the economic difficulties and the disparities between national commercial policy measures[66] which once again must be compatible with the Treaty. The view has been advanced that a serious threat of economic difficulties will suffice.[67]

9.29 Frequently situations (a) and (b) will occur at one and the same time. Yet it has been suggested that they are alternative.[68] This would appear to mean that Article 115 can be used to protect a national measure of commercial policy even in the absence of any economic difficulties or danger of such difficulties in the Member State concerned. This controversial issue will be discussed further below.

9.30 The procedure for applying Article 115 has been more stringent since the end of the transitional period. During the transitional period, Article 115(2) empowered the Member States to take measures themselves in urgent cases and then to notify them to the Commission, which could confirm them or direct that the measures be abolished. In *Amministrazione delle Finanze dello Stato* v. *Rasham*[69] the Court in effect held that during the transitional period failure by the Member State to notify such measures to the Commission did not render them invalid. The Court also ruled in that case that Decision 66/532,[70] which accelerated the abolition of most customs duties and quantitative restrictions, had no bearing on Article 115(2), which therefore continued to have effect until the end of the transitional period, namely 1 January 1970.

Since the end of the transitional period, Member States may only take measures under Article 115 on the prior authorisation of the Commission. This is shown unequivocally by the Court's case law which is discussed below. Although under Article 115 the Commission could grant such an authorisation without the Member State making a request, it is not the Commission's practice to do so.

Another feature of this provision is that before granting an authorisation for exceptional measures, the Commission is called upon to 'recommend the methods for the requisite co-operation between Member States'. Some recommendations of this kind have

---

[66] As to when such disparity exists, see Lux, *op. cit.* 362.
[67] Mégret, *op. cit.* 386.
[68] Opperman, *op. cit.* 378, Lejeune, *op. cit.* 193, Mégret, *op. cit.* 386, Börner, *op. cit.* 72, Lux, *op. cit.* 361; see generally Kretschmer, *op. cit.* (Groeben, Boeckh, *etc.*) 1971–4.
[69] Case 27/78 [1978] E.C.R. 1761, [1979] 1 C.M.L.R. 1.
[70] [1966] J.O. 165; see para. 5.01 above.

been issued,[71] but it has long been obvious that in practice they are little more than pious hopes. This is why it has become the practice of the Commission to take decisions under Article 115 without first sending recommendations.[72] In *Bock* v. *E.C. Commission*[73] Advocate General Dutheillet de Lamotte held that this practice did not constitute a defect in form such as to vitiate a decision, notably on the grounds that 'the omission of a formality which was known to be futile would not constitute . . . a defect sufficiently substantial to vitiate the contested provision'.

9.31   As regards the measures which may be taken under Article 115, paragraph 3 states that 'in the selection of such measures, priority shall be given to those which cause the least disturbance to the functioning of the common market . . .' This is merely an expression of the general principle that measures taken under exception clauses must be no more restrictive than is necessary.[74] Accordingly, an import ban may not be authorised where a less restrictive measure would suffice. For the same reason the Commission may only grant authorisation for a limited period.[75]

9.32   Can Article 115 be used to restrict exports? The classic situation envisaged is where a product is in short supply; if supplies of this product are being exported from Member State A to Member State B and then on to Ruritania (a third country); if there are no Community measures governing the exportation of these particular goods to Ruritania, then may Article 115 be relied on to restrict re-exports to Ruritiania? The Commission has been known to issue recommendations[76] under Article 115 in such cases to the effect that the Member States should prohibit re-exports to third countries, but it appears never to have applied binding measures to exports. In any case, Article 103(4) is a more appropriate basis for exceptional measures designed to cope with shortages of supply. The normal case in which Article 115 is applied concerns imports and the case law and legislation discussed below concern imports only.

9.33   Having made these general remarks, we can now turn to consider the Court's case law on Article 115 before discussing the main legislation adopted by the Commission under this provision. Of this the *Rasham* case has already been discussed and requires no further comment.

---

[71] *E.g.* Recom. 64/100 ([1964] J.O. 374); Recom. 67/80 ([1967] J.O. 272).
[72] In many decisions of this kind the Commission has explained why no prior recommendation had been made; see, *e.g.* Dec. of 5 March 1962 ([1962] J.O. 1099); Dec. of 31 July 1963 ([1963] J.O. 2338); Dec. 79/229 ([1979] O.J. L47/18).
[73] See n.65 above, at 916.
[74] See n.2 above.
[75] Lejeune, *op. cit.* 213.
[76] *E.g.* Recom. 71/108 ([1971] J.O. L50/7).

The first two cases, *Bock* v. *E.C. Commission*[77] and *Kaufhof* v. *E.C. Commission*[78] were based on remarkably similar facts, arising in each case after the end of the transitional period. The plaintiffs in *Bock* sought to import into the Federal Republic of Germany a consignment of preserved mushrooms originating in the People's Republic of China and in free circulation in the Netherlands. They therefore lodged an application for an import licence with the German authorities, as did one other prospective importer.

However, in the absence of common rules[79] the German authorities proceeded to apply to the Commission for permission to 'exclude from Community treatment' the import of preserved mushrooms originating in the People's Republic of China and in free circulation in any Member State. This authorisation was duly granted by the Commission under Article 115 with respect to such mushrooms in free circulation in the Benelux countries. The plaintiffs were therefore unable to import the mushrooms into Germany.

Consequently, they brought an action under Article 173 of the Treaty to have the Commission's Decision annulled. The Commission first argued that the Decision was not of direct and individual concern to the plaintiffs within the meaning of Article 173 so that the action was inadmissible. The Court rejected the Commission's argument in the following terms:

> 'The applicant has challenged the decision only to the extent to which it also covers imports for which applications for import licences were already pending at the date of its entry into force. The number and identity of importers concerned in this way was already fixed and ascertained before that date. The defendant was in a position to know that the contested provision in its decision would affect the interests and situation of those importers alone. The factual situation thus created differentiates the latter from all other persons and distinguishes them individually just as in the case of the person addressed.'

The action was therefore ruled to be admissible—a ruling of considerable significance to any person who finds himself in the same situation.

As to the substance, the Court began by stating that Article 115 constitutes an exception to Article 30 as well as to Article 113 on the common commercial policy so that derogations allowed under Article 115 must be strictly interpreted and applied. It continued:

> 'It appears from the file that at the date of the contested decision the German authorities were considering only two applications, amounting to a total import of some 120 metric tons, that is to say, about 0·26 per cent., according to the defendant's own statements, of the total of 46,122 metric tons of preserved mushrooms imported into Germany in 1969. In these circumstances the Commission, by extending the authorisation at issue to an application relating

---

[77] See n.65 above.

[78] Case 29/75 [1976] E.C.R. 431.

[79] Reg. 865/68 on the common organisation of the market for products processed from fruit and vegetables ([1968] O.J. Spec.Ed. 228) did not lay down common rules on quantitative restrictions with respect to third countries. Such rules did not exist until the adoption of Reg. 1927/75 ([1975] O.J. L198/7), after the material facts in the *Kaufhof* case had occurred.

to a transaction which was insignificant in terms of the effectiveness of the measure of commercial policy proposed by the Member State concerned and which in addition had been submitted at a time when the principle of the free circulation of goods applied unrestrictedly to the goods in question, has exceeded the limits of what is "necessary" within the meaning of Article 115— interpreted within the general framework of the Treaty, following the expiry of the transitional period.'

Accordingly, the contested Decision was annulled.

9.34 The *Kaufhof* case was based on virtually identical facts, with the immaterial difference that the goods in issue were preserves of beans in pods rather than preserved mushrooms. In view of the *Bock* case the Commission did not contest the admissibility of the action. Again, the Court repeated its earlier statement that since Article 115 constitutes an exception to Articles 30 and 113, derogations allowed under it are to be strictly construed and applied (a statement which also appears in the subsequent cases on Article 115). However, the Court set out rather different reasons for annulling the Commission's Decision from those given in *Bock*:

'It appears from the statements made by the defendant's Agent during the oral proceedings that it considers that the authorisation requested should be granted if the measure of commercial policy adopted by the Member State concerned is compatible with the Treaty, without having to take account of the reasons on which that measure is based, and when it involves an absolute prohibition on imports, without having to take account of the quantity, whether large or negligible, concerned in the applications already received.

By failing to review the reasons put forward by the Member State concerned in order to justify the measures of commercial policy which it wishes to introduce, the Commission was in breach of its duty under Article 115 to examine whether the measures have been "taken in accordance with this Treaty" and whether the protective measures sought are necessary within the meaning of the same provision.

By extending the authorisation to applications already received, without taking account of the size or insignificance of the quantity in question in these applications, the Commission has also exceeded the limits of its discretion.'

In *Bock* the Court had annulled the Commission's Decision because of the insignificant amount of imports involved. On the other hand, in *Kaufhof* the Court pointed to the Commission's failure to review the reasons put forward by the Member State to justify its request,[80] and to the retroactive nature of the Decision.

9.35 The next three judgments of the Court on Article 115 are rather different from *Bock* and *Kaufhof* in that they were all delivered in reply to questions put under Article 177 as to the powers which Member States may exercise under Article 115 before making an application to the Commission. Therefore the powers and duties of the Commission were not directly in issue.

---

[80] Reich, 'La politique commerciale commune de la CEE et le contrôle de l'utilisation de la clause de sauvegarde de l'article 115 du traité CEE' [1978] R.T.D.E. 33.

The first of this batch of cases is *Donckerwolcke* v. *Procureur de la République*.[81] There a reference arose out of criminal proceedings brought against a number of persons who had imported various consignments of cloth sacks from Belgium into France in 1969 (before the end of the transitional period) and in 1970 (after the end of the transitional period). In the customs documents the importers gave the Belgo-Luxembourg Economic Union as the place of origin of the goods. Subsequent inquiries revealed, however, that the goods in fact originated in Lebanon and Syria and were in free circulation in Belgium; the importers were therefore charged before the French courts with making false customs declarations. The object of the questions was essentially to ascertain whether, during and after the transitional period, it was compatible with Article 30 for a Member State to require declarations of origin to be made with respect to imports and to subject imports to a system of import licences so as to monitor them with a view to applying Article 115.

The Court began by considering the situation obtaining after the expiry of the transitional period. As explained earlier in this book, the Court held that goods in free circulation in the Community though originating in a third country were totally assimilated to goods originating in the Community[82]; that the requirement of import licences even as a pure formality was contrary to Article 30[83]; that it was compatible with Article 30 for a Member State to require an importer to make a declaration of origin of goods in so far as he knew or could reasonably be expected to know that origin[84] (probably a Member State may impose this requirement even without obtaining an authorisation under Article 115, though the Court did not spell this out); but that it was contrary to Article 30 for a Member State to impose penalties for making a false declaration, which were excessive in regard to the purely administrative nature of the contravention.[85] For the present purposes the most important passage of the judgment is the ruling to the effect that the requirement of an import licence is contrary to the Treaty unless the goods are the subject of a derogation properly authorised by the Commission under Article 115. Implied in this is the assertion that after the end of the transitional period a Member State requires authorisation from the Commission before it can take exceptional measures under Article 115. A Member State can no longer take such measures on its own and submit them to the Commission for subsequent approval.

However, the Court went on to hold that during the transitional period the Member States could do precisely this, as indeed the

---

[81] See n.57 above; case notes by Schmidt [1977] EuR 263; Usher [1977] E.L.Rev. 304.
[82] Para. 2.16 above.
[83] Para. 7.03 above.
[84] Para. 7.13 above.
[85] Para. 7.11 above.

second paragraph of Article 115 makes clear: at that time a Member State could take exceptional measures in case of urgency on condition that it notified them to the other Member States and the Commission subsequently; the Commission then had the power to require the Member State concerned to amend or abolish its unilateral measures. Without considering the requirement of urgency at all, the Court concluded that 'the obligations imposed on the importer of goods put into free circulation in another Member State to obtain an import licence was, so far as its principle is concerned, compatible with Community law in its state of development at that time'. The Court did add one rider, however: by virtue of Articles 31 and 32[86] the exceptional measures could not be more restrictive then than they were on 1 January 1958.

9.36   In *Cayrol* v. *Rivoira*[87] many of the points already decided in *Donckerwolcke* reared their heads again. In December 1970 and December 1971 Cayrol imported into France various consignments of table grapes dispatched from Italy by Rivoira. The grapes bore the Italian export mark and were accompanied by the certificate of the *Istituto Nazionale per il Commercio Estero* certifying that the goods were in conformity with the quality standards and stating that they were of Italian origin. This proved to be false: the grapes were in fact of Spanish origin and had been put into free circulation in Italy. Since the French import quota for grapes from Spain had been exhausted, both Cayrol and Rivoira were charged with and convicted of having imported prohibited goods by means of a false declaration of origin and on the basis of false or inaccurate documents. Cayrol, having reached a settlement with the French authorities as to the amount of the fine, now brought an action before the Italian courts to recover from Rivoira part of this sum on the grounds that Rivoira had deceived the customs authorities as to the origin of the grapes. The Italian court then put a series of questions to the Court of Justice as to the application of Article 115. In broad terms, the object of these questions was to establish whether Article 115 could be applied in the circumstances and whether the French measures complied with Community law.

The Court first found that it followed from a combination of Regulation 2513/69[88] on the co-ordination of treatment accorded by Member States to fruit and vegetable imports from third countries and of the Agreement concluded between the EEC and Spain on 29 June 1970[89] that table grapes from Spain were not covered by a Community import system between 1 July and 31 December. Therefore Article 115 was not ousted during that period. Thus it is

---

[86] Para. 5.01 above.
[87] Case 52/77 [1977] E.C.R. 2261, [1978] 2 C.M.L.R. 253.
[88] [1969] J.O. L318/6.
[89] See Reg. 1524/70 ([1970] J.O. L182/1).

clear beyond doubt that Community rules on imports may apply for part of the year only so that Article 115 may be applied during the rest of the year.

In so far as it concerns us in the present context, the rest of the judgment adds nothing to the *Donckerwolcke* decision.

9.37 The sequel to Cayrol was *Procureur de la République* v. *Rivoira*,[90] involving a reference from the French court seised of the criminal proceedings. Unfortunately, in Cayrol the Court had not stated in express terms that France was not entitled to prohibit the importation of the grapes without prior authorisation from the Commission under Article 115—though this is undoubtedly the effect of the judgment. This was the object of the French court's first question.

The Court began by stating that Regulation 2513/69 only restricted direct imports from third countries of the products concerned: it did not and could not restrict or prohibit inter-State trade in products in free circulation, because this would constitute a derogation from the fundamental rules of the Treaty on the free movement of goods. Only Article 115 gave the Commission power to authorise a Member State to take protective measures against products originating in third countries and in free circulation in Member States. Article 115 can only be applied if the substantive and procedural conditions set out in that provision are fulfilled. It followed that in 1970 and 1971 a Member State could not prohibit the importation of grapes in free circulation without the prior authorisation of the Commission under Article 115.

The second and final question was whether criminal penalties could be imposed on persons making false declarations of the kind in question. The Court replied that:

'although the fact that Spanish grapes imported into France from Italy have been declared as being of Italian origin may in appropriate cases give grounds for the application of the criminal penalties provided against false declarations, it would be disproportionate to apply without distinction the criminal penalties provided in respect of false declarations made in order to effect prohibited imports.'

This adds nothing to *Donckerwolcke* and *Cayrol*, but it clarifies those judgments: it shows that once a Member State has been authorised to prohibit imports under Article 115, it may impose higher penalties for false declarations than it could previously.

9.38 The plaintiffs in *Spijker Kwasten* v. *E.C. Commission*[91] were the sole regular importers into the Benelux countries of brushes originating in the People's Republic of China. They sought the annulment under Article 173 of a Commission Decision based on

---

[90] Case 179/78 [1979] E.C.R. 1147, [1979] 3 C.M.L.R. 456.
[91] Case 231/82 [1983] E.C.R. 2559, [1984] 2 C.M.L.R. 284.

Article 115 authorising those States to exclude such brushes from Community treatment. Since the Decision was not retroactive, the action was held to be inadmissible.

9.39 In its Order in *Ilford* v. *E.C. Commission*[92] the Court partially suspended the operation of a Commission Decision addressed to Italy under Article 115, which decision had authorised that country to exclude film originating in Japan from Community treatment. It did so on the basis that direct imports into Italy from Japan did not appear to be subject to any restriction under Italian law. Alternatively, if the Italian authorities had adopted such a measure, it did not appear to have been 'taken in accordance with the Treaty' as required by Article 115. The Court thus found that, *prima facie,* the conditions for applying Article 115 had not been fulfilled.

9.40 Two judgments of major importance on Article 115 were delivered in the *Tezi Textiel*[93] cases. Those cases related to textile products originating in Macao and in free circulation in Italy. These products were covered by Council Regulation 3589/82[94] on common rules for imports of certain textile products originating in third countries. That Regulation, which was based on Article 113 of the Treaty, gave effect on a provisional and autonomous basis to the Multi-Fibre Agreement. It laid down a quantitative limit for the whole Community for each year from 1983 to 1986 for each supplier country, including Macao; it then subdivided that quantitative limit between the Member States, the Benelux countries being treated as a single unit. By two successive decisions the Commission authorised the Benelux countries to exercise intra-Community surveillance of certain textile products throughout 1983, pursuant to Articles 1 and 2 of Decision 80/47 (discussed below). Consequently on 29 April 1983 Tezi applied to the Dutch authorities for licences to import such products from Italy. The applications were refused on the grounds that by Decision of 12 April 1983 based on Article 3 of Decision 80/47 the Commission had authorised the Benelux countries to exclude such goods from Community treatment, as had been requested by the Netherlands with the consent of Belgium and Luxembourg. Tezi then brought proceedings before the Dutch courts challenging this refusal to grant it licences. A reference for a preliminary ruling was then made: that case was *Tezi Textiel* v. *Ministry for Economic Affairs.* The questions posed by the national court were as follows:

'1. Must Articles 113 and 115 of the EEC Treaty, taken together, be interpreted as meaning that the Commission may still apply Article 115

---

[92] Case 1/84R [1984] E.C.R. 423, [1984] 2 C.M.L.R. 475.
[93] See n.60 above. See Usher 'The Single Market and Goods Imported from Third Countries' [1986] Y.E.L. 159.
[94] [1982] O.J. L374/106.

in relation to international trade in textiles after the conclusion of the Arrangement regarding international trade in textiles ("the Multi-Fibre Arrangement") and the adoption of Council Regulation (EEC) No. 3589/82?

2. If the answer to Question 1 is in the affirmative, must the phrase "measures of commercial policy taken in accordance with this Treaty by any Member State" contained in Article 115 of the Treaty be interpreted as including a breakdown of Community quantitative limits between the Member States, such as is provided for in Annex IV to Council Regulation (EEC) No. 3589/82?'

On 1 December 1983 Tezi submitted further applications for such licences. However, these applications were also refused since by decision of 14 December 1983 the Commission once again authorised the Benelux countries at their request to exclude such goods from Community treatment. That decision, which was also based on Article 3 of Decision 80/47, applied retroactively from 1 December to 31 December 1983. This time Tezi brought a direct action for annulment of the decision and for damages: *Tezi Textiel* v. *E.C. Commission*. The two cases were heard together although for procedural reasons they could not be joined and two separate judgments had to be given.

In both cases Tezi's principal contention was that, since the Community had adopted common measures under Article 113, recourse to Article 115 was precluded. Similarly, it claimed that the words 'measures of common policy taken in accordance with this Treaty by any Member State' in the initial limb of Article 115 referred only to national measures of commercial policy, and not to measures which Member States take to implement Community regulations. The Commission and the four governments which intervened took the converse view.

The Advocate General forcefully expressed the view that the phrase 'measures of commercial policy taken in accordance with this Treaty by any Member State' in Article 115 does not cover national sub-quotas such as those provided for in Regulation 3589/82 nor does it cover a national measure implementing that Regulation. He was surely right to point out that, if a Community Regulation or national measures implementing such a Regulation constituted 'measures of commercial policy taken in accordance with this Treaty by any Member State' in Article 115, then 'the Council could open the way indefinitely to new breaches of the principles of the customs union' and this would be contrary to the rule that Article 115 must be interpreted strictly. Consequently, in his view, the contested decisions were unlawful.

The Court found otherwise. It began[95] by confirming *E.C. Commission* v. *E.C. Council*[96] (the rum quotas case). It had held there that, while a total quota for imports into the Community from

---

[95] In its judgment in the direct action, the Court first held that action to be admissible.
[96] Case 218/82 [1983] E.C.R. 4063, [1984] 2 C.M.L.R. 350; see para. 4.11 above.

third countries may be divided into national sub-quotas, it would be contrary to the Treaty provisions on the free movement of goods to restrict the movement of such goods between Member States once they had been put into free circulation.

Yet it then went on to rule against Tezi on the grounds that Regulation 3589/82 did not introduce a 'genuine common policy' within the meaning of Article 113 for textile products originating in third countries party to the Multi-Fibre Agreement. To be sure, that Regulation constituted 'a step towards the establishment of a common commercial policy based, in accordance with Article 113(1) of the Treaty, on uniform principles'. Nevertheless, the Court went on:

> 'However, it does not appear that the system established by that Regulation has brought about complete uniformity as regards conditions of importation. The second clause of the tenth recital in the preamble to the regulation states in fact that "the extent of the disparities existing in the conditions for importation of these products into the Member States and the particularly sensitive position of the Community textiles industry mean that the said conditions can be standardised only gradually."
>
> Contrary to Tezi's contention, the disparities in question cannot therefore be attributed solely to Regulation No. 3589/82; they are the result of measures taken by the Member States, on their own initiative, but in accordance with the relevant requirements laid down by Community law. As can be seen from the passage in the tenth recital quoted above, Regulation No. 3589/82 merely maintains, to a certain extent, existing disparities, while proclaiming as its goal their gradual reduction and eventual elimination.'

This ruling is most surprising.[97] In the first place, by stating that the disparities in question could not be attributed *solely* to Regulation 3589/82, the Court conceded that they were partly attributable to the Regulation. Yet it is surely contrary to the principles established in *Ramel*[98] and *E.C. Commission* v. *E.C. Council* (rum quota) for a Community regulation to introduce any new disparities, which can then be made absolute pursuant to Article 115. Secondly, the Court's view that there were certain disparities in national measures apart from those in the Regulation is based merely on the statement to that effect in the preamble to the Regulation. The Court simply quoted the relevant passage of the preamble without making any attempt to base this crucial part of its ruling on its own findings of fact: in its judgment the Court has not even attempted to establish the nature and extent of the alleged disparities in national measures. This is surely in stark contrast to the Order in *Ilford* where, after considering the Italian legislation concerned at some length, the Court found that, *prima facie*, no national commercial policy measures existed. Equally, the Court affirmed that the national measures concerned had been taken 'in accordance with the relevant requirements laid down by Community law' without proffering any evidence to support this.

---

[97] See Timmerman's critical casenote in [1986] S.E.W. 762.
[98] Cases 80–81/77 [1978] E.C.R. 927; para. 4.09 above.

Where does this leave the Advocate General's view that the words 'measures of commercial policy taken in accordance with this Treaty by any Member State' in Article 115 do not cover disparities between Member States introduced by Community legislation nor national measures taken to implement such legislation? The Court did not expressly advert to this issue at all although it was raised in one of the questions referred in Case 242/84. Nevertheless, one can infer from the passage of the judgment already quoted that Article 115 may be applied where differences in commercial policy measures applicable to Member States result partly from purely national measures and partly from Community legislation. Happily, the Court stopped short of saying that Community legislation by itself could lawfully introduce disparities which could be rendered absolute under Article 115. Had it done so, it would plainly have driven a coach and horses through the ruling in *E.C. Commission* v. *E.C. Council*.

9.41 At all events, Tezi also argued that, in the light of Articles 5 and 7(2) of Regulation 3589/82, that Regulation leaves no further scope for the application of Article 115. These arguments were also dismissed by the Court.

Article 5 provides that in certain circumstances the quantitative limit applicable to the whole of the Community may be reduced. However, as the Court pointed out, this would 'have much more serious consequences for the non-member producer countries than a Commission decision taken under Article 115'. This is true, but it is scarcely a legal answer to Tezi's argument on this point. The Court gave no other grounds for rejecting this argument.

Article 7(2) provides that the allocation of the Community quantitative limits may be adopted 'where this proves necessary, particularly in view of trends in patterns of trade, in order to ensure their improved utilisation.' The Court stated that, if this provision were applied so as to reduce a Member State's national sub-quota, this would merely affect direct imports from third countries into that Member State, without restricting the importation of goods in free circulation in other Member States.

9.42 In *Tezi Textiel* v. *E.C. Commission* the plaintiffs claimed in the alternative that the contested decision infringed Article 115, even if recourse to that Article was not precluded.

Firstly, Tezi claimed that the contested Decision covered a somewhat wider category of textile products than was strictly necessary. This argument was also dismissed by the Court on the grounds that 'neither Decision No. 80/47 nor Article 115 exclude the possibility that such a decision may cover a large number of products falling within the same tariff category, provided that the applicant Member State can show that there is a need for protective measures of such a scope, although it is not essential for evidence to be provided for each producer.'

Yet as explained below, Decision 80/47 refers to the product for which a Member State seeks the application of Article 115 not only in terms of its tariff heading but also in terms of its NIMEXE code[99] which is more specific.[100] One would have thought then that the Member State must show the need for protective measures in relation to each NIMEXE heading concerned and not merely for each tariff heading or even sub-heading: see Articles 2(3)(a) and 3(2) of Decision 80/47.

Secondly, Tezi contested the view that economic difficulties existed such as to justify the authorisation of protective measures. Once again, the Advocate General found for the plaintiffs. In his view, 'the causal connection between the alleged disparities and the economic difficulties assumed to exist in the Netherlands . . . is by no means proved and improbable in any event'.

After referring to *Donckerwolcke,* the Court ruled that:

> 'since, as stated above, the system introduced by Regulation No. 3589/82 constitutes, in its sphere of application, a step toward the establishment of a common commercial policy based, as Article 113(1) provides, on uniform principles, the Commission must show great prudence and moderation in exercising the powers which it still has under Article 115 with regard to products covered by Regulation No. 3589/82.
>
> It follows that, in the sector in question, the Commission may, solely for serious reasons and for a limited period, effect a full examination of the situation in the Member State seeking a decision under Article 115 and having regard to the general interests of the Community, authorise, pursuant to that article, the protective measures which cause the least disruption of intra-Community trade.'

For reasons which need not be considered here the Court found that these conditions had been satisfied.

9.43 This case law has answered a number of important questions about Article 115, but not that discussed at paragraph 9.29 above: can Article 115 be used to protect a national measure of commercial policy even in the absence of any economic difficulties or danger of such difficulties in the Member State concerned? Even the *Tezi Textiel* cases do not appear to provide an answer to that crucial question. As will be seen, the Commission has taken the view that Article 115 can be applied in such circumstances.

9.44 As regards the measures adopted by the Commission under Article 115, a glance at the table of figures set out earlier in this section will suffice to show that these are legion. We can only

---

[99] See Council Reg. 1445/72 ([1972] O.J. L161/1) and Commission Reg. 3840/86 ([1986] O.J. L368/1).

[100] Since 1 January 1988 the NIMEXE and the former common customs tariff have been replaced by the combined nomenclature: see Council Reg. 2658/87 ([1987] O.J. L256/1) and Oliver and Yataganas 'The Harmonised System of Customs Classification' [1987] Y.E.L. 113

consider here the legislation of general application and certain more specific Decisions which are indicative of present trends.

The first Decision laying down general procedures and criteria for the application of Article 115 was Decision 71/202.[101] This was subsequently modified by Decision 73/55.[102] These Decisions provided for Member States to take exceptional measures without prior authorisation from the Commission. Although the *Donckerwolcke, Cayrol* and *Rivoira* judgments did not concern those Decisions, they stated that prior authorisation from the Commission is necessary for the taking of exceptional measures since the end of the transitional period. It was clear therefore that these Decisions were incompatible with the Treaty. Indeed, Advocates General Capotorti and Warner stated this expressly in the *Donckerwolcke* and *Cayrol* cases respectively.[103]

9.45 Accordingly, the Commission adopted Decision 80/47[104] which effected a fundamental reform in the application of Article 115. In view of its importance, it is necessary to reproduce in full various provisions of that Decision.

The scope of the Decision is laid down by Article 1 as follows:

'This Decision shall apply to imports into a Member State of products originating in a third country which have been put into free circulation in the Community, in cases where they are subject either to quantitative import restrictions in that Member State or to voluntary export restraint measures applied by the third country concerned by virtue of a trade agreement and are likely to be the subject of protective measures under Article 115 of the Treaty.'

The Decision then goes on to make provision for two types of exceptional measure: intra-Community surveillance (Article 2) and protective measures (Article 3).

9.46 Article 2 begins:

'1. Where there is a danger that imports into a Member State of a product referred to in Article 1 will give rise to economic difficulties, imports of that product may, following an authorisation given by the Commission for a specific period, be made subject to the issue of an import document.

2. Without prejudice to the provisions of Article 3, this document shall be issued by the Member State concerned, for any quantity requested and free of charge, within a maximum period of five working days from the date on which the application by the importer was received irrespective of where he has his place of business in the Community.'

Article 2(2) makes it clear that a Member State may not withhold an import document. Article 2(3) lays down precisely which particulars a Member State shall supply for the purpose of obtaining authorisation to apply this system of intra-Community surveillance;

---

[101] [1971] O.J. L121/26.
[102] [1973] O.J. L80/22.
[103] [1976] E.C.R. at 1948, [1977] E.C.R. at 2290 respectively.
[104] [1980] O.J. L16/14, amended by corrigendum [1980] O.J. L89/22, see Kretschmer [1981] EuR 63, *op. cit.* n.54 above.

this includes the Common Customs Tariff heading of the product, its NIMEXE code[105] and its country of origin. Article 2(4) provides that a Member State which has obtained such authorisation may only require certain specific information from an applicant for an import document.[106]

9.47   As to protective measures Article 3(1) provides:

> 'Where imports into a Member State of a product referred to in Article 1 give rise to economic difficulties, the Member State in question may take protective measures after obtaining the prior authorisation of the Commission which shall determine the conditions and details of such measures.'

Article 3(2) stipulates what information a Member State must provide to the Commission to obtain such authorisation, including: the Common Customs Tariff heading of the product in question, its NIMEXE code and its country of origin, and details for the two preceding years and the current year of the volume and quantity of imports of the product in question and of the economic difficulties in the sector. Article 3(3) and (4) provides:

> '(3)   The introduction of the request by the Member States may not prevent the issue under the conditions and within the period laid down in Article 2 of import documents for which application was made prior to the Commission's decision.
>
> (4)   However, where the Member State finds that the volume or total quantity covered by applications pending in respect of the product in question originating in the third country concerned is more than either 5 per cent. of possible direct imports from the third country concerned or 1 per cent. of the total extra-EEC imports during the latest 12 months period for which statistical information is available:
>> (i)   the maximum period for the issue of import documents shall be increased to 10 working days from the date on which the application by the importer was received;
>> (ii)   the Member State may reject the application for import documents if the Commission's decision authorises it to do so.'

Article 3(5) requires the Member State to inform applicants for import documents of the introduction of a request for protective measures and to send a copy of this request to the other Member States. Article 3(6) requires the Commission to decide on the request of the Member State within five working days of its receipt.

The crux of this system is that a Member State may no longer take exceptional measures without prior authorisation from the Commission, which principle is in keeping with the Court's case law. The only action which a Member State may take under Articles 2 and 3 without such prior authorisation is to wait an additional five working days before granting an import licence, where the conditions set out in Article 3(4) are fulfilled; but this can only be relied on where the Commission has already authorised the Member

---

[105] See nn.99 and 100 above.
[106] On surveillance measures see generally Dec. 87/61 ([1987] O.J. L32/18).

State to take intra-Community surveillance measures under Article 2.

A further important feature of this system is that it only provides for exceptional measures where economic difficulties exist actually (Article 3) or potentially (Article 2). Thus it does not allow for the protection of national measures of commercial policy where the applicant Member State is not suffering economic difficulties by virtue of the imports in question and is not in danger of doing so. As will be seen below, however, the Commission has subsequently allowed the United Kingdom to apply intra-Community protective measures to bananas originating in certain countries, although there is of course no British production of bananas.

It is not entirely clear from the wording of Decision 80/47 whether intra-Community surveillance measures must be taken under Article 2 before protective measures may be taken under Article 3. This requirement is not expressly stated, but it appears from the terms of Article 3 that it will normally be applied once intra-Community measures are in force.[107] In *Tezi Textiel* v. *E.C. Commission*,[108] the Court said somewhat equivocally that 'the link between the applicants for import licences to the authorities of the Member State which wishes to apply protective measures and the Commission's decision to authorise such measures is not so close that the measures authorised can never cover products for which no licences have been requested'.

Finally, it would seem to follow from Article 3(2) that an applicant Member State must show the need for protective measures in relating to each and every NIMEXE heading concerned. However, as already mentioned,[109] it was held in *Tezi Textiel* that it suffices for the Member State to refer more generally to the 'tariff category' concerned. Yet this could result in the measures taken being wider in scope than necessary.

9.48 Article 4 of the Decision relates to proof of origin. It will be recalled that according to the case law of the Court a Member State may require an importer of goods from another Member State to state their origin on the import document. However, so long as no authorisation has been granted by the Commission under Article 115 this information may only be required of the importer in so far as he knows or can reasonably be expected to know it. Since Article 4 applies where such authorisation has already been granted by the Commission, it is wider:

---

[107] Kretschmer, *op. cit.* n.54 above, states that the wording of the Decision does not require Art. 2 measures to have been taken before protective measures are authorised under Art. 3. However, he points out that in practice a Member State will normally need to take surveillance measures under Art. 2 so as to obtain the statistical evidence necessary for an application under Art. 3 (his n.49 in [1981] EuR 63 and his n.35 in Groeben, Boeckh, *etc.*).

[108] Case 59/84, see n.60 above.

[109] Para. 9.42 above.

'1. As part of the completion of formalities in connection with the importation of products of a type which are subject to intra-Community surveillance measures or protective measures, the relevant authorities of the importing Member State may ask the importer to state the origin of the products on the customs declaration or on the application for an import document.

2. Additional proof may be requested only in cases where serious and well-founded doubts make such proof essential in order to establish the true origin of the products in question. However, a request for such additional proof may not in itself prevent the import of the goods.'

9.49   Shortly after this, the Commission adopted Decision 80/776,[110] which shows that the procedures and conditions laid down in Decision 80/47 were not exclusive: the Commission was prepared to grant authorisations under Article 115 in cases where the conditions set out in Decision 80/47 were not satisfied. Decision 80/776 permitted the United Kingdom to take intra-Community surveillance measures under Article 2(4) of Decision 80/47 and to require proof of origin under Article 4 of Decision 80/47 with respect to bananas originating in certain third countries. As explained earlier, no such authorisation could be granted under Decision 80/47 because, in the absence of any national production, no economic difficulties were caused to the United Kingdom by banana imports. The reasoning behind the Decision is explained by the following recitals:

'Whereas the first Article of Protocol 4 to the Lomé Convention signed on 31 October 1979 and put into effect unilaterally by the Community from 1 March 1980 provides that "as regards its exports of bananas to the markets of the Community, no ACP State will be placed, as regards access to its traditional markets and its advantages on those markets, in a less favourable situation than in the past or at present";

Whereas to fulfil that requirement the United Kingdom, which constitutes a major traditional market for certain ACP States, still makes imports of bananas originating in other non-member countries subject to quantitative restrictions;

Whereas, in order to control imports of such products via the other Member States, the United Kingdom has applied to the Commission for authorisation to introduce intra-Community surveillance of such imports;

Whereas, although under Commission Decision No. 80/47/EEC, adopted by virtue of the powers conferred on the Commission by Article 115 of the Treaty, such surveillance measures can only be taken where there is a danger that the imports will give rise to economic difficulties in the Member States concerned. It does not appear necessary in these very specific circumstances to require compliance with that condition, since the surveillance measures which the United Kingdom wishes to introduce are sufficiently justified by the need to ensure the effectiveness of the commercial policy measures it has to implement to fulfil the requirements of Protocol 4 to the Lomé Convention.'

This Decision was followed first by measures authorising the United Kingdom temporarily to suspend the grant of import licences for

---

[110] [1980] O.J. L224/15.

bananas originating in certain third countries[111] and finally by a Decision[112] authorising it to impose import quotas.

9.50   This same tendency to create exceptions to the principles laid down in Decision 80/47 can be observed in the Commission's Statement concerning Article 115 made in response to the Council's Resolution of 22 July 1980 concerning access to Community public supply contracts for products originating in third countries.[113] As part of the Multilateral Agreements concluded under the auspices of the GATT and generally known as the Tokyo Round, the Community had concluded an Agreement on government procurement.[114] By its Resolution of 22 July 1980 the Council declared that 'Member States may continue to apply, in accordance with the Treaty, existing commercial policy measures in respect of public supply contracts' falling outside the Agreement on government procurement. The Resolution further noted 'the possibility referred to by the Commission of taking any necessary protective measures, under Article 115 of the Treaty, to ensure that the implementation of such provisions is not obstructed by deflection of trade'.

The Commission's Statement is in the same vein:

> 'The Commission notes the concern expressed by the Council in its Resolution.
>
> The Commission is aware that in awarding public supply contracts the Member States may still, in accordance with the Treaty, apply certain measures of national commercial policy with regard to the eligibility of products originating in third countries for such contracts. The Commission recognises that, until these national measures are harmonised within the framework of the contractual or unilateral common commercial policy and in the light of the outcome of current or future international negotiations, their application may give rise to difficulty in cases where tenders include products originating in third countries in free circulation in another Member State.
>
> The Commission would recall that Article 115 of the Treaty enables the efficacy of such national measures to be safeguarded against deflection of trade resulting from the free movement within the Community of products originating in third countries.
>
> In accordance with Article 115 of the Treaty, the Commission intends to authorise those Member States concerned which have applied for such authorisation to provide, in respect of all entities not covered by the Agreement, in respect of entities covered by the Agreement, *vis-à-vis* non-signatory countries and in respect of entities covered by the Agreement, but as regards

---

[111] Dec. 80/949 ([1980] O.J. L267/35), extended by Dec. 80/1088 ([1980] O.J. L320/35); see also Dec. 81/85 ([1981] O.J. L58/31) authorising Italy to take intra-Community surveillance measures with respect to bananas originating in certain third countries (see now [1987] O.J. C127); similar authorisation has also been granted to France ([1987] O.J. C174) and this is currently being contested in Case 206/87 *Lefebvre* v. *E.C. Commission*.

[112] Dec. 80/1158 ([1980] O.J. L343/41). That Dec. has now been extended in time most recently by Dec. of 18 December 1987 ([1987] O.J. C348/3).

[113] Both the statement and the resolution are to be found at [1980] O.J. C211. Neither has a binding effect in law: Case 59/75 *Pubblico Ministero* v. *Manghera* [1976] E.C.R. 91, [1976] 1 C.M.L.R. 557; Case 43/75 *Defrenne* v. *Sabena* [1976] E.C.R. 455, [1976] 2 C.M.L.R. 98.

[114] See Dec. 80/271 ([1980] O.J. L71/1). See para. 12.31 below.

products or contracts not covered by it, for the exclusion from their public
contracts of certain products or categories of products originating in third
countries which are in free circulation in another Member State, in all cases
where similar arrangements are made as regards directly imported products
originating in third countries . . .'[115]

There is no mention here of any economic difficulties, nor is
Decision 80/47 referred to. It would appear, however, that the
Commission has not in fact issued any decisions of the kind
envisaged in this Statement.

9.51 Decision 80/47 has now been repealed and re-enacted with
some amendments by Decision 87/443,[116] which came into force on
1 October 1987. The principal changes are to be found in a
substantial re-wording of Article 1, which defines the scope of the
Regulation, and in the introduction of a wholly new provision in
Article 5. The new Article 1 is in the following terms:

'This Decision shall apply to imports into a Member State of products
originating in a third country and put into free circulation in the Community
which are not subject to uniform conditions of import in the Member States.'

This is considerably broader than the earlier Article 1. Article 5
provides as follows:

'The procedures laid down by this Decision shall apply where the effectiveness
of commercial policy measures applied by the Member States pursuant to the
international obligations of the Community is jeopardised by deflections of
trade with the exception of the elements referred to in Article 2(4)(d) and
Article 3(3)(e).'

Article 2(4)(d) and 3(3)(e) relate to economic difficulties. Consequently, Article 5 makes it possible to base measures such as those
described in paragraphs 9.49 and 9.50 on Decision 87/433, whereas
Decision 80/47 could not constitute the basis for such measures.
Indeed, Decision 80/776 has now been extended until 31 December
1988, on the basis of Decision 87/443.[117]

Finally, the following additional recital in the preamble should
be noted:

'Whereas the Single European Act provides for the establishment, as from
1 January 1993, of an area without internal frontiers in which goods, services
and capital will be able to move freely; whereas this implies, on the one hand,
that the disparities still existing among commercial policies applied by the
Member States shall be progressively eliminated or reduced and, on the other,
that the Commission must be fully aware of these objectives when assessing
the need to authorise measures pursuant to Article 115 of the Treaty.'

---

[115] The Resolution and the Statement (both in [1980] O.J. C211), closely mirror a
Resolution and a Statement on the same subject made on 21 December 1976, when the Tokyo
Round negotiations were still under way: [1977] O.J. C11/1).
[116] [1987] O.J. L238/26.
[117] Dec. 88/21 ([1988] O.J. L9/19).

ARTICLE 222

9.52 Article 222 provides:

'This Treaty shall in no way prejudice the rules in Member States governing the system of property ownership.'

Article 222 is not one of the most straightforward provisions in the Treaty. It appears to have been conceived primarily to show that nationalisation was compatible with the Treaty.[118] However, the position of nationalised industries under Community law cannot be explored here.[119] At all events it is suggested that Article 222 does not permit discrimination by a nationalised industry against imported goods.[120]

This provision has been considered by the Court in *Consten and Grundig* v. *E.C. Commission*,[121] *Parke, Davis* v. *Centrafarm*[122] and *Italy* v. *EEC Commission*.[123] In each of these cases it held that Article 222 could not be relied on. In particular, in the first two cases it held that it was compatible with Article 222 for the general rules of the Treaty to affect the exercise of industrial property rights, so long as their existence was not affected.

Indeed, it is doubtful if Article 222 can ever constitute an exception to Articles 30 to 34.

ARTICLE 223

9.53 Article 223 provides:

'1. The provisions of this Treaty shall not preclude the application of the following rules:
(a) . . .
(b) Any Member State may take such measures as it considers necessary for the protection of the essential interests of its security which are connected with the production of or trade in arms, munitions and war material; such measures shall not adversely affect the conditions of competition in the common market regarding products which are not intended for specifically military purposes.
2. During the first year after the entry into force of this Treaty, the Council shall, acting unanimously, draw up a list of products to which the provisions of paragraph 1(b) shall apply.
3. The Council may, acting unanimously on a proposal from the Commission, make changes in this list.'

This must be read in conjunction with Article 225, which provides:

'If measures taken in the circumstances referred to in Articles 223 and 224 have the effect of distorting the conditions of competition in the common

---

[118] Neri and Sperl *Répertoire du Traité CEE* (1960), 410; see also Written Question 346/80 ([1980] O.J. C213/6).
[119] See paras. 4.05 and 9.03 and Chapter XI of this book.
[120] Such a view is suggested by para. 7 of the judgment in Case 182/83 *Fearon* v. *Irish Land Commission* [1984] E.C.R. 3677, [1985] 2 C.M.L.R. 228 which concerns establishment within the meaning of Art. 52 EEC.
[121] Cases 56 and 58/64 [1966] E.C.R. 299, [1966] C.M.L.R. 418.
[122] Case 24/67 [1968] E.C.R. 55, [1968] C.M.L.R. 47.
[123] Case 32/65 [1966] E.C.R. 389, [1969] C.M.L.R. 39.

market, the Commission shall, together with the State concerned, examine
how these measures can be adjusted to the rules laid down in this Treaty.

By way of derogation from the procedure laid down in Articles 169 and
170, the Commission or any Member State may bring the matter directly
before the Court of Justice if it considers that another Member State is making
improper use of the powers provided for in Articles 223 and 224. The Court
of Justice shall give its ruling in camera.'

9.54 'Security' in Article 223(1)(b) refers both to internal and
external threats to the State. However, the use of the terms 'war
material' and 'specifically military purposes' indicates that the provision does not cover security matters normally dealt with by the
police, such as crime detection and prevention and traffic regulation.[124]

The term 'arms, munitions and war material' is contrasted with
'products which are not intended for specifically military purposes'.
Thus supplies such as petrol, which can be used for military purposes
but are not specifically intended for them, are not arms, munitions
or war material within the meaning of Article 223. Daig suggests[125]
that 'war material' extends to items which are neither arms nor
munitions, such as military uniforms, and that it covers goods
required by the military even in peacetime. The exception clause in
Article 223(1)(b) only operates with respect to goods figuring at the
material time on the list provided for in Article 223(2). In answer
to Written Question 574/85[126] the Council has stated that such a list
was drawn up on 15 April 1958 and has not been published or
amended up to the date of that answer (November 1985).

It would seem clear that the measures which Member States may
take under Article 223(1)(b) include quantitative restrictions and
measures of equivalent effect with respect to goods figuring on the
list[127] where such measures are necessary. The wording of the
provision ('any Member State may take such measures as it considers
necessary') shows that the appreciation of the necessity lies with the
Member State, though it may be subject to the judicial control of
the Court. Article 223 does not permit any exceptional measures at
all with respect to goods not appearing on the list.[128]

9.55 Should the Commission or a Member State consider that
another Member State is making improper use of these powers, then
by virtue of Article 225 it can bring the matter to the Court without
sending the reasoned opinion required by Articles 169 and 170
respectively. This exception was presumably created in view of the

[124] Daig in Groeben, Boeckh, Thiesing, Vol. I, 663.
[125] *Op. cit.* 664; however, Matthies in Groeben, Boeckh, Thiesing, Ehlermann, *op. cit.* n.1
above, Vol. II at 1038 would exclude uniforms.
[126] [1985] O.J. C287/9.
[127] See generally the A.G. in Case 15/69 *Württembergische Milchverwerkung-Südmilch* v.
Ugliola [1969] E.C.R. at 373, [1970] C.M.L.R. 194.
[128] See generally para. 12.33 below.

likely urgency of such an action. The stipulation in Article 225(2) that proceedings are to be held in camera is an exception to the rule in Article 28 of the Protocol on the Statute of the Court of Justice of the EEC, which states that the hearings shall be in open court unless the Court 'decides otherwise for serious reasons'.[129]

ARTICLE 224

9.56 Article 224 provides:

'Member States shall consult each other with a view to taking together the steps needed to prevent the functioning of the common market being affected by measures which a Member State may be called upon to take in the event of serious internal disturbances affecting the maintenance of law and order, in the event of war, serious international tension constituting a threat of war, or in order to carry out obligations it has accepted for the purpose of maintaining peace and international security.'

At first sight this provision appears merely to impose an obligation on Member States—to consult each other on the occurrence of one of the serious events enumerated there—but not to vest any powers in the Member States. However, that Article 224 does give rise to powers on the part of the Member States is shown by the reference in Article 225 to 'the powers provided for in Articles 223 and 224'.[130]

9.57 Unlike Article 223, the exceptional measures envisaged by this provision are not limited to arms, munitions and war material. It empowers Member States to impose quantitative restrictions and measures of equivalent effect with respect to any category of goods, including the sequestration of or import bans on goods of nationals of a particular third country or territory, which is a protagonist to international tension. This is possibly the only instance in the Treaty where goods can be discriminated against by reason of the nationality of their owner, rather than their origin.[131] Indeed, if the circumstances set out in Article 224 arise, virtually any provision of the Treaty may be disregarded.[132]

What are these circumstances? Broadly speaking, they are the existence or serious threat of war, civil war or sedition or the existence of obligations which a Member State has 'accepted for the purpose of maintaining peace and international security' by which is meant primarily UN resolutions.[133] Thus a gamut of very different situations is covered. For instance, all the Member States may be affected in the same way, or only one may be affected. Again, the measures will normally be very urgent, but they need

---

[129] On Art. 225(2) proceedings generally see Gori, *op. cit.* 309.
[130] Müller-Heidelberg, *op. cit.* 315–316; for the text of Art. 225 see para. 9.53 above.
[131] See para. 2.23 above.
[132] See generally, *Ugliola*, n.127 above.
[133] Neri and Sperl, *op. cit.* n.118 above, at 412.

where measures are taken against a distant territory that constitutes no real security threat to the Member States.

9.58 It appears to follow from *Johnston* v. *Chief Constable of the Royal Ulster Constabulary*[134] that Article 224 is a residual provision and will therefore not apply where another more specific provision is applicable. In view of the troubles in Northern Ireland, the United Kingdom claimed to be entitled under Article 224 to have a policy of discriminating against women in recruitment in the RUC full-time reserve. The Court described the unrest in Northern Ireland as 'serious internal disturbances'; this could be taken to imply that in the Court's view it constituted 'serious internal disturbances affecting the maintenance of law and order' within the meaning of Article 224. However, the Court found that the circumstances concerned were covered by one of the exceptions in Council Directive 76/207[135] on the implementation of the principle of equal treatment for men and women. It concluded from this that the national court's question on Article 224 did not arise. It is not clear whether the Court merely found it unnecessary to decide the point; or whether, as a matter of substantive law, it considered Article 224 to be inapplicable. However, the latter view is consistent with the maxim *'lex specialis derogat generali'* (the specific provision ousts the general one). It would follow that, as regards the free movement of goods, one must look notably to the public security exception in Article 36 before considering Article 224.[136]

9.59 It appears to follow from *Johnston* that the existence of a situation referred to in Article 224 does not in itself give the Member State concerned unlimited powers to derogate from Community law. The United Kingdom had contended that in view of the troubles it was entitled to preclude recourse to the courts in this matter. The Court dismissed this argument on the grounds that 'none of the facts before the Court and none of the observations submitted to it suggest that the serious internal disturbances in Northern Ireland make judicial review impossible or that measures needed to protect public safety would be deprived of their effectiveness because of such review by the national courts'. Consequently, it is probable that except in cases of extreme urgency Member States are required, when applying Article 224, to ensure that the functioning of the common market is as little disturbed as possible.

Matthies[137] takes the view that the consultation provided for in Article 224 must take place before the measures concerned are

---

[134] Case 222/84 [1985] E.C.R. 1651, [1986] 3 C.M.L.R. 240.
[135] [1976] O.J. L39/40.
[136] See Matthies, *op. cit.* at 1035.
[137] *Op. cit.* 1036; see also Kuyper, 'Sanctions against Rhodesia. The EEC and the Implementation of General International Rules' [1975] C.M.L.Rev. 231; *The Implementation of International Sanctions* (1978) at 195.

adopted, thereby rejecting the view suggested in the Commission's answer to Written Question 527/75,[138] according to which such consultations may be deferred until the functioning of the common market is in fact affected. The same author maintains[139] that the Commission must be involved in those consultations since otherwise it would be unable to exercise its powers under Article 225.

Article 224 has in particular been applied by the Member States in adopting sanctions against Rhodesia[140] pursuant to a United Nations Security Council Resolution adopted after that country's Unilateral Declaration of Independence and against Iran[141] after the taking of the American hostages in Teheran. The latter case was somewhat unusual in that no resolution on sanctions was passed by the Security Council so that there was technically no obligation in international law on the Member States to impose the sanctions: the requirement that there be an 'obligation . . . accepted' was thus somewhat liberally interpreted. The sanctions adopted against Argentina following that country's invasion of the Falkland Islands were enshrined in a Council Regulation[142] based on Article 113 of the Treaty relating to the common commercial policy. However, the preamble to that Regulation states that the Member States have consulted each other pursuant to Article 224.

ARTICLE 233

9.60 Article 233 provides as follows:

'The provisions of this Treaty shall not preclude the existence or completion of regional unions between Belgium and Luxembourg, or between Belgium, Luxembourg and the Netherlands, to the extent that the objectives of these regional unions are not attained by the application of this Treaty.'

The regional unions in question are, first, the Belgo-Luxembourg Economic Union created by a Convention of 1921; and the Benelux, set up in London during the Second World War by a Convention between the Governments in exile of Belgium, the Netherlands and Luxembourg.[143]

---

[138] [1976] O.J. C89/8.
[139] *Ibid.*
[140] See Kuyper, n.137 above; Written Questions 526/75 ([1976] O.J. C89/6) and 527/75, n.137 above.
[141] E.C.Bull. 5 [1980] 26.
[142] Reg. 877/82 was extended as regards most Member States by Regs. 177/82 ([1982] O.J. L136/1) and 1254/82 ([1982] O.J. L146/1) and repeated by Reg. 1577/82 ([1982] O.J. L177/1). See Kuyper 'Community sanctions against Argentina: Lawfulness under Community and International law' in Essays in European Law and Integration ed. O'Keefe and Schermers, Netherlands 1982.
[143] See Van Damme 'Benelux and its Relationship with the EEC' in *Legal Problems of an Enlarged European Community* ed. Bathurst (1972); Van der Woude 'La libre circulation des marchandises à l'intérieur du Bénélux dans une perspective communautaire' [1987] R.M.C. 83.

In *Pakvries* v. *Minister for Agriculture and Fisheries*[144] the Court ruled that Article 233 'enables the three Member States concerned to apply, in derogation from the Community rules, the rules in force within their union in so far as it is further advanced than the common market'. It follows that by virtue of Article 233, the Member States concerned may integrate more rapidly than the Community as a whole. On the other hand, this provision does not apply where the objectives of these regional unions are attained by application of the Treaty of Rome. Both Reuter[145] and Petersmann[146] agree that within these limits Article 233 constitutes an exception to the rule against non-discrimination—a fact which is obviously of some significance for the interpretation of Articles 30 to 36. It would appear to follow that the Member States concerned, acting within these limits, may grant preferential treatment to one another pursuant to the BLEU or Benelux Conventions; the resulting less favourable treatment of other Member States would not constitute arbitrary discrimination contrary to Article 36.[147]

ARTICLE 234

9.61   The first paragraph of Article 234 provides:

> 'The rights and obligations arising from agreements concluded before the entry into force of this Treaty between one or more Member States on the one hand, and one or more third countries on the other, shall not be affected by the provisions of this Treaty.'

This is qualified by the second paragraph, which reads:

> 'To the extent that such agreements are not compatible with this Treaty, the Member State or States concerned shall take all appropriate steps to eliminate the incompatibilities established. Member States shall, where necessary, assist each other to this end and shall, where appropriate, adopt a common attitude.'

The third and final paragraph of Article 234 is not relevant for present purposes. As explained below, the Court now appears to have held in *Conegate* v. *H.M. Customs and Excise*[148] that Article 234 can never constitute an exception to Articles 30 and 34. Nevertheless, for reasons which will be expounded below, it is appropriate to consider Article 234 in detail.

By virtue of Article 5 of each of the Acts of Accession, Article 234 applies for the new Member States to agreements or conventions concluded before accession.[149]

It should also be pointed out that paragraph 5 of Article 37, which governs State monopolies, provides that 'the obligations on Member States shall be binding only in so far as they are compatible

---

144 Case 105/83 [1984] E.C.R. 2101 at 2115, [1985] 2 C.M.L.R. 602 at 613.
145 In *Les Novelles, Droit des Communautés Européennes* (1969) para. 2.13.
146 In Groeben, Boeckh, Thiesing, Ehlermann, *op. cit.* Vol. II, 1133.
147 Para. 8.05 above.
148 Case 121/85 [1986] 1 C.M.L.R. 739.
149 See generally Puissochet, *The Enlargement of the European Communities* (1975).

with existing international agreements'. This provision, which only applies to State monopolies, is generally taken to go beyond the first paragraph of Article 234. It is discussed in a later chapter of this book.[150]

9.62 The exception clause contained in the first paragraph is limited in four ways:

  (i) It only applies to agreements concluded before the Treaty came into force or, for the new Member States, before accession.

  (ii) It only applies to agreements concluded between one or more Member States on the one hand and one or more third countries on the other. It therefore does not apply to agreements between Member States.

This principle was forcefully laid down by the Court in one of its earliest judgments concerning the EEC Treaty, in Case 10/61 *EEC Commission* v. *Italy*.[151] The Commission claimed that Italy was infringing the Treaty by failing to reduce its customs duties on certain goods from other Member States in accordance with Articles 12 and 14 of the Treaty requiring the gradual abolition of customs duties between Member States. In its defence Italy claimed that it was obliged to charge the higher level of duty by virtue of the 1956 Geneva Agreements concluded under the auspices of GATT. To this end Italy invoked Article 234. However, this defence was rejected by the Court, which ruled that 'in matters governed by the EEC Treaty, that Treaty takes precedence over agreements concluded between Member States before its entry into force, including agreements made within the framework of GATT'.

9.63 Yet it is submitted that there are exceptions to this rule. If a Member State was required to carry out border controls under a prior treaty with a third State, that obligation would fall within Article 234—even as regards controls at frontiers with other Member States. Now there is no reason why the result should be different where more than one Member State is bound by a prior treaty obligation.

This question was considered by Advocate General Warner in *Henn and Darby*,[152] where the Court of Justice had been asked a series of questions by the House of Lords as to the compatibility with Community law of a prohibition on imports of indecent and obscene articles. In its seventh and final question the House of Lords asked, *inter alia*, whether this prohibition was lawful in view

---

[150] See para. 11.18 below.
[151] [1962] E.C.R. 1, [1962] C.M.L.R. 187.
[152] Case 34/79 [1979] E.C.R. 3795, [1980] 1 C.M.L.R. 246; see paras. 5.07, 8.08 and 8.26 above.

of the Geneva Convention of 1923 for the suppression of the traffic in obscene publications and of Article 234.

The Advocate General found that the 1923 Convention lent itself to two possible interpretations:

— either the Convention only created, at all events as regards imports and exports, a series of bilateral obligations between the parties; if so, the Convention had been superseded as between Member States by the EEC Treaty in line with the Court's ruling in *EEC Commission* v. *Italy*;

— alternatively, the Convention created multilateral obligations between all the parties to it, so that States which are parties to the Convention but not Members of the Community have a right to the enforcement of the Convention even as respects imports and exports between Member States on the footing that a 'flourishing trade in obscene material' within the Community could prejudice other States' efforts to suppress the traffic in it. (Although the Advocate General did not refer to illicit trafficking in drugs, the same reasoning could clearly apply to a prior multilateral convention aimed at combatting that problem.)

Since the Court of Justice had no jurisdiction to interpret the 1923 Convention, the Advocate General concluded that it was for the national court to decide which of these two interpretations was correct.

The Court, however, saw no need to enter into these finer points: it merely replied that 'in so far as a Member State avails itself of the reservation relating to the protection of public morality provided for in Article 36 of the Treaty, the provisions of Article 234 do not preclude that State from fulfilling the obligations arising from the Geneva Convention of 1923 . . .'

9.64 This issue arose again in *Conegate* which concerned imports into Britain of 'inflatable dolls of a sexual nature' from Germany. The last question posed by the English High Court was whether an import ban imposed by a Member State in accordance with the Geneva Convention of 1923 and the Universal Postal Convention was consistent with Article 234. It appeared that in fact the question was inappropriate, because the Geneva Convention only applied to 'publications' and the Universal Postal Convention did not extend to goods which were not sent by post. Nevertheless, the five-judge Chamber of the Court decided the question, holding that 'an agreement concluded prior to the entry into force of the Treaty may not be relied upon in order to justify restrictions on trade between Member States'. This appears to mean that Article 234 can never constitute an exception to Articles 30 and 34. Yet the Court did not consider the view propounded by the Advocate General Warner in *Henn and Darby* and therefore gave no reason for rejecting it.

It is submitted that his view is to be preferred, since there may indeed be prior treaties concluded with third countries which oblige the Member States to restrict trade between one another. In any event, such treaties will be the exception.

9.65   (iii) The exception clause in Article 234(1) is also subject to the limitation contained in Article 234(2): Member States are required to do all in their power to eliminate any inconsistencies between the Treaty and prior agreements. At the very least, this means that if an agreement with one or more third countries comes up for renewal after the Treaty entered into force (or, for new Member States, since accession), then no Member State may renew it unless elements incompatible with the Treaty are removed from that agreement.

(iv) The exception laid down by Article 234(1) only applies to obligations of Member States and to rights of third States, and not the other way round; thus a Member State cannot, it appears, rely on Article 234 for the continued enjoyment of rights derived from a prior treaty with a third State and which conflict with Community law: Case 10/61 *EEC Commission* v. *Italy*, already referred to.

9.66   Further light on the meaning of this exception clause has been shed by the ruling in *Attorney General* v. *Burgoa*.[153] The defendant, the skipper of a Spanish vessel, was charged with various offences under Irish fisheries legislation alleged to have been committed within the exclusive fishery limits of the Irish State. During the hearing before the Irish Circuit Court the defendant relied on the London Fisheries Convention of 1964, to which both Spain and Ireland were party. Thereupon the Irish court referred to the Court of Justice a series of questions, the bulk of which concerned Article 234. Only the first two questions are of relevance here:

(i) First, the Irish court asked whether Article 234 created rights and obligations for the Community institutions as well as for the Member States.

After confirming its ruling in *EEC Commission* v. *Italy* to the effect that the rights at issue were those of third countries only, the Court continued:

'Although the first paragraph of Article 234 makes mention only of the obligations of Member States, it would not achieve its purpose if it did not imply a duty on the part of the institutions of the Community not to impede the performance of the obligations of Member States which stem from a prior agreement. However, that duty of the Community institutions is directed only to permitting the Member State concerned to perform its obligations under

---

[153] Case 812/79 [1980] E.C.R. 2787, [1981] 2 C.M.L.R. 193.

the prior agreement and does not bind the Community as regards the non-member country in question.'

(ii) Secondly, the Irish court asked whether Article 234 or any other rule of Community law maintained or upheld rights of the beneficiaries of Treaties to which Article 234 applied, which national courts must apply.

The Court replied that:

> 'since the purpose of the first paragraph of Article 234 is to remove any obstacle to the performance of agreements previously concluded with non-member countries which the accession of a Member State to the Community may present, it cannot have the effect of altering the nature of the rights which may flow from such agreements.'

9.67   In conclusion, it is submitted that despite *Conegate* there will be exceptional cases in which a Member State should be able to rely on Article 234 as an exception to Article 30 or Article 34. The Court has not yet had to decide such a case: in *Henn and Darby* the prior treaty concerned merely covered the same ground as Article 36, whereas in *Conegate* the treaties referred to by the national court were not relevant in any case.

CHAPTER X

Agriculture

10.01 Central to the common agricultural policy is the concept of the common organisation of the market. Although Article 40(2) of the Treaty provides that:

'this organisation shall take one of the following forms, depending on the product concerned:
(a) common rules on competition;
(b) compulsory co-ordination of the various national market organisations;
(c) a European market organisation',

it has always been option (c) that has been chosen. A common market organisation will normally include rules on price formation (under which supplies will usually be bought up when prices fall below a certain level) and measures relating to imports from outside the Community coupled with export refunds for goods exported to third countries.[1] In addition, all regulations establishing common market organisations during the transitional period—and some since—have included a provision prohibiting customs duties and taxes of equivalent effect and quantitative restrictions and measures of equivalent effect between Member States. However, for reasons explained in this chapter it has become clear that such a clause is now superfluous.

In view of the fundamental importance of common market organisations this chapter is divided into two sections: the first covers the application of the prohibition on quantitative restrictions and measures of equivalent effect in the absence of such an organisation, the second deals with its application to products covered by such an organisation. It should be borne in mind that nearly all agricultural products[2] are now covered by common organisations; among the few remaining exceptions are bananas, potatoes and ethyl alcohol. Until relatively recently 'sheepmeat' and 'goatmeat' were not covered by a common organisation of the market either.[3]

I. WHERE NO COMMON MARKET ORGANISATION EXISTS

10.02 In the absence of a common market organisation for a product can a Member State maintain import or export quotas for

---

[1] See generally Waelbroeck in *Le droit de la Communauté économique européenne* (1970), Vol. 2, 59 *et seq.*; Ries, *L'ABC du Marché commun agricole* (1978); Fennell, *The Common Agricultural Policy of the European Community* (1979); Constantinides–Mégret *La politique agricole commune en question* (1982); Snyder *Law of the Common Agricultural Policy* (1985).
[2] Agricultural products are those listed in Annex II to the Treaty: Art. 38(3).
[3] See now Reg. 1837/80 ([1980] O.J. L183), as amended.

that product even after the end of the transitional period, when those quotas form part of a national market organisation? Until the Court's judgment in *Charmasson* v. *Minister of Economic Affairs*[4] it was widely thought that a Member State could maintain such quotas and indeed this was the view taken both by the Commission and by the Advocate General in that case. The Court was to reject that view in favour of a more integrationist approach.

In fact, the case concerned imports from outside the Community. The plaintiff imported bananas from a number of countries including Zaire and Somalia. Both those States were associated with the Community by the Yaoundé Convention of 1963,[5] Article 5 of which provided, *inter alia*, that 'as regards the elimination of quantitative restrictions, the Member States shall apply to goods originating in the Associated States the corresponding provisions of the Treaty.' Nevertheless, while the French authorities granted free access to bananas from certain former French colonies, banana imports from other countries such as Zaire and Somalia were subject to a system of quotas.

The plaintiff sought the annulment by the Conseil d'Etat of an official notice published in the French *Journal Officiel* opening a quota for bananas from countries other than those enjoying the privileged treatment referred to. He claimed that the system of quotas infringed the Yaoundé Convention and Article 33 EEC providing for the progressive abolition of quotas during the transitional period. The latter provision was involved because the notice appeared in October 1969 and thus before the end of the transitional period. Yet the crux of the case concerned the legality of such quotas after the end of this period.

The principal question referred to the Court of Justice was whether the existence of a national market organisation for a product not yet subject to a common organisation impeded the application of Article 33. Like the French Government, the Commission took the view that it did. It deduced this in particular from Article 45 which provides for the conclusion of long-term agreements or contracts between importing and exporting Member States 'until national market organisations have been replaced by one of the forms of common organisation referred to in Article 40(2)'; and from Article 43(3) which provides that a common organisation may replace national organisations so long as the common organisation offers 'equivalent safeguards for the employment and standard of living of the producers concerned'—it considered that such safeguards would not be offered by the mere abolition of restrictions to inter-State trade. However, it added a rider to the effect that this exception only applied to organisations which already existed when

---

[4] Case 48/74 [1974] E.C.R. 1383, [1975] 2 C.M.L.R. 208; noted by Paulin and Forman [1975] C.M.L.Rev. 399, and Wyatt [1976] E.L.Rev. 310.
[5] Now replaced by the Lomé Convention.

the Treaty came into force. The Advocate General reach the same conclusion, which was shared by the authors of the Acts of Accession: 'see Article 60(2) of that Act, which indeed would make nonsense of any other view.' As we shall see,[6] the Court subsequently held that Article 60(2) does in fact have a different meaning.

The Court swept away all these objections. Its starting-point was Article 38(2) EEC which reads: 'Save as otherwise provided in Articles 39 to 46, the rules laid down for the establishment of the common market shall apply to agricultural products.' An examination of Articles 39 to 46 led the Court to conclude that:

> 'whilst a national organisation of the market existing at the date of coming into force of the Treaty could, during the transitional period, preclude the application of Article 33 thereof, to the extent that such application would have impaired its functioning, this cannot, however, be the case after the expiration of that period, when the provisions of Article 33 must be fully effective.'

10.03 To say that Article 33 is fully effective after the end of the transitional period is not quite accurate since Article 33 provides for the progressive abolition of quotas during the transitional period and is redundant thereafter. In any case, it is clear that the Court meant that import quotas were prohibited after the end of 1969. By necessary implication, this must be so for all quantitative restrictions on imports or exports and measures of equivalent effect.

In fact, the Court has since applied its ruling in *Charmasson* to measures of equivalent effect to quantitative restrictions on exports. During a potato shortage the French Government published a Notice to Exporters in the French *Journal Officiel* requiring potato exporters to make an export declaration to be endorsed by the French authorities. In an action brought under Article 169, the Court confirmed the Commission's view that the measure infringed Article 34: Case 68/76 *E.C. Commission* v. *France*.[7]

10.04 Since in the latter case the national measure was adopted only in 1975, it was not necessary to decide whether Article 34 took effect with respect to agricultural products as from January 1962, as with other products; or whether it did not take effect until the end of the transitional period. However, the Court held that 'following the end of the transitional period, the provisions of Articles 39 to 46 cannot be relied on in justification of a unilateral derogation from the requirements of Article 34 of the Treaty.' This appears to conflict with the Court's earlier ruling in *Cadsky* v. *Istituto Nazionale per il Commercio Estero*[8] where it held that the prohibition in Article 16 on customs duties and taxes of equivalent

---

[6] Para. 10.05.

[7] [1977] E.C.R. 515, [1977] 2 C.M.L.R. 161. Wyatt [1977] E.L.Rev. 281.

[8] Case 63/74 [1975] E.C.R. 281, [1975] 2 C.M.L.R. 246; noted by Wyatt [1976] E.L.Rev. 120.

effect on exports applied as from January 1962 to agricultural products as to other products. There appears to be no reason to make a distinction in this respect between Articles 16 and 34 and it is therefore submitted that the prohibition in Article 34 has applied to agricultural products since January 1962.

10.05 The Court subsequently built on the *Charmasson* decision in two parallel cases raising the question whether, after the end of 1977, the United Kingdom could ban imports of potatoes. In the first case, *Meijer* v. *Department of Trade*,[9] the plaintiffs were seeking a declaration in the High Court that the United Kingdom was not entitled to impose this ban, a question being referred by the High Court under Article 177 of the Treaty. At the same time, the Commission brought proceedings against the United Kingdom under Article 169 EEC.[10]

Article 60(2) of the first Act of Accession constitutes a clear exception to the basic rule in Article 42[11] of the same Act, since it provides:

> 'In respect of products not covered, on the date of accession, by a common organisation of the market, the provisions of Title I concerning the progressive abolition of charges having equivalent effect to customs duties and of quantitative restrictions and measures having equivalent effect shall not apply to those charges, restrictions and measures if they form part of a national market organisation on the date of accession. This provision shall apply only to the extent necessary to ensure the maintenance of the national organisation and until the common organisation of the market for those products is implemented.'

Does Article 60(2) also constitute a special provision within the meaning of Article 9(2) of the Act which reads:

> 'Subject to the dates, time limits and special provisions provided for in this Act, the application of the transitional measures shall terminate at the end of 1977'?

This was in essence the question referred by the High Court and was also the only issue in the Article 169 proceedings: if Article 60(2) was not a 'special provision' in this sense, it was clear that the ban would be contrary to Article 30 EEC.

The root of the problem was that Article 60(2) did not expressly state that its provisions would cease to have effect on 31 December 1977. The simple reason for this was that when the Act of Accession was drafted the *Charmasson* case had not yet been decided, and it was generally thought then that quantitative restrictions forming

---

[9] Case 118/78, [1979] E.C.R. 1387, [1979] 2 C.M.L.R. 398, noted by Wyatt (n. 10 below).
[10] Case 231/78, *E.C. Commission* v. *United Kingdom* [1979] E.C.R. 1447, [1979] 2 C.M.L.R. 427, noted by Wyatt [1979] E.L.Rev. 359.
[11] Art. 42, which falls within Title I of the Act of Accession, provides:

> 'Quantitative restrictions on imports and exports shall, from the date of accession, be abolished between the Community as originally constituted and the new Member States and between the new Member States themselves.
>
> Measures having equivalent effect to such restrictions shall be abolished by 1 January 1975 at the latest.'

part of a national market organisation could be maintained until the establishment of a common market organisation. Nevertheless, the Advocate General saw great significance in this lacuna and in the fact that in his view the Act of Accession did not provide for a 'transitional period' like Article 8 of the Treaty of Rome but merely a series of 'transitional measures.' He concluded that the United Kingdom was correct in alleging that Article 60(2) was a 'special provision' within the meaning of Article 9.

Had the Court followed his conclusions, it would not only have dealt a severe blow to the principle of the free movement of goods, but it would also have removed much of the incentive for the Member States to strive for the establishment of common market organisations for products not yet subject to them. However, the Court took the opposite course.

Article 2 of the Act of Accession made it clear, the Court held, that the fundamental objective of the Act was the integration of the new Member States into the Community. This was why Article 9 of the Act stated that the special provisions were intended to 'facilitate the adjustment of the new Member States to the rules in force within the Communities.' It followed that 'the provisions of the Act of Accession must be interpreted having regard to the foundations and the system of the Community, as established by the Treaty.' After an analysis of the provisions of the Treaty concerning the abolition of quantitative restrictions and measures of equivalent effect as well as its agricultural provisions, the Court rejected the submission of the British Government. The reservation contained in Article 9(2) must be narrowly interpreted so as to include only special provisions 'which are clearly delimited and determined in time and not to a provision, such as Article 60(2), which refers to an uncertain future event.'

The Court then reached the same conclusion by a different route: it would be contrary to the principle of the equality of the Member States in Community law to allow the effects of Article 60(2) to continue for more than a provisional period, given that in this view this provision created an exception on which only the new Member States could rely. The Court gave no reasons for its view that the six original Member States could not rely on Article 60(2), which was not part of the Commission's case. Furthermore, this statement added nothing of value to its judgment.

In any event, the Court ruled that the import ban infringed Article 30.[12]

10.06 The Court subsequently confirmed these rulings in an action[13] concerning lamb, which was not yet subject to a common

---

[12] Accordingly, Art. 65(2) of the Act of Greek Accession ([1979] O.J. L291) which corresponds to Art. 60(2) of the first Act of Accession, is expressed to apply only until 31 December 1985 at the latest. Similarly, Arts. 76(2) and 244(2) of the Act of Accession of Spain and Portugal ([1985] O.J. L302/1) are expressed to apply only until 31 December 1995.

[13] Case 232/78 *E.C. Commission* v. *France* [1979] E.C.R. 2729, [1980] 1 C.M.L.R. 418.

market organisation although such an organisation has been created since then.[14] It held that French restrictions on the importation of British lamb infringed Articles 12 and 30 EEC as from 1 January 1978.[15]

Following the ruling in the potato cases that the original Member States could not rely on Article 60(2), the Commission sought to amend its submissions at the oral hearing so as to obtain a declaration that the French measures had infringed the Treaty as from January 1975 with respect to the measures of equivalent effect. Advocate General Reischl pointed out that Article 60(2) referred back to provisions of Title I of Part Four of the Act of Accession—Articles 35, 36 and 42—which laid down reciprocal obligations as between the original Member States and the new Member States. Therefore it was wrong to hold that the old Member States were unable to rely on Article 60(2) before 1978—and in his view the Court had probably not intended to convey this view in the potato cases. Accordingly he found that the infringement had only commenced in January 1978.

The Court was able to avoid ruling on the latter point by holding that the proposed amendment to the Commission's submissions was inadmissible under the Rules of Procedure of the Court.[16]

10.07 Most recently, the Court has taken this case law a step further in *E.C. Commission* v. *Greece* (bananas).[17] The Greek authorities subjected bananas to a system of import licences, which in practice were never granted. The Commission contended that this fell foul of Article 30 read with Article 65(2) of the Act of Accession, *even during* the five-year transitional period provided for in that Article.[18] In the Commission's submission, this virtually total ban was not 'strictly necessary to ensure the maintenance of a national organisation' as required by Article 65(2).

Although the Court found that the Greek measures concerning bananas amounted to a 'national market organisation' within the meaning of that provision it upheld the Commission's claim. Since Greece was in any event bound to admit imports freely as from 1 January 1986, the Court found that a virtually total ban would not

[14] See n. 3 above.
[15] The Member State concerned consistently refused to comply with the Court's judgment until the common market organisation was set up. This failure to respect a judgment of the Court caused a good deal of consternation in Community law circles; see, *e.g.* 'Editorial Comments' in [1980] C.M.L.Rev. 311. It also led to a further action by the Commission against France, this time for failure to comply with a judgment of the Court: Case 24/80R and 97/80R [1980] E.C.R. 1319, [1981] 3 C.M.L.R. 25. The infringement in question was brought to an end on the adoption of the common market organisation for sheepmeat (n. 3 above).
[16] On the other hand, this problem cannot arise in connection with the Act of Accession of Spain and Portugal, since Arts. 76(2) and 244(2) are expressed to apply in favour of all Member States.
[17] Case 194/85 (judgment of 25 February 1988).
[18] See n. 12 above.

help national producers adapt to the common market. It would have been otherwise, the Court held, if the Greek Government had gradually opened up its market to imports, possibly by means of a system of import surveillance or by quotas.

The implications for the interpretation of Articles 76(2) and 244(2) of the Act of Accession of Spain and Portugal, which are similarly worded, are obvious.

10.08 Finally, a discussion of this subject would not be complete without a brief mention of Article 46 of the Treaty. That Article provides:

> 'Where in a Member State a product is subject to a national market organisation or to internal rules having equivalent effect which affect the competitive position of similar production in another Member State, a counter-vailing charge shall be applied by Member States to imports of this product coming from the Member State where such organisation or rules exist, unless that State applies a countervailing charge on export.
>
> The Commission shall fix the amount of these charges at the level required to redress the balance; it may also authorise other measures, the conditions and details of which it shall determine.'

In *Ramel* v. *Receveur des Douanes*[19] the Court held *obiter* that Article 46 lapsed at the end of the transitional period. However, in *St. Nikolaus Brennerei* v. *Hauptzollamt Krefeld*[20] the Court ruled that Article 46 had survived the end of the transitional period. It therefore upheld the validity of Commission Regulation 851/76[21] requiring Germany and the Benelux countries to apply a countervailing charge on imports of subsidised French alcohol, which Regulation was based on Article 46. In reaching this conclusion the Court relied on the fact that the Commission disposed of no other adequate basis for action with respect to State aids for agricultural products not yet subject to a common market organisation.[22]

Although Article 46 is primarily concerned with countervailing charges, its final half-sentence would appear to contemplate the adoption of other forms of measure. Despite this, it scarcely seems conceivable that it would ever be appropriate to impose quantitative restrictions or measures of equivalent effect, since according to *St. Nikolaus Brennerei* the purpose of countervailing measures adopted pursuant to Article 46 is to 're-establish equilibrium.' It seems probable that only countervailing charges are proportionate to this aim. If that is so, then Article 46 cannot constitute an exception to Article 30.

---

[19] Cases 80–81/77 [1978] E.C.R. 927.
[20] Case 337/82 [1984] E.C.R. 1051, [1985] 3 C.M.L.R. 83; see also Cases 114/83 *Société d'Initiatives* v. *E.C. Commission* [1984] E.C.R. 2589, [1985] 2 C.M.L.R. 767 and 289/83 *GAARM* v. *E.C. Commission* [1984] E.C.R. 4295, [1986] 3 C.M.L.R. 15.
[21] [1976] O.J. L96/41.
[22] See Art. 42 EEC and Reg. 22/62 ([1962] J.O. 993)

II. WHERE A COMMON MARKET ORGANISATION DOES EXIST

10.09 In view of the *Charmasson* judgment it has become clear that, since the end of the transitional period, the provisions of Articles 30 and 34 apply to all agricultural products so that it is unnecessary to re-enact those provisions in regulations setting up a common market organisation.[23] Consequently, it has been the practice in recent years to forgo express provisions of this kind since they are superfluous. This practice was endorsed by the Court in *Kramer*.[24] It held there that after the end of the transitional period the prohibition on measures of equivalent effect applied to products covered by a common market organisation, even where the regulation establishing that organisation did not expressly lay down the prohibition.[25]

10.10 When a national measure may be contrary to Article 30 or 34 and to a regulation setting up a common market organisation, should the Treaty provisions or the regulation be considered first?[26] The Court has had occasion to rule on a considerable number of cases of this kind.[27] However, the practice of the persons bringing these matters before the Court has not been consistent: the Court has been asked to rule on the compatibility of national measures now with the Treaty provisions, now with the common market organisation, and sometimes with both. It is not surprising, then, that the Court has tended to mingle the two, with the consequence that it is often unclear whether a particular judgment is limited to the common market organisation in question or whether it is an interpretation of Articles 30 and 34 applicable to all products.

Nevertheless, in *Pigs and Bacon Commission* v. *McCarren*[28] the Court affirmed that:

---

[23] As to the situation during the transitional period, see paras. 5.01 *et seq.*, 6.02 *et seq.* above.

[24] Cases 3, 4 and 6/76 [1976] E.C.R. 1279, [1976] 2 C.M.L.R. 440.

[25] This was confirmed in Case 83/78 *Pigs Marketing Board* v. *Redmond* [1978] E.C.R. 2347, [1979] 1 C.M.L.R. 177, noted by Wyatt [1979] E.L.Rev. 115; Oliver [1980] C.M.L.Rev. 113.

[26] See generally Baumann, 'Common Organizations of the Market and National Law' [1977] C.M.L.Rev. 303; Usher, 'The Effects of Common Organisations and Policies on the Powers of a Member State' [1977] E.L.Rev. 428.

[27] In particular Case 190/73 *Van Haaster* [1974] E.C.R. 1123, [1974] 2 C.M.L.R. 521, Case 4/75 *Rewe-Zentralfinanz* v. *Landwirtschaftskammer* [1975] E.C.R. 843, [1977] 1 C.M.L.R. 599; Cases 89/74, 18–19/75 *Arnaud* [1975] E.C.R. 1023, [1975] 2 C.M.L.R. 490; Cases 10–14/75 *Lahaille* [1975] E.C.R. 1053; Cases 3, 4 and 6/76 *Kramer*, n. 24 above; Case 35/76 *Simmenthal* v. *Minister for Finance* [1976] E.C.R. 1871, [1977] 2 C.M.L.R. 1; Case 111/76 *Van den Hazel* [1977] E.C.R. 901, [1980] 3 C.M.L.R. 12; Case 154/77 *Dechmann* [1978] E.C.R. 1573, [1979] 2 C.M.L.R. 1; Case 83/78 *Pigs Marketing Board* v. *Redmond*, n. 25 above; Case 153/78 *E.C. Commission* v. *Germany* [1979] E.C.R. 2555, [1980] 1 C.M.L.R. 198; Case 5/79 *Buys* [1979] E.C.R. 3203, [1980] 2 C.M.L.R. 493; Cases 16–20/79 *Danis* [1979] E.C.R. 3327, [1980] 3 C.M.L.R. 492; Case 251/78 *Denkavit Futtermittel* v. *Minister für Ernährung* [1979] E.C.R. 3369, [1980] 3 C.M.L.R. 513; Cases 95 and 96/79 *Kefer and Delmelle* [1980] E.C.R. 103, [1982] 2 C.M.L.R. 77; Case 94/79 *Vriend* [1980] E.C.R. 327, [1980] 3 C.M.L.R. 473.

[28] Case 177/78 [1979] E.C.R. 2161, [1979] 3 C.M.L.R. 389.

'In the event of proceedings relating to an agricultural sector governed by a common organisation of the market the problem raised must first be examined from that point of view having regard to the precedence necessitated by Article 38(2) of the EEC Treaty for the specific provisions adopted in the context of the common agricultural policy over the general provisions of the Treaty relating to the establishment of the Common Market.'

Having decided that a national measure of the kind at issue contravened the regulation establishing the common market organisation, there was no need for the Court to consider its compatibility with the Treaty provisions.[29]

On this approach a national measure, like a horse in a steeplechase, must clear the fence of the common market organisation before the fence of Articles 30 and 34. If it falls at the first fence, there is no need to consider Articles 30 and 34. It is submitted that this is the most appropriate approach, because common market organisations will often contain specific provisions which have a bearing on the national measure in question, for example with respect to price formation. In the absence of such provisions, one may fall back on Articles 30 and 34.

In other, quite unrelated, matters the Court has followed a similar approach to the relationship between Community legislation and Articles 30 to 36. One instance of this is the form of words used in the *Cassis de Dijon* case:[30] 'in the absence of common rules relating to the production and marketing of alcohol . . . it is for the Member States to regulate [these] matters.' Another example is the Court's ruling to the effect that, once a Community Directive has harmonised measures necessary to protect public health, Member States can no longer adopt or maintain unilateral measures in reliance on Article 36.[31]

10.11 Consequently, it is generally considered[32] that judgments of the Court on measures of equivalent effect on imports and exports of products covered by common market organisations may be of limited significance as they may not be applicable to products not covered by such an organisation. Some of these judgments appear to be of general application; they have been discussed in Chapter VII. Other judgments appear to be interpretations of the common market organisation in question, even if they expressly refer to Articles 30 and 34. It is by no means a simple matter to decide which judgments are of general application and which are not.

---

[29] In *Kramer*, n. 24 above, the Court adopted the same approach.
[30] Case 120/78 *Rewe-Zentral* v. *Bundesmonopolverwaltung für Branntwein* [1979] E.C.R. 649, [1979] 3 C.M.L.R. 494; a similar form of words appears in Case 8/74 *Dassonville* [1974] E.C.R. 837, [1974] 2 C.M.L.R. 436.
[31] Para. 8.15 above.
[32] See, *e.g.* VerLoren van Themaat, 'De artikelen 30–36 van het EEG-Verdrag' [1980] *R.M. Themis* L4/5, 378 at 386; Barents, 'New Developments in Measures having Equivalent Effect' [1981] C.M.L.Rev. 271 at 299; *contra* the A.G. in Case 155/80 *Oebel* [1981] E.C.R. 1993, [1983] 1 C.M.L.R. 390.

The cases discussed below appear not to be of general application but deserve mention in this book precisely because this point is uncertain. The *locus classicus* on this area of the law is *Pigs Marketing Board* v. *Redmond*.[33] The facts of that case were that in January 1977 a police officer in Northern Ireland stopped a lorry containing 75 'bacon pigs,' pigs weighing more than 77 kilogrammes. By the Movement of Pigs Regulations (Northern Ireland) 1972 it was an offence to transport bacon pigs otherwise than to one of the Pigs Marketing Board's purchasing centres with a document authorising transport, so that in effect the Board had a purchasing monopoly of all bacon pigs produced in Northern Ireland. Since the lorry driver was unable to produce the requisite certificate, the owner of the pigs was charged with an offence under the Regulations. The defendant having argued that the Regulations and certain provisions relating to the establishment of the Board were contrary to Community law, the Resident Magistrate referred a number of questions to the Court. These included the compatibility of the Northern Irish provisions with Articles 30 and 34 and Regulation 2759/75[34] setting up the common organisation of the market in pigmeat.

On these points the Court held:

> 'A marketing system on a national or regional scale set up by the legislation of a Member State and administered by a body which, by means of compulsory powers vested in it, is empowered to control the sector of the market in question or a part of it by measures such as subjecting the marketing of the goods to a requirement that the producer shall be registered with the body in question, the prohibition of any sale otherwise than to that body or through its agency on the conditions determined by it, and the prohibition of all transport of the goods in question otherwise than subject to the authorisation of the body in question are to be considered as incompatible with the requirements of Articles 30 and 34 of the EEC Treaty and of Regulation 2759/75 . . .'[35]

10.12 The principle of pre-exemption is neatly illustrated by two very clear cases at opposite ends of the spectrum.

In *Apple and Pear Development Council* v. *Lewis*[36] the Court had to rule whether a Member State was entitled to set up a body laying down quality standards for fruit. It so happens that under the common market organisation for fresh fruit and vegetables highly detailed quality standards are laid down by the Community. It was little wonder then that the Court held this Community legislation to be exhaustive and that 'any attempt by such a body to impose compliance with [its recommendations as to quality] by applying any sort of penalties or by using the authority vested in it by its constitution to bring pressure to bear on growers or on traders

---

[33] See n. 25 above.
[34] [1975] O.J. L282/1.
[35] One might have thought that these measures fell under Art. 37 rather than Arts. 30 and 34: see Chap. XI, n. 1.
[36] Case 222/82 [1983] E.C.R. 4083, [1984] 3 C.M.L.R. 733.

would be unlawful.' On the other hand, such a body could lawfully give advice on the quality and presentation of fruit, it was held.

At the other end of the spectrum is *Holdijk*.[37] The defendants there were charged with keeping fatting calves in enclosures which fell below the minimum requirements stipulated in Dutch law. They contended *inter alia* that the relevant common organisation of the market precluded Member States from enacting such legislation. However, the Court found that 'as it stands at present Community law contains no specific rules for the protection of animals kept for farming purposes.' On this basis, it ruled that:

> '. . . the establishment of such an organisation pursuant to Article 40 of the Treaty does not have the effect of exempting agricultural producers from any national provisions intended to attain objectives other than those covered by the common organisation, even though such provisions may, by affecting the conditions of production, have an impact on the volume or the cost of national production and therefore on the operation of the Common Market in the sector concerned . . .
>
> In those circumstances, the absence of any provision for the protection of animals kept for farming purposes in the regulations establishing common organisations of the agricultural markets cannot be interpreted as rendering the national rules in that field inapplicable pending the possible adoption of Community provisions at a later stage.'

It is clear from other passages of the judgment that the Court was also influenced by the laudable aims of the national measure in issue.[38]

10.13   There is in addition a grey area in which it is not nearly so easy to determine whether national legislation is pre-exempted. This is illustrated by three cases delivered within a few months of one another.

The most generous approach towards the Member States was taken in *Jongeneel Kaas* v. *Netherlands*.[39] That case concerned Dutch legislation relating to the quality of cheeses produced in the Netherlands. The Court held that national legislation of this kind was lawful, since there was no Community legislation on the matter. This in itself seems wholly uncontroversial. However, the Dutch legislation also set out an exhaustive list of cheeses which could be produced in the Netherlands (this naturally included traditionally Dutch cheeses such as Gouda and Edam, but it also covered Cheddar and Feta). Even though this in no way limited the varieties which could be sold in the Netherlands, the Court's ruling that such a measure was compatible with the common market organisation for milk and milk products seems questionable. Indeed, the Advocate General was of the opposite opinion, since he considered that 'such a policy harms sales and thereby adversely affects the functioning

---

[37] Cases 141–143/81 [1982] E.C.R. 1299, [1983] 2 C.M.L.R. 635.
[38] See para. 8.54 above.
[39] Case 237/82 [1984] E.C.R. 483, [1985] 2 C.M.L.R. 53, noted by Waelbroeck [1985] C.M.L.Rev. 117.

of the common organisation of the market.' It is submitted that, once a product is covered by a common market organisation, it should not be open to any Member State to prohibit its production, subject to considerations of public health, the protection of industrial and commercial property and the like.

Next, in *Prantl*[40] the Court was called upon to decide whether a German statutory provision to the effect that only wines from certain specified regions of Germany could be marketed in bottles of a particular shape known as *Bocksbeutel* was compatible with the Community legislation forming part of the common market organisation for wine. This case concerned imports from Italy which did not comply with the German measure and was therefore different from *Jongeneel*, which related to the application of Dutch legislation to Dutch produce. The Council Regulation setting up that common market organisation stipulated that the Council 'shall adopt, as necessary, the rules relating to the designation and presentation' of wine products, but the only implementing Regulation protecting the use of particular bottles concerned the bottle known as the *flûte d'Alsace*. Since the protection of bottles was only 'of secondary importance in relation to a common organisation of the market,' the Court ruled that, by adopting a Regulation protecting the *flûte d'Alsace*, the Community had not precluded Member States from protecting other types of bottle.[41]

Finally, the accused in *Pluimveeslachterij Midden-Nederland*[42] were Dutch companies which owned slaughterhouses and which were charged with infringing the Dutch legislation on the packaging and slaughtering of poultry. They claimed that the Duch legislation was pre-exempted by the common market organisation for poultry. However, although the Council Regulation establishing that organisation provided for legislation to be adopted on these matters, no relevant Community legislation had in fact been passed. The Commission had submitted a proposal to the Council several years before, but there had been a deadlock in the Council. Accordingly, the Court found that 'there cannot in principle be any objection' to national legislation of the kind in question. However, it held that 'such measures may not be regarded as involving the exercise of the Member State's own power, but as the fulfilment of the duty to co-operate in achieving the aims of the common organisation of the market which, in a situation characterised by the inaction of the Community legislature, Article 5 of the Treaty imposes on them. Consequently, the measures adopted by the Member States may only be temporary and provisional in nature and they must cease to be applied as soon as Community measures are introduced.'

---

[40] Case 16/83 [1984] E.C.R. 1299, [1985] 2 C.M.L.R. 238.
[41] However, the Court went on to hold that such national legislation was contrary to Art. 30: see paras. 7.44 and 8.86 above.
[42] Cases 47 and 48/83 [1984] E.C.R. 1721.

While the national measures were held to be lawful in each of these cases, the fact remains that the Court's approach and reasoning have differed. Yet it seems safe to concluded with Waelbroeck[43] that 'a presumption seems to exist that Member States retain the power to regulate a subject matter falling within the scope of a common organisation of the market, but not specifically regulated by that organisation, unless there is a clear indication that the Community intended the field to remain free.'

10.14 At this stage it is appropriate to consider in turn the Court's case law relating to:
  (a) the obligation to affiliate to a particular organisation before marketing goods, and
  (b) production quotas.

As to (a) the first case was *Vriend*.[44] There the defendant had been found guilty of selling several lots of chrysanthemum cuttings in the Netherlands without being affiliated to a body which bore the acronym NAKS. By virtue of a Dutch Royal Decree a person selling such products was required to be affiliated to this body. The Dutch court hearing the case referred two questions to the Court of Justice asking whether a requirement of this kind was compatible with Articles 30 to 47 of the Treaty and with Regulation 234/68[45] on the establishment of a common organisation of the market in trees and plants.

The Court replied that:

> 'national rules of the kind referred to by the national court whereby a Member State, directly or through the intermediary of bodies established or approved by an official authority, reserves exclusively to persons affiliated to such bodies the right to market, resell, import, export and offer for export material for plant propagation such as chrysanthemum plants which are covered by the common organisation of the market in live trees and other plants . . . established by Regulation 234/68 . . . is incompatible with the said Regulation and also with Articles 30 and 34 of the EEC Treaty.'

The ruling in *Van Luipen*[46] was very much on the same lines.

On the other hand, in *Apple and Pear Development Council*[47] it was held that the obligation to become a member of a body whose activities did not relate to intra-Community trade was lawful unless the activities of that body were themselves contrary to Community law.

Finally, in *Jongeneel Kaas*[48] it was held to be compatible with the Regulation setting up the common market organisation in milk products to require cheese producers to be members of a national

---

[43] *Op. cit.*, n. 39 above at p. 123.
[44] Case 94/79 [1980] E.C.R. 327, [1980] 3 C.M.L.R. 473.
[45] [1968] J.O. L55/1.
[46] Case 29/82 [1983] E.C.R. 151, [1983] 2 C.M.L.R. 681.
[47] See n. 36 above.
[48] See n. 39 above.

body whose function was to check that nationally-produced cheese complied with national standards, provided that (a) the national standards were themselves compatible with Community law and (b) the marketing, resale, importation, exportation and offer for exportation of cheese was not reserved to members of this body.

The state of the law thus seems somewhat unclear, but the present position may perhaps be summarised as follows:

— producers of an agricultural product subject to a common market organisation may be required to affiliate to a particular national body provided that the aims and activities of that body are themselves compatible with Community law;

— sales (other than by a producer to a wholesaler in the same Member State) may not be subject to the requirement to affiliate to a national body.

10.15 As to (b) the law is also in a considerable state of uncertainty. In two early cases, *Officier van Justitie* v. *Van Haaster*[49] and *Officier van Justitie* v. *Van den Hazel*,[50] such quotas were held to contravene the two common market organisations concerned. In *Van Haaster* the accused was charged with growing hyacinth bulbs without holding a licence required under Dutch law. This licensing system was in fact tantamount to a production quota system. A reference for a preliminary ruling was made asking whether this scheme was compatible with Article 10 of Regulation 234/68[51] setting up a common market organisation in trees and plants, which Article prohibits quantitative restrictions and measures of equivalent effect. This is one of the simplest common market organisations, containing little more than rules relating to common quality standards. Nevertheless, 'in the light of the objects and purposes of the Regulation within the framework of the principles laid down by the Treaty itself' the Court found that a national system of this kind was contrary to Article 10.

The decision in *Van den Hazel* was along similar lines. There a national scheme of slaughter quotas for poultry was held to be contrary to Regulation 123/67[52] setting up a common market organisation in poultry meat.

Yet in *Procureur de la République* v. *Forest*[53] a French system of milling quotas was held to be compatible with Regulation 2727/75[54] on the common market organisation in cereals. The Court gave three reasons for this ruling: the quota system in issue did not concern the production of flour for export; the total sum of all the

---

[49] See n. 27 above.
[50] See n. 27 above.
[51] See n. 45 above.
[52] [1967] J.O. 2301.
[53] Case 148/85 [1988] 2 C.M.L.R. 577.
[54] [1975] O.J. L281/1.

quotas allocated considerably exceeded demand within France; and Regulation 2727/75 provided for the setting of prices and other matters for cereals, not flour. However, it is submitted as to the second point that the very fact that the defendants were prosecuted for exceeding their milling quotas showed that these quotas constituted a real restriction. As to the last point, one would have thought that any major interference by a Member State in the production of flour must inevitably undermine the Community market mechanisms for cereals.

10.16 In considering this area of the law, it should be remembered that in one respect common organisations of the market may go beyond Articles 30 and 34: the regulations setting up these common organisations often prohibit restrictions on trade even within each Member State.[55] This is particularly the case with respect to price controls. On the other hand, Articles 30 and 34 only apply to restrictions on trade between one Member State and another.[56]

10.17 Lastly, the importance of the recent judgment in *E.C. Commission* v. *France* (substitute milk powder)[57] cannot be sufficiently emphasised. The defendant there sought to justify its ban on the sale of substitute milk powder on the basis that it was in the interests of the Common Agricultural Policy in view of the Community's considerable surpluses of milk powder. The Court rejected this submission on two grounds: firstly, it was for the Community and not the Member States to take steps to reduce these surpluses within the framework of the CAP; and secondly, even if national measures bolstered a common policy, they could not run counter to one of the fundamental principles of the Community such as the free movement of goods, unless they were justified on grounds recognised in Community law. Accordingly, the contested measure was held to infringe Article 30.[58]

---

[55] See *e.g.* Art. 10 of Reg. 234/68, para. 10.16 above.
[56] See para. 6.74 *et seq.* above.
[57] Case 216/84 (judgment of 23 February 1988).
[58] See also Cases 407/85 *Drei Glocken* v. *USL* and 90/86 *Zoni* (judgments of 14 July 1988), which relate to the Italian prohibition on the use of soft wheat in pasta.

CHAPTER XI

State monopolies of a commercial character

11.01 Article 37 of the Treaty provides as follows:

'1. Member States shall progressively adjust any State monopolies of a commercial character so as to ensure that when the transitional period has ended no discrimination regarding the conditions under which goods are procured and marketed exists between nationals of Member States.

   The provisions of this Article shall apply to any body through which a Member State, in law or in fact, either directly or indirectly supervises, determines or appreciably influences imports or exports between Member States. These provisions shall likewise apply to monopolies delegated by the State to others.

2. Member States shall refrain from introducing any new measure which is contrary to the principles laid down in paragraph 1 or which restricts the scope of the Articles dealing with the abolition of customs duties and quantitative restrictions between Member States.

3. The timetable for the measures referred to in paragraph 1 shall be harmonised with the abolition of quantitative restrictions on the same products provided for in Articles 30 to 34.

   If a product is subject to a State monopoly of a commercial character in only one or some Member States, the Commission may authorise the other Member States to apply protective measures until the adjustment provided for in paragraph 1 has been effected; the Commission shall determine the conditions and details of such measures.

4. If a State monopoly of a commercial character has rules which are designed to make it easier to dispose of agricultural products or obtain for them the best return, steps should be taken in applying the rules contained in this Article to ensure equivalent safeguards for the employment and standard of living of the producers concerned, account being taken of the adjustments that will be possible and the specialisation that will be needed with the passage of time.

5. The obligations on Member States shall be binding only in so far as they are compatible with existing international agreements.

6. With effect from the first stage the Commission shall make recommendations as to the manner in which and the timetable according to which the adjustment provided for in this Article shall be carried out.'

This provision applies only to trading monopolies and not to monopolies of production or the provision of services. This is why it appears in the same chapter of the Treaty as the provisions relating to quantitative restrictions and measures of equivalent effect.

11.02 By virtue of Article 44 of the first Act of Accession, Denmark, Ireland and the United Kingdom were required to adjust their State monopolies in accordance with Article 37(1) EEC by 31 December 1977.[1] The six original Member States were correspondingly obliged to adjust their State monpolies with respect to goods from the new Member States by the same date. The Nine and Greece had equivalent obligations to make the necessary adjustments to their State monopolies by 31 December 1985 by virtue of Article 40 of the Act of Accession of Greece.[2] However, the same provision required Greece to abolish all exclusive export rights as from its accession, namely 1 January 1981; the same applied to exclusive import rights with respect to copper sulphate, saccharin and flimsy paper. Similarly, the Act of Accession of Spain and Portugal[3] contains transitional provisions with respect to Article 37. Those relating to trade between Spain and the Ten are to be found in Article 48 and Annexes V and VI, while trade between Portugal and the Ten is governed by Article 208; trade between Spain and Portugal is subject to Protocol No. 3 and in particular Article 2 thereof.[4] The transitional arrangements enshrined in these provisions are expressed to expire at the end of 1991 as regards Spain, and at the end of the following year as regards Portugal. Article 48(4) provides somewhat enigmatically:

> 'The adjustment of the monopoly of products indicated in the list appearing in Annex VI may not necessarily affect the functioning of the Spanish petroleum monopoly with regard to third countries. This monopoly may continue to determine the origin and the conditions of acquisition of a share of crude oil imports, from third countries, necessary to ensure availability of supply on the Spanish market, whilst complying with the provisions of the EEC Treaty, and in particular those relating to free movement contained in Articles 30 and 37 of that Treaty.'

Since exceptions to fundamental rules of Community law are to be construed restrictively, this provision presumably does not entitle Spain to impose restrictions after 1991 on imports of crude oil originating in third countries but in free circulation in another Member State in accordance with Article 9(2) of the Treaty of Rome.

11.03 Paragraphs 1 and 2 of Article 37 have both been held to be sufficiently clear and precise to be directly applicable: in *Pubblico Ministero* v. *Manghera*[5] and *Rewe-Zentral* v. *HZA Landau*[6] the

---

[1] However, in so far as they concerned producers subject to a common market organisation on the date of accession and contained customs duties and charges of equivalent effect and quantitative restrictions and measures having equivalent effect, all these charges and measures were to be abolished by 1 February 1973, by virtue of Art. 60(1) of the Act of Accession: Case 83/78 *Pigs Marketing Board* v. *Redmond* [1978] E.C.R. 2347, [1979] 1 C.M.L.R. 177; Wyatt [1979] E.L.Rev. 115; Oliver [1980] C.M.L.Rev. 113.

[2] [1979] O.J. L291/1.

[3] [1985] O.J. L302/1.

[4] See generally the Commission Recommendations to France on the adjustments as regards Spain and Portugal of the French State monopolies over potassic fertilisers ([1987] O.J. L203/53), matches ([1987] O.J. L203/56) and manufactured tobacco ([1987] O.J. L203/58).

[5] Case 59/75 [1976] E.C.R. 91, [1976] 1 C.M.L.R. 557 noted by Wyatt [1975–76] 1 E.L.Rev. 307.

[6] Case 45/75 [1976] E.C.R. 181, [1976] 2 C.M.L.R. 1 noted by Wyatt, *op. cit.*

Court ruled that Article 37(1) was directly applicable since the end of the transitional period while in *Costa* v. *ENEL*[7] Article 37(2) was held to have possessed this quality since the entry into force of the Treaty. Yet this is not an Article which is notable for its clarity. Indeed, in 1964 Colliard wrote of the 'obscure clarity' of Article 37[8] and though much water has flowed under the bridge since that time, that description still holds good today. So it is that various controversies have arisen over Article 37, which in turn have engendered an extensive literature on the subject.[9] However, in the present context is it not necessary to give a comprehensive analysis of this Article, but merely to answer the following questions: do the provisions of Article 37 oust those of Articles 30 to 34 since the end of the transitional period, and, if so, do they lead to different results?

11.04   It can be said at once that Article 37 shares two important characteristics with the Articles preceding it:

— First, it only applies to 'goods', which concept has the same meaning as in Articles 30 to 34. The Court of Justice reached this conclusion in the *Sacchi*[10] case on the basis of the position of Article 37 in the Treaty (in the chapter on quantitative restrictions) and of its use of the terms 'imports', 'exports' and 'products'. It followed that a monopoly of television advertising, being a service under Article 59 *et seq.*, did not fall within Article 37

   In *Société Coopérative du Béarn* v. *Mialocq,*[11] the Court confirmed this ruling, adding however that:

   'the possibility cannot be ruled out that a monopoly over the provision of services may have an indirect influence on trade in goods between Member States. Thus an undertaking or group of undertakings which exercises a monopoly over the provision of certain services may contravene the principle of the free movement of goods, if, for example, such

---

[7] Case 6/64 [1964] E.C.R. 585, [1964] C.M.L.R. 425.
[8] 'L'obscure clarté de l'article 37 du traité de la Communauté économique européenne' [1964] *Recueil Dalloz chronique* 266. In this article the author criticises the Conseil d'Etat for refusing to refer a question of the interpretation of Art. 37 to the Court of Justice under Art. 177, because the Conseil d'Etat considered that the point was an *acte clair* so that a reference was unnecessary (*Société des pétroles Shell Berre*—Act. Jur. 1964 II 438). Hence the ironic expression 'obscure clarity'.
[9] In addition to the articles already cited see, *inter alia*, Van Hecke, 'Government Enterprises and National Monopolies under the EEC Treaty' [1965–66] C.M.L.Rev. 450; Waelbroeck in *Le droit de la Communauté économique européenne* (1970), Vol. I; Béraud, 'L'aménagement des monopoles nationaux prévu à l'article 37 du traité CEE à la lumière des récents développements jurisprudentiels' (1979) 15 R.T.D.E. 573; Wooldridge, 'Some recent decisions concerning the ambit of Article 37 of the EEC Treaty', *Legal Issues of European Integration* (1979), 105; Wyatt and Dashwood, *The substantive Law of the EEC* (1980), Chap. II; Ross 'Article 37—Redundancy or Reinstatement' [1982] E.L.Rev. 281; Hochbaum in Groeben, Boeckh, Thiesing, Ehlermann *Kommentar zum EWG Vertrag* 3rd ed. (1983) 307; Burrows, 'State Monopolies' [1983] Y.E.L. 25.
[10] Case 155/73 [1974] E.C.R. 409, [1974] 2 C.M.L.R. 177, see para. 2.05 above.
[11] Case 271/81 [1983] E.C.R. 2057.

a monopoly leads to discrimination against imported products as opposed to products of domestic origin.'

— Secondly, it does not apply to trade with third countries. In *Hansen* v. *HZA Flensburg*[12] (Hansen II) the Court deduced this also from the position and the wording of Article 37. It concluded that 'the provisions of that Article cannot be applied to products imported from third countries since the arrangements for the importation of such products are subject not to the provisions governing the internal market but to those relating to commercial policy.[13]

11.05   Less straightforward, however, are the answers to the following questions:

— what is the precise meaning of the term 'State monopoly'?
— does the term 'discrimination regarding the conditions under which goods are procured and marketed' in Article 37(1) embrace all quantitative restrictions and measures of equivalent effect?
— what is meant by the obligation to 'adjust' the monopoly?
— which aspects of a monopoly fall under Article 37 and which under other provisions of the Treaty?
— do Articles 37(4), 37(5) and 36 constitute exceptions to the prohibitions contained in Article 37?

11.06   Before examining such case law as there is on these matters, mention should first be made of a theory put forward by the Commission, which would answer the first four of these questions in one fell swoop. It is based on the Court's ruling in *Manghera*[14] to the effect that Article 37 could be relied on before national courts to set aside an exclusive right to import held by a monopoly, since such a right constituted discrimination prohibited by Article 37(1). In the light of this the Commission has maintained in the more recent cases[15] on Article 37 discussed below that this provision also covers exclusive export rights and the exclusive right to market imported goods. The latter was included because the abolition of a monopoly's exclusive import rights would be hollow if that monopoly's exclusive right to market imported goods were maintained

---

[12] Case 91/78 [1979] E.C.R. 935, [1980] 1 C.M.L.R. 162, noted by Wyatt [1980] E.L.Rev. 213.

[13] Even this point is not free from controversy: does Art. 37 apply, like Arts. 30 to 36, to goods originating in third countries but in free circulation in the Community within the meaning of Arts. 9 and 10 (see paras. 2, 12 *et seq.*)? The passage here quoted from *Hansen II* might be read as implying that Art. 37 does apply to such goods. This would accord with the view already forcibly put forward by Waelbroeck, *op. cit.* n.9 above, at 132 and with Van Hecke *op. cit.* n. 9 above, at 460. The Commission refused to be drawn on this point in its answer to written question 51 ([1965] J.O. 391); see also para. 11.02 above as regards the Spanish oil monopoly.

[14] See n.5 above.

[15] For the Commission's earlier view see, *e.g.* Béraud, Waelbroeck and Wooldridge (all cited at n.9 above).

as, in the Court's words in the *Manghera* case, 'the free movement of goods from other Member States similar to those with which the national monopoly is concerned' would not be 'ensured'.

On the other hand, according to this view Article 37, constituting as it does an obligation on Member States to act during the transitional period, cannot be invoked for any other purpose since the end of that period. Indeed on this view, since these three exclusive rights constitute the essence of a State monopoly, a body enjoying no such rights is not a State monopoly within the meaning of Article 37 at all. Thus any other State measures or practices linked to a monopoly fall to be considered under other Articles of the Treaty, such as Articles 12, 16, 30, 34, 92 and 95. Likewise, any abuse by the monopoly of its dominant position might fall foul of Article 86. In particular, according to the Commission, a production monopoly is compatible with the Treaty by virtue of Article 222[16]; the same applies to a monopoly's exclusive right to market its own production.

This theory can thus be reduced to the following simple formula: since the end of the transitional period Article 37 can only be relied on to set aside exclusive import or export rights or the exclusive right to market imported goods and only bodies enjoying one or more of these exclusive rights are State monopolies within the meaning of Article 37. Thus all of the first four questions set out above are all answered at once.

However, the Court has never accepted this theory.

11.07 Turning, then, to the meaning of 'State monopoly', the second sub-paragraph of Article 37(1) provides a wide definition of this term, which is not limited to public bodies but extends also to monopolies delegated by the State to a private enterprise or group of enterprises.[17]

Nor is it entirely free from doubt whether the monopoly must have some institutional structure as the term 'body' in the English text and similar terms in most of the other language texts would suggest.[18] The contrary view, based on the German *Einrichtung*, which means 'arrangement' as well as 'organisation' found favour with the Commission in its Recommendation to the French Government on the allocation of import licences to private undertakings.[19] It appears that it was generally thought, at the time when

---

[16] See para. 9.52 above.
[17] See in particular Hochbaum *op. cit.* n.9 above, at 306 and Waelbroeck, *op. cit.* 9 above, at 125.
[18] See in particular Hochbaum, *op. cit.* n.9 above, at 306, Waelbroeck, *op. cit.* n.9 above, at 126, Wyatt and Dashwood, *op. cit.* n.9 above, at 116.
[19] Recommendation of 24 July 1963 ([1963] J.O. 2271).

the Treaty was drafted, that Article 37 applied to such a system.[20] However, the Court's ruling in Case 161/82 *E.C. Commission* v. *France* (artificial insemination)[21] has now established that an import licencing system does not in itself constitute a State monopoly, a point which the Commission in any event conceded. Yet that ruling left open the question whether a State monopoly within the meaning of Article 37 exists where the right to import a product is restricted by the State to a limited class of persons rather than one organisation.

On another point, in its recent judgment in *Bodson* v. *Pompes Funèbres des Régions Libérées*[22] the Court ruled that Article 37 extended to State monopolies 'exercised' by local authorities such as communes. This ruling is to be welcomed since, as the Advocate General pointed out, Member States could otherwise circumvent the prohibition in Article 37 by the simple expedient of creating a large number of local monopolies. However, the Court went on to hold that, where a certain number of communes constituting a significant proportion of the national territory had granted an exclusive concession to members of the same group of undertakings and that group was therefore able to influence patterns of trade, no State monopoly existed. The reason given by the Court for the latter conclusion was—rather surprisingly—that the position of the group was not then attributable to any act of the public authorities, but to the conduct of the group itself.

11.08 It is not clear whether the concept of 'discrimination [between nationals of Member States] regarding the conditions under which goods are procured and marketed' in Article 37(1) covers all quantitative restrictions and measures of equivalent effect. The Advocate General in *Rewe* v. *Bundesmonopolverwaltung für Branntwein*[23] (*Cassis de Dijon*) took the view that some measures of equivalent effect are not discriminatory and so fail to come under Article 37(1); indeed, that was the case with the minimum alcohol requirement at issue in those proceedings. Yet the Court held in *Manghera*[24] that the obligation laid down in Article 37(1) 'aims at ensuring compliance with the fundamental rule of the free movement of goods throughout the common market, in particular by the abolition of quantitative restrictions and measures having equivalent

---

[20] A.G. Gand in Case 20/64 *Albatros* v. *Sopéco* [1965] E.C.R. 29 at 44, [1965] C.M.L.R. 159. In this case a reference was made under Art. 177 asking in essence whether the French petroleum import licensing system was contrary to Arts. 30 to 37 as from 1959. The Court replied that there was no obligation at the time to abolish or adjust a system of this kind, which pre-dated the Treaty.

[21] [1983] E.C.R. 2079, [1984] 2 C.M.L.R. 296.

[22] Case 30/87 (judgment of 4 May 1988).

[23] Case 120/78 [1979] E.C.R. 649 at 667, [1979] 3 C.M.L.R. 494 noted by Wyatt, *op. cit.* n.12 above; see paras. 6.40 *et seq.* above.

[24] See n.5 above.

effect in trade between Member States.'[25] This may not necessarily have any bearing on the point at issue here.

The point is made no easier by the wording of Article 37(2) which applies to new measures introduced after the entry into force of the Treaty, whereas the preceding paragraph applies to pre-existing measures. Article 37(2) prohibits any new measure 'which is contrary to the principles laid down in paragraph 1 or which restricts the scope of the Articles dealing with the abolition of customs duties and quantitative restrictions between Member States'.

At all events it is not surprising that in Case 90/82 *E.C. Commission* v. *France*[26] the fixing by the French Minister for Economic Affairs and Finance of the retail prices of manufactured tobacco products (which are subject to a State monopoly in France) was 'contrary to Article 37 in as much as the fixing of a price other than that determined by the manufacturer or importer constitutes an extension to imported tobacco of a prerogative typical of the national monopoly, of such a nature as adversely to affect the marketing of imported tobacco under normal conditions of competition'.

11.09   As regards the third question, the meaning of the obligation to 'adjust', the Court has repeatedly held that it does not require the total abolition of the monopoly,[27] although, as already mentioned, it has held in the *Manghera* case that under Article 37 no State monopoly may have an exclusive import right after the end of the transitional period. For the rest, as shown below, the Court's case law on this point is far from clear.

11.10   The Court's answer to the fourth question—as to which aspects of a State monopoly fall under Article 37 and which under other provisions of the Treaty—has wavered considerably. For this reason it appears most appropriate to consider these cases in chronological order.

The first case on the matter concerning facts arising after the end of the transitional period was *Manghera*. There the national court making the reference only asked the Court of Justice to rule on the compatibility of the exclusive import rights with Article 37, and the Court limited its answer to Article 37 without mentioning Article 30.

---

[25] See also Case 86/78 *Peureux* v. *Directeur des Services Fiscaux* [1979] E.C.R. 897, [1980] 3 C.M.L.R. 337, para. 30 of the judgment, noted by Wyatt, *op. cit.* n.12 above.
[26] [1983] E.C.R. 2011, [1984] 2 C.M.L.R. 516; conversely, non-discriminatory taxation linked to a *de facto* reduction in the price of goods sold by a State monopoly was held to be compatible with Art. 37 in Case 253/83 *Kupferberg* v. *Hauptzollamt Mainz* [1985] E.C.R. 157, [1987] 1 C.M.L.R. 36.
[27] *Manghera* (see n.5 above); Case 91/75 *HZA Göttingen* v. *Miritz* [1976] E.C.R. 217; Case 91/78 *Hansen* (see n.12 above); Case 119/78 *Peureux* v. *Directeur des Services Fiscaux* [1979] E.C.R. 975, [1980] 3 C.M.L.R. 337 noted by Wyatt, *op. cit.* n.12 above.

However, in two cases decided shortly afterwards, *Hauptzollamt Göttingen* v. *Miritz*[28] and *Rewe* v. *Hauptzollamt Landau*,[29] the Court had to face the problem squarely. Although the two cases were decided on the same day and on similar facts, the approach adopted in each case was not quite the same. In the *Miritz* case the Court was asked by a German court to rule on the compatibility with Articles 12 and 37(2) of a 'special equalisation' charge imposed by a German law of 1970 on alcohol products imported into Germany with the aim of protecting national alcohol producers, all of which were subject to a State monopoly. The Court held that 'since the structure and character of the equalisation charge link it to the system of the German alcohol monopoly, the answer to the first question [on Article 12] must be ascertained from the text of Article 37, which deals specifically with the adjustment of State monopolies'. Later in the same judgment the Court added:

> 'Article 37(1) is not concerned exclusively with quantitative restrictions but prohibits any discrimination, when the transitional period has ended, regarding the conditions under which goods are procured and marketed between nationals of Member States. It follows that its application is not limited to imports or exports which are directly subject to the monopoly but covers all measures which are connected with its existence and affect trade between Member States in certain products, whether or not subject to the monopoly'.[30]

Thus, held the Court, a charge discriminating against imported products in favour of domestic products coming under a monopoly infringed Article 37(2).

11.11   The *Rewe* case also concerned the German alcohol monopoly. There the national court asked the Court of Justice to rule on the compatibility with Articles 37 and 95 of a 'monopoly equalisation duty' imposed on alcohol imports. The Court first examined the problem from the point of view of Article 95. It found that Article 95 did not prohibit a tax such as that in question if it was imposed equally on the domestic product and on the similar imported product—even if the tax on the former were paid to the monopoly, while that on imported goods were imposed for the benefit of the general budget of the State. However, the Court found it necessary to consider Article 37 in addition, stating: 'the fact that a national measure complies with the requirements of Article 95 does not imply that it is valid in relation to other provisions of the Treaty, such as Article 37'. After making the statement already quoted from the *Miritz* case to the effect that

---

[28] See n.27 above.
[29] See n.6 above.
[30] This follows the Court's judgment in Case 13/70 *Cinzano* v. *HZA Saarbrücken* [1970] E.C.R. 1089, [1971] C.M.L.R. 374, which, however, relates to facts arising during the transitional period.

Article 37 was not concerned exclusively with quantitative restrictions, the Court then reached the same conclusion with respect to Article 37 as it had in interpreting Article 95.

11.12   There then follows a gap in the case law on this subject, during which time the Commission developed its new theory already explained about the role of Article 37 since the end of the transitional period. The first case in which it expounded this theory was *Hansen v. Hauptzollamt Flensburg*[31] (Hansen I) in which the plaintiffs contested the validity of a tax on various types of alcohol from Guadeloupe and certain third countries imposed in connection with the German alcohol monopoly. In addition to a couple of questions on the territorial applicability of Article 95, the German court asked the Court of Justice whether a tax such as that in question infringed Article 37, 92 or 95.

The Court stated that it appeared from a comparative study carried out by the Commission that preferential tax arrangements of the type in question existed in several Member States, sometimes quite independently of a commercial monopoly.

> 'Accordingly' said the Court, 'it appears preferable to examine the problem raised by the national court primarily from the point of view of the rule on taxation laid down in Article 95, because it is of a general nature and not from the point of view of Article 37, which is specific to arrangements for State monopolies. This approach is further justified by the fact that Article 37 is based on the same principle as Article 95, that is the elimination of all discrimination in trade between Member States.'

The Court also considered that is was 'preferable' to examine the matter from the point of view of Article 95 rather than Article 92. The use of the word 'preferable' indicates that it was open to the Court to examine the matter under Article 37, and implies that it would have reached the same result.

11.13   Of all the cases the most straightforward in this respect is *Rewe-Zentral (Cassis de Dijon)*.[32] As already explained, the case concerned the compatibility with Articles 30 and 37 of a minimum alcohol requirement applying in the same way to domestic and imported drinks. It appears that the national court mentioned Article 37 in its reference merely because the basic rule fixing a minimum alcohol content for spirits is contained in the German Federal Law on the Monopoly in Spirits. On this point the Court's answer was that:

> 'It should be noted . . . that Article 37 relates specifically to State monopolies of a commercial character. That provision is therefore irrelevant with regard to national provisions which do not concern the exercise by a public monopoly of its specific function—namely, its exclusive right—but apply in a general

---

[31] Case 148/77 [1978] E.C.R. 1787, [1979] 1 C.M.L.R. 604, noted by Wyatt, *op. cit.* n.12 above.
[32] See n.23 above.

manner to the production and marketing of alcoholic beverages, whether or not the latter are covered by the monopoly in question. That being the case, the effect on intra-Community trade of the measure referred to by the national court must be examined solely in relation to the requirements under Article 30.'

The statement that the 'specific function' of the monopoly was its 'exclusive right' suggests a possible acceptance by the Court of the Commission's interpretation of Article 37. However, within a matter of weeks the Court was to veer away from that position once again. The change came in a batch of three cases decided on the same day, two cases entitled *Peureux* v. *Directeur des Services Fiscaux* on the French alcohol monopoly and *Hansen* v. *Hauptzollamt Flensburg* (Hansen II), which once again involved the German alcohol monopoly. What is more, the Court's approach in the two *Peureux* cases was different from that in *Hansen II*.

11.14 In the first *Peureux* case,[33] the plaintiff company was claiming that the 'cash adjustment' which French producers of certain types of alcohol had to pay to release that produce from the national alcohol marketing monopoly was contrary to Community law. The action related to two separate periods:

— the period immediately before the entry into force of French Decree 77/842, during which the plaintiffs complained that they, as national producers, had to pay the 'cash adjustment', whereas imported alcohol of the same kind was not subject to this charge; and

— the subsequent period, during which the plaintiffs' sole complaint was that they were obliged to pay this charge to which their counterparts in other Member States were not subject, so that the plaintiffs' produce was placed at a disadvantage when exported to other Member States.

The French court in effect asked the Court of Justice whether the 'cash adjustment' infringed Article 37 under these circumstances, not mentioning any other Treaty provision.

As to the earlier period the Court first held that Article 37(1) no longer constitutes an exception to Article 95 since the end of the transitional period. Having found that Article 95 did not prohibit internal taxation involving reverse discrimination, the Court then ruled that the same applied under Article 37—whether or not that provision prohibited other types of reverse discrimination.[34] This was because:

'the rules contained in Article 37 concern only activities intrinsically connected with the specific business of the monopoly and are irrelevant to national provisions which have no connection with such specific business. The fact that products are or are not subject to internal taxation according to whether they

---

[33] See n.25 above.
[34] On reverse discrimination see paras. 6.74 *et seq.* above.

are subject or not to the monopoly is not a factor which determines how the specific business of the monopoly is conducted.'[35]

Consequently, such a charge was prohibited neither by Article 37 nor by Article 95. *A fortiori* the same applied for the second of the two periods.

11.15   The Court adopted the same criteria in the second *Peureux*[36] case. As explained earlier in this book, the plaintiffs in the main action wished to distil some oranges steeped in alcohol, which they had imported from Italy. The defendant contested their right to do this, on the basis of an article in the French *Code Général des Impôts* prohibiting the distillation of all imported raw materials with the exception of certain types of fresh fruit. The French court asked whether this provision was compatible with 'Articles 10 and 37 or any other provision of the Treaty of Rome on the free movement and circulation of products coming from third countries'.

After holding that the French provision in question was a measure of equivalent effect to a quantitative restriction under Article 30, the Court went on to consider Article 37. As in the first *Peureux* case it held that:

> 'the rules contained in Article 37(1) and (2) concern only activities intrinsically connected with the specific business of the monopoly and are irrelevant to national provisions which have no connection with such specific business.'

In view of the obligation on French producers to sell their alcohol to the monopoly the Court found that there was such an intrinsic connection. It concluded that the French measure, in addition to infringing Article 30, also constituted discrimination prohibited by Article 37(1) because it treated the same kind of nationally produced alcohol differently according to whether it had been obtained from national or from imported raw material.

11.16   It is clear that the scope of Article 37 as laid down in the *Peureux* cases, though wider than that enunciated in the *Cassis de Dijon* judgment (*Rewe-Zentral*), does not constitute a major break from it. The same cannot be said of *Hansen II*.[37] In the light of the *Rewe*[38] and *Miritz* cases the Commission prevailed upon the German Government to deprive its alcohol monopoly of its exclusive rights over imports. However, the monopoly was still obliged to buy up national production at a price above that at which imported alcohol was now sold freely on the German market. The monopoly thus had to sell this national production at a loss. To raise money to pay for this loss a tax imposed on both imported and domestic alcohol

---

[35] This ruling was cited and followed in Case 17/81 *Pabst und Richarz* v. *Hauptzollamt Oldenburg* [1982] E.C.R. 1331, [1983] 3 C.M.L.R. 11.

[36] See n.27 above.

[37] See n.12 above, with a critical note by Meier in [1979] EuR 281.

[38] By this is meant Case 45/75, see n.6 above.

was increased. The plaintiffs, obliged to pay this increased tax on various quantities of alcohol of both Community and non-Community origin, claimed that the increase was contrary to Community law. The national court therefore asked the Court of Justice whether Article 37 was a *lex specialis* in relation to Articles 92 and 93, and also whether a tax increase of the kind at issue infringed Article 37(1) or (2). Although the plaintiffs also claimed that the increase was contrary to Article 95, no mention was made of that provision in the reference.

It is not without relevance that, although a measure of this kind would normally be defined as an aid, there were difficulties in the way of judging it under Articles 92 and 93. The alcohol in question is an agricultural product but no act has been adopted by the Council under Article 42[39] to apply Article 92 to it. Unlike the Commission, the Advocate General regarded this as irrelevant since the end of the transitional period and found that the tax increase infringed Article 93(3) in that the German Government had not submitted it to the Commission in sufficient time.

A desire to avoid this particular point may well explain the Court's chosen course of deciding the case on Article 37 alone. The following statement of the Court is particularly noteworthy in this context:

> 'Article 37 remains applicable wherever, *even after the adjustment prescribed in the Treaty,*[40] the exercise by a State monopoly of its exclusive rights entails a discrimination or restriction prohibited by that Article.
>
> In a case such as the present, which concerns an activity specifically connected with the exercise by a State monopoly of its exclusive right to purchase, process and sell spirits, the application of the provisions of Article 37 cannot be excluded.'

It followed, in the Court's view, that the applicability of Articles 92 and 93 need not be considered. An examination of Article 37 then led it to conclude that

> 'any practice by a State monopoly which consists in marketing a product such as spirits with the aid of public funds at an abnormally low resale price compared to the price, before tax, of comparable quality imported from another Member State is incompatible with Article 37(1) of the EEC Treaty.'[41]

Precisely because the Court avoided deciding on the applicability of Articles 92 and 93—and was not asked about the applicability of Articles 12 and 95[42]—it is impossible to know whether the Court's

---

[39] Art. 42 EEC reads:
'The provisions of the Chapter relating to rules on competition shall apply to production of and trade in agricultural products only to the extent determined by the Council within the framework of Article 43(1) and (2) . . .'

[40] The italics are those of the author.

[41] For reasons connected with Art. 92 and thus beyond the scope of this book, this statement is much criticised by Meier, *op. cit.* n.37 above.

[42] The application of either of those Arts. would have required an extension of the decisions in Case 77/76 *Cucchi* v. *Avez* [1977] E.C.R. 987 and Case 105/76 *Interzuccheri* v. *Rezzano* [1977] E.C.R. 1029. See the Commission and the A.G. in *Hansen II*. In addition the application of Art. 86 would have required the Court to decide whether this provision is applicable to State enterprises.

conclusion could only have been reached on the basis of Article 37. That is a matter that will no doubt be clarified eventually.

After this review of case law on the relationship between Article 37 and other Articles of the Treaty, it is clear that the Court's approach has not been consistent. However, the fact remains that—with the possible exception of *Hansen II*—the Court has always reached the same result whether or not it has applied Article 37.

11.17   As to the final question set out in paragraph 11.05 above, the Court held in *Miritz*[43] that Article 37(4) did not derogate from the other provisions of Article 37: on the contrary it was expressed to have effect 'in applying the rules' contained in that Article. This ruling was the almost inevitable sequel to the Court judgment in *Charmasson* v. *Minister of Economic Affairs.*[44]

11.18   On the other hand, it is clear from the express wording of Article 37(5) that that paragraph does constitute an exception to the other provisions of Article 37. This provision was added at the request of the German Government to take account of the agreement between itself and Svenska Tändsticks AB, the Swedish match concern. Accordingly, it would appear that the term 'international agreements' must be construed to cover agreements between a Member State and a private organisation of a non-Member State.[45] In this respect it is wider than Article 234[46] which is expressed to apply only to agreements between States. Mention should also be made of the theory[47] that with respect to agreements falling under Article 37(5) there is no obligation corresponding to that in Article 234(2) to renegotiate agreements to eliminate inconsistencies with the Treaty.

11.19   A further undecided question is whether Article 36 can be applied to exempt measures falling under Article 37. Article 36 is expressed only to apply to restrictions covered by Articles 30 to 34, and, as already pointed out,[48] Article 36 must be restrictively interpreted. Yet in *SAIL*[49] the Commission claimed that Article 36 could constitute an exemption from the prohibitions contained in Article 37, in view of the parallelism between that provision and Articles 30 to 34. The Advocate General considered this argument

---

[43] See n.27 above.
[44] Case 48/74 [1974] E.C.R. 1383, [1975] 2 C.M.L.R. 208, discussed at para. 10.02 above. The imposition of the charge had in fact been suggested by the Commission in its Recommendation based on Art. 37(6) to the German Government on the adjustment of its alcohol monopoly ([1970] J.O. L31/22). See Béraud, Wooldridge and Dashwood and Wyatt (all cited at n.9 above).
[45] Hochbaum, *op. cit.* n.9 above at 324.
[46] See para. 9.61 above.
[47] See Waelbroeck, *op. cit.* at 134 and the sources there cited.
[48] Para. 8.01 above.
[49] Case 82/71 [1972] E.C.R. 119, [1972] C.M.L.R. 723.

to be at least plausible, though he found the measure in question unnecessarily restrictive and thus incapable of being justified by Article 36 in any case. Béraud[50] suggests that Article 36 should apply to measures falling within the scope of Article 37—provided such measures were introduced independently of the monopoly.

Thus, apart from the effect of Article 37(4), no clear answer can be given to any of the five questions posed in paragraph 11.04.[51]

11.20   Indeed, one cannot avoid ending this chapter on a pessimistic note: despite no lack of case law on the point, it is impossible to give a clear answer to the question posed at the beginning, namely in what cases Article 37 ousts Articles 30 to 34 and whether it leads to a different result in those cases. The suspicion lingers that somewhere in the 'obscure clarity' of Article 37 the Court discerns obligations not found elsewhere in the Treaty and possibly even exemptions from other provisions in the Treaty, which it has one day to reveal—if it has not already begun to do so, in *Hansen II*. Otherwise, why not interepret Article 37 restrictively?

---

[50] *Op. cit.* n.9.
[51] A further unsettled question is the relationship between Arts. 37 and 90 and 222. On this relationship see, *e.g.* Van Hecke, *op. cit.* at 454 and Waelbroeck, *op. cit.* at 123; also the A.Gs. in *SAIL* (n.49 above) and *Manghera* (n.5 above); see also paras. 4.05, 9.03 and 9.52 above.

CHAPTER XII

Community legislation relating to the free movement of goods

12.01 A fully fledged discussion of harmonisation[1] in the Community in all its aspects falls outside the scope of this book. Rather, the intention of this chapter is more limited: to show the reader how Community legislation can set aside the obstacles to the free movement of goods discussed in previous chapters and the relationship between such legislation and Articles 30 to 36.

After a general introductory section we shall go on to consider the relationship between harmonisation and Articles 30 to 36, and finally look at the public purchasing Directives.

The provisions in the Single European Act relating to harmonisation are discussed separately in Chapter 13.

I. GENERAL

The legal basis for such legislation

12.02 The best known basis in the Treaty for this type of legislation is Article 100. This provides as follows:

'The Council shall, acting unanimously on a proposal from the Commission, issue Directives for the approximation of such provisions laid down by law,

---

[1] See generally, Leleux 'Le rapprochement des législations dans la CEE' [1968] C.D.E. 129; Beuve-Méry and Schaub, 'Die Beseitigung der Technischen Handelshindernisse zwischen den EWG-Mitgliedstaaten durch Richtlinien gemäß Art, 100 EWGV' [1970] EuR 135; Vignes in *Le droit de la CEE* (1973), Vol. 3, 152 *et seq.*; Ficker in Groeben, Boechkh, Thiesing, *Kommentar zum EWG-Vertrag* (1974), Vol. I, 1270 *et seq.*; Marx, *Funktion und Grenzen der Rechtsangleichung nach Art. 100 EWG-Vertrag* (1975); *Les instruments du rapprochement des législations dans la CEE* ed. Waelbroeck (1975); Vogelaar, 'The Approximation of the laws of the Member States under the Treaty of Rome' [1975] C.M.L.Rev. 24; Slot, *Technical and administrative obstacles to trade in the EEC* (1975); Lasnet 'L'élimination des entraves techniques aux échanges dans la CEE' [1976] C.D.E. 4; Schneider, *Die Rechtsangleichung als Integrationsmittel der Europäischen Gemeinschaft* (1977); Editorial Comments [1978] C.M.L.Rev. 389; Close, 'Harmonisation of laws: use or abuse of the powers under the EEC Treaty' [1978] E.L.Rev. 461; Seidel, 'Ziele und Ausmaß der Rechtsangleichung in der EWG— zur britischen Auffassung' [1979] EuR 171; Editorial Comments [1980] C.M.L.Rev. 463; Leleux in 'Ecrits de Droit Européen' [1980] C.D.E. at 83; Currall, 'Some Aspects of the Relation between Articles 30–36 and Article 100 of the EEC Treaty, with a closer look at Optional Harmonisation' [1984] Y.E.L. 169; Meier 'Für ein neues EG-Konzept zur Harmoniserung des Lebensmittelrechts' [1984] EuR 268; Case 148/78 *Pubblico Ministero* v. *Ratti* [1979] E.C.R. 1629, [1980] 1 C.M.L.R. 96; Case 815/79 *Cremonini and Vrankovitch* [1980] E.C.R. 3583, [1981] 3 C.M.L.R. 49.

regulation or administrative action in Member States as directly affect the establishment or functioning of the common market . . .'

The overwhelming majority of Directives are based wholly or partly on this provision. In view of its very considerable importance, many reams have been devoted to it. However, in the present context we can confine ourselves to the following remarks:

— the only category of instrument which may be based on Article 100 is the Directive;
— while the concept of provisions which 'directly affect the establishment or functioning of the common market' is a vague one, there can be no doubt that it covers national provisions creating barriers to trade which are justified under Article 36.[2] Article 100 has also been used frequently as a basis for some customs legislation;
— it is not necessary that all Member States possess measures covering the field to be harmonised. It is enough that one Member State has such a measure.[3]

The Single European Act now supplements this provision by Article 100A, which is discussed in Chapter 13.

12.03 The Treaty also contains others bases for legislation intended to remove obstacles to inter-state trade. Of these, Article 43 is an appropriate basis for harmonising legislation relating to agricultural products.[4] Unlike Article 100, it allows for legislation by means of Regulations and not only by means of Directives. The Community legislation harmonising veterinary controls on meat and livestock has been adopted on the basis, *inter alia*, of Article 43.

In two separate cases,[5] the United Kingdom has contested the validity of Directive 85/649[6] prohibiting the use in livestock of certain substances having a hormonal action and of Directive 86/113[7] laying down minimum standards for the protection of laying hens kept in battery cages, on the grounds that they are based on Article 43 alone instead of Articles 43 and 100 together. The Court rejected the United Kingdom's arguments on this point although it annulled the Directives on other grounds. It interpreted Article 43 widely, holding that 'even where the legislation in question is directed both to objectives of agricultural policy and to other objectives which, in the absence of specific provisions, are pursued on the basis of Article 100 of the Treaty, that Article, a general one under which

---

[2] See para. 12.22.
[3] Ficker, *op. cit.* 1288–1289.
[4] Agricultural products for this purpose are those listed in Annex II to the Treaty: Art. 38(3).
[5] Cases 68/86 *United Kingdom* v. *E.C. Council* [1988] 2 C.M.L.R. 543 and 131/86 *United Kingdom* v. *E.C. Council* [1988] 2 C.M.L.R. 364.
[6] [1985] O.J. L382/228.
[7] [1986] O.J. L95/45.

directives may be adopted for the approximation of the laws of the Member States, cannot be relied on as a ground for restricting the field of application of Article 43 of the Treaty.' Moreover, the plaintiff contends that the Council had departed from its consistent practice of basing measures in these fields on Articles 43 and 100 together. The Court dismissed this argument on the grounds that the practice of the Council could not alter the rules laid down in the Treaty.

12.04 Article 103 would appear to be an appropriate basis for taking 'conjunctural policy' measures or measures designed to cope with a shortfall in supplies. Examples might be legislation imposing rationing or legislation relating to price controls.[8] Such legislation could take the form of Regulations or Directives. Article 103 requires no further comment here as it has already been considered at length in an earlier chapter.[9]

12.05 Lastly, Article 235[10] provides:

'If action by the Community should prove necessary to attain, in the course of the operation of the common market, one of the objectives of the Community and this Treaty has not provided the necessary powers, the Council shall, acting unanimously on a proposal from the Commission and after consulting the Assembly, take the appropriate measures.'

It will be noted that this provision only applies if 'this Treaty has not provided the necessary powers.' Thus it will not normally be possible or necessary to rely on it with respect to the type of legislation we are concerned with here, since this is in general covered by Article 100. However, Article 100 only permits the adoption of Directives: in the past, if it was necessary to pass legislation in the form of a Regulation and neither Article 43 nor Article 103 was applicable, then it was necessary to resort to Article 235.[11] In view of the insertion of Article 100A in the Treaty by the Single European Act,[12] recourse to Article 235 will become much less frequent.

Article 235 has been used as the legal basis for legislation on the environment. However, it is now to be replaced in this rôle by the new provisions of the Single European Act.[13]

---

[8] See para. 7.84 above.

[9] Paras, 9.04 *et seq.* above.

[10] See generally Cases 8/73 *Hauptzollamt Bremerhaven* v. *Massey-Ferguson* [1973] E.C.R. 897 and 45/86 *E.C. Commission* v. *E.C. Council* 'generalised system of preferences' [1988] 2 C.M.L.R. 131 and the special issue on Art. 235 in [1976] EuR with articles by Everling (at p.1), Schwartz (at p.27) and Tomuschat (at p.45).

[11] Harmonisation of national laws has also been carried out by the Community Patent Convention, which is not based on any Treaty Art. but is expressed to be subject to the Treaty of Rome. However, the disadvantages of this method become obvious when it is realised that, although that Convention was signed in 1975, it has still not been ratified by all the Member States and is consequently not yet in force. See generally para. 8.96 above.

[12] See para. 13.06 *et seq.* below.

[13] Para. 13.25.

12.06   In addition to these legislative provisions, Article 101 provides for a special procedure for ironing out distortions caused by differences between national measures. If it finds the existence of such a distortion, the Commission is to consult the Member States concerned and, if necessary, it may propose to the Council a separate Directive which the Council may adopt by qualified majority after the end of the first stage of the transitional period. Article 102 further requires a Member State wishing to adopt a measure likely to cause such a distortion to consult the Commission, which is then required to recommend the appropriate measures to the Member States concerned. If the Member State in question adopts the measure contrary to the recommendation of the Commission, Article 102 states that other Member States cannot be required to amend their provisions under Article 101. In fact, Articles 101 and 102 have had very little impact: a handful of Commission recommendations have ensued[14] but no Directives.

Total and optional harmonisation

12.07   Having considered the various bases in the Treaty for harmonisation, it is now necessary to discuss the two basic types of harmonisation: total and optional. Total harmonisation imposes a two-fold obligation on the Member States:

— to permit goods complying with the Directive to be freely imported and marketed (the free movement clause); and
— to prohibit the sale of goods not complying with the Directive (the exclusivity clause).

On the other hand, optional harmonisation involves the first obligation only: the Member States are then free to allow the sale of goods not meeting the standards laid down in the Directive. This means that, should a Member State so wish, it can allow national norms to co-exist with the Community ones. It is then open to small producers to produce only according to national norms, although this reduces the possibility of exporting their goods.

This can best be illustrated by reference to examples. Directive 76/768[15] on the approximation of laws relating to cosmetic products provides for total harmonisation. Article 7(1) of that Directive provides:

'Member States may not, for reasons related to the requirements laid down in this Directive and the annexes thereto, refuse, prohibit or restrict the marketing of any cosmetic products which comply with the requirements of this Directive and the Annexes thereto' (the free movement clause).

In addition, Article 3 provides:

'Member States shall take all necessary measures to ensure that only cosmetic products which conform to the provisions of this Directive and its Annexes may be put on the market' (the exclusivity clause).

---

[14] Recommendations are not binding: Art. 189 EEC.
[15] [1976] O.J. L262/169.

On the other hand, Directive 71/316[16] on the approximation of laws relating to common provision for both measuring instruments and methods of methodological control provides for optional harmonisation. It contains a free movement clause (broadly similar to Article 7(1) of Directive 76/768) but no exclusivity clause.

Optional harmonisation is more flexible and less likely to stifle innovation than total harmonisation. It is also more attractive to small companies producing only for the market of their own Member State: for such companies total harmonisation entails the expense of changing over to new standards without any compensating advantage. Consequently optional harmonisation has come to be more frequently used.[17] On the other hand, optional harmonisation does not necessarily remove differences between national standards and these differences can sometimes be successfully exploited by multinationals so as to restrict parallel imports. Other weaknesses in optional harmonisation are discussed in paragraphs 12.26 and 12.27.

Safeguard Clauses

12.08 It is also quite common for a Directive to contain a safeguard clause. An example is Article 12(1) of Directive 76/768 already referred to:

> 'If a Member State notes, on the basis of a substantiated justification, that a cosmetic product, although complying with the requirements of the Directive, represents a hazard to health, it may provisionally prohibit the marketing of that product in its territory or subject it to special conditions. It shall immediately inform the other Member States and the Commission thereof, stating the grounds for its decision.'

Subsequent provisions of the Directive require the Commission to deliver an opinion on whether the product constitutes a health hazard and, if necessary, to propose the technical adaptation of the Directive.

Technical adaptation

12.09 In order to bring legislation into line with technical developments, it is obviously necessary to amend it from time to time. Clearly, it would be too cumbersome to follow the same procedure as for the basic Directive on each occasion, culminating in the adoption of an amending Directive by the Council. To avoid this it is the practice for the Council to delegate to the Commission power to elaborate technical adaptations with the assistance of a special committee consisting of representatives of the Member States and chaired by a representative of the Commission. If the representatives of the Member States approve a draft amendment by a qualified majority according to Article 148(2) of the Treaty, then it is adopted

---

[16] [1971] J.O. L202/1.
[17] Lasnet, *op. cit.* n. 1 above, at 12.

by the Commission. Should the draft not meet with this approval then it is put to the Council. If the Council fails to adopt it by a qualified majority within three months, then the Commission shall adopt it. Such a procedure is provided for, for instance, by Articles 9 and 10 of Directive 76/768.

The Council's legislative programmes

12.10 With a view to establishing timetables and priorities the Council has adopted a number of General Programmes laying down harmonisation plans for the future. The first of these, adopted on 28 May 1969,[18] consists of a bundle of resolutions notably on industrial products and on food products. This was later supplemented by the Council Resolution of 21 May 1973.[19] Also, by a Resolution of 14 April 1975,[20] the Council adopted a preliminary programme laying down a consumer protection and information policy, replaced by a second programme adopted by a Council Resolution of 19 May 1981.[21]

Notification of national measures

12.11 In order to forestall national initiatives likely to undermine the General Programme of 28 May 1969, on the same day the Member States concluded a gentlemen's agreement[22] generally known as the *status quo* agreement. By this agreement the Member States undertook to notify any draft measure relating to products covered by the General Programme. The agreement then requires the Member States in question to refrain from adopting the measures for a period of five months,[23] to give the Council the opportunity to pass a Directive on the matter. By way of exception a Member State may adopt a measure at once if this is necessary for health or safety reasons; it must then inform the Commission afterwards.

As regards measures concerning goods not covered by the General Programme, the Member States undertook in the agreement to notify to the Commission any such measures which are likely to result in obstacles to trade. The Member State concerned is then required to refrain from bringing these measures into force for a period of two months after such notification.

A similar gentlemen's agreement was concluded by the Member States on 5 March 1973[24] in connection with measures concerning the protection of the environment. This provides for the Member

---

[18] [1969] J.O. C76/1.
[19] [1973] O.J. C38/1.
[20] [1975] O.J. C92/1.
[21] [1981] O.J. C133/1.
[22] [1969] J.O. C76/9.
[23] Under the original agreement, a six-month period was laid down in certain cases, but that has now been reduced to five months: Agreement of 5 March 1973 [1973] O.J. C9/3.
[24] [1973] O.J. C9/1.

States to notify the Commission of such draft measures in certain circumstances and in particular when they may 'directly affect the functioning of the common market.'

It can of course happen that the Commission becomes aware of a measure notified under one or other of these agreements, which, if adopted, would infringe Article 30 or Article 34.[25]

12.12 These gentlemen's agreements have been partially superseded by Council Directive 83/189[26] laying down a procedure for the provision of information in the field of technical standards and regulations, which is based on Articles 100 and 213 of the Treaty. The Directive applies only to 'industrially manufactured products other than agricultural products within the meaning of Article 38(1) of the Treaty, products for human or animal consumption, medicinal products within the meaning of Directive 65/65 and cosmetic products within the meaning of Directive 76/768' (Article 1(7)). However, by virtue of Article 5 of Council Directive 87/22[27] Articles 8 and 9 of Directive 83/189 have applied since 1 July 1987 to medicinal products covered by Directive 65/65, albeit 'subject to the application of other Community provisions.'[28] What follows does not purport to be an exhaustive description of this Directive.

Article 8(1) requires the Member States to communicate immediately to the Commission any draft technical regulation. By 'technical regulation' is meant 'technical specifications, including the relevant administrative provisions, the observance of which is compulsory, *de jure* or *de facto*, in the case of marketing or use in a Member State or a major part thereof, except those laid down by local authorities' (Article 1(5)). In addition, the Member States must 'let the Commission have a brief statement of the grounds which make the enactment of such a technical regulation necessary, where these are not already made clear in the draft.' The Commission must immediately notify the other Member States of any draft it has received.

Article 9 is in the following terms:

'1. Without prejudice to paragraph 2, Member States shall postpone the adoption of a draft technical regulation for six months from the date of the notification referred to in Article 8(1) if the Commission or another Member

---

[25] In certain circumstances even a draft measure may constitute a measure of equivalent effect within the meaning of Art. 30: para. 6.13 above.

[26] [1983] O.J. L109/8. See Lecrenier 'Les articles 30 et suivants CEE et les procédures de contrôle prévues par la directive 83/189 CEE' [1985] R.M.C. 6 and McMillan 'Qu'est-ce que la normalisation?' [1985] R.M.C. 93. A particularly full and up to date account of the practice and procedure under the Directive is to be found in Lecrenier 'Vers l'achèvement du marché intérieur: l'évolution des procédures de contrôle prévues par la directive 83/189 CEE depuis quatre ans' [1988] R.M.C. 121.

[27] [1987] O.J. L15/38.

[28] Indeed, while under Dir. 83/189 itself Arts. 8 and 9 apply only to draft technical regulations on the marketing or use of a product, Art. 5 of Dir. 87/22 renders them applicable to draft technical regulations relating to 'the production and marketing' of medicinal products. The latter phrase is presumably to be construed disjunctively.

State delivers a detailed opinion within three months of that date, to the effect that the measure envisaged must be amended in order to eliminate or reduce any barriers which it might create to the free movement of goods.

2. The period in paragraph 1 shall be 12 months if, within three months following the notification referred to in Article 8(1), the Commission gives notice of its intention of proposing or adopting a Directive on the subject.

3. Paragraphs 1 and 2 shall not apply in those cases where, for urgent reasons relating to the protection of public health or safety, a Member State is obliged to prepare technical regulations in a very short space of time in order to enact and introduce them immediately without any consultations being possible. In such cases the Member State in question shall in the notification provided for in Article 8 state the grounds warranting the urgent adoption of the measures.'

Article 10 provides:

'Articles 8 and 9 shall not apply where Member States honour their obligations arising out of Community Directives or commitments arising out of an international agreement where they result in the adoption of uniform technical specifications in the Community.'[29]

12.13 The first question raised by these provisions is this: do Articles 8(1) and 9 have direct effect? In other words, can failure by a Member State to observe their provisions be relied on before a national court? It is now established that directives do not produce 'horizontal effect' so that they cannot be relied on as against a private party: *Marshall* v. *Southampton Area Health Authority*.[30] On the other hand, it would appear that these provisions may be relied on as against the Member States concerned. These provisions are clear and unconditional and require no further implementation. They are analogous to Article 93(3) of the Treaty, which requires plans to grant or alter aid to be notified to the Commission and prohibits the Member States from implementing them pending the Commission's approval. In *Costa* v. *ENEL*[31] that provision was held to have direct effect. The requirements of the Directive are to be distinguished from a mere obligation of prior consultation such as that in the Council Decision of 9 October 1961[32] on certain commercial policy measures, which has been held not to have direct effect: *Bulk Oil* v. *Sun International*.[33] Accordingly, in a communication[34] devoted to this matter the Commission has expounded the view that Articles 8 and 9 have direct effect and that therefore national technical standards and regulations adopted in breach of them may not be enforced by Member States against third parties.

---

[29] Currall, *op. cit.*, n. 1 above at pp. 203–204.
[30] Case 152/84 [1986] 1 C.M.L.R. 688.
[31] Case 6/64 [1964] E.C.R. 585, [1964] C.M.L.R. 425, reaffirmed in Case 120/73 *Lorenz* v. *Germany* [1973] E.C.R. 1471. It is true that only the final sentence of Art. 93(3), which lays down the prohibition of putting unapproved aids into effect, was held to have direct effect. Yet this can surely not be dissociated from the obligation to notify in the first place.
[32] [1961] J.O. 1273.
[33] Case 174/84 [1986] E.C.R. 723, [1986] 2 C.M.L.R. 732.
[34] [1986] O.J. C245/4.

If it is right that Articles 8 and 9 have direct effect, then they create new grounds for challenging the validity of technical regulations and thus constitute an important supplement to Article 30. Yet it may not always be easy for a private party to ascertain whether a Member State has complied with its obligations under these provisions in a particular case.

12.14 Next, what is the nature of the 'detailed opinion' referred to in Article 9(1) of the Directive? Despite being called an 'opinion' it produces legal effects for the Member State to which it is addressed and is binding on it. Thus, when a 'detailed opinion' emanates from the Commission, it arguably constitutes a decision subject to annulment pursuant to Article 173 of the Treaty.[35] Yet, there is no analogous procedure whereby a 'detailed opinion' issued by another Member State could be contested in a direct action before the Court.

The case of the notice referred to in Article 9(2) is perhaps different again. This also produces legal effects, but it would be highly unusual for a mere statement of intention to be capable of annulment under Article 173: in the absence of bad faith it is hard to imagine how an action for the annulment of such a notice could be justifiable.

12.15 It follows from Article 9(1) that in all cases other than those referred to in Article 9(3), Member States must refrain from bringing their draft technical regulations into effect for 3 months after notification. Otherwise the notifying Member State could prevent the Commission and the other Member States from exercising their powers to issue a 'detailed opinion' within 3 months. In no case is the period of restraint longer than 12 months (Article 9(2)).

Paradoxically, Article 9(2) does not apply where a draft technical regulation notified by a Member State relates to a matter which is already the subject of a draft directive proposed by the Commission to the Council. Nor is any special provision made for this case elsewhere in the Directive. One must then fall back on the *status quo* agreement of 28 May 1969. Paragraph 1(a) of that agreement as amended stipulates that, where a Member State proposes to adopt a measure relating to a product by the General Programme of 28 May 1969 and the matter is covered by a draft directive already before the Council, that Member State shall refrain from bringing the measure for a five-month period following its notification to the Council.[36] As mentioned in paragraph 12.17 below, this anomaly has now been removed with effect from 1 January 1989 by the insertion into Article 9 of the Directive of a paragraph 2a.

---

[35] See generally Cases 8 and 11/66 *Cimenteries* v. *E.C. Commission* [1967] E.C.R. 75, [1967] C.M.L.R. 77.
[36] N. 23 above.

12.16   In addition, the Directive contains provisions designed to prevent non-compulsory standards approved by recognised standards bodies from creating fresh barriers to inter-state trade. As the preamble states, such standards can in practice have the same effects on the free movement of goods as State measures.[37] Hence the requirement in Article 4 that all new draft standards be notified to the Commission and certain named standards institutions every four months. Hence also the stipulation in Article 7 that 'Member States shall take all appropriate measures to ensure that their standards institutions do not draw up or introduce standards in the field in question' for a certain period while a European standard is being drawn up at the request of the Standing Committee created by Article 5.

12.17   Council Directive 89/182[38] effects certain important changes to Directive 83/189. The new instrument, which is to be implemented by 1 January 1989, is based on Articles 43, 100A and 213 of the Treaty.

One of the most important changes is that under the new version of Article 1(7) 'product' means 'any industrial product and any agricultural product'; thus all the categories of goods excluded from the earlier definition are now brought within the Directive.

In addition, various amendments have been made to Articles 6, 8, 9, 10 and 11. Of these the most important is the insertion into Article 9 of a new paragraph 2a which provides in particular that:

'Member States shall refrain from adopting technical regulations on a subject covered by a proposal for a directive or regulation submitted by the Commission to the Council before the communication provided for in Article 8(1) for a period of 12 months from the date of its submission.'

The new approach

12.18   It was anticipated that the entry into force of Directive 83/189 would bring to light new areas in which harmonisation was needed. This, it was felt, would aggravate the pre-existing difficulties encountered in harmonising national measures according to the practice of incorporating detailed technical specifications into Directives. Thus the Directive, together with the perceived need to quicken the pace of harmonisation, has led to the adoption of the 'new approach to technical harmonisation and standards' set out in detail in the Resolution of the Council of 7 May 1985.[39] The new approach is based on various principles set out at length in the Annexes to the Resolution. According to these principles total harmonisation is to be used whenever possible and the task of

---

[37] Para. 4.20 *et seq.*
[38] [1988] O.J. L81/75; Lecrenier, 'Vers l'achèvement du marché intérieur . . .,' n. 26 above.
[39] [1985] O.J. C136/1, also written question 119/86 ([1987] O.J. C19/4), McMillan *op. cit.* n. 26 above, White Paper paras. 67–73.

drawing up standards is to be delegated to standards organisations.

This new approach is now reflected in Council Directive 87/404 on pressure vessels.[40]

The White Paper

12.19 An even more significant development has been the publication of the Commission's White Paper[41] on 'Completing the Internal Market.' This imaginative document sets as its goal the creation of a fully unified internal market by 1992. Important sections relate to the free movement of goods and the elimination of technical barriers to trade, while other sections are devoted to persons, services, capital and tax barriers to trade. The White Paper contains a specific legislative programme, setting out for each measure the year in which the Commission's draft legislation will reach the Council and the date of its expected adoption by the Council. It is the cornerstone of the Single European Act which will be discussed in Chapter 13.

The Tokyo Round

12.20 As part of the Multilateral Agreements concluded under the auspices of the GATT and generally known as the Tokyo Round, the Community has concluded an Agreement on technical barriers to trade.[42] A detailed examination of that Agreement falls outside the scope of this book but, broadly speaking, its effect is that both the Community and the Member States must ensure that technical regulations and standards adopted by them do not constitute unnecessary obstacles to international trade with the other contracting parties. That principle is subject to a number of conditions, in particular the condition of reciprocity. In implementation of these undertakings the Council adopted Decision 80/45,[43] which provides, *inter alia*, that the 'Commission shall examine the extent to which it is able to propose amendments to Directives already adopted in order to enable compliance with those Directives to be determined on the basis of test results, certificates or marks of conformity issued by the competent authorities of third countries' (Article 2(2)(a)). Title III of the Decision sets out a 'procedure for applying the condition of reciprocity.' In further implementation of the Agreement, on 11 February 1980, the Commission submitted to the Council a proposal[44] for a draft Directive concerning a special procedure for the certification of products from third countries.

---

[40] [1987] O.J. L220/48.
[41] N. 39 above.
[42] [1980] O.J. L71/29, see also Bourgeois 'The Tokyo Round Agreements on Technical Barriers and on Government Procurement in International and EEC Perspective' [1982] C.M.L.Rev. 5; Steenbergen 'Trade Regulation after the Tokyo Round' in *Protectionism and the European Community*, Deventer (1983).
[43] [1980] O.J. L14/36.
[44] [1980] O.J. C54/5.

II. COMMUNITY LEGISLATION AND ARTICLES 30 TO 36

12.21 First of all, it should be pointed out that any attempt[45] to define the scope of Articles 30 to 36 by reference to Article 100 (or other Articles providing for Community legislation) has always signally failed. The Court has always refused to find that the restriction on imports resulting from a particular measure could be set aside under Article 100 and that therefore such a measure fell outside Article 30. In Case 193/80 *E.C. Commission* v. *Italy*[46] the Court rejected this line of argument which the defendant Government had put forward in the following terms:

> 'It is apparent that the purposes of Articles 30 and 100 are different. The purpose of Article 30 is, save for certain specific exceptions, to abolish in the immediate future all quantitative restrictions on the imports of goods and all measures having an equivalent effect, whereas the general purpose of Article 100 is, by approximating the laws, regulations and administrative provisions of the Member States, to enable obstacles of whatever kind arising from disparities between them to be reduced. The elimination of quantitative restrictions and measures having an equivalent effect, which is unreservedly affirmed in Article 3(a) of the Treaty and carried into effect by Article 30, may not therefore be made dependent on measures which, although capable of promoting the free movement of goods, cannot be considered to be a necessary condition for the application of that fundamental principle.'

12.22 Frequently, Community legislation is designed to harmonise measures justified under Article 36. It will be recalled that where Community legislation provides extensive health or other guarantees, Member States may no longer rely on Article 36.[47]

Exceptionally, such Community legislation has the effect of supplementing Articles 30 to 34 and ensuring their observance. This is the case with Council Directive 83/643[48] on the facilitation of physical inspections and administrative formalities in respect of the carriage of goods between Member States, which has been considered earlier in this book.[49] A further example of such legislation is to be found in the public supply Directives discussed below.

12.23 It will be remembered[50] at the same time that Community legislation may not create or permit unnecessary restrictions to inter-State trade—though whether in this respect the Community institutions are bound by Articles 9 to 17 and 30 to 36 as such, or by the principle of the free movement of goods, is an open question. At all events, it seems clear that, in the performance of the tasks with which they are entrusted, the Community institutions have greater freedom of action than do the Member States. Furthermore,

---

[45] *E.g.* Marx, *op. cit.*, n. 1 above.
[46] [1981] E.C.R. 3019.
[47] See para. 8.15 above.
[48] [1983] O.J. L359/8.
[49] Paras. 7.09, 7.17, 7.19 and 7.21 above.
[50] See paras. 4.08 *et seq.* above.

while a norm enacted by some Member States only will restrict inter-State trade, it will cease to do so once it is introduced throughout the Community.[51]

12.24   In these circumstances, has the *Cassis de Dijon*[52] judgment, by construing Article 30 widely, undermined or restricted the Community's harmonisation programme[53]? Put more concretely, could this judgment result in the withdrawal of any draft Directives? At first sight, one might think that the judgment could have this effect. However, it is submitted that this judgment has actually acted as a catalyst to harmonisation. Evidence of this is provided by the adoption of Council Directive 83/189 laying down a procedure for the provision of information in the field of technical standards and regulations.[54]

It is suggested that the reasons for this are two-fold:

— in so far as national measures are not justified under *Cassis de Dijon*, then in some cases an analogous measure can be adopted by the Community;

— in so far as national measures are so justified, Member States still have to allow imports conforming to norms providing equivalent guarantees.[55] This means that a Member State may have to check the equivalence of other norms and, if need be, apply those other norms alongside its own. This could result in one and the same Member State applying a plethora of different norms. It is simpler to resort to harmonisation by a Community Directive.

12.25   Supposing, then, that certain barriers to inter-State trade have been removed by a harmonising Directive, it is submitted that the compatibility of a national measure with Community law should first be examined by reference to the Directive.[56] Only if the national measure is compatible with the Directive should it be examined in the light of Articles 30 to 36. This is because the Directive will contain more specific rules than Articles 30 to 36, which are, after all, generalities. Again, a Directive harmonising health or other guarantees covered by Article 36 may have exhausted the Member

---

[51] See para. 6.72 above.

[52] Case 120/78 [1979] E.C.R. 649, [1979] 3 C.M.L.R. 494, paras. 6.40 *et seq.* above.

[53] See Mattera [1980] R.M.C. 505; Masclet 'Les articles 30, 36 et 100 du Traité EEC à la lumière de l'arrêt "Cassis de Dijon"', [1980] R.T.D.E. 611; Editorial Comments in [1980] C.M.L.Rev. 463.

[54] See paras. 12.12 *et seq.* above. In 'Les entraves à la libre circulation des marchandises' [1982] *Recueil Dalloz-Sirey*, Chronique 37, Judge Touffait takes the Commission to task for implying in its Communication on *Cassis de Dijon* ([1980] O.J. C256/2—see para. 6.42 above) that that judgment widened the scope of Art. 30 and correspondingly limited the scope of Art. 100.

[55] Para. 6.55 *et seq.* above.

[56] See also para. 10.10 above.

State's right to rely on that provision.[57] This approach is also suggested by the form of words used in the *Cassis de Dijon* case: 'in the absence of common rules relating to the production and marketing of alcohol . . . it is for the Member States to regulate [these] matters.'[58] At all events, it is plain that the adoption of Community legislation does not remove a matter from the scope of Article 30.[59]

12.26 On another point, when optional harmonisation is adopted, importers of goods not conforming to the standard laid down in the Directive (standard A) may still rely on Article 30. Thus goods produced in one Member State according to the standard of that State (standard B) may be imported into another Member State which has a different standard (standard C). If standards B and C are equivalent to one another, then Article 30 precludes the latter State from restricting the importation and sale of those goods.[60]

12.27 What then if the importing Member State has rendered the Community standard (standard A) compulsory and abolished its own national standard? This delicate issue was raised in Written Question 1176/81. The question referred to Directive 80/232[61] on the ranges of nominal quantities and capacities permitted for certain prepackaged products, which provides for optional harmonisation. Belgium was apparently considering making the implementation of the provisions of the Directive mandatory so that only the ranges listed in the Directive could be marketed in Belgium. If another Member State, say France, were to proceed with optional harmonisation and allow other standards not set out in the Directive, the French goods conforming to those other standards could not then be sold in Belgium. In view of *Cassis de Dijon* the questioner asked whether Belgium would then be infringing Article 30. If so, why did the Directive provide for optional rather than total harmonisation? The very principle of optional harmonisation was thus fundamentally put in question.

In its reply,[62] the Commission stated that:

> 'arguments based on the *Cassis de Dijon* judgment cannot be used in this instance to force a Member State which has made the provisions of the Directive mandatory to accept products which do not conform to it.'

---

[57] Para. 8.15 above.
[58] A similar form of words was used in Case 8/74 *Dassonville* [1974] E.C.R. 837, [1974] 2 C.M.L.R. 436.
[59] See para. 19 of the Order of the President of the Court of 13 March 1987 in Case 45/87R *E.C. Commission* v. *Ireland* [1987] 2 C.M.L.R. 563.
[60] See Currall, *op. cit.* n. 1 and *Cremonini*, n. 1; for the principle of equivalence, see para. 6.55 *et seq.* above.
[61] [1980] O.J. L51/1.
[62] [1982] O.J. C92/2.

III. THE PUBLIC SUPPLY DIRECTIVES

12.28 Harmonising directives and regulations run into several hundreds. Consequently it would be quite impossible even to attempt to give an outline of them here. In the present context it is only possible to focus on the public supply Directives since they are linked particularly closely to Article 30.

We saw in an earlier chapter[63] how discrimination in the award of public supply contracts was contrary to Article 30. Directive 77/62,[64] based on Article 100, is designed to supplement the prohibition in Article 30

'by the co-ordination of the procedures relating to public supply contracts in order, by introducing equal conditions of competition for such contracts in all the Member States, to ensure a degree of transparency allowing the observance of this prohibition to be better supervised.'[65]

It defines public supply contracts as contracts for the delivery of products, whether or not such delivery includes siting and installation operations (Article 1(a)). It applies to the contracts entered into by the State, regional or local authorities and certain other public authorities (Article 1(b)). Certain types of contract are excluded from the Directive, such as contracts awarded by bodies administering transport services (Article 2(2)(a)) or producing, distributing and transmitting or transporting services for water or energy and telecommunications services (Article 2(2)(b)).[66] It applies in essence only to public supply contracts whose estimated value net of VAT is not less than 200,000 European units of account (Article 5(1)(a)).

12.29 The Directive does not aim to create a Community procedure for the award of public supply contracts, but requires the Member States to adapt their national procedures in accordance with its provisions (Article 2(1)). The first substantive part of the Directive is Title II entitled 'Common rules in the technical field.' Article 7(1) provides in particular that the technical specifications defined in Annex II and the description of testing, checking and acceptance methods shall figure in the general or the contractual documents relating to each contract. Article 7(2) provides in particular that

'Unless such specifications are justified by the subject of the contract, Member States shall prohibit the introduction into the contractual clauses relating to a given contract of technical specifications which mention goods of a specific make or source or of a particular process and which have the effect of favouring or eliminating certain undertakings or products . . .'

---

[63] See paras. 7.23 *et seq.*

[64] [1977] O.J. L13/1. This is only the second Dir. on public contracts, the first being Dir. 71/305 ([1971] O.J. L185/5). However, that Dir. concerns only contracts to carry out work. It therefore relates to the provision of services rather than the movement of goods and thus falls outside the scope of this book.

[65] Second recital to the Dir.; clearly this Dir. does not alter the scope of Art. 30: see n. 59 above.

[66] But see the Council Recommendation on public telecommunications contracts ([1984] O.J. L298/51).

Title III relates to common advertising rules. It provides that where a public authority intends to award a contract covered by this Directive, it must advertise its intention by a notice in the Official Journal of the European Communities.

Title IV relates to the actual award of contracts. Article 20 states that a supplier may be excluded on a number of grounds such as that he is bankrupt or that he has failed to pay social security contributions or tax due in the country where he is established or the country of the contracting authority. The following Articles relate to similar matters such as proof of the supplier's financial standing (Article 22) and of his technical ability (Article 23). Article 25 concerns the criteria for the award of public contracts, which shall be:

'(a) either the lowest price only;
(b) or, when the award is made to the most economically advantageous tender, various criteria according to the contract in question: *e.g.* price, delivery rate, running costs, cost-effectiveness, quality, æsthetic and functional characteristics, technical merit, after-sales service and technical assistance.'

12.30 Although it is not expressly stated in this Directive, it does not cover third country suppliers.[67]

The Member States were required to implement this Directive within 18 months of its notification to them, that is to say by 23 June 1978.[68]

To ensure the effective operation of this Directive, an Advisory Committee for Public Contracts was set up by Directive 77/63.[69]

12.31 Annexed to the Multilateral GATT Agreements of 1979 already referred to [70] is an Agreement on government procurement.[71] In some respects the Agreement goes further than Directive 77/62. Since the Agreement does not apply as between the Member States, Directive 80/767[72] was passed to ensure that Community suppliers had at least the same rights as suppliers from third countries under the Agreement.[73]

Perhaps the most important respect in which this Directive goes beyond Directive 77/62 is that the threshold for the application of the procedure is brought down from 200,000 to 140,000 European units of account. However, this Directive does not apply to all the

---

[67] See the Council Reg. and Commission Statements discussed at para. 9.50 above.

[68] Few Member States did in fact implement the Dir. by that date: written question 872/78 ([1979] O.J. C172/2); written question 421/79 ([1980] O.J. C110/15); written question 721/79 ([1980] O.J. C74/11); in the case of Italy this resulted in successful proceedings being brought by the Commission under Art. 169 EEC: Case 133/80 *E.C. Commission* v. *Italy* [1981] E.C.R. 457, [1981] 3 C.M.L.R. 456.

[69] [1977] O.J. L13/15.

[70] Para. 12.20 above.

[71] [1980] O.J. L71/44. See Bourgeois and Steenbergen, *op. cit.*, n. 42 above.

[72] [1980] O.J. L215.

[73] The recitals to this Dir. are highly misleading in this respect.

public authorities covered by Directive 77/62. It only applies to the entities listed in the Annex to the Directive which, in the case of the United Kingdom, range from the Royal Mint and the Imperial War Museum to Whitehall Departments. County and District Councils are not included in the list, however.

Member States were required to implement Directive 80/767 by 1 January 1981.

12.32 In its White Paper on completing the Internal market[74] the Commission admitted that the Directives on public contracts had not been a success: 'less than 1 ECU in 4 of public expenditure in the areas covered by the co-ordination Directives is the subject of publication in the Official Journal and thus, even theoretically, of Community-wide competition.' It therefore promised further action in this field to strengthen the Directives.

In a separate development, the GATT Agreement on Government Procurement has been amended and liberalised by a Protocol signed on behalf of the Community on 16 November 1987 and approved by the Council [75] on the same day. That Protocol came into force on St Valentine's Day 1988.[76]

Accordingly, the Council has now adopted Directive 88/295[77] which, as its preamble states, seeks to 'improve and extend the scope of [Directives 77/62 and 80/767] by increasing the transparency of procedures and practices for the award of public supply contracts and to make possible stricter enforcement of the prohibition on restrictions on the free movement of goods, which constitutes the basis of these Directives' and to 'amend these Directives in order to incorporate changes to the GATT Agreement on Government Procurement.' The Member States are required to implement the new Directive by 1 January 1989, except Greece, Spain and Portugal which must do so by 1 January 1992 (Article 20).

12.33 The changes effected by this Directive are both substantial and numerous and cannot be described exhaustively here. At all events, the most important amendments to Directive 77/62 are as follows:

The scope of the earlier Directive has been altered in that the definition of 'public supply contracts' in Article 1(a) has been widened and the excluded categories of contract in Article 2(2) have been varied. At the same time, an Article 2a has been inserted and this is in the following terms:

'Without prejudice to Articles 2, 3 and 5(1), this Directive shall apply to all products within the meaning of Article 1(a), including those covered by

---

[74] See para. 12.19 above.
[75] Council Dir. 87/565 ([1987] O.J. L345/24).
[76] See the Commission's communication [1988] O.J. C25/2.
[77] [1988] O.J. L127/1.

contracts awarded by contracting authorities in the field of defence, except for the products to which the provisions of Article 223(1)(b) of the Treaty apply.'[78]

Under the new Article 6, Member States are required to apply their national procedures whereby all interested parties can present an offer save in the circumstances set out in paragraphs 2 to 4. Article 7 relating to technical specifications has been replaced by a wholly new provision. The new Article 7(2) stipulates:

'Without prejudice to the legally binding national technical rules insofar as these are compatible with Community law, such technical specifications shall be defined by the contracting authorities by reference to national standards implementing European standards, or by reference to common technical specifications.'

Article 7(3) contains exceptions to this rule. According to Article 7(5), in the absence of European standards on common technical specifications, the technical specifications may be defined in relation to '(a) national standards implementing international standards accepted in the country of the contracting authority, (b) other national standards in the country of the contracting authority, (c) any other standard' in that order of preference.

Title III is also subject to substantial amendments.

A new Article 26(1) provides:

'This Directive shall not prevent, until 31 December 1992, the application of existing national provisions on the award of public supply contracts which have as their objective the reduction of regional disparities and the promotion of job creation in the most disadvantaged regions and in declining industrial regions, on condition that the provisions concerned are compatible with the Treaty and with the Community's international obligations.'

Although it is not expressly stated in the preamble to the new Directive, this provision is presumably designed to take account of Article 8C of the Treaty inserted by the Single European Act.[79]

In addition, the new Directive lowers the threshold for the application of the procedure as regards the contracting authorities covered by Directive 80/767 to 130,000 ECUs net of VAT.

12.34 The adoption of Directive 88/295 does not by any means complete the Commission's programme in this field. Thus its draft Directive[80] co-ordinating administrative and judicial procedures for enforcing rights relating to public supply and public works contracts is still before the Council. Moreover, further Commission proposals were announced in the White Paper.

Finally it should be mentioned that the Commission has published a 'guide to the Community rules on open government procurement.'[81]

---

[78] As to Art. 223 see para. 9.54 above.
[79] See para. 13.05 below.
[80] [1987] O.J. C230/6.
[81] [1987] O.J. C358/1.

CHAPTER XIII

The Single European Act

13.01 Beyond any doubt the Single European Act,[1] which was signed in February 1986 and came into force on 1 July 1987, constitutes the most important amendment to the Treaty of Rome ever made. The changes effected by the Act relate to several areas of Community law, but for obvious reasons only the provisions concerning the free movement of goods will be discussed here. Let it be said at once that Articles 30 and 36 have been left untouched and that the relevant amendments relate instead to harmonisation.

13.02 This is not the place to discuss in detail the development which led up to the adoption of the Single European Act. Nevertheless, a brief mention should be made of the draft Treaty establishing the European Union[2] drawn up by the European Parliament in February 1984. The relevant provision of the draft Treaty was Article 47 according to which the Union was to have 'exclusive competence for trade between Member States' and complete free movement of goods was to be established within two years of the Treaty's coming into force.[3]

This was perhaps too ambitious a project, being in effect a blueprint for a federal Europe. However, the Parliament's initiative created a momentum which led ultimately to the Single European Act being signed by the Member States in February 1986. This Act is very different in content from the draft Treaty, which has now been consigned to the history books although it is likely to influence amendments made to the Treaties in the future.

13.03 Section II, subsection I of the Single European Act is entitled 'Internal market.' It begins by inserting into the Treaty of Rome a new provision, which bears the number Article 8A and which reads as follows:

> 'The Community shall adopt measures with the aim of progressively establishing the internal market over a period expiring on 31 December 1992, in accordance with the provisions of this Article and of Articles 8B, 8C, 28,

---

[1] [1987] O.J. L169/1, [1987] 2 C.M.L.R. 741.
[2] [1984] O.J. C77/23.
[3] See Bieber, Jacqué and Weiler *An Ever Closer Union* (1985), 110; Capotorti, Hilf, Jacobs and Jacqué *Le Traité d'union européenne* (1985), 180; *Der Vertrag zur Gründung der Europäischen Union* (1984), 171.

57(2), 59, 70(1), 83, 99, 100A and 100B and without prejudice to the other provisions of this Treaty.

The internal market shall comprise an area without internal frontiers in which the free movement of goods, persons, services and capital is ensured in accordance with the provisions of this Treaty.'

It is no coincidence that the deadline of 31 December 1992 is also that mentioned in the Commission's White Paper on the Internal Market[4] for implementing the programme set out in that document. Indeed, the Conference adopted a declaration on Article 8A expressing its 'firm political will' to take before 1 January 1993 the decisions necessary to complete the internal market as defined in Article 8A and more particularly the decisions necessary to implement the White Paper.

Pescatore[5] is highly critical of this provision: he regards it as reopening the initial transitional period which expired at the end of 1969 by virtue of Article 8 of the Treaty. Yet Ehlermann,[6] Jacqué[7] and Glaesner[8] are surely right to say that this is not in fact the effect of Article 8A at all, since it does not purport to undermine the Treaty provisions on the free movement of goods or their direct effect.[9] Also Article 8A is expressed to apply 'without prejudice to the other provisions of this Treaty.'

The declaration on Article 8A, which has already been referred to, concludes with the following statement:

'Setting the deadline of 31 December 1992 does not create an automatic legal effect.'

For the reasons set out in paragraph 13.27 below, the better view is that this statement is without binding effect and can at most be relied on as an aid to the interpretation of the Act. Even so, Article 8A surely relates only to restrictions which are justified under Article 36 or the mandatory requirements[10] and which therefore require Community legislation for their removal. If that is right, then by definition Article 8A cannot have direct effect. The maximum that could then be achieved in the event of a failure to meet the deadline of 31 December 1992 would be to obtain a declaration under Article 175 from the Court against the relevant Community institution.[11] Such an action was already brought with partial success by the Parliament against the Council in relation to the common transport

---

[4] Para. 12.19 above.
[5] 'Die "Einheitliche Europäische Akte"': Eine ernste Gefahr für den Gemeinsamen Markt' [1986] EuR 153 at 157.
[6] 'The Internal Market Following the Single European Act' [1987] C.M.L.Rev. 361.
[7] 'L'acte unique européen' [1986] R.T.D.E. 575 at 598.
[8] 'Die Einheitliche Europäische Akte' [1986] EuR 119 at 129.
[9] The same applies to the free movement of persons and the free provision of services, but the present discussion is confined to the free movement of goods.
[10] See para. 8.02 above.
[11] Glaesner op. cit. at 133; Ehlermann op. cit. at 372; contra Gulmann 'The Single European Act: Some Remarks from a Danish Perspective' [1987] C.M.L.Rev. 31 at 36.

policy[12] but to date the practical effects of the Court's judgment in that case are generally thought to have been somewhat limited.

13.04   Next, Article 8B provides:

'The Commission shall report to the Council before 31 December 1988 and again before 31 December 1990 on the progress made towards achieving the internal market within the time limit fixed in Article 8A.

The Council, acting by a qualified majority on a proposal from the Commission, shall determine the guidelines and conditions necessary to ensure balanced progress in all the sectors concerned.'

The first paragraph is complemented by Article 100B(1), which is set out below.

The reference in the second paragraph to 'balanced progress' is said to mean that progress in enacting legislation must not show a marked difference between the various sectors governed by the Act.[13] Nevertheless, it is doubtful whether any legal consequences would flow from a failure by the Council to 'determine the guidelines and conditions necessary,' especially as no deadline is set for this in Article 8B.

13.05   Article 8C reads:

'When drawing up its proposals with a view to achieving the objectives set out in Article 8A, the Commission shall take into account the extent of the effort that certain economies showing differences in development will have to sustain during the period of establishment of the internal market and it may propose appropriate provisions.

If these provisions take the form of derogations, they must be of a temporary nature and must cause the least possible disturbance to the functioning of the common market.'

This Article must be read together with Articles 130A and 130E which are discussed below. While it provides for a 'two-speed Europe,' it applies only until the end of 1992.[14] Clear words would be needed to provide for the principle of a 'two-speed Europe' on a permanent basis, constituting as it does a departure from the fundamental principle of the unity of Community law.

As Glaesner has pointed out,[15] the reference to 'economies' would appear to allow for different regions of the same Member State to be accorded different treatment. This view is borne out by Articles 130A and 130E which relate to regional policy.

Also it has been suggested[16] that Article 8C might perhaps relate only to legislation based on the Articles referred to in Article 8A.

---

[12] Case 13/83 *European Parliament* v. *E.C. Council* [1985] E.C.R. 513, [1986] 1 C.M.L.R. 138.
[13] Glaesner *op. cit.* at 130.
[14] Ehlermann, *op. cit.* at 373; Forwood and Clough 'The Single European Act and Free Movement—Legal Implications of the Provisions for the Completion of the Internal Market' [1986] E.L.Rev. 383 at 399.
[15] *Op. cit.* at 134.
[16] Forwood and Clough, *op. cit.* at 399.

Yet, this seems unlikely since the objectives set out in Article 8A can also be achieved on the basis of other Articles of the Treaty. Indeed, this is expressly recognised by the words '. . . without prejudice to the other provisions of this Treaty' in Article 8A.

13.06 For the present purposes the most important—and the most controversial—provision is Article 100A, which is in the following terms:

'1. By way of derogation from Article 100 and save where otherwise provided in this Treaty, the following provisions shall apply for the achievement of the objectives set out in Article 8A. The Council shall, acting by a qualified majority on a proposal from the Commission in co-operation with the European Parliament and the Economic and Social Committee, adopt the measures for the approximation of the provisions laid down by law, regulation or administrative action in Member States which have as their object the establishment and functioning of the internal market.

2. Paragraph 1 shall not apply to fiscal provisions, to those relating to the free movement of persons nor to those relating to the rights and interests of employed persons.

3. The Commission, in its proposals laid down in paragraph 1 concerning the health, safety, environmental protection and consumer protection, will take as a base a high level of protection.

4. If, after the adoption of a harmonisation measure by the Council acting by a qualified majority, a Member State deems it necessary to apply national provisions on grounds of major needs referred to in Article 36, or relating to protection of the environment or the working environment, it shall notify the Commission of these provisions.

The Commission shall confirm the provisions involved after having verified that they are not a means of arbitrary discrimination or a disguised restriction on trade between Member States.

By way of derogation from the procedure laid down in Articles 169 and 170, the Commission or any Member State may bring the matter directly before the Court of Justice if it considers that another Member State is making improper use of the powers provided for in this Article.

5. The harmonisation measures referred to above shall, in appropriate cases, include a safeguard clause authorising the Member States to take, for one or more of the non-economic reasons referred to in Article 36, provisional measures subject to a Community control procedure.'

13.07 The Article is more flexible than Article 100 in two respects: it enables the Council to act by a qualified majority; and it provides for the adoption of regulations as well as directives. However, the price for this is Article 100A(4). Moreover, one of the declarations adopted by the Conference and annexed to the Act states that:

'In its proposals pursuant to Article 100A(1) the Commission shall give precedence to the use of the instrument of a directive if harmonisation involves the amendment of legislative provisions in one or more Member States.'

For the reasons explained below, it is submitted that, like all the declarations annexed to the Act, this declaration is not binding and is at most an aid to the interpretation of the Single European Act.

In any case, the declaration does not purport to lay down an absolute obligation to propose a directive in the circumstances in

347

question, but merely to 'give precedence to that type of instrument.' Such a requirement is surely so vague as to be devoid of legal effect in any event.

At all events the words 'shall apply' in the opening sentence of paragraph 1 make it clear that, where this Article is applicable, the Council may not opt to base legislation on Article 100 instead.[17] This is quite understandable since Article 100 merely requires the Parliament to be consulted, whereas proposals based on Article 100A are subject to the new co-operation procedure with the Parliament set out in the new Article 149(2).

The phrase 'save where otherwise provided in this Treaty' in the initial sentence of Article 100A(1) is important. It follows from it that a particular regulation or directive, which could have been based on, say, Article 43 alone before the Act came into force, may still have precisely the same legal basis.

13.08 Paragraph 2 excludes three areas from the scope of Article 100A, presumably because the Member States regarded them as too sensitive to be subject to majority voting. None of those areas is relevant to this book.

Paragraph 3 has been described by Ehlermann[18] as 'hardly justiciable'; the requirement to 'take as a base a high level of protection' is, in all probability, too imprecise.

13.09 Article 100A(4), which was drafted by the Heads of State and Government themselves in the European Council[19] has been the subject of tremendous controversy.[20] This is because in certain circumstances it entitles a Member State to continue to impose a particular standard even after Community harmonising legislation has come into force. It is small wonder then that Members of the European Parliament have posed a written question asking the Council whether it agrees that this paragraph 'constitutes a threat to the achievement of a genuine single Community market' and 'could make the common market more compartmentalised than it is now'; in its answer[21] the Council did not wholly reject this suggestion. While Article 100A(4) is set about with certain conditions, these are not such as to quell such fears. It should be observed, however, that it would in no way be compatible with paragraph 4 for a regulation or directive itself to stipulate that 'certain Member States may opt out.'

---

[17] Ehlermann *op. cit.* at 382.

[18] *Op. cit.* at 389.

[19] Ehlermann *op. cit.* at 381.

[20] See *e.g.* Ehlermann *op. cit.* at 389; but Jacqué, *op. cit.* at 599, says that Art. 100A(4) is not a step back from the situation obtaining beforehand in practice; also see generally Edward 'The Impact of the Single Act on the Institutions' [1987] C.M.L.Rev. 19.

[21] Written question 1893/86 ([1987] O.J. C112/39); see also written question 1864/86.

Paragraph 4 applies solely to legislation based on Article 100A and then only if the Council has acted by a qualified majority.[22] Although the point is not free from doubt, it is conceivable that a Member State may rely on paragraph 4 even if it has voted in favour of the proposal concerned.[23] An analogy can be drawn here with *Italy* v. *E.C. Council*[24] where it was held that a Member State could bring an action under Article 173 despite having voted in favour of the contested act. If the converse view were to be taken, the Member State might be deterred from adopting legislation in the first place.

A further point of controversy is whether Article 100A(4) extends to Commission acts implementing Council legislation based on Article 100A. Gulmann[25] takes the view that it does, while the opposite view is advanced by Ehlermann[26]—except, of course, where the Member State has lawfully relied on paragraph 4 with respect to the Council legislation.

13.10 It is an open question whether paragraph 4 only permits Member States to maintain national provisions which were in force before the Community legislation was adopted; or whether it also empowers Member States to introduce fresh measures at a later stage. Forwood and Clough[27] suggest that the latter view may be correct, while Gulmann[28] and Flynn[29] come out unequivocally in favour of this view. Ehlermann[30] considers that the national measures must be taken 'before the Community harmonisation decision is implemented' and this appears to contemplate their being taken between the adoption of Community legislation and its entry into force. Also, he does not rule out a Member State relying on paragraph 4 to amend a measure which has been retained in accordance with that paragraph.[31]

13.11 Since the wording of paragraph 4 plainly leaves something to be desired, a too literal interpretation could lead to difficulties in practice. Common sense would suggest that the first two paragraphs must be taken together to mean that the national measures concerned must be justified under Article 36 or the mandatory

---

[22] Gulmann's suggestion (*op. cit.* at 37–38) that Art. 100A(4) may even be relied on where an act has been adopted by unanimous vote flies in the face of its express wording, as he himself admits. Under Art. 148(3) of the Treaty a vote is considered unanimous despite one or more abstentions.

[23] Ehlermann, *op. cit.* at 394, expresses uncertainty on this point.

[24] Case 166/78 (potato starch) [1979] E.C.R. 2575, [1981] 3 C.M.L.R. 770 ([1987] O.J. C191/22).

[25] *Op. cit.* at 38.

[26] *Op. cit.* at 390.

[27] *Op. cit.* at 399–400.

[28] *Op. cit.* at 38.

[29] 'How will Article 100A(4) work? A comparison with Article 93' [1987] C.M.L.Rev. 689 at 696.

[30] *Op. cit.* at 395.

[31] *Op. cit.* at 394.

requirements and that the Commission's task is to check that this is so. Nothing would be gained by applying different rules as to justification under paragraph 4 from those normally applicable and much confusion would ensue.

On this view, Article 36 is to be applied in the normal way despite the reference to 'major needs.' That term would then be read simply as a reminder that Article 36 cannot be invoked lightly; it would not be interpreted as precluding reliance on Article 36 for 'non-major needs.'

What is the meaning of the next limb of the first sub-paragraph ('relating to protection of the environment or the working environment')? This limb could conceivably be taken as a general reference to all the mandatory requirements recognised by the Court. There is no logical reason why the other mandatory requirements should not apply in this context. This is especially true of consumer protection which is mentioned in paragraph 3 but not in paragraph 4. Yet the fact remains that this paragraph does not refer to all the mandatory requirements and, constituting an exception to a general rule, should presumably be interpreted restrictively.[32] As to the term 'working environment,' Ehlermann[33] writes that it 'becomes really understandable when one reads the new Article 118A, where improvements in the working environment are clearly meant to promote health and safety of workers.'

By the same token, there appears to be no reason why the Commission's examination of the national measures should be confined to the question whether they are a means of arbitrary discrimination or a disguised restriction on trade between Member States, as the second paragraph would appear to suggest. It seems inconceivable that the Commission should be required to confirm measures which are unjustified for some other reason—especially where the grounds of justification relied on by the Member State are in truth economic.[34]

Similarly, there is every reason to believe that the normal principle as to burden of proof applies, namely that there is a presumption that a restriction on imports or exports is not justified.[35] In Pescatore's view,[36] the burden of proof is reversed under paragraph 4 and the Commission must therefore start from the presumption that the measure is justified. Yet there is nothing in the wording of paragraph 4 to suggest this. Clear wording would surely be required to reverse the burden of proof.

13.12 Even if the normal rules as to justification apply the fact remains that to a certain extent the Commission is required under

---

[32] Ehlermann *op. cit.* at 393.
[33] *Op. cit.* at 392.
[34] Para. 8.19 above.
[35] Para. 8.03 above.
[36] *Op. cit.* at 158.

Article 100A(4) to disregard the existence of Community legislation. The key question is: to what extent?

If the national standard is lower than the Community one, then plainly imports complying with the Community norm may not be required to meet it. In those circumstances the Commission may not confirm the national measure.

Where the national standard and the Community standard are different but equivalent the same applies: the national norm cannot be applied so as to restrict imports from other Member States complying with the Community regulation or directive concerned. There is nothing in paragraph 4 to oust the principle of equivalence.[37] Accordingly, the Commission may not confirm a national measure of this kind.

In contrast, where a Member State's standard is higher than that enshrined in Community legislation based on Article 100A, that State may require imports to meet its standard. Such a measure must be confirmed by the Commission. Only to this extent does paragraph 4 derogate from the normal rules.[38] Nevertheless the significance of this derogation cannot be underestimated.

13.13 As to procedure, the prevailing view[39] is that the act whereby the Commission confirms or refuses to confirm a national measure is in the nature of a decision and is not therefore analogous to a reasoned opinion under Article 169.

On this view, the Commission's act may take effect immediately, before the Court's judgment, and can be relied on by private parties before national courts. The same reasoning leads to the conclusion that the Commission's confirmation or refusal to confirm a national measure is subject to review by the Court under Article 173 of the Treaty.[40] Naturally this does not prevent a party from challenging the Commission's decision before the national courts, which would then refer the matter in the normal way to the Court of Justice under Article 177.

13.14 The confirmation procedure under paragraph 4 is somewhat analogous to that laid down in Article 93(3) of the Treaty in relation to new State aids.[41] Article 93(3) does not stipulate precisely how long the Commission may take to conduct an initial examination of a notified State aid, but in *Lorenz* v. *Germany*[42] it was held that a

---

[37] Para. 6.55 above.

[38] Even under the normal rules, the Court has been known to go to great lengths to find that Community legislation did not afford exhaustive guarantees: Case 72/83 *Campus Oil* v. *Ministry for Industry and Energy* [1984] E.C.R. 2727, [1984] 3 C.M.L.R. 544, para. 8.16 above.

[39] Ehlermann *op. cit.* at 397–398 and see n. 40 below.

[40] Flynn *op. cit.* at 702; Forwood and Clough *op. cit.* at 403, Glaesner *op. cit.* at 135, Jacqué *op. cit.* at 600.

[41] See generally Flynn *op. cit.*

[42] Case 120/73 [1973] E.C.R. 1471.

Member State may implement an aid scheme if the Commission has not informed it of its position within two months of notification, provided that the Member State gives prior notice to the Commission of its intention to implement the aid.[43] The same principles may well be applicable here.[44]

13.15 The wording of the third sub-paragraph also raises a number of questions. It does not state at what stage this action must be lodged with the Court. Although this is not expressly stipulated, common sense would suggest that the Commission must first formally decide to refuse to confirm the national measure and inform the Member State of the decision. Moreover, if the Member State complies with the decision at that stage, the Commission need not bring the matter before the Court at all.

In contrast, it would appear to be open to another Member State to commence proceedings before the Court without waiting for the Commission to decide whether to confirm the national measure. There seems to be no reason to make the rights of action of Member States dependent on the course of events within the Commission.

If the Commission confirms the measure of one Member State but another Member State objects, the latter State would appear to be faced with a choice: it can seek the annulment of the Commission decision under Article 173; it can bring an action under the third sub-paragraph against the Member State whose measure it contests; or it can do both. It is probably open to the dissatisfied State to bring an action under the third sub-paragraph even after the date for bringing annulment proceedings under Article 173 has expired.[45]

Flynn[46] has suggested that the action under the third sub-paragraph is not available where a Member State has failed to notify its provisions altogether. This, he says, would amount to a concession that a Member State has a 'power' not to notify provisions. Yet it must not be overlooked that on this view a Member State which failed to notify provisions would gain time, since the Commission would have to send the Article 169 letter and the reasoned opinion before involving the Court (or, in the case of an action commenced by another Member State, the administrative procedure set out in Article 170 would first have to be followed). Under Article 100A(4)

---

[43] There are, however, suggestions that the two-month rule will not be applicable to every case: see para. 15 of the judgment in Case 84/82 *Germany* v. *E.C. Commission* [1984] E.C.R. 1451, [1985] 1 C.M.L.R. 153 and A.G. Slynn in Case 223/85 *RSV* v. *E.C. Commission* (judgment of 24 November 1987).

[44] Gulmann, *op. cit.* at 39, goes so far as to suggest the Commission approval need not be forthcoming before the measure is brought into force. He contrasts the wording of para. 4 with that of Arts. 93(3) and 115 of the Treaty. Yet that would surely undermine the approval procedure; see Flynn *op. cit.* at 695. The fact that para. 4 is less clear on this point than Arts. 93(3) and 115 may simply be due to inadequate drafting.

[45] See generally Case 216/82 *Universität Hamburg* v. *Hauptzollamt Hamburg Kehrwieder* [1983] E.C.R. 2771.

[46] *Op. cit.* at 701.

the only step which the Commission need take before lodging its action with the Court is to adopt the decision provided for in that paragraph and this could be done relatively speedily. A Member State which fails to abide by the procedural requirements of this paragraph surely forfeits the right to the procedural guarantees. On the other hand, as explained in paragraph 13.17 below, it will not always be clear whether national provisions need be notified. Perhaps then the Commission has a choice in respect of unnotified measures: it may either commence proceedings directly before the Court under Article 100A(4) or it may follow the procedure under Article 169. A Member State would then also be able to choose between Article 100A(4) and Article 170.

13.16 In view of the analogy with Article 93(3) relating to State aids, it would seem that failure by a Member State to notify a measure in accordance with paragraph 4 renders that measure illegal and that illegality may be relied on by individuals before national courts.[47] In that case the national court must apply the Community regulation or directive and not the illegal national measure. The same probably applies where the Member State has notified its measure but has brought it into force before the end of the two-month period. It is also conceivable that the same applies even after the expiry of the two-month period where the Member State has failed to give prior notice to the Commission of its intention to implement the measure.

As already mentioned, it would appear that the act whereby the Commission confirms or refuses to confirm a national measure is a decision having direct effect.

13.17 It will not always be clear whether a particular national measure has to be notified or not. To take a purely hypothetical example, a regulation might be adopted under Article 100A harmonising standards for building materials. The regulation might relate to the inflammability of the materials, their ability to take certain types of strain and so on, but might say nothing about their resistance to earthquakes. If a Member State deems it necessary to lay down standards for domestic and imported building materials with regard to resistence to earthquakes, is it bound to notify its measure under paragraph 4? This is a crucial question, but no general answer can be given to it. The answer in each case will turn on the scope of the regulation concerned. If it purports to cover all types of standards for building materials then paragraph 4 undoubtedly applies. On the other hand, if it only covers standards relating to certain types of danger but not earthquakes, then paragraph 4 does not apply. In practice, it will not always be easy to distinguish between the two.

---

[47] See *Lorenz*, n. 42 above. Forwood and Clough *op. cit.* at 403.

13.18   Paragraph 5 provides for harmonisation measures to contain safeguard clauses of a type which is already common.[48] It does not entail any change in practice. Glaesner[49] has expressed the view that, where a regulation or directive contains such a safeguard clause, Member States may not have recourse to paragraph 4, while Gulmann[50] takes the opposite view.

13.19   Will Article 100A continue to constitute a valid legal basis for fresh legislation after 1992? Glaesner[51] maintains that it will. He cites *European Parliament* v. *E.C. Council*,[52] where it was held that the Council had failed to fulfil its duties under Article 75 relating to the common transport policy in that it had not adopted the requisite legislation by the end of the transitional period. In his view it was tacitly assumed by the Court that such legislation could still be adopted on the basis of Article 75. He concludes that Article 100A will not lapse on 31 December 1992, the deadline set by Article 8A for adopting the relevant legislation.

If Article 100A does lapse at the end of 1992, then amendments to legislation adopted on that basis prior to that date will have to be based on Article 100 or perhaps some other provision of the Treaty.

13.20   For completeness it should be mentioned that Denmark has made the following declaration on Article 100A, which is annexed to the Act:

> 'The Danish Government notes that, in cases where a Member State is of the opinion that measures adopted under Article 100A do not safeguard higher requirements concerning the working environment, the protection of the environment or the needs referred to in Article 36, the provisions of Article 100A(4) guarantee that the Member State in question can apply national provisions. Such national provisions are to be taken to fulfil the abovementioned aim and may not entail hidden protectionism.'

It is not at all clear what this declaration is intended to achieve but for the reasons explained below it does not seem that it has any value in law.

13.21   Article 100B reads:

> 1. During 1992, the Commission shall, together with each Member State, draw up an inventory of national laws, regulations and administrative provisions which fall under Article 100A and which have not been harmonised pursuant to that Article.

---

[48] Para. 12.08.
[49] *Op. cit.* at 134.
[50] *Op. cit.* at 38; similarly Ehlermann *op. cit.* at 399. Jacqué (*op. cit.* at 599–600) leaves the point open.
[51] *Op. cit.* at 133.
[52] N. 12 above.

The Council, acting in accordance with the provisions of Article 100A, may decide that the provisions in force in a Member State must be recognised as being equivalent to those applied by another Member State.

2. The provisions of Article 100A(4) shall apply by analogy.

3. The Commission shall draw up the inventory referred to in the first subparagraph of paragraph 1 and shall submit appropriate proposals in good time to allow the Council to act before the end of 1992.'

This is supplemented by a declaration of the Conference in the following terms:

'The Conference considers that, since Article 8C of the EEC Treaty is of general application, it also applies to the proposals which the Commission is required to make under Article 100B of that Treaty.'

13.22 The meaning of the second sub-paragraph of Article 100B(1) is unclear. Legislation of the kind referred to there could in any case be adopted on the basis of Article 100 or Article 100A as the case may be. In these circumstances, does the second sub-paragraph of Article 100B(1) mean that such legislation cannot be adopted under Article 100A until 1992? Or that it may not be adopted at all until 1992? If not, what is the meaning of this provision?

In Ehlermann's view[53] Article 100B does not rule out the adoption of decisions requiring the recognition of national provisions before 1992. Indeed, he regards this provision as being otiose.

At all events, it seems clear that this sub-paragraph does not prevent the Court of Justice and the national courts from continuing to apply the principle of equivalence.[54] Firstly, there is no logical reason why, by conferring this power on the Council, Article 100B(1) should be taken to deprive the courts of the power to recognise different standards as equivalent to one another, as they have done in the past. This is all the more so since, as already mentioned, this provision merely sets out in express terms a power which the Council already enjoyed under Article 100. The rôle of the Council in adopting decisions on equivalence will therefore be to create greater legal certainty and facilitate the task of the courts. Secondly, Article 8A provides that the objectives of the internal market are to be achieved 'without prejudice to the other provisions of the Treaty,' which includes the Court's case law on the principle of equivalence in Article 30.

Another point of difficulty is whether equivalence decisions adopted by the Council may relate to national measures which have lawfully been confirmed by the Commission under Article 100A(4).

Finally, Article 100B(2) presents some difficulty: once the Council has decided that certain specified national standards are equivalent to one another, how can a Member State lawfully claim under Article 100A(4) that its standard is in fact higher? Logically one

---

[53] *Op. cit.* at 402.
[54] Forwood and Clough *op. cit.* at 402; for the contrary suggestion, see Pescatore *op. cit.* at 159. On the principle of equivalence, see para. 6.55 *et seq.*

would have thought that the only way in which a Member State could advance such a claim would be by contesting the Council's decision under Article 173. Forwood and Clough have therefore suggested[55] that Article 100B(2) may well apply to national measures adopted after the Council's decision.

13.23   According to Article 118A(1), 'Member States shall pay particular attention to encouraging improvements, especially in the working environment, as regards the health and safety of workers . . .' The meaning of 'the working environment' has already been discussed in paragraph 13.11 above. On any view, this term would appear to be wider than 'the health and safety of workers.' If that is so, then the words 'especially in the working environment' seem to make little sense. The phrase 'improvement in the working environment, especially as regards the health and safety of workers' would surely have been far more logical.

Article 118A(2) provides for directives—though not regulations—to be adopted by the Council 'in order to help achieve the objective laid down in the first paragraph.' Such directives are to be adopted according to the same procedure as under Article 100A: the Council is to act by qualified majority on a proposal from the Commission, in co-operation with the Parliament and after consulting the Economic and Social Committee. A major difference from Article 100A is that the directives based on Article 118A are merely to lay down 'minimal requirements for gradual implementation.'

There is no provision equivalent to Article 100A(4). However, Article 118A(3) stipulates: 'The provisions adopted pursuant to this Article shall not prevent any Member State from maintaining or introducing more stringent measures for the protection of working conditions compatible with this Treaty.'

It could perhaps be argued that Article 118A(2) is the proper legal basis for health and safety standards for goods used exclusively or almost exclusively in the workplace, such as tools and industrial machines. In that case, Article 100A could not be used as a legal basis for such legislation, since it is expressed to apply 'save where otherwise provided in this Treaty.'

13.24   The Act also adds to the Treaty Articles 130A to 130E, which are entitled 'economic and social cohesion.' The first of these Articles states that the Community shall strengthen its 'economic and social cohesion' in particular by 'reducing disparities between the various regions and the backwardness of the least favoured regions.' Article 130B begins: 'Member States shall conduct their economic policies and shall co-ordinate them, in such a way as, in addition, to attain the objectives set out in Article 130. The

---

[55] *Op. cit.* at 404.

implementation of the common policies and of the internal market shall take into account the objectives set out in Article 130A and in Article 130C and shall contribute to their achievement.' In view of the case law of the Court on Article 36 and Articles 103 to 105[56] it is absolutely clear that Article 130B creates no exception to Articles 30 and 34.

13.25   Articles 130R and 130T relate to the environment. Hitherto environmental legislation has been based on Article 235 but recourse to that Article for such legislation is now ousted by these new provisions. Article 130R(1) states:

'Action by the Community relating to the environment shall have the following objectives:
    (i) to preserve, protect and improve the quality of the environment;
   (ii) to contribute towards protecting human health;
  (iii) to ensure a prudent and rational utilisation of natural resources.'

The procedural and substantive requirements laid down for legislation in this field are markedly different from those in Article 100A. Thus, according to Article 130R(4) 'the Community shall take action relating to the environment to the extent to which the objectives referred to in paragraph 1 can be better attained at Community level than at the level of the individual Member States.' This appears to be a step backwards.[57] Also under Article 130S the Parliament is merely to be consulted on draft legislation on the environment and a unanimous vote of the Council is required, unless the Council has previously chosen by unanimous decision to act by qualified majority on the matter concerned. Again, Article 130T is the same *mutatis mutandis* as Article 118A(3).

To what extent environmental legislation concerning the free movement of goods is to be adopted on the basis of Article 130S rather than Article 100A is unclear.[58] In Ehlermann's view,[59] Article 100A is the provision specifically concerned with realising the objectives laid down in Article 8A and requirements concerning goods must therefore always be based on Article 100A rather than on Article 130S.

13.26   It remains only to discuss the nature of the various declarations appended to the Act. The first eleven of these declarations are stated to have been 'adopted' by the Conference 'at the time of signing this text' and to be 'annexed to this Final Act.' The declaration on Article 8A that 'setting the date of 31 December 1992 does not create an automatic legal effect' falls within this group; so does the declaration on Article 100A that 'the Commission shall give precedence to the use

---

[56] As to Art. 36, see para. 8.19; as to Arts. 103 and 104, see paras. 9.04 to 9.13.
[57] Glaesner *op. cit.* at 140–141.
[58] See generally Glaesner *op. cit.* at 131; Krämer 'The Single European Act and Environment Protection: Reflections on Several New Provisions in Community Law' [1987] C.M.L.Rev. 659.
[59] *Op. cit.* at 383.

of the instrument of a directive if harmonisation involves the amendment of legislative provisions in one or more Member States.' A further
9 declarations are simply 'noted' by the Conference and 'annexed to
this Final Act.' These are all unilateral declarations most of which have
been made by the Presidency, the Commission or the Government of
a Member State; one declaration has been made by the Governments
of all the Member States while another has been made jointly by the
President and the Commission. The Danish Government's Declaration
in Article 100A falls within this group.

13.27 Pescatore[60] and Toth[61] both take the view that, in determining
the legal value of any of these declarations, one must have regard to
international law as well as Community law. From an international
legal analysis Toth concludes that 'none of the twenty Declarations
amounts to a reservation *stricto sensu*' and this also appears to be
Pescatore's view.

Toth also refers to the requirement in Article 236 of the Treaty of
Rome that amendments to that Treaty be determined 'by common
accord.' He deduces from this that, if the unilateral declarations which
purport to restrict or amend some of the effects of the Act were
binding, that would entail the invalidity of the Act itself!

Surely the crucial part of his reasoning is the finding that none of
the declarations has been ratified. The declarations are not incorporated
into the Act by any provision corresponding to Article 239 of the
Treaty of Rome, according to which 'the Protocols annexed to this
Treaty by common accord of the Member States shall form an integral
part thereof.' Also, Article 33 of the Act provides that 'the Act will
be ratified by the High Contracting Parties' without mentioning the
declarations. Toth then goes on to find that the declarations cannot
be taken into account at all by the Court in interpreting the Act. He
bases this view on Article 31 which stipulates that 'the provisions of
. . . the Treaty establishing the European Economic Community . . .
concerning the powers of the Court of Justice of the European
Communities and the exercise of those powers shall apply only to the
provisions of Title II and to Article 32.' He therefore concludes that
none of the 20 declarations has any legal force whatever and that the
Court may not even take them into account in interpreting the Act.[62]

---

[60] *Op. cit.* at 167.
[61] 'The Legal Status of the Declarations Annexed to the Single European Act' [1986]
C.M.L.Rev. 803 *passim*.
[62] It is submitted that Toth's argument based on Art. 31 is open to question. Art. 31 does
not provide that the jurisdiction of the Court relates to Art. 31 itself! Yet common sense
suggests that it must. This means that Art. 31 is not to be interpreted too narrowly. In any
event, the Court may consider instruments which it has no jurisdiction to interpret as such:
see generally Case 44/84 *Hurd* v. *Jones* [1986] E.C.R. 29, [1986] 2 C.M.L.R. 1. Moreover,
Art. 31 says nothing of national courts: it seems inconceivable that the Court of Justice
cannot take the declarations into account if the national courts may.
Accordingly, if it is true that the declarations cannot be taken into account by the courts
at all, then that principle must rest on some basis other than Art. 31.

Glaesner[63] shares Toth's view that the declarations have not been ratified. He also considers that one may not have regard to the 9 unilateral declarations in interpreting the Act. On the other hand, he propounds the view that the 11 declarations adopted by the Conference may be taken into account for this purpose. Similarly, Ehlermann[64] states that 'the declarations made by the Intergovernmental Conference were designed as aids to interpretation and should be used as such' while 'the unilateral declarations by individual Member States . . . have no place in interpretation.'

13.28 In conclusion, while the Single European Act leaves Articles 30 to 36 intact, it has major implications for Community legislation relating to the free movement of goods.

---

[63] *Op. cit.* at 122–123.
[64] *Op. cit.* at 367.

CHAPTER XIV

Conclusion

In 1982 when the first edition of this book appeared, few would have predicted the publication of the Commission's White Paper on Completing the Internal Market and the adoption of the Single European Act. These two developments may account in part for the fact that—contrary to the expectations of some observers—the Court has not withdrawn from its broad interpretation of Article 30 in *Cassis de Dijon*.[1] On the contrary, it has repeatedly confirmed that judgment, notably in such important and sensitive cases as *E.C. Commission* v. *Germany* (beer)[2], *E.C. Commission* v. *France* (substitute milk powder)[3] and *Zoni*.[4]

On the other hand, in view of the vast number of cases relating to Articles 30 to 36 decided since 1982, it would be surprising if there were not one or two instances in which the Court has taken a step back: *Campus Oil*[5] and *Tezi Textiel*[6] are undoubtedly cases in point.

Naturally, a number of important matters remain to be decided. Thus the Court may soon have to settle the most delicate issue of whether the effect of certain measures on imports is not so remote or so tenuous that they are not caught by Article 30 at all.[7] Moreover, although the Court has decided a number of cases relating to Article 34, the scope of that provision has not yet been fully clarified. Yet probably the greatest challenge which may face the Court in the coming years is the Single European Act and notably Article 100(4). Whether that provision can be used by Member States as a major obstacle to completing the internal market may depend to a considerable extent on the Court.

---

[1] Case 120/78 [1979] E.C.R. 649, [1979] 3 C.M.L.R. 494, para. 6.40 *et seq.* above.
[2] Case 178/84 [1988] 1 C.M.L.R. 780.
[3] Case 216/84 (judgment of 23 February 1988).
[4] Case 90/86 (judgment of 14 July 1988) relating to pasta made from soft wheat.
[5] Case 72/83 [1984] E.C.R. 2727, [1984] 3 C.M.L.R. 544.
[6] Cases 59 and 242/84 [1986] E.C.R. 887, [1987] 3 C.M.L.R. 64.
[7] See para. 6.46 above.

ANNEXE I

Cases and materials

COMMISSION DIRECTIVE OF 22 DECEMBER 1969[*]

based on the provisions of Article 33(7), on the abolition of measures which have an effect equivalent to quantitative restrictions on imports and are not covered by other provisions adopted in pursuance of the EEC Treaty

(70/50/EEC)

THE COMMISSION OF THE EUROPEAN COMMUNITIES,

Having regard to the provisions of the Treaty establishing the European Economic Community, and in particular Article 33(7) thereof,

Whereas for the purpose of Article 30 *et seq.* 'measures' means laws, regulations, administrative provisions, administrative practices, and all instruments issuing from a public authority, including recommendations;

Whereas for the purposes of this Directive 'administrative practices' means any standard and regularly followed procedure of a public authority; whereas 'recommendations' means any instruments issuing from a public authority which, while not legally binding on the addressees thereof, cause them to pursue a certain conduct;

Whereas the formalities to which imports are subject do not as a general rule have an effect equivalent to that of quantitative restrictions and, consequently, are not covered by this Directive;

Whereas certain measures adopted by Member States, other than those applicable equally to domestic and imported products, which were operative at the date of entry into force of the Treaty and are not covered by other provisions adopted in pursuance of the Treaty, either preclude importation or make it more difficult or costly than the disposal of domestic production;

Whereas such measures must be considered to include those which make access of imported products to the domestic market, at any marketing stage, subject to a condition which is not laid down for domestic products or to a condition differing from that laid down for domestic products, and more difficult to satisfy, so that a burden is thus placed on imported products only;

Whereas such measures must also be considered to include those which, at any marketing stage, grant to domestic products a preference, other than an aid, to which conditions may or may not be attached, and where such measures totally or partially preclude the disposal of imported products;

Whereas such measures hinder imports which could otherwise take place, and thus have an effect equivalent to quantitative restrictions on imports;

Whereas effects on the free movement of goods of measures which relate to the marketing of products and which apply equally to domestic and imported products are not as a general rule equivalent to those of quantitative restrictions, since such effects are normally inherent in the disparities between rules applied by Member States in this respect;

---

[*] [1970] O.J. L13/29.

361

Whereas, however, such measures may have a restrictive effect on the free movement of goods over and above that which is intrinsic to such rules;

Whereas such is the case where imports are either precluded or made more difficult or costly than the disposal of domestic production and where such effect is not necessary for the attainment of an objective within the scope of the powers for the regulation of trade left to Member States by the Treaty; whereas such is in particular the case where the said objective can be attained just as effectively by other means which are less of a hindrance to trade; whereas such is also the case where the restrictive effect of these provisions on the free movement of goods is out of proportion to their purpose;

Whereas these measures accordingly have an effect equivalent to that of quantitative restrictions on imports;

Whereas the customs union cannot be achieved without the abolition of such measures having an equivalent effect to quantitative restrictions on imports;

Whereas Member States must abolish all measures having equivalent effect by the end of the transitional period at the latest, even if no Commission Directive expressly requires them to do so;

Whereas the provisions concerning the abolition of quantitative restrictions and measures having equivalent effect between Member States apply both to products originating in and exported by Member States and to products originating in third countries and put into free circulation in the other Member States;

Whereas Article 33(7) does not apply to measures of the kind referred to which fall under other provisions of the Treaty, and in particular those which fall under Articles 37(1) and 44 of the Treaty or form an integral part of a national organisation of an agricultural market;

Whereas Article 33(7) does not apply to the charges and taxation referred to in Article 12 *et seq.* and Article 95 *et seq.* or to the aids mentioned in Article 92;

Whereas the provisions of Article 33(7) do not prevent the application, in particular, of Articles 36 and 223;

HAS ADOPTED THIS DIRECTIVE:

Article 1

The purpose of this Directive is to abolish the measures referred to in Articles 2 and 3, which were operative at the date of entry into force of the EEC Treaty.

Article 2

1. This Directive covers measures, other than those applicable equally to domestic or imported products, which hinder imports which could otherwise take place, including measures which make importation more difficult or costly than the disposal of domestic production.

2. In particular, it covers measures which make imports or the disposal, at any marketing stage, of imported products subject to a condition—other than a formality—which is required in respect of imported products only, or a condition differing from that required for domestic products and more difficult to satisfy. Equally, it covers, in particular, measures which favour domestic products or grant them a preference, other than an aid, to which conditions may or may not be attached.

3. The measures referred to must be taken to include those measures which:
   (a) lay down, for imported products only, minimum or maximum prices below or above which imports are prohibited, reduced or made subject to conditions liable to hinder importation;
   (b) lay down less favourable prices for imported products than for domestic products;
   (c) fix profit margins or any other price components for imported products

only or fix these differently for domestic products and for imported products, to the detriment of the latter;

(d) preclude any increase in the price of the imported product corresponding to the supplementary costs and charges inherent in importation;

(e) fix the prices of products solely on the basis of the cost price or the quality of domestic products at such a level as to create a hindrance to importation;

(f) lower the value of an imported product, in particular by causing a reduction in its intrinsic value, or increase its costs;

(g) make access of imported products to the domestic market conditional upon having an agent or representative in the territory of the importing Member State;

(h) lay down conditions of payment in respect of imported products only, or subject imported products to conditions which are different from those laid down for domestic products and more difficult to satisfy;

(i) require, for imports only, the giving of guarantees or making of payments on account;

(j) subject imported products only to conditions, in respect, in particular of shape, size, weight, composition, presentation, identification or putting up, or subject imported products to conditions which are different from those for domestic products and more difficult to satisfy;

(k) hinder the purchase by private individuals of imported products only, or encourage, require or give preference to the purchase of domestic products only;

(l) totally or partially preclude the use of national facilities or equipment in respect of imported products only, or totally or partially confine the use of such facilities or equipment to domestic products only;

(m) prohibit or limit publicity in respect of imported products only, or totally or partially confine publicity to domestic products only;

(n) prohibit, limit or require stocking in respect of imported products only; totally or partially confine the use of stocking facilities to domestic products only, or make the stocking of imported products subject to conditions which are different from those required for domestic products and more difficult to satisfy;

(o) make importation subject to the granting of reciprocity by one or more Member States;

(p) prescribe that imported products are to conform, totally or partially, to rules other than those of the importing country;

(q) specify time limits for imported products which are insufficient or excessive in relation to the normal course of the various transactions to which these time limits apply;

(r) subject imported products to controls [or], other than those inherent in the customs clearance procedure, to which domestic products are not subject or which are stricter in respect of imported products than they are in respect of domestic products, without this being necessary in order to ensure equivalent protection;

(s) confine names which are not indicative of origin or source to domestic products only.

Article 3

This directive also covers measures governing the marketing of products which deal, in particular, with shape, size, weight, composition, presentation, identification or putting up and which are equally applicable to domestic and imported products, where the restrictive effect of such measures on the free movement of goods exceeds the effects intrinsic to trade rules.

This is the case, in particular, where:
— the restrictive effects on the free movement of goods are out of proportion to their purpose;
— the same objective can be attained by other means which are less of a hindrance to trade.

Article 4

1. Member States shall take all necessary steps in respect of products which must be allowed to enjoy free movement pursuant to Articles 9 and 10 of the Treaty to abolish measures having an effect equivalent to quantitative restrictions on imports and covered by this Directive.

2. Member States shall inform the Commission of measures taken pursuant to this Directive.

Article 5

1. This Directive does not apply to measures:
 (a) which fall under Article 37(1) of the EEC Treaty;
 (b) which are referred to in Article 44 of the EEC Treaty or form an integral part of a national organisation of an agricultural market not yet replaced by a common organisation.

2. This Directive shall apply without prejudice to the application, in particular, of Articles 36 and 223 of the EEC Treaty.

Article 6

This Directive is addressed to the Member States.

Done at Brussels, 22 December 1969.

For the Commission
The President
Jean REY

Communication from the Commission concerning the consequences of the judgment given by the Court of Justice on 20 February 1979 in Case 120/78 ('Cassis de Dijon')**

The following is the text of a letter which has been sent to the Member States; the European Parliament and the Council have also been notified of it.

In the Commission's Communication of 6 November 1978 on 'Safeguarding free trade within the Community', it was emphasized that the free movement of goods is being affected by a growing number of restrictive measures.

The judgment delivered by the Court of Justice on 20 February 1979 in Case 120/78 (the *Cassis de Dijon* case), and recently reaffirmed in the judgment of 26 June 1980 in Case 788/79, has given the Commission some interpretative guidance enabling it to monitor more strictly the application of the Treaty rules on the free movement of goods, particularly Articles 30 to 36 of the EEC Treaty.

The Court gives a very general definition of the barriers to free trade which are prohibited by the provisions of Article 30 *et seq.* of the EEC Treaty. These are taken to include 'any national measure capable of hindering, directly or indirectly, actually or potentially, intra-Community trade'.

In its judgment of 20 February 1979 the Court indicates the scope of this definition as it applies to technical and commercial rules.

Any product lawfully produced and marketed in one Member State must, in principle, be admitted to the market of any other Member State.

Technical and commercial rules, even those equally applicable to national and imported products, may create barriers to trade only where those rules are necessary to satisfy mandatory requirements and to serve a purpose which is in the general interest and for which they are an essential guarantee. This purpose must be such as to take precedence over the requirements of the free movement of goods, which constitutes one of the fundamental rules of the Community.

The conclusions in terms of policy which the Commission draws from this new guidance are set out below.

— Whereas Member States may, with respect to domestic products and in the absence of relevant Community provisions, regulate the terms on which such products are marketed, the case is different for products imported from other Member States.

Any product imported from another Member State must in principle be admitted to the territory of the importing Member State if it has been lawfully produced, that is, conforms to rules and processes of manufacture that are customarily and traditionally accepted in the exporting country, and is marketed in the territory of the latter.

This principle implies that Member States, when drawing up commercial or technical rules liable to affect the free movement of goods, may not take an exclusively national viewpoint and take account only of requirements confined to domestic products. The proper functioning of the common market demands that each Member State also gives consideration to the legitimate requirements of the other Member States.

— Only under very strict conditions does the Court accept exceptions to this principle; barriers to trade resulting from differences between commercial and technical rules are only admissible:

— if the rules are necessary, that is appropriate and not excessive, in order to satisfy mandatory requirements (public health, protection of consumers or the environment, the fairness of commercial transactions, etc.);

— if the rules serve a purpose in the general interest which is compelling enough to justify an exception to a fundamental rule of the Treaty such as the free movement of goods;

** [1980] O.J. C256/2.

— if the rules are essential for such a purpose to be attained, *i.e.* are the means which are the most appropriate and at the same time least hinder trade.

The Court's interpretation has induced the Commission to set out a number of guidelines.

— The principles deduced by the Court imply that a Member State may not in principle prohibit the sale in its territory of a product lawfully produced and marketed in another Member State even if the product is produced according to technical or quality requirements which differ from those imposed on its domestic products. Where a product 'suitably and satisfactorily' fulfils the legitimate objective of a Member State's own rules (public safety, protection of the consumer or the environment, etc.), the importing country cannot justify prohibiting its sale in its territory by claiming that the way it fulfils the objective is different from that imposed on domestic products.

In such a case, an absolute prohibition of sale could not be considered 'necessary' to satisfy a 'mandatory requirement' because it would not be an 'essential guarantee' in the sense defined in the Court's judgment.

The Commission will therefore have to tackle a whole body of commercial rules which lay down that products manufactured and marketed in one Member State must fulfil technical or qualitative conditions in order to be admitted to the market of another and specifically in all cases where the trade barriers occasioned by such rules are inadmissible according to the very strict criteria set out by the Court.

The Commission is referring in particular to rules covering the composition, designation, presentation and packaging of products as well as rules requiring compliance with certain technical standards.

— The Commission's work of harmonization will henceforth have to be directed mainly at national laws having an impact on the functioning of the common market where barriers to trade to be removed arise from national provisions which are admissible under the criteria set by the Court.

The Commission will be concentrating on sectors deserving priority because of their economic relevance to the creation of a single internal market.

To forestall later difficulties, the Commission will be informing Member States of potential objections, under the terms of Community law, to provisions they may be considering introducing which come to the attention of the Commission.

It will be producing suggestions soon on the procedures to be followed in such cases.

The Commission is confident that this approach will secure greater freedom of trade for the Community's manufacturers, so strengthening the industrial base of the Community, while meeting the expectations of consumers.

Case 8/74 *Procureur du Roi* v. *Dassonville*
[1974] E.C.R. 837 at 852, [1974] 2 C.M.L.R. 436 at 453

5. All trading rules enacted by Member States which are capable of hindering, directly or indirectly, actually or potentially, intra-Community trade are to be considered as measures having an effect equivalent to quantitative restrictions.

Case 104/75 *Officier van Justitie* v. *De Peijper*
[1976] E.C.R. 613 at 635–636, [1976] 2 C.M.L.R. 271 at 304

4. National measures of the kind in question have an effect equivalent to a quantitative restriction and are prohibited under Article 30 of the Treaty if they are likely to constitute an obstacle, directly or indirectly, actually or potentially, to imports between Member States.

Rules or practices which result in imports being channelled in such a way that only certain traders can effect these imports, whereas others are prevented from doing so, constitute such an obstacle to imports. . . .

16. Nevertheless, it emerges from Article 36 that national rules or practices which do restrict imports of pharmaceutical products or are capable of doing so are only compatible with the Treaty to the extent to which they are necessary for the effective protection of health and life of humans.

17. National rules or practices do not fall within the exception specified in Article 36 if the health and life of humans can be as effectively protected by measures which do not restrict intra-Community trade so much.

Case 120/78 *Rewe-Zentral AG* v. *Bundesmonopolverwaltung für Branntwein* (*Cassis de Dijon*)
[1979] E.C.R. 649 at 662–664, [1979] 3 C.M.L.R. 494 at 508

8. In the absence of common rules relating to the production and marketing of alcohol—a proposal for a regulation submitted to the Council by the Commission on 7 December 1976 (Official Journal C309, p. 2) not yet having received the Council's approval—it is for the Member States to regulate all matters relating to the production and marketing of alcohol and alcoholic beverages on their own territory.

Obstacles to movement within the Community resulting from disparities between the national laws relating to the marketing of the products in question must be accepted in so far as those provisions may be recognised as being necessary in order to satisfy mandatory requirements relating in particular to the effectiveness of fiscal supervision, the protection of public health, the fairness of commercial transactions and the defence of the consumer. . . .

It is clear from the foregoing that the requirements relating to the minimum alcohol content of alcoholic beverages do not serve a purpose which is in the general interest and such as to take precedence over the requirements of the free movement of goods, which constitutes one of the fundamental rules of the Community.

In practice, the principal effect of requirements of this nature is to promote alcoholic beverages having a high alcohol content by excluding from the national market products of other Member States which do not answer that description.

It therefore appears that the unilateral requirement imposed by the rules of a Member State of a minimum alcohol content for the purposes of the sale of alcoholic beverages constitutes an obstacle to trade which is incompatible with the provisions of Article 30 of the Treaty.

There is therefore no valid reason why, provided that they have been lawfully produced and marketed in one of the Member States, alcoholic beverages should not be introduced into any other Member State; the sale of such products may not be subject to a legal prohibition on the marketing of beverages with an alcohol content lower than the limit set by the national rules.

Consequently, the first question should be answered to the effect that.the concept of 'measures having an effect equivalent to quantitative restrictions on imports'

ANNEXE I

contained in Article 30 of the Treaty is to be understood to mean that the fixing of a minimum alcohol content for alcoholic beverages intended for human consumption by the legislation of a Member State also falls within the prohibition laid down in that provision where the importation of alcoholic beverages lawfully produced and marketed in another Member State is concerned.

ANNEXE II

Table of Cases

I. NUMERICAL TABLE

9 & 12/60: Société Commerciale Antoine Vloeberghs SA v. High Authority [1961]
E.C.R. 197
    2.01fn1

7/61: E.E.C. Commission v. Italy (pork imports) [1961] E.C.R. 317, [1962]
C.M.L.R. 39
    8.19

10/61: E.E.C. Commission v. Italy (radio valves) [1962] E.C.R. 1, [1962]
C.M.L.R. 187
    1.00fn3; 1.00fn4; 9.62; 9.63; 9.65; 9.66

13/63: Italy v. E.E.C. Commission (electric refrigerators) [1963] E.C.R. 165,
[1963] C.M.L.R. 289
    4.16fn48; 8.06; 9.02fn3

73–74/63: N.V. Internationale Crediet- en Handelsvereniging 'Rotterdam' v.
Minister van Landbouw en Visserij [1964] E.C.R. 1, [1964] C.M.L.R. 198
    9.01fn2; 9.02fn4

90–91/63: E.E.C. Commission v. Luxembourg and Belgium (milk products) [1964]
E.C.R. 625, [1965] C.M.L.R. 58
    4.09fn20

6/64: Costa v. Ente Nazionale per l'Energia Elettrica (ENEL) [1964] E.C.R. 585,
[1964] C.M.L.R. 425
    11.03; 12.13

20/64: Albatros Srl v. Société des Pétroles et des Combustibles Liquides (SOPECO)
[1965] E.C.R. 29, [1965] C.M.L.R. 159
    11.07fn20

56, 58/64: Ets. Consten S.A. v. Grundig-Verkaufs GmbH [1966] E.C.R. 299,
[1966] C.M.L.R. 418
    8.97fn245; 9.52

32/65: Italy v. E.E.C. Council and Commission [1966] E.C.R. 389, [1969]
C.M.L.R. 39
    9.52fn123

8–11/66: Re Noordwijks Cement Accoord: Cimenteries C.B.R. Cementsbedrijven
N.V. v. E.E.C. Commission [1967] E.C.R. 75, [1967] C.M.L.R. 77
    12.14fn35

24/67: Parke, Davis & Co. v. Probel [1968] E.C.R. 55, [1968] C.M.L.R. 47
    8.97fn245; 9.52

27/67: Fink-Frucht GmbH v. Hauptzollamt München-Landsbergerstrasse [1968]
E.C.R. 223, [1968] C.M.L.R. 228
    6.28

7/68: E.C. Commission v. Italy (art treasures) [1968] E.C.R. 423, [1969]
C.M.L.R. 1
    2.03; 2.04; 8.59

13/68: Salgoil SpA v. Italian Ministry of Foreign Trade [1968] E.C.R. 453, [1969]
C.M.L.R. 181
    5.06

2–3/69: Sociaal Fonds voor de Diamantarbeiders *v.* S.A. Ch. Brachfield & Sons and Chougol Diamond Co. [1969] E.C.R. 211, [1969] C.M.L.R. 335
    2.23

6,11/69: E.C. Commission *v.* France (export credits) [1969] E.C.R. 523, [1970] C.M.L.R. 43
    7.89; 9.21; 9.22fn52

15/69: Württembergische Milchverwertung-Südmilch AG *v.* Ugliola [1969] E.C.R. 363, [1970] C.M.L.R. 194
    9.54fn127; 9.57fn132

26/69: E.C. Commission *v.* France (Tunisian olive oil) [1970] E.C.R. 565, [1970] C.M.L.R. 444
    2.20fn58

77/69: E.C. Commission *v.* Belgium (wood) [1970] E.C.R. 237
    4.04fn6

8/70: E.C. Commission *v.* Italy (administrative levy) [1970] E.C.R. 961
    4.04fn6

13/70: Francesco Cinzano & Cia GmbH *v.* Hauptzollamt Saarbrücken [1970] E.C.R. 1089, [1971] C.M.L.R. 374
    11.10fn30

33/70: S.A.C.E. *v.* Italian Ministry of Finance [1970] E.C.R. 1213, [1971] C.M.L.R. 123
    6.04fn8

37/70: Rewe-Zentrale des Lebensmittel-Großhandels GmbH *v.* Hauptzollamt Emmerich [1971] E.C.R. 23, [1971] C.M.L.R. 238
    9.02fn3

40/70: Sirena Srl *v.* Eda Srl [1971] E.C.R. 69, [1971] C.M.L.R. 260
    8.97fn241; 8.97fn243; 8.97fn247

62/70: Werner A. Bock KG *v.* E.C. Commission [1971] E.C.R. 897, [1972] C.M.L.R. 160
    9.27fn5; 9.30; 9.33; 9.34; 9.35

78/70: Deutsche Grammophon Gesellschaft mbH *v.* Metro-SB-Großmärkte GmbH & Co. KG [1971] E.C.R. 487, [1971] C.M.L.R. 631
    2.26; 4.22; 8.97; 8.105; 8.118; 8.119

9,11/71: Cie d'Approvisionnement de Transport & de Credit S.A. *v.* E.C. Commission [1972] E.C.R. 391, [1973] C.M.L.R. 529
    9.08

10/71: Ministère Public of Luxembourg *v.* Hein née Muller [1971] E.C.R. 723
    9.03fn7

51–54/71: International Fruit Company N.V. *v.* Produktschap voor Groenten en Fruit [1971] E.C.R. 1107
    6.15; 7.03; 7.92; 7.98

82/71: Il Pubblico Ministero *v.* SpA Società Agricola Industria Latte (SAIL) [1972] E.C.R. 119, [1972] C.M.L.R. 723
    11.19

21–24/72: International Fruit Company N.V. *v.* Produktschap voor Groenten en Fruit (No. 3) [1972] E.C.R. 1219, [1975] 2 C.M.L.R. 1
    1.00fn4; 1.00fn5

29/72: Marimex SpA *v.* Ministero delle Finanze [1972] E.C.R. 1309, [1973] C.M.L.R. 486
    4.14fn42

43/72: Merkur-Aussenhandels GmbH *v.* E.C. Commission [1973] E.C.R. 1055
    9.08

2/73: Riseria Luigi Geddo *v.* Ente Nazionale Risi [1973] E.C.R. 865, [1974] 1 C.M.L.R. 13
    5.08

51/74: P.J. Van der Hulst's Zonen v. Produktschap voor Siergewassen [1975] E.C.R. 79, [1975] 1 C.M.L.R. 236
    4.05fn12

63/74: W. Cadsky SpA v. Istituto Nazionale per il Commercio Estero [1975] E.C.R. 281, [1975] 2 C.M.L.R. 246
    10.04

89/74, 18–19/75: Procureur Général Bordeaux v. Arnaud [1975] E.C.R. 1023, [1975] 2 C.M.L.R. 490
    7.51; 10.10fn27

4/75: Rewe-Zentralfinanz GmbH v. Director of the Landwirtschaftskammer [1975] E.C.R. 843, [1977] 1 C.M.L.R. 599
    6.18fn37; 7.09; 8.06; 8.16; 8.54fn136; 10.10fn27

10–14/75: Procureur de la République at the Cour d'Appel Aix-en-Provence and Fédération Nationale des Producteurs de Vins de Table et Vins de Pays v. Paul Louis Lahaille and others [1975] E.C.R. 1053
    10.10fn27

29/75: Kaufhof AG v. E.C. Commission [1976] E.C.R. 431
    9.33; 9.34; 9.35

36/75: Rutili v. Minister for the Interior [1975] E.C.R. 1219, [1976] 1 C.M.L.R. 140
    8.25

38/75: Douaneagent der N.V. Nederlandse Spoorwegen v. Inspecteur der Invoerrechten en Accijnzen [1975] E.C.R. 1439, [1976] 1 C.M.L.R. 167
    1.00fn3

43/75: Defrenne v. Sabena [1976] E.C.R. 455, [1976] 2 C.M.L.R. 98
    4.25; 9.50fn113

45/75: Rewe-Zentrale des Lebensmittel-Großhandels eGmbH v. Hauptzollamt Landau/Pfalz [1976] E.C.R. 181, [1976] 2 C.M.L.R. 1
    11.03; 11.10; 11.11; 11.16

51/75: E.M.I. Records Ltd. v. CBS United Kingdom Ltd. [1976] E.C.R. 811, [1976] 2 C.M.L.R. 235
    2.17; 8.97fn241; 8.131

59/75: Pubblico Ministero v. Manghera [1976] E.C.R. 91, [1976] 1 C.M.L.R. 557
    9.50fn113; 11.03; 11.06; 11.08; 11.09; 11.10; 11.19fn51

65/75: Tasca [1976] E.C.R. 291, [1977] 2 C.M.L.R. 183
    7.68; 7.74

86/75: E.M.I. Records Ltd. v. CBS Grammofon A/S [1976] E.C.R. 871, [1976] 2 C.M.L.R. 235
    2.17; 8.131

88–90/75: S.A.D.A.M. v. Comitato Interministeriale dei Prezzi [1976] E.C.R. 323, [1977] 2 C.M.L.R. 183
    7.68; 7.69; 7.70; 9.06

91/75: Hauptzollamt Göttingen and Bundesfinanzminister v. Wolfgang Miritz GmbH & Co. [1976] E.C.R. 217
    11.09fn27; 11.10; 11.11; 11.17

96/75: E.M.I. Records Ltd. v. CBS Schallplatten GmbH [1976] E.C.R. 913, [1976] 2 C.M.L.R. 235
    2.17; 8.131

104/75: Officier van Justitie v. De Peijper [1976] E.C.R. 613, [1976] 2 C.M.L.R. 271
    4.28fn75; 6.18fn37; 6.19; 6.20; 8.05; 8.10; 8.11; 8.17; 8.34; 8.35; 9.01fn2

118/75: The State v. Watson & Belman [1976] E.C.R. 1185, [1976] 2 C.M.L.R. 552
    2.37fn100

77/77: Benzine en Petroleum Handelsmaatschappij B.V., British Petroleum Raffi-
naderij Nederland N.V. and British Petroleum Maatschappij Nederland B.V.
v. E.C. Commission [1978] E.C.R. 1513, [1978] 3 C.M.L.R. 174
9.10fn21; 9.11

80–81/77: Société les Commissionnaires Réunis Sàrl *v.* Receveur des Douanes; Sàrl
Les Fils de Henri Ramel *v.* Receveur des Douanes [1978] E.C.R. 927
4.09; 4.11; 4.18; 9.40; 10.08

82/77: Openbaar Ministerie *v.* Van Tiggele [1978] E.C.R. 25, [1978] 2 C.M.L.R.
528
6.15; 6.24fn57; 6.31fn78; 6.42fn110; 7.73; 7.74; 7.77; 7.78; 8.14fn41

88/77: Minister for Fisheries *v.* Schonenberg [1978] E.C.R. 473, [1978] 2 C.M.L.R.
519
3.04fn27

102/77: Hoffmann-La Roche & Co. AG *v.* Centrafarm Vertriebsgesellschaft Phar-
mazeutischer Erzeugnisse mbH [1978] E.C.R. 1139, [1978] 3 C.M.L.R. 217
8.115; 8.117

148/77: H. Hansen Jun. & O.C. Balle GmbH & Co. *v.* Hauptzollamt Flensburg
[1978] E.C.R. 1787, [1979] 1 C.M.L.R. 604
3.03fn9; 11.12

154/77: Procureur du Roi *v.* Dechmann [1978] E.C.R. 1573, [1979] 2 C.M.L.R. 1
7.67fn134; 10.10fn27

2/78: E.C. Commission *v.* Belgium (spirits imports) [1979] E.C.R. 1761, [1980]
1 C.M.L.R. 216
7.07; 7.08

3/78: Centrafarm B.V. *v.* American Home Products Corporation [1978] E.C.R.
1823, [1979] 1 C.M.L.R. 326
18.116; 8.117

7/78: Regina *v.* Thompson, Johnson & Woodiwiss [1978] E.C.R. 2247, [1979]
1 C.M.L.R. 47
2.06; 2.35; 8.30

13/78: Firma Joh. Eggers Sohn & Co. *v.* Freie Hansestadt Bremen [1978] E.C.R.
1935, [1979] 1 C.M.L.R. 562
6.19; 7.33; 7.40; 7.43; 8.10

27/78: Amministrazione delle Finanze dello Stato *v.* Ditta Rasham [1978] E.C.R.
1761, [1979] 1 C.M.L.R. 1
9.30

34/78: Yoshida Nederland B.V. *v.* Kamer van Koophandel en Fabrieken voor
Friesland [1979] E.C.R. 115, [1979] 2 C.M.L.R. 747
4.10fn24

83/78: Pigs Marketing Board (Northern Ireland) *v.* Redmond [1978] E.C.R. 2347,
[1979] 1 C.M.L.R. 177
5.07; 9.04; 10.09fn25; 10.10fn27; 11.02fn1

86,119/78: S.A. Des Grandes Distilleries Peureux *v.* Directeur des Services Fiscaux
de la Haute-Sâone [1979] E.C.R. 897, [1980] 3 C.M.L.R. 337
7.22; 11.08fn25; 11.09fn27; 11.12; 11.14; 11.15

91/78: Hansen GmbH & Co. *v.* Hauptzollamt Flensburg [1979] E.C.R. 935,
[1980] 1 C.M.L.R. 162
11.04; 11.09fn27; 11.13; 11.16; 11.20

118/78: C.J. Meijer B.V. *v.* Department of Trade [1979] E.C.R. 1387, [1979]
2 C.M.L.R. 398
10.05

120/78: Rewe-Zentrale AG *v.* Bundesmonopolverwaltung für Branntwein [1979]
E.C.R. 649, [1979] 3 C.M.L.R. 494
4.16; 6.13fn27; 6.40; 6.42; 6.43; 6.46; 6.47; 6.48; 6.49; 6.50fn138;
6.51; 6.55; 6.60; 6.70; 6.71; 6.72; 7.45; 7.52; 7.59; 7.63; 7.88; 8.02;
8.10; 8.18; 8.53; 8.67; 8.70; 8.72; 8.80; 8.81; 8.83fn204; 8.89; 8.90;
8.93; 10.10; 11.08; 11.12; 11.16; 12.24; 12.25; 12.27; 14.00

32/79: E.C. Commission v. United Kingdom (fishery conservation measures) [1980] E.C.R. 2403, [1981] 1 C.M.L.R. 219
  3.03fn20

34/79: The Queen v. Henn and Darby [1979] E.C.R. 3795, [1980] 1 C.M.L.R. 246
  2.21; 2.37; 5.08; 8.08; 8.09; 8.25; 8.26; 8.27; 9.63; 9.64; 9.67

44/79: Hauer v. Land Rheinland-Pfalz [1979] E.C.R. 3727, [1980] 3 C.M.L.R. 42
  8.25fn73

52/79: Procureur du Roi v. Debauve [1980] E.C.R. 881, [1981] 2 C.M.L.R. 362
  2.05; 2.25; 2.28; 2.32; 8.07; 8.22fn68

62/79: Coditel S.A. v. Ciné Vog Films S.A. [1980] E.C.R. 833, [1981] 2 C.M.L.R. 362
  2.32; 8.22fn68; 8.119fn281

65/79: Procureur de la République v. Chatain, Laboratoires Sandoz [1980] E.C.R. 1345, [1981] 3 C.M.L.R. 418
  2.35fn96; 7.11fn26

73/79: E.C. Commission v. Italy (sugar charges) [1980] E.C.R. 1533, [1982] 1 C.M.L.R. 1
  6.24fn57

94/79: Re Pieter Vriend [1980] E.C.R. 327, [1980] 3 C.M.L.R. 473
  10.10fn27; 10.15

95–96/79: Procureur du Roi v. Kefer and Delmelle [1980] E.C.R. 103
  7.67fn134; 7.78fn157; 10.10fn27

788/79: Italian State v. Gilli and Andres [1980] E.C.R. 2071, [1981] 1 C.M.L.R. 146
  6.43; 6.48; 6.55fn148; 6.60fn157; 6.61; 7.52; 8.03; 8.53; 8.72

812/79: Attorney-General v. Burgoa [1980] E.C.R. 2787, [1981] 2 C.M.L.R. 193
  9.66

815/79: Cremonini and Vrankovich [1980] E.C.R. 3583, [1981] 3 C.M.L.R. 49
  12.01fn1; 12.26fn60

823/79: Carciati [1980] E.C.R. 2773, [1981] 2 C.M.L.R. 193
  8.68; 8.69

22/80: Boussac Saint-Frères S.A. v. Gerstenmeier [1980] E.C.R. 3427, [1982] 1 C.M.L.R. 202
  7.51fn98

24,97/80R: E.C. Commission v. France (lamb imports) [1980] E.C.R. 1319, [1981] 3 C.M.L.R. 25
  10.06fn15

27/80: Fietje [1980] E.C.R. 3839, [1981] 3 C.M.L.R. 722
  6.15; 6.55; 6.59; 7.59; 7.61; 8.14; 8.74; 8.79

32/80: Officier van Justitie v. Kortmann [1981] E.C.R. 251, [1982] 3 C.M.L.R. 46
  6.23

53/80: Officier van Justitie v. Koninklijke Kaasfabriek Eyssen B.V. [1981] E.C.R. 429, [1982] 2 C.M.L.R. 20
  7.54; 8.43

55,57/80: Musik-Vertrieb Membran GmbH v. GEMA [1981] E.C.R. 147, [1981] 2 C.M.L.R. 44
  4.26fn69; 6.23; 8.94; 8.109fn267; 8.118; 8.120; 8.121; 8.122

58/80: Dansk Supermarked A/S v. Imerco A/S [1981] E.C.R. 181, [1981] 3 C.M.L.R. 590
  4.04; 4.22; 4.26fn69; 8.84; 8.115fn275; 8.118fn279

112/80: Firma Anton Dürbeck v. Hauptzollamt Frankfurt am Main-Flughafen [1981] E.C.R. 1095, [1982] 3 C.M.L.R. 314
  1.00fn4

220/81: Robertson [1982] E.C.R. 2349, [1983] 1 C.M.L.R. 556
 7.59fn117; 8.75

245/81: Edeka Zentrale AG v. Germany [1982] E.C.R. 2745
 1.00fn4

247/81: E.C. Commission v. Germany [1984] E.C.R. 1111, [1985] 1 C.M.L.R.
 640
 7.28; 8.50

249/81: E.C. Commission v. Ireland (promoting Irish goods) [1982] E.C.R. 4005,
 [1983] 2 C.M.L.R. 104
 4.05; 6.05; 6.10; 6.18fn39; 6.25; 6.26; 6.27; 7.25; 7.26

258/81: Metallurgiki Halyps AE v. E.C. Commission [1982] E.C.R. 4261
 9.02fn3

261/81: Walter Rau Lebensmittelwerke v. De Smedt PVBA [1982] E.C.R. 3961,
 [1983] 2 C.M.L.R. 496
 7.59fn118; 8.72

262/81: Coditel SA v. Ciné Vog Films SA (No. 2) [1982] E.C.R. 3381, [1983] 1
 C.M.L.R. 49
 8.119fn281; 8.120

266/81: Società Italiana per l'Oleodotto Transalpino (S.I.O.T.) v. Ministero delle
 Finanze [1983] E.C.R. 731, [1984] 2 C.M.L.R. 231
 1.00fn4

271/81: Société Coopérative de l'Elevage et d'Insémination Artificielle du Béarn v.
 Mialocq [1983] E.C.R. 2057
 11.04

286/81: Oosthoek's Uitgeversmaatschappij B.V. [1982] E.C.R. 4575, [1983] 3
 C.M.L.R. 428
 6.76fn192; 7.32; 8.78

314–316/81 & 83/82: Procureur de la République v. Waterkeyn [1982] E.C.R.
 4337, [1983] 2 C.M.L.R. 145
 6.74fn190; 6.75

11/82: Piraiki-Patriaki Cotton Industry AE v. E.C. Commission [1985] E.C.R.
 227, [1985] 2 C.M.L.R. 4
 9.02fn3

29/82: F. Van Luipen en Zonen BV [1983] E.C.R. 151, [1983] 2 C.M.L.R. 681
 10.15

40/82: E.C. Commission v. United Kingdom (poultry meat) [1982] E.C.R. 2793,
 [1982] 3 C.M.L.R. 497, [1984] E.C.R. 283
 5.11fn31; 8.09; 8.12fn33; 8.55

42/82: E.C. Commission v. France (Italian table wines) [1983] E.C.R. 1013, [1984]
 1 C.M.L.R. 160
 7.09fn19; 7.20; 8.09; 8.12; 8.39; 8.41

59/82: Schutzverband gegen Unwesen in der Wirtschaft v. Weinvertriebs GmbH
 [1983] E.C.R. 1217, [1984] 1 C.M.L.R. 319
 5.11fn31; 7.34

74/82: E.C. Commission v. Ireland [1984] E.C.R. 317
 5.11fn31; 8.55

78/82: E.C. Commission v. Italy [1983] E.C.R. 1955
 7.74; 7.78

84/82: Germany v. E.C. Commission (State Aids to the German Textile Industry)
 [1984] E.C.R. 1451, [1985] 1 C.M.L.R. 153
 13.14fn43

90/82: E.C. Commission v. France [1983] E.C.R. 2011, [1984] 2 C.M.L.R. 516
 11.08

94/82: De Kikvorsch Groothandel-Import-Export BV [1983] E.C.R. 947, [1984]
 2 C.M.L.R. 323
 7.58fn110; 8.71

15/83: Denkavit Nederland v. Hoofdproduktschap voor Akkerbouwprodukten [1984] E.C.R. 2171
    4.12; 6.68fn175; 7.94fn202

16/83: Karl Prantl [1984] E.C.R. 1299, [1985] 2 C.M.L.R. 586
    6.45; 6.52; 7.44; 8.86; 8.88; 8.90; 10.14

36/83: Mabanaft GmbH v. Hauptzollamt Emmerich [1984] E.C.R. 2497, [1987] 1 C.M.L.R. 473
    2.01fn1

37/83: Rewe-Zentrale AG v. Director of the Landwirtschaftskammer for the Rhineland [1984] E.C.R. 1229, [1985] 2 C.M.L.R. 586
    4.12; 4.18; 8.58

47–48/83: Pluimveeslachterij Midden-Nederland B.V. [1984] E.C.R. 1721
    10.14

58/83: E.C. Commission v. Greece (cash payments for imports) [1984] E.C.R. 2027, [1986] 1 C.M.L.R. 673
    7.29fn54

63/83: R. v. Kent Kirk [1984] E.C.R. 2689, [1984] 3 C.M.L.R. 522
    8.25fn73

72/83: Campus Oil Ltd. v. Minister for Industry and Energy [1984] E.C.R. 2727, [1984] 3 C.M.L.R. 544
    6.19; 7.22; 7.83; 8.16; 8.20; 8.30; 8.33; 9.03; 9.10fn22; 13.12fn38; 14.00

94/83: Criminal proceedings against Albert Heijn B.V. [1984] E.C.R. 3263
    8.47

97/83: C.M.C. Melkunie B.V. [1984] E.C.R. 2367, [1986] 2 C.M.L.R. 318
    8.48

105/83: Pakvries B.V. v. Minister for Agriculture and Fisheries [1984] E.C.R. 2101, [1985] 2 C.M.L.R. 602
    9.60

114/83: Société d'Initiatives et de Coopération Agricoles v. E.C. Commission [1984] E.C.R. 2589, [1985] 2 C.M.L.R. 767
    9.02fn3; 10.08fn20

134/83: Criminal proceedings against Jan Gerrit Abbink [1984] E.C.R. 4097, [1986] 1 C.M.L.R. 579
    8.69

173/83: E.C. Commission v. France (waste oils) [1985] E.C.R. 491
    6.12fn23; 6.70fn182

177/83: Theodor Kohl KG v. Ringelhan & Rennett S.A. [1984] E.C.R. 3651, [1985] 3 C.M.L.R. 340
    6.53fn146; 8.90

207/83: E.C. Commission v. United Kingdom (origin marking of imports) [1985] E.C.R. 1201, [1985] 2 C.M.L.R. 259
    6.53fn146; 7.50; 8.71; 8.76

229/83: Association des Centres Distributeurs Edouard Leclerc v. Au Blé Vert Sàrl [1985] E.C.R. 1, [1985] 2 C.M.L.R. 296
    2.26; 6.31fn79; 6.52; 6.54; 6.77; 7.76; 8.93

231/83: Cullet and Another v. Centre Leclerc, Toulouse [1985] E.C.R. 315, [1985] 2 C.M.L.R. 524
    6.31fn79; 7.77; 8.31

240/83: Procureur de la République v. Association de défense des Brûleurs d'Huiles Usagées [1985] E.C.R. 53
    8.91fn220

251/83: Haug-Adrion v. Frankfurter Versicherungs-AG [1984] E.C.R. 4277, [1985] 3 C.M.L.R. 266
    4.05; 7.95

168/84: Beckholz *v.* Finanzamt Hamburg-Mitte-Altstadt [1985] E.C.R. 2251, [1985] 3 C.M.L.R. 667
   3.04fn30

174/84: Bulk Oil (Zug) AG *v.* Sun International Ltd. [1986] E.C.R. 559, [1986] 2 C.M.L.R. 732
   7.09fn23; 12.13

176/84: E.C. Commission *v.* Greece (beer) [1988] 1 C.M.L.R. 813
   7.58fn111; 8.44fn113

178/84: E.C. Commission *v.* Germany (purity requirements for beer) [1988] 1 C.M.L.R. 780
   6.43; 7.46; 8.44fn113; 8.45; 8.51fn128; 8.72fn174; 8.79; 14.00

182/84: Miro B.V. [1985] E.C.R. 3731, [1986] 3 C.M.L.R. 545
   7.45; 8.82

188/84: E.C. Commission *v.* France (woodworking machines) [1986] E.C.R. 419
   6.55; 8.34fn103; 8.51

192/84: E.C. Commission *v.* Greece (agricultural machinery credits) [1985] E.C.R. 3967, [1988] 1 C.M.L.R. 420
   6.12fn23; 6.12fn24; 7.30

199/84: Procuratore della Repubblica *v.* Migliorini [1985] E.C.R. 3317, [1987] 2 C.M.L.R. 3317
   4.11

216/84: E.C. Commission *v.* France (substitute milk powder) (judgment of 23 February 1988)
   6.43; 6.45; 6.47; 7.58fn112; 8.24; 8.49; 8.72; 10.18; 14.00

222/84: Johnston *v.* Chief Constable of the Royal Ulster Constabulary [1986] 3 C.M.L.R. 240
   9.58; 9.59

242/84: Tezi Textiel B.V. *v.* Ministry of Economic Affairs [1986] E.C.R. 933, [1987] 3 C.M.L.R. 64
   9.25fn60; 9.40; 9.41; 9.43; 14.00

247/84: State *v.* Motte [1985] E.C.R. 3887, [1987] 1 C.M.L.R. 663
   8.44fn113; 8.44fn114; 8.45

248/84: Germany *v.* E.C. Commission (judgment of 14 October 1987)
   6.24fn58

283/84: Trans Tirreno Express SpA *v.* Ufficio Provinciale IVA, Sassari [1986] E.C.R. 231, [1986] 2 C.M.L.R. 100
   3.04fn30

249/84: Ministère Public and the Ministry of Finance *v.* Profant [1985] E.C.R. 3237, [1986] 2 C.M.L.R. 378
   8.69fn163

304/84: Ministère Public *v.* Muller and Kampfmeyer France Sàrl [1986] E.C.R. 1511, [1987] 2 C.M.L.R. 469
   8.44fn113; 8.44fn114

50/85: Schloh *v.* Auto Contrôle Technique Sprl [1987] 1 C.M.L.R. 450
   2.25fn67; 8.52

54/85: Ministère Public *v.* Mirepoix [1986] E.C.R. 1067, [1987] 2 C.M.L.R. 44
   8.47; 8.91fn220

80 & 159/85: Nederlandse Bakkerij Stichting *v.* Edah B.V. [1988] 2 C.M.L.R. 113
   7.75fn147

121/85: Conegate Ltd. *v.* H.M. Customs and Excise [1986] E.C.R. 1007, [1986] 1 C.M.L.R. 739
   8.05fn11; 8.29; 9.61; 9.64; 9.67

124/85: E.C. Commission *v.* Greece (meat) [1988] 2 C.M.L.R. 518
   6.29fn70; 8.21

148/85: Directeur Général des Impôts *v.* Forest (Sangoy) [1988] 2 C.M.L.R. 577
   6.44; 6.47; 7.89; 10.16

National Courts

II. ALPHABETICAL TABLE OF EUROPEAN COURT CASES

Kramer—Cases 3–4,6/76
Krantz v. Netherlands—Case 69/88
Kupferberg v. Hauptzollamt Mainz—Case 253/83

Lahaille—Cases 10–14/75
Lambert—Case 308/86
Landwirtschaftskammer (Rewe-Zentral v.)—Case 4/75
Leclerc v. Au Blé Vert—Case 229/83
Ledoux—Case 127/86
Leeuwarder Papierwarenfabriek—Cases 296 & 318/82
Lefebvre—Case 206/87
Lefevre—Case 188/86
Lensing-Kaffee-Tee-Import v. Hauptzollamt Berlin-Packhof—Case 147/73
Linsey v. Payless DIY—Case 134/88
Livestock Sales Transport v. Intervention Board for Agricultural Produce—Case
    162/86
Lorenz v. Germany—Case 120/73
Luisi and Carbone v. Ministero del Tesoro—Cases 286/82 & 26/83

Mabanaft v. Hauptzollamt Emmerich—Case 36/83
Maize Seed—Case 258/78
Manghera—Case 59/75
Mantero (Dona v.)—Case 13/76
Marimex v. Ministero delle Finanze—Case 29/72
Marshall v. Southampton and South West Hants Area Health Authority—Case
    152/84
Massey-Ferguson (Hauptzollamt Bremerhaven v.)—Case 8/73
Meijer v. Department of Trade—Case 118/78
Melkunie BV—Case 97/83
Merck v. Stephar—Case 187/80
Merkur-Aussenhandels v. Commission—Case 43/72
Meroni (Iannelli and Volpi v.)—Case 74/76
Metallurgiki Halyps v. Commission—Case 258/81
Metro-SB-Großmärkte (D.G.G. v.)—Case 78/70
Mialocq—Case 271/81
Migliorini—Case 199/84
Minister for Fisheries v. Schonenberg—Case 88/77
Ministère Public v. Cognet—Case 355/85
——— v. Gofette and Gilliard—Case 406/85
——— v. Hein—Case 10/71
——— v. Lambert—Case 308/86
——— v. Ledoux—Case 127/86
——— v. Lefevre—Case 188/86
——— v. Mirepoix—Case 54/85
——— v. Muller and Kampfmeyer—Case 304/84
——— v. Profant—Case 249/84
Mirepoix—Case 54/85
Miritz (Hauptzollamt Göttingen v.)—Case 91/75
Miro BV—Case 182/84
Motte—Case 247/84
Muller and Kampfmeyer—Case 304/84
Musik-Vertrieb Membran v. GEMA—Cases 55,57/80

390

Public Prosecutor *v.* Grosoli—Case 223/78
Puttershoek—Cases 73–74/63

The Queen *v.* Henn and Darby—Case 34/79

Ramel *v.* Receveur des Douanes—Cases 80–81/77
Rasham (Amministrazione delle Finanze dello Stato *v.*)—Case 27/78
Ratti—Case 148/78
Rau *v.* De Smedt—Case 261/81
Receveur des Douanes (Ramel *v.*)—Cases 80–81/77
Redmond (Pigs Marketing Board *v.*)—Case 83/78
Regina *v.* Bouchereau—Case 30/77
—— *v.* Kirk—Case 63/83
—— *v.* Thompson, Johnson and Woodiwiss—Case 7/78
Rewe Zentral *v.* Hauptzollamt Kehl—Case 10/73
Rewe-Zentralfinanz eGmbH *v.* Director of the Landwirtschaftskammer—Case 4/75
Rewe-Zentralfinanz *v.* Landwirtschaftskammer für das Saarland—Case 33/76
Rewe-Zentrale des Lebensmittel-Großhandels *v.* Hauptzollamt Emerich—Case 37/70
Rewe-Zentrale des Lebensmittel-Großhandels *v.* Hauptzollamt Landau-Pfalz—Case 45/75
Rewe-Zentrale AG *v.* Bundesmonopolverwaltung für Branntwein (Cassis de Dijon)—Case 120/78
Rewe-Zentrale AG *v.* Direktor der Landwirtschaftskammer Rheinland—Case 37/83
Rezzano e Cavassa (Interzuccheri *v.*)—Case 105/76
Riseria Luigi Geddo *v.* Ente Nazionale Risi—Case 2/73
Rivoira—Case 179/78
—— (Cayrol *v.*)—Case 52/77
Robertson—Case 220/81
Roelstraete—Case 116/84
Roussel Laboratoria BV *v.* Netherlands—Case 181/82
RSV *v.* Commission—Case 223/85
Rutili *v.* Minister for the Interior—Case 36/75

S.A. Ch. Brachfeld & Sons—Cases 2–3/69
SACE *v.* Italian Ministry of Finance—Case 33/70
Sacchi—Case 155/73
SADAM *v.* Commitato Interministeriale dei Prezzi—Cases 88–90/75
SAIL—Case 82/71
Salgoil *v.* Italian Ministry of Foreign Trade—Case 13/68
Sandoz BV (Openbaar Ministerie *v.*)—Case 174/82
Saquella *v.* Ministry of Foreign Trade—Cases 206, 207, 209/80
Schloh *v.* Auto Contrôle Technique—Case 50/85
Schlüter *v.* Hauptzollamt Lörrach—Case 9/73
Schonenberg—Case 88/77
Schul *v.* Inspecteur der Invoerrechten—Case 15/81
Schutzverband gegen Unwesen in der Wirtschaft *v.* Weinvertriebs GmbH—Case 59/82
Simmenthal SpA *v.* Ministero delle Finanze—Case 35/76
S.I.O.T. *v.* Ministero delle Finanze—Case 266/81
Sirena *v.* Eda—Case 40/70
SMANOR—Case 298/87
Sociaal Fonds voor de Diamantarbeiders *v.* S.A. Ch. Brachfeld & Sons—Cases 2–3/69

Walrave & Koch *v.* Association Union Cycliste Internationale—Case 36/74
Wakefield B.C. *v.* B. & Q. plc—Case 166/88
Warner Bros. *v.* Christiansen—Case 158/86
Waterkeyn—Cases 314–316/81 & 83/82
Watson and Belman—Case 118/75
Weinvertriebs—Case 59/82
Werner A. Bock *v.* Commission—Case 62/70
Winthrop (Centrafarm *v.*)—Case 16/74
Württemburgische Milchverwertung-Südmilch *v.* Ugliola—Case 15/69

Yoshida Nederland B.V. *v.* Kamer van Koophandel en Fabrieken voor Friesland—
    Case 34/78

Zoni—Case 90/86

ANNEXE III

Selected Bibliography

Barents	'New Developments in Measures having Equivalent Effect' [1981] C.M.L.Rev. 271.
Béraud	'Les mesures d'effet équivalent au sens des articles 30 et suivants du Traité de Rome' [1968] R.T.D.E. 265.
Capelli	'Les malentendus provoqués par l'arrêt "Cassis de Dijon"' [1981] R.M.C. 421.
Daniele	'Réflexions d'ensemble sur la notion de mesures ayant un effet équivalent à des restrictions quantitatives' [1984] R.M.C. 477.
Dashwood	(1) 'The Cassis de Dijon Line of Authority' from *In Memoriam J. D. B. Mitchell* [1983].
	(2) See Wyatt below.
Dauses	'La jurisprudence de la Cour de justice en matière de libre circulation des marchandises dans la Communauté européenne' [1985] R.T.D.E. 1.
Defalque	'Le concept de discrimination en matière de libre circulation des marchandises' [1987] C.D.E. 471.
Dona	'Les mesures d'effet équivalant à des restrictions quantitatives' [1973] R.M.C. 224.
Ehlermann	(1) 'Die Bedeutung des Artikels 36 EWG für die Freiheit des Warenverkehrs' [1973] EuR 1.
	(2) Commentary on Articles 30 to 36 in Groeben, Boeckh, Thiesing, *Kommentar zum EWG-Vertrag* 2nd ed. (Baden-Baden, 1974), Vol 1.
	(3) 'Das Verbot der Maßnahmen gleicher Wirkung in der Rechtsprechung des Gerichtshofes' in *Festschrift für Ipsen* (Hamburg, 1977).
Evans	'Economic Policy and the Free Movement of Goods in EEC Law' [1983] I.C.L.Q. 577.
FIDE	'The Elimination of Non-Tariff Barriers with Particular Reference to Industrial Property Rights including Copyright' [1982].
Gormley	'Prohibiting Restrictions on Trade within the EEC' (The Hague, 1985).
Grabitz	'Das Recht auf Zugang zum Markt nach dem EWG-Vertrag', in *Festschrift für Ipsen*, (Hamburg, 1977).
Graf	'Der Begriff "Maßnahmen gleicher Wirkung wie mengenmässige Einfuhrbeschränkungen" im EWG-Vertrag' (Munich, 1972).
Gulmann	'Handelshindringer i EF-Retten' (Denmark, 1980).
Leitao	'Quelques réflexions politico-juridiques autour de l'élimination des mesures d'effet équivalent: unité du marché commun, principe logique ou principe organique?' [1986] R.M.C. 21.
Mackenzie Stuart	'The Free Movement of Goods' (1979) 12 *Bracton Law Journal European Supplement* 17.

395

Marenco   (1) 'Pour une interprétation traditionnelle de la notion de mesures d'effet équivalant à une restriction quantitative' [1984] C.D.E. 291.

(2) 'La giurisprudenza comunitaria sulle misure di effetto equivalente a una restrizione quantitativa' (1984–1986) [1988] *Il Foro Padano* IV, p. 166.

Masclet   (1) 'Les articles 30, 36 et 100 du traité CEE à la lumière de l'arrêt "Cassis de Dijon"' [1980] R.T.D.E. 611.

(2) 'La libre circulation des marchandises dans les Communautés européennes' [1986] R.T.D.E. 243.

Mattera   (1) 'Libre circulation des marchandises et articles 30 à 36 du Traité CEE' [1976] R.M.C. 500.

(2) 'L'arrêt "Cassis de Dijon": une nouvelle approche pour la réalisation et le bon fonctionnement du marché intérieur' [1980] R.M.C. 505.

(3) 'Les nouvelles formes du protectionnisme économique et les articles 30 et suivants du Traité CEE' [1983] R.M.C. 252.

Matthies   (1) 'Herkunftsangaben und Europäisches Gemeinschaftsrecht' in *Festschrift für Schiedermair* (Munich, 1976), 395.

(2) 'Die Verantwortung der Mitgliedstaaten für den freien Warenverkehr im Gemeinsamen Markt', in *Festschrift für Ipsen* (Tübingen, 1977), 669.

(3) 'Die Verfassung des Gemeinsamen Marktes' in 'Das Europa der zweiten Generation', *Gedächtnißchrift für Sasse* (Baden-Baden, 1981), Vol I, 115.

(4) Commentary on Articles 30 to 37 in 'Kommentar zum EWG-Vertrag' (ed. Grabitz) Munich, looseleaf with updates.

Meier   (1) Commentary in Ehle and Meier *EWG-Warenverkehr* (Cologne, 1971), 158 et seq.

(2) 'Zur Kombination von nationalen Lebensmittel-Begriffsbestimmungen und Vorschriften zum Schutz des Verbrauchers gegen Irreführungen als Rechtsfertigungsgründe nach Art 36 EWGV' [1980] W.R.P. 59.

(3) 'Kennzeichnung statt Verkehrsverbote—Die Rechtsprechung als Schrittmacher des Lebensmittelrechts' *Schriftenreihe des Bundes für Lebensmittelrecht und Lebensmittelkunde*, Heft 94, 47.

Meij and Winter   'Measures having an equivalent effect to quantitative restrictions' [1976] C.M.L.Rev. 79.

Mestmäcker   *Die Vereinbarkeit von Preisregelungen und dem Arzneimittelmarkt mit dem Recht der Europäischen Wirtschaftsgemeinschaft* (Baden-Baden, 1980).

Oliver   (1) A Review of the Case Law of the Court of Justice on Articles 30 to 36 EEC in 1983' [1984] C.M.L.Rev. 221.

(2) 'A Review of the Case Law of the Court of Justice on Articles 30 to 36 EEC in 1984' [1985] C.M.L.Rev. 301.

(3) 'A Review of the Case Law of the Court of Justice on Articles 30 to 36 EEC in 1985' [1986] C.M.L.Rev. 325.

Page   'The Concept of Measures having an Effect Equivalent to Quantitative Restrictions' [1977] E.L.Rev. 105

Seidel   'Der EWG-rechtliche Begriff der "Maßnahmen gleicher Wirkung wie eine mengemässige Beschränkung" [1967] NJW 2081.

Schiller   'Gewährt Art. 30 des EWG-Vertrages dem Gemeinschaftsbürger neben einem subjektiven Abwehrrecht auch ein subjektives Leistungsrecht?' [1980] R.I.W./A.W.D. 569.

Touffait   'Les entraves techniques à la libre circulation des marchandises' [1982] *Recueil Dalloz-Sirey*, Chronique 37.

Ulmer (Peter)	'Zum Verbot mittelbarer Einfuhrbeschränkungen im EWG-Vertrag' [1973] G.R.U.R.Int. 502.
Van Gerven	'The Recent Case Law of the Court of Justice concerning Articles 30 and 36 of the EEC Treaty' [1977] C.M.L.Rev. 5.
Van Rijn	'A Review of the Case Law of the Court of Justice on Articles 30 to 36 in 1986 and 1987' [1988] C.M.L.Rev. (forthcoming).
Veelken	'Maßnahmen gleicher Wirkung wie mengenmässige Beschränkungen' [1977] EuR 311.
Verloren van Themaat	(1) 'Bevat art. 30 van het EEG-Verdrag slechts een non-discriminatie-beginsel ten anzien van invoerbeperkingen?' 15 SEW 632.
	(2) 'Zum Verhältnis zwischen Artikel 30 und Artikel 85 EWG-Vertrag' in *Festschrift für Gunther* (Baden-Baden, 1976), 373.
	(3) 'De artikelen 30–36 van het EEG-Verdrag' [1980] R.M. Themis 4/5 at 378.
	(4) 'La libre circulation des marchandises après "Cassis de Dijon"' [1982] C.D.E. 123.
Waegenbaur	Commentary on Articles 30 to 36 in Groeben, Boeckh, Thiesing, Ehlermann *Kommentar zum EWG-Vertrag* 3rd ed. (Baden-Baden, 1983) Vol I.
Waelbroeck	(1) Commentary on Articles 30 to 36 in *Le droit de la Communauté économique européenne* (Brussels, 1970), Vol I.
	(2) *Les réglementations nationales de prix et le droit communautaire* (Brussels, 1975).
	(3) 'Mesures d'effet équivalent, discrimination formelle et matérielle dans la jurisprudence de la Cour de Justice' in *Liber Amicorum Frédéric Dumon*, Antwerp.
Winkel	'Die Vereinbarkeit staatlicher Preislenkungsmaßnahmen mit dem EWG-Vertrag' [1976] N.J.W. 2048.
Winter	See Meij, above.
Wyatt (with Dashwood)	*The Substantive Law of the EEC* 2nd ed. (London, 1987).

Index

STATE COMMERCIAL MONOPOLIES—*cont.*
equivalent effect, measures, 11.08
exceptions, 11.18–11.20
exclusive rights, 11.06
function, 11.13
goods, 11.04
import licensing system, 11.07
interpretation, questions, 11.05
local authorities exercising, 11.07
meaning—
  adjust, 11.09
  discrimination, 11.08
  State monopoly, 11.07
monopoly equalisation duty, 11.11
quantitative restrictions, 11.07
relationship with—
  Article 234, 9.61
  Treaty's provisions, 11.10–11.16
services, 11.04
third countries, trade with, 11.04
timetable, 11.02
transitional period, end, 11.06, 11.12, 11.14

TAXATION—
internal, 6.22, 6.28
TERRITORY—
associated overseas countries, 3.02
continental shelf, 3.06
customs territory, 3.06
fishing, 3.04, 3.05
generally, 3.01, 3.03, 3.05
overseas countries and territories, 3.02
sea and sea-bed, 3.04
THIRD COUNTRIES' GOODS—
free circulation—
  assimilation, 2.16
    exceptions, 2.18–2.22
  conditions for, 2.12
  consequence, 2.16
    exceptions, 2.18–2.22
  customs duties—
    assessment, 2.12
    certificates, 2.14
    deferred payment, 2.12
    determination, 2.12
    drawbacks, 2.13
    error, 2.14
    fraud, 2.14
    repayment, 2.13
  generally, 2.09
  national commercial policy, 2.18
  superseded measures, 2.15
  technical standards, 6.60
  trade marks, 2.17
TRADE MARKS—
affixing of mark, unauthorised, 8.116
assimilation of third countries', 2.17
common origin principle—
  generally, 8.125–8.126
  split in mark—
    act of authorities, 8.127–8.130
    voluntary assignment, 8.127

TRADE MARKS—*cont.*
Community system, 8.96
confusion between, 8.133
different for same product, 8.116, 8.117
exercise by owner of rights, 8.133
exhaustion of rights principle, 8.114–8.117
guarantee by, 8.114–8.116
harmonisation of national laws, 8.96
imports' prevention by use, 8.114–8.117
repackaging of marked goods, 8.115–8.117
restriction of trade, disguised, 8.115–8.117
subject-matter, 8.114
third country, right in, 8.131–8.132
unfair competition prevention contrasted, 8.87
see also INDUSTRIAL AND COMMERCIAL PRO-
PERTY RIGHTS
TRADE NAMES—
unfair competition prevention contrasted, 8.87
TRANSACTIONS COVERED—
advance payments, 2.36
advertising, 2.28
capital, free movement, 2.06n18, 2.35–2.36
coins, purpose of transfer, 2.35
films, imports, 2.30
generally, 2.24–2.25
mail order firms, 2.25
persons, free movement, 2.31, 2.37
political demonstrators, 2.37
printing, 2.29
re-imports, 2.26
restrictions by Member States, 2.29–2.30
services provision, relationship with—
  conflict, 2.33–3.34, 2.38
  generally, 2.27, 2.29, 2.32
  receipt of service, 2.31
  tools required, 2.30
  tourism, 2.31, 2.37
  travellers, 2.31
teaching materials, 2.30n84
tools, movement of, 2.30
transit goods, 2.25
TREASURES, *see* ARTICLE 36 EXCEPTIONS,
national treasures, protection
TREATY OF ROME—
meaning, 1.01
provisions—
  outline, 1.01
  transitional, 1.01

UNFAIR COMPETITION, PREVENTION—
bottling, 8.86–8.87
consumer protection ground contrasted, 8.70, 8.83–8.84
distinctive signs, 8.90
fair and traditional practices, 8.86, 8.88–8.89
imitation of goods, 8.85
industrial property rights contrasted, 8.87, 8.90